D0080910

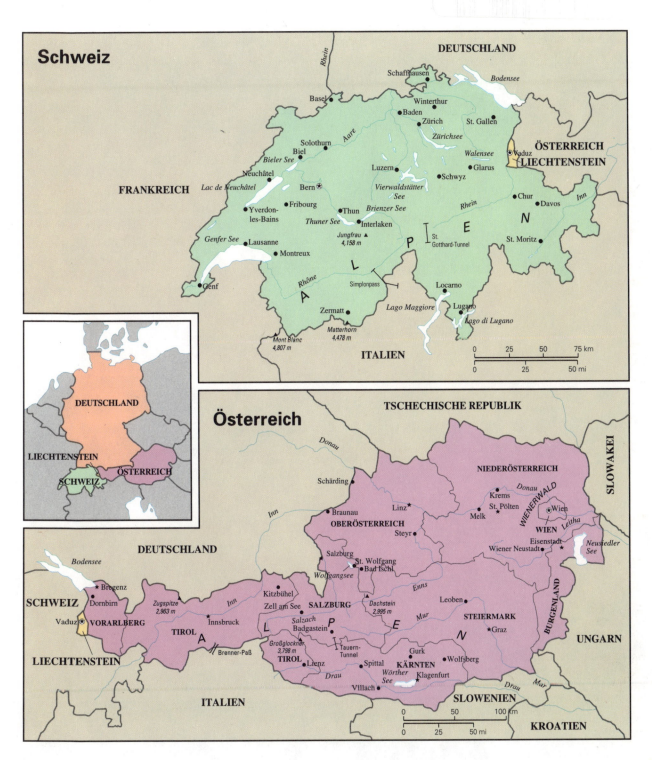

Schweiz

DEUTSCHLAND

Rhein

Schaffhausen
Bodensee

Basel
Winterthur
Baden
Zürich
St. Gallen
Zürichsee

Aare
Walensee
ÖSTERREICH
Solothurn
Vaduz ✪
LIECHTENSTEIN
Biel
Bieler See
Luzern
Glarus
Schwyz

Neuchâtel
Vierwaldstätter See

FRANKREICH
Lac de Neuchâtel
Bern ✪
Rhein
Chur
Davos
Inn

Yverdon-les-Bains
Fribourg
Thun
Brienzer See

Thuner See
Interlaken
St. Gotthard-Tunnel
St. Moritz

Genfer See
Lausanne
Jungfrau ▲ 4,158 m

Montreux

A L P E N

Rhône
Simplonpass

Genf
Locarno

Zermatt
Lugano
Lago Maggiore
Lago di Lugano

Mont Blanc 4,807 m
Matterhorn 4,478 m

ITALIEN

0   25   50   75 km
0   25   50 mi

Österreich

TSCHECHISCHE REPUBLIK

Donau
NIEDERÖSTERREICH
SLOWAKEI

Schärding
Donau
Krems
Inn
Linz ★
St. Pölten
WIENERWALD
✪ Wien

Braunau
OBERÖSTERREICH
WIEN
Leitha
Steyr
Wiener Neustadt
Eisenstadt
Neusiedler See

Salzburg
St. Wolfgang
Bad Ischl
Wolfgangsee
Enns
BURGENLAND

DEUTSCHLAND
Bodensee
Kitzbühel
SALZBURG
Dachstein 2,995 m
Leoben

Bregenz ★
Zell am See
Mur
STEIERMARK
UNGARN
SCHWEIZ
Dornbirn
Zugspitze 2,963 m
Inn
Innsbruck ★
Graz ★
Vaduz ✪ VORARLBERG
Salzach
Badgastein
A L P E N

LIECHTENSTEIN
TIROL
Großglockner 3,798 m
Tauern-Tunnel
Gurk
Wolfsberg
Brenner-Paß
TIROL
Lienz
Spittal
KÄRNTEN

ITALIEN
Drau
Villach
Wörther See
Klagenfurt
Drau
Mur

SLOWENIEN

0   50   100 Km
0   25   50 mi
KROATIEN

DEUTSCHLAND

LIECHTENSTEIN

ÖSTERREICH

SCHWEIZ

DEUTSCH HEUTE

GRUNDSTUFE

DEUTSCH HEUTE

GRUNDSTUFE • SIXTH EDITION

JACK MOELLER
Oakland University

HELMUT LIEDLOFF
Southern Illinois University

WINNIFRED R. ADOLPH
Florida State University

GISELA HOECHERL-ALDEN
University of Wisconsin-Madison

CONSTANZE KIRMSE
Goethe-Institut München

JOHN F. LALANDE, II
University of Illinois

HOUGHTON MIFFLIN COMPANY   BOSTON
Geneva, Illinois   Palo Alto   Princeton, New Jersey

Cover Designer: Diana Coe
Cover Image: Grant Taylor/Tony Stone Images
Developmental Editor: Barbara B. Lasoff
Project Management: Harriet C. Dishman/Elm Street Publications

Sponsoring Editor: E. Kristina Baer
Project Development Editor: Amy Hatch Davidson
Senior Production/Design Coordinator: Carol Merrigan
Senior Manufacturing Coordinator: Marie Barnes
Marketing Assistant: Amanda Rappaport

Printed in the U.S.A.

Library of Congress Catalog Card Number: 95-81740

Student's Edition ISBN: 0-395-74418-0

Instructor's Annotated Edition ISBN: 0-395-76686-9

23456789-DW-00 99 98 97 96

CONTENTS

KAPITEL 11   344

KAPITEL 12   378

KAPITEL   13   412

KAPITEL   14   438

REFERENCE SECTION

Deutsch heute: Grundstufe, Sixth Edition is an introductory program in German designed for college students and other adult learners. One goal of *Deutsch heute* is to provide students with a sound basis for learning German as it is used in spoken and written communication today within the context of German-speaking culture. The *Deutsch heute* program offers systematic practice in the four basic language skills of listening, speaking, reading, and writing, along with materials geared to provide a firm foundation in the basic elements of German grammar. *Deutsch heute* also provides activities that guide you in employing your skills in active personal communication and offers you opportunities to experience authentic materials likely to be encountered in a German-speaking country—materials like schedules, menus, and TV listings.

By the end of the course, you will have had the opportunity to master the basic features of the sound and writing systems, become familiar with the communicative functions of the language, role-play various situations with a partner, learn how to get the gist of various types of authentic materials, use actively many basic grammatical structures in everyday conversation and writing as well as understand material that contains grammatical features of lower frequency, use an active vocabulary of approximately 1200 words, and understand a considerable number of additional words.

Another goal of the Sixth Edition of *Deutsch heute* is to introduce you to contemporary life and culture in the three primary German-speaking countries: Germany, Austria, and Switzerland. The dialogues and readings convey important information on everyday life and culture in these countries. The readings are mature in content but simple in structure. Cultural notes *(Land und Leute)* throughout the textbook provide more in-depth information. In combination with the photographs, drawings, and ads included in the Sixth Edition of *Deutsch heute*, the readings help convey to you what life is like in the German-speaking countries today.

A further goal of *Deutsch heute, Sixth Edition* is to have you experience the relationship between culture and language, thereby making you more aware of your own native language and culture.

ORGANIZATION OF THE STUDENT TEXT

The student text contains fourteen chapters *(Kapitel)*. *Kapitel 1* is designed to get you speaking and using German for active, personal communication from the very start. It introduces you to the German sound system by means of a short dialogue *(Bausteine für Gespräche)*, the German alphabet, and numbers. You will learn to give information about yourself, to spell words, to use numbers in simple arithmetic, to give the day of the week, and to describe the contents of your room by size and color.

Each of the *Kapitel* centers on a cultural theme such as university life, shopping, leisure time, the social position of women, the German economy, Germany since 1945, Germany as a multicultural society, and the environment. There are also specific readings on Austria and Switzerland.

A typical chapter is composed of the following sections:

1. *Lernziele* are chapter objectives that summarize the content of each chapter and pro-

vide you with learning goals in five basic areas: communication tasks and purposes (*Sprechintentionen*), a reading (*Lesestück*) based on a cultural theme, additional cultural information in English (*Land und Leute*), vocabulary (*Vokabeln*), and grammar (*Grammatik*).

2. *Bausteine für Gespräche* introduce idiomatic and colloquial phrases presented in dialogue format. A section called *Brauchbares* (Useful information) follows most dialogues. This section highlights, explains, and sometimes amplifies linguistic features and cultural information from the dialogues. Communication practice and vocabulary development continue in the oral activities that follow, which include *Fragen* (Questions on the dialogues) and partner/group activities offering choices so that you can formulate your own responses. Most chapters contain sections of vocabulary expansion exercises and activities (*Erweiterung des Wortschatzes*). A list of words that you should learn and be able to use (*Vokabeln*) concludes this section.

3. *Lesestücke,* the main cultural readings, present the cultural theme of each chapter, beginning in *Kapitel 2*. Each *Lesestück* is preceded by pre-reading activities (*Vorbereitung auf das Lesen*) to give direction to your reading and help you to be successful in second-language reading: *Vor dem Lesen* (Before the reading) activities help to familiarize you with the topic of each reading by letting you discover what you may already know about the topic; *Beim Lesen* (While reading) provides specific questions to answer, words or phrases to look for, or tasks to complete (such as note-taking) as a means of aiding you in structuring your reading experience. The activities in the *Vorbereitung* are in English in *Kapitel 3–5* and in German beginning with *Kapitel 6*. A *Brauchbares* section serves the same function as that section after the dialogues. Readings are then followed by the section *Nach dem Lesen* (After the reading) which contains written and oral exercises, including *Fragen zum Lesestück* (Questions on the reading), *Erzählen wir* (Let's discuss it), partner/group activities, often a vocabulary-expansion section (*Erweiterung des Wortschatzes*), and a list of words to memorize (*Vokabeln*).

4. *Grammatik und Übungen* (Grammar and Exercises) explain grammatical concepts in concise, lucid terms and contain illustrative examples, often with equivalents in English. Grammar is explained in English to ensure immediate comprehension, and basic terms are regularly defined. German structure is often contrasted with English to clarify the structure of both languages. The grammar exercises have German titles, and the direction lines set the scene and clearly state grammatical tasks to make the communicative purpose clearer. The exercises can be completed in writing or orally in class; they can also be used for review and additional practice in combination with the Computer Study Modules and with the student audiocassettes for home or language lab study. Included in the grammar exercises are partner/group activities that provide opportunity to use "grammar" in a personal situation.

5. *Wiederholung* (Review) activities practice the content, structure, and vocabulary of the chapter in new formats and reintroduce material from earlier chapters.

6. *Grammatik: Zusammenfassung* (Grammar: Summary) provides grammatical tables, and, where useful, a brief summary of a grammatical feature introduced in the chapter. This is a reference section that is useful for review.

7. *Land und Leute* (The Country and Its People) sections provide more in-depth cultural information about many aspects of the German-speaking countries. The topics of *Land und Leute* are related to the overall chapter theme. Each *Land und Leute* is accompanied by a photo to further illustrate the cultural topic.

Partner/group activities occur throughout the chapter, in the *Bausteine* and *Lesestück* sections, as well as in the *Grammatik und Übungen* and *Wiederholung*. They are preceded by two facing arrows.

In the one type of partner/group activities, you are requested to respond to questions or statements in a way that reflects your personal opinions, attitudes, or experience. Often, varied responses are listed; these responses represent a variety of attitudes or moods. New vocabulary is marked with a raised degree mark (°). The printed variations do not represent all possible responses, but rather, they are a selection of useful conversational tools covering a range of meanings. You should choose the responses that actually express your own feelings or ideas and invent or recall other expressions from previous chapters.

In a second type of partner/group activity, called *Frage-Ecke*, both you and your partner have a chart. Your chart contains information that your partner wants and your partner's chart contains information that you want. The charts for each partner are printed near each other so when doing this exercise you will, of course, need to look only at your own chart. In addition to the information given in the chart, you are each asked to supply personal information related to the topic of the exercise. Once your partner has answered your question you should ask additional ones to elicit more information. For instance, in *Kapitel 7* your partner tells you what she/he is doing over the weekend. You may then pursue the matter in more detail by asking when, with whom, whether she/he does it often, etc. In this way the exercise leads into a genuine exchange of information.

In the third type of partner/group work you are given a situation that requires communication with a partner but no vocabulary or structures are suggested. Additional words and phrases to express notions such as skepticism, insecurity, and annoyance are found in the Supplementary Expressions of the Reference Section. You may refer to these and to the Supplementary Word Sets to approach more closely what you want to say.

Authentic materials appear at various places throughout the text. "Authentic materials or texts" is a term used to indicate such common printed material as menus, advertisements, classified ads, and television listings. These materials are part of the experience in the daily life of a native German speaker and many of them are also encountered by a visitor to a German-speaking country. You are not expected to understand each word in such a text. Rather you should try to extract only the information that interests you. For example, it is not necessary to read the entire *TV Guide* to find out what program you wish to see on a particular day at a particular time.

To help you learn to deal with such materials a variety of activities are provided that range from questions that help you get essential information and directions that help you guess meaning to opportunities to make use of the material in a role-playing situation. Definitions of all new words are provided in the Vocabulary for Authentic Text Activities in the Reference Section.

Deutsch heute, Sixth Edition is illustrated with numerous photographs, authentic materials, and line drawings. Since many of the photographs and authentic materials are closely related to the cultural notes and themes of the dialogues and core reading selections, they can be effectively used as the basis for many activities. A number of exercises are based on line drawings. Line drawings are also often used to introduce word sets and to demonstrate grammatical concepts and semantic differences explained in the grammar section. Maps of the German-speaking countries are found on the inside cover leaf at the front of the book; a map of Europe is found on the inside cover leaf at the back of the book.

The Reference Section contains the following elements:

Pronunciation and Writing Guide: This sound-symbol section gives three or four key words and simplified phonetic symbols for each German sound. Each section provides hints on how to pronounce the sound, and where useful, contrasts it with English.

Grammatical Tables: The tables in the Reference Section include the following charts: (1) paradigms for pronouns, articles, adjectives, and nouns; (2) adjectives and adverbs that are irregular in their comparative and superlative forms; (3) lists of prepositions governing the accusative, dative, or genitive case; (4) special verb + preposition combinations; (5) dative verbs; (6) examples of regular and irregular weak verbs, modals, and strong verbs, including stem-changing verbs, in the various tenses of the indicative, passive, and subjunctive; and (7) a list of the strong and irregular weak verbs used in the Sixth Edition of *Deutsch heute* with principal parts and English meanings.

Supplementary Grammar: This section contains a brief introduction into verbs in special subjunctive. The special subjunctive is used in indirect discourse, i.e., when one repeats what someone else has said.

Supplementary Expressions: This reference list of supplementary expressions helps you increase the number of things you can say and write during the course of a chapter. The list of expressions is organized according to functions and notions, for example, stalling for time; expressing skepticism, regret, or admiration; asking for favors; and making requests.

Supplementary Word Sets: This reference list of supplementary word sets offers you another opportunity to personalize vocabulary. You can consult these word lists, arranged by theme, for any topic in which you have a special interest and for which you may wish to expand your vocabulary. Many of the partner/group activities indicate where these lists may be useful, and they are often correlated with topics presented in the *Erweiterung des Wortschatzes* sections.

Vocabulary for Authentic Text Activities: All words and abbreviations that appear in authentic materials and because of their special nature are not included in the German–English Vocabulary are listed in Vocabulary for Authentic Text Activities. You may consult this section for help if you cannot guess the meaning of a word or phrase and are thus not able to get the gist of the message.

Supplementary Dialogues: This list of specific, functional phrases in dialogue format is useful for students traveling or living in German-speaking countries. These dialogues for "survival German" take place in settings such as the airport, the post office, and the hotel.

German–English Vocabulary: The German–English end vocabulary lists all words used in *Deutsch heute, Sixth Edition* except numbers. Numerals after the English definitions indicate the chapter in which words and phrases are introduced in the *Vokabeln* lists for the *Bausteine für Gespräche* and *Lesestücke*. Recognition vocabulary from readings and exercises not intended for active mastery is also included.

English–German Vocabulary: The English–German end vocabulary contains the words listed in the chapter *Vokabeln* lists. This list of approximately 1200 words constitutes the active vocabulary of a student who has successfully completed the *Deutsch heute* program.

Index: The index indicates the pages on which grammatical features and topics in the *Erweiterung des Wortschatzes* are introduced. References to the cultural notes, called *Land und Leute*, are also included.

ARBEITSHEFT: Workbook/Lab Manual/Video Workbook

The *Arbeitsheft* consists of five sections: (1) a workbook with writing exercises coordinated with each chapter of the text; (2) a lab manual that requires you to react orally or in writing to material on the recordings; (3) a video workbook that offers a number of pre- and post-viewing activities; (4) self-tests with an answer key for correction; and (5) proficiency cards, which provide tasks and problem-solving activities for in-class use. Exercises in both the Workbook and the Lab Manual parallel the presentation of content, structure, and vocabulary in the student text. Many Workbook chapters contain short reading passages based on familiar material to give you extra practice in reading German. The Sixth Edition of the *Deutsch heute Arbeitsheft* contains many communicative exercises that allow you greater freedom of expression, and a number of realia-based exercises.

The proficiency cards supplement the partner activities in the text. The cards are coordinated with each chapter and allow you to synthesize your acquired knowledge of communication tasks and purposes, vocabulary, grammar, and culture in simulations of culturally authentic situations. The proficiency cards offer activities that permit you to be creative and spontaneous in completing a specified communication task. Your instructor will generally refrain from correcting and providing any information or feedback until you have completed the task on the card.

RECORDINGS

The audio recordings that accompany **Deutsch heute, Sixth Edition** were made to provide the best possible models of German speech. Using a cast of native speakers, the recordings provide recorded versions of printed material from *Kapitel 1,* the *Bausteine,* the *Lesestücke,* exercises from the *Grammatik und Übungen,* some with additional items appearing only in the recordings, and the short story in the textbook. In addition, the recordings include the listening comprehension exercises called *Übungen zum Hörverständnis* and the pronunciation sections called *Übungen zur Aussprache* from the Lab Manual.

Sentences from the *Bausteine* are spoken once at normal speed, then modeled phrase by phrase with pauses for repetition, and finally modeled again with pauses for repetition of complete utterances. The reading selections *(Lesestücke)* are recorded without pauses. The grammar exercises are recorded in three phases: cue, pause for response, and confirmation response. Group/partner activities and activities from the *Erweiterung des Wortschatzes* and *Wiederholung* sections are not on tape. The *Übungen zum Hörverständnis* from the Lab Manual are followed by a pause to allow you to respond in writing. Longer reading passages are read twice. The *Übungen zur Aussprache* are recorded in two phases: cue and pause for response. The recordings are available for student purchase in boxed sets of cassettes.

VIDEO PROGRAM

A video program entitled *Einfach toll!* is based upon some of the topics in **Deutsch heute**. The video program consists of eight modules and a brief prelude in which the main characters introduce themselves. The scenes were shot in Germany and show experiences in the lives of young German people. In addition, there are seven short cultural interludes to increase your familiarity with the German scene. Pre-viewing and post-viewing activities in the Video Workbook section of the *Arbeitsheft* guide your viewing of the video material so that you may get the most out of the experience.

COMPUTER STUDY MODULES

Available in both IBM and Macintosh platforms, the Computer Study Modules include all the discrete-point exercises from the textbook. You can use this computerized study aid for reinforcement and practice of grammar and vocabulary or as an additional preparation for exams. Your answers will be checked by the program.

CD-ROM

The *Einfach toll!* CD-ROM is a self-study learning tool: you can use it at home or in the language lab to hone your listening skills. Based on one or two video clips, each module begins with comprehension activities, then moves to more complex manipulation activities, and concludes with a creative, freeform activity. Cultural notes within each module provide additional background information on the material presented in the video clips.

CLASSROOM EXPRESSIONS

Below is a list of common classroom expressions in German (with English equivalents) which the instructor may use. Also provided are common expressions you can use to make comments or requests and ask questions.

Terms of praise and disapproval

Gut. Das ist (sehr) gut.   Good. That is (very) good.

Schön. Das ist (sehr) schön.   Nice. That is (very) nice.

Ausgezeichnet.   Excellent.

Wunderbar.   Wonderful.

Das ist schon besser.   That's better.

Viel besser.   Much better.

Nicht schlecht.   Not bad.

Richtig.   Right.

Natürlich.   Of course.

Genau.   Exactly.

Sind Sie/Bist du sicher?   Are you sure?

Nein, das ist nicht (ganz) richtig.   No, that's not (quite) right.

Ein Wort ist nicht richtig.   One word isn't right.

Nein, das ist falsch.   No, that's wrong.

Sie haben/Du hast mich nicht verstanden. Ich sage es noch einmal.   You didn't understand me. I'll say it again.

Sie haben/Du hast den Satz (das Wort) nicht verstanden.   You didn't understand the sentence (the word).

Sagen Sie/Sag (Versuchen Sie/Versuch) es noch einmal bitte.   Say (Try) it again please.

General instructions

Nicht so laut bitte.   Not so loud please.

Würden Sie/Würdet ihr bitte genau zuhören.   Would you please listen carefully.

Stehen Sie/Steht bitte auf.   Stand up please.

Bilden Sie/Bildet einen Kreis.   Form a circle.

Arbeiten Sie/Arbeitet einen Moment mit Partnern.   Work for a minute with partners.

Bringen Sie/Bringt (Bilder) von zu Hause mit.   Bring (pictures) along from home.

(Morgen) haben wir eine Klausur.   (Tomorrow) we're having a test.

Schreiben Sie/Schreibt jetzt bitte.   Please write now.

Lesen Sie/Lest jetzt bitte.   Please read now.

Ich fange (Wir fangen) jetzt an.   I'll (We'll) begin now.

Fangen Sie/Fangt jetzt an.   Begin now.

Hören Sie/Hört bitte auf zu schreiben (lesen).   Please stop writing (reading).

Könnte ich bitte Ihre/eure Aufsätze (Klassenarbeiten, Tests, Übungsarbeiten, Hausaufgaben) haben?   Could I please have your essays (tests, tests, exercises, homework)?

Jeder verbessert seine eigene Arbeit.   Everyone should correct her or his own work (paper).

Verbessern Sie Ihre/Verbessere deine Arbeit bitte.   Please correct your work (paper).

Tauschen Sie mit Ihrem/Tausch mit deinem Nachbarn.   Exchange with your neighbor.

Machen Sie/Macht die Bücher auf (zu).   Open (Shut) your books.

Schlagen Sie/Schlagt Seite (11) in Ihrem/eurem Buch auf.   Turn to page (11) in your book.

Schauen Sie/Schaut beim Sprechen nicht ins Buch.   Don't look at your book while speaking.

Wiederholen Sie/Wiederholt den Satz (den Ausdruck).   Repeat the sentence (the expression).

Noch einmal bitte.   Once again please.

(Etwas) Lauter. (Deutlicher./Langsamer./Schneller.)   (Somewhat) Louder. (Clearer./Slower./Faster.)

Sprechen Sie/Sprich bitte deutlicher.   Please speak more distinctly.

(Jan), Sie/du allein.   (Jan), you alone.

Alle zusammen.   All (everybody) together.

Sprechen Sie/Sprecht mir nach.   Repeat after me.

(Nicht) Nachsprechen bitte.   (Don't) Repeat after me.

Hören Sie/Hört nur zu./Nur zuhören bitte.   Just listen.

Hören Sie/Hört gut zu.   Listen carefully.

Lesen Sie/Lies den Satz (den Absatz) vor.   Read the sentence (the paragraph) aloud.

Jeder liest einen Satz.   Everyone should read one sentence.

Fangen Sie/Fang mit Zeile (17) an.   Begin with line (17).

Nicht auf Seite (19), auf Seite (20).   Not on page (19), on page (20).

Gehen Sie/Geh an die Tafel.   Go to the board.

(Jan), gehen Sie/gehst du bitte an die Tafel?   (Jan), will you please go to the board?

Wer geht an die Tafel?   Who will go to the board?

Schreiben Sie/Schreib den Satz (das Wort) an die Tafel.   Write the sentence (the word) on the board.

Schreiben Sie/Schreibt ab, was an der Tafel steht.   Copy what is on the board.

Wer weiß es (die Antwort)?   Who knows it (the answer)?

Wie sagt man das auf deutsch (auf englisch)?   How do you say that in German (in English)?

Auf deutsch bitte.   In German please.

Verstehen Sie/Verstehst du die Frage (den Satz)?   Do you understand the question (the sentence)?

Ist es (zu) schwer (leicht)?   Is it (too) difficult (easy)?

Sind Sie/Seid ihr fertig?   Are you finished?

Kommen Sie/Komm (morgen) nach der Stunde zu mir.   Come see me (tomorrow) after class.

Jetzt machen wir weiter.   Now let's go on.

Jetzt machen wir was anderes. Now let's do something different.

Jetzt beginnen wir was Neues. Now let's begin something new.

Das ist genug für heute. That's enough for today.

Hat jemand Fragen? Does anyone have a question?

Haben Sie/Habt ihr Fragen? Do you have any questions?

Student responses and questions

Das verstehe ich nicht. I don't understand that.

Das habe ich nicht verstanden. I didn't understand that.

Ah, ich verstehe. Oh, I understand.

Ich weiß es nicht. I don't know (that).

Wie bitte? *(Said when you don't catch what someone said.)* Pardon./Excuse me?/I'm sorry.

Wie sagt man ... auf deutsch (auf englisch)? How do you say . . . in German (in English)?

Können Sie den Satz noch einmal sagen bitte? Can you repeat that please?

Kann sie/er den Satz wiederholen bitte? Can she/he repeat the sentence please?

Ich habe kein Papier (Buch). I don't have any paper (a book).

Ich habe keinen Bleistift (Kuli). I don't have a pencil (a pen).

Auf welcher Seite sind wir? Welche Zeile? Which page are we on? Which line?

Wo steht das? Where is that?

Ich habe eine Frage. I have a question.

Was haben wir für morgen (Montag) auf? What do we have due for tomorrow (Monday)?

Sollen wir das schriftlich oder mündlich machen? Should we do that in writing or orally?

Wann schreiben wir die nächste Arbeit? When do we have the next paper (written work)?

Wann schreiben wir den nächsten Test? When do we have the next test?

Für wann (sollen wir das machen)? For when (are we supposed to do that)?

Ist das so richtig? Is that right this way?

(Wann) Können Sie mir helfen? (When) Can you help me?

(Wann) Kann ich mit Ihnen sprechen? (When) Can I see you?

ACKNOWLEDGMENTS

The authors and publisher of *Deutsch heute, Sixth Edition,* would like to thank Renate Gerulaitis (Oakland University) for her careful reading of the manuscript. Her suggestions for idiomatic and stylistic changes, as well as cultural content have been invaluable. We are also grateful to Wolfgang Adolph (Educational Consultant) for his never-failing willingness to research cultural information and especially for his contributions to the readings. We also owe a large debt of gratitude to Alice Pfeiffer *(Bundeshandelsakademie Bregenz)* for providing cultural information about Germany, Austria, and Switzerland. This current information is reflected in the *Land und Leute* notes on these three countries.

We wish to thank especially Barbara Lasoff (Developmental Editor), who has once again guided the development of a revision of *Deutsch heute* with patience and skill. This new edition reflects in countless ways her critical judgment, insights, and editorial expertise. We are especially grateful to Barbara for her untiring efforts and devotion to the project, for they have made the timely publication of the text possible.

The authors would also like to express their appreciation to the following Houghton Mifflin editorial, art, and design staff and freelancers for their technical and creative contributions to the text: Kristina Baer, Sponsoring Editor, for her support and encouragement of the project; Linda Hadley, art editor, for her tireless efforts in finding the appropriate art; Uli Gersiek, graphics; Harriet C. Dishman and her associates at Elm Street Publications who managed the production process so well; Hildegunde Kaurisch, for her expert writing of new cultural notes *(Land und Leute)* and revision of old ones; Kirk Smith for preparing end vocabulary; Karen Hohner (copyeditor), who always discovers things the rest of us have overlooked; and Gertrud Rath-Montgomery (proofreader).

Finally we wish to thank the following people for their thorough and thoughtful review of the Fifth Edition of *Deutsch heute.* Their comments and suggestions were invaluable during the development of the Sixth Edition.

Edwin P. Arnold, Clemson University, SC

Todd C. Hanlin, University of Arkansas-Fayetteville, AR

Jeffrey L. High, University of Massachusetts-Amherst, MA; Elms College, MA, and Holyoke Community College, MA

Doreen Krueger, Concordia University, WI

Sieglinde Lug, University of Denver, CO

Mark Pearson, Cottey College, MO

Roberta Schmalenberger, Clark College, WA

Barbara Starcher, Memorial University, Newfoundland

Friederike von Schwerin-High, University of Massachusetts-Amherst, MA

Studenten nach der Vorlesung. (München)

Kapitel 1

L E R N Z I E L E *(Goals)*

■ Sprechintentionen *(Functions)*

Asking for and giving personal information: name, age, address, telephone number
Introducing oneself
Spelling
Working with numbers
Asking what day it is
Asking about colors

■ Land und Leute *(The Country and Its People)*

Writing German addresses
Registering and studying at a German university
Making and receiving telephone calls
The telephone system in the Federal Republic of Germany

■ Vokabeln *(Vocabulary)*

The alphabet
Numbers
Days of the week
Objects in a student's room
Colors

■ Grammatik *(Grammar)*

Gender of nouns
Pronouns
Noun-pronoun relationship

BAUSTEINE FÜR GESPRÄCHE

(Building Blocks for Conversation)

The dialogues in this section will help you acquire a stock of idiomatic phrases that will enable you to participate in conversations on everyday topics.

Wie heißt du?

What is your name?

While at the art department to sign up for an excursion to Florence with her art history class, Gisela runs into Alex, who is in the same class but whom she has never really met. After chatting briefly, Gisela and Alex decide to meet before the trip. Then Gisela goes into the office to sign up for the trip to Florence.

Vorm schwarzen Brett

ALEX: Ich heiße Alex. Und du – Wie heißt du?

GISELA: Ich heiße Gisela.

ALEX: Ach ja. Und deine Telefonnummer?

GISELA: 71 63 54. (Einundsiebzig, dreiundsechzig, vierundfünfzig.) Und wie ist deine Nummer?

ALEX: 34 79 01. (Vierunddreißig, neunundsiebzig, null, eins.)

GISELA: Wie bitte?

ALEX: 34 79 01.

GISELA: O.K. Also, tschüs, dann.

In front of the bulletin board

My name is Alex. How about you— What is your name?

My name is Gisela.

Oh yes. And your telephone number?

71 63 54. And what is your telephone number?

34 79 01.

I beg your pardon?

34 79 01.

O.K. Well, so long then.

Wie heißen Sie?

What is your name?

Gisela is next in line. She goes into the office to sign up for the excursion to Florence.

Im Büro

SEKRETÄRIN: Bitte? Wie heißen Sie?

GISELA: Gisela Riedholt.

SEKRETÄRIN: Wie schreibt man das?

GISELA: R-i-e-d-h-o-l-t.

SEKRETÄRIN: Und Ihre Adresse?

GISELA: Bahnhofstraße 10 (zehn), 79117 (neunundsiebzig, eins, eins, sieben) Freiburg.

SEKRETÄRIN: Danke, Frau Riedholt.

GISELA: Bitte.

In the office

Can I help you? What is your name?

Gisela Riedholt.

How do you spell (write) that?

R-i-e-d-h-o-l-t.

And your address?

10 Bahnhofstraße, 79117 Freiburg.

Thank you, Ms. Riedholt.

You're welcome.

Brauchbares   *(Something useful)*

1. How does the address (i.e., the position of the house number, the street name, and the postal code) in Germany differ from where you live?
2. Note that the telephone numbers are stated as double digits. The first two digits in the postal code are generally stated as a single number; each of the remaining digits is spoken individually.
3. **Bitte** has several English equivalents. Name three.
4. Words in different languages that are related in spelling and meaning and are derived from the same source language are called *cognates*. The words are often pronounced differently. There are hundreds of German–English cognates because the two languages have common roots. Name three cognates in the dialogues.

Activities preceded by this symbol give you the opportunity to speak with fellow students about your personal feelings and experiences and to learn how to exchange ideas and negotiate in German, either one on one or as a group. The sentences and expressions to be used by one of the partners or members of a group are in the left column; the responses to be used by the other partner or members of a different group are in the right column. Substitute your own words for those in brackets.

New vocabulary is indicated by a raised degree mark (°). The definitions of these words are found in the vocabulary lists in the sections called **Vokabeln.** In this chapter the **Vokabeln** section is on pages 16–17. Beginning with *Kapitel 2* the chapters have two **Vokabeln** sections—one in the **Bausteine für Gespräche** section and one in the reading section.

When you say or write something, you have a purpose in mind. In this sense there is a certain linguistic function or intention you are stating or performing, such as exchanging information (e.g., identifying or asking for information), evaluating (e.g., praising, criticizing), expressing emotions (e.g., pleasure, dissatisfaction), getting something done (e.g., asking for help, giving permission), using social conventions (e.g., greeting, excusing oneself). To help you know when to use the words, phrases, or sentences you are learning, the purpose or function is given in the margin.

1. Wie heißt du?   Get acquainted with members of your class. Introduce yourself to your fellow students and ask what their names are.

Getting acquainted

StudentIn° 1 (S1):   *StudentIn 2 (S2):*

Ich heiße [Dieter]. Wie heißt du?   Ich heiße [Barbara].

2. Heißt du Sarah?   See how well you remember the names of at least four fellow students. If you're wrong they will correct you.

Confirming information

StudentIn 1 (S1):   *StudentIn 2 (S2):*

Heißt du [Mark Schmidt]?   Ja°.
Du heißt [Monika], nicht°?   Nein°. Ich heiße [Karin].

3. Wie heißen Sie?   Ask your instructor for her/his name.

Asking someone's name

StudentIn: *Herr°/Frau Professor°:*
Wie heißen Sie?   Ich heiße [Lange].

Erweiterung des Wortschatzes   *(Vocabulary Expansion)*

This vocabulary expansion section contains commonly used words and phrases
that supplement those found in the dialogues **(Bausteine für Gespräche)** and
in the readings beginning in *Kapitel 2*. You are expected to learn these words
so that you will understand them in new contexts and be able to use them to
express your own thoughts. The new words and phrases in the **Erweiterung
des Wortschatzes** are included in the list of words that appear in the vocabulary sections **(Vokabeln)**.

1 The subject pronouns *du* and *Sie*

Wie heißt **du**?   What is your name? (What are *you* called?)
Wie ist **deine** Telefonnumer?   What is *your* telephone number?

Du is equivalent to *you* and is used when addressing a relative, close friend,
or person under approximately fifteen years of age. Members of groups such
as students, athletes, laborers, and soldiers also address each other as **du.** It is
used when talking to one person and is referred to as the familiar form. The
word for *you* used to address more than one friend, relative, etc., will
be explained in *Kapitel 2*.

Stuttgarts Postleitzahlen beginnen alle mit 70–.

Land und Leute

Postleitzahlen

In Germany postal codes **(Postleitzahlen)** have
five digits and in Austria and Switzerland four.
Large cities have several postal codes, each
one designating a specific district of that city.
German postal codes reveal the geographic
location of a town or city. A postal code
beginning with 2 indicates a location in
northern Germany, e.g., **27765 Hamburg.** A
postal code that begins with 8 indicates a
location in southern Germany, e.g., **80802
München.** As you noticed in the **"Wie heißen
Sie"** dialogue on page 2, German postal codes
appear before the city or town. The same is
true for Austria and Switzerland, e.g., **1080
Wien, 8027 Zürich.**

Dein(e) is equivalent to *your*. It is used with a person to whom you say **du.**

Wie heißen **Sie?**   What is your name? (What are *you* called?)
Wie ist **Ihre** Adresse?   What is *your* address?

Sie is also equivalent to *you* but is a more formal form of address, and is used when addressing a stranger or adult with whom the speaker is not on intimate terms. **Sie** is used when speaking to one person or to more than one person.

Ihr(e) is equivalent to *your* and is used with a person to whom you say **Sie.** In writing, **Sie** and **Ihr(e)** are capitalized.

Dein and **Ihr** modify masculine and neuter nouns. **Deine** and **Ihre** modify feminine nouns. See the section on Gender of nouns on pages 11–12 of this chapter.

2 Das Alphabet

The German alphabet has 26 regular letters and 4 special letters. They are pronounced as follows:

a ah	**g** geh	**l** ell	**q** kuh	**v** fau	**ä** äh (a-Umlaut)
b beh	**h** hah	**m** emm	**r** err	**w** weh	**ö** öh (o-Umlaut)
c tseh	**i** ih	**n** enn	**s** ess	**x** iks	**ü** üh (u-Umlaut)
d deh	**j** jot	**o** oh	**t** teh	**y** üppsilon	**ß** ess-tsett
e eh	**k** kah	**p** peh	**u** uh	**z** tsett	
f eff					

Capital letters are indicated by **groß: großes B, großes W.** Lower-case letters are indicated by **klein: kleines b, kleines w.**

▷◁ **1. Wie schreibt man das?**   Ask your instructor or a fellow student for her/his name. Then ask how to spell it. (Use the **Sie**-form in speaking with your instructor: **Wie heißen Sie?**)

Asking for information

▶ Wie heißt du?   *Mark Fischer.*
▶ Wie schreibt man das?   *Emm-ah-err-kah. Eff-ih-ess-tseh-hah-eh-err.*

2. Abkürzungen. *(Abbreviations.)*   Pronounce the following abbreviations and have your partner write them down.

1. Pkw (= Personenkraftwagen, *official word for automobile, e.g., on signs*)
2. VW (= Volkswagen)
3. BMW (= Bayerische Motorenwerke)
4. ADAC (= Allgemeiner Deutscher Automobil-Club)
5. WC (= Wasserklosett; *toilet*)
6. USA (= U.S.A.)
7. CDU (= Christlich-Demokratische Union)
8. FDP (= Freie Demokratische Partei)
9. SPD (= Sozialdemokratische Partei Deutschlands)
10. EU (= Europäische Union)

3.   Wie schreibt man das?   Spell the name of your hometown for your partner. See if she/he can tell where you are from.

Providing information

4. Schreiben Sie das. *(Write that.)*   Spell several German words to a partner who will write them down. Then reverse roles. You may use the words listed or choose your own.

tschüs □ danke □ bitte □ Adresse □ Telefonnummer

3 Die Zahlen von 1 bis 1.000

0 = null	10 = zehn	20 = zwanzig	30 = dreißig
1 = eins	11 = elf	21 = einundzwanzig	40 = vierzig
2 = zwei	12 = zwölf	22 = zweiundzwanzig	50 = fünfzig
3 = drei	13 = dreizehn	23 = dreiundzwanzig	60 = sechzig
4 = vier	14 = vierzehn	24 = vierundzwanzig	70 = siebzig
5 = fünf	15 = fünfzehn	25 = fünfundzwanzig	80 = achtzig
6 = sechs	16 = sechzehn	26 = sechsundzwanzig	90 = neunzig
7 = sieben	17 = siebzehn	27 = siebenundzwanzig	100 = hundert
8 = acht	18 = achtzehn	28 = achtundzwanzig	101 = hunderteins
9 = neun	19 = neunzehn	29 = neunundzwanzig	1.000 = tausend

Note the following irregularities:

1. **Eins** *(one)* becomes **ein** when it combines with the twenties, thirties, and so on: **einundzwanzig, einunddreißig.**
2. **Dreißig** *(thirty)* ends in **-ßig** instead of the usual **-zig.**
3. **Vier** *(four)* is pronounced with long [ī], but **vierzehn** *(fourteen)* and **vierzig** *(forty)* are pronounced with short [i].
4. **Sechs** *(six)* is pronounced [ẹeks], but **sechzehn** *(sixteen)* and **sechzig** *(sixty)* are pronounced [ẹeç-].
5. **Sieben** *(seven)* ends in **-en,** but the **-en** is dropped in **siebzehn** *(seventeen)* and **siebzig** *(seventy).*
6. **Acht** *(eight)* is pronounced [axt], but the final **t** fuses with initial **ts** in **achtzehn** *(eighteen)* and **achtzig** *(eighty).*
7. Numbers in the twenties, thirties, and so on follow the pattern of the nursery rhyme "four-and-twenty blackbirds":
   24 = **vierundzwanzig** *(four-and-twenty)*
   32 = **zweiunddreißig** *(two-and-thirty)*
8. German uses a period instead of a comma in numbers over 999. German uses a comma instead of a period to indicate decimals.

German	*English*
1.000 g (Gramm)	1,000 g
4,57 m (Meter)	4.57 m

9. Simple arithmetic:
   Addition (**+ = und**): **Fünf und drei ist acht.**
   Subtraction (**− = weniger**): **Fünf weniger drei ist zwei.**
   Multiplication (× or • = **mal**): **Fünf mal drei ist fünfzehn.**
   Division (÷ = [**geteilt**] **durch**): **Fünfzehn durch drei ist fünf.**

⟩ **5. Rechnen.** *(Doing arithmetic.)*   Find a partner. On a piece of paper each of you writes out five simple mathematical problems. Read your five problems to your partner and let her/him solve them; then solve your partner's five problems.

Using numbers

S1:

S2:

Wieviel° ist drei und zwei [3 + 2]?

Drei und zwei ist fünf.

Wieviel ist zehn weniger acht [10 − 8]?

Zehn weniger acht ist zwei.

⟩ **6. Deine Adresse? Deine Telefonnummer? Rollenspiel.** *(Role-play.)*
Imagine you have a job checking names for the telephone directory. Ask at least three of your fellow students for their names, phone numbers, and addresses. Then get the same information from your instructor. Remember to use **Ihre** with your instructor. Also be sure to say thank you.

Asking for personal information

S1:

S2:

Wie heißt du?

[Julia Meier].

Wie ist deine Telefonnummer?

[652-9846].

Wie ist deine Adresse?

[Park Road zehn].

Danke.

Bitte.

Land und Leute

Die Universität

The academic year at a German university has two terms: the **Wintersemester,** from mid-October to mid-February; and the **Sommersemester,** from mid-April to mid-July. Students must register each semester. The first time a student registers is called **Immatrikulation;** any subsequent registration is a **Rückmeldung.** Courses taken by the student are listed in an official transcript book (**Studienbuch),** which the student is responsible for, along with certificates signed by a professor to acknowledge the student's presence and success in the seminar (**Seminarscheine).** German students do not pay tuition, but they are required to pay a small administrative fee every time they register, and to have health insurance (**Krankenversicherung).** An ID card (**Studentenausweis)** enables a student to use university facilities such as the library and the cafeteria (**Mensa)** and to get reductions on theater and museum tickets, certain club memberships, and public transportation.

☞   **7.   Wie ist die Telefonnummer von ... ?**   At the right is part of a page from the Bonn telephone directory. The letters in parentheses indicate districts of Bonn and towns in the greater Bonn area. Note that German telephone books contain titles and professions. For example, **Neubauer, Uwe Dr.** has a doctor title and is probably a Ph.D.; **Neuber, Bruno Dr.** also has a doctor title and is a dentist, as indicated by the word **Zahnarzt; Neubauer, Heinz** is an engineer (**Ing. = Ingenieur**). **Str.** is the abbreviation for **Straße**.

Ask your partner for the addresses and phone numbers of people listed on this page of the telephone book. Exchange roles after three names.

☞   **8.   Wie alt bist du?°**   Find out the ages of four fellow students. Be sure you know their names. Write down the information.

S1:   *S2:*

Wie alt bist du?   Ich bin [19] Jahre alt.

9.   Ich heiße ...   Introduce yourself to the class by giving the information mentioned in the model.

▶   Ich heiße _____ . Ich bin _____ Jahre alt. Meine° Adresse ist _____ .
Meine Telefonnummer ist _____ .

☞   **10.   Gespräche.** *(Conversations.)*   With a partner express the following exchange of information in German. One of you should be student 1 (S1), the other, student 2 (S2). Once you have finished, exchange roles and start again from the beginning.

A

S1: Ask S2 for her/his name.
S2: Say in German: "My name is . . ."
S1: Ask S2 to repeat it.
S2: Repeat your name.
S1: Ask S2 how to spell it.
S2: Spell your last name.

B

S1: Find out S2's telephone number.
S2: Give your telephone number.
S1: Find out S2's address.
S2: Give your address, but remember to do it the German way.

C

S1: Ask S2 how old she/he is.
S2: Answer. (You may give a "creative" response if you like.) Ask S1 how old she/he is.
S1: Answer. (Feel free to give a "creative" response.)

Neubauer Harald	65 08 02
Rosental 25	
Neubauer Heinz	21 67 83
Ing.grad. Remposstr, 1	
Neubauer Heinz	32 38 87
(Bgo) Kantstr.8	
Neubauer Helmut	32 26 00
(Bgo) Tulpenbaumweg 10	
Neubauer Hermann	32 38 29
(Bgo) Akazienweg 21	
Neubauer Ines	61 22 25
1 Bahnhofstr.99	
Neubauer J.	61 45 74
Mohrstr.26	
Neubauer Josef	64 22 96
(Dui) Europaring 24	
Neubauer Karl	47 55 00
Beuel HeinrichHeineStr.27	
Neubauer Klaus	47 36 77
Beuel Geislarstr.124	
Neubauer Maria	45 00 68
(Ndk) Langgasse 91	
Neubauer Rainer	64 06 65
(Alf) Oberdorf 47	
Neubauer Sabine	67 41 70
Friedlandstr.62	
Neubauer Uwe Dr.	31 32 42
(Bgo) DechantHeimbachStr.21	
Neubauer Wilhelm	31 68 79
(Bgo) EltvillerStr.16	
Neubauer Wolf	69 14 28
1 Wolfstr.37	
Neubeck Hans Frhr.	32 35 13
von (Bgo) Rotdornweg 83	
Neuber Bruno Dr.	45 03 05
Zahnarzt	
(Ndk) Provinzialstr.103	

Asking someone's age

Land und Leute

Das Telefon

Before 1995 the telephone system in Germany was government-owned, a division of the Federal Post Office **(Bundespost)**. Today it is a public corporation—**Deutsche Telekom**.

Public telephones in Germany operate on a coin-operated message-unit system that automatically calculates charges for local or long-distance calls. Local calls cost a minimum of 30 Pfennig. Calls outside the immediate area require both an area code **(Vorwahl)** and additional 10 Pfennig, 1 Mark, or 5 Mark coins. Every post office maintains public telephones. These are either coin-operated, or one pays for the call at the counter. Phone numbers in Germany can vary in length. The following are examples of telephone numbers of two businesses in Munich: 52 60 96 and 2 18 36 75.

Plastic, non-recyclable debit cards for a specific amount of telephone charges **(Telefonkarten)** can be purchased at the post office or telephone office and used in special phones. Environmentalists have opposed these cards because their disposal adds to environmental problems. Yet, because of their varied designs, these cards have become collector's items and are traded like American baseball cards.

Germans usually identify themselves at once when they answer the phone. Callers also give their names before asking for the person they are trying to reach.

Whereas people who want to end a telephone conversation formally say **Auf Wiederhören** (literally: *Until we hear each other again*), friends typically use an informal **Tschüs** (*So long*) to say good-bye. For example:

Die neuen Telefonzellen sind nicht mehr gelb.

—Ingrid Breimann.
—Hier ist Gerda. Kann ich bitte mit Thomas sprechen?
—Hallo, Gerda. Thomas ist nicht zu Hause. Er spielt heute Fußball.
—Ach ja, richtig. Ich rufe am Montag wieder an. Bis dann, Ingrid.
—Tschüs.

—Ingrid Breimann.
—This is Gerda. Can I speak to Thomas, please?
—Hi, Gerda. Thomas is not at home. He's playing soccer today.
—Oh, that's right. I'll call back on Monday. Till later, Ingrid.
—So long.

4 Die Wochentage

Welcher Tag ist heute?	What day is it today?
Heute ist Montag.	Today is Monday.
Dienstag	Tuesday
Mittwoch	Wednesday
Donnerstag	Thursday
Freitag	Friday
Samstag *(in southern Germany)*	Saturday
Sonnabend *(in northern Germany)*	
Sonntag	Sunday

Monday (**Montag**) is considered the first day of the week in German-speaking countries. As a result, calendars begin with **Montag** rather than **Sonntag.**

11. Welcher Tag ist heute?   Ask a fellow student what day it is today.

▶ Welcher Tag ist heute?   *Heute ist [Mittwoch].*

12. Hat Dennis am° Mittwoch Deutsch? *(Does Dennis have German on Wednesday?)*   Say that the following people have German a day later than your friend thinks.

▶ Hat Dennis am Mittwoch Deutsch?   *Nein, am Donnerstag.*

1. Hat Claudia am Montag Deutsch?
2. Hat Rebecca am Donnerstag Deutsch?
3. Hat Thomas am Dienstag Deutsch?
4. Hat Kevin am Freitag Deutsch?

Junge Leute sagen fast immer „du" zueinander. (Universität Frankfurt)

5 Gender of nouns

Masculine	Neuter	Feminine
the man ← he	the baby ← it	the woman ← she
	the day ← it	
	the word ← it	
	the address ← it	

Every English noun belongs to one of three genders: masculine, neuter, or feminine. The gender of a singular English noun shows up in the choice of the pronoun that is used to refer back to it.

The English type of gender system is one of natural gender. Nouns referring to male beings are masculine. Nouns referring to female beings are feminine. Nouns referring to young beings (if thought of as still undifferentiated as to sex) are neuter, and all nouns referring to inanimate objects are also neuter. (*Neuter* is the Latin word for *neither,* i.e., neither masculine nor feminine.)

Like English, German generally uses a system of natural gender for nouns that refer to living beings. Unlike English, however, German also makes gender distinctions in nouns that do not refer to living beings. This type of gender system is one of grammatical gender.

Masculine	Neuter	Feminine
der Mann° ← er	das Kind° ← es	die Frau ← sie
der Tag ← er	das Wort° ← es	die Adresse ← sie

In German there are three groups of nouns: masculine (**der**-nouns), neuter (**das**-nouns), and feminine (**die**-nouns). The definite articles **der, das,** and **die** function like the English definite article *the.* Most nouns referring to males are **der**-nouns (**der Mann** = *man*), most nouns referring to females are **die**-nouns (**die Frau** = *woman*), and nouns referring to young beings are **das**-nouns (**das Kind** = *child*). Note that **der Junge°** (= *boy*) is a **der**-noun, but **das Mädchen°** (= *girl*) is a **das**-noun because all words ending in **-chen** are **das**-nouns. Other nouns belong to any one of the three groups: **der Tag, das Wort, die Adresse.**

■ *Signals of gender*

Like English, German signals the gender of a noun in the choice of the pronoun that is used to refer back to it: **er** is masculine, **es** is neuter, and **sie** is feminine. Unlike English, however, German also signals gender in the choice of the definite article that precedes a noun: **der** is masculine, **das** is neuter, and **die** is feminine.

The article is the most powerful signal of gender. You should always learn a German noun together with its definite article, because there is no simple way of predicting the gender of a particular noun.

6 Ein Studentenzimmer *(A student's room)*

Learn the following nouns:

1. der **Bleistift**
2. der **CD-Spieler**
3. der **Computer**
4. der **Fernseher**
5. der **Kugel-
   schreiber**
   (der **Kuli**)
6. der **Stuhl**
7. der **Tisch**

8. das **Bett**
9. das **Bild**
10. das **Buch**
11. das **Bücherregal**
12. das **Fenster**
13. das **Heft**
14. das **Kassettendeck**
15. das **Papier**
16. das **Poster**
17. das **Radio**
18. das **Telefon**
19. das **Zimmer**

20. die **Büchertasche**
21. die **Gitarre**
22. die **Lampe**
23. die **Pflanze**
24. die **Tür**
25. die **Uhr**
26. die **Wand**

*5 sentences that describe the room

13. **Groß oder klein?**   Sabine is going to help you arrange your room. She asks whether certain pieces of furniture are large **(groß)** or small **(klein).** Respond.

▶ Ist das Zimmer groß oder klein?   *Das Zimmer ist [groß].*

1. Ist das Fenster groß oder klein?
2. Ist das Bett groß oder klein?
3. Ist der Fernseher groß oder klein?
4. Wie ist der Stuhl?
5. Ist die Pflanze groß oder klein?
6. Wie ist die Uhr?
7. Und die Lampe?
8. Und der Tisch?
9. Und das Bücherregal?
10. Wie ist die Büchertasche?

14. Alt oder neu?　Tell your partner whether various things in your room are new **(neu)** or old **(alt)**.

▶ Computer　*Der Computer ist [neu].*

1. Fernseher
2. Bett
3. Lampe
4. CD-Spieler
5. Radio

6. Büchertasche
7. Buch
8. Kugelschreiber
9. Bild
10. Poster

7 Pronouns

Wie alt ist **Mark?**　How old is Mark?
Er ist zwanzig.　He is twenty.

A **pronoun** is a part of speech that designates a person, place, thing, or concept. It functions as a noun does. A pronoun can be used in place of a noun or a noun phrase.

8 Noun-pronoun relationship

Der Mann ist groß.	**Er** ist groß.	He is tall.
Der Stuhl ist groß.	**Er** ist groß.	It is large.
Das Kind ist klein.	**Es** ist klein.	She/He is small.
Das Zimmer ist klein.	**Es** ist klein.	It is small.
Die Frau ist groß.	**Sie** ist groß.	She is tall.
Die Lampe ist groß.	**Sie** ist groß.	It is large.

In German the pronouns **er, es,** and **sie** may refer to persons or things. In English the singular pronoun referring to things *(it)* is different from those referring to persons *(she, he)*.

　　Note that in referring to people, **groß** means *tall* and **klein** means *short* or *small*. In referring to things, **groß** means *large* or *big* and **klein** means *small* or *little*.

15. Wie ist das Zimmer?　Tanja is seeing your room for the first time since you made some changes. She's trying to sort out which things are new and which are old. Respond, using a pronoun instead of the noun.

▶ Ist der Tisch neu?　*Ja, er ist neu.*

1. Ist der Stuhl alt?
2. Ist die Uhr neu?
3. Ist das Radio alt?
4. Ist die Pflanze neu?
5. Ist die Lampe alt?

6. Ist die Büchertasche neu?
7. Ist das Poster neu?
8. Ist der Computer neu?
9. Ist der Fernseher alt?
10. Ist das Kassettendeck neu?

16. Groß, klein, alt. With your partner look at the pictures of people and try to decide whether they are tall, short, or old. To get each other's opinions ask the questions below.

S1: Ist die Frau alt?
S2: Nein, sie ist nicht alt.

S1:

1. Ist das Kind groß?
2. Ist der Mann alt?
3. Ist das Mädchen klein?

S2:

4. Ist der Junge groß?
5. Ist die Frau groß?
6. Ist das Kind klein?

9 Die Farben *(Colors)*

The following sentences should help you remember the colors.

Der Ozean ist **blau.**

Das Gras ist **grün.**

Die Schokolade ist **braun.**

Die Tomate ist **rot.**

Die Banane ist **gelb.**

Der Asphalt ist **schwarz.**

Die Maus ist **grau.**

Das Papier ist **weiß.**

17. Welche° Farbe? *(What Color?)* Ask your partner the colors of five items in the student room on page 12. Your partner will then ask you the color of five items.

To ask what color something is one asks:

▶ Welche Farbe hat [der Stuhl]?   *What color is [the chair]?*

To answer the question one says:

▶ [Der Stuhl] ist [braun].   *[The chair] is [brown].*

18. Welche Farbe hat ... ? Point to an object in the classroom and ask your partner what the color of the item is.

▶ Welche Farbe hat [die Wand]?   *[Die Wand] ist [weiß].*

Describing things

Vokabeln *(Vocabulary)*

The vocabulary sections in each chapter contain the words and phrases that you are expected to learn actively. You should be able to understand them in many contexts and use them to express your own thoughts.

In English, proper nouns like *Monday* or *America* are capitalized, but not common nouns like *address* or *street*. In German, all nouns are capitalized: proper nouns like **Montag** or **Amerika** as well as common nouns like **Adresse** and **Straße**. Unlike English, German does not capitalize proper adjectives.

Compare the following: **amerikanisch**   American
                          englisch   English
                          deutsch   German

The German pronoun **Sie** (you *formal*) and the possessive adjective **Ihr** (your *formal*) are capitalized in writing. The pronoun **ich** (I) is not capitalized.

Substantive *(Nouns)*

die **Adresse**   address
das **Bett**   bed
das **Bild**   picture; photo
der **Bleistift**   pencil
das **Buch**   book
das **Bücherregal**   bookcase
die **Büchertasche**   book bag
der **CD-Spieler**   CD player
der **Computer**   computer
(das) **Deutsch**   German
der **Dienstag**   Tuesday
der **Donnerstag**   Thursday
die **Farbe**   color
das **Fenster**   window
der **Fernseher**   television set
die **Frau**   woman; **Frau**   Mrs., Ms.
   (term of address for adult women)
der **Freitag**   Friday
der **Garten**   garden
die **Gitarre**   guitar
das **Heft**   notebook
der **Herr**   gentleman; **Herr**   Mr.
   (term of address)
das **Jahr**   year
der **Junge**   boy
das **Kassettendeck**   cassette deck
das **Kind**   child
der **Kugelschreiber** (der **Kuli,** *collo-quial*)   ballpoint pen
die **Lampe**   lamp
das **Mädchen**   girl
der **Mann**   man

der **Mittwoch**   Wednesday
der **Montag**   Monday
die **Nummer**   number
das **Papier**   paper
die **Pflanze**   plant
das **Poster**   poster
der **Professor** *(m.)* / die **Professorin** *(f.)*
   professor
das **Radio**   radio
der **Samstag** *(in southern Germany)*
   Saturday
der **Sekretär** *(m.)* / die **Sekretärin** *(f.)*
   secretary
der **Sonnabend** *(in northern Germany)*
   Saturday
der **Sonntag**   Sunday
die **Straße**   street
der **Student** *(m.)* / die **Studentin** *(f.)*
   student
der **Stuhl**   chair
der **Tag**   day
das **Telefon**   telephone
die **Telefonnummer**   telephone
   number
der **Tisch**   table
die **Tür**   door
die **Uhr**   clock, watch
die **Wand**   wall
die **Woche**   week
das **Wort**   word
die **Zahl**   number, numeral
das **Zimmer**   room

Verben *(Verbs)*

bin / ist / sind am / is / are
hast / hat / haben have / has / have

heißen to be named, to be called
schreiben to write

Andere Wörter *(Other words)*

ach oh
also well
alt old
bitte please; you're welcome (*after* **danke**)
blau blue
braun brown
da there
danke thanks
dann then
das that; the (*neuter*)
dein(e) your (*familiar*)
der the (*masculine*)
die the (*feminine*)
du you (*familiar*)
er he, it
es it
gelb yellow
[geteilt] durch divided by (*in division*)
grau gray
groß large, big; tall (*people*)
grün green
heute today
ich I
Ihr(e) your (*formal*)
ja yes

klein small; short (*people*)
mal times (*in multiplication*)
man one, people
mein(e) my
nein no
neu new
nicht? (*tag question*) don't you? isn't it?; **Du heißt (Sie heißen) [Monika], nicht?** Your name is [Monika], isn't it?
rot red
schwarz black
sie she, it
Sie you (*formal*)
so so; this way
tschüs so long, good-bye (*informal*)
und and; plus (*in addition*)
von of
wann when
weiß white
welch (-er, -es, -e) which
weniger minus (*in subtraction*)
wie how
wieviel how much
For the numbers 1–1000, see p. 6.

Besondere Ausdrücke *(Special expressions)*

am [Freitag] on [Friday]
Bitte? May I help you?
Du heißt (Sie heißen) [Mark], nicht? Your name is [Mark], isn't it?
Ich bin 19 Jahre alt. I'm 19 years old.
Welche Farbe hat ... ? What color is . . . ?
Welcher Tag ist heute? What day is today?
(Wie) bitte? (I beg your) pardon.
Wie alt bist du (sind Sie)? How old are you?

Wie alt ist ... ? How old is . . . ?
Wie heißt du (heißen Sie)? What's your name?
Wie ist deine (Ihre) Adresse? What's your address?
Wie ist deine (Ihre) Telefonnummer? What is your telephone number?
Wie ist die Telefonnummer von [Clemens Neumann]? What is [Clemens Neumann's] telephone number?
Wie schreibt man das? How do you spell that? (*literally*: How does one write that?)

WIEDERHOLUNG

(Review)

The **Wiederholung** is a review section in which you will have the opportunity to work again with the content, vocabulary, and structures of the current chapter and earlier chapters.

1. Studentenzimmer zu vermieten! *(Student room to rent!)*   The ad below advertises a room that is for rent. You don't have to understand every word in order to get the information you need. Read the ad and answer the following questions.

Studentenzimmer
zu vermieten!

Kleines Zimmer, großes Fenster: Fünf Minuten zur Universität.
Bett, Tisch, zwei Stühle, Bücherregal.
DM 450,- im Monat. Kurt Riedl, Schellingstraße 56, 80142 München. Tel.: 34 20 19

1. Ist das Zimmer groß oder klein?
2. Wie ist das Fenster? Groß oder klein?
3. Im Zimmer ist ein° _____ , ein _____ , ein _____ und zwei _____ .
4. Wie heißt der Vermieter°?
5. Wie ist die Adresse?
6. Wie ist die Telefonnummer?

°a
°landlord

2. Die Galerie.   Now that you have a room, you need a place to eat out occasionally. Tell what you know about the Galerie by completing the following sentences.

Die Galerie
Musik-Café
Bar
Restaurant

Der Superbrunch
jeden Sonntag
Live Musik
10-15 Uhr
Preis 20,50 DM pro Person
Schillerstr. 15
Tel. 19 57 93

1. Die Galerie ist ein _____ , eine _____ und ein _____ .
2. Der Superbrunch ist jeden° _____ .   every
3. Die Musik ist _____ .
4. Die Adresse ist _____ .
5. Die Telefonnummer ist _____ .

3. Zum Schreiben *(To be written)*

1. **Mein Zimmer.**   Identify fifteen items in your room. List them by gender. Then describe five of the items using full sentences.

▶ der Stuhl   *Der Stuhl ist braun. Er ist nicht groß.*

2. **Fragen.** *(Questions.)*   While a student at the university in Hamburg in Germany, you are involved in a minor automobile accident. You need to get the name, address, telephone number, and age of the driver of the other vehicle. Write down the questions you would ask to obtain this information.

Sagen diese Frauen „Sie" zueinander? (Ostdorf bei Balingen)

Kapitel 2

L E R N Z I E L E

■ **Sprechintentionen**

Greeting people formally
Greeting friends
Saying good-bye
Asking people how they are
Expressing likes and dislikes
Asking about personal plans
Asking what kind of person someone is
Expressing agreement and disagreement
Describing people
Telling time
Making plans

■ **Lesestück** *(Reading)*

Eine Studentin in Berlin

■ **Land und Leute**

Regional greetings and farewells
Staying in shape
Appropriate use of *du* and *Sie*
The role of sports in German-speaking countries

■ **Vokabeln**

Descriptive adjectives
Sports
Telling time

■ **Grammatik**

Pronouns and nouns as subjects
Three forms for *you:* **du, ihr, Sie**
The verb **sein**
Regular verbs
Expressing likes and dislikes with **gern**
Negation with **nicht**
Expressing future time with the present tense
Asking informational and yes/no questions
Tag questions

BAUSTEINE FÜR GESPRÄCHE

Wie geht's?

In der Bibliothek

HERR LANGE: Guten Morgen, Frau Kluge. Wie geht es Ihnen?

FRAU KLUGE: Guten Morgen, Herr Lange. Gut, danke. Und Ihnen?

HERR LANGE: Danke, ganz gut.

Im Hörsaal

ALEX: Hallo, Gisela.

GISELA: Grüß dich, Alex. Wie geht's?

ALEX: Ach, nicht so gut.

GISELA: Was ist los? Bist du krank?

ALEX: Nein, ich bin nur furchtbar müde.

How are you?

In the library

Good morning, Ms. Kluge. How are you?

Good morning, Mr. Lange. Fine, thanks. And you?

Thanks, not bad.

In the lecture hall

Hi, Gisela.

Hello, Alex. How are you?

Oh, not so well.

What's wrong? Are you sick?

No, I'm just terribly tired.

Brauchbares

In *Kapitel 1* you learned that the German words for *you* are **Sie** or **du**. In the phrases **Wie geht es Ihnen?** and **Und dir?, Ihnen** and **dir** are again different forms of *you*.

1. Guten Tag. Greet different people in the class. Choose a time of day and greet your partner, who responds appropriately.

> Greeting someone

S1:

Guten Morgen.
Guten Tag.°
Guten Abend.°

S2:

Morgen.
Tag.
Abend.
Hallo.
Grüß dich.

2. Wie geht's? Find a partner and role-play a scene between you and a friend or a professor. Assume you haven't seen your friend or the professor for several days and you run into her/him in the cafeteria. Say hello and ask how she/he is. See the top of page 23 for help in getting started.

> Asking people how they are

S1:

Hallo, [Tanja]. Wie geht's?
Guten Tag, Herr/Frau Professor°,
  wie geht es Ihnen?

S2:

Gut, danke°. (Und dir?°/Und
  Ihnen?°)
Danke, ganz gut.
Es geht.°
Nicht so gut.
Schlecht°.
Ich bin krank.
Ich bin müde.

Auf Wiedersehen auf dem Hauptbahnhof in Frankfurt.

Land und Leute

Guten Tag

Adults in German-speaking countries often greet each other with a handshake. When one is first introduced or in a formal situation a handshake is expected. Greetings vary depending on the region and the speakers.

Expressions for greeting each other:

Guten Morgen/Morgen *(informal)*
Guten Tag/Tag *(informal)*
Grüß Gott *(southern Germany, Austria)*
Grüezi *(Switzerland)*
Grüß dich *(informal; southern Germany, Austria)*
Salut *(informal; Switzerland)*
Servus *(informal; southern Germany, Austria)*
Guten Abend/n'Abend *(informal)*

Expressions for saying good-bye:

(Auf) Wiedersehen
(Auf) Wiederschauen
Tschüs *(informal)*
Adieu
Ciao *(informal)*
Ade *(informal; southern Germany, Austria)*
Servus *(informal; southern Germany, Austria)*
Salut *(informal; Switzerland)*
Gute Nacht *(at bedtime)*

Was machst du gern?

PHILIPP: Was machst du heute abend?

LINDA: Nichts Besonderes. Musikhören oder so. Vielleicht gehe ich ins Kino.

PHILIPP: Hmm. Spielst du gern Schach?

LINDA: Schach? Ja. Aber nicht so gut.

PHILIPP: Ach komm, wir spielen zusammen, ja?

LINDA: Na gut! Wann?

PHILIPP: Um sieben?

LINDA: O.K. Bis dann.

What do you like to do?

What are you doing tonight?

Nothing special. Listening to music or something like that. Maybe I'll go to the movies.

Hmm. Do you like to play chess?

Chess? Yes. But not so well.

Ah come on, we'll play together, O.K.?

All right. When?

At seven?

O.K. See you then.

das Aerobic; Aerobic machen

der Fußball; Fußball spielen

das Schach; Schach spielen

das Tennis; Tennis spielen

die Karten; Karten spielen

das Tischtennis; Tischtennis spielen

der Basketball; Basketball spielen

das Computerspiel; Computerspiel spielen

der Volleyball; Volleyball spielen

das Gewichtheben; Gewichte heben

das Videospiel; Videospiel spielen

das Golf; Golf spielen

das Jogging; joggen

When sample sentences in activities have one or more words in **boldface type,** you should replace those words in subsequent sentences with the new words provided.

3. Was spielst du gern?   Find out which activities your partner likes to do. Then respond to her/his questions. You may want to refer to the Supplementary Word Sets in the Reference Section.

Expressing likes and dislikes

S1:

Spielst du	**gern**	Schach?
	gut	
	oft°	
	viel°	

S2:

Ja. Und du?
Ja. Du auch°, nicht?
Nein. Und du?
Nein. Aber du, nicht?

4. Treibst du gern Sport?   A fellow student asks whether you like to engage in sports. Respond as in the model.

S2:

Treibst du gern Sport°?

Machst du viel Sport?

S1:

| Ja. Ich | **schwimme° gern.** |
| | wandere° gern. |

Nein. Ich mache nicht viel Sport.
Nein. Ich hebe° Gewichte.

5. Was machst du?   Think about what you are going to do today. Ask a few classmates what they are going to do in their free time. They will ask you in turn.

Asking about personal plans

S1:

Was machst du	**heute**	**morgen°?**
	heute	nachmittag°?
	heute	abend°?
	am [Montag]?	

S2:

Ich	**arbeite°.**
	mache Deutsch°.
	mache Aerobic°.
	spiele Tennis.
	höre° Musik°.
	gehe ins Kino.
	gehe tanzen°.
	gehe Jogging°.

6. Ich mache das.   Report to the class four things you do or don't do. Use **gern, viel, oft, nicht gern, nicht viel, nicht oft.**

Reporting

▶ *Ich spiele [nicht] viel Schach.*

„Gesund durch Fitneßtraining" – das glauben viele.

Land und Leute

Fit bleiben

Many people in the German-speaking countries love to go hiking **(wandern)** and walking **(spazierengehen)**. There are well-maintained trails everywhere. Some are no more than paths through local scenic spots or city parks, while others are part of a vast complex of trails.

Swimming is also a popular activity. In addition to seashore and lakeside beaches, town pools—both indoors and outdoors—provide ample opportunity for swimming. An outdoor pool **(Freibad),** with a nominal admission fee, is generally located on the outskirts of a city. It is often large and surrounded by grassy areas. People come with food and blankets to spend the day picnicking, swimming, and playing volleyball or badminton. In many cities, public indoor pools **(Hallenbäder)** have developed into public spas, offering saunas, hot tubs, massages, swimming lessons, snack bars, hair salons, and exercise machines besides several large swimming and diving pools.

One can find health clubs **(Fitneßcenter)** in most cities. There one can play squash **(Squash)** or work out **(Fitneßtraining),** which includes weightlifting **(Gewichtheben)** and aerobics **(Aerobic).**

Erweiterung des Wortschatzes

1 Was für ein Mensch sind Sie?

The following adjectives can be used to characterize people. Some of them have English cognates and can be guessed easily.

intelligent	intelligent	**nett**	nice
fleißig	industrious	**freundlich**	friendly
faul	lazy	**unfreundlich**	unfriendly
froh	happy	**tolerant**	tolerant
lustig	cheerful	**kritisch**	critical
ruhig	quiet, calm	**praktisch**	practical
ernst	serious	**natürlich**	natural

musikalisch – musical
Sportlich – sporty

1. **Frage-Ecke.** *(Question corner.)*   Below are two charts (labeled S1 and S2) with the names and characteristics of several people. Each chart has information that the other doesn't have. Without looking at your partner's chart, ask questions to determine the characteristics of the people on your chart for whom no information is given. Your partner will do the same.

Asking what kind of person someone is and describing someone

S2: Was für ein Mensch ist Lisa?
S1: Sie ist fleißig und nett.

S1:

Lisa	fleißig	nett
Philipp		
Nadine	tolerant	natürlich
Laura		
Michael	ernst	kritisch
Stefan		

S2:

Lisa		
Philipp	ruhig	freundlich
Nadine		
Laura	praktisch	ruhig
Michael		
Stefan	intelligent	unfreundlich

2. **Was für ein Mensch?**   Ask three students what kind of person they are. Then report on your findings. You may want to refer to the Supplementary Word Sets in the Reference Section.

Asking and reporting

S1: Was für ein Mensch bist du?
S2: Ich bin lustig.
S1: [Frank] ist lustig.

3. **Ja oder nein?**   In groups of three, ask your partners whether they agree with your opinions of certain people. One of them agrees, but the other doesn't and corrects your opinions with an opposite adjective. You may want to refer to the Supplementary Word Sets in the Reference Section.

Expressing agreement and disagreement

S1: [Margit] ist sehr° ernst, nicht?/Ist [Margit] sehr ernst?
S2: Ja, sehr.
S3: Nein, ich glaube nicht°. Sie° ist sehr lustig.

2 Telling time

The following methods are used to express clock time.

Wieviel Uhr ist es?°
Wie spät ist es?° } What time is it?

	Method 1	Method 2
1.00 Uhr	Es ist eins.	Es ist eins.
	Es ist ein Uhr.	Es ist ein Uhr.
1.05 Uhr	Es ist fünf (Minuten) nach eins.	Es ist ein Uhr fünf.
1.15 Uhr	Es ist Viertel nach eins.	Es ist ein Uhr fünfzehn.
1.25 Uhr	Es ist fünf (Minuten) vor halb zwei.	Es ist ein Uhr fünfundzwanzig.
1.30 Uhr	Es ist halb zwei.	Es ist ein Uhr dreißig.
1.35 Uhr	Es ist fünf nach halb zwei.	Es ist ein Uhr fünfunddreißig.
1.45 Uhr	Es ist Viertel vor zwei.	Es ist ein Uhr fünfundvierzig.
1.55 Uhr	Es ist fünf (Minuten) vor zwei.	Es ist ein Uhr fünfundfünfzig.
2.00 Uhr	Es ist zwei Uhr.	Es ist zwei Uhr.

Note that German uses a period instead of a colon in time expressions.

German has two ways to indicate clock time. With a few exceptions, they parallel the two ways English indicates clock time.

Method 1 Es ist Viertel nach acht.   It's a quarter past eight.
Method 2 Es ist acht Uhr fünfzehn.   It's eight-fifteen.

In conversational German, method 1 is used to indicate time. Notice that the **-s** of **eins** is dropped before the word **Uhr.** The expression with **halb** indicates the hour to come, not the preceding hour: **halb zwei = 1.30 Uhr.**

In official time, such as train and plane schedules and concerts, method 2 is used.

Mein Zug fährt um **7.30 Uhr [7 Uhr 30].**   My train leaves at 7:30 A.M.
Das Konzert beginnt um **19.30 Uhr [19**   The concert begins
  Uhr 30].   at 7:30 P.M.

Official time is indicated on a 24-hour basis.

Um wieviel Uhr spielen wir Tennis?   (At) what time are we playing tennis?
Um halb neun.   At 8:30.

German uses **um** + a time expression to ask or speak about the specific hour at which something will or did take place.

Wann spielen wir Tennis?   *When* are we playing Tennis?
Morgen. Um 8.30 Uhr.   Tomorrow. At 8:30.

The question word **wann** *(when)* can imply a request for a specific time (e.g., **um 8.30 Uhr**) or a general time (e.g., **morgen**).

4. Wie spät ist es?   A friend asks you what time it is. Respond using the times listed below, in German.

▶   2.00 Uhr   *Es ist zwei.*

1. 3.00 Uhr   3. 11.45 Uhr   5. 4.55 Uhr
2. 6.15 Uhr   4. 1.20 Uhr   6. 2.30 Uhr

5. Nein, später°!   Say that it is ten minutes later than your friend thinks it is.

▶   Ist es 8 Uhr?   *Nein, später! Es ist zehn nach acht.*

1. 12.00 Uhr   4. 4.20 Uhr   6. 8.40 Uhr
2. 1.05 Uhr   5. 5.30 Uhr   7. 9.45 Uhr
3. 2.10 Uhr

6. Rollenspiel. *(Role-play.)*   You and a friend have planned to do some things together on Friday, Saturday, and Sunday. Your friend can't remember when you're supposed to do what together, but you can tell her/him by consulting the list below.

> Discussing a schedule

Freitag

16.30 Uhr   Fußball spielen
19.30 Uhr   ins Kino gehen

Samstag

10.00 Uhr   Tennis spielen
21.30 Uhr   tanzen gehen

Sonntag

11.45 Uhr   schwimmen gehen
15.00 Uhr   wandern gehen

S1: Um wieviel Uhr/Wann ... ?
S2: Wir [gehen] um [halb neun] ...

1. gehen wir Freitag ins Kino?
2. gehen wir Samstag abend tanzen?
3. spielen wir Samstag nachmittag Tennis?
4. spielen wir Freitag Fußball?
5. gehen wir Sonntag wandern?
6. gehen wir schwimmen?

7. Giselas Terminkalender. *(Appointment calendar.)*   Tell what Gisela's plans are by consulting her calendar and answering the questions.

1. Welcher Tag ist heute?
2. Wann hat Gisela Deutsch?
3. Um wieviel Uhr ist Gisela in der Bibliothek?
4. Wann spielen Gisela und Alex Tennis?

5. Geht Gisela um 1 Uhr schwimmen?
6. Arbeitet sie um 5 Uhr?
7. Wann geht Gisela ins Kino?

EINE STUDENTIN IN BERLIN

Vorbereitung auf das Lesen   *(Preparation for reading)*

Beginning with this one, each chapter of *Deutsch heute* contains a reading section. The readings are designed to broaden your knowledge and familiarity with the culture, customs, history, and current life in Germany, Austria, and Switzerland.

Each reading is accompanied by pre-reading and post-reading activities. In the pre-reading activity, called **Vor dem Lesen** *(Before reading),* you will be asked to think about what you already know about the reading topic or about what information and vocabulary you would expect to encounter in a reading on the topic at hand. **Vor dem Lesen** may also include a visual (e.g., an ad or photo) for you to interpret as a way to stimulate your thinking about the upcoming reading. In the second pre-reading section activity, called **Beim Lesen** *(While reading),* you will find suggestions for things to look for as you work through the text. In the post-reading section, called **Nach dem Lesen** (*After reading*), activities such as **Fragen zum Lesestück** (*Questions about the reading*) help you check your comprehension and express your own views on the reading topic.

In the **Vor dem Lesen, Beim Lesen,** and **Nach dem Lesen** exercises, German words that are new and that you should learn and be able to use are followed by a raised degree mark°. These words and their definitions are listed in the **Vokabeln** section following the reading. Other unfamiliar words are defined in the margin.

The reading in this chapter is a letter Christin Stettner has written to her friends, Maria and Volker. Christin is from a small town in Germany and has recently moved to Berlin to study English at the university.

■ *Vor dem Lesen*

1. What would you write about your college or university and your living arrangements in your first letter to friends?
2. Glance at the form of the letter and compare it to that of a personal letter you might write. What is in the first line of the letter? What is the English equivalent of **liebe/lieber?**

■ *Beim Lesen*

1. Circle or make a list of the cognates in the letter.
2. Underline or make a list of the numbers in the letter.

Berlin, 6. Oktober°   6. Oktober: read as **den sechsten Oktober**

Liebe Maria und lieber Volker,

wie geht's? Berlin ist interessant, aber sehr groß. Meine neue Adresse ist Lepsiusstraße 27, 12163 Berlin, und meine Telefonnummer ist 030/791°   791: read as **neunundsiebzig eins** or **sieben einundneunzig**
5 23 44. Mein Zimmer ist nicht schlecht, vielleicht ein bißchen klein, aber die Universität ist furchtbar groß und hat viele Studenten.

Mein Nachbar heißt Jürgen und kommt aus° München. Er studiert auch   from
Englisch. Heute ist Samstag, und er arbeitet bis Viertel nach zwei. Ich mache nichts Besonderes, aber heute nachmittag gehen wir zusammen schwimmen
10 und heute abend tanzen. Jürgen ist sehr fleißig, freundlich und lustig, und ich glaube, er ist auch sehr intelligent und tolerant. Jedenfalls° ist er furchtbar nett.   at any rate

Viele Grüße
Eure° Christin   yours

Nach dem Lesen   *(After reading)*

1. Fragen zum Lesestück. *(Questions about the reading.)*   Answer the following questions about the reading.

1. Wie ist Christins Adresse? Wie ist die Postleitzahl?
2. Wie ist Christins Telefonnummer? Wie ist die Vorwahl für Berlin?
3. Wie ist Christins Zimmer?
4. Wie ist die Universität?
5. Was für ein Mensch ist Jürgen?
6. Was macht Jürgen heute?

2. Ergänzen Sie. *(Complete.)*   Complete the following sentences using information from the text.

1. Christins Zimmer ist ein bißchen klein aber _____ .
2. Christin glaubt, Jürgen ist _____ .
3. Heute abend gehen Christin und Jürgen _____ .
4. Die Universität _____ .
5. Christin und Jürgen studieren _____ .

3. Beschreiben Sie. *(Describe.)*   Give a brief description in German of each of the following items.

1. Berlin
2. Christins Zimmer
3. Jürgen

4. Erzählen Sie. *(Tell.)*

1. Using vocabulary from the letter, write down words or phrases that you can use when talking about the following topics in German.

   a. mein Zimmer
   b. meine Universität
   c. ein Freund° oder eine Freundin°   friend *(m.)*/friend *(f.)*

2. Using the words and phrases that you wrote down in 1, have a conversation with another student about the topics. Begin by writing two questions that you can ask your partner.

Vokabeln

Substantive

der **Abend**   evening
das **Aerobic**   aerobics
der **Basketball**   basketball
die **Bibliothek**   library
das **Computerspiel**   computer game
(das) **Deutsch**   German language
(das) **Englisch**   English language
   (academic subject)
die **Frage**   question
der **Fußball**   soccer
das **Gewichtheben**   weight lifting;
   Gewichte heben   to lift weights
das **Golf**   golf
das **Jogging**   jogging; **Jogging gehen**
   to go jogging
die **Karte**   card; postcard; die **Karten**
   (pl.)   (playing) cards
das **Kino**   movie theater
der **Mensch**   person, human being

die **Minute,** die **Minuten** *(pl.)*
   minute
der **Morgen**   morning
die **Musik**   music
der **Nachbar** *(m.)*/die **Nachbarin** *(f.)*
   neighbor
der **Nachmittag**   afternoon
die **Nacht**   night
der **Professor** *(m.)*/die **Professorin**
   (f.)   professor
das **Schach**   chess
der **Sport**   sport; **Sport treiben**
   to engage in sports
das **Tennis**   tennis
das **Tischtennis**   table tennis, Ping-
   Pong
die **Universität**   university
das **Videospiel**   video game
der **Volleyball**   volleyball

Verben

arbeiten   to work; to study
gehen   to go
glauben   to believe
hören   to hear; to listen to
joggen   to jog
kommen   to come
machen   to do; to make
schwimmen   to swim
sein   to be

spielen   to play
studieren   to study; to attend college
tanzen   to dance
wandern   to hike; to go walking

Andere Wörter

aber   but, however
auch   also
bis   until, till
bißchen: ein bißchen   a little
ein(e)   a, an
ernst   serious
faul   lazy
fleißig   industrious, hard-working
freundlich   friendly
froh   happy
furchtbar   terrible; very
ganz   complete, whole; very; **ganz
   gut**   not bad, O.K.
gern   gladly, willingly; *used with
   verbs to indicate liking, as in* **Ich
   spiele** *gern* **Tennis.**
gut   good, well; fine
halb   half
hallo   hello
heute abend   this evening
heute morgen   this morning
heute nachmittag   this afternoon
ihr   you *(familiar pl.)*
intelligent   smart, intelligent
interessant   interesting
krank   sick, ill
kritisch   critical
lieb- (-er, -e)   dear
lustig   merry, cheerful
müde   tired
nach   after
natürlich   natural
nett   nice
nicht   not
nichts   nothing

nur   only
oder   or
oft   often
praktisch   practical
ruhig   calm, easy-going, quiet
schlecht   bad, badly
sehr   very (much)
sie   she, they
so   so
spät   late; **später**   later
tolerant   tolerant
um   at; **um zehn Uhr**   at ten o'clock
unfreundlich   unfriendly
viel   much
vielleicht   maybe, perhaps
vor   before
wann   when
was   what
was für (ein)   what kind of (a)
wer   who
wir   we
zusammen   together

Besondere Ausdrücke

Auf Wiedersehen   good-bye
bis dann   see you then
Es geht.   O.K.; Not bad.; All right.
Grüß dich   hi
Gute Nacht   good night
Guten Abend/Abend   good evening
Guten Morgen/Morgen   good
   morning
Guten Tag/Tag   hello
halb   half; **halb zwei**   one-thirty
Ich glaube nicht.   I don't think so.
   Ich glaube ja.   I think so.
Ich mache Deutsch.   I'm doing
   German homework.
in der Bibliothek   in the library
ins Kino   to the movies
Musikhören   listening to music
Na gut!   All right.
nicht (wahr)? *(tag question)*   don't
   you? isn't he? isn't that so?, etc.
nichts Besonderes   nothing special
O.K.   okay, O.K.
um [sieben] Uhr   at [seven] o'clock
Um wieviel Uhr?   At what time?
Und dir?   And you? (How about
   you?) *(familiar)*

Und Ihnen?   And you? (How about
   you?) *(formal)*
viele Grüße *(closing in a letter)*
   regards
Viertel nach   quarter after
Viertel vor   quarter of, quarter to
Was ist los?   What's wrong?
Wie geht es Ihnen?   How are you?
Wie geht's?   How are you? *(literally:*
   How's it going?)
Wie spät ist es?   What time is it?
Wieviel Uhr ist es?   What time is it?

Doof bleibt doof, da helfen keine Pillen!
(Stupid remains stupid. No pills can cure that.)

GRAMMATIK UND ÜBUNGEN

(Grammar and Exercises)

1 Subject pronouns

Singular *(sg.)*	Plural *(pl.)*
1. **ich** I	**wir** we
2. **du** you	**ihr** you
(familiar sg.)	*(familiar pl.)*
3. **er** he, it	
es it	**sie** they
sie she, it	
Sie you *(formal, sg. and pl.)*	

A personal pronoun is said to have "person," which indicates the identity of the subject.

1. First person refers to the one(s) speaking *(I, we)*.
2. Second person refers to the one(s) spoken to *(you)*.
3. Third person refers to the one(s) or thing(s) spoken about *(he/it/she, they)*.

2 The subject pronouns *du, ihr, Sie*

Tag, Julia. ... Was machst **du?**
Tag, Lisa. Tag, Gerd! ... Was macht **ihr?**

In *Kapitel 1* (p. 4) you learned when to use the familiar form **du. Du** is used to address one person. The familiar form used to address more than one person is **ihr.**

Tag, Herr Wagner. ... Was machen **Sie?**
Tag, Frau Braun. Tag, Fräulein Schneider! ... Was machen **Sie?**

In *Kapitel 1* (p. 5) you learned when to use the formal form **Sie.** Like the English *you,* **Sie** can be used to address one person or more than one.

3 The meanings and use of *sie* and *Sie*

Glaubt **sie** das?	Does *she* believe that?
Glauben **sie** das?	Do *they* believe that?
Glauben **Sie** das?	Do *you* believe that?

In spoken German, the meanings of **sie** *(she),* **sie** *(they),* and **Sie** *(you)* can be distinguished by the corresponding verb forms and by context. In written German, **Sie** *(you)* is always capitalized.

sie + singular verb form = *she*
sie + plural verb form = *they*
Sie + plural verb form = *you* (formal)

14

Sagen diese Studenten „du" oder „Sie" zueinander? (Universität Frankfurt)

Land und Leute

Du vs. *Sie*

Historically speaking, **sie sind** *(they are)* and **Sie sind** *(you are)* are the same form. It was considered polite to address someone in the third-person plural and to capitalize the pronoun in writing.

The development of formal pronouns to address a person was a phenomenon common to most European languages. English used to distinguish singular *thou/thee* from plural *ye/you; thou/thee* was restricted to informal usage, and *ye/you* was used both as informal plural and formal singular and plural. Today only *you* survives as our all-purpose pronoun. In German (as well as in other European languages such as French, Spanish, and Italian) there are still distinctions between the formal and informal pronouns for *you.*

The formal pronoun **Sie** is used for everyday communication outside the realm of family and friends. Even neighbors and coworkers address each other as **Sie** (they **siezen**). **Du** (along with its plural form **ihr**) is traditionally a form of address used among relatives or close friends. An older person usually decides on the appropriateness of this form in speaking to someone younger. Most young people address each other with **du** (they **duzen**) nowadays. A step somewhere between **du** and **Sie** is to use a first name and **Sie.** This form of address expresses intimacy and respect at the same time, and is often a "warm-up" for the less formal, more friendly **duzen.**

1 Ich, du, er. Give the subject pronouns you would use in the following situations.

▶ You're talking about a female friend.   *sie*
▶ You're talking to a female friend.   *du*

1. You're talking about a male friend.
2. You're talking to a male friend.
3. You're talking about yourself.
4. You're talking about yourself and a friend.
5. You're talking to your parents.
6. You're talking to a clerk in a store.

7. You're talking about your father.
8. You're talking about your sister.
9. You're talking about a child.
10. You're talking to your professor.
11. You're talking about your friends.

4 Present tense of *sein*

sein	
ich **bin**	wir **sind**
du **bist**	ihr **seid**
er/es/sie **ist**	sie **sind**
Sie **sind**	

to be	
I am	we are
you are	you are
he/it/she is	they are
you are	

The verb **sein,** like its English equivalent *to be,* is irregular in the present tense.

2 Intelligente Menschen.   Say that the persons listed below are intelligent in their political views.

▶   Melanie   *Melanie ist intelligent.*

1. Gerd
2. du
3. Monika und Günter
4. Professor Schneider
5. ich
6. wir
7. Jens und Nadine
8. Frau Müller
9. ihr
10. das Kind

3. So ist sie/er.   Your partner will point to a person in one of the photos below and on page 39 and ask you what adjectives you would apply to that person.

> Surmising

S1: Was für ein Mensch ist die Frau?
S2: Sie ist intelligent, aber faul.

5 Infinitive

Infinitive	Stem + ending	English equivalents
glauben	glaub + en	*to believe*
heißen	heiß + en	*to be named*
arbeiten	arbeit + en	*to work; to study*
wandern	wander + n	*to hike; to go walking*

The basic form of a verb (the form listed in dictionaries and vocabularies) is the infinitive. German infinitives consist of a stem and the ending **-en** or **-n.**

6 The finite verb

Andrea **arbeitet** viel.   Andrea *works* a lot.
Arbeitest du viel?   *Do* you *work* a lot?

The term "finite verb" indicates the form of the verb that agrees with the subject.

7 Present tense of regular verbs

glauben	
ich glaub**e**	wir glaub**en**
du glaub**st**	ihr glaub**t**
er/es/sie glaub**t**	sie glaub**en**
Sie glaub**en**	

to believe	
I believe	we believe
you believe	you believe
he/it/she believes	they believe
you believe	

In the present tense, most English verbs have two different forms; most German verbs have four different forms.

The present tense of regular German verbs is formed by adding the endings **-e, -st, -t,** and **-en** to the infinitive stem. The verb endings change according to the subject. (Note that a few verbs like **wandern** add only **-n** instead of **-en: wir wandern.**) In informal spoken German, the ending **-e** is sometimes dropped from the **ich**-form: **Ich glaub' das nicht.**

jung = young

Gisela **spielt** gut Tennis.
Frank und Alex **spielen** gut Basketball.

With a singular noun subject **(Gisela)** the verb ending is **-t.** With a plural noun subject **(Frank und Alex)** the verb ending is **-en.**

arbeiten: to study; to work	
ich arbeite	wir arbeiten
du arbeit**est**	ihr arbeit**et**
er/es/sie arbeit**et**	sie arbeiten
Sie arbeiten	

In regular English verbs, the third-person singular ending is usually -s: *she works*. After certain verb stems, however, this ending expands to -es: *she teaches*.

German also has verb stems that require an expansion of the ending. If a verb stem ends in **-d** or **-t,** the endings **-st** and **-t** expand to **-est** and **-et.** The other endings are regular.

heißen: to be called, named	
ich heiße	wir heißen
du heißt	ihr heißt
er/es/sie heißt	sie heißen
Sie heißen	

If a verb stem ends in a sibilant **(s, ss, ß, z),** the **-st** ending contracts to a **-t: du heißt, du tanzt.** The other endings are regular.

4. **Das ist gesund.** *(It's healthy.)* Many people believe that working a lot is healthy. Say that the following people believe it and that they work a lot.

▶ wir: *Wir glauben das. Wir arbeiten viel.*
▶ Franziska: *Franziska glaubt das. Franziska arbeitet viel.*

1. ich
2. sie *(pl.)*
3. er
4. sie *(sg.)*
5. wir
6. Herr Müller
7. du
8. Frau Schneider
9. Christin und Jürgen
10. ihr

8 The construction verb + *gern*

Ich spiele **gern** Tennis   I like to play tennis.
Ich spiele **nicht gern** Golf.   I don't like to play golf.

The most common way of saying in German that you like doing something is to use the appropriate verb + **gern.** To say that you don't like doing something, use **nicht gern.**

5. Und du, Uwe?   Uwe is telling about the things his friend Lore does. Ask whether he enjoys the same things. Begin your question with the verb.

▶   Lore treibt gern Sport.   *Treibst du auch gern Sport?*

1. Sie macht viel Sport.
2. Sie spielt auch gern Volleyball.
3. Sie schwimmt gern.
4. Lore spielt gut Schach.
5. Und sie hört gern Musik.
6. Sie arbeitet auch viel.
7. Sie wandert gern.
8. Sie geht gern ins Kino.
9. Sie tanzt gern.

6. Was für Musik hörst du gern?   Ask four fellow students what kind of music they like.

Stating preferences

S1: Was für Musik hörst du gern?
S2: Ich höre gern [Jazz].

Jazz   **Rock**   **Pop**   **Country und Western**   **Blues**   **Rap**   **Reggae**   **klassische Musik**

7. Was machst du?   State what various people are doing by using the cues in the columns below. Answer in complete sentences.

▶   Jürgen   *Jürgen macht viel Sport. Er geht gern ins Kino.*

1	2	3	4
ich	hören	gern	Sport
Linda und ich (wir)	machen	oft	Volleyball
Christin (sie)	spielen	viel	Musik
du	gehen	gut	ins Kino
Gisela und Alex (sie)			
ihr			
Jürgen (er)			

Land und Leute

Sportvereine

As mentioned on p. 27, in Germany, Austria, and Switzerland people of all ages engage in sports. In addition to hiking **(Wandern)**, walking **(Spazierengehen)**, and swimming **(Schwimmen)**, they enjoy soccer **(Fußball)**, calisthenics **(Gymnastik)**, and aerobic exercises **(Aerobic)**. School sports are intramural rather than intermural. Athletes are not recruited by schools, and athletic scholarships are uncommon. A person who wishes to participate in competitive sports can join a sports club **(Sportverein)**. In Germany alone there are approximately 63,000 clubs with about 20 million **Sportverein** members. Even the smallest village has its own **Verein**, which also plays an important part in the social life of the town. Millions of people participate in running **(Laufen)**, swimming **(Schwimmen)**, cycling **(Radfahren)**, skiing **(Skifahren)**, and hiking **(Wandern)** competitions every year. Those who win or finish are awarded badges of merit as a sign of personal accomplishment. However, for most people who play sports the primary purpose is not to win games but to be physically active and to be with people in a social setting.

Zwei Fußballvereine spielen gegeneinander. (Weimar)

Fußball is the most popular sport in the German-speaking countries. It is played by 4.8 million Germans, of whom approximately 75,000 are women, who play on more than a thousand women's teams. Germany also has a professional women's soccer league. The 16 federal states and local governments subsidize the **Sportvereine** and contribute to the construction of sports facilities for public use.

9 Position of *nicht*

The position of **nicht** is determined by various elements in the sentence.

Herr Wagner *arbeitet* **nicht.**	Mr. Wagner doesn't work.
Mark glaubt *Sophie* **nicht.**	Mark doesn't believe Sophie.
Ich glaube *es* **nicht.**	I don't believe it.
Arbeitest du *heute* **nicht?**	Aren't you working today?

Nicht always follows:

1. the finite verb (e.g., **arbeitet**)
2. nouns used as objects (e.g., **Sophie**)
3. pronouns used as objects (e.g., **es**)
4. specific adverbs of time (e.g., **heute**)

Lukas ist **nicht** *faul.*	Lukas is not lazy.
Das ist **nicht** *Frau Wagner.*	That is not Ms. Wagner.
Wir wandern **nicht** *oft.*	We don't hike much.
Wir gehen heute **nicht** *ins Kino.*	We're not going to the movies today.

Nicht precedes most other kinds of elements:

1. predicate adjectives (a predicate adjective is an adjective that completes the meaning of a linking verb; the most frequently used linking verb is **sein,** *to be:* e.g., Mark ist nicht **faul.**)
2. predicate nouns (a predicate noun is a noun that completes the meaning of a linking verb: e.g., Das ist nicht **Frau Wagner.**)
3. adverbs, including general time adverbs (e.g., nicht **oft,** nicht **sehr,** nicht **gern**)
4. prepositional phrases (e.g., nicht **ins Kino**)

Ich gehe **nicht** *oft ins Kino.*   I don't often go to the movies.

If several of the elements occur in a sentence, **nicht** usually precedes the first one.

8. Wir nicht.   Jutta, a new acquaintance, has some questions for you and Hans-Dieter. Answer in the negative.

▶   Macht ihr viel Sport?   *Nein. Wir machen nicht viel Sport.*

1. Spielt ihr viel Basketball?
2. Spielt ihr oft Tennis?
3. Schwimmt ihr gern?
4. Arbeitet ihr viel?
5. Arbeitet ihr gern?
6. Hört ihr gern Musik?
7. Wandert ihr viel?
8. Spielt ihr gern Tischtennis?
9. Tanzt ihr gern?

9. Volker aber nicht.   Veronika makes some observations about Volker and Maria. Say that she's right about Maria, but not Volker.

▶   Volker und Maria treiben gern Sport, nicht?   *Maria treibt gern Sport, Volker aber nicht.*

1. Volker und Maria machen viel Sport, nicht?
2. Sie schwimmen gut, nicht?
3. Sie arbeiten viel, nicht?
4. Sie arbeiten gern, nicht?
5. Sie spielen oft Schach, nicht?
6. Sie spielen sehr viel Videospiele, nicht?
7. Sie hören gern Musik, nicht?
8. Sie machen auch Musik, nicht?
9. Sie tanzen gern, nicht?

10. Und das machen sie gern.   Nicole and Gustav lead an active life. Say what they like to do.

▶   Arbeiten Nicole und Gustav viel in Bremen?   *Ja, und sie arbeiten gern in Bremen.*

1. Treiben Nicole und Gustav viel Sport?
2. Sind sie oft in Basel?
3. Spielen sie viel Schach?
4. Hören sie viel Musik?
5. Hören sie oft Radio?
6. Spielen sie viel Tischtennis?
7. Tanzen sie oft?
8. Gehen sie viel ins Kino?
9. Spielen sie oft Videospiele?

▷▷ **11. Was machst du gern?** With a partner, try to find two activities you both enjoy doing and two you both dislike doing.

Finding common likes and dislikes

S1: Ich schwimme gern. Schwimmst du auch gern?
S2: Ja, ich schwimme gern./Nein, ich schwimme nicht gern.
     Ich spiele gern Tennis. Spielst du gern Tennis?

10 Present-tense meanings

Linda **arbeitet** gut. = { Linda *works* well. (plain)
  Linda *does work* well. (emphatic)
  Linda *is working* well. (progressive)

German uses a single verb form to express ideas or actions that may require one of three different forms in English.

Du **gehst** heute nachmittag   You*'re going* swimming this afternoon,
   schwimmen, nicht?   aren't you?
Ich **mache** das morgen.   I*'ll do* that tomorrow.

German, like English, may use the present tense to express action intended or planned for the future.

12. Wie sagt man das? *(How do you say that?)* Give the German equivalents of the following sentences.

▶ Frank does not work well.   *Frank arbeitet nicht gut.*

1. Karla does work a lot.   6. I'm playing tennis today.
2. I do believe that.   7. We're playing basketball today.
3. Stefan does play soccer well.   8. I believe so.
4. You're working tonight, Hannah.   9. Detlev is going to the movies.
5. You do that well, Ursula.   10. I'm going dancing.

11 Informational questions

Wann gehst du schwimmen? ⌢   *When* are you going swimming?
Wer arbeitet heute nachmittag? ⌢   *Who* is working this afternoon?

A question that asks for a particular bit of information is called an informational question. It begins with an interrogative expression such as **wann** *(when)*, **was** *(what)*, **welch(-er, -es, -e)** *(which)*, **wer** *(who)*, **wie** *(how)*, and **was für (ein)** *(what kind of)*. The interrogative is followed by the verb. In an informational question in German, the finite verb is used. In English, a form of the auxiliary verb *to be* or *to do* is often used with a form of the main verb. In German, the voice normally falls at the end of an informational question, just as it does in English.

⇨ **13. Wer? Was? Wann?** Your partner has a list showing when various people are playing particular games. Ask your partner three questions, one beginning with **wer** (*who*), one with **was,** and one with **wann.**

Asking informational questions

S1: Wer spielt heute Squash?
S2: Barbara spielt heute Squash.
S1: Wann spielt ihr Volleyball?
S2: Wir spielen um halb sechs Volleyball.
S1: Was spielt Professor Krause?
S2: Er spielt Golf.

Wer?	Wann?	Was?
Barbara	heute	Squash
Anne und Kevin	um drei	Schach
ich	um acht	Fußball
Professor Krause	heute abend	Golf
wir	um halb sechs	Volleyball

12 Yes/No questions

Gehst du heute schwimmen? ⌄   *Are* you *going* swimming today?
Treiben Sie gern Sport? ⌄   *Do* you *like to play* sports?

A question that can be answered with yes or no begins with the verb. A yes/no question in German uses the finite verb, whereas English often requires a form of the auxiliary verb *to do* or *to be* plus a form of the main verb. In German, the voice normally rises at the end of a yes/no question, just as it does in English.

⇨ **14. Ja oder nein?** Ask your partner the following questions. Your partner will then ask you the same questions. At the end make up two more questions to ask each other.

Confirming or denying

S1: Arbeitest du heute abend?
S2: Ja, ich arbeite heute abend.
     Nein, ich arbeite heute abend nicht.

1. Schwimmst du gern?
2. Spielst du oft Basketball?
3. Treibst du gern Sport?
4. Spielst du gut Fußball?
5. Spielst du viel Volleyball?
6. Machst du viel Sport?
7. Wanderst du gern?
8. Gehst du heute abend ins Kino?
9. ?
10. ?

13 Tag questions

Du hörst gern Musik, **nicht wahr?**   You like to listen to music, *don't you?*

Mark geht heute abend ins Kino, **nicht?**   Mark is going to the movies tonight, *isn't he?*

A tag question is literally "tagged on" to the end of a statement. In English the tag equivalent to **nicht wahr?** or **nicht?** depends on the subject of the sentence: *don't you?*, *aren't you?*, *isn't he?*, and *doesn't she?*, etc.

15.   Nicht?   In a conversation with a friend, ask for confirmation that what you think is correct. Use the tag question **nicht?** or **nicht wahr?**

▶   Frau Meier ist sehr nett.   *Frau Meier ist sehr nett, nicht?*
Frau Meier ist sehr nett, nicht wahr?

1. Professor Wagner arbeitet viel.
2. Sie und ihr Mann wandern gern.
3. Jürgen ist oft müde.
4. Rita macht viel Sport.
5. Sie schwimmt gut.
6. Sie ist auch sehr intelligent.
7. Wir gehen heute abend ins Kino.
8. Wir gehen um sieben.

16.   Wie sagt man das?   You overhear someone on the phone talking with Ursula. Translate the questions for Dieter, your German friend.

▶   Ursula, how are you?   *Ursula, wie geht's?*

1. What are you doing, Ursula?
2. Are you working?
3. Are you going swimming today?
4. Is Rudi going also?
5. When are you playing tennis, Ursula?
6. Does Rudi play well?
7. What kind of person is Rudi?
8. Do you like to play chess?
9. Rudi likes to play, too, doesn't he?
10. You're coming at seven, aren't you?
11. When are Rudi and Beate going to the movies?

17.   Ein Interview.   You are looking for a new roommate. Write five questions you want to ask the person about her/his likes, dislikes, and activities. Then find a partner and conduct an interview.

WIEDERHOLUNG

1. Wer ist Linda? Read the information on Linda and answer the questions.

Linda ist 19 Jahre alt und Studentin in München. Sie ist sehr fleißig, nett und lustig. Heute ist Donnerstag, und Linda macht um 8.50 Uhr° Englisch. Um 10 Uhr spielt sie mit Philipp Tennis, und um 13 Uhr schwimmt sie. Zusammen mit Philipp, Alex und Gisela geht sie um 19.15 Uhr° ins Kino.

8.50 Uhr: spoken or read **acht Uhr fünfzig**

19.15 Uhr: spoken or read **neunzehn Uhr fünfzehn**

1. Wie alt ist Linda?
2. Wo studiert sie?
3. Was für ein Mensch ist Linda?
4. Welcher Tag ist heute?
5. Um wieviel Uhr macht sie Englisch?
6. Wer spielt mit Linda Tennis? Wann?
7. Wer geht mit Linda ins Kino? Wann?

2. Ja, Veronika. Confirm Veronika's information about you and your friends.

▶ Gabi arbeitet in Basel, nicht wahr? *Ja, sie arbeitet in Basel.*

1. Du arbeitest in Zürich, nicht?
2. Wolf hört gern Musik, nicht wahr?
3. Renate und Paula spielen gut Rock, nicht?
4. Wir spielen gut Basketball, nicht?
5. Trudi macht viel Sport, nicht wahr?
6. Du und Regina, ihr spielt gern Tennis, nicht?

3. Was machen sie? Somebody you know slightly is asking about your friends. Construct sentences using the following cues.

▶ wie / heißen / der Junge / ? *Wie heißt der Junge?*

1. er / heißen / Konrad
2. er / studieren / in Berlin / ?
3. nein / er / studieren / in München
4. wie / arbeiten / er /?
5. er / sein / fleißig
6. was / machen / Martha und er / heute abend / ?
7. sie / gehen / ins Kino
8. wann / sie / gehen / ins Kino / ?
9. wer / treiben / gern / Sport / ?
10. Martha / spielen / gut / Fußball

4. Ergänzen Sie. Complete the following exchanges with appropriate words.

1. PROFESSOR: _____ heißen Sie?
   STUDENT: Ich _____ Alex Fischer.
2. HERR WAGNER: Guten Tag, Frau Schneider. Wie _____ es Ihnen?
   FRAU SCHNEIDER: Danke. Es _____ .
3. MARIA: Arbeitest _____ heute nicht?
   VOLKER: Nein, ich _____ heute Tennis.
   MARIA: _____ du viel Sport?
   VOLKER: Ja, _____ spiele gern Volleyball.
4. ALEX: _____ gehst du ins Kino?
   GISELA: _____ 7 Uhr.

5. Wie sagt man das? Give the German equivalent of the questions you ask Cornelia.

1. Cornelia, how are you?
2. What are you doing?
3. Are you working?
4. Are you going swimming today?
5. Is Michael going also?
6. When are you playing tennis?
7. Does Michael play well?
8. What kind of person is Michael?
9. He likes to play chess, doesn't he?

Was finden diese jungen Leute so lustig? (Universität Mannheim)

6. **Frage-Ecke.** Below are two schedules (labeled S1 and S2) listing some activities for Linda, Philipp, and Alex and Gisela. Each schedule has information the other does not have. First determine who will be S1 and who will be S2. Secondly, you and your partner should then fill in the "ich" column of your respective schedules with your activities for the time periods. Finally, without looking at each other's schedule, ask each other questions to determine the missing activities on your schedule. Be sure to ask your partner what she/he has planned.

S2: Was macht Linda heute morgen?
S1: Sie macht heute morgen Deutsch.
S2: Was machen Alex und Gisela Samstag?
S1: Sie spielen Samstag Schach.

S1:

	heute morgen	heute abend	Samstag	Sonntag
Linda	Deutsch machen		ins Kino gehen	
Philipp		Musik hören	in die Bibliothek gehen	
Alex und Gisela		tanzen	Schach spielen	
ich				
Partnerin/ Partner				

S2:

	heute morgen	heute abend	Samstag	Sonntag
Linda		arbeiten		Karten spielen
Philipp	Deutsch machen			Videospiele spielen
Alex und Gisela	Sport treiben			wandern
ich				
Partnerin/ Partner				

7.   Was sagen Sie? *(What do you say?)*   Respond appropriately to the expressions or questions below in German.

1. Guten Tag!
2. Wie ist Ihre Telefonnummer?
3. Welcher Tag ist heute?
4. Wie spät ist es?
5. Wie geht's?

6. Was ist los?
7. Was machen Sie heute abend?
8. Hören Sie gern Musik?
9. Treiben Sie gern Sport?
10. Was für ein Mensch sind Sie?

8.   Zum Schreiben

1. Think ahead to the weekend and, using complete sentences, write down at least three things you will do and three things you will not do. Use a separate sentence for each thing.

2. Answer the following questions about the form of a personal letter written in German.

   a. Where do you write the city and date for a personal letter?
   b. Look at the punctuation in the city/date line. Where do you find a comma? Where do you find a period?
   c. What is the salutation for a woman? For a man?
   d. How does Christin close the letter?
   e. Look carefully at the greeting and closing. What punctuation is used after the greeting? After the closing?

3. Using Christin's letter to Maria and Volker as a model, write a letter to a friend about your room, your school, and one friend. Before you write the letter, reread Christin's letter and notice how she uses the words **und, aber, auch, furchtbar**, and **jedenfalls**. Try to use some of these words in your letter. You may also want to review the vocabulary for the names of things in your room that were presented in *Kapitel 1.*

GRAMMATIK: ZUSAMMENFASSUNG

(Grammar: Summary)

Subject pronouns

Singular		Plural	
1.	**ich** I	**wir** we	
2.	**du** you *(familiar)*	**ihr** you *(familiar)*	
3.	**er** he, it		
	es it	**sie** they	
	sie she, it		
	Sie you *(formal)*		

Present tense of *sein*

sein: to be	
ich **bin**	wir **sind**
du **bist**	ihr **seid**
er/es/sie **ist**	sie **sind**
Sie **sind**	

The verb **sein,** like its English equivalent *to be,* is irregular in the present tense.

Infinitive and infinitive stem

Infinitive	Stem + ending
glauben	glaub + en
wandern	wander + n

The basic form of a verb is the infinitive. Most German infinitives end in **-en;** a few end in **-n,** such as **wandern.** In vocabularies and dictionaries, verbs are listed in their infinitive form.

Present tense of regular verbs

	glauben	arbeiten	heißen
ich	glaub**e**	arbeit**e**	heiß**e**
du	glaub**st**	arbeit**est**	heiß**t**
er/es/sie	glaub**t**	arbeit**et**	heiß**t**
wir	glaub**en**	arbeit**en**	heiß**en**
ihr	glaub**t**	arbeit**et**	heiß**t**
sie	glaub**en**	arbeit**en**	heiß**en**
Sie	glaub**en**	arbeit**en**	heiß**en**

1. German verb endings change, depending on what the subject of the verb is. The verb endings are added to the infinitive stem. There are four basic endings in the present tense of most regular verbs: **-e, -st, -t, en.**
2. If a verb stem ends in **-d** or **-t,** the endings **-st** and **-t** expand to **-est** and **-et.**
3. If a verb stem ends in a sibilant **(s, ss, ß, z),** the **-st** ending contracts to **-t.**

[handwritten margin notes:]
Studieren — to study in discipline
lernen — to look over before an exam

Position of *nicht*

The position of **nicht** is determined by the various elements in the sentence. Because of the great flexibility of **nicht,** its use is best learned by observing its position in sentences you hear and read. Here are several guidelines:

1. **Nicht** always follows the finite verb:

   Bernd arbeitet **nicht.**   Bernd is not working.

2. **Nicht** always follows:

   a. noun objects
   Ich glaube *Bernd* **nicht.**   I don't believe Bernd.

   b. pronouns used as objects
   Ich glaube *es* **nicht.**   I don't believe it.

   c. specific adverbs of time
   Bernd spielt *heute* **nicht.**   Bernd is not playing today.

3. **Nicht** precedes most other elements:

   a. predicate adjectives
   Sebastian ist **nicht** *nett.*   Sebastian isn't nice.

   b. predicate nouns
   Das ist **nicht** *Herr Schmidt.*   That isn't Mr. Schmidt.

   c. adverbs
   Er spielt **nicht** *gut* Tennis.   He doesn't play tennis well.

   d. adverbs of general time
   Er spielt **nicht** *oft* Tennis.   He doesn't play tennis often.

   e. prepositional phrases
   Ute geht **nicht** *ins Kino.*   Ute isn't going to the movies.

4. If several of the elements occur in a sentence, **nicht** usually precedes the first one.

   Ich gehe **nicht** *oft ins Kino.*   I don't often go to the movies.

Morgen, morgen, nur nicht heute, sagen alle faulen Leute.
(Tomorrow, tomorrow, not today,
That's what all lazy people say.)

Informational questions

1	2	3	
Wann	gehen	Sie?	When are you going?
Wo	arbeitest	du?	Where do you work?

In an informational question in German an interrogative is in first position and the finite verb in second position. Some common interrogatives are **wann, was, welch (-er, -es, -e), wer, wie, was für ein,** and **wo.**

Yes/No questions

1	2	3	
Bist	du	müde?	Are you tired?
Spielt	Andrea	gut?	Does Andrea play well?
Arbeitest	du	heute?	Are you working today?

In a yes/no question in German the finite verb is in first position.

Das Wetter heute in Hannover: kalt und naß.

Kapitel 3

LERNZIELE

- ### Sprechintentionen
  Talking about the weather
  Inquiring about someone's birthday
  Summarizing information
  Stating one's nationality

- ### Lesestück
  Groß oder klein? Alles ist relativ!

- ### Land und Leute
  Berlin vs. Bonn
  Birthday customs and greetings
  Development of the standard German language

- ### Vokabeln
  Weather expressions
  Months and seasons
  Suffixes *-er* and *-in*
  Names of countries and nationalities
  The question word *woher*

- ### Grammatik
  Simple past tense of *sein*
  Present tense of *haben*
  Position of the finite verb in statements
  Nominative case
  Plural of nouns
  Indefinite article *ein*
  Expressing negation by *kein* and *nicht*
  Possession with proper names
  Possessive adjectives
  Demonstrative pronouns *der, das, die*

BAUSTEINE FÜR GESPRÄCHE

Wie ist das Wetter?

Im Sommer

FRAU KÜMMEL: Schönes Wetter, nicht?

HERR ALTHAUS: Ja, aber es ist zu trocken.

FRAU KÜMMEL: Vielleicht regnet es morgen.

HERR ALTHAUS: Hoffentlich.

Im Herbst

HERR HOFER: Heute ist es wirklich kalt, nicht?

FRAU VOGEL: Ja, sehr, und gestern war es noch so schön.

HERR HOFER: Jetzt bleibt es bestimmt kalt.

FRAU VOGEL: Leider.

Im Winter

DIETER: Was für ein Wetter!

LISA: Der Wind ist furchtbar kalt. Ich glaube, es schneit bald.

DIETER: Wieviel Grad ist es?

LISA: Es ist zwei Grad.

How's the weather?

In the summer

Nice weather, isn't it?

Yes, but it's too dry.

Maybe it'll rain tomorrow.

I hope so.

In the fall

It's really cold today, isn't it?

Yes, very much so. And it was still so nice yesterday.
Now it'll stay cold for sure.

Unfortunately.

In the winter

What weather!
The wind is awfully cold. I think it's going to snow soon.
What's the temperature?
It's two degrees.

Brauchbares

1. In German an adjective that precedes a noun has an ending, e.g., **schön*es* Wetter.** If the adjective does not precede a noun it has no ending (e.g., **Es ist schön**).

2. Note that in German when the subject (e.g., **es**) does not begin the sentence it follows the verb (e.g., **Vielleicht regnet es.**).

3. German-speaking countries use the Celsius thermometer. Two degrees Celsius = 37 degrees Fahrenheit.

▷ **1. Schönes Wetter, nicht?** A fellow student comments on the weather. Agree with her/him.

Discussing the weather

S2:   *S1:*

Schönes Wetter, hm?	Ja, es ist wirklich **schön.**
Gutes	gut.
Schlechtes	schlecht.
Furchtbares	furchtbar.
	warm°.

▷ **2. Das Wetter.** Talk about the weather with two or three fellow students. Ask how it is now and then make a prediction about tomorrow. You may want to refer to the Supplementary Word Sets in the Reference Section.

Inquiring about the weather

S1:   *S2:*

Wie ist das Wetter heute?	Es ist **kalt.**
	schlecht.
	naß°.
	schön.
	heiß°.
	kühl°.

Predicting the weather

Vielleicht	**regnet** es morgen.	Ja, vielleicht.
	schneit es	Ich glaube nicht.
	scheint° die Sonne°	Hoffentlich nicht.

▷ **3. Was für ein Wetter!** A fellow student is unhappy with the weather. Respond by commenting on the weather yesterday.

Stating displeasure about the weather

S2:   *S1:*

Was für ein	**Wetter!**	Ja, und gestern war es **noch schön warm°.**
	Wind!	auch schlecht.
	Regen°!	auch kalt.
	Schnee°!	noch trocken.

▷ **4. Was sagen Sie?** Make each of the comments below to a partner. After each comment, your partner will respond with an appropriate expression from the list. Your partner should avoid using the same expression each time.

Discussing the weather

Hoffentlich. □ Leider. □ Vielleicht. □ Jetzt bleibt es so. □ Ja, sehr. □ Vielleicht schneit es bald. □ Vielleicht regnet es. □ Nein, noch nicht°.

1. Heute ist es schön warm.
2. Heute ist es wirklich heiß.
3. Es ist zu trocken.
4. Was für ein Wetter!
5. Der Wind ist furchtbar kalt.
6. Schneit es?
7. Jetzt bleibt es bestimmt kalt.

Erweiterung des Wortschatzes

1 Die Monate°

Januar	April	Juli	Oktober
Februar	Mai	August	November
März	Juni	September	Dezember

Der Mai war schön, nicht?   May was nice, wasn't it?

All the names of the months are **der**-words.

2 Die Jahreszeiten°

der **Frühling**

der **Sommer**

der **Herbst**

der **Winter**

1. **Wie heißen sie?**   Answer the following questions about the seasons.
   1. Wie heißen die Wintermonate? die Sommermonate?
   2. Wie heißen die Herbstmonate? die Frühlingsmonate?

2. Wann ist es … ?   Tell in what months the following weather conditions occur where you live.

▶ Wann ist es oft kalt?   *Im Januar und im Februar.*

1. Wann regnet es viel?
2. Wann schneit es viel?
3. Wann ist es oft heiß?
4. Wann scheint die Sonne nicht viel?
5. Wann ist es schön warm?
6. Wann ist es sehr trocken?
7. Wann ist der Wind kalt? warm? heiß?
8. Wann ist das Wetter gut – nicht heiß und nicht kalt?

3. Wie ist das Wetter in … ?   Ask your partner about the weather in two of the four cities below. Your partner will ask you about the weather in the other two cities. (Note that in German dates, the day precedes the month, e.g., 10. Mai.) Below are forms of the questions and answers you can use.

1. Wie ist das Wetter heute in [Berlin]?

   a. In [Berlin] ist das Wetter [schön]. / Das Wetter in [Berlin] ist heute [schön].
   b. Es ist [in Berlin] [warm / heiß / kalt / kühl / naß / trocken].
   c. Es [regnet / schneit] in [Berlin].
   d. Die Sonne scheint heute [in Berlin].

2. Wieviel Grad ist es?
   Es ist [18 Grad]. / Es ist [minus zwei Grad].

3. Welche Jahreszeit ist es [in Berlin]?

4. Wie ist das Wetter [hier / in Vermont] im [Winter / Sommer / Herbst / Frühling]?

Hamburg: 10°C/50°F	Zürich: -15°C/5°F	München°: 36°C/97°F	Wien°: 21°C/70°F
10. Mai	3. Januar	28. Juli	2. Oktober

Munich / Vienna

▷ **4. Wann hast du Geburtstag°?** Interview four students to find out the months of their birthdays.

S1:

Wann hast du Geburtstag?

S2:

Ich habe im [Mai] Geburtstag.

Vokabeln

Nouns whose plural forms are commonly used are listed with their plural forms: **die Jahreszeit, -en = die Jahreszeiten.**

Substantive

der **Frühling**   spring
der **Geburtstag**   birthday
der **Grad**   degree
der **Herbst**   autumn, fall
die **Jahreszeit, -en**   season
der **Monat, -e**   month
der **Regen**   rain

der **Schnee**   snow
der **Sommer**   summer
die **Sonne**   sun
das **Wetter**   weather
der **Wind**   wind
der **Winter**   winter
For the months see p. 58.

Verben

bleiben   to remain, stay
regnen   to rain
scheinen   to shine

schneien   to snow
war   was (*past tense of* **sein**)

Andere Wörter

bald   soon
bestimmt   certain(ly), for sure
furchtbar   horrible, terrible
gestern   yesterday
heiß   hot
hmm   hmm
hoffentlich   I hope so
jetzt   now
kalt   cold
kühl   cool
leider   unfortunately

morgen   tomorrow
naß   wet
noch   still; in addition; **noch nicht**
   not yet
schön   nice, beautiful
trocken   dry
warm   warm; **schön warm**
   nice and warm
wirklich   really
zu   too

Besondere Ausdrücke

Es ist [minus] [10] Grad.   It's
   [minus] [10] degrees.
Ich habe im [Mai] Geburtstag.   My
   birthday is in [May].
im [Herbst]   in the [fall]; **im [Mai]**
   in [May]
Wann hast du Geburtstag?   When is
   your birthday?

Was für ein Wetter!   What weather!
Wie ist das Wetter?   How's the
   weather?
Wieviel Grad ist es?   What's the
   temperature?

GROSS ODER KLEIN? ALLES IST RELATIV!

Vorbereitung auf das Lesen

■ *Vor dem Lesen*

1. Look at the advertisement below and answer the following questions.

   a. What does the advertisement imply about the winter weather in Germany?
   b. What is the weather like in Florida?
   c. How much does a ticket from Frankfurt to Miami cost? Do you find the price expensive **(teuer),** reasonable **(günstig),** or cheap **(billig)**?

> ✳✳✳✳✳✳✳✳✳✳✳✳✳✳✳✳✳✳✳✳✳✳✳✳
> *Wieder ein*
> *nasser, kalter Winter?*
>
> In Florida
> ist auch der Winter
> warm und s☺nnig!
>
> Täglich
> von Frankfurt nach
> Miami
> für nur DM 499.-!!!

2. Do you think the concept of cold means the same thing to inhabitants of Florida as to those of Toronto, Canada? What temperature do you personally think is cold on a winter day?
3. On a map of the world locate Berlin, the capital of Germany, and Washington, D.C. Which city is farther north?

4. Where do you think winters are colder: Minnesota (U.S.A.), Ontario (Canada), or northern Germany?

5. Where do you think winters are colder: in northern Germany (Hamburg) or in southern Germany (Munich)?

6. Germany is the third largest country of the European Union, after France and Spain. How large do you think Germany is compared to your state or province?

7. Using the map in the front of the book, locate the following cities: Frankfurt am Main, Berlin, Bonn, Dresden, Hamburg, and München.

◼ *Beim Lesen*

1. In the reading you will find data on the number of inhabitants of Germany, Germany's size, and distances within the country. As you are reading, make notes on the relevant facts about Germany.

2. Which words or concepts in the text would you consider to be relative?

Washington ist Amerikas Hauptstadt und liegt circa° 1500 Kilometer weiter südlich als unsere Hauptstadt Berlin. Also ist der Sommer in Amerika auch anders als der Sommer in Deutschland. Ein Amerikaner in Deutschland sagt: „Heute ist es schön warm." Ein Deutscher hört das und denkt: „Warm? Hier?
5 Jetzt? Nein! Furchtbar heiß." Was für Deutsche heiß ist, finden Amerikaner warm, denn das Klima ist in Amerika anders als in Deutschland. In Amerika ist das Wetter oft heiß im Sommer, aber im Winter ist es sehr kalt im Norden und warm im Süden. In Deutschland ist es dagegen° oft kühl im Sommer und nicht so kalt im Winter. Hier beeinflußt nämlich° der Ozean das Klima, und er
10 beeinflußt es mehr im Norden als im Süden und mehr im Westen als im Osten.
   Wörter wie „heiß" und „warm" sind also relativ. Auch die Wörter „groß" und „klein" sind relativ, wenigstens° in der Geographie. Für Deutsche ist Amerika sehr groß. Für Amerikaner ist Deutschland ziemlich klein. Deutschland hat etwa achtzig Millionen Einwohner, Amerika zweihundert-
15 sechzig Millionen. Dabei° ist Deutschland nur etwa halb so groß wie Texas (oder Alberta). Von Bonn im Westen nach Dresden im Osten sind es nur etwa fünfhundert Kilometer. Von Hamburg im Norden nach München im Süden sind es nur achthundert Kilometer. Das ist nur eine Tagesreise°. Von Seattle im Nordwesten nach Miami im Südosten sind es fünf bis sieben
20 Tagesreisen (5267 km)°. In Deutschland haben „groß" und „klein" also andere Dimensionen als in Amerika.

approximately

on the other hand
after all

at least

And yet

day's journey (by car)

= 3273 miles

Brauchbares

1. In *Kapitel 1* you learned that German and English have many cognates. However, there are also a number of "false" cognates, that is, words that look alike but have different meanings. **Also** in l. 2 is a common "false" cognate. In German it means *therefore* or *so*. The word for English *also* in German is **auch**.

2. Note the phrase in l. 16–17 **"sind es nur etwa fünfhundert Kilometer"** (*it is only five hundred kilometers*). In German **es** is only a "dummy" subject; the real subject, **fünfhundert Kilometer,** is plural; therefore the verb is

Auf der Autobahn sind es nur 72 Kilometer von Augsburg nach Ulm.

plural, i.e., **sind.** With a singular subject the verb would be **ist: Es ist nur ein Kilometer** (*It is only one kilometer*). The equivalent English phrase, *it is,* never changes, whether the real subject is singular or plural.

3. German-speaking countries use kilometers to measure distance. One kilometer (km) equals .62 mile.

Nach dem Lesen

1. Ergänzen Sie.   Using your notes on the size of Germany, complete the following sentences.

1. Deutschland hat _____ Einwohner.
2. Deutschland ist etwa halb so groß wie _____ .
3. Von Bonn nach Dresden sind es etwa _____ Kilometer.
4. Es ist eine Tagesreise von München im Süden nach Hamburg im _____ .

2. Fragen zum Lesestück

1. Wie heißt die deutsche° Hauptstadt?
2. Welche Stadt liegt weiter nördlich° – Berlin oder Washington, D.C.?
3. Was sagt ein Amerikaner in Deutschland im Sommer?
4. Was denkt ein Deutscher?
5. Wie ist das Klima in Amerika?
6. Warum ist der Winter in Deutschland nicht so kalt?
7. Welche Wörter sind relativ?
8. Etwa wie viele Kilometer ist die Tagesreise von Hamburg nach München?
9. Wie viele Kilometer ist für Sie eine Tagesreise?

- refer to reading passage
- bulk of answer is in the question

3. Erzählen wir. *(Let's talk about it.)*

1. Before you can talk about a topic you need to have the appropriate vocabulary. Go back to the text and write down several words in addition to the one provided that you could use when you talk about Germany.

   Klima: Sommer, _____ , _____
   Größe°: Kilometer, _____ , _____   size

2. Talk briefly about one of the following topics.

   Das Wetter in Deutschland.
   Deutschland ist klein.

Summarizing information

4. Deutschland und seine° Nachbarn.   Germany is situated in the center of   its
Europe, and it has many neighboring countries. Using the map of Europe on the inside back cover of your book fill in the missing country names in the paragraph below. Note: Certain names of countries in German are always used with a definite article. Some of these countries are: **die Schweiz** (Switzerland), **die Niederlande** (The Netherlands), and **die Tschechische Republik** (Czech Republic).

Deutschland liegt im Zentrum° Europas. Es hat neun Nachbarn: Das   center
Nachbarland im Norden ist _____ ; die Nachbarländer im Süden sind _____
und die _____ ; im Osten liegen _____ und die _____ ; im Westen _____ , _____ ,
_____ und die _____ .

Über Nacht gab's 60 Zentimeter Neuschnee in Parpan, in der Schweiz.

Land und Leute

Das Reichstagsgebäude in Berlin. Neuer Sitz des Bundestags.

Berlin vs. Bonn

At the end of World War II in 1945 the four Allies divided Germany into four zones of occupation, and its capital Berlin into four sectors: American, British, French, and Soviet. Currency reforms in the Western zones and then in the Soviet zone in 1948, the blockade of Berlin by the Soviets, and the establishment of western Germany as the **Bundesrepublik Deutschland (BRD)** (Federal Republic of Germany) and of eastern Germany as the **Deutsche Demokratische Republik (DDR)** (German Democratic Republic) in 1949 led to the separation of Berlin into two parts: a western and an eastern part. The construction of the Berlin Wall **(die Mauer)** in 1961, built by the DDR to halt the emigration of several millions of East Germans into West Germany, completed the division of Berlin.

From the end of World War II in 1945 until the unification of Germany on October 3, 1990, Berlin had a special status under international law. Legally, it belonged neither to the **Bundesrepublik Deutschland** nor to the **Deutsche Demokratische Republik.** In practice both parts of Berlin were closely connected to their respective systems, **West-Berlin** to the **BRD** and **Ost-Berlin** to the **DDR.** Many countries recognized the eastern part of Berlin as the capital of the **DDR.** The **BRD** made Bonn, a medium-sized city on the **Rhein,** its temporary capital.

On November 9, 1989, the wall that divided Berlin was opened. As of October 3, 1990, the date of unification of Germany, Berlin is again one city. It is the largest city in Germany with a population of 3.4 million. Article 2 of the **Einigungsvertrag** (Unification Treaty) states that "Berlin is the capital city of Germany." However, not all the government agencies will move from Bonn to Berlin. According to the Bonn–Berlin Act of 1995 eight of the eighteen federal ministries and 65 percent of the 21,200 civil servants are to remain in Bonn. In practice, Bonn will become a second seat of government.

Regierungsgebäude in Bonn.

Erweiterung des Wortschatzes

1 The suffix *-in*

Masculine	der Nachbar
Feminine	die Nachbar**in**
Feminine plural	die Nachbar**innen**

The suffix **-in** added to the singular masculine noun gives the feminine equivalent. The plural of a noun with the suffix **-in** ends in **-nen**.

1. Mann oder Frau? Give the other form—feminine or masculine—of the words listed below.

▶ die Professorin   *der Professor*

1. die Sekretärin
2. der Student
3. die Amerikanerin
4. der Einwohner

2 Names of countries

Wie groß ist **Deutschland?**   How large is Germany?
Existiert **das romantische Deutschland** noch?   Does romantic Germany still exist?

The names of most countries are neuter; for example **(das) Deutschland** and **(das) Amerika**. Articles are not used with names of countries that are neuter, unless the name is preceded by an adjective.

Die Schweiz ist schön.   Switzerland is beautiful.
Die USA sind groß.   The United States is large.

The names of a few countries are feminine (e.g., **die Schweiz**); some names are used only in the plural (e.g., **die USA**). Articles are always used with names of countries that are feminine or plural.

2. Andere Länder. Try to guess the English names for the countries listed below.

1. Italien
2. Spanien
3. Griechenland
4. Schweden
5. Rumänien
6. Frankreich
7. Norwegen
8. Liechtenstein
9. die Türkei
10. die Niederlande

Ein Berliner und sein Hund.

3 Nouns indicating citizenship and nationality

Berlin	der Berliner	die Berlinerin
England	der Engländer	die Engländerin
Spanien	der Spanier	die Spanierin
Norwegen	der Norweger	die Norwegerin
München	der Münchner	die Münchnerin
Kanada	der Kanadier	die Kanadierin
Deutschland	der Deutsche (Deutscher)	die Deutsche

Nouns indicating an inhabitant of a city or a citizen of a country follow several patterns. While you won't be able to predict the exact form, you will always be able to recognize it.

The noun suffix **-er** is added to the name of many cities, states, or countries to indicate a male citizen or inhabitant **(Berliner).** Some nouns take an umlaut **(Engländer).** To indicate a female citizen or inhabitant the additional suffix **-in** is added to the **-er** suffix **(Berlinerin, Engländerin).**

In some instances the **-er/-erin** is added to a modified form of the country **(Kanadier/Kanadierin).** Other countries have still other forms to indicate the citizen or inhabitant **(Deutscher/Deutsche).**

Mark ist **Deutscher.**	Mark is (a) *German.*
Anna ist **Deutsche.**	Anna is (a) *German.*

Note that to state a person's nationality, German uses the noun directly after a form of **sein.** The indefinite article **ein** is not used, whereas in English nouns of nationality may be preceded by an indefinite article.

4 The question word *woher*

Woher kommst du?	Where are you from?
Ich **komme aus** [Frankfurt/ der Schweiz/den USA].	I am from [Frankfurt/ Switzerland/the U.S.A.].

To ask in German where someone is from, use the interrogative **woher** and a form of the verb **kommen.** To answer such a question, use a form of the verb **kommen** and the preposition **aus.**

Ich komme aus (I come from)

▷   **3.   Frage-Ecke.**   Find out where the following people are from and where they live now. Obtain the missing information by asking your partner.

S2: Woher kommt Anton?
S1: Er kommt aus Deutschland.

S2: Was ist Anton?
S1: Er ist Deutscher.

S2: Wo wohnt° Anton?
S1: Er wohnt in München.

S2: Und woher kommst du?
S1: Ich komme aus ...

S1:

	Woher kommt ... ?	Was ist ... ?	Wo wohnt ... ?
Anton	Deutschland	Deutscher	München
Carmen	Spanien	Spanierin	Barcelona
Kristina			
Herr Heller			
ich			
Partnerin/Partner			

S2:

	Woher kommt ... ?	Was ist ... ?	Wo wohnt ... ?
Anton			
Carmen			
Kristina	Deutschland	Deutsche	Leipzig
Herr Heller	Österreich	Österreicher	Wien
ich			
Partnerin/Partner			

▷   **4.   Woher kommst du?**   Ask five classmates where they are from. Make notes so you can tell others where they are from.

> Stating one's nationality

Vokabeln

Substantive

(das) **Amerika** America
der **Amerikaner, -**/die **Amerikanerin,
-nen** American person
der **Deutsche** *(m.)*/die **Deutsche**
(f.)/die **Deutschen** *(pl.)* German
person
ein **Deutscher** *(m.)*/eine **Deutsche** *(f.)*
a German person
(das) **Deutschland** Germany
der **Einwohner, -**/die **Einwohnerin,
-nen** inhabitant
das **Europa** Europe
die **Hauptstadt, ̈e** capital
das **Kanada** Canada
der **Kilometer, -** kilometer
das **Klima** climate
das **Land, ̈er** country, land

die **Million, -en** million
das **Nachbarland, ̈er** neighboring
country
der **Norden** north
der **Osten** east
(das) **Österreich** Austria
der **Österreicher, -**/die
Österreicherin, -nen Austrian
person
der **Ozean** ocean
die **Schweiz** Switzerland
der **Schweizer, -**/die **Schweizerin,
-nen** Swiss person
die **Stadt, ̈e** city
der **Süden** south
die **USA** *(pl.)* U.S.A.
der **Westen** west

Verben

beeinflussen to influence
denken to think
finden to think, find
haben to have

liegen to lie, be situated, be located
sagen to say, tell
wohnen to live, reside

Andere Wörter

alles everything
als than
also therefore, so
andere other
anders different(ly)
deutsch German *(adj.)*
etwa approximately, about
für for
halb half; **halb so groß** half as large
hier here
in in
mehr more
nach to *(with cities and neuter
countries, e.g.,* **nach Berlin; nach
Deutschland)**

nördlich to the north
relativ relative
so ... wie as . . . as
sonnig sunny
südlich to the south
von from; of
weiter farther, further
wie as
wieder again
wo where
woher where from
ziemlich quite, rather, fairly;
ziemlich klein rather small

Besondere Ausdrücke

Ich bin [Schweizer/Amerikanerin].
I am [Swiss/American].
Ich komme aus ... I come/am from . . .
nicht so [kalt] not as [cold]

Woher kommst du? Where are you
from?
zum Beispiel *(abbrev.* **z.B.)** for
example *(abbrev.* e.g.)

GRAMMATIK UND ÜBUNGEN

1 Simple past tense of *sein*

Present	Heute ist das Wetter gut.	The weather is good today.
Simple past	Gestern war es schlecht.	It was bad yesterday.

The simple past tense of **sein** is **war**.

ich **war**	wir waren	I was	we were
du warst	ihr wart	you were	you were
er/es/sie **war**	sie waren	he/it/she was	they were
Sie waren		you were	

In the simple past, the **ich-** and **er/es/sie-**forms of **sein** have no verb endings.

1. Wo warst du in den Sommerferien? State where the following people spent their summer vacation.

▶ Maria / Italien   *Maria war in Italien.*

1. Harald / Dresden
2. ihr / Salzburg
3. Karl und Kristina / Österreich
4. du / Leipzig
5. wir / Zürich
6. Verena / München
7. meine Freunde / Wien
8. Alex / Dänemark
9. Und wo waren Sie in den Sommerferien?

2. Wie war das Wetter? Ask a fellow student what the weather was like on four previous days. Record the answers. You may want to refer to the Supplementary Word Sets in the Reference Section.

Discussing the weather

S1:

Wie war das Wetter [am Samstag]?

Und [am Freitag]?

S2:

Es war [schön].
[Am Samstag] war es [schön].
Es war [kalt].

2 Present tense of *haben*

haben: to have	
ich habe	wir haben
du **hast**	ihr habt
er/es/sie **hat**	sie haben
Sie haben	

The verb **haben** is irregular in the **du-** and **er/es/sie-**forms of the present tense.

3. Wann hast du Geburtstag? Frank and Gisela are updating their birthday list. Frank doesn't know the exact dates of their friends' birthdays. Take the role of Gisela and tell him in what month the following people's birthdays are. And then give the month of your own birthday.

▶ ich / Juli   *Ich habe im Juli Geburtstag.*

1. Petra / Juni
2. du / September
3. Jürgen / Februar
4. ihr / Mai
5. Ulrike und Heinz / Oktober
6. wir / April
7. Und wann haben Sie Geburtstag?

3 Position of the finite verb in statements

1	2	3	4
Der Sommer	ist	in Deutschland	anders.
In Deutschland	ist	**der Sommer**	anders.

In a German statement, the finite verb is always in second position, even when an element other than the subject (for example, an adverb or a prepositional phrase) is in first position. When an element other than the subject is in first position, the subject follows the verb.

4. Hoffentlich ist es schön. You and Sonja are discussing the weather, hoping it will be nice for an outdoor activity. Agree with her by restating her comments, beginning with the word in parentheses. Follow the model.

▶ Es ist heute schön, nicht? (heute)   *Ja. Heute ist es schön.*

1. Es bleibt hoffentlich warm. (hoffentlich)
2. Das Wetter war gestern schlecht, nicht? (gestern)
3. Das Wetter war auch am Mittwoch gut, nicht? (am Mittwoch)
4. Das Wetter bleibt jetzt bestimmt gut, nicht? (jetzt)
5. Die Sonne scheint hoffentlich. (hoffentlich)

5. Wer? Was? Wann?   You and Sabrina have been talking to your friends to find out when they are free for a get-together. By consulting your list you are able to tell Sabrina when your various friends are busy and what they are doing. Begin with the time element.

▶ *Morgen abend spielt Ramon Basketball.*

Wer?	Was?	Wann?
Ramon	Basketball spielen	morgen abend
Michael und Hans	Tennis spielen	am Montag
Anna	ins Kino gehen	heute
Carla	Geburtstag haben	am Sonntag
David und Greta	Volleyball spielen	heute abend
ich	nicht arbeiten	morgen

Land und Leute

Geburtstage

Birthdays are very important to people in German-speaking countries. They seldom forget the birthday of a family member or friend—they write, call, give flowers and/or other gifts. Birthdays are celebrated in different ways. The "birthday child" **(Geburtstagskind)** may have an afternoon coffee party **(Geburtstagskaffee)** with family members and friends or a more extensive birthday party in the evening. At the **Geburtstagskaffee** candles are placed around the edge of a birthday cake **(Geburtstagskuchen)** and blown out by the person whose birthday it is. Although the **Geburtstagskind** is often taken out by family members or friends, he or she usually gives a party or brings a cake to work. Besides giving presents **(Geburtstagsgeschenke)**, it is common to send a birthday card or make a phone call. Common greetings are: **Herzlichen Glückwunsch zum Geburtstag!** *(Happy Birthday!)* or **Alles Gute zum Geburtstag!** *(All the best on your birthday!)*, and **Ich gratuliere zum Geburtstag!** *(Congratulations on your birthday!)*.

In Austria and the predominantly Catholic regions of Germany, name days **(Namenstage)**

Herzlichen Glückwunsch zum Geburtstag!

may be celebrated with as much excitement as a birthday. **Namenstage** commemorate the feast day of one's patron saint. Florist shops in these areas typically remind people whose name day is being celebrated and newspapers often print ads **(Geburtstagsanzeigen)**, in which someone is being congratulated on her/his birthday.

6. So ist das Wetter. Tell when your birthday is and what the weather is usually like at that time of year. Make a brief report to a group of four or to the whole class.

Describing the weather in a particular season

▶ *Ich habe im Februar Geburtstag. Im Februar ist es kalt. Es schneit oft, und die Sonne scheint nicht viel.*

⇨ **7. Frage-Ecke.** Find out how old the following people are, when their birthdays are, and what the typical weather in that month is. Obtain the missing information from your partner.

S2: Wie alt ist Manfred?
S1: Manfred ist 21 Jahre alt. Wann hat er Geburtstag?
S2: Im Januar.
S1: Wie ist das Wetter im Januar?
S2: Es ist kalt.

S1:

	Wie alt?	Geburtstag	das Wetter
Manfred	21		kalt
Stefanie		Oktober	
Herr Hofer	45		
Frau Vogel		April	naß und kühl
ich			
Partnerin/Partner			

S2:

	Wie alt?	Geburtstag	das Wetter
Manfred		Januar	
Stefanie	30		kühl
Herr Hofer		Juli	heiß und trocken
Frau Vogel	39		
ich			
Partnerin/Partner			

4 The nominative case

That woman plays tennis well.
She doesn't play volleyball very well.

English uses word order to signal different grammatical functions (e.g., subject) of nouns or pronouns. In a statement in English the subject precedes the verb.

Die Frau spielt gut Tennis.
Volleyball spielt **sie** aber nicht sehr gut.

German uses a different type of signal to indicate the grammatical function of nouns and pronouns. German uses a signal called *case*. When a noun or pronoun is used as the subject of a sentence, it is in the nominative case.

Masculine	Neuter	Feminine
der	das	die

In the nominative case, the German definite article has three forms. They are all equivalent to "the" in English.

Subject	Predicate noun
Herr Lange ist **Professor.**	
Das Mädchen heißt **Gabi Fischer.**	
Das ist nicht **der Junge.**	

Subject	Predicate noun
Mr. Lange is *a professor.*	
The girl's name is *Gabi Fischer.*	
That is not *the boy.*	

The nominative case is also used for a *predicate noun*. A predicate noun designates a person, concept, or thing that is equated with the subject. A predicate noun completes the meaning of linking verbs such as **sein** and **heißen**. In a negative sentence **nicht** precedes the predicate noun.

8. Wie war das Wetter? Practice making comments about the weather. Use the cues provided. Make the comments in the past tense.

▶ Wetter / schön   *Das Wetter war schön.*

1. Morgen / kalt
2. Tag / warm
3. Wind / warm
4. Sonne / heiß

5. Abend / kalt
6. Tag / naß
7. Sommer / trocken
8. Juli / heiß

9. Wie heißen sie? Your friend can't keep people's names and objects straight. Say that she/he is wrong about each one. In your response use a pronoun and put **nicht** before the predicate noun.

▶ Heißt der Junge Mark?   *Nein, er heißt nicht Mark.*

1. Heißt der Spanier Ludwig?
2. Heißt der Nachbar Karl Schiller?
3. Heißt die Studentin Susanne?

4. Heißt die Sekretärin Neumann?
5. Heißt das Mädchen Gisela?
6. Heißt das Kind Dieter?

10. Was ist das?   See if your partner knows the German words for the following objects. Deliberately mislead your partner by asking whether the object is something it isn't. Your partner will give the correct answer.

▶ Lampe?

S1: Ist das die Lampe?
S2: Nein, das ist nicht die Lampe, das ist der Tisch.

3. Buch?

1. Stuhl?

4. Computer?

die Tafel: the Chalkboard

2. Uhr?

5. Fernseher?

5 Plural forms of German nouns

A thousand years ago English had a variety of ways to signal the plural of nouns. With some nouns it used stem changes: *mann—menn (man, men); fōt—fēt (foot, feet);* with other nouns it used endings: *stān—stānas (stone, stones); oxa—oxan (ox, oxen);* and with still other nouns it used no signal at all: *scēap—scēap (sheep, sheep).* Over the centuries the ending *-as* gradually replaced most other plural endings, and its modern development *-(e)s* is now the almost universal signal for the plural of English nouns.

Type	Plural signal	Singular	Plural
1	-	das Fenster	die Fenster
	¨	der Garten	die Gärten
2	-e	der Tisch	die Tische
	¨e	der Stuhl	die Stühle
3	-er	das Kind	die Kind**er**
	¨er	das Buch	die Büch**er**
4	-en	die Frau	die Frau**en**
	-n	die Lampe	die Lampe**n**
	-nen	die Studentin	die Studentin**nen**
5	-s	das Radio	die Radio**s** ——— *very rare*

German uses five basic types of signals to mark the plural of nouns: no ending or the endings **-e, -er, -(e)n,** and **-s.** Some of the nouns of types 1, 2, and 3 add umlaut in the plural. Nouns of type 4 that end in **-in** add **-nen** in the plural. German makes no gender distinctions in the plural; the definite article **die** is used with all plural nouns.

When you learn a German noun, you must also learn its plural form because there is no sure way of predicting to which plural-type the noun belongs. You will, however, gradually discover that there is a kind of system to the various types. This "system" depends partly on whether the noun is a **der-, das-,** or **die**-noun, and partly on how many syllables it has.

das Zimmer, - indicates that there is no change in the plural form of the noun: **das Zimmer, die Zimmer**

die Stadt, ¨e indicates that an **-e** is added in the plural, and an umlaut is added to the appropriate vowel: **die Stadt, die Städte**

In the vocabularies of this book, the plural of most nouns is indicated after the singular forms.

Die Kinder sind nett. **Sie** sind nett.
Die Lampen sind alt. **Sie** sind alt.

The personal pronoun **sie** *(they)* may refer to persons or things.

- anything that ends in -e will always add a -n

Seit Martin Luther gibt es eine deutsche Sprache.

Dat deit
mie oaver leed,
dat Du krank büst.

**Weer gau wear
gesund.**

Gode Bäterung.

Eine niederdeutsche Karte: Das tut mir aber leid, daß du krank bist. Werde schnell wieder gesund. Gute Besserung.

Land und Leute

Die deutsche Sprache

A thousand years ago there was no standard form of the German language. The large central European area from the North Sea and the Baltic Sea to the Alps in the south was inhabited by Germans who lived in many different societies and who spoke variations of the German language.

Martin Luther (1483–1546) played an important role in the development and refinement of German. For his Bible translation and other works, Luther used a form of the language spoken in east central Germany; eventually it became the spoken and written standard for all of Germany as well as Austria and Switzerland. This single standard language is called **Hochdeutsch.** It is used in all domains of public life, including newspapers, radio, TV, and film. Germans consider the German spoken in the area of Hannover, a city in northern Germany, to be the closest to pure **Hochdeutsch,** i.e., the most "accent free." Realizing that local dialects are an important part of popular culture, and concerned that some dialects may die out, many writers and singers now use their native dialects to express themselves artistically.

Approximately 98 million people in Germany, Austria, and in parts of Switzerland, Belgium, Italy, Luxembourg, France, and Liechtenstein speak German as their native language.

Dialects are often incomprehensible to people from different regions within the German-speaking countries and may even differ significantly from town to town. Complete words, intonation, and pronunciation can vary dramatically. (Different ways to say **sprechen,** for example, include **schwätzen** and **schnacken.**) Political borders also have an effect on language development. Thus, ethnic Germans living in Eastern Europe speak a different German than German speakers living in Alsace, France, or Sachsen, Germany. However, people from different German-speaking areas can always communicate with each other in **Hochdeutsch.** This way German-speaking countries are linguistically unified.

11. Der, das, die.   State the noun with the definite article and then give the plural with the definite article. Plurals are given with the nouns in the German–English vocabulary list at the end of the book.

▶ Tisch   *der Tisch / die Tische*

1. Stuhl
2. Buch
3. Bleistift
4. Kugelschreiber
5. Heft

6. Lampe
7. Radio
8. Computer
9. Gitarre
10. Sekretärin

12. Was ist hier los? *(What's going on here?)*   Talk about the people and things in a small town in Northern Germany.

▶ Stadt / sein / klein   *Die Stadt ist klein.*

1. Straße / sein / schön
2. Garten / sein / klein
3. Nachbar / sein / nett
4. Mann / spielen / gern / Fußball
5. Frau / arbeiten / viel
6. Student / sein / fleißig
7. Kind / spielen / gern

Now talk about the town in general by stating everything in the plural.

▶ Straße / sein / schön   *Die Straßen sind schön.*

6 The indefinite article *ein*

Ist das **ein** Radio oder **eine** Uhr?   Is that *a* radio or *a* clock?

The German indefinite article **ein** is equivalent to English *a* or *an*.

Masculine	Neuter	Feminine
ein Mann	ein Kind	eine Frau

In the nominative case the German indefinite article has two forms: **ein** for masculine and neuter, and **eine** for feminine. The indefinite article has no plural form.

13. Was ist das?   Jan is taking his first drawing course and is showing some of his first attempts to draw things. You're a little doubtful about the results. Use an indefinite article in the response.

▶ Das Kind ist nicht schlecht, nicht?   *Das ist ein Kind?*

1. Die Frau ist gut, nicht?
2. Der Mann ist nicht schlecht, nicht?
3. Das Kind ist schön, nicht?

4. Der Stuhl ist nicht schlecht, nicht?
5. Die Lampe ist lustig, nicht?
6. Die Uhr ist nicht schlecht, nicht?
7. Der Tisch ist schön, nicht?

7 The negative *kein*

Ist das **ein** Radio?	Is that *a* radio?
Nein, das ist **kein** Radio.	No, that's *not a* radio.
Sind die Studenten Amerikaner?	Are the students Americans?
Nein, sie sind **keine** Amerikaner.	No, they are *not* Americans.

The negative form of **ein** is **kein**. It is equivalent to English *not a, not any*, or *no*. It negates a noun that in the positive would be preceded by a form of **ein** (e.g., **ein Radio**) or no article at all (e.g., **Amerikaner**).

Masculine	Neuter	Feminine	Plural
kein Tisch	**kein** Radio	**keine** Uhr	**keine** Radios

In the nominative case **kein** has two forms: **kein** for masculine and neuter, and **keine** for feminine and plural.

14. Das ist es nicht. To get back at you Jan pretends he can't figure out what you have drawn. Tell him his guesses are wrong. Use a form of **kein** in your responses.

▶ Ist das eine Frau? *Nein, das ist keine Frau.*

1. Ist das ein Mann?
2. Ist das ein Mädchen?
3. Ist das ein Kind?
4. Ist das eine Lampe?
5. Ist das ein Zimmer?
6. Ist das ein Tisch?
7. Ist das ein Computer?
8. Ist das eine Pflanze?

8 *Kein* vs. *nicht*

Ist das **eine** Uhr?	Nein, das ist **keine** Uhr.
Sind sie Amerikaner?	Nein, sie sind **keine** Amerikaner.
Ist das **die** Uhr?	Nein, das ist **nicht die** Uhr.

Kein is used to negate a noun that in an affirmative sentence would be preceded by **ein** or no article at all. **Nicht** is used when negating a noun preceded by a definite article.

15. Nicht oder kein? Your friend is showing you photographs, and you are not always sure what you are seeing. Use **nicht** or **kein** before the predicate noun, as appropriate.

▶ Ist das die Hauptstadt? *Nein, das ist nicht die Hauptstadt.*
▶ Ist das ein Italiener? *Nein, das ist kein Italiener.*

1. Ist das der Professor?
2. Ist das ein Nachbar?
3. Ist das die Gartenstraße?
4. Ist das eine Studentin?
5. Ist das ein Amerikaner?
6. Ist das die Bibliothek?
7. Ist das Frau Weiß?

16. Kein oder nicht?   Gerd is reviewing with Tanja some basic German words. With a partner complete the following exchanges in German. Then continue on your own using the models. You may point to objects in the classroom or in the drawing of a student's room in *Kapitel 1*, or use information from the **Lesestück.**

Correcting someone

1. GERD: Ist das ein Tisch?
   TANJA: Nein. Das ist _____ . Das ist ein Stuhl.
2. GERD: Die Lampe ist schön, nicht?
   TANJA: Das ist aber _____ . Das ist eine Gitarre.
3. GERD: Ist Dresden die Hauptstadt von Deutschland?
   TANJA: Nein, Dresden ist _____ . Berlin ist _____ .

9 Showing possession with a proper name

| Das ist **Giselas** Buch. | That is *Gisela's* book. |
| Das ist **Jens'** Kuli. | That is *Jens's* ballpoint pen. |

A proper name is a word that designates a specific individual or place (e.g., Ingrid, Berlin). In German as in English, possession and other close relationships are expressed by adding **-s** to the proper names. If the name already ends in a sibilant*, no **-s** is added. In written German, an apostrophe is used only when no **-s** is added (e.g., **Jens' Kuli**).

17. Ist das Gerds Buch?   After a club meeting you and a friend are straightening up. Tell your friend to whom the various things belong. Use the possessive form of the proper name.

▶   Gerd / Buch   *Das ist Gerds Buch.*

1. Beate / Kuli
2. Bruno / Lampe
3. Franz / Radio
4. Regina / Heft
5. Thomas / Büchertasche
6. Sylvia / Uhr

10 Possessive adjectives

Mein Zimmer ist groß.	*My* room is large.
Ist **dein** Zimmer groß?	Is *your* room large?
Ist **sein** Zimmer groß?	Is *his* room large?
Ist **ihr** Zimmer groß?	Is *her* room large?
Unser Zimmer ist groß.	*Our* room is large.
Ist **euer** Zimmer groß?	Is *your* room large?
Ist **ihr** Zimmer groß?	Is *their* room large?
Ist **Ihr** Zimmer groß?	Is *your* room large?

German possessive adjectives are equivalent in meaning to the English possessive adjectives, such as *my, his,* and *her.* Context usually makes clear whether **ihr** is the subject pronoun *you,* the adjective *her* or *their,* or the adjective *your.* Note that **Ihr** *(your)* is capitalized, just as the corresponding subject pronoun **Sie** *(you)* is.

*For information on sibilants, see *Kapitel 2,* p. 40.

der Bleistift	Wo ist ein Bleistift?
	Wo ist **mein** Bleistift?
das Heft	Wo ist ein Heft?
	Wo ist **mein** Heft?
die Uhr	Wo ist eine Uhr?
	Wo ist **meine** Uhr?
die Bücher	Wo sind **meine** Bücher?

Since possessive adjectives have the same forms as **ein,** they are frequently called **ein**-words.

Wo ist **euer** Radio? Wo sind **eure** Bücher?

When **euer** has an ending, the **-e-** preceding the **-r-** is usually omitted.

■ *Negating nouns preceded by possessive adjectives*

Ist das dein Heft?   Nein, das ist **nicht** mein Heft.

Nicht is used to negate a noun that is preceded by a possessive adjective.

18. Wie sagt man das?   Complete the sentences with the German equivalents of the cued words.

▶ _____ Mann arbeitet nicht. *(her)*   *Ihr Mann arbeitet nicht.*

1. _____ Kind heißt Dieter. *(their)*
2. _____ Frau ist lustig. *(his)*
3. Barbara, Frank, was für ein Mensch ist _____ Nachbar? *(your)*
4. Wo sind _____ Kinder, Frau Neumann? *(your)*
5. Ich glaube, das ist _____ Kuli. *(my)*
6. Ist das _____ Uhr, Gisela? *(your)*

19. Wie ist dein Zimmer?   Mark has a number of assumptions about your friends' possessions. Say he is correct.

▶ Wie ist Evas Zimmer? Groß?   *Ja, ihr Zimmer ist groß.*

1. Wie ist Daniels Lampe? Schön?
2. Wie sind Ingrids Stühle? Neu?
3. Wie ist euer Garten? Groß?
4. Wie ist Lisas und Ulis CD-Spieler? Furchtbar?
5. Wie ist deine Gitarre? Alt?
6. Wie ist mein Deutsch? Gut?
7. Und wie ist Ihr Zimmer?

11 Demonstrative pronouns *der, das, die*

Lore spielt viel Tischtennis, nicht?	Lore plays a lot of table tennis, doesn't she?
Ja, **die** spielt wirklich gut.	Yes, *she* plays really well.
Mark spielt viel Fußball.	Mark plays a lot of soccer.
Ja, **der** spielt aber schlecht.	Yes, but *he* plays poorly.
Franz und Kurt spielen heute gut.	Franz and Kurt are playing well today.
Ja, **die** spielen wirklich gut.	Yes, *they* are playing really well.

Der, das, and **die** are often used as demonstrative pronouns to replace nouns. A demonstrative pronoun is used instead of a personal pronoun (**er, sie, es**) when the pronoun is to be emphasized. Demonstrative pronouns usually occur at or near the beginning of a sentence. The English equivalent is usually a personal pronoun (*he, she, it, they*).

20. Ja, so sind die. Dieter is speaking on the phone with Renate. They're discussing friends and agreeing with each other. Use a demonstrative pronoun as the subject.

▶ Barbara ist intelligent, nicht?   *Ja, die ist wirklich intelligent.*

1. Thomas war gestern fleißig, nicht?
2. Professor Müller ist freundlich, nicht?
3. Die Kinder sind heute lustig, nicht?
4. Gerd und Dieter sind faul, nicht?
5. Frau Professor Dörflinger ist nett, nicht?
6. Max und Christine waren gestern froh, nicht?

WIEDERHOLUNG

1. Singular, Plural. Give the singular and plural forms of each noun. Give the appropriate form of the definite article with each noun.

▶ Einwohner   *der Einwohner, die Einwohner*

1. Mädchen
2. Stadt
3. Wort
4. Student
5. Tag
6. Woche
7. Mann
8. Frau
9. Nachbarin
10. Stuhl
11. Kugelschreiber
12. Fenster

2. Am Telefon. Albert and Erika are talking on the phone. Complete their conversation from the notes below.

▶ ERIKA: was / du / machen / jetzt / ?   *Was machst du jetzt?*

1. ALBERT: ich / hören / Musik
2. ERIKA: ihr (du und Jens) / spielen / heute / wieder / Tennis / ?
3. ALBERT: nein / Jens / kommen / heute abend / nicht
4. ERIKA: ah / er / arbeiten / wieder
5. ALBERT: vielleicht / wir / spielen / morgen
6. ERIKA: hoffentlich / es / regnen / morgen / nicht
7. ALBERT: ich / glauben / das / nicht
8. ERIKA: vielleicht / die Sonne / scheinen
9. ALBERT: morgen / der Professor / kommen / nicht
10. ERIKA: wer / sagen / das / ?

3. Viele Fragen. Dieter and Lisa have not talked with each other in a while. Dieter has now called Lisa and has a lot of questions. Below is a list of Lisa's answers. You have to finish Dieter's questions.

Dieter	*Lisa*
▶ *Wie ist das Wetter?*	Das Wetter ist schön.
1. Regnet _____ ?	Nein, es regnet heute nicht.
2. Scheint _____ ?	Ja, die Sonne scheint.
3. Was _____ ?	Ich höre Musik.
4. Was für _____ ?	Klassische Musik.
5. Wie _____ ?	Der Professor heißt Dr. Becker.
6. Wo _____ ?	Er arbeitet in Berlin.
7. Woher _____ ?	Er kommt aus Wien.
8. Wie alt _____ ?	Professor Becker ist 43.
9. Wer _____ ?	Die Studenten sagen das.
10. Wann _____ ?	Ich schreibe morgen!

4. Und auf deutsch? Karoline, your guest from Germany, doesn't understand the conversation of your two American friends. Translate for her.

1. CHARLES: We're playing tennis today, right?
2. KATIE: No, it's too cold. We'll play tomorrow. OK?
3. CHARLES: But it's so nice (out)! The sun's shining and tomorrow it'll rain for sure.
4. KATIE: I don't think so. (Use **das**.)
5. CHARLES: By the way°, what time are we going to the movies tonight?
6. KATIE: At six-thirty. George is coming, too.
7. CHARLES: Really? Isn't he working this evening?
8. KATIE: No, he works on Monday and Tuesday.

Übrigens

By the way (handwritten note)

Unser Sohn heißt

Emanuel Gerhard

und ist am 14. Juli 1995 um 20.13 Uhr auf die Welt gekommen.
Gewicht: 3000g
Größe: 50cm

Cornelia und Gerhard Mühlhäuser
sind die überglücklichen Eltern,
Franziska ist die überglückliche Schwester.

Schönbichlstraße 14
82211 Herrsching am Ammersee
Telefon: 08152-1538

---

5. Geburtstage!   Read the birth announcement and answer the questions.
You do not need to understand all the words to get the information required.

1. Wie heißt das Baby?
2. Wie alt ist Emanuel heute?
3. Wie ist Emanuels Adresse?
4. Wie ist seine Telefonnummer?
5. Wie heißen Emanuels Mutter° und Vater°?   mother/father
6. Wer ist Franziska?

6. Wo? Wann? Wie?   Exchange information with a partner about
where you were on your last vacation, when, and what the weather was like.

▶ *Ich war im Juli in Alaska. Das Wetter war sehr schön.*

7. Woher kommst du?   Assume the role of either student 1 (S1) or student 2 (S2). When you have completed the conversation, exchange roles and try it again.

S1: Find out where your partner is from.
S2: Answer by giving your hometown.
S1: Ask what the weather is like there at this time of year.
S2: Respond.

8. Zum Schreiben

1. Imagine you have just arrived in Germany. Write a short paragraph (4–5 sentences) in German about Germany. Before you begin writing, look again at the reading on page 62 to review vocabulary and at the section on word order on page 71. Then make a list (in German) of the things you want to mention in your paragraph, e.g., weather, size, and population. Organize your comments in a paragraph. After you've written your paragraph review each sentence to be sure that each sentence has a subject and a verb and that the verb agrees with the subject. Finally, check the word order of each sentence.

2. Prepare a weather forecast that will tell your fellow students what the weather will be like for the next three days. Two or three sentences per forecast are sufficient. Watch your word order.

▶ *Am Montag scheint die Sonne. Es bleibt schön.*
Am Dienstag kommt der Wind aus dem Osten. Vielleicht regnet es.
Am Mittwoch ist es sehr kalt. Es ist zwei Grad.

GRAMMATIK: ZUSAMMENFASSUNG

Simple past tense of *sein*

sein: to be	
ich **war**	wir waren
du warst	ihr wart
er/es/sie **war**	sie waren
Sie waren	

Present tense of *haben*

haben: to have	
ich habe	wir haben
du **hast**	ihr habt
er/es/sie **hat**	sie haben
Sie haben	

Position of the finite verb in statements

	1 Subject	2 Verb	3 Adverb	4 Adjective
Normal	**Der Sommer**	ist	in Deutschland	anders.
	Adverb	**Verb**	**Subject**	**Adjective**
Inverted	In Deutschland	ist	**der Sommer**	anders.

In a German statement, the verb is always in second position. In so-called normal word order, the subject is in first position. In so-called inverted word order, something other than the subject (for example, an adverb, an adjective, or indirect object) is in first position, and the subject follows the verb. Note that both "normal" and "inverted" word order are common in German.

Plural of nouns

Type	Plural signal	Singular	Plural
1	- (no change)	das Zimmer	die Zimmer
	¨	der Garten	die Gärten
2	-e	das Heft	die Hefte
	¨e	die Stadt	die Städte
3	-er	das Kind	die Kinder
	¨er	der Mann	die Männer
4	-en	die Tür	die Türen
	-n	die Lampe	die Lampen
	-nen	die Studentin	die Studentinnen
5	-s	das Radio	die Radios

Nominative case of definite articles, indefinite articles, and *kein*

	Masculine	Neuter	Feminine	Plural
Definite article	der ⎫	das ⎫	die ⎫	die ⎫
Indefinite article	ein ⎬ Stuhl	ein ⎬ Radio	eine ⎬ Lampe	— ⎬ Bücher
kein	kein ⎭	kein ⎭	keine ⎭	keine ⎭

Kein vs. *nicht*

Ist das **eine** Uhr?	Nein, das ist **keine** Uhr.
Ist das **die** Uhr?	Nein, das ist **nicht** die Uhr.
Ist das **deine** Uhr?	Nein, das ist **nicht meine** Uhr.

Kein is used to negate a noun that would be preceded by **ein** or no article at all in an affirmative sentence. **Nicht** is used in a negative sentence when the noun is preceded by a definite article (**die**) or a possessive adjective (**meine**). (For positions of **nicht**, see *Kapitel 2*, **Grammatik und Übungen**, section 9.)

Possessive adjectives

■ *Forms and meanings*

Singular			Plural		
ich:	**mein**	my	wir:	**unser**	our
du:	**dein**	your	ihr:	**euer**	your
er:	**sein**	his, its			
es:	**sein**	its	sie:	**ihr**	their
sie:	**ihr**	her, its			
			Sie:	**Ihr** your	

■ *Nominative of possessive adjectives*

Masculine		Neuter		Feminine		Plural	
ein		ein		eine		—	
mein	} Tisch	**mein**	} Radio	**meine**	} Uhr	**meine**	} Bücher
unser		**unser**		**unsere**		**unsere**	

Demonstrative pronouns and personal pronouns

	Masculine	Neuter	Feminine	Plural
Personal Pronouns	er	es	sie	sie
Demonstrative Pronouns	der	das	die	die

Auf dem Münchener Viktualienmarkt gibt es immer frisches Obst und Gemüse.

Kapitel 4

LERNZIELE

■ **Sprechintentionen**

Talking about shopping and buying groceries
Expressing and inquiring about needs
Discussing meals
Inquiring about personal habits
Offering advice and making requests
Giving directives
Expressing likes and dislikes

■ **Lesestück**

Einkaufen am Wochenende

■ **Land und Leute**

Apotheke vs. *Drogerie*
Types of bread
Specialty stores vs. supermarkets
Outdoor markets
Typical German breakfast
Currency in German-speaking countries
Shopping hours

■ **Vokabeln**

Flavoring particles: *denn* and *doch*
Common foods
Noun compounds
Days of the week and parts of days as adverbs
Units of weight, capacity, measurement, and quantity

■ **Grammatik**

Verbs with stem-vowel change $e > i$
Word order: time and place expressions
Imperatives
Direct objects
Accusative case
Expressing likes and dislikes with *gern*
Es gibt

BAUSTEINE FÜR GESPRÄCHE

Was brauchst du?

JOCHEN: Gibt es hier eine Apotheke?
CLAUDIA: Ja, was brauchst du denn?
JOCHEN: Ich brauche etwas gegen Kopfschmerzen.
CLAUDIA: Nimmst du Aspirin? Das habe ich.

What do you need?

Is there a pharmacy (around) here?
Yes, what do you need?
I need something for a headache.

Do you take aspirin? I have that.

Gehst du heute einkaufen?

JÜRGEN: Gehst du heute nicht einkaufen?
PETRA: Doch. Warum fragst du?
JÜRGEN: Wir haben keinen Kaffee mehr.
PETRA: Ein Pfund ist genug, nicht? Sonst noch etwas?
JÜRGEN: Ja, ein Brot. Kauf das doch bei Rischart. Da ist das Brot besser.

Are you going shopping today?

Aren't you going shopping today?

Yes, I am. Why do you ask?
We don't have any more coffee.

One pound is enough, right? Anything else?
Yes, a loaf of bread. But buy that at Rischart's. The bread is better there.

Brauchbares

The words **denn** in **"Was brauchst du denn?"** and **doch** in **"Kauf das doch bei Rischart"** are called *flavoring particles*. They express a speaker's attitude about an utterance and do not have exact English equivalents. See pp. 93-95.

1. Was suchen Sie? Think of three things you need to buy. A fellow student or your instructor asks what kind of store you're looking for. Respond. You may want to refer to the Supplementary Word Sets in the Reference Section for names of specialty shops.

> Inquiring about shopping possibilities

S2:	S1:		
Was suchst° du? Was suchen Sie?	Ich brauche	**Brot.** Gibt es hier Aspirin. Wurst°. Spaghetti°. einen Kamm°.	**eine Bäckerei°?** eine Apotheke? eine Metzgerei°? einen Supermarkt°? eine Drogerie°?

Expressing needs

2. Geh doch. Your friend needs some things. Tell her/him to go to the store that sells them.

S2:   *S1:*

Ich brauche | etwas gegen Kopfschmerzen.   Geh doch° | in die Apotheke.
            | Brot für morgen. | zum Bäcker.
            | Wurst für heute abend. | zum Metzger.
            | Spaghetti. | in den Supermarkt.
            | ein Heft. | ins Kaufhaus°.
            | ein Buch über° Schach. | in die Buchhandlung°.

3. Sonst noch etwas? You've been telling a friend what you need, but there's something you've forgotten. What is it? When she/he asks whether there's anything else you need, say what it is.

S2:   *S1:*

Brauchst du sonst noch etwas?   Ja, wir haben | kein Brot mehr.
                                               | keine Spaghetti
                                               | kein Bier°
                                               | keinen Kaffee
                                               | keine Butter°

4. Rollenspiel. While on vacation in Germany, you develop a splitting headache on Sunday afternoon. You ask the desk clerk in your hotel to direct you to a drugstore. The desk clerk consults the **Notdienst** (*emergency service*) listing in the newspaper and tells you the name, address, and telephone number of a few drugstores open on the weekend. Be sure to note the information you are given.

Inquiring about needs

Notdienste

Von Samstag, 13 Uhr, bis Sonntag, 8.30 Uhr, haben folgende Apotheken Notdienst.

Victoria-Apotheke, Thomas-Mann-Str. 52, Tel. 63 25 06. Flora-Apotheke, Clemens-August-Straße 42, Tel. 22 24 85. Lessing-Apotheke, Beuel, Hermannstr. 72, Tel. 47 56 20. Hardt-Apotheke, Medinghoven, Europaring 42, Tel. 64 38 62. Apotheke am Römerplatz, Bad Godesberg, Rheinstr. 3, Tel. 36 41 04 u. 35 51 68. Martin-Apotheke, Bad Godesberg/Muffendorf, Hopmannstr. 7, Tel. 32 33 06.

Von Sonntag, 8.30 Uhr, bis Montag, 8.30 Uhr, haben folgende Apotheken Notdienst.

Einhorn-Apotheke, Poststr. 34, Tel. 65 28 33 u. 63 63 57. Adler-Apotheke, Bonner Talweg/Ecke Weberstr., Tel. 21 05 87. Apotheke im Tannenbusch, Tannenbusch, Paulusplatz 13, Tel. 66 24 56. Kreuz-Apotheke, Oberkassel, Königswinterer Str. 673, Tel. 44 12 11. Engel-Apotheke, Duisdorf, Rochusstr. 192, Tel. 62 26 18. Robert-Koch-Apotheke, Bad Godesberg, Beethovenallee 19, Tel. 35 36 69.

S1: Welche Apotheken sind offen°?
S2: Die Adler-Apotheke, Bonner Talweg/Ecke Weberstraße, Tel. 21 05 87.

Land und Leute

Apotheke vs. *Drogerie*

An **Apotheke** sells both prescription and non-prescription drugs. In every town and in each section of a large city, one **Apotheke** offers emergency service **(Notdienst)** at night and on Sunday. An **Apotheke** is staffed by a pharmacist **(ApothekerIn),** a university-trained specialist, and several trained assistants.

A **Drogerie** sells a wide variety of toiletries and often herbal remedies as well as many other items (e.g., toys, cassettes, vitamins)

Sonntags hat die Stadt-Apotheke in Offenbach am Main Notdienst.

Dieser Heidelberger Drogeriemarkt hat fast alles – von Postkarten bis Strandkleidung.

found in American drugstores. The **Drogerie** is gradually being replaced by the larger, self-service drugstore **(Drogeriemarkt).** A druggist **(DrogistIn)** is trained in a three-year apprenticeship.

There are generally fewer over-the-counter drugs in the German-speaking countries than in the U.S. Some non-prescription drugs are, nevertheless, **apothekenpflichtig,** that is, to purchase them, one must go to an **Apotheke.** They cannot be found in **Drogerien.** Regulations for particular drugs differ in each country. For example, aspirin is **apothekenpflichtig** in Germany and Austria, but not in Switzerland.

▷ **5. Frage-Ecke.** Find out why various people, including your partner, are going to certain places of business.

S2: Warum° geht Jochen ins Kaufhaus?
S1: Er geht ins Kaufhaus, denn° er braucht ein Heft.   because
S2: Warum gehst du ins Kaufhaus?
S1: Ich gehe ins Kaufhaus, denn ich brauche ein Heft./Ich gehe nicht ins
      Kaufhaus, denn ich brauche kein Heft.

S1:

	ins Kaufhaus	in die Drogerie	in die Metzgerei	in die Bäckerei	in den Supermarkt
Jochen	ein Heft		Wurst		Brötchen
Monika und Stefan		eine Kassette			
Herr Sommer		einen Kamm		Kuchen	200 Gramm Butter
Partnerin/Partner					

S2:

	ins Kaufhaus	in die Drogerie	in die Metzgerei	in die Bäckerei	in den Supermarkt
Jochen		Bleistifte		sechs Brötchen	
Monika und Stefan	zwei Kulis		250 Gramm Wurst	Brot	Kaffee
Herr Sommer	ein Radio		Salami		
Partnerin/Partner					

Erweiterung des Wortschatzes

1 Flavoring particles

"Flavoring" particles are little words used to express a speaker's attitude about an utterance. They relate the utterance to something the speaker or the listener has said or thought. Depending on the choice of the flavoring particle and sometimes on the tone of voice, the speaker expresses interest, surprise, impatience, denial, and so on. Because a particle has various shades of meaning that depend on the context, a dictionary can give only the approximate English meaning. With experience you will gain a "feel" for the meaning and use of these words, which are very characteristic of colloquial German.

Land und Leute

Das Brot

Bread plays a significant part in the daily nutrition of people in the German-speaking countries. Approximately 200 types of breads are baked in Germany alone. Names, shapes, and recipes vary from region to region. The most popular breads are baked fresh daily in one of the many bakeries (**Bäckereien**) and have a tasty crust. They also tend to have a firmer and often coarser texture than American breads.

A typical breakfast would not be complete without a crisp **Brötchen** or **Semmel**, as rolls are called in many areas. Open-faced sandwiches (**belegte Brote**) are popular for the evening meal and as a light lunch, and are often eaten with a knife and fork. Bread is made from a wide variety of grains, including rye (**Roggen**) and wheat (**Weizen**). Many types of bread are made from several kinds of grain—**Dreikornbrot, Vierkornbrot. Vollkornbrot** is made of unrefined, crushed grain. Bread with sunflower seeds (**Sonnenblumenbrot**) is also very popular. There are bread museums in Ulm, Mollenfelde, and Detmold which often

In dieser Tübinger Bäckerei gibt es über zehn verschiedene Brotsorten.

feature **Gebildbrote** (picture breads) in the shape of animals, wreaths, even violins.

Other baked goods are also popular. There are 1200 kinds of **Kleingebäck** (a term used for baked goods like rolls, soft pretzels, bread sticks, etc.). A bakery or pastry shop (**Konditorei**) always has a large selection of cookies (**Kekse**), pastries (**Gebäck**), and cakes (**Kuchen** and **Torten**).

■ *Flavoring particle* denn

DETLEV: Was brauchst du **denn**?   Tell me, what do you need?
UTE: Spaghetti.   Spaghetti.
DETLEV: Machst du **denn** wieder   You mean you're making spaghetti
Spaghetti?   again?

Denn is used frequently in questions to show the personal interest of the speaker. It softens the speaker's question and makes it less abrupt. **Denn** also refers back to a previous utterance of the speaker or listener or to a topic familiar to both.

■ *Flavoring particle* doch

The flavoring particle **doch** is used to express several shades of meaning.

Du machst **doch** heute Spaghetti,   You're making spaghetti today,
nicht?   aren't you?

Das glaubst du **doch** nicht.   { You surely don't believe that.
                                        { You can't really believe that.

The speaker uses **doch** to ask the listener for corroboration. "This is really true, isn't it?"

Geh **doch** in den Supermarkt! Why don't you go to the supermarket?
Machen Sie es **doch!** Go ahead and do it.

The speaker uses **doch** to persuade the listener to do something.

Das ist **doch** dumm. You must know that that's stupid.

The speaker uses **doch** to express slight impatience: "Come on, really . . ."

2 *Doch* as a way to correct negative false assumptions

JOCHEN: Es regnet heute nicht. It's not going to rain today.
CLAUDIA: **Doch**. Oh, yes it is.

In addition to its function as a flavoring particle, **doch** may be used to contradict the assumption contained in a previous negative assertion.

3 *Doch* as a positive response to a negative question

JÜRGEN: Gehst du heute nicht Aren't you going shopping today?
  einkaufen?
PETRA: **Doch**. Yes, I am.

Doch may be used as a positive response to a negative question.

1. Viele Fragen. Your house guest wants to know a lot of things. Respond in the positive, using **ja** or **doch** as appropriate.

▶ Gehst du heute nicht in die Bibliothek? *Doch.*
▶ Gehst du um sieben? *Ja.*

1. Gibt es hier eine Apotheke?
2. Hast du kein Aspirin?
3. Gehst du nicht in den Supermarkt?
4. Kaufst du Wurst?
5. Ist die Wurst da gut?
6. Machen wir heute abend das Essen° nicht zusammen?
7. Brauchen wir Brot?
8. Trinkst° du nicht Kaffee?

2. Was ißt du? Interview fellow students to learn what they eat at various meals.

> Talking about meals and food

S1:			S2:
Was	ißt du	**zum Frühstück°?**	Ich esse [zwei Brötchen].
	trinkst du	zum Mittagessen°?	Ich trinke [Orangensaft].
		zum Abendessen°?	

3. Essen und Trinken. Exchange information with your partner about your two favorite foods and drinks in the groups: **Lieblingsgetränke, Lieblingsobst, Lieblingsgemüse, Lieblingsfleisch.**

▶ *Meine Lieblingsgetränke sind ...*

4 Lebensmittel

das **Getränk**, -e
1. der **Apfelsaft** } der **Saft**, ⁝e
2. der **Orangensaft**
3. der **Kaffee**
4. der **Tee**
5. der **Weißwein**, -e } der **Wein**, -e
6. der **Rotwein**, -e
7. das **Bier**, -e
8. die **Milch**
9. das **Mineralwasser**
10. das **Wasser**

das **Gemüse**
11. die **Gurke**, -n
12. die **Karotte**, -n
13. die **Kartoffel**, -n
14. der **Salat**, -e
15. die **Tomate**, -n

das **Obst**
16. der **Apfel**, ⁝
17. die **Banane**, -n
18. die **Orange**, -n
19. die **Traube**, -n

das **Fleisch**
20. der **Rinderbraten**, -
21. der **Schinken**, -
22. die **Wurst**, ⁝e
23. das **Würstchen**, -

andere **Lebensmittel**
24. das **Brot**, -e
25. das **Brötchen**, -
26. das **Ei**, -er
27. der **Käse**
28. die **Nudeln** *(pl.)*
29. der **Fisch**, -e
30. das **Hähnchen**, -
31. die **Butter**
32. die **Margarine**
33. der **Kuchen**, -
34. die **Torte**, -n

die Pizza
die Cola

das Gehennesfleisch (mystery meat)

die Limonade – Lemonade

Vokabeln

Starting in *Kapitel 4* vowel changes in the present tense will be noted in parentheses following the infinitive of the verb, e.g., **essen (ißt).**

Substantive

das **Abendessen, -** evening meal
die **Apotheke, -n** pharmacy
das **Aspirin** aspirin
der **Bäcker, -** baker
die **Bäckerei, -en** bakery
das **Bier, -e** beer
das **Brot, -e** bread
die **Buchhandlung, -en** bookstore
die **Butter** butter
die **Drogerie, -n** drugstore
das **Essen, -** meal; prepared food
das **Frühstück** breakfast
der **Kaffee** coffee
der **Kamm, ¨e** comb
das **Kaufhaus, ¨er** department store
die **Kopfschmerzen** *(pl.)* headache

die **Lebensmittel** *(pl.)* food; groceries
der **Liebling, -e** favorite; das **Lieblingsgetränk** favorite drink
der **Metzger, -** butcher
die **Metzgerei, -en** butcher shop, meat market
das **Mittagessen** midday meal
das **Pfund, -e** pound (= 1.1 U.S. pounds; *abbrev.* **Pfd.**)
der **Salat, -e** lettuce; salad
die **Spaghetti** *(pl.)* spaghetti
der **Supermarkt, ¨e** supermarket
die **Wurst, ¨e** sausage, lunch meat
For additional foods, see p. 96.

Verben

brauchen to need
einkaufen to shop; **einkaufen gehen** to go shopping
essen (ißt) to eat
fragen to ask

kaufen to buy
nehmen (nimmt) to take
suchen to look for
trinken to drink

Andere Wörter

bei at; at a place of business **(beim [Metzger]);** at the home of **(bei [Ingrid])**
besser better
denn flavoring particle added to question
doch *(after a negative question or statement)* yes [I] am, [I] do; *(flavoring particle)* really; after all

ein paar a few
etwas something
gegen against
genug enough
kein not a, not any
offen open
sonst otherwise
über about
warum why

Besondere Ausdrücke

beim Bäcker at the baker's (bakery)
beim Metzger at the butcher's (butcher shop)
es gibt there is; there are
geh doch well, then go
in die Apotheke to the pharmacy

in den Supermarkt to the supermarket
kein ... mehr no more . . .
Sonst noch etwas? Anything else?
Was gibt's zum [Abendessen]? What's for [dinner/supper]?

zum Abendessen for the evening
  meal, for dinner
zum Bäcker to the baker's (bakery)
zum Frühstück for breakfast

zum Metzger to the butcher's
  (butcher shop)
zum Mittagessen for the midday
  meal, for lunch

EINKAUFEN AM WOCHENENDE

Vorbereitung auf das Lesen

■ *Vor dem Lesen*

ACHTUNG!

SIE KÖNNEN JETZT STRESSFREIER EINKAUFEN
Ab heute neue Öffnungszeiten

KRONE

Ihr Supermarkt seit 45 Jahren!

Montags bis mittwochs sind wir von 8 bis 18.30 für Sie da,
donnerstags von 9 bis 20 Uhr,
freitags von 8 bis 18.30,
und jeden Samstag von 8 bis 14 Uhr.

Look at the advertisement for the store **Krone** and answer the following
questions.

1. What kind of a store is **Krone?**
2. How long has **Krone** been in existence?
3. Why is **Krone** running this advertisement?
4. On which day is the store open the latest?
5. On which day does the store have the shortest business hours?
6. How are the following expressed in German in the ad:
   a. 8 P.M.
   b. every Saturday
   c. Wednesdays
7. Where do people in your community go shopping?

8. Where do you do most of your grocery shopping?
9. Are there many specialty shops in your area?
10. The opening times advertised here are typical of Germany. How do these times compare with the business hours of stores in your town?
11. Where do you think that shopping is less stressful—in your town or in Germany?

■ *Beim Lesen*

In the reading passage you will learn about shopping habits in Germany. As you read, make a list of the places where people go shopping and the things they buy in the various stores.

Es ist Samstag, und Monika macht Frühstück. Sie macht es heute besonders schön, denn ihre Freundinnen Diane und Joan aus Amerika sind da. Ihr Bruder° Stefan kommt in die Küche, und Monika sagt: „Du, Stefan, wir haben keinen Kaffee und keine Marmelade mehr. Geh bitte zu Meiers und kauf Kaffee und
5 Marmelade." Stefan nimmt Einkaufstasche und Geld und geht. Nebenan° ist noch ein Tante-Emma-Laden°. Da kaufen Monika und Stefan manchmal morgens ein°. Da kennt man sie. Viele Leute gehen in den Supermarkt, denn da ist es natürlich billiger. Aber bei Meiers ist es viel persönlicher°.
   Herr Meier sagt: „Guten Morgen, Herr Stamer. Was bekommen Sie denn
10 heute?"
   „Ich brauche Kaffee, ein Pfund."
   „Sonst noch einen Wunsch?"
   „Ja, ich brauche noch Marmelade. Ich nehme zwei Sorten°."
   „Haben Sie denn Besuch?"
15 „Ja, Freundinnen aus Amerika sind da. – Gut, das ist alles für heute."
Stefan nimmt noch eine Zeitung und bezahlt.
   „Auf Wiedersehen, Herr Stamer, und schönes Wochenende!"
   „Danke. Auf Wiedersehen."
   Der Bäcker ist gegenüber°. Da riecht es immer so gut. Stefan kauft Brötchen.
20 Die sind noch ganz warm.
   Das Frühstück ist wirklich sehr gut. Joan und Diane finden die Brötchen und den Kaffee besonders gut.
   Es ist jetzt schon elf Uhr, und Monika sagt: „Wir brauchen noch etwas fürs° Wochenende, und um ein Uhr schließen die Läden."
25 Die Vier gehen zusammen auf den Markt. Sie kaufen Karotten und zwei Kilo Kartoffeln fürs Mittagessen. Der Fischmann ist auch da. Hier kaufen sie frischen Fisch. Den essen sie zum Abendessen. Dann gehen sie auf den Blumenmarkt. Monika kommt oft samstags mit Blumen nach Hause. „Monika, die Blumen bezahle ich aber", sagt Diane.
30 Auf dem Weg nach Hause gehen sie noch in eine Metzgerei. Dort kaufen sie Fleisch und Wurst. „Habt ihr alles, oder braucht ihr auch noch etwas?" fragt Stefan.
   „Ich brauche Vitamintabletten", sagt Diane.
   „Warum Vitamintabletten? Bist du denn krank?" fragt Stefan.
35 „Nein, ich nehme jeden Tag Vitamintabletten."

Margin glosses:
brother
next door
mom-and-pop store
kaufen ein: shop
more personal

kinds

across from there

for the

[handwritten: We take Vitamins when we're ill.]

„Wirklich? Wir nehmen nur Vitamintabletten, <u>wenn wir krank sind.</u>* Aber gehen wir doch in die Drogerie! Dort bekommen wir Vitamintabletten", sagen Stefan und Monika.

[handwritten: Where can I get]

„Ist das dann alles?" fragt Stefan.

40 „Nein, ich brauche noch ein Buch. Wo ist eine <u>Buchhandlung</u>?" fragt Joan.   *[handwritten: book store]*

„Es ist schon nach eins, die Buchhandlung ist schon geschlossen°", erklärt   closed
Monika.

**Einige Leute kaufen
immer noch gern im
Tante-Emma-Laden ein.
(Hannover)**

Brauchbares

1. In *l. 3* Monika says: **"Du, Stefan."** Germans often get the attention of people they know well by starting their sentence with **"Du."**

2. In the sentence **"Da kaufen Monika und Stefan manchmal morgens ein"** *(l. 6),* note that the verb **einkaufen** is separated into **kaufen** and **ein**. This is called a separable-prefix verb because the prefix **ein** is separated from the verb **kaufen** in the sentence. German has many such verbs and you learn more about them in *Kapitel 5.*

3. In *l. 36* Monika and Stefan say **"Aber gehen wir doch in die Drogerie."** **Gehen wir** is the equivalent of *let's go.* The German construction is identical to the present-tense **wir**-form of the verb, but the pronoun **wir** follows the verb.

---

*l. 36: Although Germans are also concerned about health, vitamin pills as a diet supplement do not play the role they do in the United States. Vitamins are regarded more as a natural ingredient of any food.

Land und Leute

Einkaufen

Traditionally, Germans would do their food shopping in small stores **(Tante-Emma-Läden)**. However, their popularity has decreased in the last 25 years. In 1972 there were 160,400 small food stores in the Federal Republic. By 1994 there were only 76,000 and the number is expected to decrease to 55,000 by the year 2000. Today Germans do most of their food shopping in supermarkets, which tend to be smaller than American ones and are located within walking distance of residential areas. Many of the larger department stores **(Kaufhäuser)** also have complete grocery departments **(Lebensmittelabteilungen)**. There are also large discount stores **(Einkaufszentren)** on the outskirts of cities which sell not only groceries, but a wide variety of items ranging from clothing to electronic equipment, even pre-fabricated houses. Many people go shopping several times a week. Although the supermarkets are self-service stores, fresh foods such as cheeses, meats and cold cuts, bread, and vegetables may be sold by shop assistants at separate counters.

Viele Leute kaufen im Supermarkt ein. (Seewalchen, Österreich)

Customers bring their own shopping bags **(Einkaufstaschen)** to the supermarkets or buy plastic bags **(Plastiktüten)** or canvas bags at the check-out counter. Customers pack their own groceries and generally pay for their purchases with cash **(Bargeld)**, not by check or credit card.

Nach dem Lesen

1. **Wie viele Geschäfte?** *(How many stores?)* Compare your list of stores and items with a partner's list. How many stores did you find?

2. **Fragen zum Lesestück**

1. Warum macht Monika das Frühstück besonders schön?
2. Was braucht Monika für das Frühstück?
3. Was für ein Laden ist nebenan?
4. Warum kaufen Monika und Stefan gern bei Meiers?
5. Was braucht Monika für das Wochenende?
6. Wann kauft Monika oft Blumen?
7. Wer bezahlt die Blumen?
8. Warum kauft Joan heute kein Buch?

3. Vokabeln. In the reading passage, find the phrases you could use in the following situations.

1. You ask a friend if she/he needs something.
2. You ask a friend to buy some coffee for you.
3. You offer to pay for some flowers.
4. You ask if the group has everything.
5. You ask if the group needs something else.

4. Erzählen wir. How do Monika's and Stefan's shopping habits differ from Joan's and Diane's—or your own? Be prepared to say one or two sentences in class. Use the following topics to get you started.

Supermarkt □ Blumen □ Bäckerei □ Metzgerei

Erweiterung des Wortschatzes

1 Noun compounds

die **Blumen** + der **Markt** = der **Blumenmarkt**
flowers + market = flower market

kaufen + das **Haus** = das **Kaufhaus**
to buy + building = department store

A characteristic of German is its ability to form noun compounds easily. Where German uses compounds, English often uses separate words. Your vocabulary will increase rapidly if you learn to analyze the component parts of compounds.

der Kopf + **die** Schmerzen = **die** Kopfschmerzen
der Fisch + **der** Mann = **der** Fischmann
das Buch + **die** Handlung = **die** Buchhandlung

The last element of a compound determines its gender.

1. Was bedeutet das? *(What does that mean?)* The compounds listed below are made up of cognates and familiar nouns. Give the English equivalent of each.

1. der Winterabend
2. der Sommertag
3. die Marktfrau
4. der Sonnenschein
5. die Tischlampe
6. die Morgenzeitung
7. die Zimmertür

2 Days of the week and parts of days as adverbs

Noun	Adverb	English equivalent
Montag	**montags**	Mondays
Samstag	**samstags**	Saturdays
Morgen	**morgens**	mornings
Abend	**abends**	evenings

A noun that names a day of the week or a part of a day may be used as an adverb to indicate repetition or habitual action. An **-s** is added to the noun. In German, adverbs are not capitalized.

 2. Ein Interview. Interview a partner. Record her/his responses.

Wann ißt du mehr – mittags oder abends?
Wann bist du sehr müde – morgens oder abends?
Wann arbeitest du mehr – samstags oder sonntags?
Wann gehst du einkaufen – freitags, samstags oder wann?
Gehst du morgens oder abends einkaufen?

> Inquiring about
> personal habits

Fürs Wochenende: Blumen vom Frankfurter Blumenmarkt.

Land und Leute

Der Markt

Many people in the German-speaking countries prefer to buy their groceries at an outdoor market **(Markt)** because of its larger selection of fresh vegetables, fruit, and flowers grown by local farmers. There may also be stands **(Stände)** with bread, fish, sausages, eggs, herbs, and teas. Some markets are held daily, others once or twice a week; still others, like the famous **Viktualienmarkt** in Munich, have become permanent and are open the same hours as regular stores. Smaller cities, like Freiburg, often have a market right in their medieval centers, thus presenting a picturesque image of the past. Large cities, like Berlin or Vienna, offer a more cosmopolitan ambiance with their Turkish, Italian, or Eastern European markets. Hamburg's famous **Fischmarkt** in the St. Pauli harbor district opens very early on Sunday mornings and sells not only fish but a great variety of products that have just arrived from all over the world.

Land und Leute

Das Frühstück

"Ein gutes Frühstück ist die wichtigste Mahlzeit am Tag" *(A good breakfast is the most important meal of the day)* is a popular saying in the German-speaking countries. A German breakfast **(Frühstück)** can be quite extensive, especially on weekends or holidays. Usually it consists of a hot beverage, fresh rolls **(Brötchen)** or bread, butter and jam; often there are cold cuts, an egg, cheese or perhaps yogurt, whole grain granola **(Müsli)**, and juice or fruit. Pancakes are not a common breakfast food. Eggs for breakfast are usually soft-boiled **(weichgekocht)**. Scrambled eggs **(Rühreier)** and fried eggs **(Spiegeleier)** are more often served for a light meal either for lunch or in the evening. Traditionally, the main warm meal of the day was eaten at noon **(Mittagessen)**.

Zu einem gemütlichen Frühstück gehören Brötchen, Marmelade, Käse, Eier und Kaffee.

Recently, however, more and more people prefer to eat their warm meal in the evening **(Abendessen)**.

3 Units of weight and capacity

1 Kilo(gramm) (kg)	= 1000 Gramm
1 Pfund (Pfd.)	= 500 Gramm
1 Liter (l)	

In the United States a system of weight is used in which a pound consists of 16 ounces. In German-speaking countries the metric system is used: the basic unit of weight is the **Gramm,** and a thousand grams are a **Kilo(gramm).** German speakers also use the older term **Pfund** for half a **Kilo(gramm),** or 500 **(fünfhundert) Gramm.** The American *pound* equals **454 Gramm.** The basic unit of capacity in the German-speaking countries is the liter. A liter equals 1.056 quarts.

4 Units of measurement and quantity

Geben Sie mir zwei **Pfund** Kaffee.	Give me two pounds of coffee.
Ich nehme zwei **Glas** Milch.	I'll take two glasses of milk.
Er kauft zwei **Liter** Milch.	He's buying two liters of milk.
Zwei **Stück** Kuchen bitte.	Two pieces of cake, please.

In German, masculine and neuter nouns expressing measure, weight, or number are in the singular. Note that feminine nouns are in the plural: **Sie trinkt zwei Tassen Kaffee.** *(She drinks two cups of coffee.)*

3. Wieviel brauchen Sie?   You're going grocery shopping for an elderly neighbor and are finding out how much of each item she wants you to buy.

▶   Wieviel Kaffee brauchen Sie? (1 Pfd.)   *Ich brauche ein Pfund Kaffee.*

1. Wieviel Kartoffeln brauchen Sie? (5 kg)
2. Und wieviel Käse? (200 g)
3. Wieviel Milch brauchen Sie? (2 l)
4. Wieviel Fisch? (2 Pfd.)
5. Und Tee? (100 g)
6. Und wieviel Bananen brauchen Sie? (1 kg)
7. Wieviel Wurst? (150 g)

4.   Einkaufen.   You and a partner plan to go grocery shopping. You are on a tight budget and are planning to buy only the items advertised at **Preisring-Markt.** You have 50 Marks to spend. Make a list of the items you need, how much of each item you need, and what the cost of each item is. If you need help, see Vocabulary for Authentic Text Activities in the Reference Section.

Buying groceries

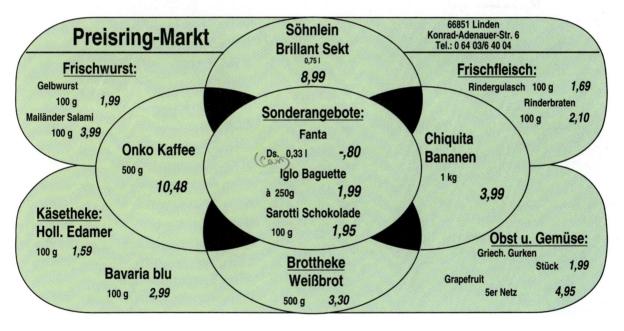

S1: Wir brauchen Kaffee, nicht?
S2: Ja. Wieviel?
S1: 500 Gramm.
S2: Gut. Wieviel kostet der?
S1: Zehn Mark° achtundvierzig.
S2: Wir brauchen Bananen, nicht?
S1: Ja. Wieviel?
S2: 2 Kilo.
S1: Gut. Wieviel macht das?
S2: Sieben Mark achtundneunzig.

Land und Leute

DM, sFr., öS

Customers in German-speaking countries almost always pay by cash in stores and restaurants. Only recently have credit cards become popular; checks, however, are uncommon.

Germany's basic monetary unit is the **Deutsche Mark (DM),** referred to as the **Mark** when speaking. There are 100 **Pfennig** in a **Mark.**

Switzerland's basic unit, the **Franken (sFr.)** is worth slightly more than the **Mark.** The Swiss **Franken** is also used by Liechtenstein as its basic monetary unit. There are 100 **Rappen (Rp.)** in a **Franken.**

Austria's basic unit is the **Schilling (öS).** The **Schilling** is a much smaller unit than the **Mark:** a piece of cake costs about 28 **Schilling,** the equivalent of 4**DM.** There are 100 **Groschen** in a **Schilling.**

In order to make identification of the different denominations clearer, each of the German-speaking countries prints the bills in various colors, and their size increases with their value. For example, the green 20**DM** bill **(Schein)** is larger than the blue 10**DM** bill.

Vokabeln

Substantive

der **Besuch, -e** visit; **wir haben Besuch** we have company
die **Blume, -n** flower
die **Einkaufstasche, -n** shopping bag

der **Freund, -e**/die **Freundin, -nen** friend
das **Geld** money
das **Glas, ¨er** glass
das **Gramm** gram (*abbrev.* **g**)

das **Haus, ̈er**   house
das **Kilo(gramm)**   kilogram (*abbrev.* **kg**)
die **Küche, -n**   kitchen
der **Laden, ̈**   store
die **Leute** (*pl.*)   people
der **Liter, -**   liter (*abbrev.* l = 1.056 U.S. quarts)
die **Mark, -**   mark; die **Deutsche Mark (DM)**   German currency
der **Markt, ̈e**   market
die **Marmelade**   marmalade, jam

die **Party, -s**   party
das **Stück, -e**   piece
die **Tablette, -n**   tablet, pill
die **Tasche, -n**   bag; pocket
die **Tasse, -n**   cup
der **Weg, -e**   way
das **Wochenende, -n**   weekend
der **Wunsch, ̈e**   wish
die **Zeitung, -en**   newspaper

Verben

bekommen   to receive
bezahlen   to pay (for); **sie bezahlt das Essen**   she pays for the meal
erklären   to explain
finden   to find; **Sie finden die Brötchen gut.**   They like the rolls.

geben (gibt)   to give
kennen   to know, be acquainted with
riechen   to smell
schließen   to close

Andere Wörter

alles   everything, all
besonders   especially, particularly
billig   cheap; **billiger**   cheaper
bitte   please
dort   there
etwas   some, somewhat
frisch   fresh
immer   always
manchmal   sometimes

mit   with
morgens   mornings, every morning
noch ein(e)   another
samstags   (on) Saturdays
schon   already
viele   many
wenn (*conj.*)   when
zu   to

Besondere Ausdrücke

auf dem Weg   on the way
auf den Markt   to the market
Besuch haben   to have company
Du, ...   Hey, . . . (*used to get someone's attention*)
nach Hause   (to go) home
noch etwas   something else (in addition)

Schönes Wochenende!   Have a nice weekend!
Sonst noch einen Wunsch?   Anything else?
Wieviel macht das?   How much does that come to?

GRAMMATIK UND ÜBUNGEN

1 Verbs with stem-vowel change *e > i*

essen: to eat	
ich esse	wir essen
du **ißt**	ihr eßt
er/es/sie **ißt**	sie essen
Sie essen	

geben: to give	
ich gebe	wir geben
du **gibst**	ihr gebt
er/es/sie **gibt**	sie geben
Sie geben	

nehmen: to take	
ich nehme	Wir nehmen
du **nimmst**	ihr nehmt
er/es/sie **nimmt**	sie nehmen
Sie nehmen	

English has only two verbs with stem-vowel changes in the third-person singular, present tense: *say > says (sezz)*, and *do > does (duzz)*.

German, on the other hand, has a considerable number of verbs with a stem-vowel change in the **du-** and **er/es/sie**-forms. Some verbs with stem vowel **e** change **e** to **i**. The verbs of this type that you know so far are **essen, geben,** and **nehmen.** The stem of **essen** ends in a sibilant; the ending **-st** therefore contracts to a **-t = du ißt** (see *Kapitel 2, Grammatik und Übungen,* section 7). **Nehmen** has an additional spelling change: **du nimmst, er/es/sie nimmt.** In the chapter vocabularies in this book, stem-vowel changes are indicated in parentheses: **geben (gibt).**

1. Was geben wir Christin?   Christin needs things for her room at the university. Tell what various friends are giving her. Use the proper form of **geben.**

▶ Jürgen / zwei alte Stühle   *Jürgen gibt Christin zwei alte Stühle.*

1. Claudia / zwei Hefte
2. Maria und Volker / ein Radio
3. wir / eine Lampe
4. ihr / eine Uhr
5. Frau Hauff / eine Büchertasche
6. du / ein Buch über Musik
7. ich / zwei Kugelschreiber

2.   Was nehmen wir?   You're in a restaurant with a group of friends. Indicate what you think each person will have. Use the proper form of **nehmen.**

▶   Claudia / Kaffee   *Claudia nimmt Kaffee, nicht?*

1. du / Tee
2. Jochen / Milch
3. ihr / etwas Obst
4. wir / Wurst und Brot
5. Volker und Maria / Käse und Brot
6. Tanja / Kuchen

3.   Was essen sie gern?   You are planning a picnic. Ask what the people listed below would like to eat. Use the proper form of **essen.**

▶   Frank   *Was ißt Frank gern?*

1. du
2. Barbara
3. Alex und Dieter
4. ihr
5. Paula
6. Sie

> Answering questions
> about eating habits

4.   Gern oder nicht gern?   Your partner wants to know what you like to eat and drink.

S2:   *S1:*

Ißt du	**viel**	**Brot?**
	oft	Kuchen?
	gern	Obst?
		Gemüse?
		Käse?

Ja,	**viel.**
	oft.
	gern.

Nein,	**nicht**	**viel.**
	nicht sehr	oft.
	nicht so	gern.

Trinkst du	**viel**	**Milch?**
	oft	Kaffee?
	gern	Tee?
		Bier?
		Wein?

2 Word order with expressions of time and place

Time	Place
Sie geht heute	in die Buchhandlung.

TMP: Comes after Verb

	Place	Time
She's going	to the bookstore	today.

When a German sentence contains both a time expression and a place expression, the time expression precedes the place expression. Note that the sequence of time and place in English is reversed.

5.   Wann gehst du?   Your friend is trying to guess when you're going to do various errands. Confirm the guesses.

▶   Wann gehst du in die Stadt? Heute morgen?   *Ja, ich gehe heute morgen in die Stadt.*

1. Wann gehst du in den Supermarkt? Um neun?
2. Wann gehst du in die Buchhandlung? Morgen?
3. Wann gehst du zum Bäcker? Später?
4. Wann gehst du in die Apotheke? Heute morgen?
5. Wann gehst du ins Kaufhaus? Jetzt?

3 Imperatives

The imperative forms are used to express commands, offer suggestions and encouragement, give instructions, and try to persuade people. In both German and English, the verb is in the first position.

Infinitive	Imperative *du*-Form	*ihr*-Form	*Sie*-Form
fragen	frag(e)	fragt	fragen Sie
arbeiten	arbeite	arbeitet	arbeiten Sie
essen	iß	eßt	essen Sie
geben	gib	gebt	geben Sie
nehmen	nimm	nehmt	nehmen Sie
sein	sei	seid	seien Sie

■ du-*imperative*

Erna. {
Frag(e) Frau List.
Arbeite jetzt, bitte.
Gib mir bitte das Brot.
Nimm doch zwei Aspirin.

Erna. {
Ask Mrs. List.
Work now, please.
Give me the bread, please.
Why don't you take two aspirin?

The **du**-imperative consists of the stem of a verb plus **-e**, but the **-e** is often dropped in informal usage: **frage > frag**. If the stem of the verb ends in **-d** or **-t,** the **-e** may not be omitted in written German: **arbeite**. If the stem vowel of a verb changes from **e** to **i**, the imperative has this vowel change and never has final **-e: geben > gib, essen > iß, nehmen > nimm**.

■ ihr-*imperative*

Günter. Peter. {
Fragt Frau List.
Gebt mir bitte das Brot.

Günter. Peter. {
Ask Mrs. List.
Give me the bread, please.

The **ihr**-imperative is identical with the **ihr**-form of the present tense.

■ Sie-*imperative*

Herr Hahn. {
Fragen Sie Frau List.
Geben Sie mir bitte das Brot.

Mr. Hahn. {
Ask Mrs. List.
Give me the bread, please.

The **Sie**-imperative is identical with the **Sie**-form of the present tense. The pronoun **Sie** is always stated and follows the verb directly. In speech, one differentiates a command from a yes/no question by the inflection of the voice. As in English, the voice rises at the end of a yes/no question and falls at the end of a command.

■ *Imperative of* sein

Anton, **sei** nicht so nervös!
Kinder, **seid** jetzt ruhig!
Frau Weibl, **seien Sie** bitte
so gut und ...

Anton, don't be so nervous!
Children, be quiet now!
Mrs. Weibl, please be
so kind and . . .

Note that the **du**-imperative (**sei**) and **Sie**-imperative (**seien Sie**) are different from the present-tense forms: **du bist, Sie sind.**

---

6. Auf einer Party: Frau Berg und Julia. The Bergs have guests. Below are some things Frau Berg says to Sarah and Martin, two people she knows well. She also knows Julia well. How would she say the same things to her?

| Giving directives |

▶ Sarah und Martin, nehmt noch etwas Käse.   *Julia, nimm noch etwas Käse.*

1. Trinkt doch noch ein Glas Wein.
2. Sagt mal, wie findet ihr die Musik?

3. Seid so nett und spielt etwas Gitarre.
4. Eßt noch etwas.
5. Kommt, hier sind unsere Fotos von Berlin.
6. Bleibt noch ein bißchen hier.
7. Seid so gut und gebt mir eure Telefonnummer.

7. Auf einer Party: Frau Berg und Herr Fromme. Herr Fromme is an acquaintance but not a personal friend of Frau Berg. Frau Berg uses **Sie** when speaking with him. How would she say the same things to him that she said to Sarah and Martin in exercise 6?

8. Macht das. Claudia and Jochen are planning a surprise party for Petra. They need your help for the final decisions. Give them your advice. Use the **ihr**-imperative.

> Offering advice

▶ Geben wir Petra ein Buch oder ein Radio? (Radio)   *Gebt Petra ein Radio.*

1. Machen wir die Party bei Monika oder bei Philipp? (Monika)
2. Kochen wir Spaghetti oder Gulasch? (Spaghetti)
3. Essen wir Brot oder Gemüse dazu°? (Brot)   with it
4. Kaufen wir das Brot im Supermarkt oder beim Bäcker? (beim Bäcker)
5. Trinken wir Wein oder Mineralwasser? (Mineralwasser)
6. Machen wir eine große oder eine kleine Party? (eine kleine Party)

9. Noch eine Party. At a very large party you hear snatches of conversation. Translate for your German friend who finds it all confusing. Use the **du-** or **ihr**-imperative as appropriate with first names and the **Sie**-imperative with last names.

▶ Stay here, Jennifer.   *Bleib hier, Jennifer.*
▶ Don't ask, Mr. Lang.   *Fragen Sie nicht, Herr Lang.*

1. Don't work too much, Julia.
2. Say something, Max.
3. Have a glass of mineral water, Christine. (Use **trinken.**)
4. Don't believe that, Mark and Tom.
5. Don't eat so much, Peter.
6. Take aspirin, Michael.
7. Be so kind, Mrs. Schulz, and stay here.
8. Michael, be quiet.
9. Please have some cake, Mrs. Klein. (Use **nehmen.**)

4 Direct object

Ich höre **Andrea** nebenan.	I hear *Andrea* next door.
Ich schließe die **Tür.**	I shut the *door.*

The direct object is the noun or pronoun that receives or is affected by the action of the verb. The direct object answers the question whom **(Andrea)** or what **(Tür).**

5 Accusative of the definite articles *der, das, die*

	Nominative	Accusative
Masculine	**Der** Kaffee ist billig.	Nehmen Sie **den** Kaffee.
Neuter	**Das** Brot ist frisch.	Nehmen Sie **das** Brot.
Feminine	**Die** Marmelade ist gut.	Nehmen Sie **die** Marmelade.
Plural	**Die** Blumen sind schön.	Nehmen Sie **die** Blumen.

The direct object of a verb is in the accusative case. In the accusative case, the definite article **der** changes to **den.** The articles **das** and **die** (*sg.* and *pl.*) do not show case change in the accusative.

10.   Einkaufen gehen.   A friend is shopping for things for her/his room. Ask whether she/he intends to buy the things. The things become direct objects in your questions.

▶   Die Lampe ist lustig.   *Kaufst du die Lampe oder nicht?*

1. Das Radio ist gut.
2. Der Stuhl ist billig.
3. Der Tisch ist schön.
4. Das Bett ist groß.
5. Die Uhr ist billig.
6. Die Blumen sind schön.

6 Word order and case as signals of meaning

Subject	Verb	Direct object
The man	visits	the professor.
The professor	visits	the man.

English usually uses word order to signal the difference between a subject and a direct object. The usual word-order pattern in statements is *subject, verb,* and *direct object.* The two sentences above have very different meanings.

Subject (nom.)	Verb	Direct object (acc.)
Der Mann	besucht	den Professor.

Direct Object (acc.)	Verb	Subject (nom.)
Den Professor	besucht	der Mann.

German generally uses case to signal the difference between a subject and a direct object. The different case forms of the definite article (e.g., **der, den**) signal the grammatical function of the noun. **Der**, in the example above, indicates that the noun **Mann** is in the nominative case and functions as the subject. **Den** indicates that the noun **Professor** is in the accusative case and functions as the direct object. The word-order pattern in statements may be *subject, verb, direct object,* or *direct object, verb, subject.* The two sentences above have the same meaning.

Since German uses cases to signal grammatical function, it can use word order for another purpose: to present information from different perspectives. A speaker may use so-called "normal" word order *(subject, verb, direct object)* or inverted word order *(direct object, verb, subject).* The English equivalents vary, depending on context and the meaning the speaker wishes to convey. The sentence **Der Mann besucht den Professor** is equivalent to *The man visits the professor.* The sentence **Den Professor besucht der Mann** is equivalent to saying something like *It's **the professor** the man is visiting.*

Der Professor fragt **die** Studentin   The professor asks the student
  etwas.   something.

When only one noun or noun phrase shows case, it may be difficult at first to distinguish meaning. In the example above, **der Professor** has to be the subject, since the definite article **der** clearly shows nominative case. By the process of elimination, therefore, **die Studentin** has to be the direct object. If **die Studentin** were the subject, the article before **Professor** would be **den**.

Die Frau fragt **das** Mädchen etwas.

Sometimes neither noun contains a signal for case. In an example like the one above, one would usually assume normal word order: *The woman asks the girl something.* Depending on context, however, it is possible to interpret it as inverted word order: *It's **the woman** the girl is asking something.*

11. Wer macht das? A number of people are having a neighborhood party. What is going on among them? Find out by identifying the subjects of the sentences.

▶ Die Frau kennt der Nachbar nicht.   *Subject: der Nachbar*

1. Das Kind sucht seine Mutter.
2. Der Junge fragt das Mädchen etwas.
3. Das Mädchen findet der Junge nett.
4. Den Rotwein trinkt der Professor gern.
5. Die Amerikaner kennt die Frau gut.
6. Die Italiener kennen die Frau aber nicht.
7. Den Kuchen essen die Kinder gern.

Land und Leute

Geschäftszeiten

For many people in the German-speaking countries, shopping is an integral part of daily life. Going shopping several times a week and walking to a store are very common. Although most food shopping is done in supermarkets, specialty stores (**Fachgeschäfte**) like the bakery, butcher shop, or fruit and vegetable store are still frequently patronized. Some customers enjoy the more personal atmosphere and the convenient location of these neighborhood stores, where they are often known and greeted by name.

Business hours for stores are regulated by law. In Germany, stores may be open from 7:00 A.M. to 6:30 P.M. on weekdays except Thursdays, when stores may be open until 8:30 P.M. Stores close no later than 2:00 P.M. on Saturday; however, on the first Saturday of each month (**langer Samstag**) and the four Saturdays before Christmas they may stay open until 6:00 P.M. Many neighborhood stores close during the early afternoon (**Mittagspause**) from about 1:00 to 3:00. On Sundays most stores are closed. Exceptions are made for flower shops (**Blumenläden**), which often open for a few hours Sunday morning. Pastry shops (**Konditoreien**) are often open on Sunday morning and afternoon as well as on Saturday afternoon. Another exception are stores which serve the traveling public in train stations and airports.

Im Winter ist diese Apotheke am langen Samstag bis 18 Uhr geöffnet.

The shop closing law (**Ladenschlußgesetz**) has been a controversial topic and various arrangements for lengthening shopping hours have been suggested and tried out. Owners of large stores and consumers generally support longer hours, but the unions strictly oppose further changes because the present law allows employees to work regular hours and have a full weekend. Owners of small stores generally contend that they do not attract enough business to make a profit from longer shopping hours.

7 Direct object vs. predicate noun

Predicate noun	Dieter Müller ist **mein Freund.**	Dieter Müller is *my friend.*
Direct object	Kennst du **meinen Freund?**	Do you know *my friend?*

The predicate noun (e.g., **mein Freund**) designates a person, concept, or thing that is equated with the subject (e.g., **Dieter Müller**). A predicate noun completes the meaning of linking verbs such as **sein** and **heißen** and is in the nominative case.

The direct object (e.g., **meinen Freund**) is the noun or pronoun that receives or is related to the action of the verb. The direct-object noun or pronoun is in the accusative case.

Predicate noun	Das ist **nicht** Gisela Meier.
Direct object	Ich kenne Gisela Meier **nicht**.

Nicht precedes a predicate noun and usually follows a noun or pronoun used as a direct object.

12. Ein kleines Interview. Here are some questions Peter was asked about his German class. Identify the direct object or predicate noun.

1. Sind das alle Studenten?
2. Kennst du die Studenten gut?
3. Ist dein Professor eine Frau oder ein Mann?
4. Ist das dein Deutschbuch?
5. Brauchst du ein Buch aus Deutschland?
6. Hast du Freunde in Deutschland oder Österreich?

13. Was kaufst du? In order to finance your summer trip to Europe you're selling things in your room or apartment. Your partner will decide which items she/he wants and asks the price. After you name the price, she/he decides whether to buy the article.

S2: Was kostet° [der Stuhl]?
S1: [Zwanzig] Mark.   cost
S2: Gut, ich kaufe/nehme [den Stuhl]./ Das ist zuviel. Ich kaufe/nehme [den Stuhl] nicht.

8 Demonstrative pronouns in the accusative case

Wie findest du **den** Kaffee?	How do you like the coffee?
Den finde ich gut.	This is (really) good!

Wie findest du **das** Fleisch?	How do you like the meat?
Das finde ich gut.	That's (really) good!

Wie findest du **die** Torte?	How do you like the cake?
Die finde ich gut.	That is (really) good!

Wie findest du **die** Eier?	How do you like the eggs?
Die finde ich gut.	Those are (really) good!

The accusative forms of the demonstrative pronouns are identical to the accusative forms of the definite articles.

14. Nein, das finde ich nicht. You and Gabi are shopping in a department store. Disagree with all of her opinions.

▶ Ich finde das Musikheft billig. Du auch?   *Nein, das finde ich nicht billig.*

1. Ich finde das Buch über Schach schlecht. Du auch?
2. Ich finde den Fernseher zu klein. Du auch?
3. Ich finde den Kugelschreiber billig. Du auch?
4. Ich finde die Lampe schön. Du auch?
5. Ich finde das Radio gut. Du auch?
6. Ich finde den Tisch zu groß für das Zimmer. Du auch?
7. Ich finde die Stühle furchtbar. Du auch?
8. Ich finde die Uhr zu groß. Du auch?

15. Im Tante-Emma-Laden. You run a small store. A customer has come to you with a shopping list. Unfortunately, your store doesn't carry these items. Send her/him to the appropriate store. You may want to refer to the Supplementary Word Sets in the Reference Section for names of specialty shops.

> Telling someone where to buy something

S2:		S1:		
Ich brauche	**Kaffee.**	Kauf	**den**	**bei Müller.**
	Butter.	Kaufen Sie	die	im Supermarkt.
	Käse.		das	beim Metzger.
	Wurst.			beim Bäcker.
	Brot.			im Kaufhaus.
	Tee.			in der Buchhandlung.
	Papier.			
	ein Buch.			

9 Accusative of *wer?*

Nominative	Accusative
Wer fragt?	**Wen** fragt sie?

The accusative case form of the interrogative pronoun **wer?** *(who?)* is **wen?** *(whom?)*.

16. Wen? You keep missing the ends of people's statements at a party. Ask whom they are talking about. Replace the direct object with **wen?** to pose your questions.

▶ Ich frage den Professor morgen. *Wen fragst du morgen?*

1. Thomas fragt Birgit heute abend.
2. Martina findet Detlev lustig.
3. Ich finde Stefan intelligent.
4. Ich frage Professor Ulmer morgen.
5. Ulrike kennt die Amerikaner gut.

10 The construction *haben + gern*

Ich **habe** Petra **gern**.	I like Petra.
Ich **habe** Mark **nicht gern**.	I don't like Mark.

In *Kapitel 2*, you learned how to say you liked to do something by using a verb plus **gern: Ich schwimme gern.** A common way of expressing fondness for someone in German is to use **haben + gern. Haben + nicht gern** is used to express dislike.

17. Wen hast du gern? Tell your partner about people you know or about famous people, such as musicians, politicians, and athletes you like or don't like and why.

Expressing likes and dislikes

▶ *Ich habe Boris Becker gern. Er spielt gut Tennis.*
▶ *Ich habe Inge nicht gern. Sie ist unfreundlich.*

11 Accusative of *ein* and *kein*

	Nominative	Accusative
Masculine	Wo ist **ein** Bleistift?	Haben Sie **einen** Bleistift?
	Da ist **kein** Bleistift.	Ich habe **keinen** Bleistift.
Neuter	Wo ist **ein** Heft?	Haben Sie **ein** Heft?
	Da ist **kein** Heft.	Ich habe **kein** Heft.
Feminine	Wo ist **eine** Uhr?	Haben Sie **eine** Uhr?
	Da ist **keine** Uhr.	Ich habe **keine** Uhr.
Plural	Sind das Kulis?	Haben Sie Kulis?
	Das sind **keine** Kulis.	Ich habe **keine** Kulis.

The indefinite article **ein** and the negative **kein** change to **einen** and **keinen** before masculine nouns in the accusative singular. The neuter and feminine indefinite articles and their corresponding negatives do not show case changes in the accusative singular. **Ein** has no plural forms. **Kein**, however, does have a plural form: **keine.**

18. Wer braucht was? There are a number of new people in your dorm and their rooms are not completely furnished. Tell what each person needs.

▶ Peter / Tisch *Peter braucht einen Tisch.*

1. Anja / Bett
2. Karin / Tisch
3. Caroline / Fernseher
4. Peter / Lampe

5. Robin / Uhr
6. Lisa / Stuhl
7. Florian / CD-Spieler

19. Ich brauche [keinen Tisch]. Ask your partner if she/he needs the things in exercise 18. She/He will reply in the negative.

S1: Brauchst du [einen Tisch]?
S2: Nein, ich brauche [keinen Tisch].

12 Accusative of possessive adjectives

	Nominative	Accusative
Masculine	Ist das **mein** Bleistift?	Ja, ich habe **deinen** Bleistift.
Neuter	Ist das **mein** Heft?	Ja, ich habe **dein** Heft.
Feminine	Ist das **meine** Uhr?	Ja, ich habe **deine** Uhr.
Plural	Sind das **meine** Kulis?	Ja, ich habe **deine** Kulis.

The possessive adjectives (**mein, dein, sein, ihr, unser, euer, Ihr**) have the same endings as the indefinite article **ein** in both the nominative and accusative cases.

20. Unsere Freunde. You're in a café having cake and coffee with Jochen. You talk about your friends. Restate, using the cued possessive adjective. The possessive adjective modifies the direct object.

▶ SIE: Martin findet die Arbeit furchtbar. (sein)   *Martin findet seine Arbeit furchtbar.*

1. SIE: Ich finde die Arbeit interessant. (mein)
2. SIE: Freitags bekomme ich Geld. (mein)
3. JOCHEN: Warum gibt Frank Andrea einen Computer? (sein)
4. SIE: Andrea gibt Frank ein Kassettendeck. (ihr)
5. JOCHEN: Patrick und Alex fragen den Professor viel. (ihr)
6. SIE: Wir brauchen heute die Bücher, nicht? (unser)
7. JOCHEN: Warum ißt du den Kuchen nicht? (dein)
8. SIE: Du, Jochen, brauchst du einen Kuli? (dein)

21. Was suchst du? Coming back from a field trip, a number of students are missing items. Tell who is looking for what by completing the sentences with the appropriate possessive adjective.

▶ Gerd sucht _____ Bleistift.   *Gerd sucht seinen Bleistift.*

1. Monika sucht _____ Buch.
2. Wir suchen _____ Kulis.
3. Katja sucht _____ Radio.
4. Jakob und Dario suchen _____ Bleistift.
5. Sarah sucht _____ Zeitung.
6. Ich suche _____ Deutschbuch.
7. Florian und Julia suchen _____ Bücher.

13 Impersonal expression *es gibt*

Gibt es hier einen Supermarkt?   Is there a supermarket here?
Es gibt heute Butterkuchen.   There's [We're having] butter cake today.

Es gibt is equivalent to English *there is* or *there are*. It is followed by the accusative case.

22. Was gibt es heute zum Abendessen? Tell what is planned for dinner tonight, and what is not.

▶ Fisch – Käse   *Es gibt Fisch, aber keinen Käse.*

1. Brötchen – Kartoffeln
2. Milch – Saft
3. Butter – Margarine
4. Gemüse – Obst
5. Tee – Kaffee
6. Mineralwasser – Wein

23. Das Essen bei Moritz.   Moritz has had success fishing and has invited his friends to a fish dinner. They discuss the preparations. Give the German equivalents. Note that the words in brackets are part of the English sentence and should not be translated.

1. Do you have the fish, Moritz?
2. Do you like cake? (Use the verb **essen** + **gern**.)
3. Do we need potatoes and carrots?
4. Where do you buy the mineral water?
5. Who's paying [for] everything? (Use the verb **bezahlen**.)
6. What kind of music do we need?
7. Whom are you asking?
8. Who is buying the wine?
   —That [is what] I'm buying.

14 Prepositions

Margot kauft die Uhr **für ihren Freund.**	Margot is buying the watch for her friend.
Margot kauft die Uhr **für ihn.**	Margot is buying the watch for him.

A preposition (e.g., **für**—*for*) is used to show the relation of a noun (e.g., **Freund**—*friend*) or pronoun (e.g., **ihn**—*him*) to some other word in the sentence (e.g., **kauft**—*buying*). The noun or pronoun following the preposition is called the object of the preposition.

15 Accusative prepositions

durch	through	Sie geht **durch** die Buchhandlung.
für	for	Sie kauft es **für** das Haus.
gegen	against	Sie hat nichts **gegen** den Mann.
ohne	without	Sie geht **ohne** das Kind.
um	around	Sie geht **um** den Tisch.

The objects of the prepositions **durch, für, gegen, ohne,** and **um** are always in the accusative case.

Er geht **durchs** Zimmer.	durch das **= durchs**
Er braucht eine Batterie **fürs** Auto.	für das **= fürs**
Er geht **ums** Haus.	um das **= ums**

The prepositions **durch, für,** and **um** often contract with the definite article **das** to form **durchs, fürs,** and **ums.** These contractions are common in colloquial German, but are not required.

24. Meine Freunde. Tell what your friends are doing. Complete the sentences by choosing an appropriate preposition and adding the correct form of the article or possessive adjective.

durch □ für □ gegen □ ohne □ um

▶ Ursel geht _____ d_____ Buchhandlung.
Ursel geht durch die Buchhandlung.

1. Walter geht _____ d_____ Garten.
2. Volker sagt etwas _____ sein_____ Professor.
3. Trudi kauft Blumen _____ ihr_____ Freundin Marta.
4. Susanne geht _____ d_ie_ Stadt.
5. Sie geht _____ ihr_____ Mann.
6. Walter kauft ein Buch _____ sein_____ Freund Jochen.

16 Accusative of masculine *N*-nouns

Nominative	Accusative
Der Herr sagt etwas.	Hören Sie **den** Her**rn?**
Der Student sagt etwas.	Hören Sie **den** Studen**ten?**

German has a class of masculine nouns that have signals for case. Not only the article, but the noun itself ends in **-n** or **-en** in the accusative. This class of nouns may be referred to as masculine **N**-nouns or "weak nouns." In the vocabularies of this book, masculine **N**-nouns will be followed by two endings: **der Herr, -n, -en.** The first ending is the singular accusative and the second is the plural ending. The masculine **N**-nouns you know so far are **der Herr, der Junge, der Mensch, der Nachbar,** and **der Student.**

25. Wie sagt man das? Give the German equivalents of the conversational exchanges below.

1. Do you like the gentleman there, Mrs. Kluge?
   —Yes. He's a neighbor.
2. Why is the neighbor going around the house?
   —Ask Mr. Heidemann.
3. Why is Mr. Leber coming without the children?
   —He's buying books for the children.
4. I have nothing against Mr. Knecht.
   —Who's Mr. Knecht?

17 Accusative of personal pronouns

Nominative	Accusative		
Subject	Object	Subject	Object
Er braucht	**mich.**	*He* needs	*me.*
Ich arbeite für	**ihn.**	*I* work for	*him.*

Pronouns used as direct objects or objects of accusative prepositions are in the accusative case.

Subject pronouns	I	you	he	she	it	we	you	they
Object pronouns	me	you	him	her	it	us	you	them

Some English pronouns have different forms when used as subject or as object.

Nominative	ich	du	er	sie	es	wir	ihr	sie	Sie
Accusative	mich	dich	ihn	sie	es	uns	euch	sie	Sie

Some German pronouns also have different forms in the nominative and accusative.

26. Nein danke! Mark wants to lend you all his things. Say you don't need them. Use a pronoun in each answer.

▶ Brauchst du mein Buch über Schach?   *Nein, danke, ich brauche es nicht.*

1. Brauchst du meinen Fußball?
2. Brauchst du mein Musikheft?
3. Brauchst du meinen Kugelschreiber?
4. Brauchst du meine Lampe?
5. Brauchst du meine Stühle?
6. Brauchst du meinen Computer?

27. Wie sagt man das? Give the German equivalents of the conversational exchanges below.

1. Who is working for us?
   —We're working for you.
2. Are you asking me?
   —Yes, I'm asking you.
3. What do you have against me?
   —I have nothing against you, Mr. Schuhmacher.
4. Do you know Uwe and Barbara?
   —Yes. I like them.

WIEDERHOLUNG

1.   Monika geht einkaufen.   Monika needs some things for supper. Tell about her shopping. Restate the sentences below, beginning with the words in italics. Make the necessary changes in word order.

▶   Monika braucht Brot *fürs Abendessen.*   *Fürs Abendessen braucht Monika Brot.*

1. Monika geht *heute morgen* einkaufen.
2. Viele Leute gehen *jetzt* in den Supermarkt.
3. Es ist aber *im Supermarkt* nicht so persönlich.
4. Monika kauft *das Brot* beim Bäcker.
5. Sie geht *dann* auf den Blumenmarkt.
6. Sie kommt oft *samstags* mit Blumen nach Hause.

2.   Essen und Trinken.   While having wine and cheese, Laura and Robert talk about eating and drinking. Form sentences, using the cues below.

▶   LAURA: wie / du / finden / der Wein / ?   *Wie findest du den Wein?*

1. ROBERT: gut // was für Wein / das / sein / ?
2. LAURA: Wein / kommen / aus Kalifornien
3. ROBERT: du / kaufen / der Käse / im Supermarkt / ?
4. LAURA: nein, / ich / kaufen / alles / auf dem Markt
5. LAURA: zum Abendessen / es / geben / Fisch
6. LAURA: du / essen / gern / Fisch / ?
7. ROBERT: nein, / ich / essen / kein Fisch / und / auch / keine Wurst
8. ROBERT: ich / essen / aber / gern / Kuchen
9. LAURA: heute / es / geben / leider / kein Kuchen

3.   Beim Frühstück.   Peter is a German exchange student who just arrived last night in New York and is staying with the Schuberts. Harry and Anna Schubert, their two children, Hannah and Frank, and Peter are sitting at the breakfast table. Give the German equivalent of their conversation.

1. MRS. SCHUBERT: Who needs the tea?
2. MR. SCHUBERT: Hannah, give Peter the coffee.
3. HANNAH: Peter doesn't drink coffee.
4. PETER: No, I always drink tea for breakfast.
5. MRS. SCHUBERT: Harry, what are you doing today?
6. MR. SCHUBERT: I'm working in the library. (in the = **in der**)
7. MRS. SCHUBERT: Aren't you buying the table?
8. MR. SCHUBERT: No, it's too small.
9. MR. SCHUBERT: Peter, whom do you know in New York?
10. PETER: I know a professor.
11. FRANK: Peter, are there many supermarkets in Germany?
12. PETER: Of course. Why do you ask, Frank?

4. **Nicht oder kein?** Answer in the negative, using **nicht** or a form of **kein**.

▶ Kauft Erika heute Kartoffeln? *Nein, sie kauft heute keine Kartoffeln.*

1. Kauft sie Kuchen?
2. Geht sie heute zum Bäcker?
3. Kauft sie das Fleisch im Super-markt?

4. Kauft Gerd heute Käse?
5. Kauft er das Brot beim Bäcker?
6. Kauft er heute Milch?
7. Gibt es hier einen Supermarkt?

5. **Wie sagt man das?** Give the German equivalents of the conversational exchanges below.

1. What color are the flowers?
   —They're red and white.
2. How are you, Mrs. Driesbach?
   —I'm fine, thanks.
3. What are you doing tonight, Iris?
   —I'm working.
4. Horrible weather today, isn't it?
   —Yes, the wind is cold. It'll certainly rain again.

6. **Frage-Ecke.** Compare the picture of your room with that of your partner.

S1: Mein Zimmer hat [eine Pflanze]. Hast du auch [eine Pflanze]?
S2: Ja, ich habe auch [eine Pflanze]./Nein, aber ich habe Blumen.

S1: Picture #1

S2: Picture #2

7. **Am Wochenende.** Exchange information with your partner about what you will do this weekend **(am Wochenende).** English equivalents of verbs you have already had and which may be useful are listed below:

~~study~~	eat	dance	listen (to)
play	drink	stay	be
buy	have	cook	go
work	look for	take	go shopping

(handwritten margin notes:)
P1: Das Zimmer hat einen Stuhl.
Mein Zimmer hat auch einen Stuhl.
Aber keinen Stuhl
(do 6 or 7 Sentences)

Pick 8 verbs

8. Zum Schreiben

1. a. Assume that you are one of the two American students, Diane or Joan, who are visiting Monika. (See **Einkaufen am Wochenende** pp. 99–100.) Write a short letter to someone you plan to visit in Austria, in which you tell what you plan to do with your German friends on the second weekend of your visit in Germany. It is O.K., incidentally, to do many of the same things that you did on the first weekend, especially if you enjoyed them.

   b. Or assume you are one of the two German students, Monika or Stefan. Write a letter to a friend in which you say you have guests from the U.S.A. and tell what you plan to do with them during the second week (end) of their visit.

   Hinweise (tips): Before you begin your letter turn back to *Kapitel 3* and review the format (opening, closing, etc.) for informal letters. Then make a list of activities you plan to write about, e.g., shopping, playing tennis.

2. Your friend Erik prefers to shop in **Supermärkte,** but your friend Monika prefers **Tante-Emma-Läden.** Write a paragraph in German in which you state your personal preference and your reasons for it.

   Hinweise: Look over the reading (pp. 99–100) and **Land und Leute: Einkaufen** (p. 101) before you begin writing. Think about which things appeal to you in the type of store you prefer. Write down your ideas and then organize them according to their order of importance. Begin your paragraph by stating which type of store you like: **Ich gehe gern [in den Supermarkt]. Da ...**

GRAMMATIK: ZUSAMMENFASSUNG

Verbs with stem-vowel change *e > i*

essen	
ich esse	wir essen
du **ißt**	ihr eßt
er/es/sie **ißt**	sie essen
Sie essen	

geben	
ich gebe	wir geben
du **gibst**	ihr gebt
er/es/sie **gibt**	sie geben
Sie geben	

nehmen	
ich nehme	wir nehmen
du **nimmst**	ihr nehmt
er/es/sie **nimmt**	sie nehmen
Sie nehmen	

Several verbs with the stem vowel **e** (including **essen, geben, nehmen**) change **e** > **i** in the **du-** and **er/es/sie**-forms of the present tense.

Word order with expressions of time and place

	Time	Place
Monika geht	heute abend	ins Kino.
Robert war	gestern	nicht hier.

In German, time expressions generally precede place expressions.

The imperative forms

	Infinitive	Imperative	Present
du	sagen	**Sag(e)** etwas bitte.	Sagst du etwas?
ihr		**Sagt** etwas bitte.	Sagt ihr etwas?
Sie		**Sagen Sie** etwas bitte.	Sagen Sie etwas?
du	nehmen	**Nimm** das Brot bitte.	Nimmst du das Brot?
ihr		**Nehmt** das Brot bitte.	Nehmt ihr das Brot?
Sie		**Nehmen Sie** das Brot bitte.	Nehmen Sie das Brot?

■ *Imperative of* **sein**

du	**Sei** nicht so nervös.
ihr	**Seid** ruhig.
Sie	**Seien Sie** so gut.

Accusative case of nouns

Nominative Subject	Accusative Direct Object
Der Kuchen ist frisch.	Er nimmt **den Kuchen**.
Die Uhr ist schön.	Sie kauft **die Uhr**.

A noun that is used as a direct object of a verb is in the accusative case.

Accusative case of masculine *N*-nouns

Nominative	der Herr	der Junge	der Mensch	der Nachbar	der Student
Accusative	den Her**rn**	den Jung**en**	den Mensch**en**	den Nachbar**n**	den Student**en**

A number of masculine nouns add **-n** or **-en** in the accusative singular.

Accusative case of the definite articles *der, das, die*

	der	das	die	Plural
Nominative	**der** ⎫ Käse	**das** ⎫ Brot	**die** ⎫ Butter	**die** ⎫ Eier
Accusative	**den** ⎭	**das** ⎭	**die** ⎭	**die** ⎭

Accusative case of demonstrative pronouns

Accusative nouns	Accusative pronouns
Ich finde **den Käse** gut.	**Den** finde ich auch gut.
Ich finde **das Brot** trocken.	**Das** finde ich auch trocken.
Ich finde **die Butter** frisch.	**Die** finde ich auch frisch.
Ich finde **die Eier** schlecht.	**Die** finde ich auch schlecht.

Accusative case of *wer*

Nominative	Accusative
Wer fragt?	**Wen** fragt er?

Accusative of *ein, kein,* and possessive adjectives

	Masculine (der Kuli)	Neuter (das Heft)	Feminine (die Uhr)	Plural (die Kulis)
Nominative	**ein** / **kein** / **dein** ⎬ Kuli	**ein** / **kein** / **dein** ⎬ Heft	**eine** / **keine** / **deine** ⎬ Uhr	**keine** / **deine** ⎬ Kulis
Accusative	**einen** / **keinen** / **deinen** ⎬ Kuli	**ein** / **kein** / **dein** ⎬ Heft	**eine** / **keine** / **deine** ⎬ Uhr	**keine** / **deine** ⎬ Kulis

Kein and the possessive adjectives (**mein, dein, sein, ihr, unser, euer, Ihr**) have the same endings as the indefinite article **ein**.

Accusative case of personal pronouns

Nominative	ich	du	er	es	sie	wir	ihr	sie	Sie
Accusative	**mich**	**dich**	**ihn**	**es**	**sie**	**uns**	**euch**	**sie**	**Sie**

Prepositions with the accusative case

durch	through	Sie geht **durch** das Zimmer. [**durchs** Zimmer]
für	for	Sie kauft die Uhr **für** das Haus. [**fürs** Haus]
gegen	against	Sie hat nichts **gegen** den Mann.
ohne	without	Sie geht **ohne** Herrn Bauer.
um	around	Sie geht **um** das Haus. [**ums** Haus]

The construction *haben + gern*

Hast du Lore **gern?** Do you like Lore?
Ich **habe** sie nicht **gern.** I don't like her.

A common way of expressing fondness for someone in German is to use **haben + gern. Haben + nicht gern** is used to express dislike.

Impersonal expression *es gibt*

Es gibt keinen Kaffee mehr. There is no more coffee.
Gibt es auch keine Brötchen? Aren't there any rolls, either?

Es gibt is equivalent to English *there is* or *there are*. It is followed by the accusative case.

Heidelberger Studenten sprechen über ihre Arbeit.

Kapitel 5

LERNZIELE

■ **Sprechintentionen**

Borrowing and lending things
Talking about student life
Offering explanations/excuses
Describing one's family, nationality, and profession
Talking about personal interests
Inquiring about abilities
Describing possibilities and probabilities
Discussing duties and requirements
Inquiring about future plans

■ **Lesestück**

Studieren in Deutschland

■ **Land und Leute**

The German university system
University admission and financial aid in Germany
The school system in Germany
Foreign students in Germany
English vs. German terms (education)
Television

■ **Vokabeln**

Professions and nationalities
Family members

■ **Grammatik**

Werden
Verbs with stem-vowel change *e* > *ie*
Wissen and *kennen*
Der-words
Modal auxiliaries
Separable-prefix verbs

BAUSTEINE FÜR GESPRÄCHE

Notizen für die Klausur

ANDREAS: Hallo, Michael. Kannst du mir bitte deine Notizen leihen?

MICHAEL: Ja, gern.

ANDREAS: Das ist nett. Für die Klausur muß ich noch viel arbeiten.

MICHAEL: Klar, hier hast du sie. Kannst du sie morgen wieder mitbringen?

Notes for the test

Hi, Michael. Can you please lend me your notes?

Yes, glad to.

That's nice [of you]. I still have to study a lot for this test.

Of course, here they are. Can you bring them back tomorrow?

Ist das dein Hauptfach?

URSEL: Grüß dich. Seit wann gehst du denn in eine Literatur-Vorlesung? Studierst du nicht Geschichte?

SABINE: Nein, nicht mehr. Ich mache jetzt Germanistik.

URSEL: Ah ja? Als Nebenfach?

SABINE: Nein, als Hauptfach.

URSEL: So? Aha. Du, möchtest du nachher Kaffee trinken gehen?

SABINE: Ich kann leider nicht, muß noch etwas lesen. Morgen habe ich ein Referat und bin nicht besonders gut vorbereitet.

Is that your major?

Hi! Since when have you been taking a literature course? Aren't you studying history?

No, not any more. I'm taking German now.

Oh yes? As a minor?

No, as a major.

Is that so? Aha. Say, would you like to go out for coffee afterwards?

Unfortunately I can't. I still have to read something. Tomorrow I have an oral report and am not especially well prepared.

Brauchbares

There are various German equivalents of the English word *study:*

a. **studieren** = *to study a subject,* e.g., **Ich studiere Geschichte** (*I'm majoring in history*). **Studieren** also means *to be a student or attend college,* e.g., **Ich studiere jetzt** (*I go to college now*).

b. **machen** = *to do homework,* e.g., **Ich mache heute abend Deutsch** (*I'm going to study German tonight*). **Machen** also means *to major in,* e.g., **Ich mache jetzt Deutsch** (*I'm majoring in German now*).

c. **lernen** = *to study in the sense of doing homework,* e.g., **ich lerne die Vokabeln** (*I'm studying the vocabulary words*).

Fragen

1. Warum möchte Andreas Michaels Notizen borgen?
2. Warum muß Andreas noch viel lernen?
3. Wann möchte Michael seine Notizen wiederhaben?
4. Warum geht Sabine jetzt in eine Literatur-Vorlesung?
5. Was ist Sabines Hauptfach?
6. Was möchte Ursel nachher machen?
7. Warum kann Sabine nicht mitgehen?

Land und Leute

Die deutsche Universität

Because students in Germany are expected to have gained a good general education in high school **(Gymnasium),** they concentrate on one major field at the university. The German university system does not have an equivalent to a Bachelor's degree. The last two years of **Gymnasium** and the first two years of the university correspond to an undergraduate degree in North America. In the arts and humanities, students usually take one major and two minor subjects, or two majors, and complete their studies with a Master of Arts **(Magister artium).** If students intend to become teachers or lawyers, they finish with state certification after passing a special comprehensive examination **(Staatsexamen).** The Ph.D. **(Doktor phil.)** is an advanced degree that requires publishing a **Dissertation. Professor** is an advanced academic title, which requires writing a postdoctoral thesis **(Habilitationsschrift).**

University students bear the responsibility for their own progress. There are few exams, papers, and daily assignments, and for many courses there are no exams. At the beginning of the semester students choose classes according to type and subject matter. A **Vorlesung** is a lecture with little discussion and no exams. An **Übung** is a course often with daily assignments, discussion, and a test

Professor und Architekturstudentin an der Technischen Hochschule in Frankfurt am Main.

(Klausur) at the end. In a **Seminar,** students write papers and discuss the material. They have to write term papers **(Seminararbeiten)** as well.

After the successful completion of a **Seminar** or **Übung,** students receive a certificate **(Schein),** which includes a grade. A minimum number of **Scheine** is necessary before a student may take the intermediate qualifying exam **(Zwischenprüfung),** which is usually taken after four to six semesters at the university. More **Scheine** are required before a student can write a Master's thesis **(Magisterarbeit)** or take a final examination such as the **Staatsexamen.**

Sun–Thurs:
3–10

1. Leihen. Try to borrow something from a fellow student. She/he responds with *yes* or *no*. Then, out of curiosity, she/he asks why you want the item you requested. You may use the questions and responses provided or make up your own. When you have finished, ask another student.

Borrowing objects/ lending objects

S1:

Kannst du mir	**deine Notizen** leihen?
	dein Referat
	deine Seminararbeit°
	deinen Kugelschreiber
	deine Disketten°

S2:

Ja, gern.
Klar.
Natürlich.
Tut mir leid°. Ich brauche den
   [das/die] selbst.

2. Hauptfach, Nebenfach. Interview four students. Find out their major and minor subjects; then ask what they like to read. To find the names of other academic disciplines, you may want to refer to the Supplementary Word Sets in the Reference Section.

Discussing college majors and minors

S1:

| Was ist dein | **Hauptfach?** |
| | Nebenfach? |

S2:

| Ich studiere | **Germanistik.** |
| | Anglistik°. |

Mein	**Nebenfach** ist	**Psychologie°.**
	Hauptfach	Philosophie°.
		Kunstgeschichte°.
		Biologie°.
		Chemie°.
		Physik°.
		Mathematik°.
		Informatik°.

Was liest du gern?

Artikel° über	Sport/Musik/Schach.
Bücher über	Psychologie.
Krimis°.	
Liebesromane°.	
Moderne° Literatur.	

Pädagogik – education
Betriebswirtschaft – business
Marketing – marketing
Sportwissenschaft – exercise science
Medien – communications

Ich studiere an der Uni Mainz
universität mainz
Medizin

Volkswirtschaft – economics
Romanistik – romance lang.
Buchhaltung – accounting

Soziologie – Sociology

Ewige Student – Prof. Student

Keine Ahnung – no idea

3. Es tut mir leid. You run into a friend in the library who wants to make plans for later. Respond that you are sorry but you can't. Explain why you are busy.

> Offering explanations/
> excuses

S2:		S1:	
Willst du nachher	**Kaffee trinken gehen?**	Ich kann leider nicht. Ich	**bereite mein Referat vor.**
	einkaufen gehen?		arbeite für die Klausur.
	fernsehen?		lese einen Artikel über Computer.
	spazierengehen?		mache heute abend Deutsch.
			muß wieder in die Bibliothek.

Was [müssen/können/sollen] wir heute abend machen?	Wir	**müssen**	**unser Referat vorbereiten, nicht?**
		sollen	unsere Notizen durcharbeiten°.
		können	die Vokabeln lernen.
			Deutsch machen.
			ein Video° sehen.

Land und Leute

Das Schulsystem in Deutschland

At the age of six all children go to a **Grundschule** (primary school, grades 1–4). After that they attend either a **Hauptschule, Realschule,** or **Gymnasium,** depending on their ability and the job or career they hope to have. The first two years (grades 5–6) are an orientation period during which the parents and child determine if the child is in a school suitable to her/his interests and abilities.

Young people preparing to work in the trades or industry (e.g., as a baker or car mechanic) go to a **Hauptschule** (grades 5–9 or 5–10). After obtaining their certificate **(Hauptschulabschluß),** they enter an apprenticeship program, which includes 3–4 days per week of work training at a small business or large company and 8–12 hours per week of study at a vocational school. One third of the young people follow this path.

Another third of the young people, those wanting a job in business or the health field, (e.g., as a bank clerk or nurse) attend a **Realschule** (grades 5–10). The certificate **(Mittlere Reife)** from a **Realschule** is a prerequisite for these positions and permits the

Zwei Schülerinnen wissen die Antwort in einem Offenbacher Gymnasium.

students to attend specialized schools for further training. Students who leave the **Gymnasium** after grade 10 also obtain the **Mittlere Reife.**

Young people planning to get a university degree attend all grades of a **Gymnasium** (grades 5–13). The **Abitur,** which is the diploma from a **Gymnasium,** is granted on the basis of grades in courses and the passing of a comprehensive exam. One third of the young people endeavor to obtain an **Abitur.**

Vokabeln

Substantive

die **Anglistik** English studies (language and literature)

die **Arbeit, -en** work; paper

der **Artikel, -** article

die **Biologie** biology

die **Chemie** chemistry

die **Diskette, -n** disk

das **Fernsehen** television (the industry); der **Fernseher** (*Kapitel 1*) television set

der **Film, -e** film

die **Germanistik** German studies (language and literature)

die **Geschichte, -n** story; history

das **Hauptfach, ⁻er** major (subject)

die **Informatik** computer science

die **Klausur, -en** test; **eine Klausur schreiben** to take a test

der **Krimi, -s** mystery (novel or film)

die **Kunstgeschichte** art history

die **Liebe** love; der **Liebesroman** romance (novel)

die **Literatur** literature

die **Mathematik** mathematics; die **Mathe** math

das **Nebenfach, ⁻er** minor (subject)

die **Notiz, -en** note

die **Philosophie, -n** philosophy

die **Physik** physics

die **Psychologie** psychology

das **Referat, -e** report

der **Roman, -e** novel

das **Seminar, -e** seminar

die **Seminararbeit, -en** seminar paper

das **Video, -s** video

die **Vorlesung, -en** lecture

Verben

Separable-prefix verbs are indicated with a raised dot: **durch·arbeiten.** (See *Grammatik und Übungen,* section 9, in this chapter.)

borgen to borrow

bringen to bring

durch·arbeiten to work through; to study

dürfen (darf) to be permitted to, to be allowed to; may

fern·sehen (sieht fern) to watch TV

können (kann) to be able to; can

leihen to lend

lernen to learn; to study

lesen (liest) to read

mit·bringen to bring along

möchte (*subjunctive of* **mögen**) would like

müssen (muß) to have to; must

sehen (sieht) to see

sollen (soll) to be supposed to

spazieren·gehen to go for a walk

vor·bereiten to prepare

wollen (will) to want to, intend to

Andere Wörter

klar clear; of course, naturally

modern modern

nachher afterwards

nicht mehr no longer, not anymore

seit since

Besondere Ausdrücke

Deutsch machen to do/study
  German (as homework); to study
  (subject at the university)
(es) tut mir leid I'm sorry
ich bin (nicht) gut vorbereitet I am
  (not) well prepared
ich kann leider nicht unfortunately,
  I can't

**kannst du mir [deine Notizen]
  leihen?** can you lend me [your
  notes]?
seit wann since when, (for) how
  long
So? Is that so? Really?

Land und Leute

N.C. und BAföG

More than 1.8 million students are enrolled in Germany's 129 universities and other institutions of higher learning and more than 350 polytechnical institutes and colleges. Enrollment has increased 75% over the last 17 years, leading to overcrowded universities throughout the country. University officials are concerned that rooms are used to 180% of their capacity, students complain about inadequate accessibility of teachers and research materials, and industry recently observed that it has 200,000 fewer apprentices than universities have students. To limit the number of students, admission is restricted under a system called **Numerus clausus (N.C.)** in 12 subjects. In these disciplines, among which are medicine, law, pharmacy, and psychology, admissions (**Studienplätze**) are distributed mainly on the basis of high school grades (**Noten**) received during the last years of the **Gymnasium** and grades on the final comprehensive examination (**das Abitur**). There can be a waiting period of up to five years for admission in some disciplines. The **Regelstudienzeit,** in effect in some states, requires that students finish their studies within a required number of semesters, on the average 9–10 semesters. In order to provide financial support for students, a law (**Bundesausbildungsförderungsgesetz,** or

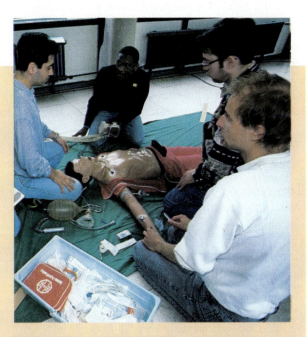

Diese Medizinstudenten haben einen Studienplatz bekommen. (Hannover)

BAföG) was passed in 1971 to give everyone an equal chance to study at a university. Today approximately 50 percent of all students are subsidized to some extent. The amount of financial support is dependent on parents' income. Upon employment, students are required to pay back one-half of the state loan, but they pay no interest.

STUDIEREN IN DEUTSCHLAND

Vorbereitung auf das Lesen

■ *Vor dem Lesen*

In this reading you will learn some basic information about the German university system and how students live in Germany. Before reading the text answer the following questions about your studies and your college or university.

1. Is your college or university a public or a private institution? What are the entrance requirements?
2. How expensive is your school? How do students pay for their education? Parents, work, scholarship, loan?
3. How is the academic year organized? What do students do on vacation?
4. How many courses are most students taking? How many subject areas are represented by the courses?
5. How long does it take to complete a Bachelor's degree?

■ *Beim Lesen*

Take notes on the following topics as you read, and compare a German university to your institution.

	meine Uni	in Deutschland
1. Studienplätze		
2. Studentenjobs		
3. Semesterferien		
4. Examen		

MÖCHTEN SIE IN DEUTSCHLAND STUDIEREN?
INFORMATIONEN FÜR AMERIKANISCHE STUDENTEN

1. Wer kann studieren?

An deutschen Universitäten studieren heute über° 1,8 Millionen Studenten. Davon° sind 113 000 Ausländer. Es gibt zu wenige Universitäten, und die meisten Kurse sind deshalb überfüllt. Deutsche können nur mit dem Abitur studieren, trotzdem° gibt es mehr Studenten als Studienplätze°. Daher haben
5 viele Fächer den N.C., den Numerus clausus°. Junge Leute wissen also, daß° es schwer ist, einen Studienplatz zu finden. Nur mit sehr guten Noten vom° Gymnasium bekommen sie einen Studienplatz. Bevor Amerikaner in Deutschland studieren können, müssen sie in Amerika schon an einer Universität oder einem College Studenten sein. Sie müssen für die deutsche Universität auch
10 eine Sprachprüfung° machen.

over
of those

in spite of that / space for students
(Latin) restricted admissions / that / **vom = von dem:** from the

language test

2. Wieviel Geld braucht man?

Die Universitäten in Deutschland sind staatlich. Steuern° finanzieren das Studium. Deshalb gibt es keine Studiengebühren°, aber die Studenten brauchen Geld für Essen und Wohnen. Leider gibt es nur wenige Studentenheime, und Studenten müssen oft Zimmer in der Stadt suchen, und die sind oft teuer. Viele
15 Studenten brauchen deshalb Geld vom Staat. Dieses Geld heißt BAföG°. Nur so kann jeder studieren. Die Hälfte° des Geldes müssen die Studenten dem Staat später zurückzahlen. Manche Studenten bekommen aber kein BAföG (z.B. wenn ihre Eltern zuviel verdienen) und brauchen deshalb Jobs. An deutschen Universitäten gibt es aber nicht viele Studentenjobs, und sie müssen
20 andere Jobs finden. Diese Studenten jobben oft auch im° Semester. Sie studieren dann länger als BAföG-Rezipienten, im Durchschnitt° vierzehn Semester. BAföG-Rezipienten studieren dagegen im Durchschnitt nur elf Semester. Zehn Prozent der ausländischen° Studenten bekommen Stipendien.

taxes
tuition

BAföG: *see p. 137*
half

im = in dem: *here* during the
im Durchschnitt: on the
 average
foreign

3. Wann studiert man?

Es gibt zwei Semester im Jahr, das Wintersemester (Mitte Oktober oder Anfang°
25 November bis Mitte oder Ende Februar) und das Sommersemester (Mitte April oder Anfang Mai bis Mitte oder Ende Juli). Die Semesterferien sind lang, aber sie sind für die meisten Studenten keine freie Zeit. Viele Studenten müssen in den Ferien jobben oder ein Praktikum° machen. Oft lesen sie in der Bibliothek, schreiben dort ihre Seminararbeiten oder bereiten sich° auf das nächste
30 Semester vor, denn sie ist in den Semesterferien nicht so überfüllt.

beginning

internship
themselves

4. Was ist anders?

Studenten studieren ein oder zwei Fächer. Ihre Kurse sind alle in diesen Fächern. Nehmen wir° zum Beispiel Klaus Brendel aus Aachen. Er studiert Physik und Informatik und möchte Ingenieur werden. Er muß keine Kurse in Englisch, Geschichte und Biologie machen, denn das hat er in der Schule
35 gemacht°. In Deutschland führen° Professoren keine Anwesenheitslisten°, und nur wenige Kurse haben jedes Semester Prüfungen. Dafür° gibt es nach vier Semestern eine Zwischenprüfung° und dann das große Examen am Ende.

nehmen wir: let's take

hat gemacht: studied / keep / attendance lists / in place of that
qualifying exam

Brauchbares

1. L. 3 **Abitur:** In Austria and Switzerland the **Matura** is the equivalent of the **Abitur.**

2. L. 5 **Numerus clausus:** A central computer administers all university admissions—primarily based on grades—for all universities. Leftover slots are assigned by lottery.

3. Note that in dependent clauses—here those beginning with **daß** (l. 5), **bevor** (l. 7), and **wenn** (l. 18)—the finite verb is at the end of the clause, e.g., **daß es schwer ist.** (See *Kapitel 6*, section 3).

4. L. 21 **vierzehn Semester:** Note that German students measure their progress at the university in semesters instead of in years.

Nach dem Lesen

1. Fragen zu dem Lesestück

1. Wie viele Studenten gibt es in Deutschland?
2. Wer kann in Deutschland studieren?
3. Warum haben viele Fächer den Numerus clausus?
4. Was müssen Amerikaner machen, bevor sie in Deutschland studieren dürfen?
5. Wieviel kostet° das Studium in Deutschland?
6. Warum müssen Studenten oft Zimmer in der Stadt suchen?
7. Was ist BAföG?
8. Was machen viele deutsche Studenten in den Ferien?
9. Was studiert Klaus Brendel? Welche Kurse macht er nicht?
10. Wann gibt es Prüfungen an deutschen Universitäten?

2. Was sagt eine Studentin/ein Student aus Deutschland? How would a German respond to the following statements by an American student? Based on the information in the reading write a logical reply.

1. AMERIKANERIN/AMERIKANER: Morgen haben wir schon wieder eine Prüfung in Mathe!
   DEUTSCHE/DEUTSCHER: _____
2. AMERIKANERIN/AMERIKANER: Die Studiengebühren sind wirklich zu hoch° hier.
   DEUTSCHE/DEUTSCHER: _____
3. AMERIKANERIN/AMERIKANER: Ich wohne sehr gern im Studentenheim.
   DEUTSCHE/DEUTSCHER: _____
4. AMERIKANERIN/AMERIKANER: Ich jobbe 10 Stunden die Woche.
   DEUTSCHE/DEUTSCHER: _____
5. AMERIKANERIN/AMERIKANER: Hoffentlich bin ich in vier Jahren mit dem Studium fertig°.
   DEUTSCHE/DEUTSCHER: _____

3. Was ist das? Match the descriptions on the right with the terms on the left.

1. BAföG
2. Numerus clausus
3. jobben
4. Studentenheim
5. Abitur

a. die Prüfung und das Diplom am Ende vom Gymnasium
b. Geld für Studenten vom Staat
c. Studentenwohnungen° an der Uni   student residences
d. Fächer mit zu wenig Studienplätzen
e. ein anderes Wort für „arbeiten"

4. Erzählen wir. Make a list of useful vocabulary and be prepared to talk to a classmate about one of the following topics as it relates to the German university system.

Studenten und Geld □ zu viele Studenten □ zu viele Prüfungen

Land und Leute

Ausländische Studenten

German universities are open to students from other countries. In western Germany alone there are more than seventy thousand foreign students. Even in the **Numerus clausus** disciplines, some places are reserved for foreigners. Like a German student, a foreigner pays no tuition **(Studiengebühren),** but all students pay thirty to eighty marks in semester fees plus about seventy marks a month for health insurance. A foreign student is generally not granted a work permit. To be admitted for study in Germany, an American must usually have had at least two years of college and must pass a language examination.

To study at a Swiss university, an American needs a Bachelor's degree and a working knowledge of the language of instruction, which may be German, French, or Italian.

An den deutschen Universitäten studieren auch ausländische Studenten. (Universität Heidelberg)

5. Zur Diskussion

1. Was finden Sie an den deutschen Universitäten gut?
2. Was finden Sie an Ihrer Universität gut?
3. Möchten Sie in Deutschland studieren? Warum (nicht)?

Erweiterung des Wortschatzes

1 Stating one's profession or nationality

Anton ist Student.	Anton is a student.
Barbara wird Ingenieurin.	Barbara is going to be an engineer.
Barbara ist Kanadierin.	Barbara is (a) Canadian.
Anton ist Deutscher.	Anton is (a) German.

Herr Becker ist **nicht (kein)** Ingenieur.	Mr. Becker is not an engineer.
Marga ist **nicht (keine)** Österreicherin; sie ist Deutsche.	Marga is not (an) Austrian; she's (a) German.

Either **nicht** or **kein** may be used to negate a sentence about someone's profession, nationality, or membership in a group. Remember that no indefinite article (**ein**) is used in the positive statement (see *Kapitel 3*). For names of additional professions, refer to the Supplementary Word Sets in the Reference Section.

1. Neue Freunde. On a plane from Toronto to Frankfurt, three young people sitting in the same row get to know each other. Give the German equivalent.

1. David is a Canadian.
2. He is a student.
3. Brigitte is not a Canadian.
4. She is also not an American; she's a German.
5. She is going to be an engineer.
6. Her brother Helmut lives in Frankfurt; he's a Frankfurter.
7. He is a pharmacist.

2. Persönliche Informationen. Prepare a brief autobiography. Give: **Name, Nationalität, Adresse und Telefonnummer, Hauptfach, Nebenfach. Was wollen Sie werden?**

> Describing one's nationality and profession

Land und Leute

Schule, Hochschule, Klasse, Student

Many words used in English to talk about university studies are not equivalent to the German words which appear to be cognates. In the German-speaking countries a greater distinction is made in words referring to education before college or university and postsecondary education.

Schüler und Schülerinnen in der ersten Klasse. (München)

- *school* / **Universität:** In German **(die) Schule** refers to an elementary or secondary school. When talking about postsecondary education German speakers use **(die) Universität** or **(die) Hochschule.** The equivalent of *What school do you go to?* is **An welcher Uni studierst du?**

- *high school* / **Hochschule:** A German equivalent of the U.S. or Canadian *high school* is **(die) Oberschule, (die) höhere Schule,** or **(das) Gymnasium.** A **Hochschule** is a postsecondary school such as a university.

- *student*: In German, **Studentin/Student** refers to someone at a post-secondary institution (i.e., at a **Universität** or **Hochschule**). The word **(die) Schülerin/(der) Schüler** is used for young people in elementary and secondary schools, much as the word *pupil* is used in English.

- *class:* The English word *class* refers to an instructional period or a group of students. The German word **(die) Klasse** refers only to a group of students (e.g., **meine Klasse** = *my class, my classmates*) or a specific grade (e.g., **die zweite Klasse** = *the second grade*). In a **Schule** the word for *class* meaning *instructional period* is **Stunde** (e.g., **die Deutschstunde** = *the German class*). At the university level in German-speaking countries there are several types of classes—**Vorlesung, Übung,** and **Seminar** (see *Land und Leute: Die deutsche Universität,* p. 133).

2 Die Familie

WILLI CLAUSEN
67 — KÄTHE CLAUSEN
63

HANS PFEIFFER
39 — KERSTEN CLAUSEN
35

VOLKER CLAUSEN
43 — RENATE CLAUSEN
40

ANGELIKA PFEIFFER
13

JÜRGEN PFEIFFER
10

CHRISTOPH CLAUSEN
7

KATRIN GUMPERT
15

use "keine" for no (siblings)

die **Mutter**, ⸚	+	der **Vater**, ⸚	= die **Eltern** (*pl.*)
(die **Mutti**,		(der **Vati**,	
die **Mama**)		der **Papa**)	
die **Tochter**, ⸚		der **Sohn**, ⸚e	
die **Schwester**, -n	+	der **Bruder**, ⸚	= die **Geschwister** (*pl.*)
die **Tante**, -n		der **Onkel**, -	
die **Kusine**, -n		der **Vetter**, -n	
die **Nichte**, -n		der **Neffe**, -n, -n	
die **Großmutter**, ⸚	+	der **Großvater**, ⸚	= die **Großeltern** (*pl.*)
(die **Oma**, -s)		(der **Opa**, -s)	

Stief-: die **Stiefmutter;** der **Stiefvater**

Refer to the Supplementary Word Sets in the Reference Section for names of additional family members.

das Einzelkind: only child

Urgroßmutter: Great Grandma

das Baby

das Kind: children

3. Die Familie. Read the following paragraph explaining the family tree on page 143.

Willi und Käthe Clausen haben eine Tochter, Kersten, und einen Sohn, Volker. Kersten und ihr Mann, Hans Pfeiffer, haben zwei Kinder, Angelika und Jürgen. Die Kinder haben eine Großmutter, Oma Clausen, und einen Großvater, Opa Clausen. Volker Clausen ist geschieden°. Renate ist seine zweite° Frau. Sie hat eine Tochter, Katrin Gumpert, von ihrem ersten° Mann. Volker ist also Katrins Stiefvater. Renate und Volker haben einen Sohn, Christoph. Angelika Pfeiffer ist seine Kusine, und Jürgen ist sein Vetter. Die Eltern von Angelika und Jürgen sind natürlich seine Tante Kersten und sein Onkel Hans.

divorced / second
first

4. Der Stammbaum. *(Family Tree.)* Answer the following questions based on the **Stammbaum**.

1. Wie heißt Jürgen Pfeiffers Vetter?
2. Wer ist Angelika Pfeiffers Onkel?
3. Wie heißen die Großeltern von Angelika und Jürgen?
4. Wie heißt Volker Clausens Frau?
5. Wie heißt Volkers Stieftochter?
6. Wie heißt Katrins Halbbruder°?

half brother

⇨ **5. Frage-Ecke.** Find out the missing information about Angelika and Christoph as well as about your partner. (S2: see page 145.)

S2: Wie heißt der Vater von Angelika?
S1: Er heißt Hans Pfeiffer.
S2: Wie alt ist Angelikas Vater?
S1: Er ist 39 Jahre alt.

S1:

	Vater	Mutter	Tante	Onkel	Großvater	Großmutter
Angelika	Hans Pfeiffer 39		Renate Clausen 40		Willie Clausen 67	Käthe Clausen 63
Christoph		Renate Clausen 40		Hans Pfeiffer 39		
ich						
Partnerin/ Partner						

S2:

	Vater	Mutter	Tante	Onkel	Großvater	Großmutter
Angelika		Kersten Clausen 35		Volker Clausen 43		
Christoph	Volker Clausen 43		Kersten Clausen 35		Willie Clausen 67	Käthe Clausen 63
ich						
Partnerin/ Partner						

Vokabeln

Substantive

das **Abitur** diploma from college-track high school [**Gymnasium**]
der **Ausländer, -**/die **Ausländerin, -nen** foreigner
das **Beispiel, -e** example; **zum Beispiel** (*abbrev.* **z.B.**) for example (*abbrev.* e.g.)
die **Eltern** (*pl.*) parents
das **Ende, -n** end, conclusion; **am Ende** at (in) the end
das **Examen, -** comprehensive exam, finals; **Examen machen** to graduate from the university
das **Fach, ˜er** (academic) subject
die **Familie, -n** family
die **Ferien** (*pl.*) vacation; **in den Ferien** on vacation; die **Semesterferien** semester break
das **Gymnasium,** *pl.* **Gymnasien** college-track high school
die **Information, -en** information
der **Ingenieur, -e**/die **Ingenieurin, -nen** engineer

der **Job, -s** job
die **Klasse, -n** class
der **Kurs, -e** course
die **Note, -n** grade; note
das **Picknick, -s** picnic; **Picknick machen** to have a picnic
der **Platz, ˜e** place; seat; space
das **Prozent** percent
die **Prüfung, -en** test, examination
die **Schule, -n** school
das **Semester, -** semester
der **Staat, -en** state, country
das **Stipendium,** *pl.* **Stipendien** scholarship
das **Studentenheim, -e** dormitory
das **Studium** study; studies
die **Zeit, -en** time
For additional family members, see p. 143.

Verben

jobben (*colloq.*)   to have a temporary
   job (e.g., a summer job)
kosten   to cost
verdienen   to earn

werden (wird)   to become
wissen (weiß)   to know (a fact)
zahlen   to pay
zurück·zahlen   to pay back

Andere Wörter

alle   all
amerikanisch   American
an   at; to
daher   therefore, for that reason
deshalb   therefore, for that reason
dies- (-er, -es, -e)   this, these
fertig   finished
frei   free
hoch   high
jed- (-er, -es, -e)   each, every; **jeder**
   everyone
jung   young
kanadisch   Canadian
lang   long; **länger**   longer

manch- (-er, -es, -e)   many a (*sg.*);
   some (*pl.*)
meist-   most; **die meisten (Leute)**
   most of (the people)
privat   private
schwer   hard, difficult
später   later
staatlich   public, government owned
teuer   expensive
wenig   little; **ein wenig**   a little;
   wenige   few
wenn (*conj.*)   if; when, whenever
zurück   back, in return
zuviel   too much

Der erste Schultag.

Ein Schachspiel im Park.

GRAMMATIK UND ÜBUNGEN

1 Present tense of *werden*

werden: to become	
ich werde	wir werden
du **wirst**	ihr werdet
er/es/sie **wird**	sie werden
Sie werden	
du-*imperative:* werde	

Werden is irregular in the **du-** and **er/es/sie-**forms in the present tense.

---

1. Sie werden anders. People are changing. Say how.

▶ Erik / leider / müde   *Erik wird leider müde.*

1. ich / auch / müde
2. Petra / besser / in Mathe
3. die Kinder / groß
4. du / leider / faul
5. wir / tolerant
6. ihr / sehr / froh
7. Hans und Karin / besser / in Deutsch
8. und Sie? / besser / in Deutsch

2 Verbs with stem-vowel change *e > ie*

sehen: to see	
ich sehe	wir sehen
du **siehst**	ihr seht
er/es/sie **sieht**	sie sehen
Sie sehen	
du-*imperative:* **sieh**	

lesen: to read	
ich lese	wir lesen
du **liest**	ihr lest
er/es/sie **liest**	sie lesen
Sie lesen	
du-*imperative:* **lies**	

Several verbs with the stem-vowel **e** change the **e** to **ie** in the **du-** and **er/es/sie-**forms of the present tense and in the **du-**imperative. Since the stem of **lesen** ends in a sibilant, the **du-**form ending contracts from **-st** to **-t** (see *Kapitel 2, Grammatik und Übungen,* section 7).

2.   Lesen und sehen.   Say what kind of films and reading matter the people mentioned below like.

▶   Erik / ernste Filme   *Erik sieht gern ernste Filme.*

1. Ingrid / lustige Filme
2. Gabi und Jürgen / amerikanische Filme
3. du / Schwarzweißfilme / ?

4. Christine / Bücher / über Sport
5. Detlev / Bücher / über Musik
6. du / Bücher / über Politik / ?
7. ihr / Bücher / über Geschichte / ?

⇨ **3.   Filme und Bücher.**   Interview three students to find out what kinds of movies they like and what books they like to read. Then report back to the class. Refer to the Supplementary Word Sets in the Reference Section for additional descriptions of film and literature.

> Talking about personal interests

S1: Was für Filme siehst du gern?
S2 [Tom]: Ich sehe gern [alte Filme, Krimis, Horrorfilme, Dokumentarfilme, Science-fiction-Filme]. → Vergnügungsfilme – disaster / Liebesfilme – love
S1: Was für Bücher liest du gern?
S3 [Linda]: Ich lese gern [Biographien, Liebesromane, Horrorgeschichten, historische Romane, Krimis, Science-fiction, Bücher über Politik/ Musik, moderne Literatur].

S1: [Tom] sieht gern [alte Filme]. [Linda] liest gern [Biographien].

3 Present tense of *wissen*

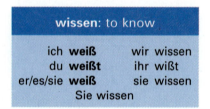

wissen: to know	
ich **weiß**	wir wissen
du **weißt**	ihr wißt
er/es/sie **weiß**	sie wissen
Sie wissen	

Mein Lieblingsfilm
My favourite movie

Wissen is irregular in the singular forms of the present tense. Note that the **du**-form ending contracts from **-st** to **-t**.

4. **Ein Picknick.**   You and your friends are going to drive in different cars to a picnic spot in the country. Inform Klaus that the people mentioned know where the picnic is. Use pronouns in your responses.

▶   Weiß Ursel, wo das Picknick ist?   *Ja, sie weiß es.*
▶   Und Andreas?   *Ja, er weiß es.*

1. Und Michael?
2. Und du?
3. Und Sabine?
4. Und Felix und Jochen?
5. Und ihr?

4 *Wissen* and *kennen*

Sie **weiß**, wer Professor Schmidt ist.	She *knows* who Professor Schmidt is.
Sie **kennt** Professor Schmidt gut.	She *knows* Professor Schmidt well.

There are two German equivalents for the English *to know:* **wissen** and **kennen. Wissen** means *to know something as a fact.* **Kennen** means *to be acquainted with a person, place, or thing.*

> **Kennen** was used as a verb in Middle English and is still used in Scottish. The noun *ken* means perception or understanding: "That is beyond my ken."

5. **Heidelberg.**   A few students are talking about the famous university town of Heidelberg. Complete the sentences with a form of **kennen** or **wissen,** as appropriate.

▶ _____ du, wo Heidelberg liegt?   *Weißt du, wo Heidelberg liegt?*
▶ Dirk _____ die Stadt gut.   *Dirk kennt die Stadt gut.*

1. _____ ihr Heidelberg gut?
2. Wir _____ die Stadt ein bißchen.
3. _____ ihr, wo die Bibliothek ist?
4. Nein, das _____ wir nicht.
5. Aber ich _____ ein Buch über Heidelberg.
6. _____ du, wo man das Buch kaufen kann?
7. Das _____ ich nicht.
8. _____ du den Autor?
9. Den _____ alle Studenten! Das ist unser Prof!

5 *Der*-words

Diese Klausur ist schwer.	*This* test is hard.
Jede Klausur ist schwer.	*Every* test is hard.
Welche Klausur hast du?	*Which* test do you have?
Manche Klausuren sind nicht schwer.	*Some* tests are not hard.
Solche Klausuren sind nicht interessant.	*Those kinds* of tests aren't interesting.

In the singular, **so ein** is usually used instead of **solcher: So eine Uhr ist sehr teuer.** *That kind of/such a watch/clock is very expensive.*

	Masculine der	Neuter das	Feminine die	Plural die
Nominative	dies**er**	dies**es**	dies**e**	dies**e**
Accusative	dies**en**	dies**es**	dies**e**	dies**e**

The words **dieser, jeder, welcher?, mancher,** and **solcher** are called **der**-words because they follow the same pattern in the nominative and accusative cases as the definite articles. **Jeder** is used in the singular only. **Welcher?** is an interrogative adjective, used at the beginning of a question. **Solcher** and **mancher** are used almost exclusively in the plural.

Der Stuhl **(da)** ist neu.   *That* chair is new.

The equivalent of *that (those)* is expressed by the definite article **(der, das, die)**. **Da** is often added for clarity.

6. **Welcher? Dieser?**   You're shopping with a friend who comments on various items. Ask which things she/he is referring to. Use the nominative of **welcher** and **dieser.**

▶   Der Kuli ist teuer.   *Welcher Kuli ist teuer? Dieser hier?*

1. Die Lampe ist schön.
2. Der Stuhl ist zu schwer.
3. Das Radio ist zu teuer.
4. Der Tisch ist zu klein.
5. Die Bleistifte sind billig.
6. Die Hefte sind teuer.

7. **Wie finden Sie diese Bilder?**   You are showing pictures of Switzerland and Austria to a friend. Restate the questions and comments, using the cued **der**-word in place of the italicized words.

▶   Findest du *die* Städte schön? (dieser)   *Findest du diese Städte schön?*

1. Kennst du *die* Städte schon? (mancher)
2. *Die* Städte kennst du gut? (welcher?)
3. Im Fenster gibt es immer *diese* Blumen. (solcher)
4. Wie heißt *die* Straße? (dieser)
5. Wie findest du *die* Bilder? (dieser)
6. *Das* Bild ist wirklich schön. (jeder)
7. *Die* Bilder möchtest du haben? (welcher?)

6 Modal auxiliaries

Ich **muß** jetzt arbeiten.   I *have to* work now.
Erika **kann** es machen.   Erika *can* do it.
Ich **darf** nichts sagen.   I *am* not *allowed* to say anything.

Both English and German have a group of verbs called *modal auxiliaries*. Modal auxiliary verbs **(muß, kann, darf)** indicate an attitude about an action; they do not express the action itself. In German, the verb that expresses the action is in the infinitive form **(arbeiten, machen, sagen)** and is in last position.

Modals are irregular in the present-tense singular. They lack endings in the **ich-** and **er/es/sie**-forms, and five of the six modals show stem-vowel change, e.g., **können > kann.**

---

können: can, to be able to, to know how to do

ich **kann** es erklären	wir **können** es erklären
du **kannst** es erklären	ihr **könnt** es erklären
er/es/sie **kann** es erklären	sie **können** es erklären
	Sie **können** es erklären

8. **Was können diese Leute?**   Say what the following people can do or know how to do.

▶ Mark schwimmt gut.   *Mark kann gut schwimmen.*

1. Karla spielt gut Tennis.
2. Wir machen Spaghetti.
3. Ich erkläre die Geschichte.
4. Du tanzt gut.
5. Herr Professor, Sie schreiben schön.
6. Karin und Peter tanzen wunderbar.
7. Ihr schwimmt gut.

9. **Was kannst du?**   Find out from several fellow students whether they know how to do certain activities.

S1: Kannst du Fußball spielen?
S2: Ja, ich kann Fußball spielen./Nein, ich kann nicht Fußball spielen.

1. schwimmen	4. gut Geschichten erzählen
2. Tennis spielen	5. Squash spielen
3. gut tanzen	6. schön schreiben

Inquiring about abilities

wollen: to want, wish; to intend to	
ich **will** arbeiten	wir **wollen** arbeiten
du **willst** arbeiten	ihr **wollt** arbeiten
er/es/sie **will** arbeiten	sie **wollen** arbeiten
Sie **wollen** arbeiten	

10. **Was wollen diese Leute?**   Say what the following people want to do or intend to do.

▶ Erich geht einkaufen.   *Erich will einkaufen gehen.*

1. Beatrice macht Musik.	4. Ich bezahle das Essen.
2. Du gehst heute abend tanzen, nicht?	5. Die Kinder essen Kuchen.
	6. Ihr macht Mathe.
3. Erich trinkt Kaffee.	7. Frau Kaiser studiert Geschichte.

11. **Willst du?**   You and your partner are planning things to do tonight and tomorrow. Suggest two things. Your partner can or cannot do them.

Making plans

S1:

Willst du	**morgen**	**ins Kino** gehen?
	heute abend	essen
	am Samstag	tanzen

S2:

Ja, | **gern.**
     | vielleicht.
Nein, ich kann nicht.

Deutsch machen □ Musik hören □ fernsehen □ spazierengehen □
Tennis spielen □ zusammen für die Klausur arbeiten?

sollen: to be supposed to	
ich **soll** morgen gehen	wir **sollen** morgen gehen
du **sollst** morgen gehen	ihr **sollt** morgen gehen
er/es/sie **soll** morgen gehen	sie **sollen** morgen gehen
Sie **sollen** morgen gehen	

12. **Wir planen eine Party.**   You and some friends are planning a party. Tell what each person is supposed to do for it.

▶ Gabi und Moritz: Musik mitbringen   *Gabi und Moritz sollen Musik mitbringen.*

1. wir: Käse kaufen
2. du: Salat machen
3. ich: Brot kaufen
4. Corinna: Wein mitbringen
5. ihr: Bier kaufen

13. **Wie wird das Wetter?**   Write down weather predictions for three days. Then ask your partner about her/his predictions.

S1:

Wie wird das Wetter morgen?
Und am [Mittwoch]?

S2:

Morgen soll es [regnen].
Am [Mittwoch] soll [die Sonne scheinen].
Es soll [schön] [bleiben/werden].

Describing possibilities and probabilities

müssen: must, to have to	
ich **muß** jetzt arbeiten	wir **müssen** jetzt arbeiten
du **mußt** jetzt arbeiten	ihr **müßt** jetzt arbeiten
er/es/sie **muß** jetzt arbeiten	sie **müssen** jetzt arbeiten
Sie **müssen** jetzt arbeiten	

14. **Was müssen diese Leute tun?**   Say what all these people have to do.

▶ Frau Professor Kluge: in die Vorlesung gehen   *Frau Professor Kluge muß in die Vorlesung gehen.*

1. wir: noch zwei Kapitel durcharbeiten
2. Karin: ein Buch über Psychologie lesen
3. ich: eine Klausur schreiben
4. ihr: in die Bibliothek gehen
5. Lukas und Lutz: ein Referat vorbereiten
6. du: für die Klausur arbeiten

15. Was mußt du machen? Ask a fellow student what she/he must do in the next few days. Use a form of the verb **müssen**.

S1:		*S2:*	
Was mußt du	**heute** machen?	**Heute** muß ich	**arbeiten.**
	morgen	Morgen	in die Bibliothek gehen.
	am Dienstag	Am Dienstag	ein Buch lesen.
			ein Referat vorbereiten.
			einen Artikel schreiben.
			Deutsch machen.

dürfen: may, to be permitted to	
ich **darf** es sagen	wir **dürfen** es sagen
du **darfst** es sagen	ihr **dürft** es sagen
er/es/sie **darf** es sagen	sie **dürfen** es sagen
Sie **dürfen** es sagen	

16. Das darf man nicht. Say what these people are not allowed to do or what is not permitted.

▶ wir: hier nicht schwimmen   *Wir dürfen hier nicht schwimmen.*

1. ich: keinen Kaffee trinken
2. du: hier nicht rauchen°   smoke
3. Eckhard: nicht so viel arbeiten
4. ihr: bei Rot nicht über die Straße gehen
5. Paul und Paula: kein Fleisch essen
6. man: hier nicht parken

7 *Mögen* and the *möchte*-forms

mögen: to like	
ich **mag** keine Tomaten	wir **mögen** Erik nicht
du **magst** keine Eier	ihr **mögt** Melanie nicht
er/es/sie **mag** kein Bier	sie **mögen** Schmidts nicht
Sie **mögen** keinen Kaffee	

Mögen Sie Frau Lenz?   Nein, ich **mag** sie nicht.

The modal **mögen** is often used to express a fondness or dislike for someone or something, much like the construction **haben** + **gern**. With this meaning it usually does not take a dependent infinitive.

17. **Was magst du?**   You are raising questions about various people's likes and dislikes. Use a form of **mögen.**

▶   du: Fisch   *Magst du Fisch?*

1. Mark: deutsches Bier
2. Ilse und Erik: Rockmusik
3. Frank: Shakespeare
4. du: moderne Musik

5. Professor Schneider: Vollkornbrot
6. ihr: Rotwein
7. Herr und Frau Braun: alte Filme

ich **möchte** gehen	wir **möchten** gehen
du **möchtest** gehen	ihr **möchtet** gehen
er/es/sie **möchte** gehen	sie **möchten** gehen
	Sie **möchten** gehen

Möchte is a different form of the modal **mögen.** The meaning of **mögen** is *to like;* the meaning of **möchte** is *would like (to).*

18. **Ja, das möchten wir.**   It's going to be a busy evening, and everything sounds good to everyone. Say what the people mentioned below would like to do.

▶   Dirk: heute abend ins Kino gehen   *Dirk möchte heute abend ins Kino gehen.*

1. wir: heute nachmittag einkaufen gehen
2. du: mehr arbeiten
3. ihr: bestimmt hier bleiben
4. Gabi: im Café essen
5. Lotte und Erika: Musik hören
6. ich: ein interessantes Buch lesen
7. Rolf: am Wochenende wandern

▷ **19.** **Was möchtet ihr machen?**   Ask three fellow students what they would like to do. Use a **möchte**-form in each question.

S1: Was möchtest du [am Wochenende/heute abend/im Sommer] machen?
S2: Ich möchte [einkaufen gehen].

> Inquiring about future plans

8 Omission of the dependent infinitive with modals

Ich **kann** das nicht.   = Ich **kann** das nicht **machen.**
Ich **muß** in die Bibliothek.   = Ich **muß** in die Bibliothek **gehen.**
Das **darfst** du nicht.   = Das **darfst** du nicht **tun.**

Modals may occur without a dependent infinitive if a verb of motion (e.g., **gehen**) or the idea of *to do* (**machen, tun**) is clearly understood from the context.

Ich **kann** Deutsch.   I can speak German. (I know German.)

Können is used to say that someone knows how to speak a language.

20. In die Bibliothek? Nein.   Christin is taking a walk with Mark, an American student she met recently. Give the English equivalents of their conversation.

1. CHRISTIN: Willst du jetzt nach Hause?
2. MARK: Nein, ich muß noch in die Bibliothek.
3. CHRISTIN: Was willst du da?
4. MARK: Ich muß Shakespeare lesen. Mußt du auch in die Uni?
5. CHRISTIN: Nein, was soll ich denn da? Heute ist Sonntag!
6. MARK: Sag mal, kannst du gut Englisch?
7. CHRISTIN: Ja, ich kann aber auch Französisch.
8. MARK: Darf hier jeder in die Bibliothek?
9. CHRISTIN: Ja, wer° will, der° darf.   whoever / (that person)

21. Wie sagt man das?

1. Can you work this afternoon?
   —No, I have to go home.
2. May I pay (for) the coffee?
   —No, you may not. [Add **das.**]
3. Dirk wants to go to the movies tonight.
   —What would he like to see?
4. Barbara intends to study German.
   —Good. She already knows German well.
5. It's supposed to rain tomorrow.
   —Really? That can't be.

22. Frage-Ecke.   Find out the information missing from your chart by asking your partner. (S2: see page 156.)

S2: Was müssen Otto und Sabine machen?
S1: Sie müssen Mathe machen.

S1:

	müssen	dürfen	wollen	sollen	können
Martina		Kaffee trinken	tanzen gehen	einen Job suchen	
Otto und Sabine	Mathe machen			Blumen mitbringen	
Udo		keine Eier essen	viel Geld verdienen		
Stefans Schwester	in die Bibliothek		fernsehen		gut Tennis spielen
ich					
Partnerin/ Partner					

S2:

	müssen	dürfen	wollen	sollen	können
Martina	jobben				gut tanzen
Otto und Sabine		Kuchen essen	ins Kino gehen		das Essen bezahlen
Udo	in die Vorlesung gehen			sein Referat vorbereiten	gut Englisch
Stefans Schwester		Bier trinken		lesen	
ich					
Partnerin/ Partner					

9 Separable-prefix verbs

to get up	I get up early.
to throw away	Don't throw away all those papers!

English has a large number of two-word verbs, such as *to get up, to throw away*. These two-word verbs consist of a verb, such as *get*, and a particle, such as *up*.

einkaufen	Monika **kauft** morgens **ein.**
mitbringen	**Bringen** Sie bitte Blumen **mit!**

German has a large number of "separable-prefix verbs" that function like certain English two-word verbs. Examples are **durcharbeiten, einkaufen, fernsehen, mitbringen, vorbereiten,** and **zurückzahlen.** In present-tense statements and questions, and in imperative forms, the separable prefix (**durch-, ein-, fern-, mit-, vor-, zurück-**) is in the last position.

Monika möchte Blumen **mit**bringen.

In the infinitive form, the prefix is attached to the base form of the verb.

Basic verb	Erik **sieht** gern lustige Filme.
	Erik likes to see amusing films.
Separable-prefix verb	Erik **sieht** gern **fern.**
	Erik likes to watch TV.

The meaning of a separable-prefix verb, such as **fernsehen,** is often different from the sum of the meanings of its parts: **sehen** (*see*), **fern** (*far off*).

Elfi will nicht **fern'**sehen.   Elfi sieht nicht **fern'**.

In spoken German, the stress falls on the prefix of separable-prefix verbs. In vocabulary lists in this textbook, separable-prefixes are indicated by a raised dot between the prefix and the verb: **durch·arbeiten, fern·sehen, ein·kaufen, mit·bringen, spazieren·gehen, vor·bereiten, zurück·zahlen.**

23.   Das mache ich.   Jürgen is telling Michael what he plans for the day. Using the cued words, repeat what Jürgen says.

▶   heute morgen einkaufen   *Ich kaufe heute morgen ein.*

1. Großmutter Blumen mitbringen
2. meine Notizen durcharbeiten
3. mein Referat vorbereiten
4. heute nachmittag spazierengehen
5. heute abend fernsehen

24.   Was ist hier los?   Describe the activities of the people mentioned below, using the cued modal verbs.

▶   Ursel kauft Samstag ein. (müssen)   *Ursel muß Samstag einkaufen.*

1. Andreas zahlt das Geld nicht zurück. (wollen)
2. Bringst du Tante Gabriele Blumen mit? (können)
3. Wir bereiten unsere Seminararbeit vor. (sollen)
4. Sabine geht Sonntag spazieren. (wollen)
5. Wir sehen heute abend fern. (möchte)

25.   Fragen.   Answer the following questions based on the listings for the German channels ZDF and SAT 1 on page 158. If you need help in reading the listings, see the Vocabulary for Authentic Text Activities in the Reference Section.

1. In den Programmen° gibt es auch amerikanische Sendungen°. Welche sind das?   (TV) channels / (TV) programs
2. Es gibt auch viele englische Wörter. Welche sind das?
3. Welches Programm hat mehr Sendungen für Kinder?
4. In Deutschland heißen die Nachrichtensendungen° „Tagesschau" und „heute". Wie viele Nachrichtensendungen gibt es in den zwei Programmen? Wann kommen sie?   news programs
5. Wo und wann gibt es Sportsendungen?
6. Wo und wann kann man eine Fitneß-Sendung ansehen?

Samstag, 4. März

ZDF

8.00 Nachbarn in Europa.
9.00 heute.
9.03 Morgenmagazin
Sport extra.
9.45 fit forever.
10.00 heute.
10.03 Globus. Natur und
Umwelt.
10.30 Info Arbeit und Beruf.
11.30 Kinderprogramm.
  11.30 Anne auf Green Gables.
  Kinderfilm (ab 4).
  11.55 Geschichten von der Straße
  (ab 4).
  12.15 Benjamin Blümchen.
  Zeichentrickserie (ab 4).
  12.40 Neue Abenteuer mit Black
  Beauty (ab 6).
12.55 Presseschau.
13.00 heute.
13.05 Mittagsmagazin.
13.25 Die fliegenden Ärzte.
14.02 Gesundheits-Tips.
14.07 Fußball.
15.40 X-Base .
Computer Future Club.
16.10 Diese Woche.
Schlagzeilen und Bilder.
16.30 Videofashion!
Internationale
Modetrends.
16.58 heute.
17.03 SOKO 5113. Krimiserie.
17.53 Sport heute.
18.00 Die Schwarzwaldklinik.
18.55 Vorschau.
19.00 heute.
19.20 Wetter.
19.25 Frauenarzt.
Familienserie.
20.15 Jede Menge Leben.
Neue Serie.
Happy Birthday,
Dorothee.
21.15 Die volkstümliche
Hitparade.
Die Hits des Monats.
21.45 heute-journal.
22.00 Die Sport-Reportage.
22.50 Willemsens Woche.
Talkshow mit Roger
Willemsen. Live aus
Hamburg.
23.20 Rob Roberts.
US-Polit-Thriller (1992)
mit Tim Robbins.
1.10 heute nacht.
Magazin mit Nina Ruge.

SAT 1

6.00 Deutschland heute
morgen.
6.40 White Fang. Serie.
7.05 Kinderprogramm.
  7.05 Grimmy (ab 6).
  7.30 James Bond (ab 8).
  7.55 Silverhawks (ab 10).
  8.20 Conan (ab 8).
8.50 Die Abenteuer des jungen Indiana Jones.
9.45 Games World. Die
Videowelt der Spiele.
10.15 jump ran.
Basketball.
11.05 Falcon Crest.
US-Familiensaga.
12.05 Unter der Sonne
Kaliforniens.
Serie.
13.05 Loving - Wege der
Liebe.
US-Familienserie.
13.30 Reiter gegen Sitting
Bull. Der US-Western
„Cavalry Scout" mit
Rod Cameron.
14.50 Das große
Wunschkonzert.
Stars der Volksmusik.
16.14 Glücksrad.
Gameshow aus Berlin.
17.00 SAT 1 Newsmagazin.
Nachrichten.
18.00 ran-SAT 1– Fußball.
19.30 Riskier' was!
Das trickreiche Quiz.
20.00 Der Bergdoktor.
Dt. Familienserie:
Schwester Namenlos.
21.00 Wolffs Revier.
Dt. Krimiserie (1994).
22.00 Chicago Hope.
Krankenhausserie.
23.00 News & Stories.
Chaos Navigation in
Rußland.
0.05 Klute.
US-Thriller (1970) mit
Jane Fonda.

26. Fernsehen.   Look at the TV guide listings and find a program for each category and what time it airs. If there is no program for a particular category, give an example of a local program. You will find the meanings of the categories in the Supplementary Word Sets in the Reference Section.

Seifenoper   Nachrichten
Fernsehserie   Spielfilm
Musiksendung   Sportsendung

27. Deine Lieblingssendung.   Find out from three people what their favorite programs are, which programs they don't like and why, and how often they watch TV.

▶ Wie oft siehst du fern? Einmal   *Ich sehe gern [...], denn es ist [lustig].*
   (zweimal, dreimal) die Woche?
   Was ist deine Lieblingssendung?

Land und Leute

Dieser Fernsehbericht handelt von Wölfen.

Fernsehen

In Germany, each community has access to two national television channels and one regional channel. These are referred to respectively as **ARD (Arbeitsgemeinschaft der öffentlich-rechtlichen Rundfunkanstalten Deutschlands)** or **Erstes Programm, ZDF (Zweites Deutsches Fernsehen)** or **Zweites Programm**, and **Drittes Programm (Regionalprogramm)**. These three channels are run as nonprofit public corporations and supervised by broadcasting councils. Their programming is financed primarily by fees collected from viewers. Commercials are usually shown in two to three clusters per evening and are restricted to a maximum of twenty minutes per workday. There are no commercials after 8 P.M. or on Sundays. Cable television is available by subscription and the new private stations have become strong competitors to the public TV stations. The major cable TV stations are **SAT 1, SAT 2, 3 SAT**, and **RTL**. Viewers find them attractive because they offer more light entertainment and more feature films. However, more and more Germans are opting for TV via satellite instead of cable.

Popular programs on German TV include news shows **(Nachrichten)**, game shows, sports **(Sportsendungen)**, movies **(Spielfilme)**, and series **(Serien)** such as situation comedies or detective shows **(Krimis)**—many of which are co-productions with Swiss and Austrian television or imported from the United States. Most movies and sitcoms are American made with dubbed voices, and many game shows are based on American models. American and other foreign films are usually broadcast with dubbed voices rather than subtitles. For many programs, stereo broadcasting makes it possible to hear the soundtrack either in the original language or in German. People who live close to a border sometimes receive broadcasts from a neighboring country.

WIEDERHOLUNG

1. Elke muß zu Hause bleiben. Elke wants to go to the movies but should stay home. Form sentences, using the cues below.

1. Elke / (möchte) / gehen / heute abend / ins Kino
2. sie / müssen / lernen / aber / noch viel
3. sie / können / lesen / ihre Notizen / nicht mehr
4. sie / müssen / schreiben / morgen / eine Klausur
5. sie / müssen / vorbereiten / auch noch / ein Referat
6. sie / wollen / studieren / später / in Kanada

2. Mach das. Tell Thomas what he must do this morning, using **du**-form imperatives.

▶ aufstehen / jetzt   *Steh jetzt auf.*

1. essen /Ei / zum Frühstück
2. gehen / einkaufen / dann
3. kaufen / alles / bei Meiers
4. kommen / gleich / nach Hause
5. vorbereiten / dein Referat
6. durcharbeiten / deine Notizen

3. Wer arbeitet für wen? You and your friends work for members of your families. Say who works for whom. Use a possessive adjective.

▶ Annette / Großmutter   *Annette arbeitet für ihre Großmutter.*

1. Felix / Tante
2. ich / Vater
3. du / Mutter / ?
4. Jürgen / Onkel
5. Karin und Sonja / Schwester
6. wir / Eltern
7. ihr / Großvater / ?

4. Wie sagt man das? Construct a dialogue between Ingrid and Christine, based on the English cues provided below.

CHRISTINE: Ingrid, may I ask something?
INGRID: Yes, what would you like to know?
CHRISTINE: What are you reading?
INGRID: I'm reading a book. It's called *Hello, Austria.*
CHRISTINE: Do you have to work this evening?
INGRID: No, I don't think so.
CHRISTINE: Do you want to go to the movies?
INGRID: Can you lend me money?
CHRISTINE: Certainly. But I would like to pay for you.

5. **Was macht Stefan?** Give an account of Stefan's day by describing in one or two sentences what he is doing in each picture.

1. 2. 3. 4.

5. 6. 7. 8.

6. **Zum Schreiben**

1. Choose one of the people in the photos on p. 146 and make up a profile about that person. Give the person a name and describe her/him:

   a. age
   b. relationship to others in the photo
   c. nationality
   d. profession (see Reference Section: Supplementary Word Sets)
   e. what the person likes to do in her/his free time
   f. what the person likes to eat and drink

   You may find it helpful to review the *Vokabeln* sections in this and prior chapters and to write a few key words next to the points mentioned in a–f before you begin writing.

2. Describe in German a typical Friday at your college or university. Before you begin your description think about what you want to mention, e.g., your classes, where you eat, your shopping habits, and your plans for the evening.

Hinweise: After you have written your description(s), check over your work, paying particular attention to the following:

- Check that each sentence has a subject and a verb and that the verb agrees with the subject.
- Check the word order of each sentence.
- Be sure you have used correct punctuation and capitalization.
- Watch for the position of the prefix in separable-prefix verbs.
- If you have used a modal auxiliary, be sure the dependent infinitive is at the end of the sentence.

Großeltern, Eltern und Enkelkinder *(grandchildren).*

GRAMMATIK: ZUSAMMENFASSUNG

Present tense of *werden*

werden	
ich werde	wir werden
du **wirst**	ihr werdet
er/es/sie **wird**	sie werden
Sie werden	

Verbs with stem-vowel change *e > ie*

sehen	
ich sehe	wir sehen
du **siehst**	ihr seht
er/es/sie **sieht**	sie sehen
Sie sehen	
du-*imperative:* **sieh**	

lesen	
ich lese	wir lesen
du **liest**	ihr lest
er/es/sie **liest**	sie lesen
Sie lesen	
du-*imperative:* **lies**	

Present tense of *wissen*

wissen	
ich **weiß**	wir wissen
du **weißt**	ihr wißt
er/es/sie **weiß**	sie wissen
Sie wissen	

Der-words

	Masculine der	Neuter das	Feminine die	Plural die
Nominative	dies**er** Mann	dies**es** Kind	dies**e** Frau	dies**e** Leute
Accusative	dies**en** Mann	dies**es** Kind	dies**e** Frau	dies**e** Leute

Der-words follow the same pattern in the nominative and accusative as the definite articles.

Meanings and uses of *der*-words

dies- (-er, -es, -e)	this; these *(pl.)*
jed- (-er, -es, -e)	each, every *(used in the singular only)*
manch- (-er, -es, -e)	many a, several, some *(used mainly in the plural)*
solch- (-er, -es, -e)	that kind of (those kinds of), such *(used mainly in the plural; in the singular **so ein** usually replaces **solch**-)*
welch- (-er, -es, -e)	which *(interrogative adjective)*

Modal auxiliaries

◼ *Present tense*

	dürfen	können	müssen	sollen	wollen	mögen	(möchte)
ich	darf	kann	muß	soll	will	mag	(möchte)
du	darfst	kannst	mußt	sollst	willst	magst	(möchtest)
er/es/sie	darf	kann	muß	soll	will	mag	(möchte)
wir	dürfen	können	müssen	sollen	wollen	mögen	(möchten)
ihr	dürft	könnt	müßt	sollt	wollt	mögt	(möchtet)
sie	dürfen	können	müssen	sollen	wollen	mögen	(möchten)
Sie	dürfen	können	müssen	sollen	wollen	mögen	(möchten)

German modals are irregular in that they lack endings in the **ich-** and **er/es/sie**-forms, and most modals show stem-vowel changes.

Stefanie muß jetzt **gehen.**   Stefanie has to leave now.

Modal auxiliaries in German are often used with dependent infinitives. The infinitive is in last position.

◼ *Meanings*

Infinitive	Meaning	Examples	English equivalents
dürfen	permission	Ich **darf** arbeiten.	I'm allowed to work.
können	ability	Ich **kann** arbeiten.	I can (am able to) work.
mögen	liking	Ich **mag** es nicht.	I don't like it.
müssen	compulsion	Ich **muß** arbeiten.	I must (have to) work.
sollen	obligation	Ich **soll** arbeiten.	I'm supposed to work.
wollen	wishing, wanting, intention	Ich **will** arbeiten.	I want (intend) to work.

Ich **mag** Paul nicht.	I don't like Paul.
Mögen Sie Tee?	Do you like tea?
Möchten Sie Tee oder Kaffee?	Would you like tea or coffee?

Möchte is a different form of the modal **mögen**. The meaning of **mögen** is *to like;* the meaning of **möchte** is *would like (to).*

Separable-prefix verbs

mitbringen	**Bring** Blumen **mit!**	Bring flowers.
fernsehen	**Siehst** du jetzt **fern?**	Are you going to watch TV now?

Many German verbs begin with prefixes such as **mit** or **fern.** Some prefixes are "separable," that is, they are separated from the base form of the verb in the imperative (e.g., **bring ... mit**) and in the present tense (e.g., **siehst ... fern**). The prefix generally comes at the end of the sentence. Most prefixes are either prepositions (e.g., **mit**) or adverbs (e.g., **fern**).

The separable-prefix verbs you have had are **durcharbeiten, einkaufen, fernsehen, mitbringen, spazierengehen, vorbereiten,** and **zurückzahlen**.

Warum **kauft** Stefan heute **ein**?	Warum will Stefan heute **einkaufen?**
Bringt er Blumen **mit**?	Kann er Blumen **mitbringen?**

The separable prefix is attached to the base form of the verb (e.g., **einkaufen, mitbringen**) when the verb is used as an infinitive.

Kloster Melk ist ein Musterbeispiel für österreichische Barockarchitektur.

Kapitel 6

LERNZIELE

■ **Sprechintentionen**

Discussing transportation
Discussing travel plans
Making plans for the weekend
Showing connections and relationships
Reporting on actions
Giving reasons
Discussing ideas for birthday presents
Making plans for a vacation

■ **Lesestück**

Eine Amerikanerin in Österreich

■ **Land und Leute**

Youth hostels
Cafés
Importance of public transportation
Vienna, a cultural city
The House of Habsburg
Austrian neutrality

■ **Vokabeln**

Means of transportation

■ **Grammatik**

Verbs with stem-vowel change *a* > *ä*
Independent clauses and coordinating conjunctions
Dependent clauses and subordinating conjunctions
Dative case
Indirect object

BAUSTEINE FÜR GESPRÄCHE

Fährst du morgen zur Uni?

PAUL: Fährst du morgen mit dem Auto zur Uni?

BIRGIT: Ja. Willst du mitfahren?

PAUL: Ja, gern. Ich hab' so viele Bücher für die Bibliothek. Kannst du mich vielleicht abholen?

BIRGIT: Ja, kein Problem. Ich komme dann um halb neun bei dir vorbei. Geht das?

PAUL: Ja, klar. Ich warte dann unten.

Are you driving to the university tomorrow?

Are you going by car to the university tomorrow?

Yes. Do you want to come along?

Yes, I'd like to. I've got so many library books. Can you pick me up maybe?

Yes, no problem. I'll come by your place at eight-thirty. Is that OK?

Yes, of course. I'll be waiting downstairs then.

Fragen

1. Wer fährt mit dem Auto zur Uni?
2. Warum möchte Paul mitfahren?
3. Wann holt Birgit Paul ab?
4. Wo wartet Paul?

In den Ferien

GERHARD: Was machst du in den Ferien?

RITA: Ich fahre nach Österreich.

GERHARD: Fährst du allein?

RITA: Nein, ich fahre mit meiner Freundin. Die kennt Österreich ziemlich gut.

GERHARD: Fahrt ihr mit dem Auto?

RITA: Nein, mit der Bahn. Wir wollen vor allem wandern.

GERHARD: Und wo übernachtet ihr?

RITA: In Wien schlafen wir bei Freunden. Und sonst zelten wir.

On vacation

What are you doing on vacation?

I'm going to Austria.

Are you going alone?

No, I'm going with my friend. She knows Austria rather well.

Are you going by car?

No, by train. Above all we want to hike.

And where are you staying?

In Vienna we're sleeping at our friends' house. And otherwise we're camping.

Fragen

1. Wohin° fährt Rita in den Ferien?
2. Warum ist es gut, daß Ritas Freundin mitfährt?
3. Wie kommen Rita und ihre Freundin nach Österreich?
4. Wo schlafen sie in Wien?
5. Wo schlafen sie, wenn sie nicht in Wien sind?

▷ **1. Interview.** Your car has broken down and you're looking for a ride. Ask three students how they get to school or work, when they leave, and when they return home.

> Discussing transportation

S1:

Fährst du mit dem Auto zur | **Uni?**
                           | Arbeit?

S2:

Ja, willst du mitfahren?

Nein, | **mein Auto ist kaputt°.**
      | ich nehme den Bus°.
      | ich gehe immer zu Fuß°.
      | ich laufe°.
      | ich fahre mit dem Rad°.

Wann | **gehst** du zur | **Uni?**
     | fährst | Arbeit?

Um | **acht.** Ist das zu | **früh?**
   | halb neun. | spät?

Wann kommst du wieder nach Hause?

Um vier. Soll ich auf dich warten?
Gegen° sechs.

▷ **2. Was machst du in den Ferien?** A friend is looking for someone to go on vacation with and asks what you're going to do during the summer vacation. Respond.

> Discussing travel plans

S2:

Hast du schon Pläne° für die Ferien?

S1:

Ja, | ich fahre nach Österreich.
    | ich möchte | **wandern.**
    | | zelten.
    | | viel schwimmen.
    | | Wasserski fahren°.
    | | schlafen°.
    | | Ski fahren°.

Nein, ich habe keine.
Ich muß arbeiten.
Nein, meine Ferien sind zu kurz°.

▷ **3. Rollenspiel.** You and your roommate are discussing plans for tomorrow. Tell her/him what you plan to do. Find out the same information from your roommate.

Land und Leute

Jugendherbergen

In German-speaking countries young people can stay inexpensively at a youth hostel (**Jugendherberge**). Germany alone has over 780 **Jugendherbergen;** Austria and Switzerland have over 120 each. Originally established in the early twentieth century, **Jugendherbergen** were located no more than a day's hike apart. They are found not only near vacation spots and national parks, but also in cities and towns. The appearance of **Jugendherbergen** varies greatly. Some are found in modern buildings while others are in small country houses or even in old fortresses. All serve a simple, cafeteria-style breakfast and provide bedding, if needed. Many have curfews and some even require their guests to help with various chores.

Traveling to other European countries is very popular among German students, particu-

Jugendherberge in Salzburg.

larly since there are special railway fares for young people under the age of 26. (North Americans in that age group can also obtain reduced fares.)

Erweiterung des Wortschatzes

1 *Wo?* and *wohin?*

Wo ist Dieter?
Where is Dieter?

Wohin geht Erika?
Where is Erika going?

English *where* has two meanings: *in what place* and *to what place*. German has two words for *where* that correspond to these two meanings: **wo** (*in what place,* i.e., position) and **wohin** (*to what place,* i.e., direction).

1. Wie bitte? You don't understand what Nicole is saying. Ask her to repeat her statements.

▶ Cornelia fährt zur Uni.   *Wohin fährt Cornelia?*
▶ Erik arbeitet im Supermarkt.   *Wo arbeitet Erik?*

1. Dieter fährt in die Schweiz.
2. Tanja arbeitet beim Bäcker.
3. Bärbel fährt nach Österreich.
4. Schmidts wandern in Österreich.
5. Fischers kaufen immer im Supermarkt ein.
6. Mark geht nach Hause.

Land und Leute

Das Kaffeehaus

The **Kaffeehaus** was first introduced to the German-speaking areas in the seventeenth century. The Viennese **Kaffeehäuser** in the late nineteenth and early twentieth centuries were especially famous as gathering places for artists, writers, and even revolutionaries like Leon Trotsky. Today, **Cafés** are still popular meeting places throughout the German-speaking countries and often provide newspapers and magazines for their customers. People from all walks of life, business people, students and artists, enjoy taking a break for coffee and perhaps a piece of cake. In addition to **Kaffee** and a wide variety of **Kuchen** and **Torten,** many **Cafés** offer a small selection of meals (hot and cold), ice cream treats, and beverages.

A cup of coffee costs around 25-30 **Schilling** in Austria, 3-4 **Franken** in Switzerland, and 3-4 **Mark** in Germany, and there are no free refills. In most Viennese **Kaffeehäuser** coffee is served with a small glass of water on a small wooden or silver tray. A spoon is placed upside down across the top of the water glass. Coffee with **Schlagobers** *(whipped cream)* is a favorite in Vienna.

Cafés are usually not open evenings, but they are open six or seven days per week. The day on which a **Café** or restaurant is closed is called its **Ruhetag.** Most **Cafés** have a sign posted in a prominent place indicating their **Ruhetag.**

In vielen Wiener Kaffeehäusern kann man auch draußen sitzen.

2 Wie fährt man? Man fährt ...

mit dem Fahrrad/Rad

mit dem Auto/mit dem Wagen

mit dem Motorrad

mit dem Bus

mit der Straßenbahn

mit der U-Bahn

mit der Bahn/mit dem Zug

mit dem Schiff

Man fliegt (mit dem Flugzeug).

2. Wie fahren Sie? Answer the following questions. For additional transportation terms, refer to the Supplementary Word Sets in the Reference Section.

Talking about transportation

1. Haben Sie ein Fahrrad? einen Wagen? ein Motorrad?
2. Ist es/er neu oder alt?
3. Wie fahren Sie zur Uni? Mit dem Bus? Mit dem Auto? Mit dem Rad? Mit der U-Bahn?
4. Fliegen Sie gern? viel?

public transportation

Land und Leute

Öffentliche Verkehrsmittel°

Die Wiener Straßenbahn ist eine praktische Alternative zum Auto.

Public transportation is efficient and much utilized by the people in German-speaking countries. Buses, streetcars, subways, and trains are owned either by the federal or local government. While the popularity of the car continues to grow, governments subsidize public transportation because public transportation is better for the environment (**umweltfreundlich**) and ensures that everyone has access to transportation. Reduced rates are available for senior citizens (**Seniorenkarten**) and for students at all levels (**Schüler-/Studentenkarten**). In towns, villages, and suburbs there is convenient bus and sometimes streetcar (**Straßenbahn**) service. Major cities have a subway (**Untergrundbahn** or **U-Bahn**) and/or a modern commuter rail system (**Schnellbahn/Stadtbahn** or **S-Bahn**). The German, Austrian, and Swiss post offices provide extensive bus service between towns. If needed, even ferries are included in the public transportation network, such as the ferry on the Alster Lake (**Alsterfähre**) in Hamburg.

Trains are still a major part of the transportation system in German-speaking countries for both long and short distance travel. Larger cities have more than one train station (**Bahnhof**), but the main train station (**Hauptbahnhof**) is usually a prominent building located in the center of town. In addition to transportation facilities, larger train stations may also have a variety of restaurants and shops to serve the traveling public. To commute, people often use short-distance trains (**Nahverkehrszüge**). Fast, comfortable **Inter-City Express (ICE)** trains run hourly between major cities. This system is being supplemented with the **Interregio-Züge,** which depart every two hours. The slightly slower "through" trains (**D-Züge**) also make long distance runs, but stop more frequently than the **ICE** trains. A network of trains known as the **Euro-City Express** connects the major cities throughout Europe. By 2005 it is expected that the **Transrapid,** a magnetic elevated train (**Magnetbahn**), will cover the 280 km distance between Berlin and Hamburg in an hour.

Vokabeln

Substantive

das **Auto, -s**   automobile, car
die **Bahn, -en**   train; railroad
der **Bus, -se**   bus
das **Fahrrad, ̈er**   bicycle
das **Flugzeug, -e**   airplane
der **Fuß, ̈e**   foot
das **Motorrad, ̈er**   motorcycle
der **Plan, ̈e**   plan
das **Problem, -e**   problem
das **Rad, ̈er** (*short for* **Fahrrad**) bike,
   bicycle; **ich fahre Rad** I ride a
   bike

das **Schiff, -e**   ship
der **Ski, -er** (**Ski** *is pronounced* **Schi**)
   ski
die **Straßenbahn, -en**   streetcar
die **U-Bahn, -en**   subway
der **Wagen, -**   car
der **Wasserski, -er**   water ski
der **Zug, ̈e**   train

Verben

ab·holen   to pick up
fahren (fährt)   to drive, to travel;
   mit (dem Auto) fahren   to go by
   (car)
fliegen   to fly
laufen (läuft)   to run; to go on foot;
   to walk
mit·fahren (fährt mit)   to drive (go)
   along
schlafen (schläft)   to sleep

Ski fahren (fährt Ski)   to ski
übernachten   to spend the night/to
   stay (*in a hotel or with friends*)
vorbei·kommen   to come by
warten (auf + *acc.*)   to wait (for)
Wasserski fahren (fährt Wasserski)
   to water ski
zelten   to camp in a tent

Andere Wörter

allein   alone
dir (*dat.*)   (to *or* for) you
früh   early
kaputt   broken; exhausted (*slang*)

kurz   short, brief
unten   downstairs; below
wem (*dat.* of **wer**)   (to *or* for) whom
wohin   where (to)

Besondere Ausdrücke

bei dir   at your place
bei mir vorbeikommen   to come by
   my place
gegen [sechs]   around, about
   [6 o'clock]
Geht das?   Is that OK?

in den Ferien   on vacation; during
   vacation
mit (dem Auto)   by (car)
vor allem   above all
zu Fuß   on foot; **Ich gehe immer zu
   Fuß.**   I always walk.

Land und Leute

Kulturstadt Wien

Austria has a very rich and diverse cultural tradition. In the late eighteenth and early nineteenth centuries, Vienna **(Wien)** was the center of a musical culture associated with such names as Haydn, Mozart, Beethoven, and Schubert. In the second half of the nineteenth century the **Operette** reached its prime with composers like Johann Strauss the Younger and Franz Lehar. At the turn of the century (referred to in French as **Fin de Siècle**), Vienna was a major intellectual and artistic center of Europe. Two important names of that time are Sigmund Freud, who established psychoanalysis, and Gustav Mahler, who continued the city's great musical tradition. Today, Vienna continues to attract well-known Austrian artists, performers, and writers, as well as creative people from Eastern European countries.

Die Wiener Oper ist in der ganzen Welt berühmt.

EINE AMERIKANERIN IN ÖSTERREICH

Vorbereitung auf das Lesen

In diesem Text lernen Sie einiges° über Österreich. — *some things*

■ *Vor dem Lesen*

Sehen Sie sich die Landkarte° von Österreich am Anfang° des Buches an°, und lesen Sie die folgende° Information. Dann beantworten Sie die Fragen.

Sehen Sie sich an: look at/map/beginning/following

- **Größe°:** 83.855 qkm°
  etwa so groß wie Maine (86.027 qkm)
  etwas größer° als Neubraunschweig° (72.000 qkm)

  size/qkm = Quadratkilometer: square kilometers
  larger/New Brunswick, Canada/population

- **Bevölkerung°:** 7,8 Millionen Einwohner
- **Regierungsform°:** Bundesstaat° mit 9 Bundesländern°
  parlamentarische Demokratie

  type of government/federation/federal states

- **Hauptstadt:** Wien (1,5 Millionen Einwohner)
- **8 Nachbarn:** Italien (I)*, Fürstentum Liechtenstein (FL), die Schweiz (CH), Deutschland (D), die Tschechische Republik (ČZ), die Slowakei (SK), Ungarn (H), Slowenien (SLO)

*The abbreviations in parentheses are the international symbols used on automobile stickers.

✈1. Ist Ihr Land oder Bundesland größer oder kleiner° als Österreich?   smaller
2. Welche anderen parlamentarischen Demokratien kennen Sie?
3. Die Österreicher sagen, Österreich liegt im Herzen° von Europa. Warum   **im Herzen:** in the heart
   sagen sie das?
4. Wie heißen Österreichs Nachbarn?
5. Wo kann man in Österreich Ski fahren?

◼ *Beim Lesen*

Machen Sie Notizen zu den folgenden Fragen:

1. Was lesen Sie über Österreichs Wirtschaft°?
2. Was lesen Sie über Petra Heller?

Petra Heller kommt aus Baltimore. Sie ist gerade mit dem Flugzeug in Wien
angekommen°, und ein Mann von dem österreichischen Fremdenverkehrsbüro°   **ist angekommen:** has
interviewt sie.   arrived/tourist office

INTERVIEWER: Willkommen in Wien, gnädige Frau°. Ich interviewe für das   **gnädige Frau:** Madam
5   österreichische Fremdenverkehrsbüro. Darf ich Sie etwas fragen?
PETRA HELLER: Aber gern. Fragen Sie!
INTERVIEWER: Woher kommen Sie?
PETRA HELLER: Aus Amerika. Ich bin Amerikanerin.
INTERVIEWER: Warum kommen Sie nach Wien? Sind Sie Touristin?
10 PETRA HELLER: Nein, ich habe seit vier Monaten mein Diplom als Ingenieurin
   und habe hier in Wien eine Stelle° bei General Motors.   position
INTERVIEWER: Darf ich fragen, wie Sie heißen?
PETRA HELLER: Heller, – Petra Heller.
INTERVIEWER: Heller – das ist ein österreichischer Name, nicht wahr?
15 PETRA HELLER: Ja, meine Eltern sind Amerikaner, aber sie kommen aus Öster-
   reich. Sie leben jetzt schon seit achtundzwanzig Jahren in Baltimore.
INTERVIEWER: Kennen Sie Österreich gut?
PETRA HELLER: Nein, leider nicht. Vor zehn Jahren war ich einmal hier in Wien
   bei meiner Großmutter zu Besuch.
20 INTERVIEWER: Sie sprechen aber gut Deutsch, Frau Heller.
PETRA HELLER: Vielen Dank für das Kompliment! Wir sprechen es natürlich zu
   Hause, aber hier lerne ich es hoffentlich wirklich gut.
INTERVIEWER: Was wissen Sie denn schon von Österreich?
PETRA HELLER: Ich weiß, daß Österreich ein Alpenland ist. Es ist ziemlich
25 klein ...
INTERVIEWER: Ja, für Amerikaner ist Österreich natürlich klein. Es hat nur 7,8
   Millionen Einwohner.
PETRA HELLER: Meine Eltern vermissen° vor allem das Österreich der° Musik.   miss/of (the)
   Für sie gehören Österreich und Musik nämlich° zusammen. Zu Hause hören   you see
30 wir viel Musik von Haydn, Mozart, Beethoven und natürlich Johann Strauß.
   Meine Mutter mag auch noch Wiener Operetten, aber ich höre lieber
   Rockmusik!
INTERVIEWER: Gut, aber die Musik, das Skifahren, das Essen und die Berge, das
   wissen die meisten Touristen auch über Österreich. Als Ingenieurin wissen
35 Sie wohl auch etwas über die österreichische Wirtschaft, nicht wahr?

PETRA HELLER: Etwas schon. Es gibt viele ausländische Firmen in Österreich. Sie wissen ja, daß ich hier für eine amerikanische Firma arbeite. Das Werk° von General Motors ist die größte° amerikanische Investition° in Österreich. In Graz gibt es auch ein Chrysler-Werk. Österreich ist für amerikanische
40 Firmen ein interessantes Land, denn die Österreicher haben viel Erfahrung° im Ost-West-Handel, nicht wahr?

company
largest/investment

experience

INTERVIEWER: Ja, das stimmt. Wir kennen und verstehen unsere östlichen° Nachbarn gut. Seit 1990 liegt Österreich ja auch nicht mehr an der Grenze von Osten und Westen, sondern im Zentrum° Europas.

eastern

center

45 PETRA HELLER: Und seit 1995 gehört Österreich auch zur Europäischen Union. Außerdem° ist das Land wirtschaftlich° sehr stark.

besides/economically

INTERVIEWER: Das kann man wohl sagen. Aber auch politisch ist Österreich wichtig, nicht wahr?

PETRA HELLER: Na ja, ich weiß, daß Wien Sitz° wichtiger° internationaler
50 Organisationen ist, und daß UNO° und OPEC° hier ihre Büros haben.

seat/of important

UNO: United Nations (Organization)/OPEC: Organization of Petroleum Exporting Countries/of the/ tried/mediate

INTERVIEWER: Richtig, und in der Zeit des° Ost-West-Konfliktes war Österreich neutral und versuchte°, kulturell, wirtschaftlich und politisch zu vermitteln°. Also wie ich sehe, wissen Sie doch einiges über unser schönes, kleines Land. Wie lange bleiben Sie denn hier?

55 PETRA HELLER: Etwa zwei Jahre. Ich will hier nicht nur arbeiten, sondern Österreich und seine Nachbarn kennenlernen. Ich möchte viel reisen, besonders mit dem Zug. Aber zuerst möchte ich Wien sehen, dann Salzburg und Innsbruck. Hoffentlich kann ich auch viel ins Theater, in die Oper und in Konzerte gehen.

60 INTERVIEWER: ... und natürlich in unsere gemütlichen Kaffeehäuser. Also vielen Dank für das Interview, Frau Heller. Ich wünsche Ihnen einen erfolgreichen° und schönen Aufenthalt° hier in Österreich!

successful
stay

Brauchbares

1. In l. 20 the interviewer says to Petra, **"Sie sprechen aber gut Deutsch."** By using the word **aber** he is expressing surprise that she speaks such good German since she has not spent much time in a German-speaking country. In addition to its usual meaning of *but,* **aber** can be used as a flavoring particle. As a particle **aber** often indicates a situation that is somewhat unexpected or gives added emphasis to the speaker's feelings about an utterance.

2. In the sentence **"Sie wissen ja, daß ich hier für eine amerikanische Firma arbeite"** (l. 37), **ja** is a flavoring particle. With the use of **ja,** Petra is reminding the interviewer that she had already told him the information. And in l. 43, **"Seit 1990 liegt Österreich ja auch nicht mehr an der Grenze von Osten und Westen,"** the interviewer uses **ja** to imply that everyone knows this about Austria. As a flavoring particle, **ja** may be used by a speaker to express the belief that an utterance is related to a condition that both the speaker and the listener are aware of, or should be aware of. In English one would say something like *You know of course, that . . .*

3. The verb **versuchte** (l. 52) is the simple past tense form. You will study these forms in *Kapitel 11.*

Nach dem Lesen

1. Fragen zum Lesestück

1. Warum kommt Petra Heller nach Österreich? → *just give the answer*
2. Für wen arbeitet der Interviewer?
3. Woher kommt Petra Heller?
4. Was machen viele Touristen in Österreich?
5. Welches Autowerk ist in Graz?
6. Warum ist Österreich für amerikanische Firmen interessant? → *just give the answer*
7. Welche internationalen Organisationen haben ihren Sitz in Wien?
8. Warum liegt Österreich jetzt wieder im Zentrum von Europa?
9. Was war Österreichs Rolle im Kalten Krieg?
10. Welche Städte will Petra Heller zuerst sehen?
11. Was möchte Petra Heller in Österreich machen?

2. Vokabeln. Welches Wort oder welche Wendung° paßt° zu welchem   phrase/fits
Thema? Ordnen° Sie das Wort zu dem Thema°, dann suchen Sie noch zwei   match/topic
Wörter oder Wendungen im Text zu den Themen.

> *Wörter/Wendungen:* neutral □ Mozart □ Ost-West-Handel
> *Themen:* Wirtschaft □ Außenpolitik° □ Musik   foreign policy

3. Petra Heller. Was wissen Sie über Frau Heller? Schreiben Sie einen
kurzen Absatz° über Petra Heller, ihre Familie, ihre Arbeit und ihre   paragraph
Interessen.

4. Erzählen wir. Sprechen Sie mit einer Partnerin/einem Partner über eines
der folgenden Themen:

Warum ich Österreich besuchen will.
Wichtiges° über Österreich.   important things
Ich möchte in Österreich arbeiten.

**Österreich ist ein Alpen-
land: Blick von Salzburg
auf die Alpen.**

Wien – Schloß Schönbrunn, die Sommerresidenz der Habsburger Kaiser.

Land und Leute

Die Habsburger

A very significant period in Austria's history is the era under the rule of the House of Habsburg. In 1273 Rudolf von Habsburg was the first member of the Habsburg family to be elected emperor of the Holy Roman Empire **(Heiliges Römisches Reich),** which existed from 962 until 1806. In the first 400 years of Habsburg rule, the empire expanded greatly. The expansion was due to wars and to a successful **Heiratspolitik,** which deliberately aimed at advantageous marriages with the ruling European houses. The success of Napoleon's wars at the beginning of the nineteenth century led to the end of the empire in 1806. Members of the House of Habsburg continued to rule the Austro-Hungarian empire until 1918, however, when Austria was declared a republic.

Vokabeln

Substantive

die **Alpen** (*pl.*)   Alps
der **Berg, -e**   mountain; **in die Berge fahren**   to go to the mountains
das **Büro, -s**   office
das **Café, -s**   café
der **Dank**   thanks; **vielen Dank** many thanks
die **Firma,** *pl.* **Firmen**   company
die **Grenze, -n**   border
der **Handel**   trade
das **Interview, -s**   interview
der **Interviewer, -/**die **Interviewerin, -nen**   interviewer

das **Kaffeehaus,** *pl.* **Kaffeehäuser** café (in Austria)
das **Konzert, -e**   concert; **ins Konzert gehen**   to go to a concert
der **Name, -n**   name
die **Oper, -n**   opera; **in die Oper gehen**   to go to the opera
die **Rockmusik**   rock (music)
das **Theater, -**   theater; **ins Theater gehen**   to go to the theater
der **Tourist, -en, -en/**die **Touristin, -nen**   tourist
die **Wirtschaft**   economy

Verben

gehören (+ *dat.*)   to belong to
interviewen   to interview
kennen·lernen   to get to know; to make the acquaintance of
leben   to live

reisen   to travel
schenken   to give (as a gift)
sprechen (spricht)   to speak
verstehen   to understand
wünschen   to wish

Andere Wörter

als as
ausländisch foreign
einige some, several
daß *(conj.)* that
denn *(conj.)* because, for
einmal once, one time
gemütlich comfortable, informal
gerade just; straight
lange *(adv.)* for a long time
lieber preferably, rather; **ich höre lieber Rock** I prefer to listen to rock

obwohl although
österreichisch Austrian
richtig correct, right
sondern *(conj.)* but (on the contrary)
stark strong
weil *(conj.)* because
wichtig important
wohl probably; indeed
zuerst first, first of all, at first

Besondere Ausdrücke

das stimmt that's right
na ja well now
nicht mehr no longer
nicht nur ... sondern auch not only . . . but also

vor [zehn] Jahren [ten] years ago
zu Besuch for a visit
zu Hause (to be) at home

Land und Leute

Neutralität

World War II ended in 1945, but because of the East-West conflict, Austria's sovereignty was not restored until 1955. The Soviet Union finally agreed to a peace treaty after Austria declared its policy of permanent neutrality (**immer-während Neutralität**). Therefore, during the Cold War, Austria was neither a member of NATO nor of the Warsaw Pact. From the end of World War II until the end of the Cold War approximately 45 years later, Austria granted temporary or permanent asylum to about two million people from more than thirty countries. In fact, its decision to allow East German refugees to enter through its border with Hungary in 1989 was a contributing factor to the fall of the government of East Germany.

Until the end of World War I in 1918, Austria included lands that today are part of eastern European countries—the Czech Republic, Romania, Hungary, and the former Yugoslavia. Because of these ties, Austria served as an important link between eastern and western

UNO-Gebäude in Wien.

Europe during the Cold War, and it continues to play an important and special role in Europe today. Austria joined the European Union (**Europäische Union**) in 1995 but has not surrendered its neutrality. It is an active member of the United Nations and serves as the site of many international congresses and conferences. Vienna ranks among the leading convention cities in the world.

GRAMMATIK UND ÜBUNGEN

1 Verbs with stem-vowel change *a* > *ä*

fahren: to drive	
ich fahre	wir fahren
du **fährst**	ihr fahrt
er/es/sie **fährt**	sie fahren
Sie fahren	
du-*imperative:* fahr(e)	

laufen: to run; to go on foot, walk	
ich laufe	wir laufen
du **läufst**	ihr lauft
er/es/sie **läuft**	sie laufen
Sie laufen	
du-*imperative:* lauf(e)	

Some verbs with stem-vowel **a** or **au** change **a** to **ä** in the **du-** and **er/es/sie-**forms of the present tense. The verbs you know with this change are **fahren, schlafen,** and **laufen.**

1. Wohin fährst du? You are discussing travel plans for the summer with a friend. Tell who is going where. Use a form of **fahren.**

▶ Birgit / Italien   *Birgit fährt nach Italien.*

1. Paul / auch / Italien
2. meine Großeltern / Spanien
3. ich / Dänemark
4. meine Schwester / Ungarn
5. wir / auch / Schweden
6. du / Österreich / ?

2. Wir laufen gern. You are discussing how and when people you know like to run or walk. Use a form of **laufen.**

▶ Rita / morgens   *Rita läuft morgens.*

1. Gisela / abends
2. ich / zur Uni
3. mein Vater / auch gern
4. wir / gern zusammen
5. du / viel / ?
6. Julia / immer / morgens

3. Restop Altea. Restop Altea Motel is in the town of Mondsee on the lake of the same name (**See** = *lake*). Tell what one can learn about the motel from its ad by answering the questions. If you need help, see Vocabulary for Authentic Text Activities in the Reference Section.

RESTOP ♿

ALTEA
M O T E L

MONDSEE
Tel. 0 62 32/28 76–28 79, Telex 63 33 57 altea
Telefax 06 2 32/28 76/5

DER MONDSEE LIEGT IHNEN ZU FÜSSEN

Idealer Ausgangspunkt für jung und alt in äußerst ruhiger Lage. Das ist unser Motel mit 46 Komfortzimmern, erreichbar von beiden Fahrtrichtungen der A-1-Autobahn. In unserem Panorama-Restaurant überraschen wir Sie mit kulinarischen Spezialitäten. Hoteleigener Badestrand!
Es lädt Sie ein:

Der Mondsee:	zum Segeln, Surfen, Wasserschilaufen und zu Schiffsrundfahrten.
Die Bergwelt:	zum Bergwandern und Bergsteigen.
Mondsee:	zum Besuch von Kulturstätten und Veranstaltungen.
Die Umgebung:	zum Tennisspielen, zum Golfen auf zwei Plätzen mit neun bzw. 18 Löchern, zu Ausflugsfahrten ins Salzkammergut.
Unser Haus:	mit dem Weekend-Hit, zahle 2 Nächte und bleibe 3!

Gute Erholung und viel Vergnügen!

1. Welche Autobahn fährt nach Mondsee?
2. Wie viele Zimmer hat das Motel?
3. Was für Sport kann man treiben?
4. Was ist der Weekend-Hit?
5. Warum schläft man in diesem Motel gut?

4. Rollenspiel. Work with a partner. You have just come across the ad for Altea Motel and want to spend a weekend there. Convince your partner to go with you and plan your activities for your time at the resort. You may use some of the phrases below to get you started:

> Making plans for the weekend

S1: Fahren wir nach Mondsee? Komm doch mit! □ Wir kommen ganz leicht° nach Mondsee. □ Ich möchte gern auf dem See° segeln°. □ Kannst du surfen? □ Und ich möchte auch gerne gut essen. □ Wir können ins Salzkammergut fahren.

easily
lake/sail

S2: Hast du denn ein Auto? □ Ich kann nicht segeln. □ Kann man da auch gut wandern? □ Gibt es in Mondsee einen Golfplatz? □ Ist das nicht zu teuer? □ Ich möchte vor allem meine Ruhe° haben.

peace and quiet

2 Independent clauses and coordinating conjunctions

Wir wollen am Wochenende zelten. Es soll regnen.
Wir wollen am Wochenende zelten, **aber** es soll regnen.

An independent (or main) clause can stand alone as a complete sentence. Two (or more) independent clauses may be connected by a coordinating conjunction (e.g., **aber**). Because coordinating conjunctions are merely connectors and not part of either clause, they do not affect word order. Thus the subject comes before the verb. The coordinating conjunctions you know are **aber, denn, oder, sondern,** and **und.**

Erika kommt morgen, **und** Christel kommt am Montag.

In written German, coordinating conjunctions are generally preceded by a comma.

Erika kommt morgen **und** Christel am Montag.
Erika kommt morgen **und** bleibt eine Woche.

Oder and **und** are not preceded by a comma when either the subject or the verb is omitted in the second clause.

5. Erika und Sabine.   Tell what Sabine and Erika are going to do this week. Combine each pair of sentences below, using the coordinating conjunctions indicated.

▶   Die Studentin heißt Erika. Ihre   *Die Studentin heißt Erika, und*
     Freundin heißt Sabine. (und)   *ihre Freundin heißt Sabine.*

1. Erika wohnt bei einer Familie. Sabine wohnt bei ihren Eltern. (aber)
2. Erika arbeitet zu Hause. Sabine muß in die Bibliothek gehen. (aber)
3. Erika arbeitet schwer. Am Mittwoch hat sie eine Klausur. (denn)
4. Sabine hat ihre Klausur nicht am Mittwoch. Sie hat sie am Freitag. (sondern)
5. Was machen die Mädchen in den Ferien? Wissen sie es nicht? (oder)

■ Sondern *and* aber

Paul fährt morgen nicht mit dem   Paul isn't going by car tomorrow,
   Auto, **sondern** geht zu Fuß.   *but (rather) is walking.*

Sondern is a coordinating conjunction that expresses a contrast or contradiction. It connects two ideas that are mutually exclusive. It is used only after a negative clause and is equivalent to *but, on the contrary, instead, rather.* When the subject is the same in both clauses, it is not repeated. This is also true of a verb that is the same; it is not repeated.

Cordelia tanzt nicht nur viel,   Cordelia not only dances a lot,
   sondern auch gut.   *but also well.*

The German construction **nicht nur ... sondern auch** is equivalent to *not only . . . but also.*

Er fährt nicht mit dem Auto, **aber**
    sein Vater fährt mit dem Auto.

He isn't going by car, *but* his father
    is.

Aber as a coordinating conjunction is equivalent to *but* or *nevertheless*. It may
be used after either positive or negative clauses.

6. Was macht Annette? Complete the sentences about Annette's activities
with **aber** or **sondern,** as appropriate.

▶   Annette spielt heute nicht Fußball, _____ Tennis.
    Annette spielt heute nicht Fußball, sondern Tennis.

1. Sie spielt Tennis nicht gut, _____ sie spielt es sehr gern.
2. Sie geht nicht zur Vorlesung, _____ in die Bibliothek.
3. Im Café bestellt sie Bier, _____ sie trinkt Eriks Kaffee.
4. Sie möchte den Kaffee bezahlen, _____ sie hat kein Geld.
5. Sie fährt nicht mit dem Bus nach Hause, _____ geht zu Fuß.

7. Meine Freunde. Your friends are all very active people. Tell what they
do using **nicht nur ... sondern auch.**

> Showing connections
> and relationships

▶   Karola studiert Musik. Sie studiert auch Sport.
    Karola studiert nicht nur Musik, sondern auch Sport.

1. Adrian lernt Deutsch. Er lernt auch Spanisch.
2. Sabine arbeitet im Café. Sie arbeitet auch im Supermarkt.
3. Bettina besucht° einen Tanzkurs. Sie besucht auch einen Karatekurs.   attends
4. Bernd spielt Fußball und Hockey. Er spielt auch Tennis.
5. Jan macht Informatik. Er macht auch Geschichte und Mathematik.

3 Dependent clauses and subordinating conjunctions

Independent Clause	Conjunction	Dependent Clause
Rita sagt,	**daß**	sie nach Österreich **fährt.**
Sie übernachtet bei Freunden,	**wenn**	sie zu Hause **sind.**

A dependent (subordinate) clause is a clause that cannot stand alone; it must
be combined with an independent clause to express a complete idea. Two signals distinguish a dependent clause from an independent clause: (1) it is introduced by a subordinating conjunction (**daß, wenn**) and (2) the finite verb
(**fährt, sind**) is at the end. In writing, a dependent clause is separated from the
independent clause by a comma. A few common subordinating conjunctions
are: **daß,** *that;* **obwohl,** *although;* **weil,** *because;* **wenn,** *if, when.*

8. Deutsche Studenten. Your friend plans to study at a German university for a year and asks you questions related to such study. Answer the questions. Use **wenn** to answer questions beginning with **wann**. Use **weil** to answer questions beginning with **warum**.

▶ Wann bekommen Studenten Geld   *Wenn sie zuwenig Geld haben.*
   vom Staat? (Sie haben zuwenig Geld.)

1. Warum jobben die Studenten nicht? (Es gibt wenige Studentenjobs.) — *weil*
2. Warum brauchen sie soviel Geld? (Wohnen und Essen sind teuer.) — *weil*
3. Wann bekommt man einen Studienplatz? (Man hat gute Noten im Gymnasium.) — *wenn*
4. Warum sollen Studenten in neun bis zehn Semestern fertig sein? (Es gibt zuwenig Studienplätze.) — *weil*
5. Wann ist es billiger zu studieren? (Man wohnt bei den Eltern.) — *wenn*

Dependent clauses and separable-prefix verbs

Statement	Monika **kauft** gern im Supermarkt **ein**.
Dependent clause	Monika sagt, **daß** sie gern im Supermarkt **einkauft**.

In a dependent clause, the separable prefix is attached to the base form of the verb, which is in final position.

9. Was sagt Gabi? You want to tell a friend about Gabi's plans. Begin each sentence with **Gabi sagt, daß ...**

Reporting on actions

▶ Sie kauft in der Stadt ein.   *Gabi sagt, daß sie in der Stadt einkauft.*

1. Renate kommt mit.
2. Renate kommt um neun bei ihr vorbei.
3. Sie kaufen auf dem Markt ein.
4. Sie bereitet dann zu Hause ein Referat vor.
5. Renate bringt ein paar Bücher mit.
6. Sie bringt die Bücher am Freitag zurück.

Dependent clauses and modal auxiliaries

Statement	Rita **möchte** in die Schweiz fahren.
Dependent clause	Rita sagt, **daß** sie in die Schweiz fahren **möchte**.

In a dependent clause, the modal auxiliary is the finite verb and therefore is in final position, after the dependent infinitive.

10. **Andreas sagt das.** Tell a friend what Andreas has told you about things he has to or would like to do.

▶ Ich möchte die Notizen von Katrin haben.   *Er sagt, daß er die Notizen von Katrin haben möchte.*

1. Ich muß die Notizen heute haben.
2. Ich muß einen Artikel lesen.
3. Ich soll eine Seminararbeit schreiben.
4. Ich will in die Bibliothek gehen.
5. Ich möchte heute abend arbeiten.

⇨ **11.** **Freizeit.** Your partner wants to know why you aren't doing certain things in your free time or on vacation. Begin your response with **weil.** You may choose one of the answers given or make up your own.

Giving reasons

S2: Warum gehst du nicht ins Kino?
S1: Weil ich kein Geld habe.

S2:

1. Warum gehst du nicht ins Kino?
2. Warum gehst du nicht mit Freunden ins Café?
3. Warum gehst du nicht in die Disco?
4. Warum läufst du nicht zur Uni?
5. Warum fährst du nicht mit dem Bus?
6. Warum machst du nicht Ferien in Italien?
7. Warum fährst du nicht in die Berge?
8. Warum fliegst du nicht nach Deutschland?
9. Warum bist du immer so müde?

S1:

Ich will zu Hause bleiben.
Ich muß eine Seminararbeit schreiben.
Ich will allein sein.
Ich muß arbeiten.
Ich will in die Bibliothek gehen.
Ich habe kein Geld.
Ich möchte mit dem Auto fahren.
Ich kann nicht tanzen.
Das interessiert mich nicht.
Ich kann nicht schlafen.

■ *Dependent clauses beginning a sentence*

	1	2	
	Paul	**fährt**	mit dem Bus.
1		2	
Weil sein Auto kaputt ist,		**fährt**	er mit dem Bus.

In a statement, the finite verb is in second position. If a sentence begins with a dependent clause, the entire clause is considered a single element, and the finite verb of the independent clause is in second position, followed by the subject.

12. Eine Radtour durch die Schweiz. Gerhard and Fabian are planning a bicycle trip through Switzerland. Combine each pair of sentences. Begin the new sentence with the conjunction indicated.

▶ (wenn) Das Wetter ist gut. Gerhard *Wenn das Wetter gut ist, wollen*
und Fabian wollen in die Schweiz. *Gerhard und Fabian in die Schweiz.*

1. (weil) Sie haben wenig Geld. Sie fahren mit dem Rad.
2. (wenn) Sie fahren mit dem Rad. Sie sehen mehr vom Land.
3. (wenn) Es ist nicht zu kalt. Sie zelten.
4. (wenn) Das Wetter ist sehr schlecht. Sie schlafen bei Freunden.
5. (obwohl) Sie haben wenig Geld. Sie können vier Wochen bleiben.
6. (weil) Sie haben nur vier Wochen Ferien. Sie müssen im August wieder zu Hause sein.

4 Dative case

Nominative	**Der** Mann heißt Falk.
Accusative	Kennst du **den** Mann?
Dative	Was weißt du von **dem** Mann?

In addition to nominative and accusative, German has a case called *dative*.

Masculine	Neuter	Feminine	Plural
dem Mann	dem Kind	der Frau	den Freunden
diesem Mann	diesem Kind	dieser Frau	diesen Freunden
einem Mann	einem Kind	einer Frau	keinen Freunden
ihrem Mann	unserem Kind	seiner Frau	meinen Freunden

The definite and indefinite articles, **der**-words, and **ein**-words change their form in the dative case. Nouns add an **-n** in the dative plural, unless the plural already ends in **-n** or **-s**: **meine Freunde** > **meinen Freunden;** but **die Frauen** > **den Frauen, die Autos** > **den Autos.**

5 Masculine N-nouns in the dative

Nominative	der Herr	der Student
Accusative	den Herr**n**	den Student**en**
Dative	dem Herr**n**	dem Student**en**

Masculine **N**-nouns, which add **-n** or **-en** in the accusative, also add **-n** or **-en** in the dative singular. The masculine **N**-nouns you know so far are: **der Herr, der Junge, der Mensch, der Nachbar, der Name, der Student,** and **der Tourist.**

6 Demonstrative pronouns in the dative

Masculine	Neuter	Feminine	Plural
dem	dem	der	denen

The dative forms of the demonstrative pronouns are identical to the dative forms of the definite articles, except that in the dative plural **den** becomes **denen.**

7 Dative of *wer?*

Nominative	**Wer** sagt das?	*Who* says that?
Dative	**Wem** sagen Sie das?	*To whom* are you saying that?

The dative form of the interrogative **wer?** *(who?)* is **wem?** *([to] whom?).*

8 Dative verbs

Das Haus **gehört meinen** Eltern.   The house belongs to my parents.
Kerstin **glaubt ihrer** Schwester nicht.   Kerstin doesn't believe her sister.

Most German verbs take objects in the accusative. However, a few verbs take objects in the dative. The dative object is usually a person. Such verbs can be classified as "dative verbs." The dative verbs in this chapter are **glauben** and **gehören.** A more complete list of dative verbs is found in section 17 of the Grammatical Tables in the Reference Section.

Daniela **glaubt ihrem** Freund Erik.   Daniela believes her friend Erik.
Erik **glaubt es** nicht.   Erik doesn't believe it.

The verb **glauben** always takes personal objects (e.g., **ihrem Freund**) in the dative case. However, impersonal objects (e.g., **es**) after **glauben** are in the accusative case.

13.   Wem gehört das?   You and a friend have returned from a bus trip to Berlin. You are the last off the bus and notice that a number of articles have been left behind. Your friend asks to whom they belong. Answer, using the cued words.

▶ Wem gehört der Roman? (der Student)   *Der Roman gehört dem Studenten.*

1. Wem gehört der Walkman? (der Junge)
2. Wem gehört die Zeitung? (der Herr)
3. Wem gehört das Buch? (die Frau)
4. Wem gehört die Gitarre? (das Mädchen)

5. Wem gehört die Tasche? (der Professor)
6. Wem gehört das Heft? (die Studentin)

14. Wer glaubt wem?   A strange story is making the rounds and everyone
has a different version of it. Tell who believes whom by using the cued
words.

▶   Wem glaubt Peter? (seine Mutter)   *Peter glaubt seiner Mutter.*

1. Wem glaubt Tamara? (ihr Bruder)
2. Wem glaubt Fabian? (seine Freundin)
3. Wem glaubt Mario? (seine Eltern)
4. Wem glaubt Hannah? (ihr Freund)
5. Wem glaubt Nadine? (ihr Vater)
6. Wem glaubt Bernhard? (seine Schwester)

9 Dative personal pronouns

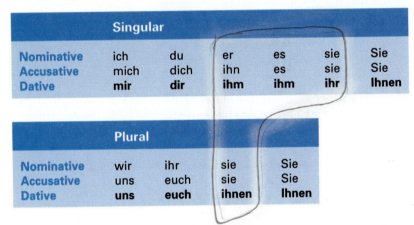

Singular						
Nominative	ich	du	er	es	sie	Sie
Accusative	mich	dich	ihn	es	sie	Sie
Dative	**mir**	**dir**	**ihm**	**ihm**	**ihr**	**Ihnen**

Plural			
Nominative	wir	ihr	sie	Sie
Accusative	uns	euch	sie	Sie
Dative	**uns**	**euch**	**ihnen**	**Ihnen**

Dative personal pronouns have different forms from the accusative pronouns,
except for **uns** and **euch.**

15. Was gehört wem?   Your friend has borrowed a number of things from
various people. Before returning them he asks you to confirm that he knows
what belongs to whom. Tell him he is correct in each instance. Use dative
pronouns in your responses.

▶   Gehört das Buch deinem Professor?   *Ja, das Buch gehört ihm.*
▶   Gehört der Kuli dir?   *Ja, der Kuli gehört mir.*

1. Gehört das Radio deiner Schwester?
2. Gehört die Gitarre dir?
3. Gehört die Diskette deinen Nachbarn?
4. Gehört die Tasche deiner Mutter?
5. Gehört der Bleistift mir?
6. Gehören die Krimis euch?

10 Indirect object

	Indirect object	Direct object
Katrin schenkt	ihrem Freund	einen CD-Spieler.
Katrin is giving	her friend	a CD-player.

In both English and German some verbs take two objects, which are traditionally called the direct object (e.g., **CD-Spieler**—*CD-player*) and the indirect object (e.g., **Freund**—*friend*). The indirect object is usually a person and answers the question *to whom* or *for whom* the direct object is intended. Some verbs that can take both direct and indirect objects are **bringen, erklären, geben, kaufen, leihen, sagen, schenken°,** and **schreiben.**

to give (as a gift)

11 Signals for indirect object and direct object

	Indirect (dative) object	Direct (accusative) object
Katrin schenkt	ihren Eltern	einen CD-Spieler.
Katrin is giving	her parents	a CD-player.

English signals the indirect object by putting it before the direct object or by using the preposition *to* or *for*, e.g., Katrin is giving a CD-player to her parents. To determine in English whether a noun or pronoun is an indirect object, add *to* or *for* before it.

German uses case to signal the difference between a direct object and an indirect object. The direct object is in the accusative, and the indirect object is in the dative. Since the case signals are clear, **German never uses a preposition to signal the indirect object.**

16. Geburtstage.   A number of people have birthdays this month. Theresa and David are discussing presents for them. Identify the indirect (dative) object and direct (accusative) object and give the English equivalent of the sentences below.

▶ DAVID: Wem schenkst du die Blumen?
indirect object: Wem
direct object: die Blumen
English equivalent: To whom are you giving the flowers?

1. THERESA: Diese Blumen bringe ich meiner Großmutter.
2. THERESA: Was kaufst du deiner Freundin?
3. DAVID: Meiner Freundin möchte ich ein Buch schenken.
4. THERESA: Ich schreibe meinem Bruder einen Brief°.
5. THERESA: Leider kann ich Christian nichts schenken. Ich habe kein Geld mehr.
6. DAVID: Das muß ich meinem Freund erklären.

letter

17. Was macht Dieter? Answer the questions below about Dieter's activities. Replace **wem** with the dative form of the pronouns or the possessive adjectives and the nouns in parentheses.

▶ Wem kauft Dieter neue Weingläser? (seine Eltern) *Seinen Eltern.*
▶ Wem leiht er sein neues Fahrrad? (ich) *Mir.*

1. Wem bringt er Blumen mit? (seine Großmutter)
2. Wem gibt er den neuen Roman? (sein Freund Erik)
3. Wem gibt er sein Radio? (du)
4. Wem leiht er etwas Geld? (ich)
5. Wem leiht er kein Geld? (ihr)
6. Wem schenkt er seinen alten Computer? (sein Bruder)
7. Wem schenkt er die schöne Tasche? (seine Tante)
8. Wem erklärt er die interessante Geschichte? (wir)
9. Wem schreibt er eine Karte? (seine Freunde Gerd und Alex)

12 Word order of direct and indirect objects

	Indirect object	Direct-object noun
Katrin leiht	*ihrem Freund*	**ihr Radio.**
Katrin leiht	*ihm*	**ihr Radio.**

The direct (accusative) object determines the order of objects. If the direct object is a noun, it usually follows the indirect (dative) object.

	Direct-object personal pronoun	Indirect object
Katrin leiht	**es**	*ihrem Freund.*
Katrin leiht	**es**	*ihm.*

If the direct (accusative) object is a personal pronoun, it always precedes the indirect (dative) object. Note that a pronoun, whether accusative or dative, always precedes a noun.

Pronoun always comes first

18. Wer bekommt das? You are moving out of town and need to get rid of some things you don't wish to move. A friend wants to know if you're giving the things to Michael, his family, and friends. Answer the questions, using accusative pronouns as in the model.

▶ Wem schenkst du den kleinen Tisch? Michaels Schwester? *Ja, ich schenke ihn Michaels Schwester.*

1. Wem schenkst du das Bett? Ihm?
2. Wem schenkst du die Pflanzen? Seinen Eltern?
3. Wem schenkst du das Poster? Seinem Bruder?
4. Wem schenkst du das Bücherregal? Seinem Freund Moritz?
5. Wem schenkst du die Bilder? Bianca?

19. Frage-Ecke. You and two friends have won a large sum of money in the lottery and are giving gifts to members of your families and friends. Find out what each person is giving to whom.

S1: Was schenkt Ralf seinen Eltern?
S2: Er schenkt ihnen zwei Wochen in Wien.

S1:

	Eltern	Schwester	Bruder	Melanie
Karsten	einen Porsche	einen Computer		
Stefanie	Winterferien in Spanien			einen Fernseher
Ralf		eine Gitarre	ein Fahrrad	
ich				
Partnerin/ Partner				

S2:

	Eltern	Schwester	Bruder	Melanie
Karsten			neue Skier	einen Kuli aus Gold
Stefanie		einen CD-Spieler	ein Kassettendeck	
Ralf	zwei Wochen in Wien			eine Uhr
ich				
Partnerin/ Partner				

20. Wie sagt man das?

1. What are you giving your mother for her birthday?
   —I'm giving her flowers and a book.
2. Whom are you writing the card to?
   —[To] my cousin Martin.
3. Are you lending your boyfriend money? He wants to buy his parents flowers.
   —No. I don't lend him money any more.
4. Is that motorcycle new? Does it belong to you?
   —No, to my sister.

▷ **21. Geburtstagsgeschenke.** You need some ideas for birthday presents for your family and relatives. Ask four fellow students what they would like to give members of their families or relatives for their birthdays.

Discussing ideas for birthday presents

S1: Was schenkst du [deiner Mutter] zum Geburtstag?
S2: Ich schenke [ihr] [ein Buch].

S1: Vater □ Bruder □ Schwester □ Großmutter □ Großvater □ Eltern

S2: Uhr □ Blumen □ Liebesroman □ Krimi □ Tasche □ Kugelschreiber □ Fernseher

13 Dative prepositions

aus	out of *(to come)* from *[cities and countries]*	Gerd geht früh **aus** dem Haus. Anna kommt **aus** Österreich.
außer	besides, except for	Wer ist **außer** den Studenten hier?
bei	with *(at the home of)* at *(a place of business)* near *(in the proximity of)*	Nils wohnt **bei** seiner Tante. Lisa arbeitet **bei** Siemens. Die Bäckerei ist **bei** der Universität.
mit	with by means of *(transportation)*	Elsa fährt **mit** ihrem Freund zur Uni. Fährst du **mit** dem Auto zur Uni?
nach	to *(with cities and countries used without an article)* after	Rita fährt im Sommer **nach** Österreich. Arno kommt **nach** dem Essen.
seit	since *(time)*	Petra ist **seit** Mittwoch in Wien.
von	from of by	Was hören Sie **von** Ihrem Freund Paul? Österreich ist ein Land **von** 7.800.000 Einwohnern. Die Oper ist **von** Mozart.
zu	to *(with people and some places)* for *(in certain expressions)*	Wir gehen gern **zu** unseren Nachbarn. Wann fährst du **zur** Uni? Was gibt's **zum** Abendessen?

The prepositions **aus, außer, bei, mit, nach, seit, von,** and **zu** are always followed by the dative. Some common translations are provided in the chart above.

■ **bei**

In addition to the meanings listed above, **bei** has many uses that are hard to translate exactly. It is used, in a general way, to indicate a situation: **beim Lesen** *(while reading)*, **bei der Arbeit** *(at work)*, **bei diesem Wetter** *(in weather like this)*.

■ bei/mit

Sarah wohnt **bei** ihren Eltern.	Sarah lives *with* her parents.
Sarah fährt morgen **mit** ihren Eltern.	Sarah's driving *with* her parents tomorrow.

One meaning of both **bei** and **mit** is *with*. However, they are not interchangeable. **Bei** indicates location. **Bei ihren Eltern** means at the home of her parents. **Mit** expresses the idea of doing something together **(mit ihren Eltern)**.

■ nach/zu

Schmidts fahren morgen **nach** Salzburg.	The Schmidts are going *to* Salzburg tomorrow.
Ich muß **zum** Bäcker.	I have to go *to* the bakery.

One meaning of both **zu** and **nach** is *to*. **Zu** is used to show movement toward people and many locations. **Nach** is used with cities and countries without an article.

■ seit

Tanja ist **seit** Montag in Hamburg.	Tanja has been in Hamburg *since* Monday.
Jürgen wohnt **seit** drei Wochen in Wien.	Jürgen has been living in Vienna *for* three weeks.

Seit plus the present tense is used to express an action or condition that started in the past but is still continuing in the present. Note that English uses the present perfect tense (e.g., *has been living*) with *since* or *for* to express the same idea.

■ *Contractions*

Brot kaufen wir nur **beim** Bäcker.	bei dem = **beim**
Jürgen kommt jetzt **vom** Markt.	von dem = **vom**
Monika geht **zum** Supermarkt.	zu dem = **zum**
Kerstin geht **zur** Uni.	zu der = **zur**

The prepositions **bei, von,** and **zu** often contract with the definite article **dem,** and **zu** also contracts with the definite article **der**. While contractions are generally optional, they are required in certain common phrases such as:

zum Frühstück/Mittagessen/Abendessen
zum Beispiel
zum Geburtstag
beim Bäcker
beim Arzt°   doctor
zum Arzt gehen
zum Bäcker gehen
zur Uni/Schule gehen
vom Arzt kommen

Contractions are not used when the noun is stressed or modified: **Gehen Sie immer noch zu dem Bäcker in der Bahnhofstraße?** (*Do you still go to the baker on Bahnhofstraße?*)

22. Nein, das ist nicht richtig.   A friend has some wrong information about Christine. Correct it. Replace the object of the preposition with the words in parentheses.

▶ Christine kommt aus Österreich, nicht? (Schweiz)   *Nein, aus der Schweiz.*

1. Sie kommt doch aus Wien, nicht? (Basel)
2. Wohnt sie bei ihren Eltern? (ihre Familie)
3. Wohnt sie seit einem Monat da? (zwei Monate)
4. Sie arbeitet bei einem Bäcker, nicht? (ein Metzger)
5. Fährt sie mit ihrem Freund Erik nach Dänemark? (ihre Freundin Petra)
6. Sie fährt mit dem Auto, nicht? (die Bahn)
7. Hörst du oft von Christine? (ihre Familie)

23. Eine Reise nach Budapest.   The ad below offers a trip from Vienna to Budapest. Tell about some of the conditions by answering the questions. If you need help see Vocabulary for Authentic Text Activities in the Reference Section.

3 Tage Budapest

1. Tag: Wien – Budapest
Wien (16.00 Uhr, Oper/Ecke Operngasse) – Budapest. Abendessen und Nächtigung in Budapest.

2. Tag: Budapest
Frühstück. Stadtrundfahrt. Mittagessen. Nachmittag und Abend zur freien Verfügung. Nächtigung in Budapest.

3. Tag: Budapest – Wien
Frühstück. Tag zur freien Verfügung. Rückreise nach Wien um 16.00 Uhr. Ankunft in Wien, Oper/Ecke Operngasse, um ca. 20.00 Uhr.

8. – 10.3.	6. – 8.12.
18 **Pauschalpreis** **1.500,–**
Einbettzuschlag   *350,–*

Unsere Leistungen:
✳ *Busreise lt. Programm*
✳ *2 Nächtigungen in Doppelzimmern mit Bad oder Dusche/WC*
✳ *Stadtrundfahrt*
✳ *Reiseleitung in Budapest*
✳ *Halbpension*
Nicht inbegriffen: Stornoschutz

1. Um wieviel Uhr fährt der Bus von Wien ab°?
2. Wo treffen° sich die Touristen in Wien?
3. Wie lange dauert° die Rückfahrt von Budapest nach Wien?
4. Was kostet die Reise nach Budapest?
5. Wieviel mehr kostet ein Einbettzimmer?

fährt ab: leaves

meet

lasts

24. Rollenspiel. Work with a partner and the ad on p. 195. While in Vienna you have decided to visit Budapest. Call a travel agent and ask for details about a short trip to the capital of Hungary. You will want to inquire about cost, length of trip, departure time, and what is included in the tour.

Making plans for a vacation

25. Verkehrsmittel°. Using the drawing below, ask your partner for the most convenient means of transportation to get from place to place. Use the questions below to get you started.

means of transportation

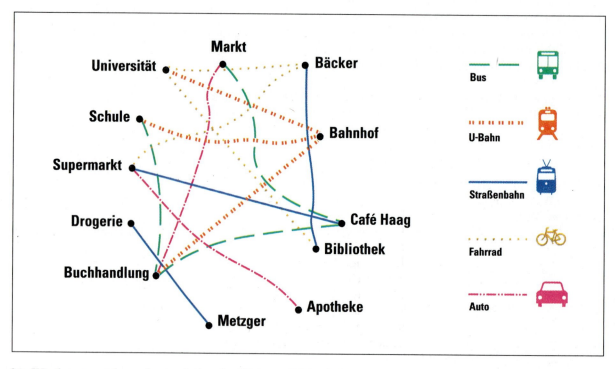

S1: Wie komme ich am besten° von der Uni zur Bibliothek?
S2: Am besten fährst du mit dem Fahrrad.

am besten: best of all

1. Wie komme ich am besten von der Schule zum Bahnhof°?
2. Wie komme ich am besten vom Markt zum Café Haag?
3. Wie komme ich am besten vom Metzger zur Drogerie?
4. Wie komme ich am besten von der Buchhandlung zum Markt?
5. Wie komme ich am besten von der Uni zum Bäcker?

train station

26. Was wissen Sie von Katrin? Tell in German what you know about Katrin.

1. Mondays Katrin does not go out of the house.
2. Tuesdays she sleeps at her girlfriend's.
3. Wednesdays she goes to the university early.
4. For breakfast she eats nothing except a roll.
5. She goes [*fahren*] to the university by streetcar.
6. I believe her friend Karoline is from Frankfurt.
7. She has been living here for a year.

WIEDERHOLUNG

1. Eine Reise nach Österreich. Tell about David's trip to Austria by forming sentences, using the cues below.

1. David / sein / Amerikaner
2. er / fliegen / nach / Österreich
3. er / fahren / mit / Zug / nach / Wien
4. er / kennenlernen / einige Studenten
5. sie / erzählen / von / diese Universität
6. nach / zwei Tage / David / fahren / nach / Salzburg

2. Was macht Monika? Complete the account of Monika's day by using the cued nouns in the proper case.

1. Monika geht aus _____ . (das Haus)
2. Sie geht zu _____ . (der Bäcker)
3. _____ Andrea arbeitet bei _____ . (ihre Freundin / der Bäcker)
4. Monika arbeitet für _____ . (ihr Onkel)
5. Sie erklärt _____ auch viel über Computer. (er)
6. Sie fährt mit _____ zur Arbeit. (das Fahrrad)
7. Nach _____ geht sie in die Buchhandlung. (die Arbeit)
8. Sie kauft _____ über Österreich. (ein Buch)
9. _____ bringt sie Blumen mit. (ihre Mutter)
10. Jeden Freitag bringt sie _____ Blumen. (sie, *sing.*)
11. Morgen schenkt sie _____ das Buch zum Geburtstag. (ihr Vater)
12. Nächstes Jahr fährt sie mit _____ nach Österreich. (ihre Freunde)
13. Das sagt sie _____ heute am Telefon. (sie, *pl.*)

3. Jetzt weiß er es. Dieter Meier sits down at Anna Müller's table in a café and they become acquainted. Read the conversation. Then summarize all the information Dieter learns about Anna. Begin each sentence with **Er weiß, daß ...**

ANNA: Ich bin Österreicherin.
DIETER: Kommst du aus Wien?
ANNA: Nein, aus Salzburg.
DIETER: Wohnst du in einem Studentenheim?
ANNA: Nein, bei einer Familie.
DIETER: Was studierst du denn?
ANNA: Wirtschaftswissenschaft° ist mein Hauptfach und Englisch mein Neben-   economics
fach. Ich möchte in Amerika arbeiten.
DIETER: Warst du schon in Amerika?
ANNA: Leider noch nicht.

4. Wie sagt man das?

1. VERENA: Would you like to go to Austria this summer?
2. CARINA: Yes. Gladly. Do you want to go by car or by train?
3. VERENA: By bike. If the weather stays nice.

4. EIN FREUND: Can you lend me your German book?
5. SIE: Of course, I can give it to you.
6. EIN FREUND: And can you also explain the dative° to me?   dative = **der Dativ**
7. SIE: Do we have enough time?

▷ **5. Wo soll ich studieren?**   Your partner wants to study in Europe, but
doesn't know whether to go to Germany or Austria. Give her/him some
facts in German about one of the two countries. You may wish to
include information on the following:

Wie groß ist das Land?   Hat es viele Berge?
Wie viele Einwohner hat es?   Hat es viel Industrie?
Wie viele Nachbarn hat es?   Wie heißt die Hauptstadt?

6. Zum Schreiben

You are studying in Vienna and wish to convince a friend to study there also.
Write a short letter in German in which you state the advantages. Begin the
letter with **Liebe** *(Dear)* [Barbara] or **Lieber** [Paul], and end with **Mit herzlichen Grüßen** *(With cordial greetings),* **Deine** or **Dein** [your name]. In a German
letter, the words **Du, Dein, Dich, Dir** are always capitalized.

    After you have finished your letter, check the following carefully:

- Subject and verb agreement
- Word order and punctuation in sentences with conjunctions
- Genders and cases of all nouns and pronouns
- Case used with each preposition

GRAMMATIK: ZUSAMMENFASSUNG

Verbs with stem-vowel change *a* > *ä*

fahren	
ich fahre	wir fahren
du **fährst**	ihr fahrt
er/es/sie **fährt**	sie fahren
Sie fahren	
du-*imperative:* fahr(e)	

laufen	
ich laufe	wir laufen
du **läufst**	ihr lauft
er/es/sie **läuft**	sie laufen
Sie laufen	
du-*imperative:* lauf(e)	

Independent clauses and coordinating conjunctions

Erik **kommt** morgen, aber Christl **muß** morgen arbeiten.

In independent (main) clauses the finite verb **(kommt, muß)** is in second position. A coordinating conjunction **(aber)** does not affect word order. The five common coordinating conjunctions are **aber, denn, oder, sondern,** and **und.**

Dependent clauses and subordinating conjunctions

Ich weiß, daß Frank morgen **kommt.**
daß Petra morgen **mitkommt.**
daß Helmut nicht **kommen kann.**

In dependent (subordinate) clauses:

1. The finite verb **(kommt)** is in final position.
2. The separable prefix **(mit)** is attached to the base form of the verb **(kommt)** in final position.
3. The modal auxiliary **(kann)** is a finite verb and therefore is in final position, after the infinitive **(kommen).**

Some common subordinating conjunctions are **daß, obwohl, weil,** and **wenn.**

Wenn du mit dem Rad fährst, **siehst** du mehr vom Land.

When a dependent clause begins a sentence, it is followed directly by the finite verb **(siehst)** of the independent clause.

Dative case

■ *Articles,* **der-** *and* **ein-***words in the dative case*

	Masculine	Neuter	Feminine	Plural
Nominative	der Mann	das Kind	die Frau	die Freunde
Accusative	den Mann	das Kind	die Frau	die Fruende
Dative	**dem** Mann	**dem** Kind	**der** Frau	**den** Freunden
	diesem Mann	**diesem** Kind	**dieser** Frau	**diesen** Freunden
	einem Mann	**einem** Kind	**einer** Frau	**keinen** Freunden
	ihrem Mann	**unserem** Kind	**seiner** Frau	**meinen** Freunden

■ *Nouns in the dative plural*

Nominative	die Männer	die Frauen	die Radios
Dative	den Männer**n**	den Frauen	den Radios

Nouns in the dative plural add **-n** unless the plural already ends in **-n** or **-s.**

■ *Masculine **N**-nouns in the dative case*

Nominative	der Herr	der Mensch
Accusative	den Herrn	den Menschen
Dative	**dem** Herrn	**dem** Menschen

For the masculine **N**-nouns used in this book, see the Grammatical Tables in the Reference Section.

■ *Dative of demonstrative pronouns*

	Masculine	Neuter	Feminine	Plural
Nominative	der	das	die	die
Accusative	den	das	die	die
Dative	**dem**	**dem**	**der**	**denen**

■ *Dative of **wer***

Nominative	wer
Accusative	wen
Dative	**wem**

Dative personal pronouns

	Singular					
Nominative	ich	du	er	es	sie	Sie
Accusative	mich	dich	ihn	es	sie	Sie
Dative	**mir**	**dir**	**ihm**	**ihm**	**ihr**	**Ihnen**

	Plural			
Nominative	wir	ihr	sie	Sie
Accusative	uns	euch	sie	Sie
Dative	**uns**	**euch**	**ihnen**	**Ihnen**

Word order of direct and indirect objects

	Indirect object	Direct-object noun
Katrin schenkt	*ihrer Schwester*	**den Kugelschreiber.**
Katrin schenkt	*ihr*	**den Kugelschreiber.**

The direct (accusative) object determines the order of objects. If the direct object is a noun, it follows the indirect (dative) object.

	Direct-object pronoun	Indirect object
Katrin schenkt	**ihn**	*ihrer Schwester.*
Katrin schenkt	**ihn**	*ihr.*

If the direct (accusative) object is a personal pronoun, it precedes the indirect (dative) object.

Dative verbs

Das Fahrrad **gehört** meinem Bruder.
Ich **glaube** dir nicht.

Most German verbs take objects in the accusative. A few verbs take objects in the dative. The dative object is usually a person. For convenience such verbs can be classified as "dative verbs."

For dative verbs used in this book, see the Grammatical Tables in the Reference Section.

Dative prepositions

aus	out of; from *(= is a native of)*
außer	besides, except for
bei	with *(at the home of)*; at *(a place of business)*; near *(in the proximity of)*; while or during *(indicates a situation)*
mit	with; by means of *(transportation)*
nach	to *(with cities, and countries used without an article)*; after
seit	since, for *(referring to time)*
von	from; of; by *(the person doing something)*
zu	to *(with people and some places)*; for *(in certain expressions)*

Contractions of dative prepositions

bei dem	=	**beim**
von dem	=	**vom**
zu dem	=	**zum**
zu der	=	**zur**

Diese jungen Leute aus Düsseldorf gehen abends zusammen aus.

Kapitel 7

LERNZIELE

■ **Sprechintentionen**

Discussing leisure-time activities
Talking about food and dining out
Expressing likes and dislikes
Discussing clothes
Expressing opinions
Talking about the past

■ **Lesestück**

Freizeitpläne

■ **Land und Leute**

Work vs. leisure time in Germany
Meals in German-speaking countries and bringing gifts
    when one is a guest
Requirements for a driver's license
Theater in the German-speaking countries
Holidays in Germany
German film

■ **Vokabeln**

Hobbies
Gefallen, mögen, gern haben
Infinitives used as nouns
Clothing

■ **Grammatik**

Present perfect tense

BAUSTEINE FÜR GESPRÄCHE

Was habt ihr vor?

DIRK: Sagt mal, was macht ihr am Wochenende?

MELANIE: Keine Ahnung.

PAUL: Ich habe am Freitag Probe mit der Band. Am Samstag spielen wir in der Musikfabrik.

DIRK: Du, Melanie, da können wir doch zusammen hingehen, oder?

MELANIE: Gute Idee. Das ist super. Vielleicht geht auch Matthias mit?

PAUL: Der kann nicht. Er muß fürs Examen arbeiten.

DIRK: Also, Melanie, ich hole dich um acht ab. In Ordnung?

What are your plans?

Say, what are you doing on the weekend?

No idea.

I've got a rehearsal with the band on Friday. On Saturday we're playing at the Musikfabrik.

Hey, you know, Melanie, we can go there together, right?

Good idea. That's great. Maybe Matthias will go along too?

He can't. He has to study for his comprehensives.

All right then, Melanie, I'll pick you up at eight. Is that all right?

Fragen

1. Was hat Paul am Wochenende vor?
2. Wohin möchte Dirk gehen?
3. Warum kann Matthias nicht mitgehen?
4. Wann holt Dirk Melanie ab?

Es hat geschmeckt.

KLAUS: Wo warst du gestern abend?

CHRISTINA: Warum?

KLAUS: Ich habe bei dir angerufen, aber da war niemand da. Ich wollte mit dir ins Kino gehen.

CHRISTINA: Gestern war ich mit Petra im Café an der Uni. Sie hat mich eingeladen.

KLAUS: Ah, das Café ist gut. Die haben tolle Salate.

CHRISTINA: Ja, genau, wir haben Fischsalat gegessen.

KLAUS: Hör auf, ich kriege gleich Hunger!

It tasted good.

Where were you last night?

Why?

I called, but there was no one there. I wanted to go to the movies with you.

I was with Petra at the Café an der Uni yesterday. She treated me.

Ah, the Café is good. They have great salads.

Yes, that's right. We had fish salad.

Stop, I'm getting hungry!

Fragen

1. Warum hat Klaus bei Christina angerufen?
2. Warum war Christina nicht zu Hause?
3. Wie findet Klaus das Café an der Uni?
4. Was haben Christina und Petra gegessen?

Brauchbares

1. In Dirk's phrase **"Sagt mal,"** **mal** is a flavoring particle. **Mal** is frequently used to soften the tone of imperatives.

2. To say they can go there Dirk uses the verb **hingehen. Hin** is used with verbs and adverbs to show direction away from the speaker. **Hin** is practiced in *Kapitel 8*.

3. To ask whether Melanie agrees with him, Dirk ends one sentence with **"oder?"** and the other with **"In Ordnung?"** These two words are common in German conversation. **Oder?** is equivalent to *Or don't you agree?* and **In Ordnung?** is equivalent to *Is that all right with you?*

4. Klaus says, **"Ich wollte ... ins Kino gehen." Wollte** is the simple past tense form of the modal **wollen** and will be practiced in *Kapitel 11*.

5. Christina uses the verb **einladen** to say Petra treated her. The basic meaning of **einladen** is *to invite*.

▷ **1. Was machst du in der Freizeit°?** Find out what a fellow student likes to do for fun. You may wish to refer to the Supplementary Word Sets on Hobbies and on Sports and Games in the Reference Section.

> Discussing leisure-time activities

S1:

Was sind deine Hobbys?

S2:

Radfahren.
Musik hören/machen.
Science Fiction lesen.
Skifahren/Wasserskifahren.
Spazierengehen.
Fotografieren°.
Jogging.
Kochen°.

Was hast du am Wochenende vor?

Ich gehe | **schwimmen.**
Ski fahren/Wasserski fahren.
windsurfen°.
tanzen.
Ich mache eine Wanderung°.
Ich muß arbeiten.
Ich will | **viel lesen.**
faulenzen°.
arbeiten.
Fußball/Tennis im Fernsehen sehen.

Land und Leute

Freizeit

Germans have a reputation for being industrious. However, for many Germans this means working hard on the job but not giving up leisure time. The average work week for German industrial workers is 37.5 hours and they have 40 days of paid vacation time (**Urlaub**) and holidays (**Feiertage**). Germany thus ranks second among the industrialized nations in paid vacation time. (Finland is first with 45.5 days. Austrian workers work 40 hours per week and have 39 days of paid vacation time. Swiss workers have a 42-hour work week with 30 days of paid vacation time.) The average work week for American workers is 40 hours, with 23 days of paid vacation time and holidays. The United States thus brings up the rear in paid free time, even less than Japan which has 25 days. On the basis of vacation days deducted from the hours worked per year, the Germans work the fewest hours

Ein Urlauber faulenzt am Bodensee.

among the industrial nations; the Japanese, followed by the Americans, work the most. The following chart shows selected countries:

Country	Hours worked per year
Japan	2080
United States	1912
Switzerland	1865
Luxembourg	1800
France	1771
Austria	1722
Germany	1667

2. Hast du Hunger oder Durst°? In groups of four, practice the questions and responses below. One person asks the question. Each of the others gives a different response. Then change roles and practice again. Ask whether a friend is hungry or thirsty.

S1:
Hast du Hunger?

Hast du Durst?

S2:
Ja, großen Hunger.
Nein, ich habe keinen Hunger.
Nein, ich habe schon gegessen°.
Ja, großen Durst.
Nein, ich habe keinen Durst.
Nein, danke. Ich habe eben° eine Cola° getrunken°.

3. Gegessen und getrunken. Answer the questions about a meal you ate yesterday. Possible answers are suggested. Then ask your partner the same questions. Note her/his answers and share them with a third person (or the class). You may also consult the menu below.

Talking about food and dining out

1. Wo hast du gestern zu Abend gegessen?

   zu Hause □ im Café an der Uni □ in ...

2. Was hast du gegessen?

   Steak° und Pommes frites° □ Spaghetti □ Wurst und Brot □ Pizza°

3. Was hast du getrunken?

   eine Cola □ ein Wasser

4. Hat es geschmeckt?

   Danke, gut. □ Ganz toll. □ Nicht besonders. □ Nein, leider nicht.

4. Ein Rollenspiel. You and your partner are in the Café an der Uni and you're treating. Using the menu from Café an der Uni, role-play a scene in which you decide what you will each order. Begin your discussion using the model below. If you need help in reading the menu, see Vocabulary for Authentic Text Activities in the Reference Section.

S1: Was ißt du?
S2: Ich nehme Wurstsalat mit Brot.
S1: Und was trinkst du?
S2: Ich trinke einen Apfelsaft. Und was ißt du?
usw.°

usw. (= und so weiter): etc. (and so on)

Café an der Uni

Getränke

Große Tasse Kaffee mit Sahne		4,20
Große Tasse Schokolade mit Sahne		4,20
Große Tasse frisch gebrühter Tee		4,20
Cappuccino		3,60
Espresso		3,30
Schweppes Sodawasser	0,2l	3,80
Schweppes Bitter Lemon	0,2l	3,80
Schweppes Ginger Ale	0,2l	3,80
Apfelsaft	0,25l	3,20
Coca-Cola	0,25l	3,20
Fanta	0,25l	3,20
Johannisbeersaft	0,2l	4,00
Pils vom Faß	0,3l	3,80
Export vom Faß	0,3l	3,50

Kuchen und Gebäck

Bitte treffen Sie an unserer Schauvitrine Ihre Wahl und bestellen Sie bei Ihrer Bedienung!

Torten	4,20
Kuchen	3,80
Croissant	2,50
Portion Schlagsahne	1,50

Eis

Kleines Eis (drei Kugeln nach Wahl)	5,00
mit Sahne	5,60
Großes Eis (fünf Kugeln nach Wahl)	7,60
mit Sahne	8,40
Eiskaffee	5,80

Toasts

„Hawaii" mit Schinken, Käse und Ananas	8,20
„Spezial" mit Schinken, Käse und Pilzen	8,90
„Farmer"-Toast mit Truthahnbrust und Spiegelei	10,20

Kalte Speisen

Baguette „Café an der Uni"	8,20
Baguette mit Thunfisch und Ei	8,20
Wurstsalat mit Brot	7,50
Käsebrot, Emmentaler oder Camembert	6,20
Wurstbrot, Salami, Bierschinken oder Leberwurst	6,20

Salate

Griechischer Salat mit Brot	12,00
Salatschüssel mit frischen Saisonsalaten, Ei, Dressing und Brot	11,50
Große Salatplatte mit Schinken, Käse, Pepperoni, Oliven, frischen Salaten und Brot	14,80

Warme Gerichte

Gebackener Camembert mit Preiselbeeren, Salatbeilage und Brot	9,70
Spaghetti „Bolognese"	9,80
Tortellini in Sahnesauce mit Salat	12,50
Pizza mit Schinken, Käse, Salami, Oliven, Pepperoni und Champignons	10,50
Schnitzel Wiener Art mit Kartoffelsalat	12,50

Geöffnet:
Montag bis Freitag 8 - 22 Uhr
Samstag und Feiertage 9 - 22 Uhr

Alle Preise sind Inklusivpreise und enthalten Bedienungsgeld und Mehrwertsteuer.

Land und Leute

Essen zu Hause und als Gast

Although a growing number of Germans eat their main hot meal in the evening (**Abendessen**), many Germans still eat their main meal at noon (**Mittagessen**). It may consist of up to three courses: appetizer (**Vorspeise**), entrée (**Hauptgericht** or **Hauptspeise**), and dessert (**Nachtisch** or **Dessert**), which is usually fruit, pudding, or ice cream. Cakes and pastries are served at afternoon coffee time (**Kaffee**).

Before a meal, it is customary to say **Guten Appetit** or **Mahlzeit**, and others may wish you the same by responding **Danke, gleichfalls.** Even in a restaurant, when sharing a table with a stranger who has asked if it is all right to sit at the table by saying **Ist hier noch frei?**, one wishes the stranger **Guten Appetit** when the meal arrives.

Most restaurants post their menus outside. After the meal, one pays the waiter (**Kellner: Herr Ober**) or waitress (**Kellnerin: Frau Ober**). A service charge (**Bedienung**) is included in the bill. However, it is customary to add a tip

Abendessen bei einer Familie in Ostdorf bei Balingen.

(**Trinkgeld**) by rounding off the bill for small amounts (e.g., 8 marks instead of 7,20) and giving a 5 to 10 percent tip for larger amounts.

When people are invited to a friend's house for dinner or for **Kaffee,** it is customary to bring a small gift. Most often the guest will bring a small bouquet, a box of chocolates, or a bottle of wine.

Vokabeln

Beginning in *Kapitel 7* the past participles of strong verbs (see p. 225) will be listed after the infinitive, e.g., **einladen, eingeladen.**

Substantive

die **Ahnung**   hunch; idea; **keine Ahnung!**   no idea!
die **Band, -s**   (musical) band
die **Cola, -s**   cola drink
der **Durst**   thirst; **Durst haben**   to be thirsty
die **Freizeit**   free time
das **Hobby, -s**   hobby
der **Hunger**   hunger; **Hunger haben** to be hungry

die **Idee, -n**   idea
die **Pizza, -s**   pizza
die **Pommes frites** *(pl.)*   French fries
die **Probe, -n**   rehearsal
das **Steak, -s**   steak
die **Wanderung, -en**   hike; **eine Wanderung machen**   to hike

Verben

an·rufen, angerufen to phone; **bei [dir] anrufen** to call [you] at home

auf·hören to stop (an activity)

ein·laden (lädt ein), eingeladen to invite; to treat

essen: gegessen

faulenzen to lounge around, be idle

fotografieren to photograph

kochen to cook

kriegen to get

mit·gehen, ist mitgegangen to go along

schmecken (+ *dat.*) to taste; **der Käse schmeckt mir** the cheese tastes good; **hat es geschmeckt?** did it taste good?

trinken: getrunken

vor·haben to intend, have in mind

windsurfen gehen to go windsurfing; **surfen** to surf

Andere Wörter

eben just

genau exact(ly); **genau!** that's right

gleich immediately; in a minute; same; similar

niemand no one

super super, great

toll great, fantastic

Besondere Ausdrücke

ein Wasser a bottle/glass of mineral water

gestern abend last night

in Ordnung? is that all right (with you)?

oder? or don't you agree?

sag/sagt mal tell me

zu Abend essen to have (eat) dinner

Fachinger: ein Mineralwasser.

FREIZEITPLÄNE

Vorbereitung auf das Lesen

■ *Vor dem Lesen**

1. Was machen Sie am liebsten° in Ihrer Freizeit?

   am liebsten: most of all

   Radfahren □ Jogging □ Fernsehen □ am Computer arbeiten° □ Lesen □
   Wandern oder Spazierengehen □ mit Freunden zusammensein □ ins
   Kino, Theater oder Konzert gehen

   Sie können diese Wörter und Wendungen° in Ihrer Antwort° gebrauchen°:   expressions

   Am liebsten ...
   In meiner Freizeit ...
   Meistens° ...   mostly
   Zur Entspannung° ...   **Zur Entspannung:** for relaxation

2. Machen Sie eine Umfrage° unter den Studentinnen/Studenten.   survey

▶ *Was machst du am liebsten in deiner Freizeit?*

Dieser junge Mann geht in seiner Freizeit gern Rollerblading.

---

*Remember, words appearing with a raised degree mark but no definition in the margin are new "active" words that you should learn and be able to use. These words and their definitions appear in the **Vokabeln** section that most closely follows the exercise.

3. Sehen Sie die Anzeigen° an, und beantworten° Sie die Fragen. ads/answer
   a. Welche Band spielt im Olympiastadion?
   b. Wo kann man ein amerikanisches Musical sehen?
   c. Wo kann man die Theaterkarten° von 10 bis 18 Uhr kaufen? theater tickets
   d. Wann endet das Musical? Kann man nach dem Musical in die Oly-Disco gehen?
   e. Wann schließt die Disco am Samstag?
   f. Wer geht in diese Disco?
   g. Welche von den drei Möglichkeiten° gefallen Ihnen? possibilities

🟧 *Beim Lesen*

Was machen die Leute im Text in ihrer Freizeit? Machen Sie eine Liste.

Peter Bosch ist Reporter bei einer Studentenzeitung und macht Straßen-interviews für die Zeitung. Seine Frage: „Was hast du letztes Wochenende in deiner Freizeit gemacht?"

Silke, 22 Jahre:

„Freizeit? Ich habe schon ewig keine richtige Freizeit mehr gehabt. Ich studiere
5 Englisch und bekomme BAföG, da möchte ich natürlich so schnell wie möglich
   mit dem Studium fertig werden. Doch am Sonntag abend hat die Jule-Neigel-
   Band im Olympiastadion gespielt; die mußte° ich hören, denn ihre Musik had to
   gefällt mir. Samstag morgen bin ich einkaufen gegangen. Ich habe nämlich
   letzten Monat gejobbt, und mit dem Geld habe ich einen Rock und eine Bluse
10 gekauft. Den Rest vom Wochenende war ich die meiste Zeit zu Hause und
   habe gelernt, denn ich habe bald mein Examen. Da bleibt leider nicht viel Zeit
   für Hobbys."

Stefan, 19 Jahre:

„Ich habe seit zwei Monaten meinen Führerschein und fahre gern mit meinem Auto spazieren. Letzten Samstag bin ich sehr früh aufgestanden. Ich bin zu meinen Großeltern gefahren und habe sie besucht. Sie wohnen etwa hundertfünfzig Kilometer nördlich von München.

Ich höre gern Rockmusik. Am Samstag sind meine Freunde und ich tanzen gegangen. Die Oly-Disco finde ich besonders toll. Mein Auto ist natürlich zu Hause geblieben, denn ich habe Bier getrunken. Ins Kino gehe ich nicht so gern. Das finde ich so passiv, denn man kann dort nicht mit Freunden sprechen. Eine Disco ist da schon viel besser, oder eine Kneipe."

Evi, 31 Jahre:

„Viele Leute sagen, Deutsche arbeiten zu viel und sind sehr fleißig. Ich denke auch manchmal, ich arbeite zu viel. Ich bin Ärztin und muß oft viele Stunden im Krankenhaus sein. Letztes Wochenende habe ich aber frei gehabt. Ich habe am Samstag zuerst mit meinem Bruder Tennis gespielt, dann bin ich mit meinem Freund radgefahren. Ich treibe gern Sport. Und außerdem ist Sport gesund. Am Abend hat meine Familie Geburtstag gefeiert, denn meine Großmutter ist 83 Jahre alt geworden! Am Sonntag sind mein Freund und ich ins Staatstheater am Gärtnerplatz gegangen. Wir haben das Musical ‚Der Fiedler auf dem Dach' gesehen. Mich hat das Stück interessiert, aber mein Freund hat es etwas langweilig gefunden. Ich gehe in meiner Freizeit gern aus. Manchmal bin ich aber ganz einfach auch gern zu Hause, sehe fern, höre Radio, lese ein Buch oder tue nichts."

Die Jule Neigel Band.

Brauchbares

1. In l. 7 Silke says, **"Die mußte ich hören."** **Mußte** is the simple past tense of **müssen,** which will be practiced in *Kapitel 11*.

2. To an American it might seem that Stefan is getting his driver's license rather late. Reasons for this are found in **Land und Leute: Führerschein,** p. 214.

Nach dem Lesen

1. Fragen zum Lesestück

1. Lesen Sie Ihre Liste von den Freizeitbeschäftigungen° im Text. Was machen Sie in Ihrer Freizeit?   *free-time activities*
2. Was studiert Silke?
3. Was macht Silke am Sonntag?
4. Warum hat Silke nicht viel Zeit für ihre Hobbys?
5. Wie alt ist Stefan?
6. Wie lange hat Stefan schon seinen Führerschein?
7. Warum geht Stefan gern in eine Disco oder Kneipe?
8. Warum bleibt Stefans Auto zu Hause?
9. Was ist Evis Beruf°?   *profession*
10. Wann hat Evi frei gehabt?
11. Mit wem geht Evi ins Theater?
12. Welches Musical spielt im Staatstheater?
13. Was macht Evi gern zu Hause?
14. Mit wem (Silke, Stefan oder Evi) möchten Sie gern ein Wochenende verbringen°? Warum?   *spend (time)*

2. Wer hätte das sagen können°?   Silke, Stefan oder Evi?
hätte sagen können: could have said

1. Ich habe wenig Freizeit. _____
2. Ich spreche gern mit meinen Freunden. _____
3. Ich studiere in München. _____
4. Ich fahre gern spazieren. _____
5. Ins Kino gehen gefällt mir nicht. _____
6. Ich muß oft lernen. _____
7. Ich muß viele Stunden arbeiten. _____
8. Ich habe neue Kleidung° gekauft. _____
9. Meine Großmutter ist 83 Jahre alt. _____
10. Ich höre gern Rockmusik. _____
11. Ich spiele gern Tennis. _____

3. Erzählen wir.   Besprechen° Sie eins der folgenden Themen° in einer Gruppe von drei Studenten.
discuss/eins ... Themen: one of the following topics

- Was ich in meiner Freizeit mache
- Warum ich keine Freizeit habe

Land und Leute

Der Führerschein

The minimum age for a driver's license in the German-speaking countries is eighteen (though exceptions are sometimes made for people as young as sixteen who need a car to make a living). To obtain a license one must attend a private driving school (**Fahrschule**). (Driver education courses are not offered in school.) In Germany a driving course consists of 18 hours of theoretical study and a minimum of 35 hours of practical driving lessons (**Fahrstunden**) as well as approximately 10 additional hours of special practice (**Sonderausbildung**), e.g., freeway (**Autobahn**) and night-time driving (**Nachtfahren**). At the end, every student must pass a theoretical test with a perfect score, and a driving test. The **Führerschein** is then issued temporarily for two years, after which time the driver can obtain it for life, if her/his driving record shows no entries for drunken driving or

Fahrschule Hahn ist nur eine der vielen Hamburger Fahrschulen.

other at-fault violations. The total cost of the driving lessons plus the 250 mark test fee (**Prüfungsgebühr**) is around 3000 marks. The failure rate is 1 in 4.

Erweiterung des Wortschatzes

1 Gefallen, mögen, gern haben

Dein Freund **gefällt** mir.	I *like* your friend. [I think your friend is O.K.]
Ich **habe** deinen Freund **gern.**	I *like* your friend. [I'm fond of him.]
Deine Freunde **gefallen** mir nicht.	I don't *like* your friends. [I don't care for them.]
Deine Freunde **mag** ich nicht.	I don't *like* your friends. [I dislike them.]

Gefallen, mögen, and **gern haben** are all equivalent to English *like.* However, they express different degrees of liking. **Mögen** and **gern haben** usually express stronger feelings of liking than **gefallen.**

Das Bild gefällt mir. ⎫ Mir gefällt das Bild. ⎭	I like the picture.
Mir gefällt es nicht, daß Mark so wenig liest.	I don't like (the fact) that Mark reads so little.

When using the verb **gefallen**, what one likes is the subject and thus in the nominative case. The person who likes something is in the dative. Note that sentences with **gefallen** often begin with the dative.

1. Was bedeutet° das?   means

1. Wie gefällt deinem Freund Mark Hamburg?
2. Ihm gefällt es sehr.
3. Diese Vorlesungen gefallen Mark auch.
4. Was gefällt deinem Freund nicht so gut?
5. Ihm gefällt es nicht, daß es so viel regnet.
6. Es gefällt Mark auch nicht, daß es so viele Autos gibt.

▷ **2. Wie gefällt dir [das Auto]?** Find out if your partner likes a certain color, car, politician, singer, TV show, college, or university. Then reverse roles. Use the verb **gefallen.**

> Expressing likes and dislikes

2 Infinitives used as nouns

Mein Hobby ist **Wandern**.   My hobby is *hiking.*
Früh morgens ist **das Joggen** toll.   *Jogging* early in the morning is great.

German infinitives may be used as nouns. An infinitive used as a noun is always neuter. The English equivalent is often a gerund, that is, the *-ing* form of a verb used as a noun.

3. In Deutschland. One often hears these opinions in Germany. Give the English equivalent.

1. Laufen ist schön.
2. Natürlichkeit in Essen und Trinken gefällt den Deutschen.
3. Es gehört zum Einkaufen am Wochenende, daß man Blumen mitbringt.
4. Schwimmen ist ein schöner Sport.
5. Skifahren ist toll.

Reden ist Silber, Schweigen ist Gold.
(Speaking is silver, silence is golden.)

3 Kleidungsstücke°

articles of clothing

1. der **Anzug,** ⸚e
2. der **Badeanzug,** ⸚e
3. der **Handschuh,** -e
4. der **Hut,** ⸚e
5. der **Pulli,** -s
6. der **(Regen)mantel,** ⸚
7. der **(Regen)schirm,** -e
8. der **Rock,** ⸚e
9. der **Schuh,** -e
10. der **Stiefel,** -

11. das **Hemd,** -en
12. das **Jackett,** -s
13. das **Kleid,** -er
14. das **Polohemd,** -en
15. das **T-Shirt,** -s

16. die **Badehose,** -n
17. die **Bluse,** -n
18. die **(Hand)tasche,** -n
19. die **Hose,** -n
20. die **Jacke,** -n
21. die **Jeans** (*pl.*)
22. die **Krawatte,** -n
23. die **Mütze,** -n
24. die **Shorts (die kurze Hose,** -n)
25. die **Socke,** -n
26. die **(Sonnen)brille,** -n
27. die **Strumpfhose,** -n

For additional articles of clothing see the Supplementary Word Sets on clothing in the Reference Section.

⇨ **4. Was tragen die Leute?** Describe the clothing of one of the persons in the pictures. Your partner will tell you whom you have described and describe another person to you.

S1: Diese Frau trägt einen Rock, eine ...
S2: Das ist ...

Herr und Frau Bosch kaufen ihrem Sohn Martin ein Mountain-Bike.

Herr König und seine Kinder Kerstin und Markus gehen spazieren.

▷ **5. Was tragen° Sie?** Answer the questions below for yourself and then ask your partner. Remember to use **du** with your partner.

Discussing clothes

1. Was tragen Sie im Winter? Im Sommer?
2. Was tragen Sie, wenn Sie in die Vorlesung gehen?
3. Was tragen Sie, wenn Sie tanzen gehen?
4. Was möchten Sie zum Geburtstag haben?
5. Welche Farben tragen Sie gern?

▷ **6. Wie gefällt es dir?** Choose a picture in this text with articles of clothing and ask several fellow students their opinion about some of the items.

Expressing opinions and likes and dislikes.

S1:

Was hältst° du von [dem Kleid]?

S2:

[Das] muß furchtbar teuer sein. Was kostet [es]?
[Das] ist schön/toll/praktisch.
[Das] sieht billig aus°.
[Das] ist nichts Besonderes.

▷ **7. Wer ist das?** With a partner, choose a person and describe what she or he is wearing, including the color. Your classmates will try to guess whom you are describing.

Vokabeln

Substantive

die **Antwort, -en**   answer
der **Arzt, ⸚e**/die **Ärztin, -nen**
   doctor, physician
die **Bluse, -n**   blouse
die **Disco, -s**   dance club
der **Führerschein, -e**   driver's license
die **Karte, -n**   ticket; die
   Theaterkarte, -n   theater ticket
die **Kleidung**   clothing
die **Kneipe, -n**   bar, pub
das **Krankenhaus, ⸚er**   hospital

das **Musical, -s**   musical
der **Reporter, -**/die **Reporterin, -nen**
   reporter
der **Rest, -e**   rest, remaining part
der **Rock, ⸚e**   skirt
das **Stück, -e**   piece (of music);
   Theaterstück   play (theater)
die **Stunde, -n**   hour
das **Thema, Themen**   topic
*For additional articles of clothing see
   p. 216.*

Verben

auf·stehen, ist aufgestanden   to get
   up; to stand up
aus·gehen, ist ausgegangen   to go
   out
aus·sehen (sieht aus), ausgesehen
   to look like, seem
beantworten   to answer (a question,
   a letter)
besuchen   to visit; **(die Universität)
   besuchen**   to attend (the university)

bleiben: ist geblieben
fahren: ist gefahren
feiern   to celebrate
gebrauchen   to use
gefallen (gefällt), gefallen (+ *dat.*)
   to please, be pleasing to; **es gefällt
   mir**   I like it
gehen: ist gegangen
halten (hält), gehalten   to hold; **halten
   von**   to think of, have an opinion

interessieren to interest
**rad·fahren (fährt Rad), ist
 radgefahren** to ride a bicycle; **ich
 fahre Rad** ride a bike
sehen: gesehen
**spazieren·fahren (fährt spazieren),
 ist spazierengefahren** to go
 for a drive

tragen (trägt), getragen to wear; to
 carry
tun (tut), getan to do
werden: ist geworden to become;
 es wird kalt it's getting cold

Andere Wörter

außerdem besides, in addition, as
 well
einfach simple; simply
ewig forever; eternally
frei: frei haben to be off from work;
 frei sein to be unoccupied

gesund healthy
langweilig boring
letzt last
möglich possible
passiv passive
schnell fast, quickly

Besondere Ausdrücke

am Computer arbeiten to work at
 the computer

**Im Deutschen Theater in München spielt eine
Operette von Johann Strauß.**

Land und Leute

Das Theater

Theater in the German-speaking countries has a long tradition. The present system of theaters with resident staffs goes back to the eighteenth century. Many theaters were founded then by local rulers to provide entertainment for the court. Today there are more than 500 theaters in the German-speaking countries. In Germany, most of the theaters are repertory theaters under the jurisdiction of city governments **(Stadttheater),** some are under the jurisdiction of an individual state **(Staatstheater),** and some are private theaters **(Privattheater).**

In addition to the repertory theaters there are also many experimental theaters **(Freie Theatergruppen).** Some of the private theaters are small stages run in conjunction with a pub **(Knelpe** or **Wirtschaft)** which helps to finance the theater. Many theaters receive government subsidies for their productions. The repertory **(Spielplan)** of German-speaking theaters usually includes a variety of German and foreign plays.

GRAMMATIK UND ÜBUNGEN

1 The present perfect tense

Ich **habe** mit Karin **gesprochen**.	I *have spoken* with Karin.
	I *spoke* with Karin.
Sie **ist** nach Hause **gegangen**.	She *has gone* home.
	She *went* home.

German has several past tenses. One of them is the present perfect tense, which is commonly used in conversation to refer to past actions or states.

The present perfect tense is made up of the present tense of the auxiliary **haben** or **sein** and the past participle of the verb. In independent clauses, the past participle is the last element. (For dependent clauses see section 10.)

2 Past participles of regular weak verbs

Infinitive	Past participle	Present perfect tense
spielen	ge + spiel + t	Tania **hat** gestern nicht **gespielt**.
arbeiten	ge + arbeit + et	Sie **hat gearbeitet**.

German verbs may be classified as weak or strong according to the way in which they form their past tenses. A German weak verb is a verb whose infinitive stem (**spiel-, arbeit-**) remains unchanged in the past tense forms.

In German, the past participle of a weak verb is formed by adding **-t** to the unchanged infinitive stem. The **-t** expands to **-et** in verbs whose stem ends in **-d** or **-t** (**arbeiten > gearbeitet**), and in some verbs whose stem ends in **-m** or **-n** (**regnen > geregnet**). Most weak verbs also add the prefix **ge-** in the past participle. In English, the past participle of corresponding verbs (called "regular" verbs) is formed by adding **-ed** to the stem, e.g., *play > played, work > worked*.

3 Auxiliary *haben* with past participles

ich **habe** etwas **gefragt**	wir **haben** etwas **gefragt**
du **hast** etwas **gefragt**	ihr **habt** etwas **gefragt**
er/es/sie **hat** etwas **gefragt**	sie **haben** etwas **gefragt**
	Sie **haben** etwas **gefragt**

The chart above shows how the present perfect tense of a weak verb is formed, using the auxiliary **haben**.

1. Wir haben es schon gehört. Your friend is eager to pass on a bit of gossip to various persons. However, you tell your friend that you and they have already heard it.

▶ Frau Fischer   *Frau Fischer hat es schon gehört.*

1. Klaus
2. ich
3. Professor Weber

4. unsere Freunde
5. wir
6. Karin

2. Ich hab's schon gemacht. Heidi wants you to do all sorts of things. Tell her you've already done what she wants.

▶ Koch jetzt Kaffee.   *Den Kaffee habe ich doch schon gekocht.*

1. Mach die Arbeit.
2. Frag den Professor.
3. Hörst du die Vorlesung?
4. Lern die Vokabeln.

5. Kauf das Buch.
6. Such das Geld.
7. Spiel heute abend Tennis.

4 Past participles of irregular weak verbs

Infinitive	Past participle	Present perfect tense
bringen	ge + brach + t	Wer **hat** die Blumen **gebracht?**
denken	ge + dach + t	Jens **hat** an den Wein **gedacht.**
kennen	ge + kann + t	Sie **hat** Thomas gut **gekannt.**
wissen	ge + wuß + t	Wir **haben** es **gewußt.**

A few weak verbs, including **bringen, denken, kennen,** and **wissen,** are irregular. They are called irregular weak verbs because the past participle has the prefix **ge-** and the ending **-t,** but the verb also undergoes a stem change. The past participles of irregular weak verbs are noted in the vocabularies as follows: **denken, gedacht.**

3. Alles vorbereiten. Gerd and his friends are getting ready for a party. Restate each sentence below in the present perfect tense.

▶ Gerd denkt an Christine.   *Gerd hat an Christine gedacht.*

1. Christine denkt an den Wein.
2. Gerd weiß den Namen.
3. Klaus weiß den Namen nicht.
4. Gerd kennt das Weingeschäft°.   wine shop
5. Klaus kennt es nicht.
6. Kennst du den Namen?
7. Wer bringt das Essen?
8. Was bringst du?

4. Was wollen Sie sagen?   The verbs listed below are most of the regular weak verbs you have learned so far. Choose ten of these verbs and use them in the present perfect tense.

arbeiten □ brauchen □ faulenzen □ feiern □ fragen □ glauben □ hören □ jobben □ kaufen □ kochen □ kosten □ kriegen □ lächeln □ leben □ lernen □ machen □ regnen □ sagen □ schenken □ schmecken □ schneien □ spielen □ suchen □ tanzen □ wandern □ warten □ wohnen □ zahlen □ zelten

5 Use of the present perfect tense

In English, the present perfect tense and the simple past tense have different meanings.

Where are you going?
Gerd has invited me to dinner (and we're going this evening).

The present perfect tense (e.g., *has invited*) in English refers to a period of time that continues into the present and is thus still uncompleted.

What did you do today?
Gerd invited me to dinner (and we went).

The simple past tense (e.g., *invited*) in English, on the other hand, refers to a period of time that is completed at the moment of speaking.

Gerd hat mich zum Essen eingeladen. $\begin{cases}\text{Gerd has invited me to dinner.} \\ \text{Gerd invited me to dinner.}\end{cases}$

In German, the present perfect tense (e.g., **hat eingeladen**) refers to all actions or states in the past, whereas in English the simple past tense is used for completed actions and the present perfect tense for uncompleted actions. Context usually makes the meaning clear.

In German, the present perfect tense is most frequently used in conversation to refer to past actions or states, and is therefore often referred to as the "conversational past." German also has a simple past tense (see *Kapitel 11*) that is used to narrate connected events in the past, and which is, therefore, frequently called the "narrative past."

5. Ich hab' das nicht gewußt.   Answer the following questions for yourself and then ask your partner the same questions. Remember to use **du**.

Talking about the past

1. Wo hast du als Kind gewohnt?
2. Wie viele Bücher hast du für deine Kurse gekauft?
3. Wieviel haben die Bücher gekostet?
4. Hast du schon viel Deutsch gelernt?
5. Bis wann hast du gestern abend gearbeitet?
6. Wie hat das Essen gestern abend geschmeckt?
7. Was hast du letzte Woche in deiner Freizeit gemacht?

6. **Wie sagt man das?**   Give the German equivalents of the conversational exchanges below, using the present perfect tense.

▶ What did Erik say?   *Was hat Erik gesagt?*
▶ —I didn't hear it.   *—Ich habe es nicht gehört.*

1. Christel bought a jacket.
   —What did it cost?
2. Why didn't the men work yesterday?
   —It rained.
3. Why didn't Barbara buy the purse?
   —She didn't have any money. → *gehabt*
4. Markus cooked the meal.
   —Really? I didn't know that.
5. Who brought the wine?
   —I don't know. I didn't ask.

Land und Leute

Feiertage

Prost Neujahr! — Feuerwerk in Mittenwald.

Germany celebrates both secular and religious holidays. Among the secular holidays are New Year's Eve **(Silvester)**, New Year's Day **(Neujahr)**, and **Tag der Arbeit** on May 1, which is celebrated in honor of workers. The newest holiday is the national holiday, **Tag der deutschen Einheit** (Day of Unity), celebrated on October 3 to commemorate the unification of East and West Germany in 1990.

   The following Christian holidays are observed throughout the country: Good Friday **(Karfreitag)**; Easter **(Ostern**—both **Ostersonntag** and **Ostermontag)**; Ascension Day **(Christi Himmelfahrt)**, the sixth Thursday after Easter; Pentecost **(Pfingsten)**, the seventh Sunday and Monday after Easter; and December 25 and 26 **(erster Weihnachtstag** and **zweiter Weihnachtstag)**. Four other Christian holidays are observed in some states, but not all.

7. Einkaufen bei Konen. Answer the following questions about the ad from the **Konen** clothing store in Munich.

1. Welche englischen Wörter finden Sie?
2. Wann schließt Konen am Donnerstag?
3. Für wen gibt es Sonderangebote°?
4. Finden Sie die Jeans teuer?

specials

⬦ **8. Rollenspiel.**   You meet a friend (your partner) who is wearing some new clothes. You like them very much and want to know where your friend got them, how much they cost, and what other articles of clothing the store has. It turns out that your friend was shopping at **Konen.** Have a conversation with her/him using the following questions and comments to get started. You may want to refer to the Vocabulary for Authentic Text Activities and the Supplementary Word Sets in the Reference Section for additional vocabulary.

S1: Du, das T-Shirt ist toll!
S2: Der Mantel gefällt mir auch.
S1: Wieviel hat er gekostet?
S2: Hundertachtundneunzig Mark.
S1: Hast du sonst noch etwas gekauft?
S2: Ja, [...].
S1: Wo hast du die Sachen° gekauft?   things
S2: Bei Konen.

6 Past participles of strong verbs

Infinitive	Past participle	Present perfect tense
sehen	ge + seh + en	Ich **habe** es **gesehen.**
finden	ge + fund + en	Ich **habe** es **gefunden.**
nehmen	ge + nomm + en	Ich **habe** es nicht **genommen.**

The past participle of a strong verb ends in **-en.** (Note the exception **getan.**) Most strong verbs also add the **ge-** prefix in the past participle. Many strong verbs have a stem vowel of the past participle **(gefunden)** that is different from that of the infinitive, and some verbs also have a change in the consonants **(genommen).** Past participles of strong verbs are noted in the vocabularies as follows: **schreiben, geschrieben.**

For a list of strong verbs, see #23 of the Grammatical Tables in the Reference Section.

Infinitive	Past participle
halten	gehalten
schlafen	geschlafen
tragen	getragen
tun	getan

9. **Pizza machen.** Tell about Peter's pizza-making experience. Restate in the present perfect tense.

▶ Warum schläft Peter heute so lange? *Warum hat Peter heute so lange geschlafen?*

1. Er tut heute nicht viel.
2. Er macht nur eine Pizza.
3. Was halten die Freunde von seinem Plan?
4. Sie machen auch eine Pizza.
5. Dann tragen sie die Pizzas zu den Nachbarn.
6. Was tun die Nachbarn dann?

Infinitive	Past participle
geben	gegeben
lesen	gelesen
sehen	gesehen
essen	gegessen
liegen	gelegen

10. **Ein Abend bei mir.** You invited Klaus over for a relaxing evening. Restate the sentences below in the present perfect tense.

▶ Ein Buch über die Schweiz liegt da. *Ein Buch über die Schweiz hat da gelegen.*

1. Was machst du mit dem Buch?
2. Ich gebe es Klaus.
3. Zuerst liest er das Buch.
4. Dann essen wir ein Wurstbrot.
5. Ich esse auch einen Apfel.
6. Später sehen wir einen Film im Fernsehen.

Infinitive	Past participle
helfen	geholfen
nehmen	genommen
sprechen	gesprochen
finden	gefunden
trinken	getrunken
leihen	geliehen
schreiben	geschrieben

11. Was haben sie getan? Restate the conversational exchanges below in the present perfect tense.

▶ Nehmen Paul und Manuel den Zug?

— Nein, ich leihe ihnen mein Auto.

Haben Paul und Manuel den Zug genommen?

— Nein, ich habe ihnen mein Auto geliehen.

1. Trinken Sie Kaffee?
   —Nein, ich nehme Tee.
2. Schreibst du die Karte?
   —Nein, ich finde sie nicht.
3. Sprechen Gerd und Susi Englisch mit euch?
   —Ja, wir finden das toll.

12. Mein Tag war langweilig/interessant. With a partner or in a group discuss your activities in the last 24 hours using the following questions as a guide. Then decide whose day was interesting and whose boring. You may want to exaggerate a bit to make your day more interesting. Then report to the class on your activities.

S1:

Hast du gut geschlafen?

S2:

Ja.
Nein, ich habe die ganze Nacht getanzt.

1. Bis wann hast du geschlafen?
2. Was hast du zum Frühstück gegessen?
3. Was hast du zum Frühstück getrunken?
4. Was für Kleidung hast du getragen?
5. Was hast du gelesen?
6. Wen hast du heute auf der Uni gesehen?
7. Mit wem hast du heute gesprochen?

13. Wie sagt man das? Give German equivalents of each of the two-line dialogues below.

▶ Did you take my ballpoint, Gabi?

—No, I haven't seen it.

Hast du meinen Kuli genommen, Gabi?

—Nein, den habe ich nicht gesehen.

1. Have you eaten already, Susanne?
   —No, I haven't had time.
2. Did you sleep well, Benno?
   —No, I drank too much coffee last night.
3. Have you spoken with Mrs. Danziger, Tanja?
   —No, but I wrote her daughter.

7 Separable-prefix verbs in the present perfect tense

Infinitive	Past participle	Present perfect tense
anrufen	an + **ge** + rufen	Kirstin **hat** gestern **angerufen**.
einkaufen	ein + **ge** + kauft	Ingrid **hat** heute **eingekauft**.

The prefix **ge-** of the past participle comes between the separable prefix and the stem of the participle. Some separable-prefix verbs are weak; others are strong. In spoken German the separable prefix receives stress: **an'gerufen**. A list of some separable-prefix verbs you have encountered follows.

Infinitive	Past participle
anrufen	angerufen
aussehen	ausgesehen
einkaufen	eingekauft
einladen	eingeladen
fernsehen	ferngesehen
kennenlernen	kennengelernt

14. **Studentenleben.** Restate the conversational exchanges below in the present perfect tense.

▶ Lädt Klaus für Samstag einige Freunde ein?
—Natürlich. Er lädt alle seine Freunde ein.

Hat Klaus für Samstag einige Freunde eingeladen?
—Natürlich. Er hat alle seine Freunde eingeladen.

1. Kauft er auch Wein ein?
—Na klar. Er kauft auch Käse, Wurst und Brot ein.
2. Bringen seine Freunde etwas mit?
—Natürlich. Sie bringen viel mit.
3. Lernt Evi seine Freunde kennen?
—Nein. Klaus lädt sie nicht ein.
4. Wann hörst du mit deiner Arbeit auf?
—Um acht. Dann rufe ich Sigrid an.

Ruf doch mal an!

Die Telefon-Information für Österreich-Reisende

So einfach ist es, zu Hause anzurufen:
Von allen öffentlichen Telefonen. Ausgenommen sind Ortsmünztelefone.

8 Past participles without the *ge-* prefix

◼ *Verbs ending in* -ieren

Infinitive	Past participle	Present perfect tense
studieren	studiert	Dirk **hat** in München **studiert**.
interessieren	interessiert	Der Film **hat** mich nicht **interessiert**.

Verbs ending in **-ieren** do not have the prefix **ge-** in the past participle. They are always weak verbs whose participle ends in **-t**. These verbs are generally based on words borrowed from French and Latin; they are often similar to English verbs.

15. Was hat man diskutiert°? Restate the conversational exchanges below   discussed
in the present perfect tense.

▶ Wo studierst du?   *Wo hast du studiert?*
    —Ich studiere in München.   *—Ich habe in München studiert.*

1. Mit wem telefoniert Gerd?
    —Mit Laura. Er gratuliert ihr zum Geburtstag.
2. Dirk diskutiert ein Problem mit seinem Freund.
    —Warum diskutieren sie so lange?
3. Die Professoren plädieren für mehr Mathematik.
    —Die Studenten protestieren gegen diesen Plan, nicht?

◼ *Verbs with inseparable prefixes*

Infinitive	Past participle	Present perfect tense
bekommen	bekommen	Ich **habe** nichts **bekommen**.
besuchen	besucht	Paul **hat** seine Tante **besucht**.
bezahlen	bezahlt	Wer **hat** das **bezahlt**?
erklären	erklärt	Ich **habe** es schon **erklärt**.
erzählen	erzählt	Erik **hat** es **erzählt**.
gefallen	gefallen	**Hat** es dir **gefallen**?
gehören	gehört	Wem **hat** diese alte Uhr **gehört**?
verstehen	verstanden	Inge **hat** es nicht **verstanden**.

Some prefixes are never separated from the verb stem. These prefixes are **be-, emp-, ent-, er-, ge-, ver-,** and **zer-**. Inseparable-prefix verbs do not add the prefix **ge-** in the past participle. Some inseparable-prefix verbs are weak; others are strong.

An inseparable prefix is not stressed in spoken German: **bekom'men.**

16. Petra erzählt von ihrer Reise.   Petra went to Switzerland. Tell about her trip. Restate each sentence in the present perfect tense.

▶ Petra erzählt von ihren Ferien.   *Petra hat von ihren Ferien erzählt.*

1. Sie bezahlt die Reise selbst.
2. Die Schweiz gefällt Petra sehr.
3. Sie besucht da Freunde.
4. Sie bekommt da auch guten Käse.
5. Sie versteht die Schweizer ziemlich gut.
6. Ein Schweizer erklärt ihr vieles.
7. Er erzählt viel Lustiges.

9 Auxiliary *sein* with past participles

ich **bin gekommen**	wir **sind gekommen**
du **bist gekommen**	ihr **seid gekommen**
er/es/sie **ist gekommen**	sie **sind gekommen**
	Sie **sind gekommen**

Some verbs use **sein** instead of **haben** as an auxiliary in the present perfect.

Warum **ist** Silke so früh **aufgestanden?**	Why did Silke get up so early?
Sie **ist** nach Freiburg **gefahren.**	She drove to Freiburg.

Verbs that require **sein** must meet two conditions. They must:

1. be intransitive verbs (verbs without a direct object) and
2. indicate a change in condition (e.g., **aufstehen**) or motion to or from a place (e.g., **fahren**).

Infinitive	Past participle	Infinitive	Past participle
aufstehen	⎧ aufgestanden	laufen	⎧ gelaufen
fahren	⎪ gefahren	reisen	⎪ gereist
fliegen	ist ⎨ geflogen	schwimmen	ist ⎨ geschwommen
gehen	⎪ gegangen	wandern	⎪ gewandert
kommen	⎩ gekommen	werden	⎩ geworden

Wer **ist** wieder so lange bei Helmut **geblieben?**	Who stayed so late at Helmut's again?
Ich **bin** es nicht **gewesen.**	It wasn't I.

The verbs **bleiben** and **sein** require **sein** as an auxiliary in the present perfect tense, even though they do not indicate a change in condition or motion to or from a place.

Wie **war** der Kaffee?	How was the coffee?
Der Kuchen **war** gut.	The cake was good.

The simple past tense of **sein (war)** is used more commonly than the present perfect tense of **sein (ist gewesen),** even in conversation.

17. So war es. Restate the conversational exchanges below in the present perfect tense.

▶ Fährst du mit dem Auto? *Bist du mit dem Auto gefahren?*
　—Nein, ich fliege. 　*—Nein, ich bin geflogen.*

1. Fährst du nach Österreich?
　—Nein, ich bleibe auch in den Ferien zu Hause.
2. Gehen Müllers auch schwimmen?
　—Ja, aber sie kommen erst später.
3. Warum geht ihr nicht schwimmen?
　—Es wird zu kalt.
4. Stehst du jeden Tag früh auf?
　—Ja. Ich laufe im Park mit meinem Hund.

18. Frage-Ecke. Exchange information with your partner about the weekend activities of various people.

S1: Was hat Evi gemacht?
S2: Evi ist spazierengegangen und hat einen Roman gelesen.

S1:

	Evi	Dirk	Stefan	Silke	ich	Partnerin/Partner
im Restaurant essen				X		
spazierengehen						
fernsehen						
radfahren		X				
faulenzen		X				
in die Kneipe gehen						
einen Roman lesen				X		
mit Freunden telefonieren						

S2:

	Evi	Dirk	Stefan	Silke	ich	Partnerin/Partner
im Restaurant essen						
spazierengehen	X					
fernsehen			X			
radfahren						
faulenzen						
in die Kneipe gehen			X			
einen Roman lesen	X					
mit Freunden telefonieren						

19. **Was haben Sie gemacht?** Discuss with your partner what you've both been doing lately. You may use some of the questions below and make up your own.

Talking about past activities

■ Wann bist du gestern aufgestanden? Am Sonntag?
■ Wohin bist du nach dem Frühstück gegangen? Oder bist du [zu Hause/im Studentenheim] geblieben?
■ Wo hast du gestern abend gegessen?
■ Was hast du gestern abend getrunken?
■ Wann bist du heute zur Uni gefahren?
■ Wie viele Vorlesungen hast du gehabt?
■ Wann bist du gestern wieder nach Hause gegangen?
■ Was hast du im Fernsehen gesehen?
■ Was hast du letzte Woche gekauft?
■ Wann bist du am Samstag ins Bett gegangen?

10 Dependent clauses in the present perfect tense

Silke erzählt, daß sie gestern einen guten Film gesehen **hat.**
Sie sagt, daß sie mit Freunden ins Kino gegangen **ist.**

In a dependent clause, the present-tense form of the auxiliary verb **haben** or **sein** follows the past participle and is the last element in the clause.

20. **Nicole und ihr Studium.** A friend who knows Nicole slightly asks you questions about her. Answer using the cues. Begin the clauses with **weil.**

▶ Warum hat Nicole im Sommer keine Reise° gemacht? (Sie hat bei einer Computerfirma gearbeitet.)
Weil sie bei einer Computerfirma gearbeitet hat.

trip

1. Warum hat Nicole in den Ferien gearbeitet? (Sie hat das Geld fürs Studium gebraucht.)
2. Warum hat sie soviel Geld gebraucht? (Alles ist so teuer geworden.)
3. Warum ist sie in die Buchhandlung gegangen? (Sie hat ein Buch gesucht.)
4. Warum hat sie dieses Buch gekauft? (Es hat ihr gefallen.)
5. Warum hat sie Deutsch gelernt? (Sie hat die Sprache° interessant gefunden.)   language
6. Warum ist sie noch nicht nach Deutschland gefahren? (Sie hat nicht genug Geld gehabt.)

21. **Wer hat was gemacht?** Find six fellow students who have done any one of the activities listed below in the past week.

▶ arbeiten   *Hast du letzte Woche gearbeitet?*

einkaufen gehen	[Tennis] spielen	zu Hause bleiben
Referat vorbereiten	mit Freunden wandern	zuviel essen
Notizen durcharbeiten	ins Kino gehen	neue Schuhe kaufen
viel schlafen	schwimmen gehen	Buch lesen
Deutsch machen	Videospiele spielen	Geburtstag feiern

WIEDERHOLUNG

1. Das gefällt ihnen nicht. You're trying to decide what books, CDs, and videos to give your friends as gifts. Sandra is trying to help and offers suggestions. Answer her questions in the negative.

▶ Liest Kevin gern klassische Literatur?   *Nein, klassische Literatur gefällt ihm nicht.*

▶ Liest Claudia gern Krimis?   *Nein, Krimis gefallen ihr nicht.*

1. Hört Anna gern klassische Musik?
2. Hört Benjamin gern Rockmusik?
3. Sieht Marion gern Actionfilme?
4. Sehen Hans und Lisa gern Dokumentarfilme?
5. Liest Alex gern Romane?
6. Und du: Hörst du gern Jazz?
   Liest du gern Liebesromane?
   Siehst du gern alte Filme?

Land und Leute

Der deutsche Film

Going to the movies is a favorite pastime of people in the German-speaking countries. Movies were invented over 100 years ago. Some of the earliest film premieres were in Germany. In Berlin in 1885 Max and Emil Skladanowsky produced a seven-minute film which is still in existence. The German movie industry flourished during the era of silent films and early "talkies" (1919–1932). Directors like Fritz Lang, F. W. Murnau, and F. W. Pabst were considered among the finest in the world, and the German use of the "moving camera" influenced many directors.

During the Nazi era (1933–1945), many great German and Austrian filmmakers emigrated to the United States and other countries. Some of them never returned; this loss led to a period of mediocrity in German filmmaking that lasted until the mid-sixties. At that point a generation of young filmmakers began to introduce the New German Cinema (**Neuer deutscher Film**). Many of those directors are now famous, including the late Rainer Werner Fassbinder, Werner Herzog, Wim Wenders, and Wolfgang Petersen.

Einer von Wim Wenders Filmen ist „Der amerikanische Freund".

Since then other directors such as Margarethe von Trotta, Volker Schlöndorff, Doris Dörrie, and Percy Adlon have gained international recognition. However, 80% of the films shown in German movie theaters today are American, with dubbed voices.

2. Frank hat Freunde zum Essen eingeladen. Tell about Frank's experience preparing a meal for friends. Supply the missing prepositions.

1. Frank lebt _____ zwei Monaten in Bremen.
2. Er arbeitet _____ einer amerikanischen Firma.
3. _____ Samstag hat er einige Freunde _____ Essen eingeladen.
4. Am Wochenende kommen seine Freunde oft _____ ihm.
5. Sie sind _____ zwölf gekommen.
6. Frank hat _____ seine Freunde einen Fisch gegrillt.
7. _____ dem Wein trinken sie eine ganze Flasche.
8. Der Wein kommt _____ Italien.
9. _____ dem Essen gehen sie _____ einem Fußballspiel.

3. Pizza oder Spaghetti? Write a paragraph about Renate's experience preparing a meal for guests. Use the present perfect tense, and the cues provided below.

1. Renate / einladen / am Samstag / Freunde / zum Essen
2. sie / machen / eine Pizza
3. sie / haben / keinen Käse // und / ihre Freundin Monika / laufen / zu / Supermarkt
4. die Pizza / aussehen / ein bißchen schwarz
5. dann / sie / kochen / Spaghetti

4. Wie sagt man das?

1. —Why did you come by bus?
   —My car is broken down.
   —I'm sorry.
2. —Did you like Denmark?
   —Yes. We hiked a lot.
   —Did you camp (in a tent)?
   —No. It rained too much. We slept at friends' (houses).
3. —Would you like a piece (of) cake?
   —Gladly. I'm hungry.
   —How does it taste?
   —Very good.

5. Fragen über die Uni. Tell what David discovered about going to a German university. Combine the sentences with the conjunction indicated.

1. David hat viele Fragen. (weil) Er möchte in Deutschland studieren.
2. Er studiert vielleicht vier Semester dort. (wenn) Die Uni ist nicht zu teuer.
3. Nicole sagt ... (daß) Es kostet nichts.
4. Dann studiert er. (wenn) Er kann einen Studentenjob finden.
5. Nicole sagt ... (daß) Es gibt leider wenige Studentenjobs.

6. Zum Schreiben

1. Two students, Michael and Sabine, are discussing various topics. Select one of the topics below and write the dialogue that takes place between them.

   das Wetter □ einkaufen □ die Vorlesung □ eine Seminararbeit vorbereiten □ das Essen □ das Wochenende □ Ferien

2. Keep a diary **(Tagebuch)** in German for a week in which you record each day's activities. Some verbs you may wish to use are: **aufstehen, arbeiten, besuchen, fernsehen, kaufen, gehen, spielen, sprechen (mit), lernen.**

3. Assume you are attending a German university for a year. Write a letter in German to a friend telling about the last few weeks. Possible topics are the weather, classes, people you've met, free-time activities, e.g., sports, TV, music, concerts, bars, movies.

4. **Ein Werbespot°.** Using the ad from **Konen** on page 224, write copy for a radio advertisement. Below are some phrases you may want to use.

   short ad

   heute bei Konen … □ Popeline-Mäntel … □ gut einkaufen … □ jeden Donnerstag bis 20.30 geöffnet°

   öffnen: to open

Hinweise: After you have completed the writing assignment, check over your work, paying particular attention to the following:

- agreement between subject and verb
- gender and case of all nouns and pronouns (see all chapters, especially *Kapitel 1, 4, 6*)
- choice of prepositions and correct case used with the prepositions (see *Kapitel 4* and *6*)
- choice of auxiliary verb in the present perfect tense (see this chapter)
- word order in sentences with dependent and independent clauses (see *Kapitel 6*)
- word order in sentences with the present perfect tense (see this chapter)

Hier gibt es Sachen für den *Neuen Mann.* (Stuttgart)

GRAMMATIK: ZUSAMMENFASSUNG

The present perfect tense

Hast du gestern abend **ferngesehen?**	Did you watch TV last night?
Nein, ich **bin** ins Kino **gegangen.**	No, I went to the movies.

The German present perfect tense, like the English present perfect, is a compound tense. It is made up of the present tense of the auxiliary **haben** or **sein** and the past participle. In independent clauses, the past participle is in final position. (For dependent clauses, see below.)

Past participles of regular weak verbs

Infinitive	Past participle	Present perfect tense	
sagen	ge + sag + t	Er **hat** es **gesagt.**	
arbeiten	ge + arbeit + et	Sie **hat** schwer **gearbeitet.**	
baden°	ge + bad + et	Er **hat** gestern nicht **gebadet.**	to bathe
regnen	ge + regn + et	Es **hat** gestern **geregnet.**	

The past participle of a weak verb is formed by adding **-t** to the unchanged infinitive stem. The **-t** expands to **-et** in verbs like **arbeiten, baden,** and **regnen.** In the past participle, most weak verbs also have the prefix **ge-.**

Past participles of irregular weak verbs

Infinitive	Past participle	Present perfect tense
bringen	ge + brach + t	Wer **hat** das **gebracht?**
denken	ge + dach + t	Sie **hat** nicht an die Zeit **gedacht.**
kennen	ge + kann + t	Sie **hat** deinen Freund gut **gekannt.**
wissen	ge + wuß + t	Sie **hat** es **gewußt.**

A few weak verbs are irregular. The past participle has the prefix **ge-** and the ending **-t;** there is also a change in the stem vowel and in the consonants of several verbs.

Past participles of strong verbs

Infinitive	Past participle	Present perfect tense
nehmen	ge + nomm + en	Ich **habe** das Brot **genommen.**
essen	ge + gess + en	Ich **habe** heute wenig **gegessen.**
tun	ge + ta + n	Ich **habe** das nicht **getan.**

The past participle of a strong verb ends in **-en.** (Note the exception **getan.**) Most strong verbs also add the **ge-** prefix in the past participle. Many strong verbs have a stem vowel of the past participle that is different from that of the infinitive, and some verbs also have a change in the consonants.

For a list of strong verbs, see #23 of the Grammatical Tables in the Reference Section.

Past participles of separable-prefix verbs

Infinitive	Past participle	Present perfect tense
aufhören	auf + **ge** + hört	Lisa **hat** mit der Arbeit **aufgehört.**
anrufen	an + **ge** + rufen	Gerd **hat** sie **angerufen.**

The prefix **ge-** of the past participle comes between the separable prefix and the stem of the participle. Some separable-prefix verbs are weak (e.g., **aufhören**); others are strong (e.g., **anrufen**).

Past participles without the *ge-* prefix

■ *Verbs ending in* **-ieren**

Present tense	Present perfect tense
Jutta **studiert** in Heidelberg.	Jutta **hat** in Heidelberg **studiert.**
Jens **repariert** sein Auto.	Jens **hat** sein Auto **repariert.**

Verbs ending in **-ieren** do not have the prefix **ge-** in the past participle. They are always weak verbs whose participle ends in **-t.** These verbs are generally based on words borrowed from French and Latin; they are often similar to English verbs.

■ *Verbs with inseparable prefixes*

Present tense	Present perfect tense
Birgit **erzählt** von ihrer Arbeit.	Sie **hat** von ihrer Arbeit **erzählt.**
Martin **versteht** sie nicht.	Er **hat** sie nicht **verstanden.**

Some prefixes are never separated from the verb stem. These prefixes are **be-, emp-, ent-, er-, ge-, ver-,** and **zer-.** Inseparable-prefix verbs do not add the prefix **ge-** in the past participle. Some inseparable-prefix verbs are weak (e.g., **erzählen**); others are strong (e.g., **verstehen**).

Use of the auxiliary *haben*

Christine **hat** heute schwer **gearbeitet.**   Christine worked hard today.
Sie **hat** ein Referat **geschrieben.**   She wrote a report.

Haben is used to form the present perfect tense of most verbs.

Use of the auxiliary *sein*

Schmidts **sind** spät nach Hause   The Schmidts came home late.
   gekommen.
Sie **sind** dann spät **aufgestanden.**   Then they got up late.

The auxiliary **sein** is used to form the present perfect tense of intransitive verbs (i.e., verbs that do not have a direct object) when these verbs denote a change in condition (e.g., **aufstehen**) or motion to or from a place (e.g., **kommen**).

Warum **bist** du so lange **geblieben?**   Why did you stay so long?
Es ist so schön **gewesen.**   It was so nice.

The intransitive verbs **bleiben** and **sein** require the auxiliary **sein,** even though they do not indicate a change in condition or motion to or from a place.

Musiker proben.

Verbs using the auxiliary *sein*

You have already encountered some verbs that take the auxiliary **sein** in the present perfect tense. They are shown in the table below.

Infinitive	Auxiliary	Past participle
aufstehen	ist	aufgestanden
bleiben	ist	geblieben
fahren	ist	gefahren
fliegen	ist	geflogen
gehen	ist	gegangen
kommen	ist	gekommen
laufen	ist	gelaufen
reisen	ist	gereist
schwimmen	ist	geschwommen
sein	ist	gewesen
wandern	ist	gewandert
werden	ist	geworden

Use of the present perfect tense in dependent clauses

Klaus sagt, daß David ihm eine Karte geschrieben **hat.**
Er sagt, daß David nach Österreich gefahren **ist.**

In a dependent clause, the auxiliary **haben** or **sein** follows the past participle and is the last element in the clause, because it is the finite verb.

Regensburger Wohnhäuser mit Blick auf die Donau.

Kapitel 8

LERNZIELE

■ **Sprechintentionen**

Making plans and preparations
Discussing and scheduling household chores
Seeking information about someone
Discussing cultural differences

■ **Lesestück**

Andere Länder – Andere Sitten

■ **Land und Leute**

Pedestrian zones
Germans in the U.S.A.
Freunde vs. *Bekannte*
Homes and apartments in German-speaking countries
Closed doors

■ **Vokabeln**

Furniture
Kitchen appliances
Verbs *legen/liegen, stellen/stehen, setzen/sitzen, hängen, stecken*

■ **Grammatik**

Hin and *her*
Two-way prepositions
Special meanings of prepositions
Time expressions in dative and accusative
Da-compounds
Wo-compounds
Indirect questions

BAUSTEINE FÜR GESPRÄCHE

Was machst du nach dem Seminar?

ALEX: Was machst du nach dem Seminar? Gehst du in die Bibliothek?

LENA: Nein, ich treffe Claudia im Altstadtcafé.

ALEX: In der Fußgängerzone?

LENA: Ja, gehst du mit?

ALEX: Nein, danke, ins Altstadtcafé gehe ich nicht so gern. Da ist immer so schlechte Luft. Alles ist voll Rauch.

LENA: Gehst du vielleicht mit in einen Biergarten? Im Waldgarten sitzt man schön draußen.

ALEX: Aber du, ich bin pleite.

LENA: Macht nichts. Ich lade dich ein.

What are you doing after the seminar?

What are you doing after the seminar? Are you going to the library?

No, I'm meeting Claudia in the Altstadtcafé.

In the pedestrian mall?

Yes, are you coming?

No, thanks, I don't like going to the Altstadtcafé. The air is always so bad there. Everything is full of smoke.

Maybe you'll go along to a beer garden? You can sit outside at the Waldgarten.

But, hey, I'm broke.

Doesn't matter. I'm treating you.

Fragen

1. Wen trifft Lena? Wann? Wo?
2. Wo ist das Altstadtcafé?
3. Wohin geht Alex nicht so gern? Warum nicht?
4. Warum findet Alex einen Biergarten bestimmt besser?
5. Leiht Lena Alex Geld? Warum (nicht)?

Vorbereitungen für ein Fest

JULIA: Sag, willst du nicht endlich mal das Wohnzimmer aufräumen? Da liegen überall deine Bücher herum.

LUKAS: Muß das sein?

JULIA: Klar, wir müssen das Essen vorbereiten und den Tisch decken. In einer Stunde kommen die Leute.

LUKAS: Was? Schon in einer Stunde? Du meine Güte! Und wir müssen noch staubsaugen, Staub wischen, abwaschen, abtrocknen, die Küche sieht aus wie …

JULIA: Jetzt red nicht lange, sondern mach schnell. Ich helf' dir ja.

Preparations for a party

Say, don't you want to straighten up the living room, finally? Your books are lying around everywhere.

Do I have to?

Of course, we have to prepare the food and set the table. People are coming in an hour.

What? In an hour? Good heavens! And we still have to vacuum, dust, do the dishes, dry them, the kitchen looks like . . .

Now stop talking so much and hurry up. You know I'm going to help you.

Fragen

1. Warum soll Lukas das Wohnzimmer aufräumen?
2. Wann kommen die Gäste°?
3. Was müssen Julia und Lukas noch machen?

Brauchbares

1. In the first conversation Lena says, **"Gehst du vielleicht mit in einen Biergarten?"** In the German construction expressing *to go along somewhere,* the **mit** precedes the place one is going to.

2. When Alex objects to the Altstadtcafé, Lena suggests a beer garden. Outdoor cafés and restaurants are very common in German-speaking countries. Even restaurants at rest stops on the **Autobahn** have patios so patrons can eat outside. The moderate climate of the summers lends itself to pleasant outdoor dining.

3. In the second conversation Julia says, **"Sag, willst du nicht endlich mal das Wohnzimmer aufräumen?"** **Mal** is a flavoring particle used to soften the intensity of expressed needs—wishes, obligations, or commands—and leaves the time for carrying out the needs vague.

4. Julia's last sentence is **"Ich helf' dir ja."** In colloquial German the ending **e** is often dropped from the verb in the **ich**-form. **Ja** is a flavoring particle here.

Land und Leute

Fußgängerzonen

The physical layout of cities in the German-speaking countries is generally different from that of cities in the United States. The concept of building large suburbs and shopping malls around a city is uncommon in most of Europe. A city **(Großstadt)** or town **(Stadt)** in German-speaking countries has a center containing office buildings as well as apartment buildings, stores, and places for cultural events. Many downtown areas have been converted to traffic-free pedestrian zones **(Fußgängerzonen)**. A typical pedestrian zone has large department stores as well as small specialty stores and street vendors, restaurants, and outdoor cafés. The streets are often lined with flowers, bushes, and trees and sometimes lead into small squares, where people can rest on benches. The downtown shopping areas are used not only by people who live in the city, but also by people who live in the outskirts or in nearby villages.

In der Heidelberger Fußgängerzone kann man gemütlich einkaufen.

1. Was machst du? A fellow student would like to do something and asks what your plans are at various times.

Making plans

S1:

Was machst du? | **nach dem Seminar?**
nach der Vorlesung?
heute nachmittag?
am Wochenende?

S2:

Ich gehe | **in einen Biergarten.**
in die Bibliothek.
ins Café.
nach Hause.

Ich treffe [Alex] | **im Café.**
in einem Biergarten.
in der Bibliothek.

2. Ein Fest. A friend has invited you to a party. Ask about the plans and what you should bring.

Preparing for a party

S1:

Was macht ihr auf dem Fest?

S2:

Wir | **tanzen.**
hören Musik.
essen viel.
trinken etwas.
reden viel.

Was soll ich zu dem Fest mitbringen?

Bring doch | **die Bilder von deiner Ferienreise°** mit.
etwas zu | **essen**
trinken
ein paar | **Flaschen° Cola**
CDs
Kassetten
einen Kassettenrecorder

Diese Studenten aus Hannover feiern ein Fest.

3. **Hausarbeit°.** Find out from several fellow students which chores they do or don't do at home. You may wish to refer to the Supplementary Word Sets in the Reference Section for additional chores.

Talking about household chores

S1:   S2:

Welche Arbeiten machst du zu Hause?	Ich	**wasche ab.**
		decke den Tisch.
		trockne ab.
		wische Staub.°
		mach' [die Wohnung] sauber°.

Welche Arbeiten machst du nicht?	Ich	**räume nicht auf.**
		koche nicht.
		putze° [das Bad°] nicht.
		wasche die Wäsche° nicht.
		spüle° kein Geschirr°.

4. **Frage-Ecke.** You and your partner need to complete the schedules for weekend chores. Find the missing information.

Scheduling chores

S1: Was macht Julia am Freitag?
S2: Sie kocht das Abendessen.

S1:

	Freitag	Samstag
Julia		das Wohnzimmer aufräumen
Lukas	das Abendessen kochen	
Alex		die Küche saubermachen
Lena	abwaschen	
ich		
Partnerin/ Partner		

S2:

	Freitag	Samstag
Julia	das Abendessen kochen	
Lukas		staubsaugen
Alex	das Bad putzen	
Lena		Geschirr spülen
ich		
Partnerin/ Partner		

Vokabeln

Substantive

das **Bad, ̈er** bath, bathroom
der **Biergarten, ̈** beer garden
die **Ferienreise, -n** vacation trip
das **Fest, -e** party; celebration; feast;
  auf dem Fest at the party; **ein
  Fest geben** to give a party
die **Flasche, -n** bottle; **eine Flasche
  Mineralwasser** a bottle of
  mineral water
die **Fußgängerzone, -n** pedestrian
  zone

der **Gast, ̈e** guest
das **Geschirr** dishes
die **Hausarbeit** housework; chore
die **Luft** air
der **Rauch** smoke
die **Reise, -n** trip, journey
der **Staub** dust
der **Wald, ̈er** forest
die **Wäsche** laundry
das **Wohnzimmer, -** living room

Verben

ab·trocknen to dry dishes; to wipe
  dry
**ab·waschen (wäscht ab),
  abgewaschen** to do dishes
auf·räumen to straighten up
  (a room)
decken to cover; **den Tisch decken**
  to set the table
helfen (hilft), geholfen (+ *dat.*)
  to help; **hilf mir** help me
putzen to clean
reden to talk

sitzen, gesessen to sit
spülen to rinse; to wash; **Geschirr
  spülen** to wash dishes
staubsaugen to vacuum; **ich
  staubsauge** I vacuum; **ich habe
  staubgesaugt** I vacuumed
Staub wischen to dust; **ich wische
  Staub** I'm dusting; **ich habe
  Staub gewischt** I dusted
treffen (trifft), getroffen to meet
waschen (wäscht), gewaschen
  to wash

Andere Wörter

draußen outside
endlich finally
herum around; **herum·liegen**
  to be lying around
pleite broke, out of money

sauber clean; **sauber·machen**
  to clean
überall everywhere
voll full

Besondere Ausdrücke

Du meine Güte! Good Heavens!
Er geht mit in einen Biergarten. He
  is going along to a beer garden.

Mach schnell! Hurry up!
Macht nichts! Doesn't matter!

Land und Leute

Das Pastorius-Haus in Germantown.

Die Deutschen in Amerika

German immigration in the New World began on an organized basis in 1683 when 33 Germans from Krefeld arrived in Philadelphia on the ship Concord. They were looking for religious and political freedom and came to Pennsylvania through the auspices of William Penn and a German named Franz Daniel Pastorius. The settlers called the community they built Germantown, which in 1854 became a part of Philadelphia. Seven million German emigrants have come to the U.S.A. Between 1820 and 1920 alone, more than six million German immigrants arrived, many of them farmers and artisans.

Today approximately 58 million Americans, out of a total population of 248 million, claim German ancestry. The states with the largest German ancestry are: Wisconsin (52% of the total population claim full or part German ancestry); South Dakota and North Dakota (47% each); Nebraska and Iowa (46% each); Minnesota (43%); Kansas (35%); and Indiana, Montana, Ohio, and Pennsylvania (33% each).

ANDERE LÄNDER – ANDERE SITTEN

Vorbereitung auf das Lesen

■ *Vor dem Lesen*

1. Die Leute sprechen gern über ihre Zeit im Ausland. Mögliche Themen sind das Essen oder die Reise selbst°, z.B. der Flug°. Welche anderen Themen können Sie nennen°? — itself / flight, name
2. Denken Sie an° ein Land – Kanada, Deutschland, die USA. Was assoziieren Sie mit diesem Land? Was ist typisch oder stereotyp für das Land? — **Denken Sie an:** think of

■ *Beim Lesen*

1. Machen Sie eine Liste von den Themen, über die° Monika und Peter sprechen. — which
2. Welche Bemerkungen° von Peter und Monika finden Sie stereotyp? — observations

Der Austauschstudent° Peter Clason studiert seit einem Jahr an einer deutschen Universität. Er sitzt mit Monika, einer deutschen Studentin, in einer Studentenkneipe. Monika ist ein Jahr in Amerika gewesen. Mit ihr kann man deshalb gut über die Unterschiede zwischen Deutschland und Amerika reden.
5 Monika fragt: „Du, Peter, sag mal, was ist für dich hier in Deutschland eigentlich anders? Was hast du beobachtet?"

PETER: Vieles ist ja genauso wie in Amerika. Aber vieles ist doch auch anders. Da war zum Beispiel meine erste° Fahrt° auf der Autobahn. Furchtbar, sag' ich dir. Die fahren wie die Wilden, hab' ich gedacht. Seitdem° fahr' ich
10 richtig gern mit dem Zug. Außerdem hat fast jede größere° Stadt einen Bahnhof, und es gibt genug Züge. Sie sind sauber. Sie fahren pünktlich ab, und sie kommen pünktlich an. Überhaupt° funktioniert alles.

MONIKA: Ja, das habe ich in Amerika vermißt° – die öffentlichen Verkehrsmittel. Es gibt zwar Busse, aber die fahren nicht so oft. Alles ist auch so weit aus-
15 einander°. Deswegen° braucht man wirklich ein Auto. – Aber Peter, es tut mir leid, ich habe dich unterbrochen°. Was ist sonst noch anders in Deutschland?

PETER: Also mit den Bussen hast du ja recht. Was noch? Vielleicht die Parks in jeder Stadt, die vielen Blumen in den Fenstern, auf den Märkten, in den
20 Restaurants. Und dann das Essen. Erstens° ist das Essen selbst anders – anderes Brot und Bier, mehr Wurst und so. Dann wie man ißt – wie man Messer und Gabel benutzt, meine ich. Und schließlich° hab' ich auch gefunden, daß das Essen mehr ein Ereignis° ist. Man sitzt länger° am Tisch und spricht miteinander.

25 **MONIKA:** Ja, da hast du auch wieder recht. Aber ich weiß nicht, ob das in allen Familien so ist. In vielen Familien arbeiten beide Eltern. Da bleibt auch nicht mehr so viel Zeit fürs Reden.

PETER: Ach ja, und noch etwas. Alles ist so sauber in Deutschland, aber manchmal gehen die Deutschen ein bißchen zu weit. Ich habe einmal im Dezember
30 eine Frau in Gummistiefeln° gesehen. Sie hat eine öffentliche Telefonzelle° geputzt. Das, liebe Monika, kann wohl nur in Deutschland passieren! Aber nun mal zu dir. Was hast du denn in Amerika so beobachtet?

MONIKA: Einige Sachen haben mir ausgesprochen° gut gefallen. Zum Beispiel kann man in Amerika auch abends und am ganzen Wochenende einkaufen
35 gehen. Das finde ich toll. In Deutschland gibt es den Donnerstagabend und dann nur einmal im Monat den langen Samstag.

PETER: Und was hat dir weniger° gefallen?

MONIKA: Na ja, also bitte, sei mir nicht böse. Ich finde die Amerikaner unglaublich freundlich. Das mag ja zunächst° sehr schön sein. Aber diese
40 Freundlichkeit° erscheint° mir doch sehr oberflächlich. Einmal war ich zum Beispiel beim Arzt, und die Krankenschwester hat „Monika" zu mir gesagt und nicht „Miss" oder „Ms. Berger". Sie hat mich doch gar nicht gekannt! Wir benutzen den Vornamen nur unter guten Freunden.

PETER: Das sehen wir eben° anders. Ein nettes Lächeln und ein freundliches
45 Wort im Alltag° machen das Leben eben einfacher.

Marginal glosses (right column):
- exchange student
- first / ride
- since then
- larger
- in general
- missed
- apart / therefore
- interrupted
- first of all
- finally
- event / for a long time
- rubber boots / telephone booth
- really
- less
- at first
- friendliness / appears
- simply
- everyday life

**Im Münchener
Hauptbahnhof.**

Brauchbares

1. l. 9, **"Die fahren wie die Wilden … "**: On much of the **Autobahn** there is no speed limit **(die Geschwindigkeitsbegrenzung).**

2. l. 21, **"Dann wie man ißt … "**: If only a fork or spoon is needed, the other hand rests on the table next to the plate. If both a knife and fork are used, the knife is held in the right hand all during the meal. Open-faced sandwiches are common and eaten with a knife and fork.

3. l. 40–41, **"Einmal war ich zum Beispiel beim Arzt … "**: Another example of American "friendliness" that would be rare in German culture is the supermarket cashier who greets the customer with a "Hi, how are you?", perhaps makes an additional comment, and then says, "Have a good day."

4. l. 43, **"Wir benutzen den Vornamen nur unter guten Freunden."**: Adult Germans use **du** and first names only with close friends. In some businesses there is an attempt to reduce the distance between one's associates by using first names while maintaining a certain degree of formality by addressing them with the formal **Sie.** Although students use **du** with each other immediately, it is still prudent in most situations for a foreign visitor to let a German-speaking person propose the use of the familiar **du.**

5. In l. 44 Peter says, **"Das sehen wir eben anders." Eben** is a flavoring particle that can be used by a speaker in a discussion in a final or closing statement to imply that she/he has no desire or need to discuss the point further. In other contexts it is used to support or strengthen a previous statement or idea or even to express strong agreement with what someone has said.

Nach dem Lesen

1. Fragen zum Lesestück

1. Über welche Themen haben Monika und Peter gesprochen?
2. Wie fahren die Deutschen auf der Autobahn?
3. Mit welchem Verkehrsmittel fährt Peter gern?
4. Wie sind die Züge in Deutschland?
5. Warum ist Monika in Amerika nicht gern mit dem Bus gefahren?
6. Peter findet, daß die Deutschen vielleicht zu sauber sind. Warum glaubt er das?
7. Wie ist das Einkaufen anders in Amerika?
8. Was hat Monika bei dem amerikanischen Arzt nicht gefallen?
9. Findet Peter, daß die Amerikaner zu freundlich sind?

2. Vokabelnsammeln. *(Gathering vocabulary.)* Suchen Sie Wörter und Wendungen° im Text zu den folgenden Themen:

expressions

das Essen
Verkehrsmittel
Einkaufen

3. Positives und Negatives. Peter und Monika machen Notizen über ihre Erlebnisse° im Ausland. Was steht° auf den Listen?

experiences / **steht:** stands, *here:* is

	Positives	Negatives
Peter über Deutschland		
Monika über Amerika		

4. Zur Diskussion. Sind Amerikaner freundlich oder zu freundlich? Geben Sie Beispiele, warum Ausländer sagen, daß Amerikaner freundlich sind. Geben Sie Beispiele, wann Amerikaner vielleicht oberflächlich sind.

5. Erzählen wir. Sprechen Sie über eines der folgenden° Themen. Was ist in Deutschland anders als hier? Was ist genauso wie hier?

following

Autofahren
Blumen
Essen
Einkaufen
Fernsehen
Freundlichkeit
Vornamen
Züge

Land und Leute

Freunde vs. Bekannte

Germans do not use the word **Freundin/Freund** as freely as Americans use *friend.* A **Freundin/ Freund** is a person with whom one is on intimate terms, a person who is often called "a very good friend" by Americans. Germans tend to have fewer **Freunde** and a larger circle of acquaintances **(Bekannte).** Even acquaintances of years' standing, e.g., neighbors and co-workers, do not necessarily become **Freunde.**

   Most teenagers and young adults in German-speaking countries spend their free time with a group of friends, rather than with one friend or a date. This is true for single men and women as well as for many couples in that age group. While an American college student might say

Mitarbeiter und Mitarbeiterinnen bei der Kaffeepause.

"I'm going on a date," a German student is more likely to say **Ich treffe mich mit meinen Freunden** (*I'm meeting with my friends*).

Erweiterung des Wortschatzes

1 Die Möbel und Küchengeräte°

kitchen appliances

das Wohnzimmer
1. der **Couchtisch, -e**
2. der **Schreibtisch, -e**
3. der **Sessel, -**
4. das **Sofa, -s**
5. der **Teppich, -e**

die Boxen: speakers

die Stereoanlage: record, cd, or tape player, radio

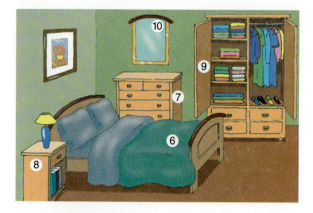

das Schlafzimmer
6. das **Bett, -en**
7. die **Kommode, -n**
8. der **Nachttisch, -e**
9. der **Schrank, -̈e**
10. der **Spiegel, -**

der Wecker: alarm clock

die Küche
11. der **Herd, -e**
12. der **Kühlschrank, -̈e**
13. die **Spülmaschine, -n**

1. Was findet man wo? You're moving. Make a list of what goes into which room. Use the items pictured above and add other things you may own. See also *Kapitel 1,* **6 Ein Studentenzimmer.**

die Küche	das Wohnzimmer	das Eßzimmer°	das Schlafzimmer

Was gibt es alles in diesem Wohnzimmer?

▷ **2. Frage-Ecke.** Various people, including your partner, have new furnishings in some rooms of their homes. Find out what they are.

S2: Was ist neu in der Küche und im Eßzimmer von Herrn Becker?
S1: In der Küche ist der Herd und im Eßzimmer der Tisch neu.

S1:

	in der Küche	im Wohnzimmer	im Eßzimmer	im Schlafzimmer
Herr Becker	Herd		Tisch	
Frau Hauff		Sofa	4 Stühle	
Andrea	Geschirr			Schreibtisch
Jens		Bücherregal		Kommode
ich				
Partnerin/ Partner				

S2:

	in der Küche	im Wohnzimmer	im Eßzimmer	im Schlafzimmer
Herr Becker		Pflanze		Schrank
Frau Hauff	Kühlschrank			Nachttisch
Andrea		Sessel	Teppich	
Jens	Spülmaschine		Bild von den Großeltern	
ich				
Partnerin/ Partner				

▷ **3. Meine Wohnung°.** Choose a room in your house or apartment and describe it to your partner. If you wish, give a few more details, e.g., size, color, new or old.

▶ *Im Schlafzimmer habe ich ein Bett, einen Schreibtisch, ein Bücherregal und eine Lampe. Der Schreibtisch ist modern und groß. Das Bücherregal ist …*

Land und Leute

Häuser und Wohnungen

Most people in German-speaking countries live in apartments, either rented (**Mietwohnung**) or owned (**Eigentumswohnung**). Inhabitants of **Mietwohnungen** share the cleaning of the stairway, attic, and basement, unless the owner has hired a superintendent (**Hausmeisterin/ Hausmeister**).

Only 41 percent of the people in western Germany and 24 percent in eastern Germany own a single family home (**Einfamilienhaus**)— compared to more than 80 percent of the people in the U.S. Even though the federal government, cities, and counties have tried to make it easier and more affordable to become a homeowner, land remains limited and expensive; construction materials and wages remain costly; planning, licensing, and building codes are complex; and mortgages still require very large down payments.

A typical house has stucco-coated walls and a tile or slate roof. Normally there is a full basement (**der Keller**) that is used primarily for storage or as a work area. The first floor (**erster Stock** or **erste Etage**) is what is usually considered the second story in American homes. The ground floor is called **das Erdgeschoß** or **Parterre**. Privacy is assured not only by closed doors but also by window curtains (**Gardinen**) and drapes (**Vorhänge**). Many homes and apartments are equipped with outdoor shutters (**Rolläden**) that unfold vertically over the windows.

In addition to the modern houses, each region of Germany has its own traditional architecture. **Fachwerkhäuser** (half-timbered houses) lend charming character to many town centers.

Einfamilienhäuser haben oft einen Garten.

2 The verbs *legen/liegen, stellen/stehen, setzen/sitzen, hängen, stecken*

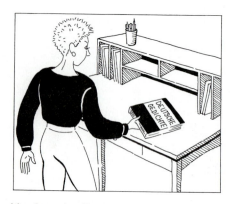

Lisa **legt** das Buch auf den Schreibtisch.

lay
(accusative)

Das Buch **liegt** auf dem Schreibtisch.

lie
(dative)

Herr Schumann **stellt** die Lampe in die Ecke°.

(handwritten: (accusative) ↓ put something in vertical position)

Die Lampe **steht** in der Ecke.

(handwritten: ↓ stands (dative))

(handwritten right margin: action is accusative! location is dative! ↓ Dative is already done)

Anna **setzt** die Katze° auf den Boden°.

(handwritten: set down (accusative))

Die Katze **sitzt** auf dem Boden.

(handwritten: sits (dative))

Felix **hängt** das Poster an die Wand.

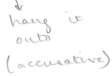

(handwritten: ↓ hang it onto (accusative))

Das Poster **hängt** an der Wand.

(handwritten: ↓ hanging (dative))

Jessica **steckt** die Zeitung in die Tasche.   Die Zeitung **steckt** in der Tasche.

[handwritten: ↓ to stick into (accusative)]   *[handwritten: sticking there (dative)]*

In English, the all-purpose verb for movement to a position is *to put,* and the all-purpose verb for the resulting position is *to be.* German uses several verbs to express the meanings *put* and *be.*

Position			
to put		*to be*	
legen, gelegt	*to lay*	liegen, gelegen	*to be lying*
stellen, gestellt	*to place upright*	stehen, gestanden	*to be standing*
setzen, gesetzt	*to set*	sitzen, gesessen	*to be sitting*
stecken, gesteckt	*to stick (into)*	stecken, gesteckt	*to be inserted (in)*
hängen, gehängt	*to hang*	hängen, gehangen	*to be hanging*

The German verbs expressing *to put* all take direct objects and are weak.

Ich **habe** das Buch auf den Tisch **gelegt.**

The German verbs expressing position *(be)* do not take direct objects and, except for **stecken,** are strong.

Das Buch **hat** auf dem Tisch **gelegen.**

4.   **Wir räumen auf.**   You and Elisabeth are straightening up your room. Describe what you do. Use the appropriate verbs from the chart above.

▶   Elisabeth _____ das Buch auf den Tisch.   *Elisabeth legt das Buch auf den Tisch.*

1. Ich _____ das Poster an die Wand.
2. Elisabeth _____ den Sessel in die Ecke.
3. Die Lampe muß über dem Tisch _____ .
4. Die Hefte _____ auf der Kommode.
5. Ich _____ das Geld in die Tasche.
6. Der Fernseher _____ unter dem Fenster.
7. Ich _____ die Schuhe in den Schrank.
8. Der Mantel _____ schon in dem Schrank.

9. Der Regenschirm _____ auch in dem Schrank.
10. Die Katze _____ auf dem Schreibtisch.
11. Elisabeth _____ die Katze auf den Boden.
12. Die Bücher müssen in dem Bücherregal _____ .
13. Ich _____ die Vase° auf das Bücherregal.

Vokabeln

Substantive

das **Ausland** (*no pl.*) foreign countries; **im Ausland** abroad
die **Autobahn, -en** freeway, expressway
der **Bahnhof, ⸚e** train station
der **Boden, ⸚** floor
die **Ecke, -n** corner
das **Eßzimmer, -** dining room
die **Gabel, -n** fork
der **Hund, -e** dog
die **Katze, -n** cat
die **Krankenschwester, -n** nurse
das **Leben, -** life
der **Löffel, -** spoon
das **Messer, -** knife

die **Möbel** (*pl.*) furniture; das **Möbelstück** piece of furniture
der **Park, -s** park
das **Restaurant, -s** restaurant
die **Sache, -n** thing; (*pl.*) clothes
das **Schlafzimmer, -** bedroom
der **Unterschied, -e** difference
die **Vase, -n** vase
das **Verkehrsmittel, -** means of transportation
der **Vorname, -ns, -n** first name
die **Wohnung, -en** dwelling, apartment
For items of furniture and kitchen appliances see pp. 251–252.

Verben

ab·fahren (fährt ab), ist abgefahren to depart (by vehicle)
an·kommen, ist angekommen (in + *dat.*) to arrive (in)
benutzen to use
beobachten to observe
hängen to hang (something), put
hängen, gehangen to be hanging
lächeln to smile
legen to lay, put (horizontal)
meinen to mean; to think, have an opinion; **was meinst du?** what do you think?

passieren, ist passiert (+ *dat.*) to happen; **was ist dir passiert?** what happened to you?
setzen to set, put
stecken to stick, put into, insert
stehen, gestanden to stand; to be located
stellen to place, put (upright)

Andere Wörter

beide both
böse (auf + *acc.*) angry (at)
eigentlich actually
einander one another, each other; **miteinander** with each other

fast almost
gar: gar nicht not at all
genauso exactly the same
nächst next
ob (*conj.*) whether, if

oberflächlich superficial
öffentlich public
pünktlich punctual
selbst oneself, myself, itself, etc.
unglaublich unbelievable

unter (+ *acc. or dat.*) under; among
weit far
zwar it's true; to be sure; indeed
zwischen (+ *acc. or dat.*) between

Besondere Ausdrücke

recht haben to be right; **Du hast
recht.** You're right.
sei [mir] nicht böse don't be mad
[at me]

was noch? what else?

GRAMMATIK UND ÜBUNGEN

1 *Hin* and *her*

Meine Tante wohnt nicht hier, sondern
  in Hamburg.
Wir fahren einmal im Jahr **hin.**
Und zweimal im Jahr kommt sie **her.**

My aunt doesn't live here, but
  rather in Hamburg.
Once a year we go *there.*
And twice a year she comes *here.*

Hin and **her** are used to show direction. **Hin** shows motion away from the
speaker, and **her** shows motion toward the speaker. **Hin** and **her** occupy last
position in the sentence.

Er war letztes Jahr in Europa. Er
  möchte wieder **dorthin.**
Kommen Sie mal **herauf.**

He was in Europe last year. He
  wants to go there again.
Come on up here.

Hin and **her** may be combined with several parts of speech, including adverbs,
prepositions, and verbs.

Woher kommen Sie?   **Wo** kommen Sie **her?**   Where are you from?
Wohin fahren Sie?   **Wo** fahren Sie **hin?**   Where are you going?

In spoken German, **hin** and **her** are often separated from **wo. Hin** and **her** occupy last position in the sentence.

1. Ilse und Axel. Ask questions about Ilse and Axel, using **wo, wohin,** or **woher.**

▶ Ilse und Axel wohnen bei München.   *Wo wohnen sie?*
▶ Sie fahren jeden Morgen nach   *Wohin fahren sie? / Wo fahren*
    München.   *sie hin?*

1. Sie arbeiten in einer Buchhandlung.
2. Sie gehen am Samstag in den Supermarkt.
3. Die Blumen kommen vom Markt.
4. Sie fahren am Sonntag in die Berge.
5. Sie wandern gern in den Bergen.
6. Nach der Wanderung gehen sie in ein Restaurant.
7. Sie essen gern im Restaurant.
8. Nach dem Essen fahren sie wieder nach Hause.
9. In den Ferien fahren sie in die Schweiz.
10. Axel kommt aus der Schweiz.

2 Two-way prepositions

Dative: **wo?**   *Accusative:* **wohin?**

Monika arbeitet **in der Küche.**
Monika is working *in the kitchen.*

Stefan kommt **in die Küche.**
Stefan comes *into the kitchen.*

German has nine prepositions that take either the dative or the accusative. The dative is used when position *(place where)* is indicated, answering the question **wo?** (e.g., **in der Küche**). The accusative is used when a change of location *(place to which)* is indicated, answering the question **wohin?** (e.g., **in die Küche**).

   In their basic meanings, the two-way prepositions are "spatial," referring to positions in space (dative) or movements through space (accusative). To distinguish place *where* from place *to which*, German uses different cases; English sometimes uses different prepositions (e.g., *in* vs. *into*).

look up prepositions!

Preposition	Meaning	*Wo?* (Preposition + dative)	*Wohin?* (Preposition + accusative)
an	on (vertical surfaces)	Das Bild hängt **an der** Wand.	Sabine hängt das Bild **an die** Wand.
	at (the side of)	Ute steht **am (an dem)** Fenster.	
	to		Benno geht **ans (an das)** Fenster.
auf	on top of (horizontal surfaces)	Kurts Buch liegt **auf dem** Tisch.	Sabine legt ihr Buch **auf den** Tisch.
	to		Ich gehe **auf den** Markt.
hinter	behind/in back of	Inge arbeitet **hinter dem** Haus.	Nils geht **hinter das** Haus.
in	in, inside (of)	Paula arbeitet **im (in dem)** Wohnzimmer.	
	into		Jürgen geht **ins (in das)** Wohnzimmer.
	to		Wir gehen **ins (in das)** Kino.
neben	beside, next to	Ritas Stuhl steht **neben dem** Fenster.	Jan stellt seinen Stuhl **neben das** Fenster.
über	over, above	Eine Lampe hängt **über dem** Tisch.	Hugo hängt eine andere Lampe **über den** Tisch.
	across (direction)		Ich gehe **über die** Straße.
unter	under	Ein Schuh steht **unter dem** Bett.	Kurt stellt den anderen Schuh **unter das** Bett.
vor	in front of	Ilses Auto steht **vor dem** Haus.	Armin fährt sein Auto **vor das** Haus.
zwischen	between	Eine Blume liegt **zwischen den** Büchern.	Judith legt noch eine Blume **zwischen die** Bücher.

3 Prepositional contractions

Er geht **ans** Fenster.	an das = **ans**	
Er steht **am** Fenster.	an dem = **am**	*not truly important as those above*
Sie geht **ins** Zimmer.	in das = **ins**	
Sie ist **im** Zimmer.	in dem = **im**	

The prepositions **an** and **in** often contract with **das** and **dem**. Other possible contractions are **aufs, hinters, hinterm, übers, überm, unters, unterm, vors,** and **vorm.**

Action = Accusative!

Location = Dative!

→ indicates dative

2. Was ist wo? Describe the picture above by completing the sentences
with appropriate prepositions, articles, and nouns.

▶ Der Hund liegt _____ . *Der Hund liegt unter dem Tisch.*

1. Der Stuhl steht _____ .
2. Die Vase steht _____ .
3. Die Bücher stehen _____ .
4. Der Tisch steht _____ .
5. Das Bild hängt _____ .
6. Die Katze sitzt _____ .
7. Der Sessel steht _____ .
8. Die Lampe hängt _____ .

→ accusative

3. Das habe ich gemacht. Tell what you did to get some of the items in the
room where they are. Complete the sentences.

▶ Ich habe das Bild _____ Wand gehängt. *Ich habe das Bild an die
Wand gehängt.*

1. Ich habe den Stuhl _____ Tisch gestellt.
2. Ich habe die Vase _____ Bücherregal gestellt.
3. Ich habe die Bücher _____ Bücherregal gestellt.
4. Ich habe den Tisch _____ Bücherregal gestellt.
5. Ich habe die Lampe _____ Tisch gehängt.
6. Ich habe den Sessel _____ Bücherregal und _____ Tür gestellt.
7. Der Hund ist _____ gegangen.
8. Die Katze ist _____ gegangen.

4. **Aufräumen.** You and your brother are getting your house ready for a guest. Answer his questions, using the cued expressions in accusative or dative.

▶ Wohin stell' ich das Radio? (auf / Nachttisch).   *Auf den Nachttisch.*

1. Wohin stell' ich die Bücher? (in / Bücherregal)
2. Wo sind meine Schuhe? (unter / Bett)
3. Wohin soll ich sie stellen? (in / Schrank)
4. Wo hängt meine Jacke? (hinter / Tür)
5. Wohin stell' ich diesen Sessel? (an / Fenster)
6. Wo soll der Teppich liegen? (vor / Sessel)
7. Wohin leg' ich die Zeitung? (auf / Schreibtisch)
8. Wohin stecke ich das Papier? (in / Tasche)
9. Wohin häng' ich den Spiegel? (an / Wand)
10. Wo soll das Bild hängen? (neben / Spiegel)

[handwritten: dative dem dem, der accusative den, das, die]

Land und Leute

Zimmertüren bleiben meistens geschlossen.

Geschlossene Türen

An American visiting a business or a home in a German-speaking country will be struck by the fact that inside doors are mostly closed. Doors to offices in American businesses, public buildings, and universities tend to be open. An open door in a German, Austrian, or Swiss firm, however, might bother the employee. Open doors imply lack of privacy. If the door has a glass pane it is usually of milk glass so that one can't see through it.

Doors also tend to be shut in private homes. When one enters a typical German home there is an entrance hall **(die Diele/der Flur).** From this hall, doors lead into the living room, kitchen, bathroom, and bedrooms. These doors remain closed so that a visitor cannot look into the rooms.

The people in German-speaking countries take their privacy seriously. They feel their privacy is violated if they can be seen or if outside noise disturbs them in their homes. Therefore, while Americans tend to solve noise problems by sound-proofing, most people in German-speaking countries observe regulations that require a quiet time around mid-day **(Ruhezeit)** and after 10 P.M. During these hours, people try not to engage in activities that might disturb the neighbors. In a country like Germany that is half the size of Texas but with a population of 80 million and where most people live in apartment houses, the need to preserve privacy is understandable.

4 *An* and *auf* = on

Der Spiegel hängt **an der Wand.** The mirror is hanging on the wall.
Mein Buch liegt **auf dem** My book is lying on the desk.
  Schreibtisch.

An and **auf** can both be equivalent to *on.* **An** = *on (the side of)* is used in reference to vertical surfaces. **Auf** = *on (top of)* is used in reference to horizontal surfaces.

5 *An, auf,* and *in* = to

Veronika geht **an** die Tür. Veronika goes to the door.
Bernd geht **auf** den Markt. Bernd goes to the market.
Lore geht **in** die Stadt. Lore goes to town.

The prepositions **an, auf,** and **in** can be equivalent to the English preposition *to.*

5. **Julia hat endlich ein Zimmer.** Julia is arranging her new room. Complete the sentences by adding the appropriate preposition **an** or **auf** and the article.

▶ Julia stellt den Schreibtisch _____ Fenster.
  Julia stellt den Schreibtisch ans Fenster.

1. Den Stuhl stellt Julia _____ Schreibtisch.
2. Sie hängt das Bild _____ Wand.
3. Sie legt die Bücher _____ Schreibtisch.
4. Der Schirm hängt _____ Tür. Das gefällt ihr nicht und sie legt ihn _____ Schrank.
5. _____ Stuhl liegt ihr Mantel. Den hängt sie _____ Tür.
6. Die Blumen stellt sie _____ Bett.
7. Und jetzt geht sie _____ Markt und kauft ein.

6. **Am Wochenende.** Susan is spending a year in Germany as an exchange student. She lives with Erika. Tell about her weekend, using the cues below.

▶ Susan / gehen / auf / Markt
  Susan geht auf den Markt.

1. auf / Markt / sie / kaufen / Blumen / für / ihr Zimmer
2. dann / sie / gehen / in / Buchhandlung
3. Erika / arbeiten / in / Buchhandlung
4. Susan / müssen / in / Drogerie
5. in / Drogerie / sie / wollen / kaufen / Kamm
6. sie / gehen / dann / in / Café
7. in / Café / sie / treffen / Erika
8. sie / sitzen / an / Tisch / in / Ecke

Study for final!!!

(accusative) Ich gehe auf die Party

(dative) Ich war auf der Party

6 Special meanings of prepositions

go to → accusative

to be in → dative

In addition to their basic meanings, prepositions have special meanings when combined with specific verbs (e.g., **denken an**, *to think of*) or with certain nouns (e.g., **Angst vor**, *fear of*). Each combination should be learned as a unit, because it cannot be predicted which preposition is associated with a particular verb or noun. The prepositions **durch, für, gegen, ohne, um** and **aus, außer, bei, mit, nach, seit, von, zu** take the accusative and dative respectively. The case of the noun following two-way prepositions must be learned. When **über** means *about/concerning*, it is always followed by the accusative case. A few combinations are given below.

denken an (+ *acc.*) Ich **denke** oft **an** meine Freunde.	*to think of/about* I often *think of* my friends.
schreiben an (+ *acc.*) Martina **schreibt an** ihren Vater.	*to write to* Martina *is writing to* her father.
studieren an/auf (+ *dat.*) Mark **studiert an/auf** der Universität München.	*to study at* Mark is *studying at* the University of Munich.
warten auf (+ *acc.*) Wir **warten auf** den Bus.	*to wait for* We're *waiting for* the bus.
helfen bei (*dative*) **Hilf** mir bitte **bei** meiner Arbeit.	*to help with* Please *help* me *with* my work.
fahren mit (*dative*) Wir **fahren mit** dem Auto nach Ulm.	*to go by (means of)* We're *going* to Ulm *by* car.
reden/sprechen über (+ *acc.*) Meine Eltern **sprechen** oft **über** das Wetter.	*to talk/speak about* My parents often *talk about* the weather.
reden/sprechen von (*dative*) Kevin **redet** wieder **von** seinem Porsche.	*to talk/speak about/of* Kevin *is talking about* his Porsche again.
schreiben über (+ *acc.*) Anna **schreibt über** ihre Arbeit.	*to write about* Anna *is writing about* her work.
halten von (*dative*) Sarah **hält** nicht viel **von** dem Plan.	*to think of, have an opinion of* Sarah doesn't *think* much *of* the plan.
Angst haben vor (+ *dat.*) Tobias **hat Angst vorm** Fliegen.	*to be afraid of* Tobias *is afraid of* flying.

7. **Mein Bruder.** Your friend Lukas is telling you about his brother. Give the English equivalents of his statements. Note especially the verb–preposition combinations.

1. Mein Bruder geht auf die Universität.
2. Oft schreibt er Briefe° an mich und meine Eltern.

letters

3. Ich denke oft an ihn, weil er mir immer bei meinen Hausaufgaben° geholfen   homework
   hat.
4. Wie oft haben wir stundenlang über Politik, Sport und Frauen gesprochen!
5. In seinem letzten Brief hat er mir von seiner Freundin Cornelia erzählt.
6. Soll ich ihm auch von meiner Freundin erzählen?

8. Was macht Dennis am Samstag?   Tell what Dennis did on Saturday by
using the phrases below with appropriate verbs. You may use more than one
phrase in a sentence. Vary the verbs as much as possible. You may also tell
what he didn't do.

▶   in die Bibliothek   *Dennis geht in die Bibliothek.*

1. in der Bibliothek *dative*
2. auf dem Markt *dative*
3. mit dem Auto *dative*
4. in die Berge *accusative*
5. in einem Café *dative*
6. auf der Autobahn *dative*
7. über Musik *accusative*
8. im Restaurant *dative*

accusative = use action verbs
dative: use (location verbs)
pg-12

9. Ein Jahr in Deutschland.   Below are some statements about Peter's stay
in Germany. Give the German equivalents.

1. Peter lives behind a supermarket.
2. There are parks in every city.
3. In the restaurants there are flowers on every table.
4. Peter goes to the university by bus.
5. He doesn't like to drive on the freeway.
6. One can buy aspirin only in the pharmacy.
7. After a meal his friends sit at the table a long time. (*Word order:* long time /
   table)
8. They talk about sports, books, and their seminar reports.

7 Time expressions in the dative

Am Montag bleibt Karla immer zu Hause.	On Monday Karla always stays home.
Philipp kommt **in** einer Woche.	Philipp's coming in a week.
Ich lese gern **am** Abend.	I like to read in the evening.
Marcel arbeitet **vor** dem Essen.	Marcel works before dinner.
Laura war **vor** einer Woche hier.	Laura was here a week ago.

With time expressions, **an, in,** and **vor** take the dative case. The use of **am** + a
day may mean *on that one day* or *on all such days.*

10.   **Wann machst du das?**   A friend is making comments about your activities. Correct her/him, using the cues provided in dative time expressions.

▶   Du arbeitest nur am Morgen, nicht? (Abend)   *Nein, nur am Abend.*

1. Frank kommt in fünf Minuten, nicht? (zwanzig Minuten) *: in*
2. Sollen wir vor dem Seminar Kaffee trinken gehen? (Vorlesung) *: vor der*
3. Du gehst am Donnerstag schwimmen, nicht? (Wochenende) *: am*
4. Du fährst am Samstag nachmittag nach Hause, nicht? (Sonntag abend) *: am*
5. Rita kommt in zwei Wochen, nicht? (eine Woche) *: in einer*
6. Du mußt die Arbeit vor dem Wintersemester fertig haben, nicht? (Sommer-semester) *: vor dem*
7. Im Sommer fährst du in die Berge, nicht? (Herbst) *: im*
8. Du gehst nur einmal im Monat in die Bibliothek, nicht? (Woche) *: in der*

8 Time expressions in the accusative

Definite point	Martin kommt **nächsten Sonntag.**	Martin is coming next Sunday.
Duration	Er bleibt **einen Tag.**	He's staying (for) one day.

Nouns expressing a definite point of time or a duration of time are in the accusative, and do not use a preposition.

11.   **Wann und wie lange?**   Michael wants to know details about the visit of a pianist. Complete the answers, using the English cues.

▶   Wann war die Pianistin in Hamburg? — Sie war *letzten Mittwoch* in Hamburg. *(last Wednesday)*

1. Wann kommt sie zu uns? — Sie kommt _____ zu uns. *(this weekend)*   *dieses Wochenende*
2. Wie lange bleibt sie? — Sie bleibt _____ . *(a day)*   *einen Tag*
3. Wie oft übt° sie? — Sie übt _____ . *(every morning)*   *jeden Morgen*
4. Wann fährt sie wieder weg°? — Sie fährt _____ wieder weg. *(next Monday)*   *nächsten Montag*   practice
5. Wann kommt sie wieder? — Sie kommt _____ wieder. *(next year)*   *nächstes Jahr*   away
6. Wie lange bleibt sie dann? — Dann bleibt sie _____ . *(a month)*   *einen Monat*

12.   **Pläne.**   Discuss weekend or vacation plans with a partner. A few suggestions for times and activities are given.

S2: Was machst du [am Wochenende]?
S1: Ich will [nichts tun].

Times: am Wochenende □ am Mittwoch □ nach dem Abendessen □
im Sommer □ in den Ferien

Activities: ins Kino gehen □ mit Freunden kochen □ lesen □
auf ein Fest gehen □ Freunde treffen □ tanzen gehen □
eine Wanderung machen

9 *Da*-compounds

Erzählt Lisa **von ihrem Freund?**	Ja, sie erzählt viel **von ihm.**
Erzählt Lisa **von ihrer Arbeit?**	Ja, sie erzählt viel **davon.**

In German, pronouns used after prepositions normally refer only to persons **(Freund).** To refer to things and ideas **(Arbeit),** a **da**-compound consisting of **da** + a preposition is generally used: **dadurch, dafür, damit,** etc. **Da-** expands to **dar-** when the preposition begins with a vowel: **darauf, darin, darüber.**

13. **Was hält Monika von Amerika?**   Monika and Peter are back in the U.S.A. Monika's friend Alex is asking about her activities and reactions in the United States. Answer Alex's questions in the affirmative. Use a **da**-compound or a preposition + a pronoun.

▶ Gefällt es Monika bei ihren amerikanischen Freunden?
   Ja, es gefällt Monika bei ihnen.
▶ Hat sie Hunger auf deutsches Brot?
   Ja, sie hat Hunger darauf.

1. Redet sie gern mit Peter?
2. Reden sie oft über kulturelle Unterschiede?
3. Hilft sie Peter oft mit seinem Deutsch?
4. Geht sie gern mit ihren Freunden essen?
5. Denkt Monika oft an zu Hause?
6. Erzählt sie gern von ihrem Leben in Deutschland?
7. Fährt sie oft mit dem Fahrrad?
8. Erzählt sie oft von ihren Freunden?

10 *Wo*-compounds

Von wem spricht Lisa?	Sie spricht **von ihrem Freund.**
Wovon (Von was) spricht Lisa?	Sie spricht **von ihrer Arbeit.**

The interrogative pronouns **wen** and **wem** are used with a preposition to refer only to persons. The interrogative pronoun **was** refers to things and ideas. As an object of a preposition, **was** may be replaced by a **wo**-compound consisting of **wo** + a preposition: **wofür, wodurch, womit,** etc. **Wo-** expands to **wor-** when the preposition begins with a vowel: **worauf, worin, worüber.** A preposition + **was (von was, für was)** is colloquial.

Matthias wohnt seit September in München.	**Seit wann** wohnt er in München?

Wo-compounds are not used to inquire about time. To inquire about time, **wann, seit wann,** or **wie lange** is used.

14. **Wie bitte?** Rolf mumbles because he's tired, so you don't hear about what or whom he is speaking. Ask what he said, using a **wo-**compound or a preposition + a pronoun to replace the boldfaced words, as appropriate.

▶ Klaus hat die Arbeit **mit dem Kugelschreiber** geschrieben.   *Womit hat er sie geschrieben?*

▶ Er hat sie **mit Annette** geschrieben.   *Mit wem hat er sie geschrieben?*

1. Susanne hat **von ihrer Vorlesung** erzählt.   Wovon hat sie erzählt?
2. Sie hat auch **von Professor Weiß** erzählt.   Von wem hat sie erzählt?
3. Udo arbeitet **für Frau Schneider.**   Für wen arbeitet er?
4. Sabine ist **mit Gerd** essen gegangen.   Mit wem ist sie essen gegangen?
5. Beim Essen hat sie **von ihrer Arbeit** erzählt.   Wovon hat sie beim Essen erzählt?
6. Nachher hat sie **mit Udo** Tennis gespielt.   Mit wem hat sie nachher Tennis gespielt?
7. Sie hat nur **über das Tennisspiel** geredet.   Worüber hat sie geredet?
8. Sie denkt nur **an Tennis.**   Woran denkt sie nur?
9. Sie wohnt jetzt wieder **bei ihren Eltern.**   Bei wem wohnt sie jetzt wieder?
10. Sie denkt nicht mehr **an eine eigene° Wohnung.** Woran denkt sie nicht mehr?   her own

15. **So bin ich.** Your partner wishes to know you better and will ask you five questions about your interests and reactions (e.g., **Woran denkst du oft?**). To prepare for this conversation complete the sentences below. Your partner will then tell a third person about your answers.

> Getting to know someone better

S2: Woran denkst du oft?
S1: Ich denke oft an die Sommerferien.
S2: [Rita/Thomas] denkt oft an die Sommerferien.

1. Ich denke oft an _____ .
2. Ich spreche gern über _____ .
3. Ich weiß viel/wenig über _____ .
4. Ich halte nicht viel von _____ .
5. Ich rede oft mit _____ .
6. Ich schreibe oft an _____ .
7. Ich habe oft Probleme mit _____ .
8. Ich muß oft über _____ lächeln.

11 Indirect questions

Direct question	Indirect question
Wann kommt Paul nach Hause?	Weißt du, **wann Paul nach Hause kommt?**
When is Paul coming home?	Do you know *when Paul is coming home?*
Kommt er vor sechs?	Ich möchte wissen, **ob er vor sechs kommt.**
Is he coming before six?	I'd like to know *whether (if) he's coming before six.*

An indirect question (e.g., **wann Paul nach Hause kommt; ob er vor sechs kommt**) is a dependent clause. It begins with a question word **(wann)** or, if there is no question word, with the subordinating conjunction **ob.** The finite verb **(kommt)** is therefore in final position.

An indirect question is introduced by an introductory clause such as:

Weißt du, … ?
Ich möchte wissen, …
Kannst du mir sagen, … ?
Ich weiß nicht, …

■ *Indirect informational questions*

Direct informational question	Wann fährt Birgit zur Uni?
Indirect informational question	Ich weiß nicht, wann Birgit zur Uni fährt.

Indirect informational questions are introduced by the same question words that are used in direct informational questions (**wer, was, wann, wie lange, warum,** etc.). The question word functions as a subordinating conjunction.

16. **Lia hat einen neuen Freund.** Barbara and Gerd are talking about Lia's new friend. Continue their conversation following the model below.

▶ BARBARA: Wie heißt er?   GERD: *Ich weiß nicht, wie er heißt.*

1. Was macht er?
2. Wie lange kennt sie ihn schon?
3. Wo wohnt er?
4. Wie alt ist er?
5. Wo arbeitet er?
6. Warum findet sie ihn so toll?
7. Wann sieht sie ihn wieder?

■ *Indirect yes/no questions*

Yes/No question	Fährt Birgit heute zur Uni?
	Is Birgit driving to the university today?
Indirect question	Weißt du, **ob** Birgit heute zur Uni fährt?
	Do you know *if/whether* Birgit is driving to the university today?

Indirect yes/no questions are introduced by the subordinating conjunction **ob.** **Ob** has the meaning of *if* or *whether* and is used with main clauses such as **Sie fragt, ob …** and **Ich weiß nicht, ob …**

■ ob *vs.* wenn

Paul fragt Birgit, **ob** sie zur Uni fährt.	Paul is asking Birgit *if/whether* she's driving to the university.
Er möchte mitfahren, **wenn** sie zur Uni fährt.	He would like to go along, *if* she's driving to the university.

Both **wenn** and **ob** are equivalent to English *if*. However, they are not interchangeable. **Wenn** begins a clause that states the condition under which some event may or may not take place. **Ob** begins an indirect yes/no question.

17. Ob Birgit zur Uni fährt? Gerd would like to drive to the university with Birgit and asks Paul whether he knows about her plans. Complete their conversation with **ob** or **wenn**.

1. GERD: Weißt du, _ob_ Birgit morgen zur Uni fährt?
2. PAUL: Ich glaube, sie fährt, _wenn_ ihr Auto wieder läuft.
3. GERD: Ich muß sie dann fragen, _ob_ das Auto wieder in Ordnung ist.
4. PAUL: Ich weiß aber nicht, _ob_ sie um acht Uhr oder erst° um neun fährt.   not till
   Weißt du, _ob_ sie manchmal mit dem Rad in die Uni fährt?
5. GERD: Nein, und ich frage mich, warum sie immer mit dem Auto fährt, _wenn_ sie immer lange suchen muß, bis sie endlich parken kann.
6. PAUL: Ich habe sie mal gefragt, _ob_ wir vielleicht zusammen mit dem Rad fahren sollen, aber ich denke, das macht sie erst°, _wenn_ ihr Auto total   only
   kaputt ist.

18. Was weißt du? Ask your partner if she/he knows the answers to questions you have about a professor. Don't hesitate to ask about your German professor.

> Seeking information

▶ Wann hat Professor [Meyer] Sprechstunde°?   office hours
  Weißt du, wann Professor [Meyer] Sprechstunde hat?

1. Wie lange arbeitet sie/er schon hier an der Uni?
2. Warum ist sie/er Hochschullehrerin/Hochschullehrer° geworden?   **Hochschul(e)** = university
3. Wo hat sie/er studiert?
4. Was interessiert sie/ihn besonders?
5. Wo wohnt sie/er?
6. Ist sie/er verheiratet°?   married
7. Hat sie/er Kinder?

Juraprofessor und Student nach einer Vorlesung an der Berliner Humboldt Universität.

WIEDERHOLUNG

1. Das hat Mark in Deutschland beobachtet. Tell about Mark's experiences in Germany, using the cued words in the perfect tense.

1. Mark / fahren / nicht gern / auf / Autobahn
2. Leute / fahren / wie die Wilden
3. viele Kinder / sehen / im Fernsehen / *Sesamstraße*
4. die vielen Blumen und Parks / gefallen / er
5. viele Leute / trinken / an / Sonntag / um vier / Kaffee
6. man / benutzen / Messer und Gabel / anders
7. man / sitzen / nach / Essen / lange / an / Tisch

2. Ferien. Complete the sentences about vacations in Germany and Switzerland, using one of the cued prepositions.

1. Im Sommer kommen viele Ausländer _____ Deutschland. (an, nach, zu)
2. Viele kommen _____ ihre Kinder. (mit, ohne, von)
3. Sie fahren natürlich _____ der Autobahn. (an, über, auf)
4. Junge Leute wandern gern _____ Freunden. (bei, ohne, mit)
5. Einige fahren _____ dem Fahrrad. (bei, an, mit)
6. Engländer fahren gern _____ die Schweiz. (an, in, nach)
7. _____ den Märkten kann man schöne Sachen kaufen. (auf, an, in)
8. Zu Hause erzählen die Engländer dann _____ ihrer Reise. (über, von, um)

3. Etwas über Musik. Answer the questions according to the cues. Use pronouns—alone or with prepositions—or **da**-compounds, as appropriate.

▶ Hast du gestern mit deiner Freundin gegessen? (Ja)
   Ja, ich habe gestern mit ihr gegessen.

▶ Habt ihr viel über Musik geredet? (Ja)
   Ja, wir haben viel darüber geredet.

1. Kennst du viel von Schönberg? (Ja)
2. Hältst du viel von seiner Musik? (Nein)
3. Möchtest du Frau Professor Koepke kennenlernen? (Ja)
4. Sie weiß viel über Schönberg, nicht? (Ja)
5. Liest sie° dieses Semester über seine Musik? (Ja)
6. Meinst du, ich kann die Vorlesung verstehen? (Nein)

Liest sie: Is she lecturing

4. Wie sagt man das? Erik Schulz goes to the University of Zürich. Tell a little about his experiences there.

1. Erik Schulz goes to the University of Zürich°.   **Universität Zürich**
2. In the summer he works for his neighbor.
3. On the weekend he goes with his girlfriend Karin to the mountains.
4. They drive her car.
5. They like to hike.
6. Afterwards they are hungry and thirsty.
7. They go to a café, where they have coffee and cake. (Use **trinken** and **essen.**)

5. Wer weiß das? Ask each of the following questions of a different member of the class and record who does or doesn't know the answers.

▶ *Mark weiß, wie die Hauptstadt der° Schweiz heißt.*   of the
▶ *Tom weiß nicht, wo Mozart gelebt hat.*

Fragen:

1. Wie heißt die Hauptstadt der Schweiz?
2. Wo hat Mozart gelebt?
3. In welchem Land liegt Konstanz?
4. In welchen Ländern machen die Deutschen gern Ferien?
5. Was trinken die Deutschen gern?
6. Wie viele Sprachen spricht man in der Schweiz?
7. Wie viele Nachbarländer hat Österreich?

6. Rollenspiel. Assume that your partner is an Austrian friend who comments on some things that strike her/him in the United States. Agree or express some doubts about her/his views, using some of the words and phrases below.

> Discussing cultural differences

Richtig. □ Genau. □ Natürlich. □ Eben. □ Du hast recht. □
Wirklich? □ Meinst du? □ Ja, vielleicht. □ Vielleicht hast du recht. □
Das finde ich gar nicht. □ Was hast du gegen [Freundlichkeit]? □
Ich sehe das ganz anders. □ Das siehst du nicht richtig.

Amerikaner sind zu freundlich. Das kann nicht echt° sein.   genuine
Das amerikanische Fernsehen ist toll.
Rock ist besser als klassische Musik.
Die Amerikaner gehen zuwenig zu Fuß.
Die Amerikaner essen zu viele Hamburger und Pommes frites.

7. Zum Schreiben

1. Choose one of the following topics and write several sentences in German, relating them to **Deutschland** and to your country.

   Blumen □ Wetter □ Autofahren □ Fernsehen □ Essen □
   Universität □ Einkaufen

2. Assume the identity of Monika Berger and write a letter to your friend Kerstin telling her about Peter Clason, the American exchange student. Some possible bits of information to include are:

   a. wo Sie Peter getroffen haben
   b. wie Peter aussieht
   c. woher er kommt
   d. worüber Sie und Peter geredet haben
   e. was Sie und Peter am Wochenende machen

Hinweise: Before beginning the writing assignments, make notes of the points you want to mention. Try to use two-way prepositions and some of the verbs that require special prepositions. Pay close attention to the case used with two-way prepositions.

For a list of other things to pay attention to when writing or reviewing your writing, see *Hinweise,* p. 235.

GRAMMATIK: ZUSAMMENFASSUNG

Hin and *her*

Komm bitte **her.**   Please come here.
Fall nicht **hin!**   Don't fall down.

Hin and **her** are used to show direction. **Hin** indicates motion in a direction away from the speaker, and **her** shows motion toward the speaker. **Hin** and **her** function as separable prefixes and therefore occupy final position in a sentence.

Komm mal **herunter!**   Come on down here.
Wann gehen wir wieder **dorthin?**   When are we going there again?

In addition to verbs, **hin** and **her** may be combined with other parts of speech such as adverbs (e.g., **dorthin**) and prepositions (e.g., **herunter**).

Two-way prepositions and their English equivalents

an	at; on; to
auf	on, on top of; to
hinter	behind, in back of
in	in, inside (of), into; to
neben	beside, next to
über	over, above; across; about
unter	under; among
vor	in front of; before; ago
zwischen	between

Nine prepositions take either the dative or the accusative. The dative is used for the meaning *place where*, in answer to the question **wo?** The accusative is used for the meaning *place to which*, in answer to the question **wohin?** The English equivalents of these prepositions may vary, depending on the object with which they are used. For example, English equivalents of **an der Ecke** and **an der Wand** are *at the corner* and *on the wall*.

Prepositional contractions

am = an dem	**im** = in dem
ans = an das	**ins** = in das

The prepositions **an** and **in** may contract with **das** and **dem**. Other possible contractions are **aufs, hinters, hinterm, übers, überm, unters, unterm, vors,** and **vorm.**

Special meanings of prepositions

Prepositions have special meanings when combined with specific verbs (e.g., **denken an**) or with certain nouns (e.g., **Angst vor**).

denken an (+ *acc.*)	to think of/about
schreiben an (+ *acc.*)	to write to
studieren an/auf (+ *dat.*)	to study at
warten auf (+ *acc.*)	to wait for
helfen bei	to help with
fahren mit	to go by (means of)
reden/sprechen über (+ *acc.*)	to talk/speak about
reden/sprechen von	to talk/speak about/of
schreiben über (+ *acc.*)	to write about
halten von	to think of, have an opinion of
Angst haben vor (+ *dat.*)	to be afraid of

Time expressions in the dative

am Montag	on Monday, Mondays
am Abend	in the evening, evenings
in der Woche	during the week
in einem Jahr	in a year
vor dem Essen	before the meal
vor einem Jahr	a year ago

In expressions of time, the prepositions **an, in,** and **vor** are followed by the dative case.

Time expressions in the accusative

Definite point	Katrin kommt **nächsten Freitag.**	Katrin is coming *next Friday.*
Duration	Sie bleibt **einen Tag.**	She's staying *(for) one day.*

Nouns expressing a definite point in time or a duration of time are in the accusative. No preposition is used in these expressions. Note that words such as **nächst** and **letzt** have endings like the endings for **dies: diesen / nächsten / letzten Monat; dieses / nächstes / letztes Jahr.**

Da-compounds

Spricht Sabrina gern **von ihrem Freund?**   Ja, sie spricht gern **von ihm.**
Spricht Sabrina oft **von der Arbeit?**   Ja, sie spricht oft **davon.**

In German, pronouns after prepositions normally refer only to persons. German uses a **da**-compound, consisting of **da** + preposition, to refer to things or ideas.

Wo-compounds

Von wem spricht Sabrina?   Sie spricht **von ihrem Freund.**
Wovon (Von was) spricht Sabrina?   Sie spricht **von der Arbeit.**

The interrogative pronoun **wen** or **wem** is used with a preposition to refer to persons. The interrogative pronoun **was** refers to things and ideas. As an object of a preposition, **was** may be replaced by a **wo**-compound consisting of **wo** + a preposition. A preposition + **was** is colloquial: **von was.**

Patrick wohnt seit September in   **Seit wann** wohnt er in München?
  München.

Wo-compounds are not used to inquire about time. To inquire about time, **wann, seit wann,** or **wie lange** is used.

Indirect questions

Weißt du, **warum** Petra heute nicht kommt?   Do you know *why* Petra isn't coming today?

Ich weiß auch nicht, **ob** sie morgen kommt.   I also don't know *if/whether* she's coming tomorrow.

An indirect question is a dependent clause. The finite verb is therefore in last position. An indirect question is introduced by an introductory clause such as: **Weißt du, … ?; Ich möchte wissen, … ; Kannst du mir sagen, … ?; Ich weiß nicht, …**

An indirect informational question begins with the same question words that are used in direct informational questions (**warum, wann, wer, was, wie lange,** etc.).

An indirect yes/no question begins with **ob. Ob** can always be translated as *whether.*

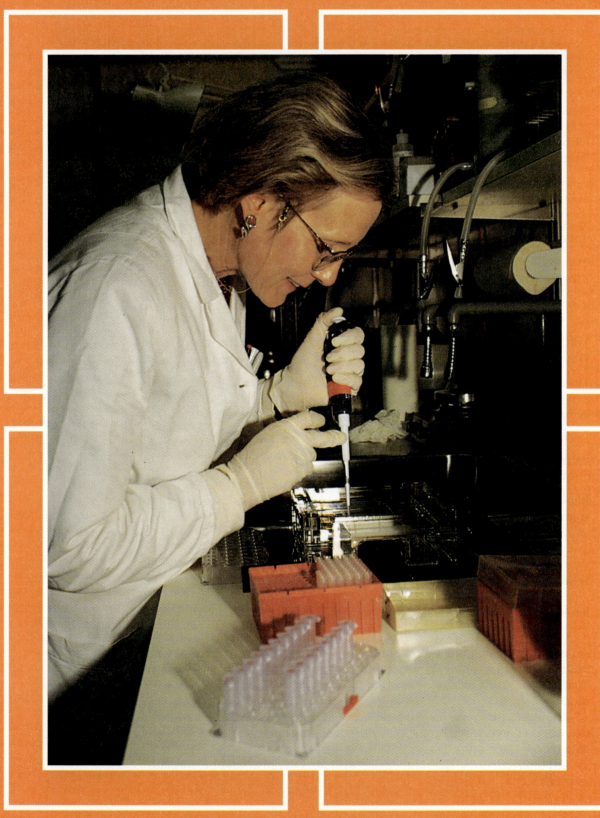

Naturwissenschaftlerin im Basler Institut für Immunologie. (Schweiz)

Kapitel 9

L E R N Z I E L E

■ **Sprechintentionen**

Telling about one's qualifications for a job
Talking about future goals
Discussing friends and family
Describing things
Stating wants/desires
Asking for personal information

■ **Lesestück**

Zwei Frauenporträts

■ **Land und Leute**

Two female German film directors
Women honored on German bank notes
Milestones in the progress toward equal rights for women
German federal policy toward women
Women in the workforce

■ **Vokabeln**

Professions
Word families
Noun suffixes *-heit* and *-keit*

■ **Grammatik**

Genitive case
Adjectives
Ordinal numbers
Dates

BAUSTEINE FÜR GESPRÄCHE

Ein Ferienjob

PERSONALCHEFIN: Herr Ohrdorf, Sie studieren jetzt im achten Semester Informatik und wollen drei Monate bei uns arbeiten.

HERR OHRDORF: Ja, richtig.

PERSONALCHEFIN: Haben Sie schon als Informatiker gearbeitet?

HERR OHRDORF: Ja, ich habe letztes Jahr auch einen Ferienjob gehabt, und da habe ich ganz gute praktische Erfahrungen gesammelt.

PERSONALCHEFIN: Und was wollen Sie später damit machen?

HERR OHRDORF: Ich möchte eine Stelle bei einer Bank, eine Aufgabe mit viel Verantwortung, hoffe ich.

A summer job

Mr. Ohrdorf, you're now in your eighth semester of computer science and want to work here for three months.

Yes, that's right.

Have you already worked as a computer specialist?

Yes, I also had a summer job last year and I got some good practical experience there.

And what do you want to do with it later on?

I would like a position with a bank, an assignment with lots of responsibility, I hope.

Fragen*

1. Was studiert Herr Ohrdorf? Warum?
2. Was für einen Ferienjob hat er schon einmal gehabt?
3. Wie hat der Job ihn auf die neue Stelle vorbereitet?
4. Wo möchte er später eine Stelle finden?
5. Was erwartet° er von dieser Stelle?

Der Computer ist nur die Maschine. Erst die Software ist das Werkzeug, das den Computer zum Arbeitsgerät macht.

Wir führen Programme für die meisten Einsatzgebiete eines Personalcomputers.

HANNES KELLER
COMPUTERZENTRUM AG
EIDMATTSTRASSE 36
8032 ZÜRICH
TELEFON 01 69 36 33

*Reminder: Words appearing with a raised degree mark but no definition in the margin are new "active" words that you should learn and be able to use. These words and their definitions appear in the **Vokabeln** section that most closely follows the exercise.

1. Eine neue Stelle. Take the part of one of the participants in a job interview. The interviewee should decide beforehand what she/he knows.

Talking about one's qualifications for a job

S1 (Personalchefin/Personalchef):

S2 (Bewerberin/Bewerber)°: applicant

Können Sie | **Schreibmaschine schreiben°?**
mit Wortprozessoren arbeiten°?
mit dem Computer arbeiten?

Ja. Sehr gut.
Nein, tut mir leid.

Haben Sie schon praktische Erfahrung als Informatikerin/Informatiker?

Ja, | **ich habe bei einer kleinen Firma gearbeitet.**
ich habe letztes Jahr einen Ferienjob gehabt.

Warum wollen Sie die Stelle wechseln°?

Ich möchte | **neue Erfahrungen sammeln.**
mehr Verantwortung bekommen.
mehr verdienen.
bei einer großen Firma arbeiten.
Ich finde die Arbeit nicht mehr interessant.

2. Berufe°. Ask four fellow students what profession they would like to pursue. For additional professions, see Supplementary Word Sets in the Reference Section.

professions

Talking about future goals

S1: Was möchtest du werden?
S2: Ich möchte [Ingenieurin/Ingenieur] werden.
S1: Ich [arbeite gern mit Maschinen°].

der **Lehrer**/die **Lehrerin**

die **Journalistin**/der **Journalist**

die **Geschäftsfrau**/
der **Geschäftsmann**

der **Rechtsanwalt/**
die **Rechtsanwältin**

der **Musiker/**die **Musikerin**

die **Ärztin/**der **Arzt**

der **Informatiker/**die **Informatikerin**

der **Zahnarzt/**die **Zahnärztin**

die **Politikerin/**der **Politiker**

die **Architektin/**der **Architekt**   der **Ingenieur/**die **Ingenieurin**

---

3. Wo möchten Sie lieber arbeiten – in einem Büro oder im Freien°?   outdoors

Answer the following questions for yourself and then compare your answers
with those of your classmates.

1. Was studierst du?
2. Arbeitest du lieber allein oder mit anderen zusammen?
3. Wo möchtest du lieber arbeiten? In einem Büro oder im Freien?
4. Wie soll die Arbeit sein? Interessant? Leicht°? Schwer?

5. Wie wichtig ist dir das Geld? Ein sicherer° Arbeitsplatz?
6. Kannst du mit einem Computer arbeiten?
7. Kannst du mit Wortprozessoren arbeiten?
8. Tippst° du deine Arbeiten selbst?

Using the information from your answers to the above questions, choose professions you might like to pursue and tell your classmates why you think your choices are appropriate.

4. Stellenangebote. *(Job opportunities.)* Look through the ads for jobs and answer the questions. If you need help to get the gist, see Vocabulary for Authentic Text Activities in the Reference Section.

1. Welche Stellen sind für eine Studentin/einen Studenten praktisch?
2. Welche Stelle ist nicht in Deutschland?
3. Welche Stellen sind nur für eine Frau? Für eine Frau oder einen Mann? Woher wissen Sie das? Was halten Sie davon?

Kindermädchen

f. 3jhr. Zwillingsmädchen von italienischer Familie auf dem Lande gesucht. Separates Zimmer mit Bad. Bewerbung mit Lebenslauf, Foto und Zeugnissen an **G. Vrafino, 10034 Boschetto-Chivasso (Turin)**

Wir suchen im Raum Südosten eine/n tüchtige/n u. aufgeschlossene/n

Elektroinstallateur/in

Muß selbständig arbeiten können.

Elektro Hiering, ☎ 6116659

Studentenjob

Taxifahrer/in auch als Festfahrer/Aushilfen. Gute Konditionen, Ausbildung im Schnellkurs.

☎ **4484770, 17-19 U.**

Exportfirma sucht ab sofort eine/n

Sekretär/in

mit Sprachkenntnissen in Italienisch u. Englisch. Zuschr. u. ✉ ZS9800194

Wir suchen für unser Fotofachlabor eine/n

Fotolaborant/in

ganz- od. halbtags, auf Wunsch Schichtdienst. ☎ **47 20 91**

⇨ **5. Eine neue Stelle.**   Work in two groups of three. One group works in an employment agency that has been asked to interview applicants for the positions advertised. Choosing one ad from the ones in this chapter, the group decides which skills and qualifications are important for the job and develops questions for a job interview, using the questions in exercises 1 and 3 but developing its own questions as well. The group then holds interviews with three people from the other group, who act as applicants. The employment agency group decides whom it will hire and why.

Land und Leute

Margarethe von Trotta, Filmregisseurin.

Zwei Filmregisseurinnen

Two of Germany's leading film directors are women—Margarethe von Trotta (b. 1942) and Doris Dörrie (b. 1955). Von Trotta's stature as a director was given additional recognition during the 45th **Internationale Filmfestspiele** in Berlin **(die Berlinale)** in 1995, which celebrated the 100th anniversary of the movies. Her movie, *Das Versprechen* (The Promise), opened the festival. Although von Trotta now resides in Italy, her films are "German" with German themes. The plot of *Das Versprechen* is an East German–West German love story that culminates in the night of the fall of the Berlin Wall on November 9, 1989. Many of her movies make political statements.

Dörrie's *Keiner liebt mich* was also a box office hit in 1995. Dörrie had made a name for herself with her early movie *Männer*, a clever and amusing story that nevertheless is critical of traditional gender roles. She has continued to fulfill the promise of *Männer* with many well-received movies since.

Doris Dörrie, Filmregisseurin.

Vokabeln

Substantive

der **Arbeitsplatz, ˸e** job, position; workplace
der **Architekt, -en, -en**/die **Architektin, -nen** architect
die **Aufgabe, -n** assignment; task, set of duties; die **Hausaufgaben** homework
die **Bank, -en** bank
der **Beruf, -e** profession, occupation
der **Chef, -s**/die **Chefin, -nen** boss
die **Erfahrung, -en** experience
das **Geschäft, -e** store; business

die **Geschäftsfrau, -en** businesswoman/der **Geschäftsmann, -leute** businessman
die **Informatik** computer science
der **Informatiker, -/**die **Informatikerin, -nen** computer specialist
der **Ingenieur, -e**/die **Ingenieurin, -nen** engineer
der **Journalist, -en, -en**/die **Journalistin, -nen** journalist

der **Lehrer, -**/die **Lehrerin, -nen**
   teacher
die **Maschine, -n** machine
der **Musiker, -**/die **Musikerin, -nen**
   musician
der **Personalchef, -s**/die
   Personalchefin, -nen head of the
   human resources (personnel)
   department
der **Politiker, -**/die **Politikerin, -nen**
   politician
der **Rechtsanwalt, -anwälte**/die
   Rechtsanwältin, -nen lawyer,
   attorney

die **Schreibmaschine, -n** typewriter;
   Schreibmaschine schreiben
   können to be able to type
die **Stelle, -n** position, job; place
die **Verantwortung** responsibility
der **Wortprozessor, -en** word processor; **mit dem Wortprozessor**
   arbeiten to do word processing
der **Zahnarzt, ¨e**/die **Zahnärztin,**
   -nen dentist

Verben

erwarten to expect
hoffen to hope
sammeln to collect
tippen to type; **er tippt seine**
   Arbeiten he types his papers

verdienen to earn
wechseln to change

Besondere Ausdrücke

bei einer Firma arbeiten to work
   for a company; **bei [Siemens]**
   arbeiten to work for [Siemens]
mit dem Computer arbeiten to do
   work (on) a computer

mit Wortprozessoren arbeiten to do
   word processing

Andere Wörter

best- (-er, -es, -e) best
leicht light; easy
sicher safe; secure; certain(ly)

**Dieser Informatiker
arbeitet bei der Firma
Hewlett-Packard in
Sindelfingen.**

ZWEI FRAUENPORTRÄTS

Vorbereitung auf das Lesen

■ *Vor dem Lesen*

1. Machen Sie eine Liste von berühmten Frauen. Nennen Sie mindestens°   at least
   eine Naturwissenschaftlerin° und eine Dichterin°. Welche berühmten   natural scientist / poet
   deutschen Frauen kennen Sie?
2. In der deutschen Verfassung° steht: „Männer und Frauen sind gleich-
   berechtigt°." Was verstehen Sie persönlich unter „gleichberechtigt"?
       Welche der folgenden Ideen sind wichtig für die Gleichberechtigung°?
   Welche nicht?

   a. Männer und Frauen sind gleich.
   b. Männer und Frauen sollen das gleiche Gehalt° für die gleiche Arbeit   salary
      bekommen.
   c. Männer sollen bei der Hausarbeit helfen.
   d. Frauen müssen berufstätig° sein.
   e. Gleichberechtigung ist nur für Frauen.

■ *Beim Lesen*

Dieser Text beschreibt° zwei deutsche Frauen. Eine ist berufstätig, die andere
ist Hausfrau°. Machen Sie Notizen zu diesen Fragen:

1. In welchen Punkten° sind die Frauen gleich?
2. In welchen Punkten sind sie ungleich? Denken Sie dabei an ihr Alter°, ihre   age
   Arbeit, ihre Familie.

In der deutschen Verfassung heißt es: „Männer und Frauen sind gleichberechtigt." (ARTIKEL 3,2) Die Verfassung ist also klar und eindeutig°. Da gibt   unambiguous
es kein Wenn und Aber. Aber die Wirklichkeit ist etwas komplizierter. Hier
sind zwei Beispiele von zeitgenössischen° Frauen in Deutschland.   contemporary

GISELA ANTON – Ehefrau°, Mutter, Physikerin, Privatdozentin°   wife / lecturer (not on tenure track)

5   Dr. Gisela Anton ist Privatdozentin für Physik an der Universität Bonn. 1994
hat sie den Leibniz-Preis° bekommen, und das bedeutet, daß sie für die näch-   prize
sten drei Jahre Forschungsgelder° in Höhe von° drei Millionen Mark für ihre   research money / **in Höhe von**: in the sum of / **besteht aus**: consists of / recipe for success
Arbeit hat. Gisela Antons Stelle besteht nicht nur aus° Schreibtischarbeit. Das
Erfolgsrezept° der Wissenschaftlerin ist Spaß an der Arbeit. „Das ist ganz
10   wichtig. Die Motivation gehört dazu. Die Physik ist schon ein hartes Studium.
Aber wenn man Motivation hat, und es macht Freude, das wird schon laufen°."   **das ... laufen**: it'll work
    Die 40jährige° Physikerin hat drei Kinder. Ihr Mann ist auch Physiker, aber   40-year-old
nicht an der Universität. Er arbeitet in der Industrie. Zum Glück wohnen Frau

Antons Eltern im gleichen Haus. Tagsüber° passen sie auf die Kinder auf.
15 Trotzdem ist die Doppelrolle für Gisela Anton nicht einfach: „Beruf und Familie
unter einen Deckel° zu kriegen, ist sicher eine der schwierigsten Komponenten
für Frauen. Ich arbeite ca.° 45 Stunden in der Woche im Institut und abends
und am Wochenende zu Hause. Auch wenn ich am Kochtopf° stehe, geht mir
die Physik durch den Kopf°."

during the day

*unter ... Deckel: under one
hat / **ca.** = circa:
approximately / **am
Kochtopf:** at the stove
head*

20   Oft aber geben Frauen ihren Beruf für ihre Familie auf, um Hausfrau und
Mutter zu sein. Unser nächstes Beispiel illustriert so einen Fall°.

case

HELGA KRAUSS – Ehefrau, Hausfrau, Krankenschwester, Mutter

„In der Zeitung habe ich gelesen: Eine Hausfrau arbeitet 75 Stunden in der
Woche", sagt die 58jährige Hausfrau Helga Krauß. „Das ist sicher richtig, denn
man hat ja nicht nur den Haushalt – die Kinder, das Kochen, das Putzen, das
25 Waschen, den Mann, den Garten – die meisten Frauen meiner Generation
helfen ihren Männern auch oft im Geschäft." Helga Krauß ist gelernte°
Krankenschwester. Ihr Mann ist Arzt. Sie haben vier Kinder. Wegen der Kinder
ist sie zu Hause geblieben und hat ihren Beruf als Krankenschwester aufgegeben. „Heute mache ich zum Beispiel die Buchhaltung° für die Praxis°
30 meines Mannes. Außerdem bin ich nicht nur Hausfrau und Mutter, sondern
auch Großmutter. Meine Tochter und auch meine Schwiegertochter° sind beide
berufstätig. Und tagsüber passe ich auf die Kinder auf. Die beiden jungen
Frauen haben lange nach einem Kindergartenplatz für ihre Kinder gesucht. Sie
haben jedoch keinen gefunden, denn sie sind verheiratet. Kindergartenplätze
35 gibt es fast nur für alleinstehende° Mütter und sehr wenige für verheiratete
Mütter mit berufstätigen Männern."

trained

bookkeeping / practice

daughter-in-law

single

Im Beruf gibt es also eine Entwicklung° zu mehr Gleichberechtigung. Das ist
gar keine Frage. Vor der Frauenbewegung° der 70er Jahre waren weniger
Frauen in akademischen° Berufen. Und sobald sie Kinder bekamen°, haben die
40 Frauen oft ihren Beruf aufgegeben. Ein Beispiel dafür ist Helga Krauß. Heute
aber wollen immer mehr Frauen im Beruf bleiben oder wieder in den Beruf
zurückgehen, wenn die Kinder ein bißchen älter° sind. Für Gisela Anton ist es
immer klar gewesen, daß sie auch als Mutter weiter an der Universität arbeitet.
Sie ist jedoch trotz ihres Erfolges° keine Professorin, sondern Privatdozentin.
45 An den deutschen Universitäten gibt es noch sehr wenig wirkliche Gleichberechtigung. Zwar sind über 43% aller Studierenden° Frauen, aber nur 5,5%
sind Professorinnen. Frauen werden nicht so schnell zu Professorinnen wie
ihre männlichen° Kollegen.
      Konkret heißt das: Frauen sind heute zwar in der Wahl° eines Berufes frei
50 und gleichberechtigt, doch wenn sie Familie haben, ist ihre Freiheit oft illu-
sorisch°. Sie haben fast immer mehr Arbeit als ihre Kollegen und Ehemänner°.
Denn die Statistik zeigt, daß nur jeder dritte Mann seiner Frau regelmäßig° im
Haushalt und mit den Kindern hilft.

development
women's movement
*professional / **Kinder
bekamen:** had children*

older

success

students

male

choice

illusory / husbands
regularly

Brauchbares

1. l. 1, **Verfassung:** The general word for *constitution* is **Verfassung.** Germany's constitution is called **"Das Grundgesetz."**

2. l. 6, **Leibniz-Preis:** The prize is named in honor of Gottfried Wilhelm Leibniz or Leibnitz (1646–1716), a German philosopher and mathematician. He developed the infinitesimal calculus (1675–76) independently of Newton, and published his work three years before Newton.

3. l. 34, **Kindergartenplätze:** In Germany only 79% of children over the age of 3 are in publicly financed day care facilities, compared to 100% in France, 95% in Belgium, and 92% in Italy. In Germany only 3% of children under the age of 3 are in day care facilities. In Denmark it is 48% and in France 20%.

4. l. 50, **doch:** Besides being a flavoring particle, **doch** also means *but still, yet.* It emphasizes a contrast to a previous statement.

Nach dem Lesen

1. Fragen zum Lesestück

1. Beschreiben Sie Gisela Anton: ihren Beruf, ihre Familie, ihre Arbeit zu Hause.
2. Welche Bedeutung° hat der Leibniz-Preis für Gisela Anton?   significance
3. Warum ist es ein Glück, daß Giselas Eltern im gleichen Haus wohnen?
4. Woran denkt Gisela beim Kochen?
5. Warum geben manche Frauen ihren Beruf auf?
6. Beschreiben Sie Helga Krauß: ihren Beruf, ihre Familie, ihre Arbeit zu Hause.
7. Wie steht es mit der Gleichberechtigung an vielen deutschen Universitäten?
8. Warum ist die Freiheit der Berufswahl° für Frauen oft illusorisch?   choice of occupation
9. Wie hat die Frauenbewegung das Leben der Frauen in Deutschland verändert°?   changed

2. Was machen Gisela Anton und Helga Krauß? Suchen Sie die Stellen im Text, die° die Arbeit der beiden Frauen beschreiben. Dann beschreiben Sie ihre Arbeit: which

1. Was machen die zwei Frauen tagsüber?
2. Welche Arbeit finden Sie interessanter°? Warum?   more interesting
3. Welche Arbeit finden Sie schwerer°? Warum?   more difficult
4. Hat die eine Frau mehr Arbeit als die andere?

3. Probleme der Frauen. Suchen Sie Informationen im Text zum Thema Kinder und der Doppelrolle der Frau. Beantworten Sie dann die Fragen:

1. Was bedeutet im Text Doppelrolle?
2. Welche Probleme haben berufstätige Frauen in Deutschland?

4. Erzählen wir. Sprechen Sie etwa eine Minute über eines der folgenden
Themen:

Die Doppelrolle der Frau
Die Arbeit von Frauen heute
Eine Frau, die° ich kenne   whom

Land und Leute

Vier berühmte Frauen

When Germany introduced new bank notes
(1990–1992), it chose to honor four great
women of its history: one musician, one scientist, and two authors. Clara Wieck (1819–1896),
who later married Robert Schumann and whose
portrait is on the 100 DM-note, performed her
first concert at the age of nine. In the course
of her career her interpretation of classical and
romantic piano pieces (including works by her
husband Robert Schumann) set the standard
for several decades. She also gained fame as
a composer and teacher.

On the 500 DM-note is the portrait of the
artist and biologist, Maria Sibylla Merian
(1647–1717). Merian wrote and illustrated
several volumes of natural history; her main
interest was the insect world.

Two writers, Bettina von Arnim (1785–1859)
and Annette von Droste-Hülshoff (1797–1848)
are represented on the 5 DM-note and 20 DM-
note, respectively. Von Arnim was a writer in
the Romantic period who was also active in
the political life of her time. Droste-Hülshoff
wrote poems and novellas **(Novellen)** that are
recognized as among the best of the nine-
teenth-century realist literature.

**Annette von Droste-Hülshoff
(1797–1848).**

**Clara Wieck Schumann
(1819–1896).**

**Bettina von Arnim
(1785-1859).**

Erweiterung des Wortschatzes

1 Word families

arbeiten	*to work*
die **Arbeit**	*the work*
der **Arbeiter**/die **Arbeiterin**	*the worker*

Like English, German has many words that belong to families and are derived from a common root.

1. Noch ein Wort. Complete the sentence with a related word and give the meanings for all the boldfaced words.

1. München hat 1,3 Millionen **Einwohner.** Viele Münchner _____ in kleinen **Wohnungen.**
2. —Haben Sie Zeit für ein **Gespräch?** Ich muß mit Ihnen _____ .
   —Auf Deutsch? Oh, das ist so eine schwere **Sprache.**
3. Der **Koch** und die **Köchin** in diesem Restaurant benutzen nie ein **Kochbuch,** aber sie _____ sehr gut.
4. Auf unserer **Wanderung** haben wir viele **Wanderer** getroffen. Der **Wanderweg** war schön. Wir _____ wirklich gern.
5. —Ich muß jetzt zum **Flughafen.**
   —Wann geht dein **Flugzeug?**
   —Ich _____ um 10 Uhr 30.
6. In dieser **Bäckerei backen** sie gutes Brot. Ich finde, der _____ macht auch guten Kuchen.

2 Noun suffixes *-heit* and *-keit*

die **Freiheit**	*freedom*	die **Wirklichkeit**	*reality*
frei	*free*	**wirklich**	*really*

Nouns ending in **-heit** and **-keit** are feminine nouns. Many nouns of this type are related to adjectives. The suffix **-keit** is used with adjectives ending in **-ig** or **-lich**.

2. Dieses Wetter! Complete Sandra's comments about the weather by using a noun ending in **-heit** that is related to the boldfaced adjective.

1. Der Garten ist sehr **trocken.** Wie lange dauert° diese _____ noch?   lasts
2. Dieses Wetter ist nicht **gesund.** Es ist nicht gut für die _____ .
3. Ich werde ganz **krank.** Hoffentlich ist es keine ernste _____ .
4. Aber die Natur ist immer **schön.** Mir gefällt ihre _____ .
5. In der Natur lebt man **frei.** Da ist die _____ groß.

3. Was für ein Mensch ist Johann? Tell what Johann is like by using a noun ending in **-keit** that is related to the boldfaced adjective.

1. Für Johann muß alles **natürlich** sein. Auch bei Mädchen findet er _____ besonders schön.
2. Johann ist besonders **freundlich.** Die Mädchen mögen seine _____ .
3. Er findet es **wichtig,** daß man sehr nett ist. Es ist für ihn von großer_____ .

Land und Leute

Gleichberechtigung: Wichtige Daten

A few milestones in the progress of women toward equality:

1901   German universities begin to admit women.

1918   German women receive the right to vote and to be elected to parliament.

1949   The Basic Law of the Federal Republic **(Grundgesetz)** guarantees the right of a person to decide on her or his role in society.

1955   The Federal Labor Court **(Bundesarbeitsgericht)** states that there should be no discrimination on the basis of sex in compensation for work performed.

1977   Women and men are judged by law to be equal in a marriage. Either can take the surname of the other, or a combination of both names. A divorce may now be granted on the principle of irreconcilability rather than guilt, and all pension rights that the spouses accrued during marriage are equally divided.

1979   Women are entitled to a six-month leave to care for a newborn child. By 1990 the leave-time had increased to 12 months and was available to women or men.

1980   The law prohibits sex discrimination in hiring practices, wages, working conditions, opportunities for advancement, and termination policies.

Vielleicht hat diese Mutter Erziehungsurlaub genommen.

1986   Years spent raising children are included in the calculation of retirement pensions.

1991   Women have the option of keeping their maiden names. Children may have the name of either parent.

1993   Either parent may stay home to care for a child until the child turns three years old.

Vokabeln

Substantive

der **Beruf, -e** profession, occupation
die **Freiheit** freedom
die **Freude, -n** pleasure; **Freude machen** to give pleasure
die **Gleichberechtigung** equal rights
das **Glück** luck; **zum Glück** fortunately
die **Hausfrau, -en** housewife
der **Haushalt** household; **den Haushalt machen** to take care of the house
die **Industrie, -n** industry
der **Kindergarten, ̈** nursery school
der **Kollege, -n, -n**/die **Kollegin, -nen** colleague

der **Physiker, -**/die **Physikerin, -nen** physicist
der **Punkt, -e** point
der **Spaß, ̈e** enjoyment; fun; joke; **an der Arbeit Spaß haben** to enjoy one's work; **das macht Spaß** that is fun
die **Verfassung, -en** constitution
die **Wirklichkeit** reality
die **Wissenschaft, -en** science
der **Wissenschaftler, -**/die **Wissenschaftlerin, -nen** scientist

Verben

auf·geben (gibt auf), aufgegeben to give up
auf·passen to watch out; **aufpassen auf** + *acc.* to take care of
bedeuten to mean

beschreiben, beschrieben to describe
lehren to teach
nennen, genannt to name
zeigen to show

Andere Wörter

berufstätig employed
berühmt famous
doch but still, yet
dritt- (-er, -es, -e) third
gleichberechtigt having equal rights
hart hard; difficult
jedoch *(conj. or adv.)* however
kompliziert complicated
schlank slender
schwierig difficult

sobald *(conj.)* as soon as
trotz (+ *gen.*) in spite of
trotzdem nevertheless
verheiratet married
wegen (+ *gen.*) on account of, because of

Besondere Ausdrücke

das heißt that means
es heißt it says
immer mehr more and more

Land und Leute

Frauenpolitik

In Germany federal policy concerning women **(Frauenpolitik)** covers a number of areas in women's lives. One aim is to help both women and men reconcile their professional and personal lives. In recent years opportunities for flexible work hours, part-time work **(Teilzeitbeschäftigung)** with full benefits, or sharing jobs have improved. Many single mothers receive financial aid, and every woman has the right to a maternity leave of six weeks preceding and eight weeks after the birth of the child while receiving her full salary **(Mutterschutz)**, the cost of which is shared by the government and her employer. Another benefit is the child-rearing leave **(Erziehungsurlaub)**, which allows either parent to stay home until the child turns three. During that time the parent on leave receives DM 600 monthly **(Erziehungsgeld)** for the first six months. After that the amount depends on the

Diese Frau hat Recht auf sechs Wochen Schwangerschaftsurlaub.

parents' income and is paid for up to two years. Mothers with no outside job are also entitled to receive this support. Mothers-to-be receive a "family benefit" **(Familiengeld)** of DM 1,000, of which the mother receives DM 500 six weeks before the birth of the child and an additional DM 500 after the birth.

GRAMMATIK UND ÜBUNGEN

1 Genitive case

■ *Showing possession and close relationships*

Ich habe mit dem Sohn **des Bäckers** gesprochen.	I talked to *the baker's* son.
Das ist die Frage **eines Kindes.**	That is *a child's* question.
Die Farbe **der Wände** gefällt mir.	I like the color *of the walls.*

English shows possession or other close relationships by adding *'s* to a noun or by using a phrase with *of*. English generally uses the *'s* form only for persons. For things and ideas, English uses the *of*-construction.

German uses the genitive case to show possession or other close relationships. The genitive is used for things and ideas as well as for persons. The genitive generally follows the noun it modifies **(die Frage eines Kindes).**

die Freundin **von meinem Bruder** (meines Bruders)
zwei **von ihren Freunden** (ihrer Freunde)
ein Freund **von Thomas** (Thomas' Freund)

In spoken German the genitive of possession is frequently replaced by **von** + *dative.*

ein Freund **von mir**
ein Freund **von Nicole**

Von + *dative* is also used in phrases similar to the English *of mine, of Nicole,* etc.

■ *Masculine and neuter nouns*

Hast du den Namen **des Kindes** verstanden?	Did you understand *the child's name?*
Das ist die Meinung **meines Professors.**	That is *my professor's* opinion.

Masculine and neuter nouns of one syllable generally add **-es** in the genitive; nouns of two or more syllables add **-s.** The corresponding articles, **der**-words, and **ein**-words end in **-es** in the genitive.

■ *Masculine N-nouns*

Die Frau **des Herrn** da kommt aus Österreich.	The wife *of the man* there is from Austria.
Haben Sie die Frage **des Jungen** verstanden?	Did you understand *the boy's* question?

Masculine nouns that add **-n** or **-en** in the accusative and dative singular also add **-n** or **-en** in the genitive. A few masculine nouns add **-ns: des Namens.**

For a list of masculine **N**-nouns, see Reference Section, Grammatical Tables, #9.

1. **Wie sagt man das?**   Give the German equivalents, using the genitive case.

   1. the man's plan
   2. the color of the house
   3. the car of the year
   4. the child's bicycle
   5. the boy's story
   6. Mr. Schmidt's car
   7. the name of the country
   8. the color of the shirt

■ *Feminine and plural nouns*

Die Farbe **der Bluse** gefällt mir.	I like the color *of the blouse.*
Schmidts sind Freunde **meiner Eltern.**	Schmidts are friends *of my parents.*

Feminine and plural nouns do not add a genitive ending. The corresponding articles, **der**-words, and **ein**-words end in **-er** in the genitive.

2. Hast du die Adresse? Your friend is getting settled near where you live and needs the addresses of various places. Help her/him.

▶ Kennst du eine Apotheke? *Hier ist die Adresse einer Apotheke.*

1. Kennst du eine Bäckerei?
2. Und eine Metzgerei?
3. Wo ist eine Drogerie?
4. Gibt es hier eine Buchhandlung?
5. Wo ist die Bibliothek?

■ *The interrogative pronoun* **wessen?**

Wessen CD-Spieler ist das?   *Whose CD player is that?*
Wessen CDs sind das?   *Whose CD's are those?*

The question word to ask for nouns or pronouns in the genitive is **wessen.** It is the genitive form of **wer** and is equivalent to English *whose.*

■ *Possessive adjectives*

Theresa ist die Freundin **meines Bruders.**

Theresa is *my brother's* girlfriend.

Hast du die Telefonnummer **seiner Freundin?**

Do you have *his girlfriend's* telephone number?

Possessive adjectives take the case of the noun they modify. Even though a possessive adjective already shows possession (**mein** = my, **sein** = his), it must itself be in the genitive case when the noun it goes with is in the genitive (**meines Bruders** = of my brother); **die Freundin meines Bruders** shows *two* possessive relationships.

3. Wessen Telefonnummer ist das? Answer the questions using the genitive case. Follow the model.

▶ meine Eltern   *Wessen Telefonnummer ist das?*
              Das ist die Telefonnummer meiner Eltern.

1. meine Tante
2. sein Bruder
3. ihr Freund Mark
4. seine Schwester
5. ihre Großeltern
6. unser Nachbar

4. Eine Fußballmannschaft plant ihr Jahresfest. A soccer team is planning its anniversary celebration and everybody's talking at once. Restate the sentences, replacing the genitive expressions with the genitive form of the cued words.

▶ KEVIN: Der Termin° des Festes ist   *Der Termin der Party ist*   date
      nächsten Samstag. (die Party)   *nächsten Samstag.*

1. MARTIN: Wie ist die Adresse des Biergartens? (das Café)
2. DOMINIK: Kennst du die Ideen seiner Freundin? (unser Nachbar)
3. STEFAN: Wie heißt die Freundin deines Bruders? (deine Schwester)
4. ALEX: Kennst du den Namen dieser Firma? (dieses Geschäft)
5. MARIO: Das ist die Telefonnummer meines Vetters. (meine Kusine)
6. PATRICK: Ich hole dich mit dem Auto meines Vaters ab. (meine Mutter)

5. Wer ist das? Take turns with your partner asking her/him to identify the relationship you describe.

S1: Wer ist der Vater meines Vaters?
S2: Dein Großvater.

S2: Wer ist die Tochter meines Bruders?
S1: Deine Nichte.

S1: Wer sind die Kinder meiner Großeltern?
S2: Deine Eltern.

 6. Familie und Freunde. Ask your partner how much she/he knows about her/his family, relatives, and friends.

Discussing friends and family

1. Wo wohnt der Freund deiner Schwester?
2. Wo wohnt die Freundin deines Bruders?
3. Wie ist die Telefonnummer deines Freundes? deiner Freundin?
4. Hast du die Adresse deiner Tante? deines Onkels? deiner Großeltern?
5. Was für ein Auto hat der Freund deiner Schwester? die Freundin deines Bruders?
6. Wie heißen die Bekannten deiner Eltern?

2 Genitive of time

Indefinite past	**Eines Tages** hat mir Melanie alles erklärt.	*One day* Melanie explained everything to me.
Indefinite future	**Eines Tages** mache ich das vielleicht.	*Someday* maybe I'll do that.

Nouns expressing an indefinite point in time are in the genitive.

3 Prepositions with the genitive

(an)statt	*instead of*	Kommt Anna **(an)statt** ihrer Schwester?
trotz	*in spite of*	**Trotz** des Wetters fahren wir in die Berge.
während	*during*	**Während** des Sommers bleiben wir nicht in Hamburg.
wegen	*on account of*	**Wegen** des Wetters gehen wir nicht schwimmen.

The prepositions **anstatt** or **statt, trotz, während,** and **wegen** require the genitive case.

wegen **dem Wetter** (des Wetters)
trotz **dem Regen** (des Regens)

In colloquial usage many people use the prepositions **statt, trotz, wegen,** and sometimes **während** with the dative.

trotz **ihm**
wegen **dir**

In colloquial usage dative pronouns are frequently used with the prepositions:
statt ihr, trotz ihm, wegen mir.

7. **Eine Wanderung.**   The company your father works for occasionally spon-
sors a hike. Your friend asks how the last one was. Answer the questions
using the cues.

▶   Bist du auch mitgegangen?   *Ja, trotz des Wetters.*
     (ja, trotz / das Wetter)

1. Warum ist dein Bruder zu Hause geblieben? (wegen / seine Arbeit)
2. Ist deine Schwester mitgegangen? (ja, statt / mein Bruder)
3. Sind die Leute lange gewandert? (nein, nur während / der Nachmittag)
4. Sind viele Leute gekommen? (nein, wegen / das Wetter)
5. Wann macht ihr Pläne für die nächste Wanderung? (während / diese
   Woche)
6. Warum gehen die Leute eigentlich wandern? (wegen / das Café)

4 Adjectives

◼ *Predicate adjectives*

Die CD ist **toll.**
Der Wein wird sicher **gut.**
Das Wetter bleibt jetzt **schön.**

Predicate adjectives are adjectives that follow the verbs **sein, werden,** or
bleiben and modify the subject. Predicate adjectives do not take endings.

◼ *Attributive adjectives*

Das ist eine **tolle** CD.
Das ist ein **guter** Wein.
Wir haben jetzt **schönes** Wetter.

Attributive adjectives are adjectives that precede the nouns they modify.
Attributive adjectives have endings.

5 Preceded adjectives

◼ *Adjectives preceded by a definite article or* **der-word**

	Masculine	Neuter	Feminine	Plural
Nom.	der alte Mann	das kleine Kind	die junge Frau	die guten Freunde
Acc.	den alten Mann	das kleine Kind	die junge Frau	die guten Freunde
Dat.	dem alten Mann	dem kleinen Kind	der jungen Frau	den guten Freunden
Gen.	des alten Mannes	des kleinen Kindes	der jungen Frau	der guten Freunde

	M.	N.	F.	Pl.
Nom.	e	e	e	en
Acc.	en	e	e	en
Dat.	en	en	en	en
Gen.	en	en	en	en

Definite articles and **der**-words indicate gender and/or case. Therefore, attributive adjectives do not have to. Their endings are simply **-e** or **-en.**

Diese Handschuhe sind **teuer.**   Willst du diese **teuren** Handschuhe wirklich kaufen?

Adjectives ending in **-er** may omit the **-e** when the adjective takes an ending.

8.   Noch einmal.   Restate the model sentences, using the cued adjectives in the nominative singular.

▶   Ist dieser Pulli noch gut? (alt)   *Ist dieser alte Pulli noch gut?*

1. rot
2. grün
3. schwer
4. leicht

▶   Wem gehört dieses Radio? (klein)   *Wem gehört dieses kleine Radio?*

5. toll
6. neu
7. kaputt
8. teuer

▶   Wie teuer war diese CD? (neu)   *Wie teuer war diese neue CD?*

9. furchtbar
10. schlecht
11. toll
12. interessant

9.   Welche meinst du?   In a department store Franziska comments on a number of items. Ask which she is referring to. Use adjectives in the accusative singular.

▶   Der rote Pulli ist toll, nicht?   *Meinst du diesen roten Pulli?*

1. Der leichte Regenmantel ist praktisch, nicht?
2. Der kurze Rock ist schön, nicht?
3. Das grüne Kleid ist sehr lang, nicht?
4. Das gelbe Hemd ist toll, nicht?
5. Die kleine Handtasche ist praktisch, nicht?
6. Die weiße Bluse ist wirklich schön, nicht?
7. Die schwarzen Schuhe sind furchtbar, nicht?
8. Die kurzen Handschuhe sind billig, nicht?

10.   Woher hast du das?   Ask four students or your instructor where they got a particular thing (e.g., a piece of clothing, a book bag). Be sure to identify it (color, size, etc.).

Describing things

S1:

Woher hast du/haben Sie [die schöne braune Büchertasche]?

S2:

[Die] habe ich [von meiner Mutter].
[Die] habe ich [in einem kleinen Geschäft gekauft].

11.   Bist du gern da?   A friend wonders whether you like to do things in various places. Say she/he is correct. Use adjectives in the dative singular.

▶ Wo ißt du gern? In dem Café an der Uni? Es ist billig.
Ja, in dem billigen Café an der Uni.

1. Wo läufst du gern? In dem Park? Er ist groß.
2. Wo sitzt du gern? In dem Biergarten? Er ist schön.
3. Wo kaufst du gern Bücher? In der Buchhandlung? Sie ist modern.
4. Wo sitzt du gern? In dem Café am Markt? Es ist klein.
5. Wo ißt du gern? In der Kneipe? Sie ist gemütlich.
6. Wo arbeitest du gern? In dem Musikgeschäft? Es ist neu.
7. Wo liest du gern? In der Bibliothek? Sie ist ruhig.

12.   Viele Fragen.   Peter has lots of questions. Rephrase them by combining the sentences in each pair below. Use the boldfaced adjectives with the plural nouns.

▶ Warum trägst du immer noch diese Schuhe? Sie sind schon **alt.**
Warum trägst du immer noch diese alten Schuhe?

1. Wer hat diese Handschuhe gekauft? Sie sind schön **warm.**
2. Wann hast du diese Hemden bekommen? Sie sind wirklich **toll.**
3. Warum hast du diese Schuhe gekauft? Sie sind wirklich **furchtbar.**
4. Was hältst du von diesen Kassetten? Sie sind **neu.**
5. Wohin hängst du diese Poster? Sie sind **lustig.**
6. Wer hat dir diese Bücher geliehen? Sie sind sehr **interessant.**

13.   Hier ist alles klein.   Add the adjective **klein** with the correct ending to each noun.

▶ Das Haus steht in der Sonnenstraße.
Das kleine Haus steht in der kleinen Sonnenstraße.

Der Junge wohnt in dem Haus. Hinter dem Haus ist der Garten. In dem Garten steht die Bank°. Auf der Bank sitzt der Junge. Unter der Bank liegt der Ball von dem Jungen. Er will mit dem Ball spielen. Er nimmt den Ball in die Hand und kickt ihn durch das Fenster. Peng! Da ist das Fenster kaputt.

bench

■ *Adjectives preceded by an indefinite article or **ein-word***

	Masculine	Neuter	Feminine	Plural
Nom.	ein alt**er** Mann	ein klein**es** Kind	eine jung**e** Frau	meine gut**en** Freunde
Acc.	einen alt**en** Mann	ein klein**es** Kind	eine jung**e** Frau	meine gut**en** Freunde
Dat.	einem alt**en** Mann	einem klein**en** Kind	einer jung**en** Frau	meinen gut**en** Freunden
Gen.	eines alt**en** Mannes	eines klein**en** Kindes	einer jung**en** Frau	meiner gut**en** Freunde

	M.	N.	F.	Pl.
Nom.	er	es	e	en
Acc.	en	es	e	en
Dat.	en	en	en	en
Gen.	en	en	en	en

Adjectives preceded by an indefinite article or an **ein-**word have the same endings as those preceded by **der-**words (**-e** or **-en**), except when the **ein-**word itself has no ending. These are **-er** for masculine nominative and **-es** for neuter nominative and accusative. Since in these instances **ein** does not indicate the gender of the noun, the adjective has to take on that function. Note the following table.

Nom.	ein alt**er** Mann	ein klein**es** Kind
Acc.	—	ein klein**es** Kind

14. Du hast recht. Regina comments on class work. Agree with her. Use adjectives in the nominative case.

▶ Professor Schmidts Musikvorlesung war trocken, nicht?

Ja, das war wirklich eine trockene Vorlesung.

1. Das Buch ist auch trocken, nicht?
2. Aber das Bier nachher war gut, nicht?
3. Die Klausur in Deutsch war lang und schwer, nicht?
4. Professor Langes Seminar ist interessant, nicht?
5. Eriks Referat war ziemlich kurz, nicht?
6. Das Referat war auch ziemlich schlecht, nicht?
7. Professor Memmels Kurs ist leicht, nicht?

15. Ein neues Zimmer. Your friend Robert, who is a student at a Swiss university, has moved to a new room. Describe his new surroundings. Use the cued adjectives in the accusative case.

▶ Robert hat ein Zimmer. (groß, modern)   *Robert hat ein großes, modernes Zimmer.*

1. Das Zimmer hat eine Eßecke. (gemütlich)
2. Es hat ein Sofa. (neu, klein)
3. Robert hat eine Lampe. (modern, lustig)
4. Er hat ein Bücherregal. (klein, praktisch)
5. Er hat einen Sessel. (alt, unpraktisch)
6. Er hat ein Bild. (groß, furchtbar)

16. Frage-Ecke. You and your partner are picking each other's brains for ideas for birthday presents. Find out what your friends are giving to whom and then what your partner is giving them.

S2: Was möchte Gerhard seinen Eltern schenken?
S1: Er möchte seinen Eltern einen teuren Videorecorder schenken.

S1:

	Eltern	Schwester	Bruder	Freundin/Freund
Gerhard	ein teurer Videorecorder	eine blaue Bluse		
Susi			ein neues Fahrrad	eine heiße CD
Anna		eine kleine Katze	ein australischer Hut	
ich				
Partnerin/Partner				

S2:

	Eltern	Schwester	Bruder	Freundin/Freund
Gerhard			ein neuer Krimi	ein schönes Bild
Susi	ein neuer Computer	ein roter Mantel		
Anna	ein guter CD-Spieler			ein gutes Buch
Ich				
Partnerin/Partner				

17. Ich habe gewonnen. You just won some money in the lottery and you're feeling generous. Tell four people what you're going to buy for yourself and ask what you can buy for them.

S1: Ich kaufe mir [einen neuen, teuren CD-Spieler]. Was kann ich dir kaufen?
S2: Du kannst mir [ein neues Radio] kaufen.

Dinge: Auto □ Fahrrad □ CD □ Kassette □ Radio □ Buch □ Jacke □ Pullover

Adjektive: besser □ gut □ interessant □ neu □ rot □ schnell □ schön □ teuer □ toll □ warm

18. Alles ist neu. In Andrea's life there are at the moment many new things and people. Ask for more details about them.

▶ Ich hab' ein neues Auto. *Erzähl mal von deinem neuen Auto.*

1. Ich hab' eine neue Freundin.
2. Ich hab' einen neuen Kassettenrecorder.
3. Ich hab' ein neues Fahrrad.
4. Ich hab' eine neue Wohnung.
5. Ich hab' neue Freunde.
6. Ich hab' einen neuen Deutschprofessor.
7. Ich hab' neue Vorlesungen.

19. Träume°. Form a group of four. One person begins by telling what she/he is dreaming about having or doing and then asks the next person what she/he is dreaming of. A few possibilities are given.

dreams

Stating wants/desires

S1: Ich träume° von [einem schönen Wochenende]. Wovon träumst du?
S2: Ich träume von [einem tollen Motorrad].

dream

Träume: Reise □ Auto □ Frau □ Haus □ Mann □ Motorrad □ Wochenende

Adjektive: schnell □ klein □ reich° □ schön □ interessant □ weiß □ groß □ toll □ lang

rich

6 Unpreceded adjectives

	Masculine	Neuter	Feminine	Plural
Nom.	guter Wein	gutes Brot	gute Wurst	gute Brötchen
Acc.	guten Wein	gutes Brot	gute Wurst	gute Brötchen
Dat.	gutem Wein	gutem Brot	guter Wurst	guten Brötchen
Gen.	guten Weines	guten Brotes	guter Wurst	guter Brötchen

	M.	N.	F.	Pl.
Nom.	er	es	e	e
Acc.	en	es	e	e
Dat.	em	em	er	en
Gen.	en	en	er	er

Adjectives not preceded by a definite article, a **der**-word, an indefinite article, or an **ein**-word must indicate the gender and/or case of the noun. They have the same endings as **der**-words, with the exception of the masculine and neuter genitive.

20. Peter ißt gern. Make each of Peter's comments more descriptive by using the appropriate unpreceded form of the cued adjective.

▶ Brötchen schmecken gut. (frisch)   *Frische Brötchen schmecken gut.*

1. Bier schmeckt auch gut. (deutsch)
2. Ich trinke gern Wein. (trocken)
3. Blumen auf dem Tisch gefallen mir. (frisch)
4. In vielen Städten kann man Fisch kaufen. (frisch)
5. Ich koche gern mit Wein. (deutsch)
6. Ich habe Hunger. (groß)
7. Zum Mittagessen esse ich gern Steak. (amerikanisch)
8. Zum Abendessen esse ich gern Wurst. (deutsch)

21. Ein Geburtstagsfest. You and your partner are planning to give a friend a birthday party. Plan the menu from the list below. Although each of you has an initial preference, agree on the final menu.

S1: Ich möchte ungarischen Käse servieren.
S2: Ich möchte lieber holländischen Käse servieren.

Lebensmittel: der Wein □ das Bier □ die Salami □ der Fisch □ das Steak □ das Brot □ der Käse □ der Tee □ der Kuchen □ der Kaffee □ die Orangen

Adjektive: italienisch □ türkisch □ englisch □ ungarisch □ brasilianisch □ französisch □ amerikanisch □ deutsch □ holländisch □ spanisch

Hier gibt es deutsches und türkisches Essen.

7 Ordinal numbers

1. erst-	**6.** sechst-	**21.** einundzwanzig**st**-	
2. zweit-	**7.** siebt-	**32.** zweiunddreißig**st**-	
3. dritt-	**8.** acht-	**100.** hundert**st**-	
		1000. tausend**st**-	

An ordinal number is a number indicating the position of something in a sequence (e.g., the first, the second). In German, the ordinal numbers are formed by adding **-t** to numbers 1–19 and **-st** to numbers beyond 19. Exceptions are **erst-, dritt-, siebt-,** and **acht-.**

Die neue Wohnung ist im **dritten** Stock.
Am **siebten** Mai habe ich Geburtstag.

The ordinals take adjective endings.

8 Dates

Der wievielte ist heute?	What is the date today?
Heute ist **der 1. (erste)** März.	Today is March first.
Den wievielten haben wir heute?	What is the date today?
Heute haben wir **den 1. (ersten)** März.	Today is March first.

In German, there are two ways to express dates. Dates are expressed with ordinal numbers preceded by the masculine form of the definite article referring to the noun **Tag.** A period after a number indicates that it is an ordinal. The day always precedes the month.

Hamburg, **den 2. März 1996.**

Dates in letter headings or news releases are always in the accusative.

22. Zwei Tage später. Frank has forgotten the exact date of his friends' birthdays. The birthdays are two days later than he thinks. Correct him.

▶ Hat Inge am neunten Mai Geburtstag? *Nein, am elften.*

1. Hat Gisela am dreizehnten Juli Geburtstag?
2. Hat Willi am ersten Januar Geburtstag?
3. Hat Uwe am zweiten März Geburtstag?
4. Hat Elke am sechsten November Geburtstag?
5. Hat Claudia am achtundzwanzigsten April Geburtstag?
6. Hat Gerd am fünfundzwanzigsten Dezember Geburtstag?

23. Zwei Fragen. Find out from four fellow students when their birthdays are and in what year or semester they are.

Asking for personal information

S1: Wann hast du Geburtstag?
S2: Am [siebten Juni].
S1: In welchem Semester/Jahr bist du?
S2: [Im zweiten.]

Land und Leute

Berufstätige Frauen

Erika Emmerich, Präsidentin des Verbands der deutschen Autoindustrie.

The report on progress toward equality in the professional life of men and women is a mixed one. The number of German women with positions of responsibility in business and public life has risen in the past years. Among these some names stand out. Rita Süßmuth became President of the **Bundestag** in 1988. Erika Emmerich is President of the Automobile Industry Association. In 1994 Jutta Limbach became the President of the Federal Constitutional Court **(Bundesverfassungsgericht)**. But women still have a long way to go to achieve true equality with their male counterparts.

Of the 672 representatives in the **Bundestag,** 176 are women. This 26% is better than the 20% representation in the previous **Bundestag.** But the fact that 53% of all eligible voters are women highlights the inadequacy of the 26%.

The statistics from the business world are mixed. One out of four business enterprises in Germany is led by a woman (figures from 1995). But on the boards of the top 600 German stock companies there are a total of only 12 women. In 1980 the average gross monthly income for men in all types of work was about 900 marks higher than that of women. By 1993 the gap had grown to a difference of 1400 marks. Men in white collar jobs earn an average of 2300 marks per month more than women employees.

German women do not lack educational opportunities or qualifications. But the burden of family and career has not been solved. The German government views the inflexible working hours of companies and the lack of part-time jobs with benefits as a major impediment to combining family and career. Jutta Limbach has stated that for women between the ages of 20 to 30 the **"Frauenfrage"** (women's question) is a **"Kinderfrage"** (children's question). Over half of the German population lives in a household with children (57% in 1992). Only 1.4% of fathers take advantage of the **Erziehungsurlaub,** the leave that permits a parent to take care of a child until her/his third birthday.

WIEDERHOLUNG

1. Vorbereitungen. Form sentences to tell about the arrangements for getting the house in shape before guests arrive, using the cues below.

1. du / wollen / abwaschen / jetzt / ?
2. ich / können / abtrocknen / dann
3. ich / müssen / saubermachen / Küche / nachher
4. du / möchten / aufräumen / Wohnzimmer / ?
5. wer / sollen / saubermachen / Badezimmer / ?
6. nachher / ich / wollen / noch / staubsaugen

2. Ein Amerikaner in Deutschland. Complete the paragraph by supplying the correct adjective endings where necessary.

Ein amerikanisch_____ Student studiert an einer deutsch_____ Universität. Er wohnt in einem schön_____ , hell_____° Zimmer bei einer nett_____ Familie. In seinem Zimmer gibt es alles – ein bequem_____° Bett, eine groß_____ Kommode, einen modern_____ Schreibtisch, Platz für viel_____ Bücher auf einem groß_____ Bücherregal – aber keinen Fernseher. Im ganz_____ Haus ist kein Fernseher. Im Wohnzimmer steht neben dem grün_____ Sofa eine toll_____ Stereoanlage°, in seinem Zimmer hat er ein klein_____ Radio, aber das ganz_____ Haus hat nicht einen einzig_____° Fernseher. Das gibt es!°

bright
comfortable

stereo system
single / **Das gibt es!:** There is such a thing!

3. Eine Schweizerin in Deutschland. Tell where Susanne studies and what she does during her summer vacation by completing the sentences. Use the cued words.

1. Susanne studiert an _____ . (die Universität Göttingen)
2. Sie wohnt in _____ . (ein großes Studentenheim)
3. Sie denkt oft an _____ . (ihre Freunde zu Hause)
4. Sie kommt aus _____ . (die Schweiz)
5. In _____ fährt sie nach Hause. (die Sommerferien)
6. Sie arbeitet bei _____ . (ihre Tante)
7. Sie fährt mit _____ zur Arbeit. (der Bus)
8. Am Sonntag macht sie mit _____ eine kleine Wanderung. (ihr Freund)
9. Nach _____ gehen sie in ein Café. (die Wanderung)
10. Leider hat sie _____ . (kein Geld)
11. Ihr Freund muß _____ etwas Geld leihen. (sie)
12. Nachher gehen sie auf _____ . (ein Fest)

4. Wie sagt man das?

1. —My friend Karin is studying at the University of Göttingen.
   —Does she live with a family?
   —Yes. The family is nice, and she likes her large room.
2. What's the date today?
   —It's February 28.
   —Oh oh. Karin's birthday was yesterday.
3. Awful weather today, isn't it?
   —Yes, but I'm going hiking, in spite of the weather.

5. Letzte Woche. Tell what various people did last week.

▶ Stefanie macht Hausarbeit.   *Stefanie hat Hausarbeit gemacht.*

1. Sie räumt ihr Schlafzimmer auf.
2. Gerd wäscht jeden Tag ab.
3. Stefanie trocknet manchmal ab.
4. Ich kaufe ein.
5. Ich fahre mit dem Fahrrad auf den Markt.
6. Gerd kocht am Wochenende.
7. Stefanie putzt das Badezimmer.

6. Was weißt du über Karin Meier?   Your friend is filling you in about Karin Meier, who moved away a number of years ago. Review information on stating one's profession in *Kapitel 5,* **Erweiterung des Wortschatzes,** and then give the German equivalents.

1. Karin is a doctor.
2. Her husband is a lawyer.
3. Karin's brother Max is a teacher.
4. Her sister Lisa is a student.
5. Lisa would like to become an engineer.

7. Was meinst du?   Answer the following questions and then find out how your partner answered them. You may wish to ask additional questions about some of your partner's answers.

1. Wer macht den Haushalt bei dir zu Hause?
2. Welchen Beruf hat deine Mutter? Was macht sie da? (Hausfrau ist auch ein Beruf.)
3. Wie gleichberechtigt sind Männer und Frauen hier in diesem Land? In der Wirtschaft? Zu Hause?
4. Was hältst du von einer Frau, die kleine Kinder hat und berufstätig ist?
5. Wann sitzt die erste Frau auf dem Präsidentenstuhl in den USA?

Drei Generationen: Enkelin, Mutter und Großmutter.

8. Zum Schreiben

1. Using your imagination, write in German a short biography of either Gisela Anton or Helga Krauß, describing details of her life that were not mentioned in the reading. Some of the points you might wish to mention are:

   - wo sie ihren Mann kennengelernt hat
   - was ihr an ihrem Mann besonders gefallen hat
   - inwiefern° sie mit ihrem Leben zufrieden° ist und inwiefern nicht   to what extent / satisfied
   - was sie in ihrer Freizeit gern macht

2. The reading mentions **alleinstehende Mütter.** Do you think it is difficult to be a single mother or father? Explain in German why or why not. Possible points to include are:

   - Zeit
   - Geld
   - Disziplin°   discipline

3. Describe in German a woman who has influenced your life and what her influence has been.

Hinweise: Before beginning your German paragraph, make notes for each point you wish to include. Try to make your account more graphic and descriptive by using attributive adjectives. After you have finished writing, check the case endings of each adjective. Also pay particular attention to the case used with each preposition. For other things to watch for in your writing, refer to p. 235.

GRAMMATIK: ZUSAMMENFASSUNG

Forms of the genitive

■ *Forms of articles,* der-*words, and* ein-*words*

	Masculine	Neuter	Feminine	Plural
Definite article	des Mannes	des Kindes	der Frau	der Freunde
Der-words	dieses Mannes	dieses Kindes	dieser Frau	dieser Freunde
Indefinite article	eines Mannes	eines Kindes	einer Frau	—
Ein-words	ihres Mannes	unseres Kindes	seiner Frau	meiner Freunde

■ *Forms of nouns*

Masculine/Neuter	Feminine/Plural
der Name **des Mannes**	der Name **der Frau**
ein Freund **des Mädchens**	ein Freund **der Kinder**

Masculine and neuter nouns of one syllable generally add **-es** in the genitive; masculine and neuter nouns of two or more syllables add **-s**. Feminine and plural nouns do not add a genitive ending.

■ *Forms of masculine* **N-***nouns*

Nom.	der Herr	der Student
Acc.	den Her**rn**	den Student**en**
Dat.	dem Her**rn**	dem Student**en**
Gen.	des Her**rn**	des Student**en**

■ *The interrogative pronoun* **wessen?**

Nom.	wer?
Acc.	wen?
Dat.	wem?
Gen.	wessen?

Uses of the genitive

■ *Possession and other relationships*

das Buch **meines Freundes**	my friend's book
die Mutter **meines Freundes**	my friend's mother
die Farbe **der Blumen**	the color of the flowers

■ *Prepositions*

(an)statt	*instead of*	Kommt Erika **(an)statt** ihrer Freundin?
trotz	*in spite of*	**Trotz** des Wetters wandern wir.
während	*during*	**Während** der Ferien wandern wir.
wegen	*on account of*	**Wegen** des Wetters bleiben sie zu Hause.

■ *Genitive of time*

Indefinite past	**Eines Tages** hat mir Julia alles erklärt.	*One day* Julia explained everything to me.
Indefinite future	**Eines Tages** mache ich das vielleicht.	*Someday* maybe I'll do that.

Adjectives

■ *Adjectives preceded by a definite article or **der**-word*

	Masculine	Neuter	Feminine	Plural
Nom.	der alte Mann	das kleine Kind	die junge Frau	die guten Freunde
Acc.	den alten Mann	das kleine Kind	die junge Frau	die guten Freunde
Dat.	dem alten Mann	dem kleinen Kind	der jungen Frau	den guten Freunden
Gen.	des alten Mannes	des kleinen Kindes	der jungen Frau	der guten Freunde

	M.	N.	F.	Pl.
Nom.	e	e	e	en
Acc.	en	e	e	en
Dat.	en	en	en	en
Gen.	en	en	en	en

■ *Adjectives preceded by an indefinite article or **ein**-word*

	Masculine	Neuter	Feminine	Plural
Nom.	ein alter Mann	ein kleines Kind	eine junge Frau	meine guten Freunde
Acc.	einen alten Mann	ein kleines Kind	eine junge Frau	meine guten Freunde
Dat.	einem alten Mann	einem kleinen Kind	einer jungen Frau	meinen guten Freunden
Gen.	eines alten Mannes	eines kleinen Kindes	einer jungen Frau	meiner guten Freunde

	M.	N.	F.	Pl.
Nom.	er	es	e	en
Acc.	en	es	e	en
Dat.	en	en	en	en
Gen.	en	en	en	en

■ *Unpreceded adjectives*

	Masculine	Neuter	Feminine	Plural
Nom.	guter Wein	gutes Brot	gute Wurst	gute Brötchen
Acc.	guten Wein	gutes Brot	gute Wurst	gute Brötchen
Dat.	gutem Wein	gutem Brot	guter Wurst	guten Brötchen
Gen.	guten Weines	guten Brotes	guter Wurst	guter Brötchen

	M.	N.	F.	Pl.
Nom.	er	es	e	e
Acc.	en	es	e	e
Dat.	em	em	er	en
Gen.	en	en	er	er

Ordinal numbers

1. erst-   **6.** sechst-   **21.** einundzwanzig**st**-
2. zweit-   **7.** siebt-   **32.** zweiunddreißig**st**-
3. dritt-   **8.** acht-   **100.** hundert**st**-
                                   1000. tausend**st**-

The ordinals (numbers indicating position in a sequence) are formed by adding **-t** to the numbers 1–19 and **-st** to numbers beyond 19. Exceptions are **erst-, dritt-, siebt-,** and **acht-.**

Dies ist mein **drittes** Semester.   This is my third semester.

The ordinals take adjective endings.

Die Bahnhofstraße in Zürich ist eine elegante Einkaufsstraße.

Kapitel 10

LERNZIELE

■ **Sprechintentionen**

Inquiring about someone's health
Expressing regret
Talking about injuries
Discussing wants
Describing one's daily routine
Talking about household chores
Making comparisons
Stating preferences
Discussing personal information

■ **Lesestück**

Ein Brief aus der Schweiz

■ **Land und Leute**

Switzerland
Languages
A song in dialect
History
Government

■ **Vokabeln**

Parts of the body
Hygiene
Adjectives used as nouns
Viel and *wenig*

■ **Grammatik**

Reflexive constructions
Definite article with parts of the body
Infinitives with *zu*
The construction *um ... zu* + infinitive
Comparison of adjectives and adverbs

BAUSTEINE FÜR GESPRÄCHE

Hast du dich erkältet?

ELISABETH: Du hustest ja fürchterlich.
RAINER: Ja, ich habe mich erkältet.
Der Hals tut mir furchtbar weh.
ELISABETH: Hast du Fieber?
RAINER: Ein bißchen – 38.
ELISABETH: Du siehst ganz schön
blaß aus.
RAINER: Ich fühle mich auch krank.
Vielleicht ist es besser, wenn ich
zum Arzt gehe.
ELISABETH: Ja, wir wollen doch am
Samstag in den Alpen Ski fahren.

Have you caught a cold?

You're coughing terribly.
Yes, I've caught a cold. My throat's
hurting a lot.
Do you have a fever?
A little—38 [= 100.4°F].
You look pretty pale.

I do feel pretty sick. Maybe I'd
better go to the doctor.

Yes, after all we do want to go
skiing in the Alps on Saturday.

Brauchbares

In Rainer's two sentences, **"ich habe mich erkältet"** and **"Ich fühle mich auch krank"** note that in German there is the pronoun **mich.** These pronouns are reflexive pronouns and the verbs that use them are called reflexive verbs. The English equivalents of these two verbs have no reflexive pronouns. For more discussion of reflexive verbs see p. 325.

Fragen

1. Beschreiben Sie Rainers Krankheit.
2. Warum ist es besser, wenn er zum Arzt geht?

 1. Was hast du? A fellow student looks pale. Ask what the matter is.

> Inquiring about someone's health

S1:

Du siehst blaß aus. Was hast du°?

S2:

Mir geht es nicht gut°.
Ich fühle mich nicht wohl°.
Mir ist schlecht°.
Ich habe | **Kopfschmerzen.**
Zahnschmerzen°.
Magenschmerzen°.
Rückenschmerzen°.
Ich bin erkältet.

2. Geht es dir besser? Ask a friend about her/his cold.

S1:

Was macht deine Erkältung°?

S2:

Es geht mir | **besser.**
            | schon besser.
            | schlechter°.

Ich fühle mich | **krank.**
               | schwach°.
               | schwächer als gestern.

 3. Das tut mir leid. You can't join in various plans because of a cold. Your friend expresses regret.

> Expressing regret

S1:

Ich bin furchtbar erkältet.
Ich kann heute nicht | **Ski fahren.**
                       | zum Fest kommen.
                       | ins Kino gehen.

S2:

Schade°.
Das tut mir leid.
Hoffentlich fühlst du dich morgen besser.

 4. Wie fühlst du dich? Ask a fellow student about health matters.

1. Was machst du, wenn du Fieber hast?
2. Was machst du, wenn du dich erkältet hast?
3. Wie oft gehst du zum Zahnarzt?

Erweiterung des Wortschatzes

1 Der Körper°

1. der **Hals,** ¨e
2. der **Arm,** -e
3. die **Hand,** ¨e
4. der **Finger,** -
5. der **Bauch,** *pl.* **Bäuche**
6. das **Bein,** -e
7. das **Knie,** -
8. der **Fuß,** ¨e
9. der **Rücken,** -

2 Der Kopf

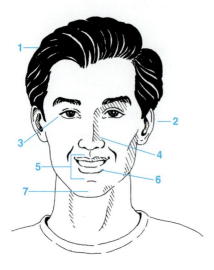

1. das **Haar, -e**
2. das **Ohr, -en** ⎫
3. das **Auge, -n** ⎬
4. die **Nase, -n** ⎬ das **Gesicht, -er**
5. der **Mund, ¨-er** ⎬
6. die **Lippe, -n** ⎬
7. das **Kinn, -e** ⎭

1. Jeder ist verletzt°. Alexander's soccer team has not only lost the game but has also incurred a number of injuries. Ask your partner where the injury is for each team member.

> Talking about injuries

S1: Wo ist Nummer 1 verletzt?
S2: Der Arm tut ihm weh.

2. **Hilfe°! Ein Dieb°!**   While you were sitting reading in the park you   *help/thief*
saw someone ride off with your bicycle before you could stop him. Describe
him to the police (your partner). Your partner will pick him out of the four
pictures of known bicycle thieves. Some possible traits are:

groß/klein; schlank/dick°; attraktiv/unattraktiv
Haare: blond°, dunkel°, lang/kurz, hellbraun°
Nase: groß/klein, dünn°, lang
Mund: groß/klein
Brille?

S1: Der Mann ist groß, schlank, …

3. **Wer ist es?**   Choose a fellow student in your German class. Your
partner will guess whom you have chosen by asking questions about her/his
appearance.

S2: Ist sie/er groß oder klein?
   Hat sie/er blonde/schwarze/braune/rote Haare?
   Sind die Haare kurz/lang?
   Trägt sie/er eine Brille?

Vokabeln

Substantive

die **Erkältung**   cold *(illness)*
das **Fieber**   fever
das **Gesicht, -er**   face
der **Hals, ̈e**   throat, neck
der **Kopf, ̈e**   head
der **Körper, -**   body
die **Krankheit, -en**   illness
der **Magen, -**   stomach; die
   Magenschmerzen *(pl.)*
   stomachache

der **Rücken, -**   back; die
   Rückenschmerzen   back pain
der **Schmerz, -en**   pain
der **Zahn, ̈e**   tooth; die
   Zahnschmerzen *(pl.)* toothache
For additional parts of the body,
   see pp. 313–314.

Verben

sich erkälten to catch a cold; **erkältet:**
   ich bin erkältet I have a cold
sich fühlen to feel *(ill, well, etc.)*
husten to cough

verletzen to injure, hurt; **ich habe**
   mir den Arm verletzt I've
   injured/hurt my arm; **ich habe**
   mich verletzt I hurt myself

Andere Wörter

blaß pale
blond blond
dick fat
dunkel dark
dünn thin
fürchterlich horrible, horribly

hell light; **hellbraun** light brown
schade that's too bad, a pity, a
   shame
schlecht bad; **schlechter** worse
schwach weak; **schwächer** weaker
wohl well

Besondere Ausdrücke

ganz schön really quite; **ganz schön**
   blaß pretty pale
Mir geht es (nicht) gut. I am (not)
   well.
Mir ist schlecht. I feel nauseated.
Was hast du? What is wrong with
   you? What's the matter?

Was macht deine Erkältung? How's
   your cold?
weh tun (+ *dat.*) to hurt; **Die Füße**
   tun mir weh. My feet hurt.

Land und Leute

Die viersprachige Schweiz

Invasions by different ethnic tribes over a
period of many hundred years shaped Switzerland's linguistic character. Today there are four
national languages, each one spoken in a
specific region or regional pocket. More than
64% of the population speak German, about
19% speak French, over 7% speak Italian. The
fourth national language, Rhaeto-Romanic
(**Rätoromanisch**) is in danger of dying out since
less than 1% of the population speaks it. Experts
predict that it may be extinct by the year 2005
unless there is a more conscious effort to preserve it. German, French, and Italian are the
official languages (**Amtssprachen**) used to conduct business and political affairs. Every Swiss
can learn these languages at school, and usually gains at least a passive understanding of
them. Each of the four national languages
has many dialects: Rhaeto-Romanic alone
has five dialects, Swiss German has many
more. Although High German (**Hochdeutsch**)
is taught in the schools, the primary language

**Deutsch, Französisch, Italienisch und Rätoro-
manisch sind die vier Sprachen der Schweiz.**

of German-speaking Swiss is a local dialect
(**Schwyzerdütsch**).
   Considering the small size—the longest
North–South distance is 137 miles (220 km)
and the longest East-West distance is 216 miles
(348 km)—and considering the multitude of
languages and dialects, Switzerland is linguistically and culturally a highly diversified country.
Only in a political sense do the Swiss see themselves as a unity.

EIN BRIEF AUS DER SCHWEIZ

Vorbereitung auf das Lesen

■ *Vor dem Lesen**

1. Viele Leute haben Brieffreunde°. Was schreibt man einer Brieffreundin oder einem Brieffreund im ersten Brief°?
2. Was möchten Sie Ihren Brieffreunden über Ihre Stadt oder Ihr Land erzählen? Nennen Sie zwei Dinge°. — *things*
3. Welche Stichwörter° assoziieren Sie mit der Schweiz? — *key words*
4. Sehen Sie sich die Landkarte° von der Schweiz am Anfang° des Buches an, und lesen Sie die folgende Information. — *map/beginning*

- **Größe°:** 41.288 qkm°; etwa halb so groß wie Österreich (83.855 qkm) oder Maine (86.027 qkm)
  etwas kleiner als Neuschottland° (52.841 qkm)
  — *size/**qkm = Quadratkilometer:** square kilometers*
  — *Nova Scotia*
- **Bevölkerung°:** ca.° 7 Millionen Einwohner
  — *population/**ca.** (abbrev. for **circa**): approximately*
- **Regierungsform°:** Bundesstaat° mit 26 Kantonen° parlamentarische Demokratie
  — *type of government/federal state/cantons*
- **Hauptstadt:** Bern
- **5 Nachbarn:** Frankreich (F)**, Deutschland (D), Österreich (A), Fürstentum Liechtenstein (FL), Italien (I)

a. Ist Ihr Land oder Bundesland° größer° oder kleiner° als die Schweiz? — *state, province/larger/smaller*
b. Ist die Schweiz größer als Österreich oder nur halb so groß?
c. Hat die Schweiz mehr Einwohner als Österreich oder weniger°? — *fewer*
d. Wie heißen die Nachbarn der Schweiz?

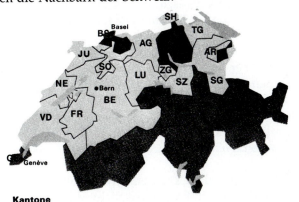

Kantone

ZH	Zürich	FR	Freiburg	AG	Aargau
BE	Bern	SO	Solothurn	TG	Thurgau
LU	Luzern	BS	Basel-Stadt	TI	Tessin
UR	Uri	BL	Basel-Land	VD	Waadt
SZ	Schwyz	SH	Schaffhausen	VS	Wallis
OW	Obwalden	AR	Appenzell A.-Rh.	NE	Neuenburg
NW	Nidwalden	AI	Appenzell I.-Rh.	GE	Genf
GL	Glarus	SG	St. Gallen	JU	Jura
ZG	Zug	GR	Graubünden		

*Remember, words that appear with a raised degree mark (°) but for which no definition is given in the margin are active words you should learn and be able to use. These words and their definitions are listed in the **Vokabeln** section that most closely follows the exercise.
**The abbreviations in parentheses are the international symbols used on automobile stickers.

■ *Beim Lesen*

Beantworten Sie diese Fragen:

1. Schreibt Claudia „du" oder „Sie" in ihrem Brief an Thomas?
2. Welche Fragen stellt° Claudia an Thomas?
3. Machen Sie Stichwörter zu Claudias wichtigen Themen.

Viele Schweizer sind nach Amerika ausgewandert°. Deswegen gibt es in Amerika   emigrated
auch einige Orte mit Schweizer Namen. Einige amerikanische und Schweizer
Städte haben Partnerschaften° und organisieren Brieffreundschaften° mit dem   partnership / pen pals
Ziel, junge Amerikaner und Schweizer zusammenzubringen. Thomas Wild aus   (correspondence friendship)
5 New Glarus in Wisconsin und Claudia Handschin aus Glarus in der Schweiz
möchten eine Brieffreundschaft beginnen. In ihrem ersten Brief an Thomas
beschreibt Claudia ihr Land:

Lieber Thomas,

mein Name ist Claudia Handschin und ich bin 22 Jahre alt. Ich studiere Chemie
10 in Basel, aber ich komme aus Glarus. Ich interessiere mich für Amerika. Da
unsere zwei Städte eine Partnerschaft haben, habe ich Deine Adresse und ein
bißchen Information über Dich bekommen. Deine Urgroßeltern° sind voriges°   great-grandparents / last
Jahrhundert von Glarus nach Amerika ausgewandert, nicht wahr? Du studierst
Deutsch, nicht wahr? Sprichst Du auch Deutsch zu Hause oder sprechen nur
15 die älteren Leute in New Glarus noch Deutsch? Hast du Verwandte hier in
Glarus?

65% aller° Schweizer sprechen Deutsch. Deutsch ist jedoch nur eine   of all
von den offiziellen Sprachen unseres Landes. Italienisch, Französisch und
Rätoromanisch° sind die anderen. Deswegen hat unser Land auch offiziell   Rhaeto-Romanic
20 keinen deutschen, französischen oder italienischen Namen, sondern einen
lateinischen: „Confoederatio Helvetica". Das heißt auf deutsch, „Schweizerische
Eidgenossenschaft°". Unsere kleine Schweiz hat nämlich 26 autonome Kantone,   Confederation
und Bern ist die Hauptstadt.

Glarus liegt in der deutschen Schweiz. Wir sprechen zu Hause Schwei-
25 zerdeutsch. Das ist ein deutscher Dialekt, aber er ist dem Hochdeutschen°   High German
nicht sehr ähnlich. Im Kindergarten sprechen wir noch Dialekt, und erst in der
Schule lernen wir Hochdeutsch. So sagen wir zum Beispiel zu einem Bekannten:
„Grüetzi! Woane gaasch?" für „Grüß dich! Wohin gehst du?" Außer in der
Schule sprechen wir Hochdeutsch noch mit Ausländern, unter mehr formellen
30 Umständen°, und oft im Radio und Fernsehen. Wenn wir schreiben, benutzen   circumstances
wir selten Dialekt.

Was kann ich Dir weiter von der Schweiz erzählen? Du weißt wohl, daß
die Schweiz eine starke Wirtschaft hat. Aber Du weißt vielleicht nicht, daß
unser kleines Land fast keine Rohstoffe hat. Wir müssen Rohstoffe und
35 Lebensmittel importieren. Um die bezahlen zu können, müssen wir auf den
Weltmärkten konkurrieren können. Das können wir nur durch Qualität. Wir
Schweizer machen alles sehr präzis: Maschinen, Instrumente, chemische
Produkte und Apparate. Diese Qualitätsprodukte sind zusammen mit dem
Tourismus die Basis für die starke Wirtschaft der Schweiz. Eine starke
40 Wirtschaft ist wiederum° die Basis für unseren hohen Lebensstandard, und sie   in turn

macht auch die Neutralität der Schweiz möglich. Die Schweiz ist politisch neutral. Doch sie kann nur dann neutral bleiben, wenn sie wirtschaftlich stark ist. Viele junge Leute finden, daß unser Land Mitglied der EU werden soll. Sonst könnte° die Wirtschaft schwächer werden. Schließlich werden Welt und   *could*
45 Wirtschaft immer internationaler. Konservativere und ältere Leute argumentieren dagegen. Für sie ist die Mitgliedschaft° in der EU das Ende der Schweizer   *membership* Neutralität. Wie wir aus zwei Weltkriegen wissen, ist Neutralität eine gute Politik. Neutralität hat in der Schweiz auch eine lange Tradition: Unser Land ist seit fast fünfhundert Jahren neutral. Die jungen Leute fürchten aber, die Schweiz
50 bleibt zwar neutral aber auch isoliert von der Welt. Wer weiß, was richtig ist?

So, lieber Thomas, für heute ist das alles aus der Schweiz. Bitte schreibe mir bald etwas über Amerika. Ich freue mich schon auf Deinen Brief!

Liebe Grüße

Deine Claudia

Brauchbares

1. Nouns ending in **-schaft** designate a group or condition. English equivalents often end in *-ship*: **Partnerschaft** (l. 3), *partnership*; **Brieffreundschaft** (l. 3), *pen pals (correspondence friendship)*; **Mitgliedschaft** (l. 46), *membership*. Note also **Eidgenossenschaft** (l. 22), *confederation*. Nouns ending in **-schaft** are feminine and their plural ending is **-en**.

2. The adjective **hoh-** in "**für unseren hohen Lebensstandard**" (l. 40) is the form of **hoch** *(high)* that is used before nouns. Note: **Unser Lebensstandard ist hoch,** but **unser hoher Lebensstandard.**

3. The verb **könnte** in l. 44 is a subjunctive form of **können** and is equivalent to English *could*. Subjunctive is treated in *Kapitel 12*.

Nach dem Lesen

1. Fragen zum Lesestück

1. Warum schreibt Claudia Handschin an Thomas?
2. Warum interessiert sich Thomas wohl für die Schweiz?
3. Welcher Prozentsatz° von Schweizern spricht Deutsch?   *percentage*
4. Warum ist der offizielle Name der Schweiz ein lateinischer Name?
5. Wann lernen Kinder Hochdeutsch?
6. Warum schreibt Claudia den Brief auf Hochdeutsch?
7. Was importieren und was exportieren die Schweizer?
8. Was ist die Basis für die starke Wirtschaft der Schweiz?
9. Wie lange ist die Schweiz schon neutral?

2. Claudia Handschin.   Ergänzen° Sie die fehlende° Information über   complete / missing
Claudia, und dann schreiben Sie einen kurzen Absatz° über sie.   paragraph

Alter° _____   age
Wohnort _____
Universität _____
Hauptfach _____

3. Die Schweizer Neutralität.   Suchen Sie im Text die Stellen über Wirtschaft
und Neutralität. Dann sagen Sie, wer laut° Claudia die folgenden Bemer-   according to
kungen° machen könnte° – ein junger Schweizer oder ein älterer, konserva-   comments / could
tiver Schweizer.

1. Wir dürfen nicht Mitglied der EU werden. Da verlieren° wir unsere   lose
   Neutralität.
2. Unsere Wirtschaft wird schwächer, wenn wir nicht Mitglied der EU
   werden.
3. Wir wollen uns nicht von der Welt isolieren.
4. Wir brauchen eine starke Wirtschaft, um neutral zu bleiben.
5. Wir wissen aus der Geschichte, daß Neutralität das Beste für uns ist.

Land und Leute

Die Schweiz: Ein Lied im Dialekt

How much the German Swiss dialect (**Schwyzer-dütsch**) differs from High German (**Hochdeutsch**) can be seen in comparing a song by the Swiss singer Mani Matter with a High German version. The title of the song is *Heidi* and is in the dialect spoken in Bern, the capital of Switzerland.

Heidi

Är wont a dr glyche gass
und i bin mit dir i d'klass
so ischs cho, das mir grad beidi
ds härz a di verlore hei.
  Heidi, mir wei di beidi,
  beidi, Heidi, hei di gärn.

The High German translation is:

Er wohnt in der gleichen Gasse*,
und ich bin mit dir in der Klasse.
So ist es, daß wir gerade beide
das Herz** an dich verloren** haben.
  Heidi, wir wollen dich beide,
  beide, Heidi, haben dich gern.

Der Berner Kabarettist Mani Matter (1936-1972).

*street
**heart/lost

Erweiterung des Wortschatzes

1 Adjectives used as nouns

Herr Schmidt ist **ein Bekannter** von mir.	Mr. Schmidt is *an acquaintance* of mine.
Frau Schneider ist **eine Bekannte** von mir.	Ms. Schneider is *an acquaintance* of mine.
Thomas hat **keine Verwandten** mehr in der Schweiz.	Thomas has *no relatives* in Switzerland any more.

Many adjectives can be used as nouns. They retain the adjective endings as though a noun were still there: **ein Deutscher (Mann), eine Deutsche (Frau).** In writing, adjectives used as nouns are capitalized.

1. Ein guter Bekannter. You and a friend are at a party where there are also some exchange students. Two German exchange students are discussing someone in German. Since your friend doesn't speak German, translate the comments for her/him.

1. Kennst du den großen Blonden dort?
2. Er ist ein guter Bekannter von mir.
3. Er ist Arzt. Er ist immer sehr freundlich zu den Kranken.
4. Seine Tochter ist drei Jahre alt. Die Kleine ist wirklich süß°.   sweet, nice
5. Er lebt in den USA, aber er ist Deutscher.
6. Hier leben viele Deutsche.

Das Gute daran ist, daß es billig ist.	*The good [thing]* about it is that it is cheap.
Hast du **etwas Neues** gehört?	Have you heard *anything new?*
Ja, aber **nichts Gutes.**	Yes, but *nothing good.*

Adjectives expressing abstractions (**das Gute,** the good; **das Schöne,** the beautiful) are neuter nouns. They frequently follow words such as **etwas, nichts, viel,** and **wenig,** and take the ending **-es (etwas Schönes).** Note that **anderes** is not capitalized in the expression **etwas anderes.**

2. Wie war das Wochenende? At the same party, a German and an American are discussing their weekend. Once more you have to translate for your friend.

1. ANDREA: Hast du am Wochenende etwas Schönes gemacht?
2. MICHAEL: Nein. Ich habe nichts Besonderes gemacht.
3. ANDREA: Dann erzähle ich dir etwas Interessantes.
4. Ich habe einen neuen deutschen Film gesehen. Und das Beste war: mein Freund hat mich eingeladen.
5. MICHAEL: War der Film auf deutsch?
6. ANDREA: Ja! Das war ja das Gute daran!
7. Und ich habe sogar fast alles verstanden.
8. MICHAEL: Ach, schön für dich. Aber so etwas Langweiliges wie dieses Wochenende habe ich lange nicht gehabt. Können wir jetzt von etwas anderem reden?

Land und Leute

Schweizer Geschichte

Switzerland's roots reach back more than 2,000 years, when a Celtic people called the Helvetians lived in the area that is now Switzerland. Over the course of several hundred years, the Alemanni, the Burgundians, and the Franks settled there as well. The Holy Roman Empire came into existence in A.D. 962. Most of this area became part of it in A.D. 1033. In the 13th century, the Habsburg family, the ruling house of Austria (1282–1918) and rulers of the Empire, gained control over these regions. The cantons **(Kantone)** Schwyz, Uri, and Unterwalden started the Swiss Confederation (1291) and fought for their independence. August 1 is now a national holiday celebrating the alliance of the three cantons. Between 1315 and 1388 Switzerland defeated Austria in three different wars and finally gained independence from the Holy Roman Empire in 1499. The period of greatest expansion came to an end in the 16th century. From that point on the Swiss Confederation began to embrace a policy of neutrality which was internationally recognized by the Congress of Vienna in 1815. Switzerland never participated in World War I or World War II. During the Nazi era in Germany, many refugees sought exile there.

Ein Beispiel für Schweizer Architektur aus dem Kanton Schwyz.

Today Switzerland is composed of 23 cantons, three of which are divided into half-cantons. It remains independent and neutral. It has an army to defend these principles, if necessary. Military service is compulsory for all men. After completing their service, soldiers take home their rifles and uniforms for they are still obligated to spend several weeks at regular intervals retraining. They remain members of the armed forces and on inactive status.

2 The adjectives *viel* and *wenig*

Wir haben **wenig** Geld, aber **viel** Zeit.

We have *little* money but *lots of* time.

When used as adjectives, **viel** and **wenig** usually have no endings in the singular.

Dieter hat **viele** Freunde.
Das kann man von **vielen** Menschen sagen.

Dieter has *lots* of friends.
You can say that about *many* people.

In the plural, **viel** and **wenig** take regular adjective endings.

3. **Viel oder wenig?** Choose several words from the list below. Ask your partner about the quantity she/he has **(Wieviel?/Wie viele?)** Then depending on the answer, ask for details **(Warum? Welche?)**.

Freunde □ Freundinnen □ Kurse dieses Semester □ CDs □ Kassetten □ Freizeit □ Geld

Land und Leute

Die politischen Institutionen der Schweiz

Although political life in Switzerland is essentially based in the cantons (comparable to states in the USA and provinces in Canada), federal affairs are represented by several constitutional bodies.

Swiss citizens who are 18 years and older have the right to vote for the National Council **(Nationalrat)**. Each citizen can vote for a party and a candidate. Elections for the Council of States **(Ständerat)** vary according to cantonal law. The National Council and the Council of States form the Federal Assembly **(Bundesversammlung)**, which elects a cabinet of Federal Ministers **(Bundesrat)** and the Federal President **(Bundespräsident)**. Although the President is the head of state, his duties are largely ceremonial and he does not hold special power within the government.

The Federal Assembly decides on new or amended laws. However, if within three months of such a decision, 50,000 signatures are collected from voters, the law must be put to the Swiss people for a vote. The law then only takes effect if the majority vote in favor. Some selected recent referenda: (1) In 1992 voters approved Switzerland joining the

Der Nationalrat tagt in Bern.

International Monetary Fund and the World Bank. (2) In 1993 voters approved a rise in the price of gasoline and the introduction of a value-added tax to replace the sales tax. They rejected an initiative to ban ads for alcohol and tobacco products. (3) In 1994 the people approved a referendum for an outright ban in 10 years on all heavy trucks traveling through Switzerland to other European countries. Such vehicles will have to be hauled by rail. No new major highways may be built.

Despite its long democratic tradition, it was not until 1971 that a referendum gave women the right to vote in federal elections and to hold federal office. In 1981 a referendum was passed that bars discrimination against women under canton as well as federal law.

Vokabeln

Substantive

der **Apparat, -e** apparatus, appliance
der/die **Bekannte** (*noun declined like adj.*) acquaintance
der **Brief, -e** letter
der **Brieffreund, -e**/die **Brieffreundin, -nen** pen pal
der **Dialekt, -e** dialect
der **Gruß, ̈e** greeting; **viele/liebe Grüße** (*closing of a letter*) best regards
das **Instrument, -e** instrument
das **Jahrhundert, -e** century
der **Kindergarten, ̈** nursery school; kindergarten

der **Lebensstandard** standard of living
das **Mitglied, -er** member
der **Ort, -e** place (geographical)
das **Produkt, -e** product
die **Qualität, -en** quality
der **Rohstoff, -e** raw material
die **Situation, -en** situation
die **Sprache, -n** language
der/die **Verwandte** (*noun declined like adj.*) relative
die **Welt, -en** world
der **Weltkrieg, -e** world war
das **Ziel, -e** goal

Verben

beginnen, begonnen   to begin
sich **freuen** (**auf** + *acc.*)   to look
  forward to; **sich freuen** (**über** +
  acc.)   to be pleased (about/with)

fürchten   to fear
(**sich**) **interessieren** (**für**)   to be
  interested (in)

Andere Wörter

ähnlich (+ *dat.*)   similar
alle   all
alt: älter   older
da (*conj.*)   since, because
deswegen   therefore, for that reason
erst   first; not until, only, just
falsch   wrong, false
hoch: hoh- (**-er, -es, -e**)   high (**hoch**
  loses the "c" when it takes endings
  as in **ein hoher Lebensstandard.**)

schließlich   finally, after all
Schweizer (*adj.*)   Swiss
selten   seldom
stark: stärker   stronger
wahr   true; **nicht wahr?**   isn't that
  so?
wirtschaftlich   economic

Besondere Ausdrücke

auf [**deutsch**]   in [German]
schreiben an + *acc.*   to write to
  someone; **sie schreibt einen Brief
  an ihn**   she writes a letter to him
  (Also: **sie schreibt ihm einen
  Brief.**)

[**sie**] **stellt Fragen an** [**ihn**]   [she]
  asks questions of [him] (Also: **sie
  stellt ihm Fragen.**)
um ... zu (+ *infinitive*)   (in order) to;
  um neutral zu bleiben   in order
  to remain neutral

**Kapellbrücke mit
Wasserturm (1333) in
Luzern.**

GRAMMATIK UND ÜBUNGEN

1 Reflexive constructions

| Accusative | Ich habe **mich** gewaschen. | I washed *(myself)*. |
| Dative | Kaufst du **dir** einen neuen Farbfernseher? | Are you buying *(yourself)* a new color TV? |

A reflexive pronoun indicates the same person or thing as the subject. A reflexive pronoun may be in either the accusative or the dative case, depending on its function in the sentence.

2 Forms of reflexive pronouns

	ich	du	er/es/sie	wir	ihr	sie	Sie
Accusative	mich	dich	**sich**	uns	euch	**sich**	**sich**
Dative	mir	dir	**sich**	uns	euch	**sich**	**sich**

Reflexive pronouns differ from personal pronouns only in the **er/es/sie, sie** *(pl.)*, and **Sie** forms, which are all **sich.**

■ *Use of accusative reflexive pronouns*

| Direct object | Ich habe **mich** schnell gewaschen. | I washed *(myself)* in a hurry. |
| Object of preposition | Max erzählt etwas über **sich.** | Max is telling something about *himself.* |

A reflexive pronoun is in the accusative case when it functions as a direct object or as the object of a preposition that requires the accusative.

1. Sie fühlen sich heute besser. You and your friends had the same virus. Say that everyone is feeling better today. Use the appropriate accusative reflexive pronoun in each instance.

▶ *Veronika fühlt sich heute besser.*

1. Gabi und Rolf
2. du
3. ich
4. wir
5. Philipp
6. ihr

■ *Use of dative reflexive pronouns*

Indirect object	Kaufst du **dir** einen neuen Computer?	Are you going to buy *yourself* a new computer?
Dative verb	Ich kann **mir** nicht helfen.	I can't help *myself*.
Object of preposition	Sprichst du von **dir**?	Are you talking about *yourself?*

A reflexive pronoun is in the dative case when it functions as an indirect object, the object of a dative verb, or the object of a preposition that requires the dative case.

2. Was kaufen sie sich? Say what the people mentioned would like to buy for themselves on their next shopping trip. Use the dative reflexive pronoun.

▶ Margot / ein neues Fahrrad   *Margot möchte sich ein neues Fahrrad kaufen.*

1. Schmidts / einen neuen Computer
2. ich / ein neues Kassettendeck
3. wir / einen kleinen Farbfernseher
4. Paul / eine Schweizer Armbanduhr°   wristwatch
5. Brauns / einen neuen Küchentisch
6. ich / einen teuren CD-Spieler
7. du / ein amerikanisches Auto
8. ihr / einige CDs
9. du / ein lustiges Poster

3. Was möchtest du dir kaufen? You would like to buy some new piece of clothing. What will it be? Ask four other persons what they would like to buy.

                                                     Discussing wants

S1: Ich möchte mir [eine neue Jacke] kaufen. Was möchtest du dir kaufen?
S2: Ich möchte mir ...

3 Verbs of personal hygiene

Wann badest du?
Ich bade abends.

Wann duschst du?
Ich dusche morgens.

Wann putzt du dir die Zähne?
Ich putze mir morgens die Zähne.

Wann rasierst du dich?
Ich rasiere mich morgens.

Wann schminkst du dich?
Ich schminke mich morgens.

Wann ziehst du dich an?
Ich ziehe mich morgens an.

Wann kämmst du dich?
Ich kämme mich morgens.

Wann ziehst du dich aus?
Ich ziehe mich abends aus.

Wann wäschst du dir Gesicht und
    Hände?
Ich wasche mir abends Gesicht
    und Hände.

■ *Verben*

sich an·ziehen, angezogen   to get dressed; **ich ziehe mich an**   I get
    dressed

sich aus·ziehen, ausgezogen   to get undressed; **ich ziehe mich aus**   I get
    undressed

baden   to take a bath; **ich bade**   I take a bath

(sich) duschen   to shower; **ich dusche (mich)**   I take a shower (**Duschen**
    can be used with or without the reflexive pronoun; the meaning is the
    same.)

sich kämmen   to comb; **ich kämme mich**   I comb my hair; **ich kämme mir
    die Haare**   I comb my hair

putzen   to clean; **ich putze mir die Zähne**   I brush/clean my teeth

sich rasieren   to shave; **ich rasiere mich**   I shave

sich schminken   to put on make-up; **ich schminke mich**   I put on make-
    up; **ich schminke mir die Lippen/Augen**   I put on lipstick/eye make-up

sich waschen (wäscht), gewaschen   to wash; **ich wasche mich**   I wash
    myself; **ich wasche mir die Hände**   I wash my hands

4.   Wann machst du das?   Ask your partner about her/his daily routine.

Describing one's daily routine

S1:   *S2:*

Wann	stehst du auf?	Um (sieben).
	duschst du?	Morgens.
	ziehst du dich an?	Abends.
	putzt du dir die Zähne?	Vor/Nach dem Frühstück.
	kämmst du dir die Haare?	Vorm Schlafengehen.
	wäschst du dir die Hände?	Vor/Nach dem Essen.
	ziehst du dich aus?	Nach einer schmutzigen° Arbeit.
	badest du?	[Drei]mal° am Tag.
	gehst du schlafen?	

dirty
times

4 Reflexive verbs in German vs. English

Setz dich.	Sit down.
Fühlst du **dich** nicht wohl?	Don't you feel well?
Hast du **dich** gestern **erkältet?**	Did you catch a cold yesterday?
Hast du **dich** zu leicht **angezogen?**	Did you dress too lightly?
Mark hat **sich** heute nicht **rasiert.**	Mark didn't shave today.
Ich **freue mich** auf deinen Brief.	I'm looking forward to your letter.
Anna **interessiert sich** für Musik.	Anna is interested in music.

In German, some verbs regularly have a reflexive pronoun as part of the verb pattern. The English equivalents of these verbs do not have reflexive pronouns. In general, the reflexive construction is used more frequently in German than in English. In the vocabularies of this book, reflexive verbs are listed with the pronoun **sich: sich fühlen.**

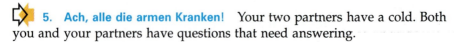 **5.   Ach, alle die armen Kranken!**   Your two partners have a cold. Both you and your partners have questions that need answering.

1. *S1:* Fühlst du dich nicht wohl?
2. *S1:* Wann hast du dich erkältet?
3. *S2:* Hat Kevin sich auch erkältet?
4. *S3:* Hat er sich nicht warm genug angezogen?
5. *S1:* Wollt ihr euch zu mir setzen? Ich werde bestimmt nicht krank!
6. *S2:* Freust du dich auf warmes Wetter?

6.   Wie sagt man das?

1. Do you feel better today, Mr. Meier?
   —No, I don't feel well.
2. How did Astrid catch cold?
   —I don't know. Did she catch cold again?
3. Lotte, why haven't you dressed yet?
   —It's still early. I'll get dressed later.
4. Please sit down, Erna.
   —Thanks, I'll sit on this chair.
5. Are you interested in old films?
   —Yes, I'm looking forward to Casablanca on TV. (*on* = **im**)

5 Definite article with parts of the body

Ich habe **mir die** Hände gewaschen.   I washed *my* hands.
Hast du **dir die** Zähne geputzt?   Did you brush *your* teeth?

In referring to parts of the body, German uses a definite article (e.g., **die**) and a reflexive pronoun (e.g., **mir**) where English uses a possessive adjective (e.g., *my*).

Ich muß **mir die** Schuhe anziehen.   I have to put on *my* shoes.

In German the definite article is also often used with clothing.

7. Schon fertig.   Say that you have washed and dressed and are ready to go out.

▶   Gesicht waschen   *Ich habe mir das Gesicht gewaschen.*

1. Hände waschen
2. Haare waschen
3. Haare kämmen

4. Zähne putzen
5. saubere Jeans anziehen
6. ein sauberes Hemd anziehen

8. Was mache ich?   With a partner take turns miming an action. One partner says what the other is doing.

▶   *Du putzt dir die Zähne.*

9. Was sagen Sie?   Answer the following questions for yourself and then compare your answers to those of a classmate.

1. Wann duschst oder badest du?
2. Wäschst du dir abends oder morgens die Haare?
3. Mit was für einem Shampoo wäschst du dir die Haare?
4. Wann putzt du dir die Zähne?
5. Mit welcher Zahnpasta° putzt du dir die Zähne?   toothpaste
6. Ziehst du dir die Schuhe aus, wenn du fernsiehst?
7. Ziehst du dir alte Sachen an, wenn du abends nach Hause kommst?

6 Infinitives with *zu*

Infinitives with *zu*	Ich brauche heute nicht **zu** arbeiten.	I don't have to [need to] work today.
Modals and infinitive	Mußt du morgen arbeiten?	Do you have to work tomorrow?

In English, dependent infinitives used with most verbs are preceded by *to*. In German, dependent infinitives used with most verbs are preceded by **zu**. Dependent infinitives used with modals are not preceded by **zu.**

Du brauchst nicht mit**zu**kommen.   You don't need to come along.
Wir haben vor, übers Wochenende   We're planning to stay here over
   da**zu**bleiben.   the weekend.

When a separable-prefix verb is in the infinitive form, the **zu** comes between the prefix and the base form of the verb.

If an infinitive phrase contains **zu** + an infinitive and modifiers (e.g., **übers Wochenende**), it is set off by commas. Note that an infinitive phrase after **brauchen** (e.g., **Ich brauche heute nicht zu arbeiten**) is not set off by commas.

Some verbs you know that can be followed by **zu** + an infinitive are **aufhören, beginnen, brauchen, lernen, scheinen, vergessen,** and **vorhaben.**

10. Das haben wir vor.   Dieter has recently passed his exams at the university and you and your friends are giving a party to celebrate. Restate the account of your preparations by combining the sentences into one.

▶ Wir laden 20 Gäste ein. Das haben wir vor.
   Wir haben vor, 20 Gäste einzuladen.

1. Ich bereite das Essen vor. Das muß ich noch.
2. Ich koche Spaghetti. Das habe ich vor.
3. Dieter geht einkaufen. Das will Dieter.
4. Er kauft eine besonders gute Torte. Das hat er vor.
5. Ich räume (nicht) auf. Das brauche ich nicht. (In your answer, omit the **nicht** in parentheses.)
6. Dieter macht alles. Das muß Dieter.
7. Er putzt das Bad (nicht). Das braucht er nicht. (In your answer, omit the **nicht** in parentheses.)

11. Hausarbeit.   You and a friend are comparing notes about all the housework you do. Use the list of chores below to continue your conversation.

Talking about household chores

einkaufen □ kochen □ das Bett machen □ [bei der Hausarbeit] helfen □ abwaschen □ abtrocknen □ aufräumen □ [die Küche] sauber machen □ Fenster putzen □ [die Wäsche/das Auto] waschen □ [im Garten] arbeiten

S1:
Ich muß [jeden Tag] [abwaschen], und du?

S2:
Ja, ich muß auch [abwaschen].
Ich brauche nicht [abzuwaschen].

Glücklich ist, wer vergißt, was nicht mehr zu ändern ist.

(Don't worry about what you can't change.)

■ *Expressions requiring infinitives with* **zu**

Es ist schön, früh morgens zu joggen.   It's nice to jog early in the morning.
Aber es ist schwer, früh aufzustehen.   But it's hard to get up early.

Infinitives with **zu** are used after a number of expressions, such as **es ist schön, es ist schwer, es macht Spaß, es ist leicht,** and **es ist Zeit.**

12.   Nicole studiert in Hamburg.   Tell about some of Nicole's experiences at the University of Hamburg.

▶   Sie steht früh auf. Es ist schwer.   *Es ist schwer, früh aufzustehen.*

1. Sie fährt mit dem Zug. Es macht Spaß.
2. Sie versteht die Vorlesungen. Es ist nicht leicht.
3. Sie sitzt mit Freunden im Biergarten. Es ist gut.
4. Sie findet einen Studentenjob. Es ist schwer.
5. Sie wandert am Wochenende mit Freunden. Es ist schön.

13.   Es macht Spaß ...   You and your partner can get better acquainted by telling each other what you find to be fun, difficult, easy, good, and nice.

S1: Es ist schön, [am Sonntag nichts zu tun].
S2: Es ist schwer [zu schlafen].

Es macht Spaß ...
Es ist schön ...
Es ist schwer ...
Es ist leicht ...
Es ist gut ...
Ich habe keine Zeit ...

7 The construction *um ... zu* + infinitive

Die Schweiz muß wirtschaftlich   Switzerland has to remain
   stark sein, **um** neutral **zu**   economically strong *in order*
   bleiben.   *to* remain neutral.

The German construction **um ... zu** + infinitive is equivalent to the English construction *(in order) to* + infinitive.

14.   Was meinen Sie?   Complete the sentences and compare your ideas with those of your partner. Then make up one or two of your own sentences using **um ... zu.**

▶   *Um gesund zu bleiben, [muß man viel Sport treiben].*

Um schöne Ferien zu haben, ...	Um glücklich° zu sein, ... happy
Um gute Noten zu bekommen, ...	Um reich° zu werden, ... rich
Um ein gutes Examen zu machen, ...	[Um ... zu ... , ...]
Um viele Freunde zu haben, ...	

8 Comparison of adjectives and adverbs

■ *Comparison of equality*

Die Schweiz ist halb **so** groß **wie** Österreich.	Switzerland is half *as* large *as* Austria.
Erik schwimmt nicht **so** gut **wie** Klaus.	Erik doesn't swim *as* well *as* Klaus does.
Diese Reise ist genau**so** schön **wie** die letzte.	This trip is just *as* nice *as* the last one.

The construction **so** … **wie** is used to express the equality of a person, thing, or activity to another. It is equivalent to English *as . . . as*.

15. Ich kann das auch. Say that you have some of the same qualities as your friends and can do things as well.

▶ Franz ist intelligent.   *Ich bin genauso intelligent wie er.*

1. Klaus ist freundlich.
2. Martha arbeitet viel.
3. Frank spielt gut Gitarre.

4. Rita kann schnell schwimmen.
5. Christian kann gut kochen.
6. David spricht gut Deutsch.

■ *Comparative forms*

Base form	**klein**	Österreich ist **klein**.	Austria is *small.*
Comparative	**kleiner**	Die Schweiz ist noch **kleiner**.	Switzerland is even *smaller.*

The comparative of an adjective or adverb is formed by adding **-er** to the base form.

Lore arbeitet **schwerer als** Kai.	Lore works *harder than* Kai.
Lore ist **fleißiger als** Kai.	Lore is *more industrious than* Kai.

The comparative form plus **als** is used to compare people, things, or activities. **Als** is equivalent to English *than*.

Base form	dunkel	teuer
Comparative	**dunkler**	**teurer (teuerer)**

Adjectives ending in **-el** drop the final **-e** of the base form before adding **-er.** Adjectives ending in **-er** may follow the same pattern.

Base form	**groß**	Hamburg ist **groß**.
Comparative	**größer**	Hamburg ist **größer** als Bremen.

Many common one-syllable words with stem vowel **a, o,** or **u** add an umlaut in the comparative form, including **alt, dumm, jung, kalt, kurz, lang, oft, rot,** and **warm.** Adjectives and adverbs of this type are indicated in the vocabularies of this book as follows: **kalt (ä).**

16. Wie ist die neue Wohnung? Your friend wants to know what your new apartment is like. Say that it is the opposite of what she/he is supposing.

Making comparisons

▶ Ist deine neue Wohnung kleiner als die alte? *Nein, sie ist größer.*

1. Ist sie billiger als die alte Wohnung?
2. Ist die Küche größer als die alte?
3. Ist diese Wohnung neuer als die andere?
4. Sind die Türen leichter als die in der alten Wohnung?
5. Ist die neue Wohnung wärmer als die andere?
6. Ist der Weg zur Uni länger als vorher°?
7. Also mußt du für die Vorlesungen nicht früher aufstehen?

previously

Base form	gern	gut	hoch	viel
Comparative	lieber	besser	höher	mehr

A few adjectives and adverbs have irregular comparative forms.

Jörg sieht **gern** fern.   Jörg likes to watch TV.
Karin liest **lieber.**   Karin prefers [likes more] to read.

The English equivalent of **lieber** is *to prefer,* or *preferably,* or *rather* with a verb.

17. In einem Möbelgeschäft. You and a friend are browsing in a furniture store, comparing items you see.

▶ Die Kommode ist groß. *Aber diese Kommode ist größer.*

1. Der Couchtisch ist billig.
2. Das Sofa kostet viel.
3. Der Teppich sieht gut aus.
4. Der Sessel ist teuer.
5. Der Schrank ist hoch.
6. Die Preise° sind hoch.

prices

18. Was machst du lieber? Your partner asks which chores and leisure activities you prefer.

Stating preferences

S2: Was machst du lieber? | **Laufen oder radfahren?**
Zeitungen oder Bücher lesen?
Klassische Musik oder Rock hören?
Das Badezimmer saubermachen oder das Wohnzimmer aufräumen?
Abwaschen oder abtrocknen?
Gartenarbeit oder Hausarbeit?
Ins Kino oder zu einer Party gehen?
Italienisch oder chinesisch essen gehen?

S1: Ich fahre lieber Rad.

■ *Preceded comparative adjectives*

Das ist kein besser**er** Plan.	That's not a better plan.
Hast du eine besser**e** Idee?	Do you have a better idea?

Comparative adjectives that precede nouns take adjective endings.

19. Es ist alles besser. Two friends are talking about things they have or experience. One tries to oudo the other.

▶ Ich habe ein großes Auto.   *Ich habe ein größeres Auto.*

1. Ich habe eine schöne Wohnung.
2. Ich wohne in einem hohen Haus.
3. Ich kaufe ein teures Kleid.
4. Ich habe einen guten Professor.
5. Ich habe einen Freund/eine Freundin mit einem großen Auto.
6. Ich wohne in einem alten Haus.
7. Ich trage einen warmen Pulli.

■ *Superlative forms*

Base form	**alt**	Trier ist sehr **alt.**	Trier is very *old.*
Superlative	**ältest-**	Es ist die **älteste** Stadt in Deutschland.	It is the *oldest* city in Germany.

The superlative of an adjective is formed by adding **-st** to the base form. The **-st** is expanded to **-est** if the adjective stem ends in **-d, -t,** or a sibilant. The superlative of **groß** is an exception: **größt-.** The words that add umlaut in the comparative also add umlaut in the superlative. Superlative adjectives that precede nouns take adjective endings.

20. Was weißt du über Deutschland? Your friend is checking on her/his facts about Germany. Tell your friend that the places she/he asks about are actually the oldest, largest, and so on.

▶ Trier ist eine alte Stadt, nicht?   *Ja, Trier ist die älteste Stadt*
                                                    Deutschlands.

1. Die Universität Heidelberg ist eine alte Universität, nicht?
2. Bayern ist ein großes Land, nicht?
3. Bremen ist ein kleines Land, nicht?
4. Berlin ist sicher eine sehr große Stadt.
5. Der Rhein ist bestimmt ein langer Fluß°.   river

Im Winter arbeitet Frau Greif **am schwersten.**	In the winter Mrs. Greif works *(the) hardest.*
Im Winter sind die Tage **am kürzesten.**	In the winter the days are *(the) shortest.*

The superlative of adverbs (e.g., **am schwersten**) and predicate adjectives (e.g., **am kürzesten**) is formed by inserting the word **am** in front of the adverb or adjective and adding the ending **-(e)sten** to it.

21. Alles ist am größten. Claudia speaks in superlatives. When someone says something, she repeats it and makes it the greatest, coldest, slowest, etc. Take her role.

▶ Im Sommer sind die Tage lang.   *Im Sommer sind die Tage am längsten.*

1. Im Herbst sind die Farben interessant.
2. Im Frühling sind die Blumen schön.
3. Im Winter sind die Tage kalt.
4. Regina fährt langsam°.   slowly
5. Hans-Jürgen arbeitet schwer.
6. Ingrid und Thomas tanzen schön.

Lukas ist der jüngste Sohn, und   Lukas is the youngest son and
   Fabian ist **der älteste (Sohn).**   Fabian is *the oldest (son).*

The superlative of attributive adjectives (with a following noun expressed or understood) is formed by inserting **der/das/die** in front of the adjective and adding the appropriate ending to the superlative form of the adjective.

Wanderer mit Blick auf das Matterhorn (4.477 Meter).

1. Im Juni sind die Rosen **am schönsten.**
2. Diese Rose ist **die schönste.**
   Diese Rosen sind **die schönsten.**

The above chart shows the two patterns of superlative predicate adjectives. The adjectives preceded by **der/das/die** have **-e** in the singular and **-en** in the plural.

22. Die schönsten, neuesten Sachen.   Like Claudia, Peter finds everything the greatest. Take his role.

▶ Diese Schuhe sind sehr billig.   *Diese Schuhe sind die billigsten.*

1. Diese Blumen sind sehr schön.
2. Dieses Auto ist sehr teuer.
3. Diese Jacke ist sehr warm.
4. Dieses T-Shirt ist toll.

5. Dieser CD-Spieler ist billig.
6. Dieses Kassettendeck ist ziemlich teuer.

Base form	gern	gut	hoch	viel
Comparative	lieber	besser	höher	mehr
Superlative	liebst-	best-	höchst-	meist-

The adjectives and adverbs that are irregular in the comparative are also irregular in the superlative. Irregular forms are indicated in the vocabularies of this book as follows: **gern (lieber, liebst-).**

23. Was sind das alles für Leute in diesem Sportclub?   Answer the questions about the sports club, using the superlative.

▶ Frank spielt lieber Tennis als Basketball. Und Fußball?
   Fußball spielt er am liebsten.

1. Peter spielt aber besser als Frank. Und Georg?
2. Inge treibt mehr Sport als ihr Bruder. Und ihre Schwester?
3. Gudrun schlägt° den Ball höher als Lisa. Und Karoline?   hits
4. Julians Tennisschuhe kosten mehr als Ullis Schuhe. Und Marks Schuhe?
5. David joggt lieber morgens als mittags. Und abends?
6. Nach dem Sport hören sie lieber Reggae als klassische Musik. Und Rockmusik?

▷ **24. Was meinst du?**   Answer the questions for yourself and then compare your answers with those of your partner.

Discussing personal information

1. Was trinkst du am liebsten?
2. Was ißt du am liebsten?
3. An welchem Tag gehst du am spätesten ins Bett?
4. Welche Sprache sprichst du am besten?
5. Was studierst du am liebsten?
6. Wer arbeitet in deiner Familie am schwersten?
7. Welchen Sport treibst du am liebsten?
8. Welcher amerikanische Politiker spricht am besten?
9. Welche amerikanische Stadt ist die schönste?

25. Was wissen Sie über diese Länder? With your partner look at the information below and the map of Europe at the very end of your book. Take turns making comparisons using **groß, so groß wie, größer als, am größten.** Other useful adjectives are **klein, viel,** and **wenig.**

Land	Größe (qkm)	Einwohner
Deutschland	357.048	81.200.000
Italien	301.278	57.200.000
Österreich	83.855	7.800.000
Portugal	92.075	9.900.000
die Schweiz	41.288	7.000.000
Spanien	504.750	39.200.000

S1: Ich denke, Italien ist kleiner als Deutschland.
S2: Ja, das stimmt. Es hat auch weniger Einwohner als Deutschland. Aber Italien hat mehr Einwohner als Portugal, und es ist auch größer als Portugal.
S1: Ja, Portugal ist klein, es ist auch kleiner als Spanien ...
    etc.

WIEDERHOLUNG

1. Erik fühlt sich nicht wohl. Karoline thinks Erik doesn't look well. Give the German equivalents.

KAROLINE: Why did you get up so late?
ERIK: I don't feel well.
KAROLINE: Do you have a fever?
ERIK: No. I caught a cold. My throat hurts.
KAROLINE: You look pale. Maybe it's better if you go to the doctor.
ERIK: You're right. I do feel weak.

2. So beginnt mein Tag. Describe the beginning of your day. You may use the expressions provided below and add some of your own.

   aufstehen □ baden oder duschen □ sich anziehen □ tragen □ etwas trinken und essen □ sich die Zähne putzen □ sich die Haare kämmen

3. In Deutschland ist es anders. Join the sentences below, using a conjunction from the list.

aber □ da □ daß □ denn □ ob □ oder □ und □ weil □ wenn

▶ Diane Miller studiert in Deutschland. Sie möchte mehr Deutsch lernen.
Diane Miller studiert in Deutschland, denn sie möchte mehr Deutsch lernen.

1. Sie geht mit ihrer Freundin Nicole. Ihre Freundin geht einkaufen.
2. Diane ist erstaunt°. Nicole geht jede Woche dreimal einkaufen.   surprised
3. Nicole kauft fast alles im Supermarkt. Die Sachen sind da oft billiger.
4. Sie kauft Tabletten in der Apotheke. Sie kauft einen Kamm in der Drogerie.
5. Beim Bäcker kauft sie frischen Kuchen. Sie kauft kein Brot.
6. Diane ist erstaunt. Nicole geht in so viele Geschäfte.

4. Bei Beckers in Zürich. Robert is an American student staying with the Becker family in Zürich. In the following dialogue Anja Becker and her friend Bianca invite Robert to join them on a trip. Complete each sentence with an appropriate possessive adjective.

1. ANJA: Komm, Robert, wir machen gerade _____ Ferienpläne. Wir fahren nach Österreich zu _____ Freunden. Du kommst doch mit, oder?
2. ROBERT: Ja, gern. Wie lange bleibt ihr denn bei _____ Freunden.
3. BIANCA: Eine Woche. Du kannst _____ Arbeit mitnehmen.
4. ROBERT: Ja, das muß ich. Ich muß _____ Referat vorbereiten.
5. ANJA: Das Schöne ist, daß Vater gesagt hat, wir können _____ Auto nehmen.
6. ROBERT: Das finde ich sehr nett von _____ Vater, Anja.
7. BIANCA: Ja, das ist toll! Ich wollte schon _____ Schwester fragen, ob sie uns _____ Wagen gibt.
8. ANJA: Na, den brauchen wir jetzt nicht. Ich glaube, _____ Reise wird super!

5. Mein Bruder. Sebastian tells about his brother. In his account are sentences with words that are related to each other. Some of them may be new to you but you can guess their meaning from the familiar words. Give the English equivalents of the sentences.

1. Ich habe meinem Bruder geholfen. Er hat meine Hilfe gebraucht.
2. Er ist Student. Er studiert in Leipzig. Mit dem Studium ist er erst in vier Jahren fertig.
3. Weil er Geld braucht, will er sein Motorboot verkaufen. Dann will er sich ein Motorrad kaufen.
4. Motorrad fährt er sehr gern. Aber der Fahrschulkurs war teuer. Die Fahrschule hat er letztes Jahr besucht.
5. Im Sommer will er dann durch Deutschland reisen. Die Reise wird bestimmt ganz toll.
6. Wenn das Wetter gut ist, will er zelten. Sein Zelt ist klein und praktisch.

⟐ **6. Sie/Er geht mir auf die Nerven.** *(She/He is getting on my nerves).*
Your roommate's faults are getting on your nerves. Write a letter to **Tante Margo,** who gives advice in the newspaper. Tell her the problem. Your partner will play **Tante Margo** and give you advice orally or in writing.

Some problems could be that your roommate watches TV all day or never:

washes □ combs her/his hair □ brushes her/his teeth □
cleans up the room □ has time

7. Wie sagt man das?

1. Dietmar is taller than his brother.
   —Yes, but still shorter than his father.
2. I work best in the mornings.
   —Really? I prefer to work evenings.
3. Today is the coldest day of the year.
   —Yes, and it isn't getting warmer.
4. Do you like to work with younger people?
   —Yes. But I like to work with older people most of all.

8. Eine Wohnung im Tessin. A Swiss family living in Zürich would like to have a home in another part of Switzerland. In the newspaper they find three ads that interest them, one in French, one in German, and one in Italian. Because they want to be where it is warmer, they are attracted to the place in Tessin, a canton on the Italian border. Show what one can learn from the ad by answering the questions. If you need help, see Vocabulary for Authentic Text Activities in the Reference Section.

1. An welchem See° liegt die Wohnung?   lake
2. Wie groß ist die Wohnung?
3. Wo hat man Platz für Boot° und Auto?   boat
4. Was kann man in seiner Freizeit machen?
5. Wie teuer ist die Wohnung?
6. Was nimmt der Verkäufer° in Zahlung?   seller
7. Wie kann man den Eigentümer° erreichen°?   owner/reach

Westschweiz (inkl. Wallis) EL

Occasion unique
à Yverdon

Une villa de maitre, début XIXᵉ, comprenant propriété attenante de 16 317 m², ainsi qu'une ferme à rénover. Situation dominante avec vue imprenable sur la ville et sur le lac de Neuchâtel, à 2 minutes en voiture du centre ville.
Pour plus de renseignements, écrire sous chiffre 22-120-5843, Est Vaudois, 1820 Montreux.   ELX977 855M

Tessin EE

Bootsgarage
am Luganersee

in **Maroggia,** direkt am See, 3½-Zimmer-Wohnung inkl. Bootsgarage mit Aufzug, Parkplatz in Einstellhalle, Lift, Anteil an Aussenbad, Hallenbad, Sauna, Pergola mit Cheminée. Fr. 720 000.–. Nehme Ferrari oder Porsche in Zahlung.

Tel. (045) 21 71 77
     (045) 51 25 43
Fax (045) 21 67 07
                                    EEX977 676L

**Pian San Giacomo/
San Bernardino GR, 1000 s/m**
Vendo

Chalet

composto da:
1 appartamento con grande soggiorno, camino, 3 camere, servizi, grande terrazza
1 appartamento con soggiorno, camera, servizi legnaia, lavanderia, riscaldamento elettrico
Grazioso giardino con tavolo in granito, posteggi, tranquillità, soleggiato, vista aperta, completamente arredato.
5 min. dalle piste di S. Bernardino, 40 min. di autostrada N 13 da Lugano o Locarno.
Prezzo Fr. 395 000.–. Tel. sera (091) 54 20 21.
                                    EKX977 509G

9.   Rollenspiel.   Assume you and your partner are members of the Swiss family who want the place in Tessin. Discuss the pros and cons of buying it and decide whether you will make an offer.

10.   Zum Schreiben

1. Pretend that you are the Thomas to whom Claudia wrote the letter about Switzerland on pages 318–319. Reply to Claudia's letter. In your reply be sure to:

   - thank her for her inquiry
   - provide some basic information about yourself (much in the same way she did in her opening paragraph)
   - answer the questions she posed in her first paragraph
   - tell her a little about your home state or province (e.g., its location, major cities, main products or services
   - tell her why you like or dislike where you live
   - ask her to write you back
   - say you are looking forward to her reply

2. In her letter Claudia told a little about herself. Make up more information about her, for example, her family, what she likes to do.

3. You have received an internship at a Swiss firm in Zürich. The firm has arranged for you to share an apartment with another intern from Zürich, and you've just received a letter from your new roommate describing herself/himself. Reply to her/his letter. You may wish to include:

   - a physical description of yourself
   - what you are studying and where
   - a list of your favorite leisure-time activities
   - questions about Zürich and what life is like there
   - and, most importantly, your morning routine

Hinweise: As you write your letter, remember to capitalize all **du**-forms and to give your letter the proper German heading, salutation, and closing.

   After you have written your letter, or description, review it, paying particular attention to the following:

   - subject-verb agreement
   - word order
   - case used with prepositions
   - adjective endings
   - reflexive pronouns

GRAMMATIK: ZUSAMMENFASSUNG

Reflexive constructions

■ *Forms of reflexive pronouns*

	ich	du	er/es/sie	wir	ihr	sie	Sie
Accusative reflexive	mich	dich	sich	uns	euch	sich	sich
Dative reflexive	mir	dir	sich	uns	euch	sich	sich

Use of reflexive constructions

■ *Accusative reflexive pronouns*

Direct object	Ich habe **mich** gewaschen.	I washed *(myself)*.
Object of preposition	Hast du das für **dich** gemacht?	Did you do that for *yourself?*

■ *Dative reflexive pronouns*

Indirect object	Hast du **dir** ein neues Auto gekauft?	Did you buy *yourself* a new car?
Dative verb	Ich kann **mir** nicht helfen.	I can't help *myself.*
Object of preposition	Spricht Edith von **sich** selbst?	Is Edith talking about *herself?*

■ *Reflexive vs. personal pronouns*

Reflexive	Max hat das für **sich** gemacht.	Ich kann **mir** nicht helfen.
	Max did it for *himself.*	I can't help *myself.*
Personal	Max hat das für **ihn** gemacht.	Max kann **mir** nicht helfen.
	Max did it for *him.*	Max can't help *me.*

Definite articles with parts of the body

Ich habe **mir die** Hände gewaschen.	I washed *my* hands.
Sophia hat **sich die** Haare gekämmt.	Sophia combed *her* hair.

In referring to parts of the body, German often uses a definite article and a dative pronoun. English uses a possessive adjective.

Infinitives with *zu*

Theo versucht, alles **zu** verstehen.	Theo tries to understand everything.
Er kann alles verstehen.	He can understand everything.

Dependent infinitives used with most verbs are preceded by **zu.** Dependent infinitives used with modals are not preceded by **zu.**

Hannah hat keine Zeit, die Arbeit **zu** machen.	Hannah has no time to do the work.
Es war schwer, die Vorlesung **zu** verstehen.	It was difficult to understand the lecture.

Infinitives with **zu** are also used after a large number of expressions like **sie hat keine Zeit** and **es ist schwer.** If an infinitive phrase contains **zu** + infinitive and modifiers, it is set off by commas.

Es ist schwer, so früh auf**zu**stehen.
Es ist Zeit, jetzt auf**zu**hören.

When a separable prefix is in the infinitive form, the **zu** comes between the prefix and the base form of the verb.

The construction *um ... zu* + infinitive

Amerikaner kommen oft nach Deutschland, **um** dort **zu** studieren.	Americans often come to Germany *in order to* study there.

The German construction **um ... zu** + infinitive is equivalent to the English construction *(in order) to* + infinitive.

Comparison of adjectives and adverbs

■ *Forms of the comparative and superlative*

Base form	klein	*small*	schön	*beautiful*
Comparative	**kleiner**	*smaller*	**schöner**	*more beautiful*
Superlative	**kleinst-**	*smallest*	**schönst-**	*most beautiful*

German forms the comparative by adding the suffix **-er** to the base form. It forms the superlative by adding the suffix **-st** to the base form. The ending **-est** is added to words ending in **-d (gesündest-)**, **-t (leichtest-)**, or a sibilant **(kürzest-)**. An exception is **größt-**.

Base form	alt	groß	jung
Comparative	**älter**	**größer**	**jünger**
Superlative	**ältest-**	**größt-**	**jüngst-**

Many one-syllable adjectives and adverbs with stem vowel **a, o,** or **u** add an umlaut in the comparative and the superlative.

Base form	gern	gut	hoch	viel
Comparative	**lieber**	**besser**	**höher**	**mehr**
Superlative	**liebst-**	**best-**	**höchst-**	**meist-**

A few adjectives and adverbs are irregular in the comparative and superlative forms.

■ *Special constructions and uses*

Bernd ist nicht **so groß wie** Jens.	Bernd is not *as tall as* Jens.
Es ist heute **so kalt wie** gestern.	Today it is just *as cold as* yesterday.

In German the construction **so ... wie** is used to make comparisons of equality. It is equivalent to English *as . . . as.*

Erika ist **größer als** ihre Mutter.	Erika is *taller than* her mother.
Es ist **kälter als** gestern.	It is *colder than* yesterday.

The comparative form of an adjective or adverb is used to make comparisons of inequality. **Als** is equivalent to English *than.*

Verena singt **am schönsten.**	Verena sings *the best.*
Im Frühling ist das Wetter hier **am schönsten.**	The weather here is *nicest* in the spring.
Die kleinsten Blumen sind **die schönsten.**	The smallest flowers are *the prettiest* (flowers).

The pattern **am** + superlative with the ending **-en** is used for adverbs (as in the first example above), and for predicate adjectives (as in the second example). The superlative of attributive adjectives, with a following noun that is expressed or understood, is preceded by the article **der/das/die** (as in the third example). The superlative form of the adjective therefore has an ending.

Das Brandenburger Tor steht im Zentrum eines vereinten Berlin.

Kapitel 11

L E R N Z I E L E

- ### Sprechintentionen
  Talking about cultural events
  Making and responding to an invitation
  Asking about cultural interests
  Asking someone where she/he was
  Asking someone about her/his past

- ### Lesestück
  Deutschland: 1945 bis heute

- ### Vokabeln
  The suffix *-ung*
  Immer + comparative
  City names used as adjectives
  Dates

- ### Land und Leute
  Bertolt Brecht
  Two German states
  After unification
  Germany: The government

- ### Grammatik
  Simple past tense
  Past perfect tense
  Conjunctions *als, wenn,* and *wann*

BAUSTEINE FÜR GESPRÄCHE

Wie war's?

ADRIAN: Wo warst du gestern abend?

BETTINA: Ich war mit Ludwig im Theater.

ADRIAN: Ah, und was gab es? Wie war es?

BETTINA: Man spielte ein Brecht-Stück, *Leben des Galilei.* Es war sehr interessant.

ADRIAN: Hattet ihr gute Karten?

BETTINA: Ja, wir hatten ganz prima Plätze. Wir hatten sogar Studentenkarten. Die kosteten nur zehn Mark, und wir konnten wirklich gut sehen.

ADRIAN: Würdest du das Stück empfehlen?

BETTINA: Ja, unbedingt. Ich wollte es zuerst gar nicht sehen, aber dann fand ich es absolut toll.

ADRIAN: In der Zeitung stand ja eine gute Kritik.

BETTINA: Naja, und danach gingen wir noch in die Wunder-Bar, tranken etwas und unterhielten uns lange über das Stück.

ADRIAN: Du, ich habe Karten für die Oper nächste Woche. Hättest du Lust mitzugehen?

How was it?

Where were you last night?

I was at the theater with Ludwig.

Ah, what were they playing? How was it?

They performed a play by Brecht, *Galileo.* It was very interesting.

Did you have good tickets?

Yes, we had really first-rate seats. We even had student tickets. They cost only 10 marks, and we could really see well.

Would you recommend the play?

Yes, without reservation. At first I didn't want to see it, but then I found it absolutely great.

There was a good review in the paper.

Yes, well, and afterwards we went to the Wunder-Bar, drank something and talked a long time about the play.

Hey, I have tickets for the opera next week. Would you like to come along?

Fragen

1. Wo war Bettina gestern abend?
2. Mit wem war sie dort?
3. Was haben sie gesehen?
4. Was für Karten hatten sie?
5. Wie war das Stück?
6. Was würde Adrian gern tun?

Brauchbares

1. When Adrian asks, **"Würdest du das Stück empfehlen?"** he is using a common German construction that consists of a form of **würde** and the infinitive of a verb. It is equivalent to **would** + a verb in English. This **würde**-construction will be practiced in *Kapitel 12*.

2. Note that to say something is written or printed somewhere, e.g., in a newspaper or sentence, German uses the verb **stehen**. Thus Adrian says, **"In der Zeitung stand ja eine gute Kritik."**

3. In Adrian's question, **"Hättest du Lust mitzugehen?"** **hättest** is the subjunctive form of **haben.** The subjunctive is used to make a statement more polite and will be presented in *Kapitel 12*.

⇨ **1. Wo warst du?** Your partner was at a cultural event last night. Find out what event she/he went to and how it was.

> Talking about cultural events

S1:	S2:
Wo warst du gestern abend?	**Im Theater.**
	Im Konzert.
	Im Kino.
	In der Oper.
Was gab es?	*Die Dreigroschenoper [The Threepenny Opera].*
	Goethes *Faust.*
	Ende gut, alles gut.
	Die Zauberflöte [The Magic Flute].
	Fidelio.
	Lohengrin.
	Beethovens *Neunte.*
	Schumanns *Klavierkonzert°.*
Hattet ihr gute Karten?	**Ja, wir bekamen sogar Studentenkarten.**
	Ja, und die kosteten nur [zwanzig] Mark.
	Ja, wir konnten wirklich gut [sehen/hören].
	Ja, wir hatten ganz prima Plätze.
	Leider nein, die guten waren zu teuer.

⇨ **2. Hast du Lust?** Invite your partner to attend an event with you. She/He may or may not accept your invitation.

> Making and responding to an invitation

S1:		S2:
Hast du Lust **in die Oper** zu gehen?		**Ja, gern.**
	ins ⎪ Musical	In welche?/In welches?
	Theater	Oh ja, das interessiert mich sehr.
	Konzert	Wenn du mich einlädst, schon.
	Pop-Konzert	Nein, ich habe leider keine Zeit.
	Open-Air Konzert	Nein, ich habe wirklich keine Lust.
	Kino	

▷ **3. Gehst du mit?** In a group of four decide what you want to do on the weekend (go to the theater, a concert, the opera, or a musical). After you agree on what to see, decide how much you want to spend for a ticket. Then decide what you want to do afterwards. You may wish to use the following sentences to get you started.

Ich möchte ins [...].
Ich würde lieber [...].
Das ist [...].

▷ **4. Interview.** Interview a fellow student about his/her taste in entertainment. Keep track of your findings and report them.

Asking about cultural
interests

Fragen Sie Ihre Partnerin/Ihren Partner,

1. ob sie/er oft ins Theater geht.
2. was für Theaterstücke sie/er gern sieht.
3. ob sie/er lieber ins Kino geht.
4. wie oft sie/er ins Kino geht – einmal in der Woche, zweimal im Monat.
5. welche neuen Filme sie/er gut findet.
6. ob sie/er manchmal in die Oper geht.
7. welche Opern sie/er kennt.
8. ob sie/er oft ins Konzert geht.
9. was für Musik sie/er gern hört.
10. welche Rockbands sie/er gut findet.
11. welche Fernsehsendungen sie/er gut findet.

Erweiterung des Wortschatzes

The suffix *-ung*

wandern	*to hike*	**die Wanderung, -en**	*hike*
wohnen	*to live*	**die Wohnung, -en**	*dwelling; apartment*

The suffix **-ung** may be added to a verb stem (e.g., **wander-, wohn-**) to form a noun. All nouns ending in **-ung** are feminine.

1. Eine Einladung. Katja is telling about Rolf Braun's model car collection. Complete the sentences by forming nouns from the boldfaced verbs. Give the English equivalents of the nouns.

1. Rolf Braun hat mich für Samstagabend **eingeladen.** Habt ihr auch eine _____ bekommen?
2. Ja, aber Mark hat sich vor einer Woche **erkältet,** und seine _____ wird einfach nicht besser.
3. Vielleicht hast du Glück. Du weißt, Rolf **sammelt** schon seit Jahren Automodelle, und er möchte uns seine _____ zeigen.

4. Und er **beschreibt** jedes Modell sehr genau. Solche _____ finde ich langweilig.
5. Du, er **erzählt** oft Anekdoten von den Modellen. Seine _____ sind immer interessant.
6. **Meinst** du? Ich habe eigentlich eine andere _____ .

Bertolt Brecht.

Land und Leute

Bertolt Brecht

Bertolt Brecht (1898–1956) is one of the most important figures of the twentieth-century theater. His dramatic theories have influenced many playwrights and theater directors throughout the world. As a young playwright during the twenties, Brecht took the German theater by storm with *The Threepenny Opera (Die Dreigroschenoper);* it shocked and fascinated audiences with its depiction of London's criminal underworld and the social and political forces underlying it. Brecht's critical focus on society and his dramatic theories revolutionized the German stage and made him a celebrity.

As an outspoken opponent of National Socialism, however, Bertolt Brecht had to flee Germany in 1933. He lived temporarily in several European countries until he settled down in California. Like many other German emigrants, he found refuge in the United States until the end of World War II and the end of the National Socialist regime. Brecht wrote some of his major plays in exile: *Mutter Courage und ihre Kinder* (1941), *Der gute Mensch von Sezuan* (1942), *Leben des Galilei* (1943).

In 1947, after he had been called before the House Committee on Un-American Activities, he moved back to Europe and eventually chose the German Democratic Republic as his home. With his wife, Helene Weigel, he founded the *Berliner Ensemble,* a theater in former East Berlin that continues to perform Brecht's plays and tries to put his theories into practice.

Das Berliner Ensemble spielt *Der gute Mensch von Sezuan.* (Theater am Schiffbauerdamm)

Vokabeln

Beginning with the **Vokabeln** of *Kapitel 11*, the simple past tense of irregular weak and strong verbs (e.g., **empfahl**) is given.

Substantive

die **Bar, -s**   bar, pub; nightclub
die **Hausaufgabe, -n**   homework; **Hausaufgaben machen**   to do homework
das **Klavier, -e**   piano; das **Klavierkonzert**   piano concerto
die **Kritik**   criticism; review
die **Lust**   desire; pleasure; **Lust haben** (+ **zu** & *infinitive*)   to be in the mood, feel like; **ich habe keine Lust das zu tun**   I don't feel like doing that

die **Sendung, -en**   radio or TV program; die **Fernsehsendung, -en** TV program

Verben

empfehlen (empfiehlt), empfahl, empfohlen   to recommend
sich unterhalten (unterhält), unterhielt, unterhalten   to talk; **sich unterhalten über** (+ *acc.*)   to talk about

würde   would; **ich würde das nicht empfehlen**   I wouldn't recommend that

Andere Wörter

absolut   absolutely, completely
danach   afterwards
prima   fantastic, great (**prima** *takes no adj. endings*)

sogar   even
unbedingt   without reservation, absolutely

Besondere Ausdrücke

es stand in der Zeitung   it said in the newspaper

was gab es?   what was playing? what was offered?

BURGTHEATER

SPIELZEIT

PREMIEREN   **PLÄNE**

Bertolt Brecht
BAAL
Regie: Manfred Karge, Bühnenbild und
Kostüme: Heidi Brambach

DEUTSCHLAND: 1945 BIS HEUTE

Vorbereitung auf das Lesen

■ *Vor dem Lesen**

1. Sie lesen hier über Deutschlands Geschichte zwischen 1945 und 1994. Was wissen Sie schon über diese Zeit?
2. Machen Sie eine Liste von Daten, Wörtern oder Namen zu den folgenden Themen. Versuchen° Sie mindestens° drei Stichwörter° für jeden Punkt aufzuschreiben°.

    at least / key words

    a. der Zweite Weltkrieg°
    b. Berlin
    c. der Kalte Krieg
    d. die Europäische Union (EU)

3. Berichten Sie einer kleinen Gruppe, was Sie aufgelistet haben.

■ *Beim Lesen*

Machen Sie Notizen von allen Ereignissen°, die° mit dem Kalten Krieg zu tun haben.

    events / that

Über vier Jahrzehnte° lang gab es praktisch° zwei deutsche Hauptstädte: Bonn und Ost-Berlin. Theoretisch blieb Berlin jedoch immer die Hauptstadt. Als 1994 die letzten alliierten° Soldaten die Stadt verließen, war Berlin erst seit vier Jahren wieder die offizielle Hauptstadt von Deutschland, aber Bonn war noch
5 immer der Sitz° der Regierung. 1945 hatten die Alliierten die ehemalige° Hauptstadt des Dritten Reiches° in vier Sektoren aufgeteilt und kontrollierten Berlin bis zur Wiedervereinigung. Wenn die Hauptstadt und Deutschland geteilt waren – so argumentierte man – konnte das Land nie wieder stark genug werden, um einen neuen Krieg anzufangen.
10   Europa hatte Angst vor einem starken Deutschland, denn es war im 20. Jahrhundert für zwei Weltkriege verantwortlich gewesen. Deutsche Soldaten hatten zwischen 1938 und 1944 außer der Schweiz alle Nachbarländer zumindest° eine Zeitlang° besetzt°. Außerdem hatten die Nationalsozialisten nicht nur im eigenen Land, sondern auch in allen besetzten Nachbarländern sy-
15 stematisch die jüdische° Bevölkerung° verfolgt° und in Konzentrationslager° gebracht. Im Holocaust starben über sechs Millionen Juden°. Außer den Juden verfolgten die Nationalsozialisten auch noch Zigeuner°, Behinderte°, Homosexuelle sowie° ihre politischen Gegner° – die Kommunisten, Sozialisten und Sozialdemokraten.

decades / for all practical purposes

Allied

seat / former

das Dritte Reich: the Third Reich

at least / a while / occupied

Jewish / population / persecuted / concentration camps / Jews
gypsies / the handicapped / as well as / opponents

---

*Reminder: Words appearing with a raised degree mark but with no definition in the margin are new "active" words that you should learn and be able to use. These words and their definitions appear in the **Vokabeln** section that most closely follows the exercise.

Während der Luftbrücke 1948 landet in Berlin alle paar Minuten ein Flugzeug.

20　　Nach dem Ende des Krieges wurden die Spannungen° zwischen den Russen und den drei westlichen Siegermächten° (England, Frankreich und den USA) immer stärker. Sie kulminierten schließlich 1948 in der Berliner Blockade. Die Russen wollten die westlichen Soldaten zwingen, Berlin zu verlassen und blockierten die Straßen von und nach Berlin. Unter Führung° Amerikas or-
25　ganisierten die westlichen Alliierten die Berliner Luftbrücke°. Ein Jahr lang versorgten° die Flugzeuge die Stadt mit allem, was die Leute zum Leben brauchten – von Rosinen° bis Kohle°. Und deshalb nannten die Berliner die Flugzeuge der Luftbrücke „Rosinenbomber". Doch als die Blockade 1949 zu Ende war, gab es zwei souveräne deutsche Staaten: die Bundesrepublik
30　Deutschland (BRD) mit der provisorischen Hauptstadt Bonn und die Deutsche Demokratische Republik (DDR) mit der Hauptstadt Ost-Berlin. Der Kalte Krieg hatte begonnen. Die neuen Fronten waren der Ostblock und der Westblock. Die neue Grenze hieß „der Eiserne Vorhang°". Nicht alle Ostdeutschen waren für den Kommunismus. Da es dem Westen auch wirtschaftlich besser ging als
35　dem Osten, versuchten viele Ostdeutsche nun°, ihr Land zu verlassen. Um den Exodus zu beenden, baute die DDR-Regierung 1961 die Mauer. Mit den Worten: „Ich bin ein Berliner!" demonstrierte der Präsident John F. Kennedy die Solidarität des Westens mit den Berlinern, als er die geteilte Stadt 1963 besuchte.

　　　In dieser Zeit war die Angst vor dem Kommunismus größer als die Angst
40　vor einem starken Deutschland. Ein wirtschaftlich und politisch starkes West-europa sollte vor dem Kommunismus schützen. Besonders Westdeutschland wollte nach dem Krieg wirtschaftlich, politisch und kulturell mit seinen Nachbarn zusammenarbeiten, um wieder ein Teil Europas zu werden. Es wollte seinen Nachbarn zeigen, daß es wirklich für den Frieden war. So
45　entstand° die Europäische Gemeinschaft° (EG), und ihre ersten Mitglieder waren außer Deutschland noch Belgien, Frankreich, Italien, Luxemburg und die Niederlande. In den nächsten Jahrzehnten bekam die EG immer mehr

tensions
victorious powers

leadership
airlift
provided
raisins / coal

der Eiserne Vorhang: the Iron Curtain
accordingly

was established / community

Mitglieder. Heute heißt die Organisation die Europäische Union (EU), und zu ihr gehören auch Dänemark, Finnland, Griechenland, Großbritannien, Irland,
50 Österreich, Portugal, Schweden und Spanien.

Ende der 80er Jahre gab es in der wirtschaftlichen Union der Ostblock-staaten (COMECON) wirtschaftliche und politische Reformen. In der ehe-maligen DDR, besonders in Leipzig, kam es 1989 zu großen, friedlichen° De-   peaceful
monstrationen. Die Menschen wollten mehr individuelle Freiheit, und am 9.
55 November 1989 mußte die Regierung der DDR die Mauer öffnen; endlich war die Mauer gefallen. Tausende von Ostberlinern kletterten° über die Mauer in   climbed
den Westen, und zusammen mit den Westberlinern zerstörten sie das verhaßte°   hated
Symbol des Kalten Krieges.

Seit dem 3. Oktober 1990 sind West- und Ostdeutschland wieder ein Land.
60 Mit ihren 80 Millionen Einwohnern ist die neue Bundesrepublik jetzt der größte Staat in der EU. Das vereinte° Berlin ist mit über drei Millionen Ein-   unified
wohnern die größte deutsche Stadt. Der Kalte Krieg war endgültig° vorbei, als   definitely
1994, nach 49 Jahren, die Alliierten Berlin offiziell verließen.

Brauchbares

1. l. 6, **das Dritte Reich:** Hitler declared that he would build a third em-pire, successor to the Holy Roman Empire (962–1806) and the Empire (1871–1918) established under William I of Prussia. William I was pro-claimed Emperor of Germany in 1871.
2. l. 13, **Nationalsozialisten:** National Socialists (Nazis) were members of the party of the **Nationalsozialistische Deutsche Arbeiterpartei** that ruled Germany under Adolf Hitler from 1933 to 1945. The policies of the party were anti-democratic, extremely nationalistic, imperialistic, and virulently anti-Semitic.
3. l. 19, **Sozialdemokraten:** Social Democrats were members of the labor-oriented Social Democratic party **(Sozialdemokratische Partei Deutsch-lands).** The party was outlawed by Hitler.
4. l. 22, **immer stärker:** For more information on the construction **immer** + comparative, see p. 355.
5. l. 25, **Berliner Luftbrücke:** During the blockade of Berlin **(Berliner Blockade)** the Allies supplied over 2 million West Berliners with food and fuel by a round-the-clock air lift. There were 277,264 flights made at 3.5-minute intervals. By the end of the lift in 1949, 8,000 tons of goods (⅔ of it coal) were flown in daily. A monument commemorating the U.S. and British airmen who died during the airlift stands at Tempelhof Field, the airport in former West Berlin that was the main terminal of the airlift.

6. l. 32, **Ostblock:** The eastern block was made up of nations under communist domination and the influence of the Soviet Union. COMECON (Council for Mutual Economic Assistance) was founded in 1949 but was only active between the years 1956–1991. COMECON was controlled by the heads of state and was a vehicle for organizing industrial production and coordinating economic policy.

7. l. 33, **der Eiserne Vorhang:** The Iron Curtain was the name for the political and ideological barrier that prevented understanding between the Soviet bloc and western Europe after World War II. The expression became current after it was used by Winston Churchill in a speech at Fulton, Missouri, in 1946.

8. l. 37, **Worten:** The German word **Wort** has two plurals. The plural form, **Worte,** is used for words in context. The other plural, **Wörter,** is used for isolated words as in a dictionary or list.

Nach dem Lesen

1. Fragen zum Lesestück

1. Wie viele Jahre gab es zwei deutsche Hauptstädte?
2. Warum teilten die Alliierten Berlin auf?
3. Gebrauchen Sie eine Landkarte° und machen Sie eine Liste von den Ländern, die° Deutschland im Zweiten Weltkrieg besetzt hat. — map / which
4. Die Nazis verfolgten viele Gruppen. Nennen Sie diese Gruppen.
5. Welche Gruppe verfolgten die Nazis am konsequentesten?
6. Was ist im Holocaust passiert?
7. Warum blockierten die Russen im Jahre 1948 Berlin?
8. Was nannten die Berliner „Rosinenbomber"? Warum?
9. Zwischen welchen Jahren gab es zwei deutsche Staaten?
10. Was wollte John F. Kennedy zeigen, als er sagte: „Ich bin ein Berliner"?
11. Warum wollte Deutschland Mitglied der Europäischen Gemeinschaft werden?
12. Wer waren die ersten Mitglieder der westlichen Wirtschaftsunion?
13. Warum demonstrierten viele Menschen 1989 in der DDR?
14. Mit welchem Wort beschreibt das Lesestück die Revolution in Leipzig?

2. Der Kalte Krieg

1. Viele Historiker sagen, daß Deutschland ein wichtiger Schauplatz° des Kalten Krieges war. Beim Lesen des Textes haben Sie Notizen zum Thema Kalter Krieg gemacht. Vergleichen° Sie Ihre Notizen mit der Liste unten. Was haben Sie aufgeschrieben, was nicht auf dieser Liste steht? — scene / compare

2. Ordnen Sie die folgenden Ereignisse° chronologisch ein°, und geben Sie
ein Jahr oder eine Zeit an°.

events / **ordnen ein:** arrange
geben an: give

Chronologie	Jahr	Ereignis	
_____	_____	der Zweite Weltkrieg	
_____	_____	Gründung° der BRD und der DDR	establishment
_____	_____	die alliierten Truppen verlassen Berlin	
_____	_____	Bau° der Mauer	construction
_____	_____	Aufteilung° Berlins	division
_____	_____	Vereinigung Deutschlands	
_____	_____	Fall der Mauer	
_____	_____	die Luftbrücke	
_____	_____	Reformen in den Ostblockländern	
_____	_____	Demonstrationen in Leipzig	
_____	_____	Gründung einer Wirtschaftsunion im Westen	

3. **Erzählen wir.** Erklären Sie in einfachen Worten die folgenden Ereignisse
oder Daten. Ihr Publikum spricht nur wenig Deutsch.

der Holocaust
die Luftbrücke
der 3. Oktober 1990
die EU

Erweiterung des Wortschatzes

1 *Immer* + comparative

Nach dem Krieg leben die Deutschen
   immer besser.

Ever since the war Germans
   have been living *better and better.*

The construction **immer** + comparative indicates an increase in the quantity,
quality, or degree expressed by the adjective or adverb. In English, the comparative is repeated (e.g., *better and better*).

1. **Wie geht es den Deutschen heute?** Frau Weiß, who was a young woman
during the war, is telling you and a friend how she perceives life in Germany since the end of the war. Translate her statements into English for your
friend.

1. Der Lebensstandard der Deutschen wird immer höher.
2. Die Wohnungen werden immer größer.
3. Sie tragen immer bessere Kleidung.
4. Die Arbeitszeit wird immer kürzer.
5. Die Ferien werden immer länger.
6. Immer weniger Leute bleiben während der Ferien zu Hause.
7. Das Leben wird immer schöner.

Land und Leute

Zwei deutsche Staaten

Two German states existed from 1949–1990. In the later years of the separation, West Germany (The Federal Republic of Germany/ **Die Bundesrepublik Deutschland**) referred to this situation as "two states, but one nation" **(zwei Staaten, eine Nation)**, and its constitution assumed a future reunification. East Germany (The German Democratic Republic/ **Die Deutsche Demokratische Republik**), in contrast, was increasingly dedicated to building an independent, separate country. While West Germany developed a market economy, East Germany followed an economic system of central planning wherein 220 state conglomerates **(Kombinate)** controlled 85 percent of the economy and farms were collectivized (1960). While the citizens of East Germany liked the fact that there was no unemployment, that government subsidies kept rents and prices of food staples low, and that the government provided health care and a pension system, they found that the political system restricted individual freedom, and the scarcity of non-staple consumer goods was a daily irritant.

The construction of the Berlin Wall **(Mauerbau)** in 1961 was the most dramatic attempt to stop the wave of people leaving East Germany. In addition, the gradual build-up of the border system of fences, dogs, and minefields between the two states had made the border practically impenetrable.

In the early seventies, Willy Brandt, Chancellor of the Federal Republic of Germany, made the first open overtures to East Germany (part of his **Ostpolitik**) and thereby laid the groundwork for cooperation with East Germany. West Germany supplemented diplomacy with hard currency by establishing special trade regulations for importing East German goods and granting credits **(Kredite)** to East Germany. In the course of the years the climate between the two countries improved. At first retirees

August 1961: Bau der Berliner Mauer.

(Rentner) and later others from East Germany were allowed to visit West Germany, permanent representations similar to embassies **(ständige Vertretungen)** were established, and West Germans living in border areas were allowed to travel more freely across the border **(grenznaher Verkehr)**.

In 1989, the overall political climate in eastern European countries began to change. Hungary was the first to open the Iron Curtain by taking down the barbed wire and letting vacationing East Germans cross into Austria. A democratic movement spread throughout the Warsaw Pact countries, of which East Germany was a member. Throughout East Germany there were large demonstrations and in November 1989, the government opened the Berlin Wall and subsequently resigned. The freedom movement culminated in free elections in March 1990.

2 City names used as adjectives

1948 organisierten die Alliierten die **Berliner** Luftbrücke.	In 1948 the Allies organized the *Berlin* airlift.
Das Café Demel ist ein sehr bekanntes **Wiener** Kaffeehaus.	The café Demel is a very well-known *Viennese* coffee house.

Names of cities used as adjectives end in **-er.** The **-er** ending is never declined, i.e., no additional adjective endings are used to indicate gender or case.

3 Dates

1945 teilten die Alliierten Berlin in vier Sektoren auf.	*In 1945* the Allies divided Berlin into four sectors.
Im Jahre 1963 besuchte Präsident Kennedy Berlin.	*In 1963* President Kennedy visited Berlin.

In dates that contain only the year, German uses either the year by itself (e.g., **1945**) or the phrase **im Jahr(e) 1945.** English uses the phrase *in* + the year (e.g., *in 1945*).

Vokabeln

Substantive

die **Angst, ̈e (vor** + *dat.*)   fear (of); **Angst haben**   to be afraid
die **Brücke, -n**   bridge
die **Bundesrepublik Deutschland**   Federal Republic of Germany *(the name of West Germany from 1949 to 1990; today the official name for all of Germany)*
die **Demonstration, -en**   demonstration
der **Frieden**   peace
die **Gefahr, -en**   danger

die **Grenze, -n**   border, boundary; limit
der **Krieg, -e**   war; der **Weltkrieg, -e**   world war
die **Mauer, -n**   wall
der **Präsident, -en, -en**/die **Präsidentin, -nen**   president
die **Regierung, -en**   government
der **Soldat, -en, -en**/die **Soldatin, -nen**   soldier
der **Teil, -e**   part
die **Wiedervereinigung**   reunification

Verben

an·fangen (fängt an), fing an, angefangen   to begin
auf·schreiben, schrieb auf, aufgeschrieben   to write down
bauen   to build
berichten   to report
fallen (fällt), fiel, ist gefallen   to fall
öffnen   to open
schützen   to protect
sterben (stirbt), starb, ist gestorben   to die

teilen   to divide; **auf·teilen (in** + *acc.*)   to split up (into)
verlassen (verläßt), verließ, verlassen   to leave, abandon
versuchen   to try
zerstören   to destroy
zwingen, zwang, gezwungen   to force, compel

Andere Wörter

als *(conj.)* when	**politisch** political(ly)
eigen own	**verantwortlich (für)** responsible (for)
nie never	**vorbei** over; gone
noch immer still	**westlich** Western

Besondere Ausdrücke

immer mehr   more and more
zu Ende   over, finished

Land und Leute

Nach der Einigung

When the Berlin Wall fell (9 November 1989), few observers believed that East and West Germany would be unified less than a year later. Unification came about in two major stages. In July 1990, economic union occurred when the **Deutsche Mark** became the common currency of East and West Germany. On 3 October 1990, political unification was completed and the districts of former East Germany were regrouped into five new states **(Länder)**, referred to as **FNL (Fünf Neue Länder): Mecklenburg-Vorpommern, Brandenburg, Sachsen-Anhalt, Sachsen,** and **Thüringen**. Berlin also acquired the full status of a **Bundesland**. The first all-German elections followed in December 1990. For the most part, unification meant that West German laws applied in the new states.

Economic unification revealed that the economy of East Germany, the strongest in Eastern Europe and supporting the highest living standard in that area, was by western standards in a shambles. Unemployment grew rapidly. To facilitate the conversion to a market economy, the German government established a trustee agency **(Treuhandanstalt)**. It broke up the state-owned combines **(Kombinate)** and helped establish 30,000 private businesses, arranging for new or restructured ownership. West Germans have been paying a surtax to finance these changes. So far, unification has cost Germans hundreds of billions of marks, resulting in a substantial budget deficit.

Unification also called for coordination of social and governmental services in the east and

Wo einmal die Mauer war, stehen ab 1998 Büros, Geschäfte und Restaurants.

west. Generally, for former East Germans, it meant fewer social benefits and government services than before unification. At the same time consumer prices rose substantially.

In addition to these political and economic considerations, the two parts of Germany were faced with the necessity of adjusting to each other on a personal level. The social division was reflected in the terms **"Ossis"** (eastern Germans) and **"Wessis"** (western Germans). **Wessis** accused the **Ossis** of being lazy while the **Ossis** perceived the **Wessis** as arrogant and unfriendly.

GRAMMATIK UND ÜBUNGEN

1 The simple past tense vs. the present perfect tense

The simple past tense, like the present perfect (see *Kapitel 7*), is used to refer to events in the past. However, the simple past and the present perfect are used in different circumstances.

■ *Uses of the simple past*

Als ich zehn Jahre alt **war, wohnten** wir in Berlin. Da **stand** die Mauer noch. Die Leute aus Ostberlin **konnten** nicht zu uns in den Westen kommen. Das **verstand** ich nicht.

When I *was* ten years old, we *lived* in Berlin. The wall *was* still *standing* then. The people from East Berlin *could*n't come to us in the West. I *did*n't *understand* that.

The simple past tense (e.g., **wohnten, stand**) is often called the narrative past because it narrates a series of connected events in the past.

■ *Uses of the present perfect tense*

MONIKA: **Hast** du gestern abend **ferngesehen?**

Did you *watch* TV last night?

DIETER: Nein, ich **habe** ein paar Briefe **geschrieben.**

No, I *wrote* a few letters.

The present perfect tense (e.g., **hat ferngesehen, hat geschrieben**) is also called the conversational past because it is used in conversational contexts and in informal writing such as personal letters, diaries, and notes, all of which are actually a form of written "conversation."

 Note that English always uses the simple past (e.g., *did you watch, wrote*) when referring to an action completed in the past.

■ *Uses of* **sein, haben,** *and modals in the simple past*

MONIKA: Jürgen **konnte** am Freitag nicht kommen.
DIETER: **War** er krank, oder **hatte** er keine Zeit?
MONIKA: Er **war** leider krank.

The simple past tense forms of **sein (war), haben (hatte),** and the modals (e.g., **konnte**) are used more frequently than the present perfect tense, even in conversation.

2 *Sein* and *haben* in the simple past tense

sein	
ich war	wir war**en**
du war**st**	ihr war**t**
er/es/sie war	sie war**en**
Sie war**en**	

haben	
ich hatte	wir hatt**en**
du hatt**est**	ihr hatt**et**
er/es/sie hatte	sie hatt**en**
Sie hatt**en**	

You learned in *Kapitel 3* that the simple past tense of **sein** is **war.** The simple past tense of **haben** is **hatte.** In the simple past, all forms except the **ich-** and **er/es/sie**-forms add verb endings.

1. Noch einmal.   Restate the conversational exchanges below in the simple past.

▶ Wie ist das neue Musical?   *Wie war das neue Musical?*
   —Ach, es ist nichts Besonderes.   *—Ach, es war nichts Besonderes.*

1. Bist du in den Ferien zu Hause?
    —Nein, ich bin bei meinem Onkel.
2. Seid ihr heute in der Bibliothek?
    —Ja, wir sind den ganzen Tag da.
3. Ist das Buch interessant?
    —Nein, es ist furchtbar langweilig.

2. In den Bergen.   Tell a friend why you and various people didn't go on the mountain climbing excursion.

▶ Dennis / keine Zeit   *Dennis hatte keine Zeit.*

1. Irma / kein Geld   4. wir / schlechtes Wetter
2. ich / viel Arbeit   5. Nils und Anke / eine Vorlesung
3. Simon / Angst   6. ich / kein Auto

3. Rollenspiel.   Assume a friend (your partner) did not call you yesterday as promised. Ask where she/he was. If appropriate ask a follow-up question such as **Wie war es denn?**

Asking someone where she/he was

S1:   *S2:*

Wo warst du gestern?   Ich war | im Kino.
                                | auf einem Fest.
                                | bei Freunden.
                                | in der Stadt.
                                | in der Bibliothek.
                                | in einer Vorlesung.

3 Modals in the simple past

Infinitive	Past stem	Tense marker	Simple past	English equivalent
dürfen	durf-	-te	**durfte**	was allowed to
können	konn-	-te	**konnte**	was able to
mögen	moch-	-te	**mochte**	liked
müssen	muß-	-te	**mußte**	had to
sollen	soll-	-te	**sollte**	was supposed to
wollen	woll-	-te	**wollte**	wanted to

In the simple past tense, most modals undergo a stem change. The past tense marker **-te** is added to the simple past stem. Note that the past stem has no umlaut.

können	
ich konnte	wir konnten
du konntest	ihr konntet
er/es/sie konnte	sie konnten
Sie konnten	

In the simple past, all forms except the **ich-** and **er/es/sie**-forms add verb endings to the **-te** tense marker.

4. Auf einem Geburtstagsfest. You and your friends planned a birthday party. Recall what happened, using the simple past of the modals.

▶ Ich will meine Freunde einladen.   *Ich wollte meine Freunde einladen.*

1. Klaus kann die CDs nicht mitbringen.
2. Katja muß noch abwaschen.
3. Frank will abtrocknen.
4. Michael soll das Wohnzimmer saubermachen.
5. Die Gäste sollen in zwei Stunden kommen.
6. Wir müssen daher schnell aufräumen.
7. Jens kann leider nicht lange bleiben.

5. Frage-Ecke. Last week you, your partner, and some other people had things to do. Find out who *was able to, wanted to, was supposed to,* and *had to* do something.

S1: Was wollte Adrian tun?
S2: Er wollte mehr Sport treiben.

S1:

	konnte	wollte	sollte	mußte
Bettina		mit ihrer Diät beginnen	ein Referat schreiben	
Adrian	seine Arbeit fertig machen			die Garage aufräumen
Frau Müller	sich mit Freunden unterhalten	eine kurze Reise nach Paris machen		
Herr Meier			seinem Sohn bei der Arbeit helfen	sich einen neuen Computer kaufen
ich				
Partnerin/ Partner				

S2:

	konnte	wollte	sollte	mußte
Bettina	jeden Tag genug schlafen			die Fenster putzen
Adrian		mehr Sport treiben	seine Großeltern besuchen	
Frau Müller			mit ihren Freunden Golf spielen	Babysitting bei ihrer Tochter machen
Herr Meier	jeden Tag spazierengehen	einen neuen Krimi lesen		
ich				
Partnerin/ Partner				

⬦ **6. Meine Kindheit.** Compare your childhood with that of your partner. Answer the following questions for yourself. Then, using the questions, have a conversation with your partner. Finally, tell the class about your childhood experiences and your partner's.

Asking someone about her/his past

1. Mußtest du deinen Eltern viel helfen?
2. Durftest du viel fernsehen?
3. Mußtest du sonntags Hausaufgaben machen?
4. Wie lange durftest du abends ausbleiben?
5. Um wieviel Uhr mußtest du ins Bett gehen?
6. Konntest du machen, was du wolltest?
7. Was durftest du nicht machen?

4 Regular weak verbs in the simple past

Infinitive	Stem	Tense marker	Simple past
machen	mach-	-te	machte
sagen	sag-	-te	sagte
reden	red-	-ete	redete
arbeiten	arbeit-	-ete	arbeitete
regnen	regn-	-ete	regnete

In the simple past tense, regular weak verbs add the past-tense marker **-te** to the infinitive stem. Regular weak verbs with a stem ending in **-d (reden)** or **-t (arbeiten)** and verbs like **regnen** and **öffnen** insert an **-e** before the tense marker. The addition of the **-e** ensures that the **-t,** as a signal of the past, is audible. This is parallel to the insertion of the extra **-e** in the present tense (**er arbeitet;** past tense **er arbeitete**).

machen	
ich machte	wir machte**n**
du machte**st**	ihr machte**t**
er/es/sie machte	sie machte**n**
Sie machte**n**	

reden	
ich redete	wir redete**n**
du redete**st**	ihr redete**t**
er/es/sie redete	sie redete**n**
Sie redete**n**	

In the simple past, all forms except the **ich-** and **er/es/sie-**forms add verb endings to the **-te** tense marker.

7. So war es früher.   Prepare a report about what you and your friend Michael did a few years ago. Use the simple past tense.

▶   Ich arbeite in einem Supermarkt.   *Ich arbeitete in einem Supermarkt.*

1. Ich verdiene natürlich sehr wenig.
2. Mein Freund Michael lernt nicht genug Mathe.
3. Aber er baut die besten Flugzeugmodelle.
4. Er sammelt viele davon.
5. Sein Vater kritisiert° ihn oft.   criticizes
6. Die beiden reden nicht wirklich miteinander.
7. Michael und ich machen nicht genug Hausaufgaben°.   homework
8. Wir hören zuviel Rockmusik.

8. Wir fahren zelten.   Report on an outing. Use the simple past.

▶   Am Samstag regnet es nicht.   *Am Samstag regnete es nicht.*

1. Gerd arbeitet nur bis 12 Uhr.
2. Gerd und Klaus machen eine Wanderung.
3. Sie zelten in den Bergen.
4. Susi und Alex warten am Campingplatz auf ihre Freunde.
5. Alle baden im See°.   lake
6. Am Abend öffnen sie eine Flasche Bier.
7. Sie reden über dies und das.

5 Irregular weak verbs in the simple past

Infinitive	Past stem	Tense marker	Simple past	Examples
bringen	brach-	-te	**brachte**	Peter brachte die Blumen nach Hause.
denken	dach-	-te	**dachte**	Jutta dachte an ihre Arbeit.
kennen	kann-	-te	**kannte**	Wir kannten ihre Chefin.
nennen	nann-	-te	**nannte**	Sie nannten das Kind nach dem Vater.
wissen	wuß-	-te	**wußte**	Du wußtest das schon, nicht?

German has a few weak verbs that have a stem vowel change in the simple past. (For this reason they are called *irregular* weak verbs.) The verbs **bringen** and **denken** also have a consonant change. The tense marker **-te** is added to the simple past stem. Several of the most common irregular weak verbs are listed in the chart on page 363.

bringen	
ich brachte	wir brachten
du brachtest	ihr brachtet
er/es/sie brachte	sie brachten
Sie brachten	

In the simple past, all forms except the **ich-** and **er/es/sie-**forms add verb endings to the **-te** tense marker.

9. Vor Jahren. This report tells how people regarded the role of women a few years ago. Restate it in the simple past.

▶ Viele Leute haben wenig über die Emanzipation gewußt.
Viele Leute wußten wenig über die Emanzipation.

1. Sie haben nur typische Rollen von Mann und Frau gekannt.
2. Viele Frauen haben aber anders gedacht.
3. Sie haben neue Ideen gehabt.
4. Die Kinder haben so wie die Eltern gedacht.
5. Wir haben auch die Probleme gekannt.
6. Die Frau hat oft nur die Hausarbeit gekannt.
7. Sie haben berufstätige Frauen „Rabenmütter°" genannt.   unfit mothers

10. Eine Reise in die USA. Tell about Bettina's experiences. Use the simple past.

1. Last summer Bettina made a trip to the U.S.A.
2. She traveled to Boston. [use **reisen**]
3. She thought Boston was [use **sein**] great.
4. She could speak English well.
5. She wanted to study at a university there.
6. The semester cost a lot of money.
7. At a party, she talked with a German student. [use **reden**]
8. They talked about life in America. [use **reden**]
9. He knew a lot about Boston.
10. Bettina had many questions.

6 Separable-prefix verbs in the simple past

Present	Simple past
Wolf **kauft** für seine Freunde **ein**.	Wolf **kaufte** für seine Freunde **ein**.
Er **bringt** für alle etwas zu trinken **mit**.	Er **brachte** für alle etwas zu trinken **mit**.

In the simple past, as in the present, the separable prefix is separated from the base form of the verb and is in final position.

11. Eine Party. Tell how three friends prepared for a party by using the cues. Use the simple past.

▶ Lilo / aufräumen / die Wohnung   *Lilo räumte die Wohnung auf.*

1. Ralf / einkaufen
2. er / mitbringen / vom Markt / Blumen
3. Lilo und Theo / zurückzahlen / es / ihm
4. Theo / vorbereiten / das Essen
5. erst um sechs / sie / aufhören / zu arbeiten

7 Strong verbs in the simple past

Infinitive	Simple past stem	Examples
sprechen	sprach	Adrian sprach mit Bettina.
gehen	ging	Bettina ging ins Theater.

A strong verb undergoes a stem change in the simple past. The tense marker **-te** is not added to a strong verb in the simple past tense.

sprechen	
ich sprach	wir sprach**en**
du sprach**st**	ihr sprach**t**
er/es/sie sprach	sie sprach**en**
Sie sprach**en**	

In the simple past, all forms except the **ich-** and **er/es/sie-**forms add verb endings to the simple past stem. The stem change of strong verbs cannot always be predicted, but you will probably not have trouble guessing the infinitive form and thus the meaning of most of the verbs. While there are thousands of weak verbs, the number of strong verbs in German is fortunately relatively small. This book uses approximately 60 strong verbs. The list of these verbs is found in the Grammatical Tables in the Reference Section. In the vocabularies of this book, the simple past stem is printed after the infinitive, followed by the past participle: **liegen, lag, gelegen.**

12. Ein Gespräch mit der Nachbarin. Say that the people mentioned below spoke with a neighbor. Use the cued subjects and the simple past.

▶ Frau Berger spricht oft mit der Nachbarin.   *Frau Berger sprach oft mit der Nachbarin.*

1. Herr Wagner
2. Michael und Anja
3. ich
4. du
5. unsere Großeltern
6. Katja

13. Berlin. Reread the information about the division and reunification of Berlin (lines 1–9, page 351). Note each verb in the simple past, give the English equivalent, and then give the German infinitive.

Land und Leute

Deutschland: Die Regierung

In the Federal Republic of Germany each state **(Bundesland)** has a constitution. However, the central government is strong.

National elections to the House of Representatives **(der Bundestag)** take place every four years. All German citizens over 18 have a "first vote" **(Erststimme)** and a "second vote" **(Zweitstimme),** which permits them to vote for a particular candidate as well as for a political party. The representative one votes for need not belong to the party one votes for. The constitution **(Grundgesetz)** of the Federal Republic stipulates that a political party has to have a minimum of 5% of all the votes cast to be represented in the **Bundestag.**

The **Bundestag** is the only federal body elected directly by the people. The Federal Council **(Bundesrat,** comparable to the U.S. Senate) consists of delegates of the states. The President **(Bundespräsident)** is elected by the Federal Convention (comparable to the U.S. Electoral College). The President's tasks are mainly ceremonial in nature.

Eine Sitzung des Bundestags im Bonner Bundeshaus.

The head of the government in the Federal Republic of Germany is the Federal Chancellor **(Bundeskanzler),** who is nominated by the President and elected by the **Bundestag.**

■ *Verbs with past-tense vowel long ā and short ă*

Infinitive	Simple past stem *(ā)*
empfehlen	empfahl
essen	aß
geben	gab
kommen	kam
lesen	las
liegen	lag
nehmen	nahm
sehen	sah
sitzen	saß
sprechen	sprach
treffen	traf
tun	tat

Infinitive	Simple past stem *(ă)*
finden	fand
helfen	half
stehen	stand
trinken	trank

14. Die Sommerarbeit. Peggy, an American, has written to a German friend about her summer internship for a German company. Read the account and answer the questions.

Samstag, den 1. Oktober

Liebe Marga,

Du wolltest etwas über meinen Sommerjob wissen. Also, ich kam am 5. Juni in München an. Viele Menschen waren auf dem Flughafen°. Zuerst verstand ich nur wenig. Aber die Deutschen waren sehr nett, vor allem meine Chefin Frau Volke. Sie half mir auch sehr bei der Arbeit. Ich fand die Arbeit dann viel leichter. Um 10 Uhr morgens machten wir immer Pause und tranken Kaffee. Manchmal waren unsere Gespräche so interessant, daß wir nicht pünktlich wieder an die Arbeit gingen. Aber Frau Volke sagte nichts. Wie Du siehst, kann ich jetzt viel mehr Deutsch. Schreib bald.

airport

Herzliche Grüße°

Deine *Peggy*

Herzliche Grüße: kind regards

1. Wann kam Peggy in München an?
2. Was sah sie auf dem Flughafen?
3. Wer war besonders nett?
4. Warum fand Peggy die Arbeit im Büro leicht?
5. Was machte man um 10 Uhr morgens?
6. Warum ging man manchmal im Büro nicht wieder pünktlich an die Arbeit?

■ *Verbs with past-tense vowel* ie, u, *and* i

Infinitive	Simple past stem *(ie)*
bleiben	blieb
fallen	fiel
gefallen	gefiel
halten	hielt
laufen	lief
schlafen	schlief
schreiben	schrieb
verlassen	verließ

Infinitive	Simple past stem *(u or i)*
fahren	fuhr
tragen	trug
gehen	ging

15. Die Reise nach Frankfurt. Jürgen has written to Rainer about his trip to Frankfurt. Read his letter and then answer the questions.

Dienstag, den 10. Juli

Lieber Rainer,

Du wolltest wissen, was ich letzte Woche gemacht habe. Nun, ich fuhr mit dem Zug nach Frankfurt. Meine Freundin Julia fuhr natürlich mit. Es war heiß, und wir trugen Shorts. Wir liefen ein bißchen in der Fußgängerzone herum und gingen schließlich ins Kino. Wir blieben nur eine halbe Stunde. Der Film gefiel uns nämlich nicht. Dann gingen wir ein Glas Apfelwein trinken. Am Abend fuhren wir dann wieder nach Hause. Julia schrieb Briefe, aber ich habe den ganzen Weg geschlafen.

Herzliche Grüße

Dein *Jürgen*

1. Wie war das Wetter?
2. Wohin fuhren Jürgen und Julia?
3. Was für Hosen trugen sie?
4. Wo liefen sie ein bißchen herum?
5. Warum blieben sie nur eine halbe Stunde im Kino?
6. Was machten sie nach dem Kino?
7. Was tat Julia auf der Rückreise° nach Hause?   return trip
8. Was tat Jürgen?

16.   Eine Nacht im Leben von Herrn Zittermann.   Read the anecdote and answer the questions. Then make up an ending to the story.

Herr Zittermann war allein im Haus. Er lag im Bett, aber er schlief noch nicht. Er hatte die Augen offen. Plötzlich° sah er unter der Tür Licht°. Starr° blieb er liegen. Was war los? Er bekam Angst. Er stand auf und nahm den Revolver, der° natürlich auf dem Nachttisch lag. Fest° hielt er den Revolver in der Hand. Er ging zur Tür und sah …

suddenly / light / motionless

which / firmly

1. Wo lag Herr Zittermann?
2. Wie viele Leute waren im Haus?
3. Schlief Herr Zittermann?
4. Was sah er plötzlich?
5. Was war seine Reaktion?
6. Was lag auf dem Nachttisch?
7. Wohin ging er?

17.   Ein Unfall° in der Herzogstraße.   You are a journalist writing about an accident. Use the cues to write your report. Unfortunately the cues cover only the time until the woman is carried to the bench. You will have to finish the report on your own.

accident

▶   ein blauer Wagen / schnell um die Ecke / fahren
Ein blauer Wagen fuhr schnell um die Ecke.

1. eine alte Frau / über die Straße / laufen

2. sie / nicht / das Auto / sehen

3. dann / sie / auf der Straße / liegen

4. ein Fußgänger / zu der Frau / kommen

5. er / die Frau / zu einer Bank° / tragen   bench

6. Wie ging die Geschichte weiter?

■ *Past tense of* **werden**

Infinitive	Simple past stem
werden	wurde

18. **Berufe.** State the occupation of various people. Use the simple past.

▶ Erika wird Ingenieurin.   *Erika wurde Ingenieurin.*

1. Du wirst Lehrer.
2. Wir werden Journalisten.
3. Inge wird Geschäftsfrau.
4. Klaus wird Apotheker.
5. Marion und Monika werden Ärztinnen.
6. Gerd wird Rechtsanwalt.
7. Karen wird Informatikerin.

8 Past perfect tense

Thomas **war** noch nie in Köln
  gewesen.

Er **hatte** noch nie den Rhein
  gesehen.

Thomas *had* never *been* in
  Cologne.

He *had* never *seen* the
  Rhine.

The English past perfect tense consists of the auxiliary *had* and the past participle of the verb. The German past perfect tense consists of the simple past of **haben** (e.g., **hatte**) or **sein** (e.g., **war**) and the past participle of the verb. Verbs that use a form of **haben** in the present perfect tense also use a form of **haben** in the past perfect; those that use a form of **sein** in the present perfect also use a form of **sein** in the past perfect.

9 Use of the past perfect tense

Edith konnte am Montag nicht
  anfangen, weil sie am Sonntag
  krank **geworden war.**

Edith couldn't begin on Monday,
  because she *had gotten* sick
  on Sunday.

The past perfect tense is used to report an event or action that took place before another event or action that was itself in the past. The following time-tense line will help you visualize the sequence of tenses.

2nd point earlier in past	1st point in past time	Present time	Future time
Past perfect	Present perfect or simple past		

19. Der Fall der Mauer. Herr Weiß, who has always lived in East Germany, makes comments related to the fall of the Berlin Wall. Give the English equivalents of his comments.

1. Zuerst konnte niemand glauben, daß die DDR das Reisen nach Westdeutschland erlaubt° hatte.

2. Als die Mauer gefallen war, fuhren unglaublich viele DDR-Bürger° in den Westen.

3. Nachdem° sie diese Reise gemacht hatten, kamen die meisten wieder nach Hause zurück.

4. Sie hatten ein Stück vom Westen gesehen und wollten dann einfach wieder zu Hause sein.

5. Wer nie selbst in der Bundesrepublik gewesen war, kannte sie doch ein wenig aus dem Fernsehen.

6. Viele gingen aber zurück, weil sie eine andere Idee des Westens gehabt hatten.

erlauben: to permit

citizens

after

10 Uses of *als, wenn,* and *wann*

Als, wenn, and **wann** are all equivalent to English *when,* but they are not interchangeable in German.

Als Paula gestern in Hamburg war, ging sie ins Theater.	When Paula was in Hamburg yesterday, she went to the theater.
Als Paula ein Teenager war, ging sie gern ins Theater.	When Paula was a teenager, she liked to go to the theater.

Als is used to introduce a clause concerned with a single event in the past or with a block of continuous time in the past.

Wenn Renate in Hamburg ist, geht sie ins Theater.	When Renate is in Hamburg, she goes to the theater.
Wenn Erik in Hamburg war, ging er jeden Tag ins Theater.	When (whenever) Erik was in Hamburg, he went (would go) to the theater every day.

Wenn is used to introduce a clause concerned with events or possibilities in present or future time. **Wenn** is also used to introduce a clause concerned with repeated events *(whenever)* in past time.

Wann gehen wir ins Kino?	When are we going to the movies?
Ich habe keine Ahnung, **wann** wir ins Kino gehen.	I have no idea when we're going to the movies.

Wann is used only for questions. It is used to introduce both direct and indirect questions.

20.   Wann ... ?   A friend is asking you a lot of questions. Respond, changing the direct questions into indirect ones. Use one of the phrases listed.

> Ich weiß nicht, ... □ Ich frage mich auch, ...
> □ Ich möchte auch wissen, ... □ Ich habe keine Ahnung, ...

▶ Wann beginnt der Film?   *Ich habe keine Ahnung, wann der Film beginnt.*

1. Wann beginnt das Konzert?
2. Wann ruft Moritz an?
3. Wann fährt Anja in die Ferien?
4. Wann wird das Wetter besser?
5. Wann kommt das Taxi?
6. Wann können wir Pause machen?
7. Wann kommt der Briefträger°?   letter carrier

21.   Bernd und der Fall der Mauer.   Tell what Bernd did after the fall of the Berlin Wall by joining the sentences with **als, wenn,** or **wann** as appropriate.

▶ Die Mauer stand noch. Bernd wohnte in Dresden.
   Als die Mauer noch stand, wohnte Bernd in Dresden.

1. Seine Tante schrieb ihm aus Köln. Er wurde immer ganz traurig°.   sad
2. Die Mauer fiel. Ein großes Chaos begann.

3. Die Tante fragte Bernd am Telefon: „Wann kommen die Eltern?"
4. Auch Bernd setzte sich ins Auto. Er hörte die Nachricht°.   news
5. Er fuhr dann nach Köln. Er war sehr neugierig°.   curious
6. Seine Tante hat ihm gesagt: „Die Eltern kommen in Köln an. Wir haben dann ein großes Fest." (*Do not change the introductory sentence:* Seine Tante hat ihm gesagt.)

WIEDERHOLUNG

1. Eine Reise nach Paris. Read the following account about Kristina's trip to Paris and answer the questions.

Kristina wohnte in Leipzig. Sie war Ingenieurin. Sie wollte immer gern Paris sehen. Aber als es noch die Grenze in Deutschland gab, konnte sie natürlich nicht nach Frankreich reisen. Sie fuhr in alle Länder von Osteuropa und kam sogar bis nach China. Doch in Wirklichkeit träumte° sie immer von Paris. Als   **träumen:** to dream
dann die Grenze fiel, konnte sie es kaum glauben. Sofort° kaufte sie sich eine   immediately
Fahrkarte für die Eisenbahn° und machte die lange Reise nach Paris. Die Stadt   railroad
fand sie ganz toll, aber unglaublich teuer. Solche Preise kannte sie nicht! Da war sie dann ganz froh, daß sie wieder nach Hause fahren konnte. Aber – sie hatte Paris gesehen!

1. Was war Kristina von Beruf?
2. Wovon träumte sie immer?
3. In welche Länder konnte sie früher nur reisen?
4. Wohin fuhr sie, als die Grenze fiel?
5. Wie fand sie die Stadt?
6. Warum war sie froh, wieder nach Hause zu fahren?

2. Ergänzen Sie. Be sure to use the correct form of a verb from the list in each sentence.

aufstehen □ stehen □ verstehen

1. Sonntags _____ ich immer sehr spät _____ .
2. Meistens° _____ dann das Frühstück schon auf dem Tisch.   most of the time
3. Mein Vater kann nicht _____ , wie man so lange schlafen kann.

ankommen □ bekommen □ kommen

4. „Wann sind Sie denn in München _____ ?"
5. „Vor einer Stunde. Ich bin dieses Mal mit dem Zug _____ , nicht mit dem Flugzeug."
6. „Ah, also haben Sie meinen Brief noch früh genug _____ ."

3.   Erzählen Sie von gestern.   Tell what you did yesterday morning. Use appropriate expressions from the list; add other expressions, if you wish.

> aufstehen □ sich baden □ sich die Haare kämmen □ sich anziehen □
> Kaffee kochen □ ein Stück Toast essen □ Kaffee trinken □ Zeitung
> lesen □ sich die Zähne putzen □ in die Vorlesung gehen

4.   Was bedeutet das?   Form compounds using the following words. Give the English equivalents of the compounds.

1. die Bilder + das Buch
2. die Farb(e) + der Fernseher
3. die Blumen + das Geschäft
4. die Kinder + der Garten
5. die Geschicht(e) + s + der Lehrer
6. das Hotel + der Gast

5.   Was für Leute wohnen in diesem Haus, und was machen sie?   Give the German equivalents.

1. Helga Nolte is a doctor. Her husband is a lawyer.
2. Christa is an engineer. Her brother is a student.
3. Christine is a computer scientist. Her father is a journalist.
4. Mrs. Brown is a professor. Her son is a teacher.

6.   Ferienpläne.   Talk with your partner about several things you wanted to do on one of your vacations and why. Be sure to include which of the things you actually were able to do. Remember, in conversation you should use the present perfect tense, except for **sein, haben** and modals, which are in the simple past.

▶ *Ich wollte jeden Tag mit Jürgen Tennis spielen.*
   Aber er ist selten gekommen, und so habe ich wenig gespielt.

> *Themen:* reisen □ [Tennis] spielen □ nach [Europa] fliegen □
> [einem Freund] helfen □ eine Arbeit suchen □ [Freunde] besuchen □
> einen Film sehen □ [ein Buch] lesen □ spät aufstehen □ schwimmen □
> einkaufen gehen

7.   Zum Schreiben

1. Choose two of the opening statements below, one beginning with **als** and one with **wenn,** or make up one of your own. Then write a short paragraph based on each. Be sure to write the paragraph beginning with **als** in the simple past tense.

   - Als ich vier Jahre alt war, ...
   - Als ich noch in die Schule ging, ...
   - Als ich das letzte Mal auf einem Fest war, ...
   - Als ich ...
   - Wenn ich [müde/glücklich/deprimiert°/nervös/böse] bin, ...   depressed
   - Wenn ich Hausarbeit machen muß, ...
   - Wenn ich ...

2. Finish the story about Mr. Zittermann in exercise 16 on page 369.

Hinweise: After you have written your paragraph or story ending, check the following:

- Choice of past tenses
- Form of the past tenses
- Use of **als, wenn, wann**

GRAMMATIK: ZUSAMMENFASSUNG

Sein and *haben* in the simple past

Infinitive	Simple past
sein	war
haben	hatte

sein			
ich war		wir waren	
du warst		ihr wart	
er/es/sie war		sie waren	
	Sie waren		

haben			
ich hatte		wir hatten	
du hattest		ihr hattet	
er/es/sie hatte		sie hatten	
	Sie hatten		

Modals in the simple past

Infinitive	Simple past
dürfen	durfte
können	konnte
mögen	mochte
müssen	mußte
sollen	sollte
wollen	wollte

Simple past of regular weak verbs

Infinitive	Stem	Tense marker	Simple past
glauben	glaub-	-te	glaubte
spielen	spiel-	-te	spielte
baden	bad-	-ete	badete
arbeiten	arbeit-	-ete	arbeitete
regnen	regn-	-ete	regnete

Irregular weak verbs in the simple past

Infinitive	Simple past
bringen	brachte
denken	dachte
kennen	kannte
nennen	nannte
wissen	wußte

In the simple past tense, modals, weak verbs, and irregular weak verbs have the past-tense marker **-te.** In verbs with a stem ending in **-d** or **-t,** and in some verbs ending in **-n** or **-m,** the tense marker **-te** expands to **-ete.** Like **hatte,** all forms except the **ich-** and **er/es/sie**-forms add endings to the past-tense marker **-te.**

Simple past of strong verbs

Infinitive	Simple past
gehen	ging
sehen	sah
schreiben	schrieb

Strong verbs undergo a stem vowel change in the simple past. Like **sein,** they do not take the past tense marker **-te.** The **ich-** and **er/es/sie**-forms have no verb endings.

Selected strong verbs

Below is a table of selected strong verbs. For a more complete list see the Grammatical Tables, #23, in the Reference Section.

Infinitive	Simple past stem	Infinitive	Simple past stem
anfangen	fing an	liegen	lag
anziehen	zog an	nehmen	nahm
bleiben	blieb	schlafen	schlief
empfehlen	empfahl	schreiben	schrieb
essen	aß	sehen	sah
fahren	fuhr	sein	war
fallen	fiel	sitzen	saß
finden	fand	sprechen	sprach
geben	gab	stehen	stand
gefallen	gefiel	tragen	trug
gehen	ging	treffen	traf
halten	hielt	trinken	trank
helfen	half	tun	tat
kommen	kam	verlassen	verließ
laufen	lief	werden	wurde
lesen	las		

Separable-prefix verbs in the simple past

Present tense	Simple past
Sie **kauft** immer im Supermarkt **ein.**	Sie **kaufte** immer im Supermarkt **ein.**
Er **kommt** immer **mit.**	Er **kam** immer **mit.**

In the simple past tense, as in the present tense, the separable prefix is separated from the base form of the verb and is in final position.

Past perfect tense

Ich **hatte** vor zwei Tagen **angefangen** zu arbeiten.

I *had started* working two days before.

Gerd **war** am Montag **angekommen.**

Gerd *had arrived* on Monday.

The German past perfect is a compound tense that consists of the simple past of either **haben** or **sein** plus the past participle of the main verb. It is used to report an event or action that took place before another past event or action.

Uses of *als, wenn,* and *wann* meaning when

Als, wenn, wann are used as follows:

1. **als**—a single event in past time

   Als Katrin Dieter gestern sah, sprachen sie über Politik.

   When Katrin saw Dieter yesterday, they talked about politics.

2. **als**—a block of continuous time in the past

   Als Katrin jung war, sprach sie gern über Politik.

   When Katrin was young, she liked to talk about politics.

3. **wenn**—repeated events (whenever) in past time

   Früher **wenn** sie Dieter sah, redete sie immer über Politik.

   In the past, *when* (whenever) she used to see Dieter, she always spoke about politics.

4. **wenn**—present or future time

   Wenn wir in München sind, gehen wir ins Konzert.

   When (whenever) we are in Munich, we go to a concert.

5. **wann**—introduces direct questions

   Wann beginnt das Konzert?

   When does the concert begin?

6. **wann**—introduces indirect questions

   Ich weiß nicht, **wann** das Konzert beginnt.

   I don't know *when* the concert begins.

Das BMW-Hochhaus in München.

Kapitel 12

L E R N Z I E L E

- ### Sprechintentionen
  Giving factual information
  Expressing importance
  Presenting yourself for an appointment
  Inquiring about and expressing wishes
  Discussing goals
  Stating preferences

- ### Lesestück
  Probleme mit der Wirtschaft

- ### Vokabeln
  Suffix *-lich*

- ### Land und Leute
  Social legislation in Germany
  Codetermination in Germany
  The European Union
  The apprenticeship system in Germany

- ### Grammatik
  Subjunctive of the main verb
  The *würde*-construction
  Conditional sentences

BAUSTEINE FÜR GESPRÄCHE

Stellenanzeigen

SIMON: Na, was gibt's Neues in der Zeitung?

VIKTOR: Ich weiß nicht. Ich hab' bis jetzt nur die Anzeigen durchgesehen.

SIMON: Welche? Die Heiratsanzeigen?

VIKTOR: Quatsch. Die Stellenanzeigen! Ich suche Arbeit. Ich hätte gern einen interessanten Job, wo man gut verdient.

SIMON: Ja, das wäre toll. Du suchst ja schon eine ganze Weile. Viel Glück!

Want ads

Well, what's new in the newspaper?

I don't know. Up to now I have only looked through the classified ads.

Which ones? The ones for marriage partners?

Nonsense. The want ads! I'm looking for work. I would like an interesting job where you can earn a lot of money.

Yes, that would be great. You've been looking a long time already. Lots of luck!

Ein Termin

VIKTOR: Guten Tag. Graf ist mein Name, Viktor Graf. Ich würde gern Frau Dr. Ziegler sprechen. Ich habe einen Termin bei ihr.

SEKRETÄRIN: Guten Tag, Herr Graf. Ja bitte, gehen Sie doch gleich hinein. Sie erwartet Sie schon.

An appointment

Hello. My name is Graf, Viktor Graf. I would like to speak to Dr. Ziegler. I have an appointment with her.

Hello, Mr. Graf. Yes, please go right in. She's expecting you.

Brauchbares

1. In **Ein Termin** Viktor says, **"Ich würde gern Frau Dr. Ziegler sprechen."** All forms of formal social address begin with **Frau** or **Herr.** Titles such as **Doktor** or **Professor** follow. The family name comes last.
2. Note in the same sentence that to request to speak to someone officially, the construction in German is **sprechen** + direct object. In English one might say *I would like to speak with* or *to Dr. Ziegler.*

Fragen

1. Warum weiß Viktor nicht, was in der Zeitung steht?
2. Was für einen Job sucht er?
3. Wen möchte Viktor sprechen?
4. Warum soll Viktor gleich hineingehen?

▷ **1. Die Zeitung.** Ask three fellow students about their newspaper reading habits. Take notes and report on your findings.

Giving factual information

S1:

Welche Zeitung liest du?

Warum liest du Zeitung – wofür interessierst du dich?

S2:

Ich lese [*Die Zeit*].

Für | **Politik.**
Wirtschaft.
Sport.
Musik.
Theater.
Literatur.
Comics.

▷ **2. Was ist wichtig?** Ask four classmates to name one or two things that are important to them in a job. Some possibilities are given.

Expressing importance

interessante oder leichte Arbeit □ gut verdienen □ sicherer Arbeitsplatz □ den Menschen helfen □ viel Freizeit

▷ **3. Im Büro.** Take the role of one of the people involved in a business conversation.

Presenting yourself for an appointment

Frau/Herr Richter:

Ich würde gern Frau/Herrn Dr. Schulze sprechen.

Sekretärin/Sekretär:

Es tut mir leid. Sie/Er ist im Moment beschäftigt°.

Sie/Er telefoniert gerade, und um drei hat sie/er einen Termin.

Haben Sie einen Termin?

Gehen Sie bitte gleich hinein. Sie/Er erwartet Sie.

Heiraten/Bekanntschaften

SOS! Wo finde ich eine treue, lustige Partnerin bis 35 J. zum Verlieben, bin 40 J., schlank, jugendl. Erscheinung, etwas schüchtern, reiselustig, selbständig u. Tierliebhaber. Bildzuschr. u. Nr. 764/G an diese Zeitung.

2 junggebliebene Freundinnen, verwitwet. 60 u. 65 J., suchen 2 nette Herrn. mögl. mit Auto. die mit ihnen Tanzen, Schwimmen und gemeinsame. nette Stunden verbringen. Zuschr. mögl. mit Bild unt. Nr. 2/835083/G-Z.

ER, 28 J.. 189 cm. schlank. sucht nette SIE. meine Hobbys sind Bodybuilding. Motorrad fahren. Kino u. Essen gehen. Bitte schreibe mir an WT 1/167

Wo ist der liebenswerte, gebildete Mann, großzügig im Denken und Handeln. kein Opatyp. ca. 180 groß? Eine attraktive, symp. Sie. mit Herz. Hirn und Niveau. 47 J.. schlk.. 167 groß. würde Ihn gerne kennenlernen. Freundl. Zuschr. m. Tel.-Ang. unt. Nr. 2/835181/G-S.

Elfi ist von Beruf Küchenhilfe und ist **21 J.** alt. Sie hat blonde Haare, geht gerne schwimmen und spazieren. Wenn Du sie kennenlernen möchtest, dann schreibe unter AA 2154.

---

4. Heiraten/Bekanntschaften°. In the dialogue on p. 380 Simon asked Viktor if he was reading the **"Heiratsanzeigen."** Above are the types of ads Simon was referring to. Answer the questions on p. 382 based on the ads. If you need help with vocabulary, see Vocabulary for Authentic Text Activities in the Reference Section.

acquaintances

1. Wie alt sind die Leute, die die Anzeigen aufgegeben° haben?   placed
2. Wie alt sollen die Partnerinnen/Partner sein?
3. Wer möchte mit der Antwort zusammen ein Bild?
4. Was bedeutet „Opatyp"?
5. In welchen Anzeigen ist das Aussehen wichtig?
6. Was für Menschen finden Sie sympathisch°?   appealing

Vokabeln

Substantive

die **Anzeige, -n**   announcement, ad
die **Comics** (*pl.*)   comics
die **Heirat**   marriage
der **Moment, -e**   moment; **im Moment**   at the moment
die **Politik**   politics; political science
der **Quatsch**   nonsense; **Quatsch!** nonsense!

der **Termin, -e**   appointment; **einen Termin bei (jemandem) haben** to have an appointment with (someone)
die **Weile**   while; **eine ganze Weile** a long time

Verben

beschäftigen   to occupy, keep busy; **beschäftigt sein**   to be busy; **sich beschäftigen (mit)**   to be occupied (with)
durch·sehen (sieht durch), sah durch, durchgesehen   to look through; to glance over; to examine
haben: hätte   would have
heiraten   to marry, get married
sein: wäre   would be

telefonieren (mit jemandem)   to telephone (someone)
werden: würde   would

Andere Wörter

hinein   in (*as in* **hineingehen**   to go in)

Besondere Ausdrücke

Viel Glück!   Good luck!
Was gibt's Neues?   What's new?

PROBLEME MIT DER WIRTSCHAFT

Vorbereitung auf das Lesen*

Dieser Text kommt aus einem Artikel der *Süddeutschen Zeitung*. Er beschreibt die Sorgen° eines Angestellten° in der Zeit wirtschaftlicher Probleme.

■ *Vor dem Lesen*

Lesen Sie die folgende Liste, und gruppieren Sie die Wörter unter eine oder mehr der drei Kategorien:

	Wirtschaft allgemein°	Firma	Mitarbeiter	
Angst				in general
Familienprobleme				
Arbeitssuche				
Depression				
mehr Freizeit				
Finanzprobleme				
Profit				
Kündigung°				dismissal
Streiks°				
Inflation				
Sorgen				
sinkende Produktion				
Kosten sparen				
weniger Arbeitsplätze				
teure Rohstoffe°				
Konkurrenz°				competition

*Reminder: Words appearing with a raised degree mark but with no definition in the margin are new "active" words that you should learn and be able to use. These words and their definitions appear in the **Vokabeln** section that most closely follows the exercise.

■ *Beim Lesen*

Dieser Text zeigt die Konsequenzen wirtschaftlicher Probleme für das Leben von Mitarbeitern. Was für Probleme haben die Wirtschaft und die Firma? Was für Probleme haben die Mitarbeiter? Beim Lesen machen Sie zwei Listen:

Probleme	
Wirtschaft/Firma	Mitarbeiter

Heute ist Montag und ich bin wieder im Büro. Wie immer, wenn ich weg war, liegen Berge von Post auf meinem Schreibtisch. Letzte Woche war ich auf einer Geschäftsreise in San Francisco. Jetzt muß ich erst einmal° alles durcharbeiten. Dazwischen° klingelt immer wieder das Telefon. Wie soll ich denn da den
5   Postberg nur vom Tisch kriegen? Diesmal ist es das Büro des Personalchefs. Seine Assistentin fragt: „Herr Gartner, hätten Sie in einer halben Stunde Zeit? Herr Sundmann möchte Sie sprechen." „Ja, kein Problem, wenn's nicht zu lange dauert", antworte ich und merke, daß ich blaß werde. Schließlich weiß ich ja, was das heißt. Jetzt bin ich dran. Ich versuche, klar zu denken und nicht
10   in Panik zu geraten°.

Herr Sundmann ist unser Personalchef. Wenn er anruft, oder seine Assistentin, dann weiß jeder in der Firma, was das heißt. In drei Jahren haben dreihundertfünfzig Mitarbeiter ihre Stelle verloren. Die Büros links und rechts von mir sind eins nach dem anderen leer geworden. Die Krise betrifft° natür-
15   lich nicht nur uns allein. Heute gibt es mehr Streiks als früher. Neue Technologie und Veränderungen° auf dem Markt betreffen heute die ganze deutsche Wirtschaft. Wie die meisten deutschen Firmen, so lebt auch unsere vom Außenhandel. Deutschland muß viele Rohstoffe importieren. Früher hatte Deutschland eine niedrige Inflationsrate. Da konnten unsere Kunden mit stabilen
20   Preisen rechnen°. Heute wird jedoch alles immer teurer. Aber jetzt gibt es auch immer mehr Länder, die die gleichen Waren billiger herstellen. Mit ihnen kann Deutschland immer weniger konkurrieren. Das haben wir hier in unserer Firma gemerkt. Also weiß ich, daß der Besuch beim Personalchef in diesen Tagen Kündigung° bedeutet. Beim Gespräch mit ihm wird es auch vor allem
25   um Geld gehen°. Ich muß mich gut darauf vorbereiten. Susanna, meine Exkollegin, hat dies alles vor einem halben Jahr durchgemacht. Sie ist immer noch arbeitslos und meist zu Hause, wenn ich sie anrufe.

erst einmal: first of all
in between

to get into

affects

changes

rechnen mit: count on

dismissal
um ... gehen: revolve around
money

Münchener gehen zur Arbeit.

Oh je!° Warum muß mir das jetzt passieren? Wenn ich etwas jünger wäre, dann fände ich sicher leichter eine neue Stelle. Aber mit fünfundvierzig? Es
30 würde mir auch nichts ausmachen, weniger zu verdienen. Wer weiß, vielleicht bin ich am Ende der Glücklichere°? Vielleicht finde ich schnell eine neue Stelle, und ich bekomme ja auch meine Abfindung° von der Firma. Da ich zwölf Jahre lang hier gearbeitet habe, müßte meine Abfindung ein Jahresgehalt sein. Aber mein jetziges hohes Gehalt ist bei der Bewerbung° sicher ein Problem. Und
35 wenn ich in einem Jahr keine neue Stelle finden kann, muß ich vielleicht meine Wohnung verkaufen. Aber Moment mal! Wäre es denn wirklich das Ende der Welt? Ich hätte doch auch mehr Zeit für die Kinder und meine Hobbys! Ich könnte endlich Bücher lesen oder die Wohnung renovieren. Alles Dinge, die ich immer schon machen wollte, für die ich aber früher nie Zeit hatte. Aber
40 würde ich diese Dinge wirklich alle tun? Hätte ich wirklich Freude daran? Ich glaube nicht, denn ich mache mir jetzt schon große Sorgen um meine berufliche° Zukunft. Unsichere Zeiten zur Zeit!

Oh je: Oh dear!

the more fortunate one
severance pay

(job) application

related to one's job or career

Brauchbares

1. l. 15, **Streiks:** In the over 50 years of its existence the Federal Republic of Germany has had relatively few labor strikes. Employer- and union-representatives of the major industries usually meet once a year to modify existing industry-wide work agreements **(Tarifverträge).** If they cannot agree, both parties accept an independent negotiator. It is only in exceptional cases that unions organize strikes, for which they need the votes of 75% of their members.

2. l. 17–18, **Außenhandel:** The most important German exports are machinery, automobiles, chemical products, and electronics. For a number of years Germany has ranked number one or two among exporting nations in the world. In 1990 Germany exported goods in the amount of 421 billion

dollars, the U.S.A. 394 billion. In 1991 the U.S.A. led with 422 billion (12% of the entire world trade); Germany was second with 403 billion (11.4%). Germany's principal trading partners are France, the Netherlands, the United Kingdom, Italy, and the U.S.A.

3. l. 21, **Waren billiger herstellen:** Of the industrial nations of the world, Germany has the highest labor costs per hour, $26.23, Switzerland is second with $24.50, Austria seventh with $20.71, and the U.S.A. is fifteenth with $15.49. (Figures are from 1992.)

Nach dem Lesen

1. Fragen zum Lesestück

1. Warum war Herr Gartner in San Francisco?
2. Was liegt auf seinem Schreibtisch?
3. Wer ruft Herrn Gartner an?
4. Warum wird Herr Gartner blaß?
5. Wer ist Herr Sundmann?
6. Wie viele Leute haben schon ihre Stelle in der Firma verloren?

Land und Leute

Das Arbeitsamt kann helfen, wenn man eine Stelle sucht.

Das soziale Netz

The foundations of German social legislation were laid during the time that Otto von Bismarck (1815–1898) was chancellor. Statutory health insurance **(Krankenversicherung),** workers compensation **(Unfall- und Invalidenversicherung),** and retirement benefits **(Rentenversicherung)** were introduced at that time. The costs were to be shared by the employer, the employee, and the state. Retirement age was set at 65.

In Germany today these kinds of insurance are still statutory. All employed people below a certain income must belong to a **Krankenkasse,** which takes care of basic health costs. There is also unemployment insurance **(Arbeitslosenversicherung)** and insurance for long-term nursing care **(Pflegeversicherung).** The entire social "safety net" **(soziales Netz)** includes further benefits such as **Kindergeld,** a monthly payment to parents to offset child-rearing expenses, low-income rent allowances **(Wohngeld),** compensation for the victims of war, financial aid for students, subsidized child care, and others. The state also provides social welfare **(Sozialhilfe)** for those in need.

These benefits come at a cost to the taxpayer. Taxes and benefits constitute 43.6% of the gross domestic product in Germany, in comparison to 30.7% in the U.S.A.

7. Wovon lebt die deutsche Wirtschaft?
8. Warum ist die deutsche Wirtschaft in einer Krise? Geben Sie mindestens zwei Gründe an.
9. Wie hoch könnte Herrn Gartners Abfindung sein?
10. Was wird das Thema sein, wenn Herr Gartner mit dem Personalchef spricht?
11. Was für Probleme sieht Herr Gartner bei der Bewerbung um eine neue Stelle?
12. Wofür hätte Herr Gartner Zeit, wenn er arbeitslos° würde?
13. Wie sieht Herr Gartner seine Zukunft?

2. Unsichere Zukunft. In diesem Text gibt es viele Stellen, wo der Mitarbeiter über seine Zukunft nachdenkt°. Suchen Sie fünf Stellen im Text   thinks about mit den Wörtern: **vielleicht, könnte, müßte, würde.** Benutzen Sie jeden Ausdruck in einem Satz°.

3. Zum Schreiben. Lesen Sie die folgenden Sätze zur Situation der   combine Wirtschaft, der Firma und der Mitarbeiter. Verbinden° Sie Sätze der ver-   various / connections schiedenen° Gruppen und zeigen Sie Zusammenhänge°. Viele Variationen sind möglich.

    Konjunktionen: weil □ aber □ denn □ und

    Adverbien: deshalb □ später □ dann □ leider □ in einem Jahr

▶ *Weil die Inflation höher ist, kann die Firma keine stabilen Preise garantieren.*

Wirtschaft

1. Die Wirtschaft ist in einer Krise.
2. Viele Länder stellen die Waren billiger her.
3. Die Rohstoffe werden teurer.
4. Die Inflation ist höher.
5. Es gibt mehr Streiks.

Firma

1. Die Firma verkauft nicht mehr so viele Waren.
2. Die Firma kann keine stabilen Preise garantieren.
3. Die Firma reduziert ihr Personal.
4. Die Firma muß/will sparen.
5. Die Firma verdient weniger Profit.

Mitarbeiter

1. Der Mitarbeiter verliert seine Stelle.
2. Der Mitarbeiter hat mehr Zeit für seine Kinder.
3. Der Mitarbeiter muß eine neue Stelle suchen.
4. Der Mitarbeiter hat Angst vor der Zukunft.

4. Erzählen wir. Benutzen Sie die Notizen, die Sie beim Lesen gemacht haben, und sprechen Sie über ein Thema:

1. Stellen Sie sich vor°, Sie verlieren vielleicht Ihre Stelle. Was sagen Sie zu   **stellen ... vor:** imagine Ihrer Familie oder Ihren Freunden? Versuchen Sie eine Minute zu sprechen.
2. Sprechen Sie kurz über die deutsche Wirtschaft.

Erweiterung des Wortschatzes

The suffix *-lich*

der Beruf	occupation	**beruflich**	career-related
der Freund	friend	**freundlich**	friendly
fragen	to ask	**fraglich**	questionable
krank	ill, sick	**kränklich**	sickly

German adjectives and adverbs may be formed from some nouns or verbs by adding the suffix **-lich**. The suffix **-lich** may also be added to other adjectives. Some stem vowels are umlauted: **ä, ö,** and **ü.** The English equivalent is often an adjective or adverb ending in *-ly*, e.g., *sick* and *sickly*.

1. Kurzgeschichten. Last night a short story writer gave a public reading of his works and is reading again tonight. Gerd and Anna are discussing the readings. Give the English equivalents of the sentences. Then identify verbs, nouns, or adjectives that are related to the boldfaced words.

1. GERD: Eva sagt, daß die Geschichten **sprachlich** sehr schön sind, aber sie weiß nicht, was sie bedeuten.
2. ANNA: Daß Eva das gesagt hat, ist wirklich **unglaublich.**
3. Hat sie das wirklich **öffentlich** gesagt?
4. GERD: Nein, sie hat mir das privat gesagt. Wußtest du eigentlich, daß Hans-Jürgen gestern abend **schließlich** doch noch gekommen ist?
5. ANNA: Ja, aber es ist **fraglich,** ob er heute abend hingeht.
6. GERD: Der Abend hat mir richtig Spaß gemacht. Alle Leute waren sehr **freundlich.**
7. ANNA: Das ist **natürlich verständlich.** Sie haben alle dieselben Interessen.

Land und Leute

Die Mitbestimmung

Democratic codetermination (**Mitbestimmung**) is a right guaranteed by law in Germany. **Mitbestimmung** gives workers the right and the responsibility to participate in important decisions about their company. Employees of the company have representatives on special councils. These councils ensure that wage agreements, laws, and regulations are carried out. They also participate in decisions about work shifts, overtime, personnel changes, continuing education, and other internal policies.

For companies with more than 2,000 employees, the law requires that an equal number of representatives of shareholders and of employees sit on the board of directors

Was wollen diese Metallarbeiter?

(**Aufsichtsrat**). In Austria, the ratio of employees to shareholders on the board is 1:3. Switzerland does not require **Mitbestimmung**; however, some companies have internal councils that function like those in German companies.

Vokabeln

Substantive

der/die **Angestellte** (*noun decl. like adj.*) salaried employee, white-collar worker

der **Außenhandel** foreign trade

das **Ding, -e** thing

das **Gehalt, ̈er** salary

der **Kunde, -n, -n**/die **Kundin, -nen** customer, client

der **Mitarbeiter, -**/die **Mitarbeiterin, -nen** employee

die **Post** mail; post office

der **Preis, -e** price

der **Rohstoff, -e** raw material

der **Satz, ̈e** sentence

die **Sorge, -n** care, worry; **sich Sorgen machen (um)** to worry (about)

der **Streik, -s** strike

die **Ware, -n** wares, merchandise, goods

die **Zukunft** future

Verben

antworten (+ *dat.*) to answer (*as in* **ich antworte der Frau**); **antworten auf** (+ *acc.*) to answer (*as in* **ich antworte auf die Frage**)

aus·machen to matter; **es macht mir nichts aus** it doesn't matter to me

dauern to last; to require time

finden: fände would find

her·stellen to produce; to manufacture

klingeln to ring

konkurrieren to compete

können: könnte would be able to

merken to notice; to realize

müssen: müßte would have to

sparen to save

verkaufen to sell

verlieren, verlor, verloren to lose

sich vor·bereiten (**auf** + *acc.*) to prepare oneself (for)

wollen: wollte would want

Andere Wörter

arbeitslos unemployed, out of work

diesmal this time

jung (ü) young

leer empty

links on/to the left

niedrig low

rechts on/to the right

unsicher insecure; unsafe

weg away

Besondere Ausdrücke

[**ich bin**] **dran** it is [my] turn

Moment mal! Just a minute!

wie immer as always

zur Zeit at the moment

Land und Leute

Die Europäische Union

The European Union (**Europäische Union**) strives for economic and political union of its member countries. Since its beginning as the European Community (**Europäische Gemeinschaft**), it has made considerable progress in creating a single market without internal borders. Goods, services, and capital can move freely without custom regulations within the EU. Citizens of EU countries can, without restrictions, travel, live, and work anywhere within the EU.

The European Union now stretches from the Arctic Circle to the island of Crete in the Mediterranean. Over 370 million people live in the EU and its gross domestic product is the largest in the world.

In spite of its successes, many problems and goals remain. Working hours, wages, extended

Europäische Union: Ein deutsches Nummernschild.

benefits, and the introduction of a common currency are issues that need to be resolved. The goal of a political confederation of states with common foreign and defense policies and common laws seems to be even more difficult to obtain.

GRAMMATIK UND ÜBUNGEN

1 Subjunctive mood vs. indicative mood

Indicative	Kerstin kommt heute nicht.	*Kerstin is not coming today.*
	Vielleicht kommt sie morgen.	*Perhaps she'll come tomorrow.*

In *Kapitel 1–11* you have primarily been using verbs in sentences that make statements and ask questions dealing with "real" situations. Verb forms of this type are said to be in the indicative mood. The indicative is used in statements that are factual (*Kerstin is not coming today*) or likely (*Perhaps she'll come tomorrow*).

Subjunctive	Ich **würde** das nicht **tun.**	*I would not do that.*
	Ich **täte** das nicht.	
	Hätte Stefan das **getan?**	*Would Stefan have done that?*

When we talk about "unreal" situations we may use verbs in the subjunctive mood. The subjunctive is used in statements that are hypothetical, uncertain, potential, unlikely, or contrary to fact. When a speaker says "I wouldn't do that," she/he means "I wouldn't do that if I were you (or she, he, or someone else)," because she/he thinks it is not a good idea. When the speaker asks "Would Stefan have done that?", she/he is postulating a hypothetical situation.

Wishes	Ich **möchte** eine Tasse Kaffee.	I *would like* a cup of coffee.
Polite requests	**Würden** Sie das bitte **tun?**	*Would* you *do* that, please?

The subjunctive is also used to express wishes and polite requests. You have been using **möchte** to express wishes since *Kapitel 5*. **Möchte** *(would like)* is the subjunctive form of **mögen** *(to like)*.

German has two ways to express the subjunctive mood. One way is to use the **würde**-construction (Ich **würde** das nicht **tun**.). The other way is to use the subjunctive form of the main verb (Ich **täte** das nicht.). The meaning of both ways is the same (I *would* not *do* that.). In conversational German the **würde**-construction is used much more frequently than the subjunctive form of main verbs, with the exception of a few verbs that are commonly used in the subjunctive (**hätte, wäre,** and the modals).

Present-time	Wenn ich nur Zeit **hätte.**	If only I *had* time.
Past-time	Wenn ich nur Zeit **gehabt hätte.**	If only I *had had (would have had)* time.

Subjunctive forms express two time categories: present time which also can refer to the future *(if only I had time now or in the future)* and past time *(if only I had had time in the past).*

2 The *würde*-construction

Ich **würde** das nicht **machen.**	I *would*n't *do* that.
Max **würde** uns bestimmt **helfen.**	Max *would* certainly *help* us.

To talk about "unreal" situations in the present, German often uses a **würde**-construction. English uses a *would*-construction.

ich **würde** es **machen**	wir **würden** es **machen**
du **würdest** es **machen**	ihr **würdet** es **machen**
er/es/sie **würde** es **machen**	sie **würden** es **machen**
Sie **würden** es **machen**	

The **würde**-construction consists of a form of **würde** plus an infinitive. **Würde** is the subjunctive form of **werden.** It is formed by adding an umlaut to **wurde,** the simple past of **werden.**

1. Würden Sie mitfahren?   Schmidts are not having much luck in planning an outing. Tell who would not go along. Restate, using each of the cued subjects and the **würde**-construction.

▶ Ich würde nicht mitfahren. (Andrea)   *Andrea würde nicht mitfahren.*

1. Christoph
2. ihr
3. Eva und Hilde
4. du

5. mein Großvater
6. deine Tante
7. Christiane
8. wir

3 Uses of the *würde*-construction

Hypothetical statements	Ich **würde** ihm **helfen.**	I *would help* him.
Wishes	Wenn er mir nur **helfen würde.**	If only he *would help* me.
Polite requests	**Würden** Sie mir bitte **helfen?**	*Would* you please *help* me?

The **würde**-construction is used in hypothetical statements, in wishes, and in polite requests.

2. Sabine würde das auch gern haben.   Say that Sabine would like to have and do things Susanne has and does. Use the **würde**-construction.

▶ Susanne hat einen guten Job.   *Sabine würde auch gern einen guten Job haben.*

1. Susanne verdient viel.
2. Sie fährt dreimal im Jahr in die Ferien.
3. Sie kauft sich jetzt eine Wohnung.
4. Sie hat viel Freizeit.
5. Am Wochenende ist sie immer in den Bergen.

3. Beim Kaffee.   The Bergers have invited their neighbors for coffee. Restate the sentences below as polite requests, using the **würde**-construction.

▶ Kommen Sie bitte herein°.   *Würden Sie bitte hereinkommen?*   in

1. Gehen Sie bitte ins Wohnzimmer.
2. Setzen Sie sich bitte.
3. Nehmen Sie bitte von dem Kuchen.
4. Erzählen Sie bitte von Ihrer Reise.
5. Bleiben Sie bitte noch ein wenig.

4. Was würden Sie gern machen?   Answer the following questions for yourself. Then compare your answers with two other members of the class.

▶ Was würdest du nach der Deutschstunde am liebsten machen?
Ich würde am liebsten nach Hause gehen/einen Kaffee trinken/schlafen.

1. Was würdest du heute abend gern machen?
2. Was würdest du am Freitagabend am liebsten machen?

> Inquiring about someone's wishes

3. Was würdest du im Sommer gern machen?
4. Was würdest du nach dem Studium gern machen?
5. Was würdest du jetzt am liebsten machen?

4 Present-time subjunctive of the main verb

Wenn Alex besser Golf **spielte,** würden wir mit ihm spielen.	If Alex *played* better golf, we'd play with him.
Wenn ich das **könnte**, würde ich es tun.	If I *could* (do that), I would (do it).
Wenn sie müde **wäre,** würde sie ins Bett gehen.	If she *were* (colloquial: *was*) tired, she would go to bed.

Notice that in English the subjunctive forms of main verbs are often identical with the past tense [e.g., *played, could, were* (colloquial: *was*)]. In German the same principle applies. For weak verbs, the present-time subjunctive is identical to the simple past tense (e.g., **spielte**); for modals and strong verbs, the subjunctive is based on the simple-past tense form of the verb (e.g., **konnte > könnte, war > wäre**). German uses the present-time subjunctive to express subjunctive for present and future time.

Land und Leute

Berufliche Ausbildung

Despite high income-tax rates and high labor costs, Germany has a very productive economy. Experts attribute this in large measure to the fact that Germany has a well-trained labor force.

Most young people who finish the **Hauptschule** (*see* **Das Schulsystem in Deutschland,** p. 135) or have a **Mittlere Reife** enter an apprenticeship (**Ausbildung**) program. There are approximately 400 such **Ausbildungsberufe.** An **Ausbildung** generally lasts three years. During this time the trainees (**Auszubildende,** also called **Lehrlinge**) work three to four days a week in a company and attend vocational school (**Berufsschule**) one to two days a week. Large companies have special workshops and staffs for trainees; in small businesses trainees often learn directly from the boss. **Auszubildende** receive benefits and a salary that increases every year. At the end of their **Ausbildung** trainees take exams both at the workplace and the **Berufsschule.** By passing the exam a

Eine Wissenschaftlerin mit einer Auszubildenden im European Space Operations Center in Darmstadt.

woman becomes a journeywoman (**Gesellin**) and a man becomes a journeyman (**Geselle**). After five more years of work and additional schooling a **Geselle** may become a **Meister,** a person who is qualified to train **Auszubildende** (**Azubis**).

5 Present-time subjunctive of the main verb vs. the *würde*-construction

Present-time subjunctive	*Würde*-construction
Wenn er nur besser **spielte**.	Wenn er nur besser **spielen würde**.
Wenn sie nur etwas **täte**.	Wenn sie nur etwas **tun würde**.
Wenn er nur **ginge**.	Wenn er nur **gehen würde**.

In present-time either the **würde**-construction or the subjunctive form of the main verb can be used. However, for the verbs **sein, haben,** and the modals, the present-time subjunctive is generally used instead of the **würde**-construction.

6 Present-time subjunctive of *sein* and *haben*

sein	
ich wäre	wir wären
du wärest	ihr wäret
er/es/sie wäre	sie wären
Sie wären	

haben	
ich hätte	wir hätten
du hättest	ihr hättet
er/es/sie hätte	sie hätten
Sie hätten	

The verbs **haben** and **sein** are more commonly used in their subjunctive forms, **wäre** and **hätte,** than as part of the **würde**-construction. Notice that the subjunctive of **haben** is identical to the simple past tense (i.e., **hatte**) except that an umlaut has been added.

In strong verbs like **sein** the endings **-est** and **-et** often contract to **-st** and **-t: wärest > wärst, wäret > wärt.** Note that the endings above are used on all verbs in the subjunctive.

5. Alle wären froh. Some politicians are talking about setting speed limits on all of the **Autobahn.** Say that the following people would certainly be happy if there were speed limits.

▶ Roland   *Roland wäre sicher froh.*

1. Ria
2. du
3. wir
4. Corinna und Rafael
5. ich
6. ihr
7. die Grünen
8. Sie

6. Alle hätten Angst. A friend asks how the same people would feel if there were a leak in one of the atomic power plants. Say they would all be afraid, of course.

▶ Roland   *Roland hätte natürlich Angst.*

1. Ria
2. du
3. wir
4. Corinna und Rafael
5. ich
6. ihr
7. die Grünen
8. alle

7. **Hättest du Lust?**   Decide what you would like to do in your free time. Then try to find three classmates who would like to do the same thing.

S1:

Hättest du Lust,

	S2:
schwimmen zu gehen?	Das wäre schön.
ins Kino zu gehen?	Wenn es nur wärmer wäre.
eine Party zu geben?	Das würde ich gern machen.
eine Radtour zu machen?	Das würde Spaß machen.
Musik zu hören?	Wenn ich nur Zeit hätte.
fernzusehen?	Dazu hätte ich keine Lust.
Russisch zu lernen?	

8. **Wenn ich nur ...**   You get to make two wishes. Tell your partner what they are and she/he will tell you her/his wishes. Some suggestions are given below.

> Expressing wishes

1. Wenn ich nur [...] hätte.

   mehr Geld □ Zeit □ mehr Freunde □ weniger Probleme □ Arbeit □ keine Hausaufgaben

2. Wenn ich nur [...] wäre.

   toleranter □ fleißiger □ ruhiger □ nicht so müde □ nicht so faul

7 Conditional sentences

A conditional sentence contains two clauses: the condition (**wenn**-clause) and the conclusion. The **wenn**-clause states the conditions under which some event may or may not take place.

■ *Conditions of fact*

Wenn ich Zeit **habe, komme** ich **mit.**	If I *have* time (maybe I will, maybe I won't), I'll *come* along.

Conditions of fact are conditions that can be fulfilled. Indicative verb forms are used in conditions of fact.

■ *Conditions contrary to fact*

Wenn ich Zeit **hätte, würde** ich **mitkommen.**	If I *had* time [but I don't], I *would come along*.
Wenn ich Zeit **hätte, käme** ich mit.	

A sentence with a condition contrary to fact indicates a situation that will not take place. The speaker only speculates on how some things could or would be under certain conditions (if the speaker had time, for example).

   To talk about the present, a speaker uses present-time subjunctive of the main verb (e.g., **hätte**) in the condition clause (**wenn**-clause) and in the conclusion a **würde**-construction (e.g., **würde mitkommen**) or the present-time subjunctive of the main verb (e.g., **käme**). Formal written German tends to avoid the **würde**-construction in the **wenn**-clause. Subjunctive forms of strong and weak verbs are discussed under headings 9-11 in this section.

⇨ **9. Frage-Ecke.** What would the following people do under certain conditions? Find out the missing information from your partner.

S2: Was würde Frau Müller machen, wenn sie mehr Zeit hätte?
S1: Wenn sie mehr Zeit hätte, (dann) würde sie öfter Tennis spielen.

S1:

	arbeitslos wäre	krank wäre	mehr Zeit hätte	viel Geld hätte
Frau Müller	Zeitung lesen		öfter Tennis spielen	in die Schweiz reisen
Herr Schäfer		viel schlafen		
Susanne und Moritz	spazieren gehen		Auto fahren	
ich				
Partnerin/Partner				

S2:

	arbeitslos wäre	krank wäre	mehr Zeit hätte	viel Geld hätte
Frau Müller		zum Arzt gehen		
Herr Schäfer	eine neue Stelle suchen		seine Freunde besuchen	ein neues Auto kaufen
Susanne und Moritz		nichts essen		ihr Haus renovieren
ich				
Partnerin/Partner				

⇨ **10. Was wäre, wenn ... ?** Answer the following questions for yourself, then ask your partner the same questions. Share your answers with the entire class.

Was würdest du tun,

1. wenn du 10 Jahre älter wärest?
2. wenn du sehr reich° wärest?   rich
3. wenn du Deutschlehrerin/Deutschlehrer wärest?
4. wenn du Präsidentin/Präsident der USA wärest?
5. wenn du kein Geld fürs Studium hättest?
6. wenn deine Freunde keine Zeit für dich hätten?
7. wenn du morgen frei hättest?
8. wenn du kein Auto hättest?
9. wenn dein Fernseher kaputt wäre?
10. wenn du morgen krank wärest?
11. wenn wir morgen 30°C hätten?

S1: Was würdest du tun, wenn du 10 Jahre älter wärest?
S2: Ich würde ein Haus kaufen/ein Buch schreiben/heiraten.

8 Modals in present-time subjunctive

Infinitive		Simple past	Present-time subjunctive
dürfen		durfte	**dürfte**
können		konnte	**könnte**
mögen	er/es/sie	mochte	**möchte**
müssen		mußte	**müßte**
sollen		sollte	**sollte**
wollen		wollte	**wollte**

The present-time subjunctive of modals is identical to the simple-past tense except that the modals that have an umlaut in the infinitive also have an umlaut in the subjunctive.

Müßtest du die Arbeit allein machen?   *Would* you *have* to do the work alone?

Like **sein (wäre)** and **haben (hätte),** the modals are generally used in their subjunctive form rather than as infinitives with the **würde-**construction.

Dürfte ich auch mitkommen?   *Might* I come along, too?
Könntest du noch etwas bleiben?   *Could* you stay a while?
Müßte sie vor allen Leuten   *Would* she *have to* speak in front
   sprechen?   of all the people?
Möchten Sie in einer Stunde essen?   *Would* you *like to* eat in an hour?
Solltet ihr jetzt nicht gehen?   *Should*n't you be going now?

The subjunctive forms of the modals are frequently used to express polite requests or wishes.

Ich wollte, ich hätte Zeit.   *I wish* I had time.
Ich wollte, sie käme bald.   *I wish* she would come soon.

The expression **ich wollte** is used frequently to introduce wishes. Note that the verb **wollte** is subjunctive. Thus, strictly, **ich wollte** is equivalent to *I would wish.*

11. Etwas höflicher°, bitte! You and some friends are getting ready to go out for the evening. You express some concerns and some orders. Soften the tone of the statements and questions by using the present-time subjunctive of the modals.

more politely

▶ Können wir das Restaurant allein finden?   *Könnten wir das Restaurant allein finden?*

1. Können wir nicht bald gehen?
2. Du mußt noch abwaschen.
3. Kann ich dir helfen?
4. Dürfen Susi und Christiane mitkommen?
5. Sollen wir Gerd nicht auch einladen?
6. Darf ich für euch alle etwas zu trinken kaufen?
7. Kannst du für das Essen zahlen?

12.   Wenn es nur anders wäre.   Express wishes to a friend about many things in your dormitory you would like to be different.

Expressing wishes

▶   Klaus kocht immer Spaghetti.   *Ich wollte, Klaus würde
                                          nicht immer Spaghetti kochen.*

▶   Michael macht das Zimmer nicht   *Ich wollte, Michael würde
      sauber.   das Zimmer saubermachen.*

1.   Martin spielt den ganzen Tag Computerspiele.
2.   Christoph hört immer Musik.
3.   Bernd redet so viel.
4.   Wolfgang kommt immer zu spät.
5.   Stefan schließt die Tür nicht.

13.   Ich wollte, ich könnte ...   Complete the following sentences for yourself. Then find out from your partner how she/he completed the sentences and what she/he would like to do.

1.   Ich wollte, ich könnte _____ .
2.   Wenn ich Zeit hätte, _____ .
3.   Wenn meine Eltern viel Geld hätten, _____ .
4.   Ich sollte _____ .
5.   Ich würde gern _____ .

14.   Was ist dir im Leben am wichtigsten?   Find out from your partner which of the following goals in life are of most importance to her/him. She/He will name 3–4 of the following goals.

Discussing goals

S1: Was ist dir im Leben wichtig?
S2: Ich möchte vor allem [einen guten Job haben].
      Dann möchte ich [einen Sinn° im Leben finden].   meaning
      Drittens möchte ich [gesund sein].

Lebensziele:

heiraten und Kinder haben
viel Geld verdienen
gesund sein
schöne Dinge haben wie ein tolles Auto, teure Kleidung
ein schönes/großes Haus haben
einen guten Job haben
Glück haben
Spaß und Freude am Leben haben
einen Sinn im Leben finden
anderen Menschen helfen

9 Present-time subjunctive of strong verbs

Infinitive	Simple past	+ umlaut for a, o, u	+ subjunctive ending	Present-time subjunctive
kommen bleiben	er/es/sie { kam blieb	käm blieb	-e -e	**käme** **bliebe**

kommen	
ich **käme**	wir **kämen**
du **kämest**	ihr **kämet**
er/es/sie **käme**	sie **kämen**
Sie **kämen**	

The present-time subjunctive of strong verbs is formed by adding subjunctive endings to the simple-past stem of the verb. An umlaut is added to the stem vowels **a**, **o**, or **u**. For a list of subjunctive forms of strong verbs, see #23 of the Grammatical Tables in the Reference Section. Although the **würde**-construction and the subjunctive form of the main verb are equivalent in meaning, the **würde**-construction is more common in spoken German.

15.   An einem langweiligen Arbeitstag.   The following are some thoughts that go through Frau Müller's mind on a boring day in the office. The sentences contain the subjunctive forms of strong verbs. Choose the appropriate English equivalents.

▶   Das ginge.   *That would work.*

1. Das täte ich gern.
2. Wir kämen gern zu der Konferenz.
3. Ich schliefe aber gern länger.
4. Frau Lange ginge sicher mit zum Chef.
5. So etwas gäbe es bei mir nicht.
6. Wenn Herr Berg nur länger bliebe.
7. Das wäre ein gutes Geschäft.
8. Und wenn die Sekretärin krank würde?

a. That would be a good deal.
b. Such a thing would never happen with me.
c. But I would like to sleep longer.
d. And (what) if the secretary would get sick?
e. I would do that gladly.
f. If only Herr Berg would stay longer.
g. We would be glad to come to the conference.
h. Frau Lange would certainly come along to [see] the boss.

16. In den Ferien. Frank is thinking about all the things he would do if the conditions were different. Complete Frank's sentences using the subjunctive of the main verb for the condition and the **würde**-construction for the conclusion.

▶ Leider habe ich kein Auto, aber wenn _____. (in die Schweiz fahren)
Leider habe ich kein Auto, aber wenn ich ein Auto hätte, würde ich in die Schweiz fahren.

1. Es gibt keinen Schnee, aber wenn _____ . (Ski fahren)
2. Leider habe ich kein Geld, aber wenn _____ . (nach Hawaii fliegen)
3. Es ist nicht warm genug, aber wenn _____ . (zelten)
4. Dieses Buch ist nicht interessant, aber wenn _____ . (lesen)
5. Ich habe keine Lust, aber wenn _____ . (ins Kino gehen)

10 Present-time subjunctive of regular weak verbs

Infinitive		Simple past	Present-time subjunctive
spielen		spielte	**spielte**
kaufen	er/es/sie	kaufte	**kaufte**
arbeiten		arbeitete	**arbeitete**
baden		badete	**badete**

The present-time subjunctive forms of regular weak verbs are identical to the simple-past forms.

17. Wenn Susanne das nur machte! Susanne plays guitar in a small band. Her friends have invited her to spend the weekend. Complete the sentences by supplying the present-time subjunctive form of the verb in parentheses. Then translate the sentences for one of the guests who knows no German.

▶ Wenn Frank nicht so oft _____ (telefonieren), könnte Susanne uns anrufen.
Wenn Frank nicht so oft telefonierte, könnte Susanne uns anrufen. (If Frank wouldn't telephone so often, Susanne would be able to call us.)

1. Wenn Susanne uns _____ (besuchen), dann könnte sie nicht arbeiten.
2. Wenn ihre Freunde mitkämen, _____ (brauchen) sie nicht allein zu spielen.
3. Wenn ihre Freunde _____ (mitmachen°), könnten wir die Nachbarn einladen.   joined in
4. Wenn Dieter eine Gitarre _____ (kaufen), müßte er auch mitspielen°.   play with (them)
5. Wenn die Gitarre nicht soviel _____ (kosten), könnten wir sie ihm kaufen.

Frankfurt am Main ist das deutsche Bank-zentrum.

11 Present-time subjunctive of irregular weak verbs

Infinitive		Simple past	Present-time subjunctive
bringen		brächte	brächte
denken	er/es/sie	dachte	dächte
wissen		wußte	wüßte

The present-time subjunctive forms of irregular weak verbs are like the simple-past forms, but with an umlaut added.

18. Ein Picknick.   Adrian is talking with Stefanie about plans for a picnic. Give the English equivalents.

ADRIAN: Hättest du Zeit mitzukommen?
STEFANIE: Ich dächte schon.
ADRIAN: Ich wüßte nicht, wen wir sonst einladen sollten.
STEFANIE: Vielleicht Onkel Max und Tante Gabi.
ADRIAN: Vielleicht könnten wir alle zusammen fahren?
STEFANIE: Schön. Das könnten wir.
ADRIAN: Wenn ich nur wüßte, wo die beiden sind!
STEFANIE: Was meinst du, was brächte Onkel Max mit?
ADRIAN: Caviar, wie immer. Ich brächte etwas zu trinken mit.

12 Past-time subjunctive

Wenn sie das **gewußt hätte, hätte** sie mir **geholfen.**	If she *had known* that, she *would have helped* me.
Wenn sie das **gewußt hätte, wäre** sie nicht **mitgekommen.**	If she *had known* that, she *would* not *have come* along.

The past-time subjunctive consists of the subjunctive forms **hätte** or **wäre** + past participle. The past-time subjunctive is used to express hypothetical statements, wishes, and contrary-to-fact conditions in past time.

19. Wenn sie das gewußt hätte ... Restate the sentences below, telling what Ursel would or would not have done if only she had known that the weather was going to be nice over the weekend.

▶ Sie ist übers Wochenende nicht weggefahren.	*Wenn sie das gewußt hätte, wäre sie übers Wochenende weggefahren.*
▶ Sie ist zu Hause geblieben.	*Wenn sie das gewußt hätte, wäre sie nicht zu Hause geblieben.*

1. Sie ist nicht an den See° gefahren.   lake
2. Sie hat ihre Freunde nicht zum Picknick eingeladen.
3. Sie hat nicht gezeltet.
4. Sie ist nicht schwimmen gegangen.
5. Sie ist ins Kino gegangen.
6. Sie hat soviel geschlafen.

20. Sie hätten es anders gemacht. No one is happy with what she/he did yesterday. Complete the sentences below to include what the people would rather have done.

▶ Karin ist schwimmen gegangen, aber _____ (lieber ins Theater gegangen).	*Karin ist schwimmen gegangen, aber sie wäre lieber ins Theater gegangen.*
▶ Marc hat gearbeitet, aber _____ (lieber geschlafen).	*Marc hat gearbeitet, aber er hätte lieber geschlafen.*

1. Ich habe in der Mensa° gegessen, aber _____ (lieber in einem eleganten   university cafeteria
   Restaurant gegessen).
2. Hanna hat an einem Referat gearbeitet, aber _____ (lieber im Garten gearbeitet).
3. Heike und Horst haben Tennis gespielt, aber _____ (lieber gewandert).
4. Klaus hat ferngesehen, aber _____ (lieber ins Kino gegangen).
5. Susanne hat klassische Musik gehört, aber _____ (lieber Hard Rock gehört).
6. Dirk hat sich aufs Examen vorbereitet, aber _____ (lieber eine Radtour gemacht).

⮕ **21. Eine schwere Woche.** Your partner has complained about a hard week. Choose a day and ask your partner what she/he did on that day. Then ask what she/he would have preferred doing. She/He will then ask you. You may choose one of the cues below.

Stating preferences

S1: Was hast du am Mittwoch gemacht?
S2: Am Mittwoch habe ich den Chef zum Flughafen° gebracht.   airport
S1: Was hättest du lieber gemacht?
S2: Ich wäre lieber auf eine Party gegangen. Und du, was hast du … ?

1. Am Montagabend bin ich lange [im Büro/in der Bibliothek] geblieben.
2. Am Dienstag bin ich zu [einem Kunden/Freund] nach [Frankfurt] gefahren.
3. Am Mittwoch habe ich [den Chef/meine Mutter] zum Flughafen gebracht.
4. Am Donnerstag habe ich den ganzen Tag am Computer gearbeitet.
5. Am Freitag bin ich mit meinen [Kollegen/Freunden] essen gegangen.
6. Am Samstag habe ich [meine Wohnung/mein Zimmer] aufgeräumt.
7. Am Sonntag habe ich alle neuen Zeitschriften durchgesehen.

   Stichwörter: ins Kino gehen □ meinen Freund besuchen □ ein gutes Buch lesen □ im Garten sitzen □ in der Sonne liegen □ zu meiner Freundin fahren □ auf eine Party gehen

13 Modals in past-time subjunctive

Das **hättest** du **wissen sollen.**   You *should have known* that.
Ich **hätte** dir **helfen können.**   I *could have helped* you.

When a modal is used in the past-time subjunctive with another verb, the infinitive of the modal is used instead of the past participle. This is called the "double infinitive" construction. The modal always occurs at the very end of the clause.

22. Was wäre passiert, wenn … ? Dieter's company had been expecting a foreign visitor. However, the visit did not take place. Dieter explains what would have happened if the visit had taken place. Give the English equivalents of his remarks.

1. Ich hätte Englisch sprechen müssen.
2. Die Besucherin hätte mein Englisch nicht verstehen können.
3. Ich hätte ihr Deutsch nicht verstehen können.
4. Wir hätten einander kaum verstehen können.
5. Ich hätte ihr die Firma zeigen müssen.
6. Wir hätten uns auch die Stadt ansehen° können.   look at
7. Wir hätten in einem teuren Restaurant essen können.
8. Wir hätten mit dem Taxi fahren dürfen.
9. Ich hätte sie zum Bahnhof bringen müssen.

23. **Was hätte Schiller machen können?** Answer the questions about the ad that invokes the name of Friedrich Schiller (1759–1805), one of the most famous figures in German literature. Schiller was a dramatist, historian, and philosopher concerned with the themes of personal and political freedom. You may refer to the Vocabulary for Authentic Text Activities in the Reference Section if you have trouble getting the gist of the ad.

1. Was hätte Schiller gemacht?
2. Wann hätte Schiller sich einschreiben° können?   register
3. Wann hätte er beginnen können?
4. Wo hätte er Auskunft° bekommen können?   information

WIEDERHOLUNG

1. Was sagen Sie? Say what you would do under certain conditions. Then think of two or more things and ask your partner.

Was würdest du tun, …

1. wenn du viel Geld bekämest?
2. wenn heute Sonntag wäre?
3. wenn du heute Geburtstag hättest?
4. wenn du jetzt zwei Wochen Ferien hättest?
5. wenn du das teure Essen im Restaurant nicht bezahlen könntest?
6. wenn Freunde dich zu einem Fest nicht einladen würden?

2. Meine Freundin Susanne. Tell about your friend Susanne by completing each sentence below with an appropriate preposition.

1. Habe ich dir _____ meiner Freundin Susanne erzählt?
2. Mit 19 Jahren hat sie _____ dem Studium angefangen.
3. Jetzt arbeitet sie _____ Siemens.
4. Sie arbeitet den ganzen Tag _____ Computer.
5. Sie und ihre Kollegen bereiten sich _____ eine Konferenz vor.
6. Sie erzählt ihrem Freund _____ ihrer Arbeit.
7. In ihrer Freizeit schreibt sie einen Roman. Sie spricht gern mit Hans _____ ihr Projekt.

3. Was möchten Sie? Tell what you would like by using one or more of the adjectives in parentheses—or by supplying your own—to modify the boldfaced nouns.

1. Wenn ich Geld hätte, würde ich mir ein _____ **Auto** kaufen. (klein, groß, billig, teuer)
2. Ich wollte, man würde mich zu einem _____ **Fest** einladen. (nett, toll, klein, laut°, interessant)   loud
3. Ich möchte einen _____ **Pulli** kaufen. (warm, blau, leicht, toll)
4. Ich würde gern mal einen _____ **Film** sehen. (toll, interessant, schön, modern, klassisch, gut)
5. Ich möchte eine _____ **Reise** nach Deutschland machen. (lang, kurz, billig)
6. Ich möchte einen Computer haben, aber es müßte ein _____ **Computer** sein. (billig, teuer, klein, einfach, groß, schnell, bedienungsfreundlich°)   user-friendly

4. Was hat er gemacht? Read the account of what Klaus did yesterday. Then answer the questions.

Klaus ging morgens für eine Stunde zu einer Vorlesung. Nachmittags saß er in der Bibliothek und arbeitete. Den Abend hatte er frei. Er ging mit Freunden in eine Kneipe. Da war die Musik live. Es war eine Volksliedgruppe°. Alle Studenten sangen mit. Das hat viel Spaß gemacht.

folk song group

1. Wohin ging Klaus morgens?
2. Was machte er nachmittags?
3. Wohin ging er abends?
4. Warum gingen Klaus und seine Freunde in die Kneipe?
5. Wer sang mit?

5. Wie sagt man das?

1. I have nothing planned for the weekend. (*use* **vorhaben;** for = **am**)
   —Would you like to go hiking?
2. Could it be that Erik is ill?
   —I don't know. You could ask him.
3. Would you like to go for a walk?
   —Gladly. How would it be this afternoon?
4. Could you help me, please?
   —I wish I had (the) time.
5. Would you like to watch TV?
   —No. I don't feel like it.

6. Zur Diskussion. Discuss the following questions in a small group. The members of your group should ask each other the questions. Try to think of follow-up questions.

1. Arbeitest du während der Ferien oder während des Semesters bei einer Firma?
2. Wo arbeitest du? Wie gefällt dir deine Arbeit?
3. Wie ist das Arbeitsklima da, wo du arbeitest?
4. Gehörst du zu einer Gewerkschaft°?

labor union

5. Was ist für dich wichtig? (Möchtest du mehr verdienen? Möchtest du längere Ferien haben?)
6. Wie könnten die Gewerkschaften mehr gegen die Arbeitslosigkeit tun?

7. Zum Schreiben

1. Write a paragraph in German about some of the differences between the economies of your country and Germany. Use the questions below as a guideline.

   - In welchem Land spielt der Außenhandel eine größere Rolle? Warum?
   - Welches Land hat mehr Rohstoffe?
   - Welche Produkte exportieren diese Länder vor allem?
   - In welchem Land sehen die Chancen für eine gesunde Wirtschaft besser aus? Warum?

2. Imagine you could spend a day with someone from either the past or the present. Write a short paragrah about this day.

   ■ Was würden Sie machen?
   ■ Worüber würden Sie sprechen?
   ■ Warum möchten Sie den Tag mit diesem Menschen verbringen°?   spend (time)

Hinweise:

1. Use the subjunctive when expressing hypothetical statements, suppositions, wishes.
2. In expressing hypothetical situations or giving reasons for your comments, you will be using dependent clauses. Be sure to watch the position of the verbs.

GRAMMATIK: ZUSAMMENFASSUNG

Subjunctive mood

Indicative	Ich **komme** nicht zur Party.	I'*m* not *coming* to the party.
	Was **hast** du **gemacht?**	What *did* you *do?*
	Kannst du mir **helfen?**	*Can* you *help* me?
Subjunctive	Ich **käme** nicht zur Party.	I *would*n't *come* to the party.
	Was **hättest** du **gemacht?**	What *would* you *have done?*
	Könntest du mir **helfen?**	*Could* you *help* me?

In both English and German, the indicative mood is used to talk about "real" conditions or factual situations. The subjunctive mood is used to talk about "unreal," hypothetical, uncertain, or unlikely events as well as to express wishes and polite requests.

| Present-time subjunctive | Wenn ich heute (oder morgen) nur mehr Zeit **hätte.** | If only I *had (would have)* more time today (or tomorrow). |
| Past-time subjunctive | Wenn ich gestern nur mehr Zeit **gehabt hätte.** | If only I *had had (would have had)* more time yesterday. |

Subjunctive forms express two time categories: present time (which can refer to the future as well) and past time.

The *würde*-construction

■ *Forms*

ich **würde** es **machen**	wir **würden** es **machen**
du **würdest** es **machen**	ihr **würdet** es **machen**
er/es/sie **würde** es **machen**	sie **würden** es **machen**
	Sie **würden** es **machen**

The **würde**-construction consists of a form of **würde** + infinitive. **Würde** is the subjunctive form of **werden.** It is formed by adding an umlaut to **wurde,** the simple past of **werden.**

■ *Uses*

Hypothetical statement	Ich **würde** das nicht **machen.**	I *would* not *do* that.
Wishes	Wenn er mir nur **helfen würde.**	If only he *would help* me.
Polite requests	**Würdest** du mir bitte **helfen?**	*Would* you please *help* me?

To talk about "unreal" situations or hypothetical statements in the present, to express wishes, and to make polite requests, German may use a **würde**-construction. The **würde**-construction is the most common way to express subjunctive mood in conversational German.

Present-time subjunctive of main verbs

Ich **täte** das nicht.
Ich **würde** das nicht **tun.** } I *would*n't *do* that.

The subjunctive form of the main verb (e.g., **täte**) and the **würde**-construction (e.g., **würde tun**) are equivalent in meaning. However, the **würde**-construction is more common in conversation for most verbs.

Present-time subjunctive of *sein* and *haben*

sein	
ich **wäre**	wir **wären**
du **wärest**	ihr **wäret**
er/es/sie **wäre**	sie **wären**
	Sie **wären**

haben	
ich **hätte**	wir **hätten**
du **hättest**	ihr **hättet**
er/es/sie **hätte**	sie **hätten**
	Sie **hätten**

The verbs **haben** and **sein** are more commonly used in their subjunctive forms, **wäre** and **hätte,** than in the **würde**-construction.

Modals in present-time subjunctive

Infinitive	Simple past	Present-time subjunctive
dürfen	durfte	**dürfte**
können	konnte	**könnte**
mögen	mochte	**möchte**
müssen	mußte	**müßte**
sollen	sollte	**sollte**
wollen	wollte	**wollte**

The modals are generally used in their subjunctive form rather than as infinitives with the **würde-**construction.

Present-time subjunctive of strong verbs

Infinitive	Simple past	Present-time subjunctive
bleiben	blieb	**bliebe**
geben	gab	**gäbe**
gehen	ging	**ginge**
kommen	kam	**käme**
tun	tat	**täte**

The present-time subjunctive forms of strong verbs are formed by adding subjunctive endings to the simple-past stem. An umlaut is added to the stem vowels, **a, o,** and **u.**

Subjunctive verb endings

ich käm**e**	wir	käm**en**
du käm**est**	ihr	käm**et**
er/es/sie käm**e**	sie	käm**en**
Sie käm**en**		

The subjunctive endings above are used for all verbs. The subjunctive verb endings **-est** and **-et** often contract to **-st** and **-t: kämest > kämst, kämet > kämt.**

Present-time subjunctive of regular weak verbs

Infinitive	Simple past	Present-time subjunctive
kaufen	kaufte	**kaufte**
arbeiten	arbeitete	**arbeitete**

The present-time subjunctive forms of weak verbs are identical to the simple-past forms.

Present-time subjunctive of irregular weak verbs

Infinitive	Simple past	Present-time subjunctive
bringen	brachte	**brächte**
denken	dachte	**dächte**
wissen	wußte	**wüßte**

Past-time subjunctive

Wenn ich Zeit **gehabt hätte, wäre** ich **gekommen.**

If I *had had* time, I *would have come.*

Wenn sie hier **gewesen wäre, hätte** ich sie **gesehen.**

If she *had been* here, I *would have seen* her.

The past-time subjunctive consists of the subjunctive forms **hätte** or **wäre** + a past participle. A **würde**-construction exists in past-time, but it is not commonly used: **Ich würde es nicht getan haben.**

Modals in past-time subjunctive

Das **hättest** du **wissen sollen.**   You *should have known* that.
Ich **hätte** dir **helfen können.**   I *could have helped* you.

When a modal is used in the past subjunctive with another verb, the infinitive of the modal is used instead of the past participle. This construction is called the "double infinitive" construction. The modal always occurs at the very end of the clause.

Uses of the *würde*-construction and the subjunctive of the main verb

■ *Hypothetical statements*

Ich **würde** das nicht **tun.**
Ich **täte** das nicht.   I *wouldn't do* that [if I were you].
Ich **hätte** das auch **getan.**   I *would have done* that too.

■ *Wishes*

Wenn Inge das nur **tun würde.**
Wenn Inge das nur **täte.**   If only Inge *would do* that.
Wenn Gabi das nur **getan hätte.**   If only Gabi *had done* that.

■ *Polite requests*

Würden Sie das für mich **tun?**
Täten Sie das für mich?   *Would* you *do* that for me?
Könnten Sie das für mich **tun?**   *Could* you *do* that for me?

■ *Conditions contrary to fact*

Present time	
Wenn ich Zeit **hätte, käme** ich.	If I *had* time [but I don't],
Wenn ich Zeit **hätte, würde** ich **kommen.**	I *would come.*

Past time	
Wenn ich Zeit **gehabt hätte, wäre** ich **gekommen.**	If I *had had* time [but I didn't], I *would have come.*

Contrary-to-fact sentences consist of two clauses: the condition (**wenn**-clause) and the conclusion. Conditions contrary to fact cannot be fulfilled. Conditions contrary to fact are expressed in the subjunctive mood.

The *würde*-construction vs. present-time subjunctive of the main verb

Wenn Jutta nicht so fleißig **wäre, hätte** sie mehr Freizeit und **könnte** ein Hobby **haben.**	If Jutta *were* not so diligent, she *would have* more time and *could have* a hobby.

In conversational German the **würde**-construction is frequently used instead of the subjunctive of the main verb. However, the subjunctive of the main verb is preferred to the **würde**-construction for **sein (wäre), haben (hätte),** and the modals, e.g., **könnte.**

Wenn Gerd täglich Zeitung **läse,** würde er alles besser verstehen.	If Gerd *read* the newspaper daily, he would understand everything better.

Formal written German tends to avoid the **würde**-construction in the **wenn**-clause.

An dieser Offenbacher Schule lernen die Kinder neben Deutsch auch ihre Muttersprache.

Kapitel 13

L E R N Z I E L E

■ **Sprechintentionen**

Talking about future plans
Talking about cultural events
Making suggestions
Discussing post-graduation plans
Stating intention
Suggesting things to do together
Announcing decisions

■ **Lesestück**

Die multikulturelle Gesellschaft

■ **Land und Leute**

Other nationalities in Germany

■ **Grammatik**

Future time: present tense
Future time: future tense
Constructions with *lassen*
Relative clauses
Relative pronouns

BAUSTEINE FÜR GESPRÄCHE

Rockfans gegen Ausländerhaß

STEFANIE: David, hast du Lust am Wochenende zu dem Open-Air-Konzert in Frankfurt zu gehen?

DAVID: Ich weiß nicht. Ich fliege in zwei Wochen nach Amerika zurück und wollte mir noch Freiburg ansehen.

STEFANIE: Ach, komm' doch. Nach Freiburg kannst du auch nächstes Wochenende noch fahren.

DAVID: Aber ich kenne keinen einzigen von den Rockmusikern, die da spielen werden!

STEFANIE: Es geht ja gar nicht nur um die Musik. Das Motto ist „Heute die! Morgen du!"–Mit dem Konzert demonstrieren wir gegen Rassismus und Ausländerhaß.

DAVID: Glaubst du denn, daß da viele Leute kommen werden?

STEFANIE: Oh ja! Stell' dir vor, man erwartet ungefähr 150.000 Menschen.

DAVID: Gut, dann laß uns gehen und auch demonstrieren!

Rock fans against xenophobia

Do you feel like going to the outdoor concert in Frankfurt on the weekend?

I don't know. I'm flying back to America in two weeks and I still wanted to have a look at Freiburg.

Oh, come on. You can still go to Freiburg next weekend.

But I don't know a single one of the rock musicians who are going to play there!

It's not only about the music, of course. The slogan is "Today them! Tomorrow you!"—With the concert we're demonstrating against racism and xenophobia.

Do you think that many people will come?

Oh yes! Just imagine, about 150,000 people are expected.

OK, then let's go and demonstrate also.

Brauchbares

1. **Frankfurt** with a population of 647,200 is Germany's fourth largest city, after **Berlin,** 3,437,900; **München,** 1,236,500; **Köln,** 955,500. It is an industrial city and banking center.

2. **Freiburg** is a popular tourist town because of its location at the foot of the Black Forest **(Schwarzwald)** mountains. There are numerous ski slopes, mountain trails for hiking, and lakes for boating, windsurfing and swimming. **Freiburg** has a famous cathedral and an excellent university, which many Americans attend.

3. **Demonstrieren:** In the 1990's Germany has been the scene of many events that give people the chance to voice their opposition to the hostility toward foreigners expressed by groups such as skinheads. These events have included rock concerts, each attended by as many as 150,000 people, as well as **Lichterketten** (chains of people holding candles) with as many as 300,000 participants each.

Fragen

1. Warum wollte David zuerst nicht zu dem Open-Air-Konzert gehen?
2. Für Stefanie geht es nicht um die Musik. Worum geht es ihr?
3. Wie viele Leute erwartet man zu dem Konzert?

▷ **1. Nächste Woche.** Ask three fellow students what they intend to do next week.

Talking about future plans

S1:   *S2:*

Was machst du nächste Woche?   **Ich fahre nach [Freiburg].**
Ich fliege nach [Europa].
Ich fange einen neuen Job an.
Ich bereite ein Referat vor.

▷ **2. Kennst du das?** Take the role of two people talking about coming cultural events.

Talking about cultural events

S1:   *S2:*

Kennst du | **die Rockband, die heute [in der Stadt] spielt?**   **Ja, sehr gut sogar.**
den Film, der diese Woche im [Odeon] spielt?   Ja, aber das interessiert mich nicht.
die Oper, die heute abend im Fernsehen kommt?   Nein, leider nicht.
den neuen Roman, den ich lesen sollte?   Nein, warum fragst du?

▷ **3. Laß uns ins Konzert gehen.** Talk together in a group about what you want to do. Each person in the group suggests something different.

Making suggestions

▶ *Laß uns ...*

essen gehen ☐ unsere Freunde anrufen ☐ unseren Freunden helfen ☐ Tennis oder Fußball spielen ☐ joggen gehen ☐ den ganzen Tag faulenzen

Vokabeln

Substantive

der **Ausländerhaß** xenophobia, hatred of foreigners
der **Fan, -s** fan; supporter (sport)
der **Haß** hate
das **Motto, -s** motto
das **Open-Air-Konzert, -e** outdoor concert

der **Rassismus** racism
der **Rockfan, -s** rock fan
der **Rockmusiker, -/**die **Rockmusikerin, -nen** rock musician

Verben

an·sehen (sieht an), sah an, angesehen   to look at; **ich sehe es mir an**   I'm having a look at it
demonstrieren   to demonstrate
lassen (läßt), ließ, gelassen   to leave; to let, permit; to have something done; **laß uns gehen**   let's go

sich (*dat.*) **vor·stellen**   to imagine; **stell dir vor/stellen Sie sich vor**   just imagine
zurück·fliegen, flog zurück, ist zurückgeflogen   to fly back

Andere Wörter

einzig   only, sole, single

ungefähr   approximately

Besondere Ausdrücke

es geht nicht nur um [die Musik]   it's not just about [the music]

DIE MULTIKULTURELLE GESELLSCHAFT

Vorbereitung auf das Lesen

Sie lesen in diesem Text von Ausländern in Deutschland, ihrem Einfluß° auf die deutsche Kultur° und ihren Problemen.   influence

■ *Vor dem Lesen*

1. Die Kultur jedes Landes zeigt Elemente von anderen Ländern und Kulturen. Versuchen Sie in Gruppenarbeit, die Tabelle zu ergänzen°. Mit welcher Kultur oder welchem Land verbinden° Sie diese Dinge oder Ideen?   complete / connect

Idee/Ding	Wo findet man sie/es?	Woher kommt sie/es?
Jeans	fast überall°	Amerika
Kartoffeln		
Kaffee		
Football		
Fußball		
Demokratie		
Papier		
Kindergarten		

2. Listen Sie fünf Elemente Ihrer Kultur auf°. Wissen Sie, woher sie kommen? **listen auf:** list

   ▶ *Jazz   Der Jazz kommt aus Amerika.*

3. Sehen Sie sich die Tabelle unten an, und schreiben Sie drei Sätze über die Tabelle.

   ▶ *Mehr Ausländer kommen aus Italien als aus Griechenland.*

4. Was für Probleme könnten Ausländer in einer fremden Kultur haben? Machen Sie in Gruppenarbeit eine Liste von vier oder mehr Problemen.

■ *Beim Lesen*

1. Schreiben Sie für jeden Absatz° einen Titel.   paragraph
2. Markieren Sie die Zeilen°, wo man die folgende Information findet.   lines

   a. _____ Asylbewerber aus Osteuropa
   b. _____ Asylgesetze in Deutschland
   c. _____ Ausländerhaß
   d. _____ ausländische Kinder und Jugendliche
   e. _____ Demonstrationen gegen Intoleranz
   f. _____ Football in Deutschland
   g. _____ Prozent von Ausländern in Deutschland

Ausländer in Deutschland

**6,88 Millionen Anfang 1994
aus:**

der Türkei	1.918.000
Jugoslawien	930.000
Italien	563.000
Griechenland	352.000
Polen	261.000
Österreich	186.000
Rumänien	163.000
Kroatien	153.000
Bosnien	139.000
Spanien	133.000
Holland	114.000
Großbritannien	112.000
USA	108.000
Portugal	106.000
Iran	102.000
anderen Ländern	1.540.000

David kommt aus Chicago und ist seit einigen Wochen in Frankfurt, wo er seine Kusine Stefanie und seinen Vetter Rolf besucht. Sie möchten essen gehen und sprechen gerade darüber, in welches Restaurant sie gehen sollen. „Wohin möchtest du gern gehen, David?" fragen sie ihn. „Ihr wißt, welche Lokale hier
5 gut sind, und ich esse fast alles gern." „Na gut", sagt Rolf, „ich habe Lust, heute griechisch oder türkisch zu essen." „Ich würde lieber spanisch essen gehen", antwortet Stefanie. „Im Don Quichotte ist das Essen gut, und da gibt es Flamenco-Musik."

Beim Essen im Restaurant fragt Rolf: „David, möchtest du am Wochenende
10 zu einem Football-Spiel gehen?"

„Du meinst Fußball, nicht?"

„Nein, ich meine amerikanischen Football."

„Was, ihr habt Football in Deutschland?"

„Ja, es gibt ungefähr 130 deutsche Klubs, wo man amerikanischen Football
15 spielt."

„Ja, David, wenigstens im Essen und im Sport ist Deutschland multikulturell", lacht Stefanie. Während die drei essen, sprechen sie über die vielen internationalen Aspekte Deutschlands.

Im ganzen° wohnen über 6, 8 Millionen Ausländer in Deutschland. Das   **im ganzen:** altogether
20 sind etwa acht Prozent der Einwohner Deutschlands. Zwischen 1955 und 1973 brauchte Westdeutschland Arbeiter, die es vor allem aus Italien, Spanien, Griechenland und der Türkei rekrutierte. Zuerst wollten die Ausländer nur ein paar Jahre in Deutschland bleiben, um genug Geld für sich und ihre Familien zu Hause zu verdienen. Als ihr Aufenthalt° immer länger wurde, brachten die   stay
25 meisten nach einigen Jahren auch ihre Familie nach Deutschland. Seit dem Fall der kommunistischen Regierungen in Osteuropa Ende der achtziger Jahre kamen zu den ausländischen Arbeitnehmern auch viele Asylbewerber° hinzu°.   applicants for political asylum/ in addition / **nahm auf:** Deutschland nahm die meisten auf°, denn es hatte neben seinem hohen   accepted / laws governing Lebensstandard bis 1993 auch die liberalsten Asylgesetze° Europas.   political asylum

Diese Türkinnen bereiten das Essen für ein Grillfest vor.

30 Ob Asylanten° oder ausländische Arbeitnehmer – kulturelle Unterschiede   political refugees
machen den Ausländern die Integration in die deutsche Gesellschaft nicht im-
mer leicht. Im allgemeinen° funktioniert die Integration von Ausländern unter   **im allgemeinen:** in general
Kindern und Jugendlichen viel besser als unter Erwachsenen. Da heute zwei
Drittel° von allen ausländischen Kindern in Deutschland geboren sind,   thirds
35 sprechen sie perfekt Deutsch, sind mit der Kultur vertraut° und tragen mei-   familiar
stens auch die gleiche Kleidung wie ihre Schulfreunde. Die jungen Leute werden in Deutschland bleiben, denn das Land ihrer Eltern ist ihnen oft fremd.
Schwieriger ist es für Ausländer, die weniger gut Deutsch sprechen oder auch
in Deutschland die Kultur und Tradition ihrer Heimat beibehalten° wollen. Sie   keep
40 werden leicht das Opfer° von Ausländerhaß.   victim

Denn auch in Deutschland gibt es eine Minderheit° von Einwohnern, die   minority
gegen alles Ausländische ist. Ihr Motto ist „Ausländer raus°", und sie verüben°   out / commit
sogar Gewalttätigkeiten° gegen Ausländer. Viel mehr Deutsche protestieren je-   acts of violence
doch gegen die Intoleranz und stehen auf der Seite der Ausländer. Die
45 Regierung, die Kirchen, die Medien, die Gewerkschaften und auch große Rock-
und Sportstars sprechen immer wieder offen gegen Ausländerfeindlichkeit°.   hostility toward foreigners
Seit 1992 haben in mehreren deutschen Städten hunderttausende von
Einwohnern gegen Intoleranz und Fremdenhaß demonstriert.

David, Stefanie und Rolf sind inzwischen mit dem Essen fertig und un-
50 terhalten sich mit dem Besitzer° des Lokals. In den sechziger Jahren war er aus   owner
Spanien gekommen, um bei Opel in Rüsselsheim zu arbeiten. Vor ein paar
Jahren hat er dann das Restaurant aufgemacht. „Natürlich bin ich Spanier",
sagt er stolz, „aber Frankfurt ist jetzt mein Zuhause." Nur seine Kinder machen
ihm Sorgen, denn ihr Spanisch ist nicht so gut, und Spanien ist für sie ein
55 fremdes Land.

Brauchbares

1. **Don Quichotte** (l. 7) is the German for Don Quijote, the protagonist of a
   novel by Miguel de Cervantes (1547–1616) and one of the most famous
   characters in Spanish literature. The German word is pronounced
   [dōki′chŏt]. The English word *quixotic* is related to this character (Don
   Quixote).

2. **Flamenco-Musik** (l. 8), along with flamenco dancing, is a popular entertainment form. Flamenco dancing is characterized by colorful costumes,
   stamping of the feet, and clapping of the hands.

Nach dem Lesen*

1. Fragen zum Lesestück

1. Wen besucht David?
2. Warum will David nicht das Restaurant wählen°?   choose
3. In was für ein Restaurant gehen die drei?
4. Worüber sprechen die drei beim Essen?
5. Wann kamen die ersten ausländischen Arbeitnehmer nach Deutschland?
6. Warum waren die ersten ausländischen Arbeitnehmer sehr willkommen?
7. Warum kamen so viele Asylbewerber nach Deutschland?
8. Warum ist es leichter für Jugendliche, sich in die deutsche Kultur zu integrieren?
9. Was machen einige Deutsche, die gegen Ausländer sind?
10. Wie zeigen viele Deutsche, daß sie gegen die Intoleranz sind?

2. Einige Themen.
Lesen Sie den Text noch einmal°. Machen Sie eine Liste von Stichwörtern° zu den folgenden Themen.   key words

1. Geschichte der Ausländer in Deutschland
2. Probleme der Ausländer in Deutschland
3. Deutschland: eine internationale Gesellschaft

3. Zur Diskussion.
Machen Sie eine Liste: Was sollte eine Ausländerin/ein Ausländer von der deutschen Kultur wissen? Was sollte eine Ausländerin/ein Ausländer von Ihrer Kultur wissen?

4. Erzählen wir.

1. Stellen Sie sich vor, daß Sie als Ausländerin/Ausländer in Deutschland leben. Erzählen Sie etwas von sich. Woher kommen Sie? Warum sind Sie nach Deutschland gekommen? Wie gefällt es Ihnen in Deutschland?
2. **Rollenspiel.** Eine Reporterin/Ein Reporter interviewt eine ausländische Arbeitnehmerin/einen ausländischen Arbeitnehmer in Ihrem Land.

Vokabeln

Substantive

der **Arbeiter, -**/die **Arbeiterin, -nen**
  worker
der **Arbeitnehmer, -**/die
  Arbeitnehmerin, -nen employee,
  worker

der/die **Erwachsene** (*noun decl. like
  adj.*) adult
die **Gesellschaft, -en** society;
  company
die **Gewerkschaft, -en** labor union

---

*Remember, words that appear with a raised degree mark (°) but for which no definition is given in the margin are active words you should learn and be able to use. Their definitions appear in the **Vokabeln** section that most closely follows the word.

die **Heimat**   native country
die **Intoleranz**   intolerance
der/die **Jugendliche** *(noun decl. like adj.)*   young person
die **Kirche, -n**   church
der **Klub, -s**   club

die **Kultur, -en**   culture
das **Lokal, -e**   restaurant; bar
das **Prozent, -e**   percent
die **Seite, -n**   side; page
das **Spiel, -e**   game
die **Tradition, -en**   tradition

Verben

auf·machen   to open
geboren   born

lachen   to laugh

Andere Wörter

denen *(dat. pl. of relative pronoun)* them; which
fremd   foreign, strange; **das ist mir fremd** *(dat.)*   that is strange to me
inzwischen   in the meantime, meanwhile
kulturell   culture, culturally

mehrere   several; various
multikulturell   multicultural
noch einmal   again, once more
stolz   proud; **stolz auf** *(+ acc.)* proud of
während *(conj.)*   while
wenigstens   at least

Besondere Ausdrücke

die [sechziger/achtziger] Jahre   the [1960s/1980s]

GRAMMATIK UND ÜBUNGEN

1 Future time: present tense

Ich **helfe** dir morgen bestimmt.

> *I'll help* you tomorrow for sure.
> *I'm going to help* you tomorrow for sure.

Arbeitest du heute abend?

> *Are you working* tonight?
> *Are you going to work* tonight?

German generally uses the present tense (e.g., **ich helfe, arbeitest du?**) to express future time. English expresses future time by the future tense (e.g., *I'll help*), with a form of *go* (e.g., *I'm going to help*), or with the present progressive tense *(are you working?)*.

1. Was für Pläne hast du? Erzähl mal! You and a friend are talking about your plans. Give the German equivalents of the sentences below. Use the present tense to express future time.

1. Are you going to watch TV tonight?
2. No, I'm going to the movies.
3. What are you going to do tomorrow?
4. My vacation starts tomorrow.
5. Are you going to Zürich again?
6. No, we'll go there next summer.

2 Future time: future tense

Wir **werden** unsere Freunde **einladen.**	We *will invite* our friends.
Jutta **wird** es allein **machen.**	Jutta *will do* it alone.

German, like English, does have a future tense, although in German it is not used as often as the present tense to express future time. The future tense in German is used primarily if it is not clear from the context that future time is meant.

Katrin **wird** wohl zu Hause **sein.**	Katrin *is probably* at home.
Das **wird** sicher falsch **sein.**	That's *probably* wrong.

In addition to expressing future time, the future tense may be used to express an assumption (present probability) when it is used with adverbs such as **wohl, sicher,** or **schon.** These adverbs all mean *probably* in English.

ich **werde** es sicher **finden**	wir **werden** es sicher **finden**
du **wirst** es sicher **finden**	ihr **werdet** es sicher **finden**
er/es/sie **wird** es sicher **finden**	sie **werden** es sicher **finden**
Sie **werden** es sicher **finden**	

In both English and German, the future tense is a compound tense. In English, the future tense is a verb phrase consisting of *will* or *shall* plus the main verb. In German, the future tense is also a verb phrase and consists of a form of **werden** plus an infinitive in final position.

2. Kein Streik. The union leader is reporting on what the union intends to get out of the negotiations with management. Express the union's intentions by restating the sentences in the future tense.

▶ Wir verdienen bestimmt mehr. *Wir werden bestimmt mehr verdienen.*

1. Wir arbeiten wohl 38 Stunden die Woche.
2. Bei Krankheit zahlt die Firma ja weiter.
3. Wir bekommen ja sechs Wochen bezahlten Urlaub°.   vacation
4. Der Arbeitstag fängt wohl um halb acht an.
5. Das Arbeitsklima wird doch besser.
6. Wir streiken bestimmt nicht.

Michael weiß nicht, ob Ursel ihn **besuchen wird.**	Michael doesn't know whether Ursel *will visit* him.
Hans sagt, daß sie sicher **kommen wird.**	Hans says she*'ll come* for sure.

The auxiliary **werden** is in final position in a dependent clause because it is the finite verb. It follows the infinitive.

3. Ein tolles Wochenende. Erik is telling what Inge and several of their Turkish friends will probably do over the weekend. Begin each sentence with **Erik sagt, daß _____ .**

▶ Inge wird wohl mit Gülay Hausaufgaben machen.
Erik sagt, daß Inge wohl mit Gülay Hausaufgaben machen wird.

1. Erkan wird wohl seinem Vater im Geschäft helfen.
2. Am Sonntag werden alle drei wohl aufs Schulfest gehen.
3. In der Schulband wird Erkan wohl Gitarre spielen.
4. Hinterher° werden sie wohl in ein türkisches Lokal gehen.   *afterward*
5. Sie werden dort wohl andere Freunde treffen.

4. Was für Pläne hast du für die Zeit nach dem Studium? Form a small group and take turns asking about plans after graduation. The first time use one of the cues below. The second time make up your own answer.

Discussing post-graduation plans

S1: Weißt du schon, was du nach dem Studium machen wirst?
S2: Ich werde wohl bei einer Computer-Firma arbeiten. Und du?

ein Jahr ins Ausland gehen
bei einer [spanischen/deutschen/großen/kleinen/Computer-/Auto-] Firma
    arbeiten
mit meinem italienischen Freund ein Lokal aufmachen
eine Stelle in [Brüssel/Straßburg/Berlin] suchen
in die Politik gehen
weiterstudieren
bei einem Forschungslaboratorium° arbeiten   *research lab*
erst mal nichts tun

3 Constructions with *lassen*

■ *Forms of* **lassen**

Present tense	
ich lasse	wir lassen
du läßt	ihr laßt
er/es/sie läßt	sie lassen
Sie lassen	

***du*-imperative:**	laß
Simple past stem:	ließ
Past participle:	gelassen

Land und Leute

Ausländer

Germany is home to more than 6.8 million foreigners. Almost 2 million are from Turkey, around 1 million are from the former Yugoslavia, and many have come from Italy, Greece, and Poland.

In the 1960s, West Germany sought many "guest workers" (**Gastarbeiter**) to relieve the labor shortage of the post-war economic boom, especially in the construction and steel industries. The early workers came from Italy, Greece, Spain, and Turkey. In 1961 there were 700,000 foreigners living in Germany; by 1970 there were 2.6 million. Even though many of the foreign workers (**ausländische Arbeitnehmer**) returned to their home countries, many others have stayed and raised their children in Germany. Today foreign workers are still an important factor in the German economy. In spite of this, German laws make it difficult for resident foreigners (**ausländische Mitbürger**) to obtain citizenship, and children born to foreigners in Germany are not automatically German citizens. However, foreigners are eligible to receive all social benefits and in some cities they have obtained the right to vote and to run for local office.

In the late 1980s and early 1990s, the number of ethnic German resettlers (**Aussiedler**) coming from the former Soviet Union and Eastern Europe increased dramatically. During the Cold War the **Aussiedler** were considered courageous people who had escaped a totalitarian regime. During the time of economic recession in the years after unification in 1990, the **Aussiedler** were seen as competition for jobs, housing, and social benefits. At the same time, a large number of refugees seeking political asylum arrived in Germany. Between 1989 and 1992 more than 1 million people applied for political asylum. These asylum seekers (**Asylanten**) receive financial aid while waiting for their cases to be heard and further benefits

Asylanten vor dem Asylbewerberheim in Rostock.

to help get started if asylum is granted. A 1993 amendment to the asylum law (**Asylgesetz**) reduced the number of people granted asylum.

In the first half of the 1990s radical groups such as the neo-Nazis and skinheads gave vent to a virulent xenophobia (**Ausländerhaß**) and committed numerous hate crimes against them. A large segment of the public protested against these acts of violence. While xenophobia and "excessive population" of foreigners (**Überfremdung**) remain issues, there is increasing public debate in the second half of the 1990s about how Germany can become a true multicultural society (**multikulturelle Gesellschaft**).

■ *Uses of* lassen

Laß deinen Schirm nicht zu Hause.	Don't leave your umbrella at home.
Laß mich dir helfen.	Let me help you.

Lassen is a commonly used verb that occurs in a variety of constructions. Like the modals, **lassen** can stand alone or take a dependent infinitive (e.g., **helfen**) without **zu.**

Hast du deinen Bruder zu Hause **gelassen?**	Did you leave your brother at home?
Hast du ihn fahren **lassen?**	Did you let him drive?

In the present perfect and past perfect tenses the participle **gelassen** is used when the verb occurs without a dependent infinitive. When the verb occurs with a dependent infinitive (e.g., **fahren**), the infinitive form **lassen** is used instead of the past participle. The infinitive **lassen** is always at the very end of the clause. This construction is called the "double infinitive" construction.

■ *Meanings of* lassen

Lassen has four basic meanings.

1. **lassen** = *to leave*

Laß das Buch hier.	Leave the book here.
Ich habe meine Tasche zu Hause **gelassen.**	I've left my bag at home.

2. **lassen** = *to let* or *to permit*

Lassen Sie mich die Arbeit machen.	Let me do the work.
Wie lange **läßt** du ihn arbeiten?	How long are you going to let him work?

3. **lassen** = *let's*

Gerd, **laß** uns jetzt gehen.	Gerd, let's go now.
Freunde, **laßt** uns essen.	Let's eat, folks.

The imperative form of **lassen** plus the pronoun **uns** is often used in place of the first-person plural imperative: **Gehen wir. Essen wir.** In talking to a person you address with **du,** use **laß;** with **ihr** use **laßt.**

4. **lassen** = *to have someone come to do something* or *to have something done*

Frau Lange **läßt** den Elektriker kommen.	Ms. Lange is sending for the electrician.
Wir **lassen** unser Auto reparieren.	We're having our car repaired.

5. Ein neues Projekt. Several young social workers are meeting to discuss a new project. One of them, Ahmed, comes in late and has to leave early. Give the English equivalents of their conversation. Some of the unfamiliar words are guessable; others are defined in the margin. Remember, **lassen** has four basic meanings.

1. LISA: Laßt uns jetzt mal den Plan durchsprechen.
2. ANDREAS: Ich glaube, Ahmed ist gekommen. Läßt du ihn mal rein, Dieter?
3. LISA: Tag, Ahmed. Wo hast du den Wagen gelassen?
4. AHMED: Auf der Straße. Habt ihr schon den Computer reparieren lassen?
5. LISA: Ja, alles in Ordnung. Also, jetzt laßt uns in Ruhe° über die Sache reden.   *in Ruhe:* without rushing
6. AHMED: Laß mal sehen, was du da aufgeschrieben hast.
7. LISA: Laßt mich das mal genau erklären.
8. ANDREAS: Roberto, bitte laß das Fenster offen. Hier ist es so warm!
9. LISA: Ahmed, laß die Bücher hier, wenn du gehst.
10. AHMED: Soll ich euch auch die Fotokopien da lassen?
11. Laßt ihr mich dann wissen, wie ihr euch entschieden° habt?   decided
12. Oh je, wo hab ich nur meine Schlüssel° gelassen?   keys
13. ANDREAS: Vielleicht hast du sie im Copy-Shop liegengelassen.
14. AHMED: Ich lasse euch jetzt allein. Tschüs.
15. LISA: Laßt ihn jetzt gehen. Er kriegt sonst Streß.

6. Noch einmal. Some students are in the office of an international student association. They are talking about their day and their assignments. One of them is on the phone. Restate the sentences below, using the cued subjects with the verb **lassen.**

▶ Wie lange lassen Sie die Leute da   *Wie lange läßt du die Leute da*
stehen? (du)   *stehen?*

1. Wann lassen Sie uns wissen, wann Sie kommen? (du)
2. Wo habt ihr euer Auto gelassen? (Sabine)
3. Bei wem läßt du deinen Wagen waschen? (ihr)
4. Andrea läßt dich aber lange warten. (deine Eltern)
5. Ich lasse die Spülmaschine reparieren. (wir)
6. Wann lassen Sie Tanja mit der Arbeit anfangen? (du)
7. Warum hat er uns so lange arbeiten lassen? (du)
8. Ich muß das Auto reparieren lassen? (Sie)

7. Wo lasse ich das? You and a friend (your partner) are planning a three-month vacation trip and are therefore giving up your apartments. You are discussing what possessions you will leave with whom. | Stating intention |

S1: Ich lasse meine CDs bei meinem Freund.
S2: Ich lasse ...

Was?: Computer □ Fernseher □ Pflanzen □ CD-Spieler □ Katze □ Hund □ Fahrrad

Bei wem?: Eltern □ Nachbarin □ Bruder □ Freundin □ Freund □ Onkel □ Kusine □ Nachbar □ Schwester □ Großmutter

8. Laß uns schwimmen gehen. Suggest an activity to your partner who will then suggest what to do afterward. Take turns suggesting other activities to each other. You may use the cues or make up your own. Follow the models.

S1: Laß uns schwimmen gehen.
S2: Ja, und dann gehen wir Kaffee trinken.

im Garten sitzen
die Stellenanzeigen durchsehen
Bernd und Ute anrufen
ein Computerspiel spielen
im Stadtpark joggen
ein bißchen fernsehen
endlich den Brief schreiben

9. Ich lasse alles machen. Tell your partner three things you will not do for yourself but will have done for you. You may wish to use the following suggestions.

Bett machen □ [Frühstück] machen □ Auto waschen □
Hausaufgaben machen □ [Fernseher] reparieren □ [Briefe] schreiben □
[Gartenarbeit] machen □ Fenster putzen

▶ *Ich wasche mein Auto nicht. Ich lasse mein Auto (von meiner Schwester) waschen.*

4 Relative clauses

Ist das **der Mann, den** Sie meinen?	Is that *the man (whom)* you mean?
Das ist **das Auto, das** ich kaufen möchte.	That's *the car (that)* I'd like to buy.
Wer ist **die Frau, die** gerade hereinkommt?	Who is *the woman (who* is) just coming in?

A relative clause provides additional information about a previously mentioned noun or pronoun. The clause is introduced by a relative pronoun (e.g., **den, das, die**) that refers back to the noun, which is the antecedent (e.g., **Mann, Auto, Frau**). Since a relative clause is a dependent clause, the finite verb (e.g., **meinen, möchte, hereinkommt**) stands in last position.

In English, the relative pronoun may or may not be stated. In German, the relative pronoun must always be stated. In written German, relative clauses are set off from main clauses by commas.

5 Relative pronouns

	Masculine	Neuter	Feminine	Plural
Nominative	der	das	die	die
Accusative	den	das	die	die
Dative	dem	dem	der	**denen**
Genitive	**dessen**	**dessen**	**deren**	**deren**

The forms of the relative pronoun are the same as the forms of the definite articles, except for the dative plural and all genitive forms.

Masculine	Das ist der Mann, **der** uns gefragt hat.
Neuter	Das ist das Kind, **das** uns gefragt hat.
Feminine	Das ist die Frau, **die** uns gefragt hat.
Plural	Das sind die Leute, **die** uns gefragt haben.

The *gender* (masculine, neuter, or feminine) of the relative pronoun depends on the gender of the noun to which it refers. In the examples above, **der** is masculine because it refers to **der Mann** and **die** is feminine because it refers to **die Frau**. Whether a pronoun is singular or plural also depends on the noun to which it refers. The pronoun **die** that refers to **die Leute** is plural and therefore requires the plural verb **haben**.

Nominative	Ist das der Mann, **der** hier war?
Accusative	Ist das der Mann, **den** Sie meinen?
Dative	Ist das der Mann, **dem** Sie es gesagt haben?
Genitive	Ist das der Mann, **dessen** Auto Sie gekauft haben?

The *case* (nominative, accusative, dative, or genitive) of a relative pronoun depends on its grammatical function in the relative clause. In the examples above, **der** is nominative because it is the subject of its clause; **den** is accusative because it is the direct object of the verb **meinen** in that clause; **dem** is dative because it is an indirect object in the clause; and **dessen** is genitive because it shows possession.

Wie heißt die Frau, **für die** Sie arbeiten?	What is the name of the woman *for whom* you work?
Wo ist die Firma, **bei der** Sie arbeiten?	Where is the firm *(that)* you work *for?*

A relative clause can also be introduced by a preposition followed by a relative pronoun. The case of the relative pronoun then depends on what case the preposition takes. In **für die, die** is accusative because of **für;** in **bei der, der** is dative because of **bei.**

In German, whenever a relative pronoun is the object of a preposition, the preposition precedes the pronoun. In colloquial English the preposition is usually in last position [*(that) you work for*].

10. Die deutsche Wirtschaft.   Below are sentences on the German economy. Identify the relative pronouns. Indicate the case and function of each relative pronoun, and name its antecedent.

▶ Die Regierung arbeitet für einen Welthandel, der wirklich frei ist.
der = nominative, subject, Welthandel

1. Ein Land wie Deutschland, das wenig Rohstoffe hat, lebt vom Handel.
2. Die Produkte, die man produziert, müssen von bester Qualität sein.
3. Denn es gibt mehrere Länder, mit denen Deutschland konkurrieren muß.
4. In der Zukunft ändert sich° wohl der Markt, für den Deutschland pro-   **ändert sich:** changes
   duzieren muß.
5. Einige Firmen, die Dinge produzieren, die man nicht mehr kauft, werden bankrott machen.
6. Das bedeutet, daß die Arbeiter, deren Firmen bankrott sind, arbeitslos werden.
7. Die Arbeitslosigkeit ist ein Problem, das nur schwer zu lösen° ist.   solve

11. Die sind doch gar nicht kaputt.   Your friend is good at fixing electrical and audio equipment, only he can't seem to find the right ones to fix. Tell him the things he wants to fix for you aren't the ones that are broken. Use the nominative of the relative pronoun.

▶ Ich repariere jetzt diesen Computer, ja?
Das ist doch nicht der Computer, der kaputt ist.

1. Ich repariere jetzt diesen Fernseher.
2. Ich repariere jetzt dieses Telefon, ja?
3. Ich repariere jetzt dieses Kassettendeck.
4. Ich repariere jetzt dieses Radio.
5. Ich repariere jetzt diese Lampen, ja?
6. Ich repariere jetzt diese Uhren.

12. Die Sachen sind toll.   Gabi shows you various articles of clothing. Show your interest by asking whether they are the ones she got for her birthday. Use the accusative of the relative pronoun.

▶ Wie gefällt dir diese Jacke?
Toll. Ist das die Jacke, die du zum Geburtstag bekommen hast?

1. Wie gefällt dir diese Hose?
2. Wie gefällt dir dieses Hemd?
3. Wie gefällt dir dieser Rock?
4. Wie gefällt dir dieser Pulli?
5. Wie gefallen dir diese Jeans?
6. Wie gefallen dir diese Schuhe?

13. David schreibt über die Ausländer. David writes to his friend Thomas about how foreigners get along in Germany. Complete the sentences below with appropriate relative pronouns.

1. In dem Brief, ———— David an seinen Freund Thomas schreibt, berichtet er über die Ausländer.
2. In Deutschland sind viele Ausländer, ———— in den großen Industriestädten leben.
3. In manchen Vierteln°, in ———— die Ausländer wohnen, wohnen nur wenige Deutsche.　　　　*quarters, sections (of a city)*
4. Dort gibt es Läden, in ———— die Ausländer die Lebensmittel kaufen können, ———— sie von ihrer Heimat her kennen.
5. Es sind meistens die Kinder, ———— es in dem fremden Land ganz gut gefällt.
6. Die Kinder lernen Deutsch, ———— sie dann oft besser sprechen als die Eltern.
7. Die Ausländer, ———— die Deutschen bei der Integration im allgemeinen° wenig helfen, bleiben oft unter sich.　　　　**im allgemeinen:** *in general*

14. Wer sind diese Leute? Veronika is a guest at a party where she knows no one. Your friend tells her something about the people. But, since she knows no German, you must translate.

▶ Frau Meier, deren Sohn in Marburg studiert, ist Rechtsanwältin.
　Mrs. Meier, whose son is studying in Marburg, is a lawyer.

1. Herr Schnell, dessen Tochter bei Volkswagen arbeitet, fährt einen Golf.
2. Herr und Frau Gescheit, deren Kinder gut Englisch können, haben ein großes Haus.
3. Der alte Herr, dessen Sohn arbeitslos ist, hat vor ein paar Wochen bankrott gemacht.
4. Herr Ettel, dessen Frau Chefärztin ist, studiert noch.
5. Diese junge Frau, deren Vater ein bekannter° Rechtsanwalt ist, hat letzte Woche geheiratet.　　　　*well-known*
6. Und dieser junge Mann, dessen Eltern sehr reich° sind, ist der Glückliche°.　　　　*rich / fortunate one*

15. Frage-Ecke. Take turns with your partner to find out who the following people are. You and your partner may identify the people differently.

S1: Wer ist Herr Rot?
S2: Das ist der Journalist, der für die *Times* arbeitet. Und wer ist Frau … ?
S1: Das ist …

Frau Blau	der Professor	Sie/Er schreibt an einem Roman.
Herr Klein	die Studentin	Sie/Er trägt immer komische° Hüte.　　*funny*
Herr Rot	der Ingenieur	Alle mögen sie/ihn.
Dr. Kühler	der Journalist	Ihr Mann ruft sie jeden Tag an.
Herr Hamburger	die Sekretärin	Ihr/Ihm gefällt es gut hier.
Frau König	der Arzt	Sie/Er arbeitet für die *Times*.
Frau Kaiser	der Musiker	Sie/Ihn sieht man nur mit der Zeitung unterm Arm.
Herr Bass	die Lehrerin	Sie/Er lächelt immer so viel.

   16. Erzähl mal.   In groups of three take turns completing each of the sentences.

▶   Wien ist eine Stadt, ...   [*die sehr alt ist*].
                                   [*die ich besuchen möchte*].
                                   [*in der ich leben möchte*].

1. Die Schweiz ist ein Land, ...
2. Österreich ist ein Land, ...
3. Volkswagen ist eine Firma, ...
4. Ich hätte gern eine Präsidentin/einen Präsidenten, ...
5. Ich habe einen Freund, ...
6. Ich habe eine Freundin, ...
7. Ich habe eine Professorin/einen Professor, ...
8. Der Juli ist ein Monat, ...

WIEDERHOLUNG

1. Eine bekannte Autorin.   Read the following account about Kirsten Elsner's start as an author. Answer the questions.

Herr Elsner bekam eine neue Stelle in einer anderen Stadt. Weil Frau Elsner dort keine Arbeit fand, blieb sie zu Hause und sorgte° für die Kinder. Am Anfang machte sie alles gern. Sie kochte, putzte, ging einkaufen und half den Kindern bei den Schulaufgaben. Um etwas für die Kinder zu tun, fing sie an, kurze Geschichten für sie zu schreiben. Sie wurde durch die Kindergeschichten bald bekannt°. Jetzt nennt man sie nicht mehr Kirsten Elsner, die Frau von Herrn Elsner. Jetzt heißt sie Kirsten Wiener, und Herr Elsner ist der Mann von der bekannten Autorin.

cared

well known

1. Warum wohnten Elsners in einer neuen Stadt?
2. Warum blieb Frau Elsner zu Hause?
3. Was machte sie zu Hause?
4. Warum fing sie an, Kindergeschichten zu schreiben?
5. Wie nennt man Herrn Elsner jetzt?

2. Gabi weiß jetzt mehr. Tanja wants to know whether you helped Gabi understand some facts about the economic situation in Germany. Answer the questions below. Replace the boldfaced words with a pronoun or use a **da**-compound.

▶ Wollte Gabi etwas über **die deutsche Wirtschaft** wissen?
Ja, sie _____ .

Ja, sie wollte etwas darüber wissen.

1. Hast du ihr von **der Rolle des Außenhandels** erzählt?
Ja, ich _____ .
2. Hat sie **die Rolle** verstanden?
Ja, sie _____ .
3. Ein Land wie Deutschland lebt vom **Handel,** nicht?
Ja, es _____ .
4. Interessiert sich Gabi auch für **die Rolle der Gewerkschaften?**
Ja, sie _____ .
5. Weiß sie etwas von **den Zielen der Gewerkschaften?**
Ja, sie _____ .
6. Haben die Deutschen große Angst vor **Inflation?**
Ja, sie _____ .
7. Findet Gabi **den Lebensstandard der Deutschen** hoch?
Ja, sie _____ .

3. Ein Student an der Uni. Bernd wonders how Peter is getting along at the university. Tell him things are not going well, but that Peter doesn't seem to mind. Complete the sentences below with adjective endings, where necessary. Then answer the questions in the negative, using adjectives from the list as antonyms for the adjectives in the questions.

alt □ dumm □ faul □ groß □ lustig □ leicht □ schlecht □ teuer

▶ Studiert Peter an einer klein_____ Universität?

Studiert Peter an einer kleinen Universität? Nein, an einer großen.

1. Ist er ein fleißig_____ Student?
2. Ist er intelligent_____ ?
3. Liest er gern ernst_____ Geschichten?
4. Wohnt er in einer modern_____ Wohnung?
5. Wohnt er in einem klein_____ Zimmer?
6. Hat er ein schwer_____ Leben?
7. Hat er einen gut_____ Studentenjob?
8. Findet er Wohnen und Essen billig_____ ?

4. Markus schreibt über Frauen. Markus has written some brief comments about women in Germany. Complete his work by supplying appropriate relative pronouns.

1. Viele Frauen sind mit dem Frauenbild, _____ in vielen Schulbüchern noch zu finden ist, unzufrieden°.

dissatisfied

2. In diesen Büchern ist es immer ein Junge, _____ etwas baut oder Fußball spielt.

3. Und es ist immer ein Mädchen, _____ zusieht° und weniger gefährliche° Sachen macht. watches / dangerous

4. Die Frauen, _____ Berufe wie Elektrikerin und Mechanikerin gelernt haben, haben es besonders schwer.

5. Man nennt eine Frau, _____ wegen der Arbeit vier Tage von zu Hause weg ist, eine Rabenmutter°. unfit mother

6. Ein Mann, _____ dieselbe Arbeit macht, ist aber kein Rabenvater°. unfit father

7. Es gibt also noch traditionelle Rollen, von _____ Männer und Frauen sich emanzipieren müssen.

5. Ihre Meinung. Express your opinion by answering one or more of the questions below.

1. Möchten Sie in einem anderen Land studieren? Warum (nicht)?
2. Möchten Sie während des Sommers in einem anderen Land arbeiten? Warum (nicht)?
3. Möchten Sie in einem anderen Land leben? In welchem Land? Warum?
4. Möchten Sie in einem Land leben, dessen Sprache Sie nicht können? Warum (nicht)?
5. Würden Sie in einem anderen Land für weniger Geld als in Amerika arbeiten? Warum (nicht)?

6. Erzählen Sie mal.

1. Erzählen Sie mal von einem Buch, das Sie gern kaufen würden.
2. Erzählen Sie mal von einer Reise, die Sie gern machen würden.
3. Erzählen Sie mal von Ferien, die Sie gern machen würden.
4. Erzählen Sie mal von Politikern, die Sie gern reden hören würden.
5. Erzählen Sie mal von einem Film, den Sie gern sehen würden.

Diese Gymnasiasten diskutieren in ihrer Arbeitsgruppe.

Ausländische Arbeitnehmer beim Straßenbau in der Schweiz.

7. Zum Schreiben

1. In a paragraph describe in German in what kind of family or world you would like to live. Use at least two relative pronouns in your paragraph.

2. In German list some difficulties or problems that foreign workers or a minority group face in any country. Then in groups of four discuss your lists. Try to make one list that all agree upon, ranking the problems. Share your list with the class.

3. Write a paragraph in German to support or refute the following statement: **Kinder, die in zwei Sprachen und zwei Kulturen aufwachsen, haben viele Vorteile°.**   advantages

Hinweise: In a relative clause the finite verb is in final position. The gender of the relative pronoun depends on the gender of the noun to which it refers. Its case depends on its function in the clause.

GRAMMATIK: ZUSAMMENFASSUNG

The future tense

ich **werde** es **machen**	wir **werden** es **machen**
du **wirst** es **machen**	ihr **werdet** es **machen**
er/es/sie **wird** es **machen**	sie **werden** es **machen**
	Sie **werden** es **machen**

The German future tense consists of the auxiliary **werden** plus an infinitive in final position.

Erika sagt, daß sie es sicher **machen wird.**

In a dependent clause, the auxiliary **werden** is in final position because it is the finite verb.

Future time: present tense

Ich **komme** morgen bestimmt.	I'll come tomorrow for sure.
Fahren Sie nächstes Jahr nach Deutschland?	Are you going to Germany next year?

German uses the future tense less frequently than English. German generally uses the present tense if the context clearly indicates future time.

Uses of the future tense

Future time	Frank **wird** mir **helfen.**	Frank *will help* me.

Future tense is used to express future time if the context doesn't make it clear that the events will take place in the future.

Assumption	Anna **wird** uns sicher **glauben.**	Anna *probably believes* us.
	Das **wird** wohl **stimmen.**	That *is probably correct.*

The future tense may also be used to express an assumption (present probability) when it is used with adverbs such as **sicher, schon,** and **wohl.**

Constructions with *lassen*

Present tense	
ich lasse	wir lassen
du läßt	ihr laßt
er/es/sie läßt	sie lassen
Sie lassen	
du-imperative:	laß
Simple past stem:	ließ
Past participle:	gelassen

■ *Uses of* lassen

Lisa **ließ** ihren Bruder zu Hause.	Lisa left her brother at home.
Lisa **ließ** ihre Schwester fahren.	Lisa let her sister drive.

Lassen behaves like the modals, in that it can stand alone or take a dependent infinitive without **zu.**

Hast du deinen Bruder zu Hause **gelassen?**	Did you leave your brother at home?
Hast du ihn fahren **lassen?**	Did you let him drive?

In the present perfect and past perfect tenses the participle **gelassen** is used when the verb occurs without a dependent infinitive. When the verb occurs with a dependent infinitive (e.g., **fahren**), the infinitive form, **lassen,** is used instead of the past participle. The infinitive **lassen** is always at the very end of the clause. This construction is called the "double infinitive" construction.

■ *Meanings of* **lassen**

Lassen is one of the most commonly used verbs in German. **Lassen** has four basic meanings.

1. **lassen** = *to leave*

Uwe **hat** seinen Freund allein **gelassen.**	Uwe left his friend alone.
Hast du deine Jacke zu Hause **gelassen?**	Did you leave your jacket at home?

2. **lassen** = *to let* or *to permit*

Wir **lassen** euch arbeiten.	We'll let you work.
Lassen Sie mich Ihnen helfen.	Let me help you.

3. **lassen** = *let's*

Daniela, **laß** uns essen.	Daniela, let's eat.
Kinder, **laßt** uns gehen.	Children, let's go.

   In talking to a person you address with **du**, use **laß**; with **ihr**, use **laßt**.

4. **lassen** = *to have something done* or *to have someone come to do something*

Sarah **läßt** ihre Uhr reparieren.	Sarah is having her watch repaired.
Haben Sie den Elektriker kommen **lassen?**	Did you send for the electrician?

Relative clauses

Wie teuer ist **der Fernseher, den** du kaufen willst?	How expensive is *the television (that)* you want to buy?
Wie alt ist **das Auto, das** du verkaufen möchtest?	How old is *the car (that)* you want to sell?
Ist das **die CD, die** du gestern gekauft hast?	Is that *the CD (that)* you bought yesterday?

A relative clause provides additional information about a previously mentioned noun or pronoun. The clause is introduced by a relative pronoun, which refers back to the noun or pronoun (called an antecedent). A relative clause is a dependent clause, and thus the verb is in final position.

Relative pronouns

	Masculine	Neuter	Feminine	Plural
Nominative	der	das	die	die
Accusative	den	das	die	die
Dative	dem	dem	der	**denen**
Genitive	**dessen**	**dessen**	**deren**	**deren**

Nominative	Ist das der Mann, **der** immer so viel fragt?
Accusative	Ist das der Mann, **den** Sie meinen?
	für den Sie arbeiten?
Dative	Ist das der Mann, **dem** Sie oft helfen?
	von dem Sie erzählt haben?
Genitive	Ist das der Mann, **dessen** Auto Sie gekauft haben?

The *gender* (masculine, neuter, or feminine) and *number* (singular or plural) of the relative pronoun are determined by its antecedent, i.e., the noun to which it refers. The *case* (nominative, accusative, dative, or genitive) of the relative pronoun is determined by its function within its clause (subject, direct object, object of a preposition, etc.).

Diese Heidelberger Radfahrer und die Straßenbahn sind umweltfreundlich.

Kapitel 14

LERNZIELE

■ **Sprechintentionen**

Discussing ways to protect the environment
Discussing who invented, wrote, or discovered something

■ **Lesestück**

Die Umwelt

■ **Land und Leute**

Packaging ordinance
Die Grünen

■ **Kurzgeschichte**

Der Verkäufer und der Elch – Franz Hohler

■ **Grammatik**

Passive voice
Summary of uses of **werden**
Alternatives to the passive voice

BAUSTEINE FÜR GESPRÄCHE

Vorbereitungen für ein Picknick

ALEX: Rebecca, Lukas, haben wir jetzt alles?

REBECCA: Ja, bis auf die Pappteller und die Plastikbestecke. Die können wir aber auf dem Weg kaufen.

ALEX: Na gut. Und ich habe hier noch ein paar Saftflaschen.

LUKAS: Sagt mal, ihr zwei. Wo ist eigentlich euer Umweltbewußtsein? Einwegflaschen, Plastikbestecke und Pappteller! Das ist hinterher alles Müll.

ALEX: Lukas, du machst mich noch verrückt. Das bißchen Müll! Außerdem ist das so viel praktischer.

REBECCA: Ja, da muß hinterher nicht abgewaschen werden, und man braucht keine Pfandflaschen zurückzutragen. Das ist viel zu umständlich.

LUKAS: Machen wir einen Kompromiß! Ihr kauft umweltfreundlich ein, und ich helfe euch. Abgewaschen wird zusammen, und ich bringe die Flaschen zurück.

REBECCA: In Ordnung! Laßt uns jetzt gehen. Sonst wird es zu spät.

Preparations for a picnic

Rebecca, Lukas, do we have everything now?

Yes, except for the paper plates and plastic knives, forks, and spoons. We can buy those on the way.

Fine. And I have a few bottles of juice here.

Listen, you two. Really, where is your environmental awareness? Non-returnable bottles! Plastic knives, forks, and spoons and paper plates! That will be trash later.

Lukas, you'll drive me crazy yet. That little bit of trash! Besides it's so much more practical.

Yes, there's no washing up afterwards and you don't need to take back the returnable bottles. That's too much trouble.

Let's compromise! You shop environment-friendly and I'll help you. Washing up will be done together, and I'll take back the bottles.

All right! Let's go now. Otherwise it'll get too late.

Fragen

1. Was muß Rebecca noch kaufen?
2. Was hat Lukas gegen die Vorbereitungen und Pläne?
3. Warum möchte Rebecca lieber Plastikbestecke und Pappteller benutzen?
4. Welchen Kompromiß machen die drei?

⊳ **Umweltbewußtsein.**   Find out from fellow students what they do for the environment.

Discussing ways to protect the environment

S1:

Was machst du für die Umwelt?

S2:

Ich fahre | **langsam.**
| mehr Fahrrad.
| öfter mit dem Bus.

Ich recycle | **Zeitungen.**
| Zeitschriften°.
| Glas.
| Plastik.
| Dosen°.

Ich benutze keine | **Pappteller.**
| Plastikbestecke.

Ich rauche° nicht.

S1:

Was wird in Ihrer Stadt für die Umwelt gemacht?

S2:

Bei uns wird weniger Wasser verbraucht°.
Bei uns werden | **nur Pfandflaschen verkauft.**
| Papier und Glas recycelt.
| neue Fahrradwege gebaut.

Vokabeln

Substantive

das **Besteck, -e**   a setting of knife, fork, and spoon; flatware
das **Bewußtsein**   consciousness, awareness
die **Dose, -n**   can, tin; box
die **Einwegflasche, -n**   non-returnable bottle
der **Kompromiß,** *pl.* **Kompromisse** compromise
der **Müll**   garbage, trash
die **Pappe**   cardboard
der **Pappteller, -**   paper plate
die **Pfandflasche, -n**   returnable bottle

das **Plastik**   plastic
das **Plastikbesteck, -e**   a setting of plastic knife, fork, and spoon
die **Saftflasche, -n**   bottle of juice
die **Umwelt**   environment
das **Umweltbewußtsein** environmental awareness
die **Vorbereitung, -en**   preparation
die **Zeitschrift, -en**   magazine; journal

Verben

rauchen   to smoke
recyceln   to recycle
verbrauchen   to use up (water, gasoline, etc.)

zurück·tragen (trägt zurück), trug zurück, zurückgetragen   to take or carry back

Andere Wörter

bis auf (+ *acc.*)   except for
hinterher   afterwards
langsam   slow(ly)
umständlich   involved; **das ist [mir]
zu umständlich**   that's too much
bother/trouble

umweltfreundlich   environment-
friendly, eco-friendly
verrückt   crazy

DIE UMWELT

Vorbereitung auf das Lesen

■   *Vor dem Lesen**

1.   Eine Umweltumfrage°.   Beantworten Sie diese Fragen auf einer Skala von   environmental survey
1 bis 5.

1 = immer   4 = selten
2 = oft   5 = nie
3 = manchmal

1. Wie oft recyceln Sie Zeitungen und Altpapier?   _____
2. Wie oft recyceln Sie Flaschen und Altglas?   _____
3. Wie oft kaufen Sie Pfandflaschen?   _____
4. Wie oft werfen° Sie alte Batterien in den Müll?   _____
5. Wie oft fahren Sie allein in Ihrem Auto?   _____
6. Wie oft fahren Sie schneller als das Tempolimit°?   _____
7. Wie oft fahren Sie nicht mit dem Auto zur Arbeit
   oder zur Uni?   _____
8. Wie oft gibt es bei Ihnen Smog-Alarm?   _____
9. Wie oft bezahlen Sie mehr für ein Produkt, weil es
   umweltfreundlich ist?   _____

2.   Eine Umweltdiskussion.   Besprechen° Sie die Ergebnisse° Ihrer   discuss / results
Umfrage zu dritt. Gebrauchen Sie diese Fragen als Inspiration. Berichten Sie
der Gruppe über Ihre Diskussion.

■ Wer von Ihnen ist am umweltfreundlichsten?
■ Machen Sie etwas für die Umwelt, was nicht in der Umfrage steht? Was?
■ Könnten Sie mehr für die Umwelt tun? Was?
■ Könnte Ihre Regierung mehr für die Umwelt tun? Was?

*Remember, words that appear with a raised degree mark (°) but no definition in the margin are
words you should learn and be able to use. These words are listed in the **Vokabeln** section that
most closely follows their appearance.

■ *Beim Lesen*

Notieren Sie beim Lesen, was die Deutschen für die Umwelt tun. Denken Sie an die folgenden Themen:

    Auto □ Luft □ Recycling/recyceln

In ihren Küchenkalender schreibt Cornelia Meister alle Pflichten, die ihre Familienmitglieder im Haushalt haben. Neben dem Putzen, Geschirrspülen, Wäschewaschen und der Gartenarbeit gehört auch das Recycling dazu. Das heißt, daß der Müll sortiert werden muß. Haushaltsmüll, der nicht wieder ver-
5 wertet werden kann, kommt in eine normale Mülltonne. Der organische Müll wird in die grüne Tonne geworfen. Altpapier, leere Glas- und Plastikflaschen und Metalldosen werden gesammelt und in spezielle Container geworfen. Geschäfte, die Batterien verkaufen, müssen leere Batterien zurücknehmen.

    Alle Produkte, die man in Deutschland wieder verwerten kann, haben
10 einen grünen Punkt auf der Packung°, und Produkte mit diesem grünen Punkt   package
sind ungefähr 40 Pfennig teurer. So wird das Recycling finanziert. Heute re-
cyceln 95 Prozent der deutschen Haushalte. Das macht die Deutschen zu Weltmeistern im Recycling. Doch damit steht die Industrie vor einem neuen Problem: Jährlich produzieren deutsche Haushalte zusammen 400.000 Tonnen°   tons
15 sortierten Müll, aber nur 125.000 Tonnen können jedes Jahr wieder verwertet werden.

    Neben dem Müllberg gibt es auch andere Umweltprobleme. Ob in Frankfurt, Rom, Mexiko City, Los Angeles oder Tokio – in vielen Großstädten gibt es jeden Sommer Probleme mit dem Smog. Wenn die Tage heißer werden,
20 dann wird auch der Smog stärker. Je industrialisierter ein Land ist, desto größer ist die Luftverschmutzung, und je wärmer das Wetter wird, desto schlechter wird die Luft. Die Bäume sterben, die Kinder kommen mit roten Augen vom Spielplatz nach Hause, und die Jogger müssen stehenbleiben, weil sie nicht mehr atmen können – alles wegen der hohen Ozonwerte° in der Luft.   ozone levels
25 In Mitteleuropa werden die hohen Ozonwerte durch Abgase° verursacht. Die   exhaust fumes
Industrie mit ihren Fabriken tut zwar auch ihren Teil dazu, aber allein in der Bundesrepublik werden 70 Prozent der Abgase von Personenautos und Lastwagen produziert.

    Umweltsünder° Nummer Eins scheint also das Auto zu sein, und seine   environmental culprit
30 Abgase sind nicht das einzige Umweltproblem. Um Autos zu bauen, zu reparieren und zu verschrotten°, braucht man Energie und Rohstoffe. Außerdem   turn to scrap
verbraucht das Auto selber viel Energie. Man hat kalkuliert, daß ein einziges Auto während seiner Lebensdauer° soviel Energie verbraucht, wie ein Deutscher   lifetime of operation
ohne Auto in sechs Jahren für Heizung°, Strom° und Transport zusammen.   heat/electricity
35   Wie schwer es ist, Umweltprobleme zu lösen, kann man gut am Beispiel des Autos sehen: Die meisten Deutschen sehen im Autoverkehr die größte Gefahr für die Umwelt, gleichzeitig° ist aber das Autofahren für drei Viertel   at the same time
der Deutschen die wichtigste Freizeitbeschäftigung°. Seit 1995 gibt es zwar   leisure-time activity
ein Ozongesetz mit Fahrverbot° und Tempolimit, wenn die Ozonwerte zu   driving ban
40 hoch sind. Aber jedes Land regelt° das Gesetz verschieden°, es gibt viele   applies/differently
Ausnahmen°, und viele Autofahrer sind gegen ein Tempolimit. Auch zur   exceptions
Reduzierung des Müllberges gibt es viele verschiedene Pläne: „Null-Verpak-
kung" ist eine Idee, das heißt, man will keine oder nur minimale Verpackung

für Produkte. Die Getränkeindustrie soll nur noch Pfandflaschen benutzen. In
45 Ländern wie Rheinland-Pfalz und Baden-Württemberg werden schon jetzt
über 80 Prozent der Getränke in Pfandflaschen verkauft. Das Argument gegen
Pfandflaschen sind die größeren Kosten für Reinigung° und Transport. Die   cleaning
Diskussion um die Lösung° des Umweltproblems geht also weiter, aber es gibt   solution
auch schon Erfolge°. Strengere Kontrollen für die Industrie und Umweltgesetze   successes
50 haben dazu geführt°, daß viele deutsche Seen und Flüsse, sogar der Rhein,   led
wieder sauberes Wasser haben.

**Diese junge Frau recycelt
ihre Zeitungen und
Altglas. (München)**

Nach dem Lesen

1. Fragen zum Lesestück

1. Was tut Familie Meister für die Umwelt? Machen Sie eine Liste.
2. Wie finanziert Deutschland das Recycling?
3. Warum nennt man die Deutschen „die Weltmeister im Recycling"?
4. Wann ist die Luftverschmutzung besonders groß?
5. Geben Sie zwei Beispiele, wie hohe Ozonwerte das tägliche Leben beeinflussen.
6. Warum nennt man das Auto „Umweltsünder Nummer Eins"? Geben Sie
   zwei Gründe° dafür.   reasons
7. Für wen ist das Autofahren die wichtigste Freizeitbeschäftigung?
8. Was regelt° das Ozongesetz von 1995?   regulates
9. Welche Argumente gibt es gegen Pfandflaschen?
10. Warum hat der Rhein wieder sauberes Wasser?

2. Vokabeln definieren.   Unten stehen einige Wörter aus dem Text und einige Definitionen. Welche Wörter werden hier definiert?

> die Abgase □ die Gesetze □ der Grüne Punkt □ der Müll □
> die Null-Verpackung □ ein Umweltsünder

1. Sie sollen die Umwelt schützen°.   protect
2. Keine oder minimale Verpackung.
3. Alles, was man wegwirft.
4. Luftverschmutzung, die von Autos und Fabriken produziert wird.
5. Er ist das Symbol für Produkte, die wieder verwertet werden.
6. Jemand, der, oder etwas, was der Umwelt schadet°.   harms

3. Zur Diskussion.   Was machen Sie für die Umwelt? Vergleichen° Sie   compare
das Recycling und die Gesetze in Ihrem Land mit dem Recycling und die
Gesetze in Deutschland. Was ist anders in Ihrem Land, und was ist ähnlich?
Benutzen Sie Ihre Notizen von „Beim Lesen".

4. Werbung° für die Umwelt.   Arbeiten Sie in einer Gruppe und   advertising
produzieren Sie einen Werbespot° oder ein Poster für eine der folgenden   advertising spot
Situationen.

1. *Smog-Alarm:* Sie leben in einer Großstadt. Es ist ein heißer Sommertag,
   und die Ozonwerte sind sehr hoch. Sie müssen den Einwohnern der Stadt
   Ratschläge° geben, was sie machen oder nicht machen sollten.   advice

2. *Umweltsünder Nummer Eins:* Die Luft in der Stadt ist sehr schlecht, weil die
   Leute zu viel Auto fahren. Geben Sie den Einwohnern der Stadt Ratschläge,
   wie sie das Autofahren reduzieren können.

3. *Den Müllberg abbauen°:* Die Leute in Ihrer Stadt produzieren zu viel Müll,   reduce
   und die Mülltonnen sind zu voll. Geben Sie den Leuten Ratschläge, wie
   sie ihren Müll reduzieren können.

Vokabeln

Substantive

der **Baum**, ⸚e   tree
die **Energie**   energy
die **Fabrik**, -en   factory
der **Fluß**, *pl.* **Flüsse**   river
das **Gesetz**, -e   law
die **Großstadt**, ⸚e   city
der **Kalender**, -   calendar
der **Lastwagen**, -   truck
die **Meinung**, -en   opinion; **meiner
 Meinung nach**   in my opinion

das **Metall**, -e   metal
die **Pflicht**, -en   chore; duty
das **Recycling**   recycling
der **See**, -n   lake
der **Smog**   smog
das **Tempolimit**   speed limit
die **Tonne**, -n   drum, container; ton
der **Verkehr**   traffic
die **Verpackung**   packaging
die **Verschmutzung**   pollution

Verben

atmen to breathe	**verursachen** to cause
lösen to solve	**verwerten** to make use of
produzieren to produce	**weg·werfen (wirft weg), warf weg,**
reparieren to repair	**weggeworfen** to throw away
scheinen, schien, geschienen to	**werfen (wirft), warf, geworfen** to
appear, seem	throw
stehen·bleiben, blieb stehen, ist	**zurück·nehmen (nimmt zurück),**
stehengeblieben to stop	**nahm zurück, zurückgenommen**
sterben (stirbt), starb, ist gestorben	to take back
to die	

Andere Wörter

dazu in addition	**leer** empty
jährlich yearly	**pro** per
je ... desto *(conj.)* the . . . the *(with*	**selber** oneself
comparative); **je größer desto**	**streng** strict
besser the larger the better	

Land und Leute

Einige Produkte mit dem Grünen Punkt.

Die Verpackungsverordnung

Between 1991 and 1993 Germany implemented the Packaging Ordinance (**die Verpackungsverordnung**) which obliges both the manufacturers and the retailers to take back, reuse, and recycle packaging materials from toothpaste tubes to shipping crates. This collection of materials is separate from the public waste disposal system. In 1991, 600 private firms formed a non-profit venture, **Duales System Deutschland (DSD),** to help companies comply with the ordinance. **DSD** trucks collect product containers like yogurt cartons, shampoo bottles, and cans at the households. The materials are sorted and returned to the manufacturers who are responsible for recycling them. Each packaging material has a green dot (**Grüner Punkt**) as a licensing symbol, which indicates that the owner has paid **DSD** to recycle it. The average cost per **Grüner Punkt** is 40 Pfennig. Besides household packaging materials, the manufacturers pick up materials from the retailers—secondary packaging materials like foil, styrofoam, and cardboard cartons as well as transport wrappings like boxes and crates. The intent of the **Verpackungsverordnung** is to make the users of packaging financially and logistically responsible for recycling it so that they will use less. Between 1991 and 1993, the total volume of packaging did in fact decrease by one million tons. However, with over 95% of German households participating in the program, the **DSD** and industry have been able to recycle only about one third of the collected waste. The rest is exported, a practice that has met with harsh criticism from environmentalists and the consumers, who ultimately pay 3 to 4 billion marks per year for the **Duales System.**

GRAMMATIK UND ÜBUNGEN

1 The passive voice

Active voice	
Helga Klein schreibt das Buch.	*Helga Klein* is writing the book.
Hoffentlich lesen **viele** das Buch.	Let's hope that *many* read the book.

Passive voice	
Das Buch wird von Helga Klein geschrieben.	*The book* is being written by Helga Klein.
Hoffentlich wird **es** gelesen.	Let's hope *it* will be read.

In the active voice, the subject is "active": the subject is the agent that performs the action expressed by the verb. Active voice focuses attention on the agent. The attention in the active sentences above is focused on Helga Klein, who is writing a book, and on the many people who will read it.

In the passive voice, the subject is "passive": the subject is acted upon by an expressed or unexpressed agent. Passive voice focuses attention on the receiver of the action. The attention in the passive sentences above is focused on the book, which is being written by Helga Klein or read by the public.

The subject (e.g., **Buch**) of a passive sentence corresponds to the object of an active sentence. The agent (e.g., **Helga Klein**) of a passive sentence corresponds to the subject of an active sentence.

In everyday conversation, speakers of German use the active voice much more often than the passive voice. The passive is used in instructions, recipes, and technical and scientific manuals, where, as in English, an impersonal style is preferred.

2 Tenses in the passive voice

Present	Das Buch **wird geschrieben.**	The book *is being written.*
Simple past	Das Buch **wurde geschrieben.**	The book *was being written.*
Perfect	Das Buch **ist geschrieben worden.**	The book *has been written.*
Past perfect	Das Buch **war geschrieben worden.**	The book *had been written.*
Future	Das Buch **wird geschrieben werden.**	The book *will be written.*

In English, a passive verb phrase consists of a form of the auxiliary verb *to be* and the past participle of the verb. In German, the passive verb phrase consists of a form of the auxiliary **werden** and the past participle of the main verb (e.g., **geschrieben**). In active voice, the present perfect and past perfect tenses of **werden** are **ist geworden** and **war geworden,** respectively. In the passive voice, **geworden** is replaced by **worden.** The past participle of the main verb remains unchanged (e.g., **geschrieben**).

3 *Von* + agent

Without agent	Zuviel Müll wird produziert.	Too much garbage is being produced.
With agent	Zuviel Müll wird **von jedem Haushalt** produziert.	Too much garbage is being produced *by every household.*

In the passive voice, the agent is often omitted. If the agent (e.g., **Haushalt**) is expressed, in most passive sentences it is the object of the preposition **von** and thus in the dative case.

4 *Durch* + means

Das Geld wurde **durch schwere Arbeit** verdient.

The money was earned *through hard work.*

Die Nachbarn wurden **durch die laute Musik** gestört.

The neighbors were disturbed *by the loud music.*

The means by which something is brought about (e.g., **Arbeit, Musik**) is most often the object of the preposition **durch** and therefore in the accusative case.

1. Die grüne Tonne. Cornelia Meister has written to her aunt in Canada how garbage is recycled in Germany. Give the English equivalent.

In den meisten Haushalten wird der Müll sortiert. Der organische Müll wird in die grüne Tonne geworfen. Das Altpapier wird gesammelt und zu einem Container getragen. Auch leere Glas- und Plastikflaschen werden in speziellen Containern gesammelt. Diese Container werden dann geleert, und die Materialien werden recycelt.

1994 war der Wahlslogan der Grünen: „Die Zeit ist einfach reif."

Land und Leute

Die Grünen

Germany was the first European country to have a political party with an environmental agenda as its top priority. The Green Party (**die Grünen**) was established at a national level in 1979, and was first elected to the **Bundestag** in 1983. **Die Grünen** integrated many political groups of the 1970s, such as citizens' action groups (**Bürger-initiativen**), ecologists (**Ökologen**), peace groups (**Friedensgruppen**), and women's groups (**Frauen-gruppen**) into a viable political alternative. They first gained prominence through such issues as their opposition to nuclear power and support of a speed limit (**Tempolimit**) on German express-ways (**Autobahnen**). A speed limit, it is believed, would help reduce the increasing damage to the forests (**Waldsterben**) caused by air pollu-tion. Today their efforts encompass working for protection of the ozone layer, elimination of chemical and nuclear weaponry, international cooperation to save the environment, and re-shaping the market economy so that ecological concerns become a major priority.

Because environmental concerns have be-come important to a large number of Germans, the established political parties have followed the Greens in developing comprehensive envi-ronmental policies. For their part, with the larger political parties becoming more environmentally oriented, **die Grünen** have developed a broader political agenda and address such issues as uni-fication and German asylum laws.

2. Von wem wird das gemacht? State by whom the following things are done in your household. Use the passive voice.

▶ Von wem wird das Essen gekocht?   *Das Essen wird von [meinem Vater] gekocht.*

1. Von wem wird das Auto gewaschen?
2. Von wem wird das Brot gekauft?
3. Von wem wird das Haus saubergemacht?
4. Von wem wird das Geschirr gespült?
5. Von wem wird die Wäsche gewaschen?
6. Von wem wird die Gartenarbeit gemacht?

⇨ **3. Wer war das?** With a partner take turns asking each other who did what.* Use the cues below and the appropriate verb. Then come up with your own cues. Use the passive voice.

Discussing who invented, wrote, or discovered something

S1: Von wem wurde das Telefon erfunden?
S2: Das Telefon wurde von Alexander Graham Bell erfunden.

der Film *Jurassic Park*	gebaut
Mickey Mouse	geschrieben
die Brooklyn Bridge	gemacht
Hamlet	entdeckt°
die amerikanische Verfassung	erfunden°
der Eiffelturm	
die Röntgen-Strahlen°	
Amerika	
der Tuberkelbazillus°	
das erste deutsche Auto	
die Relativitätstheorie	

discovered
invented

X-rays

tuberculosis bacillus

4. Gleichberechtigung gab es früher nicht. Mark listened to a discussion about the former position of women in society. Give the English equivalents of his notes.

1. Warum wurde Frau Meier denn eigentlich immer schlechter bezahlt als ihr Mann?
   —Na ja, eine Erklärung ist, daß die besseren Stellen immer den Männern gegeben wurden.
2. Die Kinder von Speemanns sind durch die Vorurteile° der Kinderbücher beeinflußt° worden, nicht?
   —Ja, in ihren Büchern ist eben immer nur das traditionelle Frauenbild gezeigt worden.

prejudices
influenced

3. Von wem wurde denn bei Gardes das Geld verdient?
   —Von Herrn Garde. Und die Hausarbeit wurde natürlich von Frau Garde gemacht.
   —Ja, für sie war das immer ein langer Tag. Nachdem° abends die Kinder ins Bett gebracht worden waren, war ihr Tag immer noch nicht zu Ende.

after

4. Und bei den jungen Kortes, von wem wird da die Wäsche gewaschen und das Haus geputzt?
   —Oft von der ganzen Familie. Schließlich wird ja ein Teil des Geldes auch von Frau Korte verdient.
5. Ganz allgemein° kann man sagen, daß früher die Probleme der Gleichberechtigung anders gesehen wurden als heute.
   —Schon die Kinder wurden auf eine traditionelle Rolle als Mann oder Frau vorbereitet.

generally

---

*Antworten: der Film *Jurassic Park:* Steven Spielberg; Mickey Mouse: Walt Disney; die Brooklyn Bridge: Johann Roebling; *Hamlet:* William Shakespeare; die amerikanische Verfassung: Thomas Jefferson; der Eiffelturm: Alexandre Eiffel; die Röntgen-Strahlen: Wilhelm Conrad Röntgen; Amerika: Christopher Columbus; der Tuberkelbazillus: Robert Koch; das erste deutsche Auto: Carl Friedrich Benz; die Relativitätstheorie: Albert Einstein

5 Impersonal passive construction

Abgewaschen wird zusammen. ⎫
Es wird zusammen abgewaschen. ⎬   Washing up will be done together.

In German it is possible to use passive without having a subject or an agent. Such a construction is called an impersonal passive construction.

    The pronoun **es** begins an impersonal passive construction if no other words precede the verb. **Es** is a dummy subject.

Es wird jetzt gearbeitet. ⎬   There is work going on now.
                         People are working now.

An English equivalent of the impersonal passive often uses an introductory phrase such as *there is* or *there are.*

▷   **5.**   **Was wird hier gemacht?**   There is a lot of activity in this apartment building. With a partner, take turns asking each other what is being done in each apartment.

S1: Was wird in Wohnung Nummer 2 gemacht?
S2: In Wohnung Nummer 2 wird gespielt *or* Es wird gespielt.

6 Modals and the passive infinitive

Unser Computer **kann** nicht mehr   Our computer *can* not *be fixed*
  repariert werden.   anymore.
Müssen die Disketten neu   Do the diskettes *have to be redone?*
  gemacht werden?

Modals are frequently used with a passive infinitive. The passive infinitive (e.g., **repariert werden** and **gemacht werden**) consists of a past participle plus **werden.**

6.   Die deutsche Wirtschaft.   Below are statements from a report on the German economy. Give the English equivalents.

1. In Deutschland müssen viele Rohstoffe importiert werden.
2. Von den Firmen sollen Qualitätsprodukte produziert werden.
3. Qualitätsprodukte können meistens gut verkauft werden.
4. Die Inflationsrate soll niedrig gehalten werden.
5. Das Problem der Arbeitslosigkeit muß gelöst werden.
6. Für alle Leute soll Arbeit gefunden werden.

7.   Das muß gemacht werden.   Compare your "to do" list with that of a fellow classmate. Use the cues provided and add your own.

▶ Referat schreiben   *Mein Referat muß noch geschrieben werden.*

1. Hausaufgaben machen
2. Fernseher reparieren
3. Briefe schreiben
4. Autorate° bezahlen
5. Garage aufräumen

die Autorate = car payment

8.   Neues aus der Stadtpolitik.   The mayor of a small city in Austria is proudly reporting at a press conference what he and the city council have accomplished in the last year. Give his remarks in English. Note that verbs that may be unfamiliar to you are given in the margin in their infinitive forms with their meanings.

1. Ich wurde gebeten°, einiges über unsere Arbeit im letzten Jahr zu berichten.
2. Viele Probleme unserer Stadt konnten gelöst werden.
3. Die Fußgängerzone wurde durch viel Grün verschönert°.
4. In der Mozartstraße wurden 40 neue Bäume gepflanzt.
5. Im Park wurden neue Wege für die Radfahrer gebaut.
6. Der Bau eines neuen Kindergartens im Zentrum konnte begonnen werden.
7. Leider wurden ungefähr 230 Fahrräder gestohlen°, aber einige konnten wieder gefunden werden.

bitten: to request

verschönern: to beautify

stehlen: to steal

7 Summary of the uses of *werden*

■ *Active voice: main verb*

Herr Heller **wird** alt.	Mr. Heller *is growing* old.
Die Kinder **wurden** müde.	The children *were getting* tired.
Frau Ullmann **ist** Chefin der Firma **geworden.**	Ms. Ullmann *has become* head of the company.

Werden as a main verb is equivalent to English *to grow, get,* or *become.*

■ *Auxiliary verb in future tense*

Er **wird** hoffentlich mehr **arbeiten.**	I hope he *will work* more.
Du **wirst** das wohl **wissen.**	You *probably know* that.

Werden is used with a dependent infinitive to form the future tense.

■ *Passive voice: auxiliary verb*

Der organische Müll **wurde** in die grüne Tonne **geworfen.**	Organic garbage *was thrown* into the green bin.
Die leeren Flaschen **sind** in Glascontainern **gesammelt worden.**	The empty bottles *were collected* in glass containers.

Werden is used with a past participle to form the passive voice. The passive voice can occur in any tense. In place of **geworden,** the participle **worden** is used in the present perfect and past perfect tenses.

9. Die deutsche Wirtschaft. A German businesswoman is talking to some foreign journalists about the economic situation in Germany. Identify the verb phrase with **werden** in each sentence. Tell whether **werden** is being used (a) as a main verb in the active voice (give the tense), (b) to express future, or (c) as a tense of the passive voice (give the tense). Then give English equivalents for the sentences.

▶ Viele alte Fabriken müssen modernisiert werden.
müssen modernisiert werden / *present passive with modal* /
Many old factories must be modernized.

1. Hier muß noch viel gemacht werden.
2. Die Situation wird im nächsten Jahr sicher besser.
3. Der Export wird langsam weniger.
4. Wer wird dem Land helfen?
5. Werden die Waren auf dem Weltmarkt eine Zukunft haben?
6. Man meint, daß das Land immer weniger Rohstoffe haben wird.
7. Das Leben ist in letzter Zeit teurer geworden.
8. Die Industrie wird sich wohl neue Märkte suchen.
9. Manche Arbeiter wollen einfach nicht arbeiten. Was soll aus ihnen werden?
10. Die Situation wird hoffentlich in den nächsten Jahren besser.
11. Die Arbeit muß noch gemacht werden.

8 Alternatives to the passive voice

In German, other constructions are frequently used instead of passive voice. Three possible alternatives follow.

■ man *as subject*

Man sagt das oft.	*One* often says that.
(Das wird oft gesagt.)	That's often said.
Wie kann **man** das machen?	How can *people* do that?
(Wie kann das gemacht werden?)	How can that be done?

In German, the pronoun **man** is used frequently instead of the passive voice, whenever there is no expressed agent. English has several possible equivalents of **man:** *one, you, we, they,* or *people.*

10. Die Universität in der Schweiz. Diane has many questions about universities in Switzerland. Give the English equivalents of the sentences below.

1. Wie lange geht man auf die Universität?
2. Wieviel bezahlt man dafür?
3. Muß man viel lernen?
4. Wie lange darf man studieren?
5. Was kann man später machen?
6. Wie viele Klausuren muß man im Semester schreiben?
7. Soll man mehrere Fächer auf einmal studieren?

11. Eine neue Kollegin. A new employee has a few questions for her colleagues in the environmental office of the city administration. She gets all sorts of information. Restate the questions and statements below using **man.**

▶ Der Computer soll wohl viel benutzt werden?
Den Computer soll man wohl viel benutzen?

1. Muß alles auf Computer gemacht werden?
2. Wie oft soll dem Chef über die Arbeit berichtet werden?
3. Könnte dieses alte Büro nicht mal modernisiert werden?
4. Darf im Büro geraucht werden?
5. Wann wird Kaffee getrunken?
6. Hm, zuerst muß die Kaffeemaschine repariert werden.

■ sein ... zu + *infinitive*

Das **ist** leicht **zu verstehen.**	That's easy to understand.
(Das kann leicht verstanden werden.)	That can be understood easily.
Die Arbeit **ist** noch **zu machen.**	The work is still to be done.
(Die Arbeit muß noch gemacht werden.)	The work must still be done.

A form of **sein ... zu** + infinitive is often used in German instead of a passive verb phrase. The **sein ... zu** + infinitive construction expresses the possibility or necessity of doing something, just as the English construction does, using a form of *be* and an infinitive (e.g., *is [easy] to understand*).

12. Dieter geht ins Theater. Dieter asks questions about the play you want to see. Respond as suggested, using **sein ... zu** + infinitive.

▶ Kann man das Theater leicht finden? (Ja) *Ja, das Theater ist leicht zu finden.*

1. Muß man die Karten vorher° kaufen? (Ja) ahead (of time)
2. Kann man noch gute Plätze haben? (Ja)
3. Kann man noch billige Karten bekommen? (Ja)
4. Kann man die Handlung° leicht erklären? (Nein) plot
5. Kann man das Stück leicht verstehen? (Nein)

13. Was können wir für die Umwelt tun? Using the cues below, tell someone what things must be done to protect the environment.

▶ die Fabriken modernisieren *Die Fabriken sind zu modernisieren.*

1. Abgase der Autos reduzieren
2. neue Wege für die Radfahrer bauen
3. die Häuser besser isolieren° insulate
4. mehr Geld in die öffentlichen Verkehrsmittel investieren
5. Altpapier recyceln

■ **sich lassen** + *infinitive*

Das **läßt sich** machen. That can be done.
(Das kann gemacht werden.)

Läßt sich dieser Fernseher noch reparieren? Can this TV still be repaired?
(Kann dieser Fernseher noch repariert werden?)

A form of **sich lassen** + infinitive can be used in place of a passive verb phrase. This construction expresses the possibility of something being done.

14. Läßt sich das Auto reparieren? Daniel is telling Anna that they have to do something about their old car. Translate his remarks into English.

1. Hoffentlich läßt sich der Motor noch reparieren.
2. Aber es läßt sich noch nicht sagen, wieviel das kostet.
3. Leider lassen sich die Türen nicht so gut öffnen.
4. Vielleicht läßt sich ein Weg finden, wenigstens die linke Tür zu reparieren.
5. Ich weiß nicht, wie sich das Problem mit unserem alten Auto lösen läßt.
6. Wenn das Auto repariert ist, läßt es sich sicher verkaufen.

15. Alles läßt sich machen. In a business conference, Ms. Hohner asks whether most matters are taken care of. Answer her questions, using a form of **sich lassen** + infinitive.

▶ Kann man einen Weg finden? *Oh ja! Ein Weg läßt sich finden.*

1. Kann man die Ware billig produzieren?
2. Kann man das Problem lösen?
3. Kann man darüber reden?
4. Kann man das bezahlen?
5. Kann man das leicht erklären?
6. Kann man die Ware gut verkaufen?

EINE KURZGESCHICHTE *(A short story)*

Der Verkäufer und der Elch
Eine Geschichte mit 128 deutschen Wörtern

von Franz Hohler

Kennen Sie das Sprichwort° „Dem Elch° eine Gasmaske verkaufen?" Das sagt man bei uns von jemandem°, der sehr tüchtig° ist, und ich möchte jetzt erzählen, wie es zu diesem Sprichwort gekommen ist. — proverb / moose — someone / capable

Es gab einmal einen Verkäufer°, der war dafür berühmt°, daß er allen alles verkaufen konnte. — salesman / famous

Er hatte schon einem Zahnarzt eine Zahnbürste° verkauft, einem Bäcker ein Brot und einem Blinden einen Fernsehapparat. — toothbrush

„Ein wirklich guter Verkäufer bist du aber erst", sagten seine Freunde zu ihm, „wenn du einem Elch eine Gasmaske verkaufst."

Da ging der Verkäufer so weit nach Norden, bis er in einen Wald kam, in dem nur Elche wohnten.

„Guten Tag", sagte er zum ersten Elch, den er traf, „Sie brauchen bestimmt eine Gasmaske."

„Wozu°?" fragte der Elch. „Die Luft ist gut hier." — what for

„Alle haben heutzutage° eine Gasmaske", sagte der Verkäufer. — nowadays

„Es tut mir leid", sagte der Elch, „aber ich brauche keine."

„Warten Sie nur", sagte der Verkäufer, „Sie brauchen schon noch eine."

Und wenig später begann er mitten° in dem Wald, in dem nur Elche wohnten, eine Fabrik zu bauen. — in the middle

„Bist du wahnsinnig°?" fragten seine Freunde. — crazy

„Nein", sagte er, „ich will nur dem Elch eine Gasmaske verkaufen." Als die Fabrik fertig war, stiegen° soviel giftige° Abgase aus dem Schornstein°, daß der Elch bald zum Verkäufer kam und zu ihm sagte: „Jetzt brauche ich eine Gasmaske." — rose / poisonous / smokestack

„Das habe ich gedacht", sagte der Verkäufer und verkaufte ihm sofort° eine. „Qualitätsware!" sagte er lustig. — immediately

„Die anderen Elche", sagte der Elch, „brauchen jetzt auch Gasmasken. Hast du noch mehr?" (Elche kennen die Höflichkeitsform° mit „Sie" nicht.) — polite form

„Da habt ihr Glück", sagte der Verkäufer, „ich habe noch Tausende."

„Übrigens°", sagte der Elch, „was machst du in deiner Fabrik?" — by the way

„Gasmasken", sagte der Verkäufer.

P.S. Ich weiß doch nicht genau, ob es ein schweizerisches oder ein schwedisches Sprichwort ist, aber die beiden Länder werden ja oft verwechselt°. — confused

GRAMMATIK: ZUSAMMENFASSUNG

Tenses in the passive voice

Present	Der Brief **wird geschrieben.**	The letter *is being written.*
Simple past	Der Brief **wurde geschrieben.**	The letter *was being written.*
Perfect	Der Brief **ist geschrieben worden.**	The letter *has been written.*
Past perfect	Der Brief **war geschrieben worden.**	The letter *had been written.*
Future	Der Brief **wird geschrieben werden.**	The letter *will be written.*

NOTE: In the present perfect and past perfect tenses the participle **worden** is used in place of **geworden.**

Agent or means expressed

von + agent

Das Geld wurde **von den Arbeitern** verdient.	The money was earned *by the workers.*

durch + means

Das Geld wurde **durch schwere Arbeit** verdient.	The money was earned *through hard work.*

In passive voice the agent is the object of the preposition **von** and thus in the dative case. The means is the object of the preposition **durch** and therefore in the accusative case. The agent or means may be omitted **(Viel Geld wurde verdient.).**

Modals + passive infinitive

Der Brief muß **geschrieben werden.**	The letter must be written.
Kann diese Arbeit schnell **gemacht werden?**	Can this work be done quickly?

The passive infinitive consists of the past participle of a verb plus **werden.** Modals are often used with a passive infinitive.

Alternatives to the passive voice

Passive Voice	Deutsch **kann** leicht **gelernt werden**.	German can be learned easily.
1. *man*	Deutsch kann **man** leicht lernen.	One can learn German easily.
2. *sein ... zu* + infinitive	Deutsch **ist** leicht **zu lernen**.	German is easy to learn.
3. *sich lassen* + infinitive	Deutsch **läßt sich** leicht **lernen**.	German can be learned easily.

Ende gut, alles gut.

Reference Section

■ Contents

PRONUNCIATION AND WRITING GUIDE

The best way to learn to pronounce German is to imitate speakers of German, as completely and accurately as you can. Some of the sounds of German are just like those of English and will cause you no trouble. Others may sound strange to you at first and be more difficult for you to pronounce. With practice, you will be able to master the unfamiliar sounds as well as the familiar ones.

Though imitation is the one indispensable way of learning to pronounce any language, there are two things that should help you in your practice. First, you should learn how to manipulate your vocal organs so as to produce distinctly different sounds. Second, you should learn to distinguish German sounds from the English sounds that you might be tempted to substitute for them.

As you learn to pronounce German, you will also start to read and write it. Here a word of caution is in order. The writing system of German (or any language) was designed for people who already know the language. No ordinary writing system was ever designed to meet the needs of people who are learning a language. Writing is a method of reminding us on paper of things that we already know how to say; it is not a set of directions telling us how a language should be pronounced.

This Pronunciation and Writing Guide will give you some help with the German sound system. Further practice with specific sounds will be given in the Lab Manual section of the *Arbeitsheft*.

Stress

Nearly all native German words are stressed on the "stem syllable," that is, the first syllable of the word, or the first syllable that follows an unstressed prefix.

Without prefix		*With unstressed prefix*	
den'ken	to think	**beden'ken**	to think over
kom'men	to come	**entkom'men**	to escape

In the end vocabulary of this book, words that are not stressed on the first syllable are marked. A stress mark follows the stressed syllable.

German Vowels

German has short vowels, long vowels, and diphthongs. The short vowels are clipped, and are never "drawled" as they often are in English. The long vowels are monophthongs ("steady-state" vowels) and not diphthongs (vowels that "glide" from one vowel sound toward another). The diphthongs are similar to English diphthongs except that they, like short vowels, are never drawled. Compare the English and German vowels in the words below.

English (with off-glide)	*German (without off-glide)*
bait	Beet
vein	wen
tone	Ton
boat	Boot

R-3

Spelling as a reminder of vowel length

By and large, the German spelling system clearly indicates the difference between long and short vowels. German uses the following types of signals:

1. A vowel is long if it is followed by an **h** (unpronounced): **ihn, stahlen, Wahn.**
2. A vowel is long if it is double: **Beet, Saat, Boot.**
3. A vowel is generally long if it is followed by one consonant: **den, kam, Ofen, Hut.**
4. A vowel is generally short if it is followed by two or more consonants: **denn, Sack, offen, Busch, dick.**

Pronunciation of vowels

Long and short a

Long [ā] = **aa, ah, a (Saat, Bahn, kam, Haken):** like English *a* in *spa,* but with wide-open mouth and no off-glide.
Short [a] = **a (satt, Bann, Kamm, Hacken):** between English *o* in *hot* and *u* in *hut.*

Long and short e

Long [ē] = **e, ee, eh, ä, äh (wen, Beet, fehlen, gähnt):** like *ay* in English *say,* but with exaggeratedly spread lips and no off-glide.
Short [e] = **e, ä (wenn, Bett, fällen, Gent):** Like *e* in English *bet,* but more clipped.

Unstressed [ə] *and* [ər]

Unstressed [ə] = **e (bitte, endet, gegessen):** like English *e* in *begin, pocket.*
Unstressed [ər] = **er (bitter, ändert, vergessen):** When the sequence [ər] stands at the end of a word, before a consonant, or in an unstressed prefix, it sounds much like the final *-a* in English *sofa;* the **-r** is not pronounced.

Long and short i

Long [ī] = **ih, ie (ihn, Miete, liest):** like *ee* in *see,* but with exaggeratedly spread lips and no off-glide.
Short [i] = **(in, Mitte, List):** like *i* in *mitt,* but more clipped.

Long and short o

Long [ō] = **oh, o, oo (Sohne, Ofen, Tone, Moos):** like English *o* in *so,* but with exaggeratedly rounded lips and no off-glide.
Short [o] = **o (Most, Tonne, offen, Sonne):** like English *o* often heard in the word *gonna.*

Long and short u

Long [ū] = **uh, u (Huhne, schuf, Buße, Mus):** like English *oo* in *too,* but with more lip rounding and no off-glide.
Short [u] = **u (Hunne, Schuft, Busse, muß):** like English *u* in *bush,* but more clipped.

Diphthongs

[ai] = **ei, ai, ey, ay (nein, Kaiser, Meyer, Bayern):** like English *ai* in *aisle,* but clipped and not drawled.
[oi] = **eu, äu (neun, Häuser):** like English *oi* in *coin,* but clipped and not drawled.
[au] = **au (laut, Bauer):** like English *ou* in *house,* but clipped and not drawled.

Long and short ü

Long [ǖ] = **üh, ü (Bühne, kühl, lügen):** To pronounce long [ǖ], keep your tongue in the same position as for long [ī], but round your lips as for long [ū].
Short [ü] = **ü (Küste, müssen, Bünde):** To pronounce short [ü], keep your tongue in the same position as for short [i], but round your lips as for short [u].

Long and short ö

Long [ȫ] = **ö, öh (Höfe, Löhne, Flöhe):** To pronounce long [ȫ], keep your tongue in the same position as for long [ē], but round your lips as for long [ō].
Short [ö] = **ö (gönnt, Hölle, Knöpfe):** To pronounce short [ö], keep your tongue in the same position as for short [e], but round your lips as for short [o].

Consonants

Most of the German consonant sounds are similar to English consonant sounds. There are four major differences.

1. German has two consonant sounds without an English equivalent: [x] and [ç]. Both are spelled **ch.**
2. The German pronunciation of [l] and [r] differs from the English pronunciation.
3. German uses sounds familiar to English speakers in unfamiliar combinations, such as [ts] in an initial position: **zu.**
4. German uses unfamiliar spellings of familiar sounds.

The letters **b,** *d,* *and* g

The letters **b, d,** and **g** generally represent the same consonant sounds as in English. German **g** is usually pronounced like English *g* in *go.* When the letters **b, d,** and **g** occur at the end of a syllable, or before an **s** or **t,** they are pronounced like [p], [t], and [k] respectively.

b = [b] **(Diebe, gaben)**   b = [p] **(Dieb, Diebs, gab, gabt)**
d = [d] **(Lieder, laden)**   d = [t] **(Lied, Lieds, lud, lädt)**
g = [g] **(Tage, sagen)**   g = [k] **(Tag, Tags, sag, sagt)**

The letter j

The letter **j (ja, jung)** represents the sound *y* as in English *yes.*

The letter l

English [l] typically has a "hollow" sound to it. When an American pronounces [l], the tongue is usually "spoon-shaped": It is high at the front (with the tongue tip pressed against the gum ridge above the upper teeth), hollowed out in the middle, and high again at the back. German [l] **(viel, Bild, laut)** never has the "hollow" quality. It is pronounced with the tongue tip against the gum ridge, as in English, but with the tongue kept flat from front to back. Many Americans use this "flat" [l] in such words as *million, billion,* and *William.*

The letter r

German [r] can be pronounced in two different ways. Some German speakers use a "tongue-trilled [r]," in which the tip of the tongue vibrates against the gum ridge above the upper teeth—like the *rrr* that children often use in imitation of a telephone bell or police whistle. Most German speakers, however, use a "uvular [r]," in which the back of the tongue is raised toward the uvula, the little droplet of skin hanging down in the back of the mouth.

You will probably find it easiest to pronounce the uvular [r] if you make a gargling sound before the sound [a]: ra. Keep the tip of your tongue down and out of the way; the tip of the tongue plays no role in the pronunciation of the gargled German [r].

r = [r] + vowel **(Preis, Jahre, Rose):** When German [r] is followed by a vowel, it has the full "gargled" sound.

r = vocalized [r] **(Tier, Uhr, Tür):** When German [r] is not followed by a vowel, it tends to become "vocalized," that is, pronounced like the vowel-like glide found in the final syllable of British English *hee-uh* (here), *thay-uh* (there).

The letters s, ss, ß

s = [ṣ] **(sehen, lesen, Gänse):** Before a vowel, the letter **s** represents the sound [ṣ], like English *z* in *zoo*.

s = [s] **(das, Hals, fast):** In most other positions, the letter **s** represents the sound [s], like English [s] in *so*.

[s] = **ss, ß** **(wissen, Flüsse, weiß, beißen, Füße):** The letters **ss** and **ß** (called **ess-tsett**) are both pronounced [s]. When they are written between vowels, the double letters **ss** signal the fact that the preceding vowel is short, and the single letter **ß** signals the fact that the preceding vowel is long (or a diphthong). The letter **ß** is also used before a consonant and at the end of a word.

The letter v

v = [f] **(Vater, viel):** The letter **v** is generally pronounced like English [f] as in *father*.

v = [v] **(Vase, November):** In words of foreign origin, the letter **v** is pronounced [v].

The letter w

w = [v] **(Wein, Wagen, wann):** Many centuries ago, German **w** (as in **Wein**) represented the sound [w], like English *w* in *wine*. Over the centuries, German **w** gradually changed from [w] to [v], so that today the **w** of German **Wein** represents the sound [v], like the *v* of English *vine*. German no longer has the sound [w]. The letter **w** always represents the sound [v].

The letter z

z = final and initial [ts] **(Kranz, Salz, Zahn, zu):** The letter **z** is pronounced [ts], as in English *rats*. In English, the [ts] sound occurs only at the end of a syllable; in German, [ts] occurs at the beginning as well as at the end of a syllable.

The consonant clusters gn, kn, pf, qu

To pronounce the consonant clusters **gn, kn, pf, qu** correctly, you need to use familiar sounds in unfamiliar ways.

gn: pronunciation is [gn]   **pf:** pronunciation is [pf]
kn: pronunciation is [kn]   **qu:** pronunciation is [kv]

gn = [gn-] **(Gnade, Gnom)**
kn = [kn-] **(Knie, Knoten)**
pf = [pf-] **(Pfanne, Pflanze)**
qu = [kv-] **(quälen, Quarz, quitt)**

The combination ng

ng = [ŋ] (Finger, Sänger, Ding): The combination ng is pronounced [ŋ], as in English *singer*. It does not contain the sound [g] that is used in English *finger*.

The combinations sch, sp, *and* st

sch = [š] (Schiff, waschen, Fisch)
sp = [šp] (Spaten, spinnen, Sport)
st = [št] (Stein, Start, stehlen)

Many centuries ago, both German and English had the combinations **sp, st, sk,** pronounced [sp], [st], [sk]. Then two changes took place. First, in both languages, [sk] changed to [š], as in English *ship, fish,* and German **Schiff, Fisch.** Second, in German only, word-initial [sp-] and [st-] changed to [šp-] and [št-]. The *sp* in English *spin* is pronounced [sp-], but in German **spinnen** it is pronounced [šp-]. The *st* in English *still* is pronounced [st-], but in German **still** it is pronounced [št-]. Today, German **sch** always represents [š] (like English *sh,* but with more rounded lips); **sp-** and **st-** at the beginning of German words or word stems represent [šp-] and [št-].

The letters ch

The letters **ch** are usually pronounced either [x] or [ç]. The [x] sound is made in the back of the mouth where [k] is produced.

If you have ever heard a Scotsman talk about "Lo*ch* Lomond," you have heard the sound [x]. The sound [x] is produced by forcing air through a narrow opening between the back of the tongue and the back of the roof of the mouth (the soft palate). Notice the difference between [k], where the breath stream is stopped in this position and [x], where the breath stream is forced through a narrow opening in this position.

To practice the [x] sound, keep the tongue below the lower front teeth and produce a gentle gargling sound, without moving the tongue or lips. Be careful not to substitute the [k] sound for the [x] sound.

ck, k = [k] (Sack, pauken, Pocken, buk)
ch = [x] (Sache, hauchen, pochen, Buch)

The [ç] sound is similar to that used by many Americans for the *h* in such words as *hue, huge, human.* It is produced by forcing air through a narrow opening between the front of the tongue and the front of the roof of the mouth (the hard palate). Notice the difference between [š], where the breath stream is forced through a wide opening in this position and the lips are rounded, and [ç], where the breath stream is forced through a narrow opening in this position and the lips are spread.

To practice the [ç] sound, round your lips for [š], then use a slit-shaped opening and spread your lips. Be careful not to substitute the [š] sound for [ç].

sch = [š] (misch, fischt, Kirsche, Welsch, Menschen)
ch = [ç] (mich, ficht, Kirche, welch, München)

Note two additional points about the pronunciation of **ch:**

1. ch = [x] occurs only after the vowels **a, o, u, au.**
2. ch = [ç] occurs only after the other vowels and **n, l,** and **r.**

The combination chs

chs = [ks] (**sechs, Fuchs, Weichsel**)
chs = [xs] or [çs] (**des Brauchs, du rauchst, des Teichs**)

The fixed combination **chs** is pronounced [ks] in words such as **sechs, Fuchs,** and **Ochse**. Today, **chs** is pronounced [xs] or [çs] only when the **s** is an ending or part of an ending (**ich rauche, du rauchst; der Teich, des Teichs**).

The suffix -ig

-ig = [iç] (**Pfennig, König, schuldig**): In final position, the suffix **-ig** is pronounced [iç] as in German **ich**.
-ig = [ig] (**Pfennige, Könige, schuldige**): In all other positions, the **g** in **-ig** has the sound [g] as in English *go*.

The glottal stop

English uses the glottal stop as a device to avoid running together words and parts of words; it occurs only before vowels. Compare the pairs of words below. The glottal stop is indicated with an *.

an *ice man   a nice man
not *at *all   not a tall
an *ape   a nape

German also uses the glottal stop before vowels to avoid running together words and parts of words.

Wie *alt *ist *er?
be*antworten

The glottal stop is produced by closing the glottis (the space between the vocal cords), letting air pressure build up from below, and then suddenly opening the glottis, resulting in a slight explosion of air. Say the word *uh-uh*, and you will notice a glottal stop between the first and second *uh*.

The Writing System

German punctuation

Punctuation marks in German are generally used as in English. Note the following major differences.

1. In German, dependent clauses are set off by commas.
   German   Der Mann, der hier wohnt, ist alt.
   English   The man who lives here is old.

2. In German, independent clauses joined by **und** (*and*) or **oder** (*or*) are set off by commas only if the second clause contains both a different subject and a different verb.
   German   Robert singt, und Karin tanzt.
   English   Robert is singing and Karin is dancing.

3. In German, a comma is not used in front of **und** in a series as is often done in English.

   German   Robert, Ilse und Karin singen.
   English   Robert, Ilse, and Karin are singing.

4. In German, opening quotation marks are placed below the line.

   German   Er fragte: „Wie heißen Sie?"
   English   He asked, "What is your name?"

   Note that a colon is used in German before a direct quotation.

5. In German, commas stand outside of quotation marks.

   German   „Meyer", antwortete sie.
   English   "Meyer," she answered.

German capitalization

1. In German, all nouns are capitalized.

   German   Wie alt ist der Mann?
   English   How old is the man?

2. Adjectives are not capitalized, even if they denote nationality.

   German   Ist das ein amerikanisches Auto?
   English   Is that an American car?

3. The pronoun **ich** is not capitalized, unlike its English counterpart *I*.

   German   Morgen spiele ich um zwei Uhr Tennis.
   English   Tomorrow I am playing tennis at two o'clock.

GRAMMATICAL TABLES

1. Personal pronouns

Nominative	ich	du	er	es	sie	wir	ihr	sie	Sie
Accusative	mich	dich	ihn	es	sie	uns	euch	sie	Sie
Dative	mir	dir	ihm	ihm	ihr	uns	euch	ihnen	Ihnen

2. Reflexive pronouns

	ich	du	er/es/sie	wir	ihr	sie	Sie
Accusative	mich	dich	sich	uns	euch	sich	sich
Dative	mir	dir	sich	uns	euch	sich	sich

3. Interrogative pronouns

Nominative	wer	was
Accusative	wen	was
Dative	wem	
Genitive	wessen	

4. Relative and demonstrative pronouns

	Masculine	Neuter	Feminine	Plural
Nominative	der	das	die	die
Accusative	den	das	die	die
Dative	dem	dem	der	denen
Genitive	dessen	dessen	deren	deren

5. Definite articles

	Masculine	Neuter	Feminine	Plural
Nominative	der	das	die	die
Accusative	den	das	die	die
Dative	dem	dem	der	den
Genitive	des	des	der	der

6. *Der*-words

	Masculine	Neuter	Feminine	Plural
Nominative	dieser	dieses	diese	diese
Accusative	diesen	dieses	diese	diese
Dative	diesem	diesem	dieser	diesen
Genitive	dieses	dieses	dieser	dieser

The **der**-words are **dieser, jeder, mancher, solcher,** and **welcher.**

7. Indefinite articles and *ein*-words

	Masculine	Neuter	Feminine	Plural
Nominative	ein	ein	eine	keine
Accusative	einen	ein	eine	keine
Dative	einem	einem	einer	keinen
Genitive	eines	eines	einer	keiner

The **ein**-words include **kein** and the possessive adjectives: **mein, dein, sein, ihr, unser, euer, ihr,** and **Ihr.**

8. Plural of nouns

Type	Plural signal	Singular	Plural	Notes
1	Ø (no change)	das Zimmer	**die Zimmer**	Masculine and neuter nouns
	¨ (umlaut)	der Garten	**die Gärten**	ending in **el, -en, -er**
2	-e	der Tisch	**die Tische**	
	¨e	der Stuhl	**die Stühle**	
3	-er	das Bild	**die Bilder**	Stem vowel **e** or **i** cannot take umlaut
	¨er	das Buch	**die Bücher**	Stem vowel **a, o, u** takes umlaut
4	-en	die Uhr	**die Uhren**	
	-n	die Lampe	**die Lampen**	
	-nen	die Freundin	**die Freundinnen**	
5	-s	das Radio	**die Radios**	Mostly foreign words

9. Masculine *N*-nouns

	Singular	Plural
Nominative	der Herr	die Herren
Accusative	den Herrn	die Herren
Dative	dem Herrn	den Herren
Genitive	des Herrn	der Herren

Some other masculine N-nouns are **der Journalist, der Junge, der Kollege, der Mensch, der Nachbar, der Pilot, der Präsident, der Soldat, der Student, der Tourist.**

A few masculine N-nouns add **-ns** in the genitive: **der Name > des Namens.**

10. Preceded adjectives

	Singular			Plural
	Masculine	**Neuter**	**Feminine**	
Nom.	der **alte** Tisch ein **alter** Tisch	das **alte** Buch ein **altes** Buch	die **alte** Uhr eine **alte** Uhr	die **alten** Bilder keine **alten** Bilder
Acc.	den **alten** Tisch einen **alten** Tisch	das **alte** Buch ein **altes** Buch	die **alte** Uhr eine **alte** Uhr	die **alten** Bilder keine **alten** Bilder
Dat.	dem **alten** Tisch einem **alten** Tisch	dem **alten** Buch einem **alten** Buch	der **alten** Uhr einer **alten** Uhr	den **alten** Bildern keinen **alten** Bildern
Gen.	des **alten** Tisches eines **alten** Tisches	des **alten** Buches eines **alten** Buches	der **alten** Uhr einer **alten** Uhr	der **alten** Bilder keiner **alten** Bilder

11. Unpreceded adjectives

	Masculine	Neuter	Feminine	Plural
Nominative	kalt**er** Wein	kalt**es** Bier	kalt**e** Milch	alt**e** Leute
Accusative	kalt**en** Wein	kalt**es** Bier	kalt**e** Milch	alt**e** Leute
Dative	kalt**em** Wein	kalt**em** Bier	kalt**er** Milch	alt**en** Leuten
Genitive	kalt**en** Weines	kalt**en** Bieres	kalt**er** Milch	alt**er** Leute

12. Nouns declined like adjectives

■ *Nouns preceded by definite articles or* **der**-*words*

	Masculine	Neuter	Feminine	Plural
Nominative	der Deutsche	das Gute	die Deutsche	die Deutschen
Accusative	den Deutschen	das Gute	die Deutsche	die Deutschen
Dative	dem Deutschen	dem Guten	der Deutschen	den Deutschen
Genitive	des Deutschen	des Guten	der Deutschen	der Deutschen

■ *Nouns preceded by indefinite article or* **ein**-*words*

	Masculine	Neuter	Feminine	Plural
Nominative	ein Deutsch**er**	ein Gut**es**	eine Deutsche	keine Deutschen
Accusative	einen Deutsch**en**	ein Gut**es**	eine Deutsche	keine Deutschen
Dative	einem Deutsch**en**	einem Gut**en**	einer Deutschen	keinen Deutschen
Genitive	eines Deutsch**en**	—	einer Deutschen	keiner Deutschen

Other nouns declined like adjectives are **der/die Bekannte, Erwachsene, Fremde, Jugendliche, Verwandte.**

13. Irregular comparatives and superlatives

Base form	bald	gern	gut	hoch	nah	viel
Comparative	eher	lieber	besser	höher	näher	mehr
Superlative	ehest-	liebst-	best-	höchst-	nächst-	meist-

14. Adjectives and adverbs taking umlaut in the comparative and superlative

alt	jung	oft
arm	kalt	rot
blaß (blasser or blässer)	krank	schwach
dumm	kurz	schwarz
gesund (gesünder or gesunder)	lang	stark
groß	naß (nässer or nasser)	warm

15. Prepositions

With accusative	With dative	With either accusative or dative	With genitive
bis	aus	an	(an)statt
durch	außer	auf	trotz
für	bei	hinter	während
gegen	mit	in	wegen
ohne	nach	neben	
um	seit	über	
	von	unter	
	zu	vor	
		zwischen	

16. Verbs and prepositions with special meanings

abhängen von
anfangen mit
anrufen bei
antworten auf (+ *acc.*)
arbeiten bei *(at a company)*
aufhören mit
beginnen mit
sich beschäftigen mit
danken für
denken an (+ *acc.*)
sich erinnern an (+ *acc.*)
erzählen über (+ *acc.*) *or* von
fahren mit *(by a vehicle)*
fragen nach
sich freuen auf (+ *acc.*)
sich freuen über (+ *acc.*)
sich fürchten vor (+ *dat.*)
halten von
helfen bei

hoffen auf (+ *acc.*)
sich interessieren für
lächeln über (+ *acc.*)
lachen über (+ *acc.*)
reden über (+ *acc.*) *or* von
riechen nach
schreiben an (+ *acc.*)
schreiben über (+ *acc.*)
sprechen über (+ *acc.*), von, *or* mit
sterben an (+ *dat.*)
studieren an *or* auf (+ *dat.*)
suchen nach
sich vorbereiten auf (+ *acc.*)
warnen vor (+ *dat.*)
warten auf (+ *acc.*)
wissen über (+ *acc.*) *or* von
wohnen bei
zeigen auf (+ *acc.*)

17. Dative verbs

antworten
danken
fehlen
gefallen
gehören
glauben
helfen
leid tun
passieren
schmecken
weh tun

The verb **glauben** may take an impersonal accusative object: **ich glaube es.**

18. Present tense

	lernen[1]	arbeiten[2]	tanzen[3]	geben[4]	lesen[5]	fahren[6]	laufen[7]	auf·stehen[8]
ich	lerne	arbeite	tanze	gebe	lese	fahre	laufe	stehe … auf
du	lernst	arbeitest	tanzt	gibst	liest	fährst	läufst	stehst … auf
er/es/sie	lernt	arbeitet	tanzt	gibt	liest	fährt	läuft	steht … auf
wir	lernen	arbeiten	tanzen	geben	lesen	fahren	laufen	stehen … auf
ihr	lernt	arbeitet	tanzt	gebt	lest	fahrt	lauft	steht … auf
sie	lernen	arbeiten	tanzen	geben	lesen	fahren	laufen	stehen … auf
Sie	lernen	arbeiten	tanzen	geben	lesen	fahren	laufen	stehen … auf
Imper. sg.	lern(e)	arbeite	tanz(e)	gib	lies	fahr(e)	lauf(e)	steh(e) … auf

1. The endings are used for all verbs except the modals, **wissen, werden,** and **sein.**
2. A verb with a stem ending in **-d** or **-t** has an **e** before the **-st** and **-t** endings. A verb with a stem ending in **-m** or **-n** preceded by another consonant has an **e** before the **-st** and **-t** endings, e.g., **atmen** > **du atmest, er/es/sie atmet; regnen** > **es regnet.** Exception: If the stem of the verb ends in **-m** or **-n** preceded by **-l** or **-r**, the **-st** and **-t** do not expand, e.g., **lernen** > **du lernst, er/es/sie lernt.**
3. The **-st** ending of the **du**-form contracts to **-t** when the verb stem ends in a sibilant (**-s, -ss, -ß, -z,** or **-tz).** Thus the **du-** and **er/es/sie**-forms are identical.
4. Some strong verbs have a stem-vowel change **e** > **i** in the **du-** and **er/es/sie**-forms and the imperative singular.
5. Some strong verbs have a stem-vowel change **e** > **ie** in the **du-** and **er/es/sie**-forms and the imperative singular. The strong verbs **gehen** and **stehen** do not change their stem vowel.
6. Some strong verbs have a stem-vowel change **a** > **ä** in the **du-** and **er/es/sie**-forms.
7. Some strong verbs have a stem-vowel change **au** > **äu** in the **du-** and **er/es/sie**-forms.
8. In the present tense, separable prefixes are separated from the verbs and are in last position.

19. Simple past tense

	Weak verbs		Strong verbs
	lernen[1]	arbeiten[2]	geben[3]
ich	lernte	arbeitete	gab
du	lerntest	arbeitetest	gabst
er/es/sie	lernte	arbeitete	gab
wir	lernten	arbeiteten	gaben
ihr	lerntet	arbeitetet	gabt
sie	lernten	arbeiteten	gaben
Sie	lernten	arbeiteten	gaben

1. Weak verbs have the past-tense marker **-te** + endings.
2. A weak verb with a stem ending in **-d** or **-t** has a past-tense marker **-ete** + endings. A weak verb with a stem ending in **-m** or **-n** preceded by another consonant has a past-stem marker **-ete** plus endings, e.g., **er/es/sie atmete; es regnete.** Exception: If the stem of the verb ends in **-m** or **-n** preceded by **-l** or **-r**, the **-te** past-tense marker does not expand, e.g., **lernte.**
3. Strong verbs have a stem-vowel change + endings.

20. Auxiliaries *haben, sein, werden*

ich	habe	bin	werde
du	hast	bist	wirst
er/es/sie	hat	ist	wird
wir	haben	sind	werden
ihr	habt	seid	werdet
sie	haben	sind	werden
Sie	haben	sind	werden

21. Modal auxiliaries: present, simple past, and past participle

	dürfen	können	müssen	sollen	wollen	mögen	(möchte)
ich	darf	kann	muß	soll	will	mag	(möchte)
du	darfst	kannst	mußt	sollst	willst	magst	(möchtest)
er/es/sie	darf	kann	muß	soll	will	mag	(möchte)
wir	dürfen	können	müssen	sollen	wollen	mögen	(möchten)
ihr	dürft	könnt	müßt	sollt	wollt	mögt	(möchtet)
sie	dürfen	können	müssen	sollen	wollen	mögen	(möchten)
Sie	dürfen	können	müssen	sollen	wollen	mögen	(möchten)
Simple past	durfte	konnte	mußte	sollte	wollte	mochte	
Past participle	gedurft	gekonnt	gemußt	gesollt	gewollt	gemocht	

22. Verb conjugations: strong verbs *sehen* and *gehen*

■ *Indicative*

	Present		Simple past	
ich	sehe	gehe	sah	ging
du	siehst	gehst	sahst	gingst
er/es/sie	sieht	geht	sah	ging
wir	sehen	gehen	sahen	gingen
ihr	seht	geht	saht	gingt
sie	sehen	gehen	sahen	gingen
Sie	sehen	gehen	sahen	gingen

	Present perfect				Past perfect			
ich	habe		bin		hatte		war	
du	hast		bist		hattest		warst	
er/es/sie	hat		ist		hatte		war	
wir	haben	gesehen	sind	gegangen	hatten	gesehen	waren	gegangen
ihr	habt		seid		hattet		wart	
sie	haben		sind		hatten		waren	
Sie	haben		sind		hatten		waren	

	Future			
ich	werde		werde	
du	wirst		wirst	
er/es/sie	wird		wird	
wir	werden	sehen	werden	gehen
ihr	werdet		werdet	
sie	werden		werden	
Sie	werden		werden	

■ *Imperative*

Imperative		
Familiar singular	sieh	geh(e)
Familiar plural	seht	geht
Formal	sehen Sie	gehen Sie

■ *Subjunctive*

Present-time subjunctive		
ich	sähe	ginge
du	sähest	gingest
er/es/sie	sähe	ginge
wir	sähen	gingen
ihr	sähet	ginget
sie	sähen	gingen
Sie	sähen	gingen

Past-time subjunctive				
ich	hätte		wäre	
du	hättest		wärest	
er/es/sie	hätte		wäre	
wir	hätten	gesehen	wären	gegangen
ihr	hättet		wäret	
sie	hätten		wären	
Sie	hätten		wären	

■ *Passive voice*

Present passive		Past passive	
ich	werde	wurde	
du	wirst	wurdest	
er/es/sie	wird	wurde	
wir	werden	gesehen	wurden	gesehen
ihr	werdet	wurdet	
sie	werden	wurden	
Sie	werden	wurden	

Present perfect passive		Past perfect passive	
ich	bin	war	
du	bist	warst	
er/es/sie	ist	war	
wir	sind	gesehen worden	waren	gesehen worden
ihr	seid	wart	
sie	sind	waren	
Sie	sind	waren	

23. Principal parts of strong and irregular weak verbs

The following list includes all the strong and irregular verbs from the **Vokabeln** lists. Compound verbs like **herumliegen** and **hinausgehen** are not included, since the principal parts of compound verbs are identical to the basic forms: **liegen** and **gehen**. Separable-prefix verbs like **einladen** are included only when the basic verb (**laden**) is not listed elsewhere in the table. Basic English meanings are given for all verbs in this list. For additional meanings, consult the German-English vocabulary on pages R-43–R-63. The number indicates the chapter in which the verb was introduced.

Infinitive	Present-tense vowel change	Simple past	Past participle	Subjunctive	Meaning
anfangen	fängt an	fing an	angefangen	finge an	*to begin* 11
anrufen		rief an	angerufen	riefe an	*to telephone* 7
sich anziehen		zog an	angezogen	zöge an	*to get dressed* 10
sich ausziehen		zog aus	ausgezogen	zöge aus	*to get undressed* 10
beginnen		begann	begonnen	begönne *or* begänne	*to begin* 10
bleiben		blieb	ist geblieben	bliebe	*to stay* 3
bringen		brachte	gebracht	brächte	*to bring* 5
denken		dachte	gedacht	dächte	*to think* 3
einladen	lädt ein	lud ein	eingeladen	lüde ein	*to invite; to treat* 7
empfehlen	empfiehlt	empfahl	empfohlen	empföhle	*to recommend* 11
essen	ißt	aß	gegessen	äße	*to eat* 4
fahren	fährt	fuhr	ist gefahren	führe	*to drive, travel* 6
fallen	fällt	fiel	ist gefallen	fiele	*to fall* 11
finden		fand	gefunden	fände	*to find* 3
fliegen		flog	ist geflogen	flöge	*to fly* 6
geben	gibt	gab	gegeben	gäbe	*to give* 4
gefallen	gefällt	gefiel	gefallen	gefiele	*to please* 7
gehen		ging	ist gegangen	ginge	*to go* 2
haben	hat	hatte	gehabt	hätte	*to have* 3
halten	hält	hielt	gehalten	hielte	*to hold; to stop* 7
hängen		hing	gehangen	hinge	*to be hanging* 8
heißen		hieß	geheißen	hieße	*to be called, named* 1
helfen	hilft	half	geholfen	hülfe *or* hälfe	*to help* 8
kennen		kannte	gekannt	kennte	*to know* 4
kommen		kam	ist gekommen	käme	*to come* 2
lassen	läßt	ließ	gelassen	ließe	*to let, allow* 13
laufen	läuft	lief	ist gelaufen	liefe	*to run* 6
leihen		lieh	geliehen	liehe	*to lend* 5
lesen	liest	las	gelesen	läse	*to read* 5
liegen		lag	gelegen	läge	*to lie* 3
nehmen	nimmt	nahm	genommen	nähme	*to take* 4
nennen		nannte	genannt	nennte	*to name* 9

Infinitive	Present-tense vowel change	Simple past	Past participle	Subjunctive	Meaning
riechen		roch	gerochen	röche	to smell 4
scheinen		schien	geschienen	schiene	to shine 3; to seem 10
schlafen	schläft	schlief	geschlafen	schliefe	to sleep 6
schließen		schloß	geschlossen	schlösse	to close 4
schreiben		schrieb	geschrieben	schriebe	to write 1
schwimmen		schwamm	ist geschwommen	schwömme or schwämme	to swim 2
sehen	sieht	sah	gesehen	sähe	to see 5
sein	ist	war	ist gewesen	wäre	to be 2
sitzen		saß	gesessen	säße	to sit 8
sprechen	spricht	sprach	gesprochen	spräche	to speak 6
stehen		stand	gestanden	stände or stünde	to stand 8
sterben	stirbt	starb	ist gestorben	stürbe	to die 11
tragen	trägt	trug	getragen	trüge	to wear; to carry 7
treffen	trifft	traf	getroffen	träfe	to meet; to hit 8
treiben		trieb	getrieben	triebe	to engage in 2
trinken		trank	getrunken	tränke	to drink 4
tun		tat	getan	täte	to do 7
vergessen	vergißt	vergaß	vergessen	vergäße	to forget 10
verlieren		verlor	verloren	verlöre	to lose 12
waschen	wäscht	wusch	gewaschen	wüsche	to wash 8
werden	wird	wurde	ist geworden	würde	to become 5
werfen	wirft	warf	geworfen	würfe	to throw 14
wissen	weiß	wußte	gewußt	wüßte	to know 5
zwingen		zwang	gezwungen	zwänge	to compel 11

SUPPLEMENTARY GRAMMAR: INDIRECT DISCOURSE

Indirect discourse

Direct discourse	Theo sagte: „**Ich habe keine Zeit.**"	Theo said, *"I have no time."*
Indirect discourse	Theo sagte, **daß er keine Zeit hätte.** ⎫	Theo said that he *had* (colloquial: *has*)
	Theo sagte, **daß er keine Zeit habe.** ⎬	no time.

Direct discourse is used to repeat the exact words of another person. Indirect discourse is used to report what someone else has said. The conjunction **daß** may or may not be stated in indirect discourse: **Theo sagte, er hätte/habe keine Zeit.** To report what someone else has said, German speakers may use one of two possible subjunctive forms: general subjunctive (e.g., **er hätte**) or special subjunctive (e.g., **er habe**).

General subjunctive

Present time	Erika sagte, sie **schriebe** einen Brief.	Erika said she *was* (colloquial: *is*) *writing* a letter.
Past time	Erika sagte, sie **hätte** den Brief gestern geschrieben.	Erika said she *had written* (colloquial: *wrote*) the letter yesterday.

The subjunctive form presented in *Kapitel 12* is the general subjunctive. It is based upon the simple past tense form (e.g., **schrieb**). The general subjunctive is also called subjunctive II because the simple past tense is the second principal part of verbs.

Special subjunctive

■ *Present-time special subjunctive*

schreiben	
ich schreib**e**	wir schreib**en**
du schreib**est**	ihr schreib**et**
er/es/sie schreib**e**	sie schreib**en**
Sie schreib**en**	

The present-time special subjunctive is based on the infinitive stem (e.g., **schreib-**) to which the subjunctive endings are added. Most of the forms of the special subjunctive are basically the same as the indicative forms. Use of the special subjunctive is generally limited to the **er/es/sie**-form, since it is the only form that is clearly different from the indicative. Because it is based on the infinitive, the first principal part of verbs, special subjunctive is also called subjunctive I.

Infinitive	Special subjunctive: *er/es/sie*-form	Indicative: *er/es/sie*-form
fahren	**fahre**	fährt
lesen	**lese**	liest
werden	**werde**	wird
können	**könne**	kann
haben	**habe**	hat
sein	**sei**	ist

Verbs that have a vowel change in the **du-** and **er/es/sie-**forms of the indicative do not undergo a vowel change in the special subjunctive because these forms are based on the infinitive.

■ *Special subjunctive of* **sein**

ich	**sei**	wir	**seien**
du	**seiest**	ihr	**seiet**
er/es/sie	**sei**	sie	**seien**
	Sie	**seien**	

Sei occurs frequently in its several forms in indirect discourse, since the forms are clearly different from the indicative. **Sei** does not have the **-e** ending characteristic of the **ich** and **er/es/sie-**forms in the special subjunctive.

■ *Past-time special subjunctive*

Anna sagte, sie **habe** einen Job **gefunden.**

Anna said she *had found* (colloquial: *found*) a job.

Tobias sagte, er **sei** allein **gefahren.**

Tobias said he *had driven* (colloquial: *drove*) alone.

Past-time special subjunctive is composed of the special subjunctive forms of the auxiliaries **haben** (e.g., **habe**) or **sein** (e.g., **sei**) plus the past participle of the main verb. Note that English uses a past perfect when referring to past time in indirect discourse (e.g., *she had found*).

Use of the general subjunctive and special subjunctive

General subjunctive	Karin sagte, sie **wüßte** es nicht.	Karin said she *did*n't (colloquial: *doesn't*) *know.*
Special subjunctive	Karin sagte, sie **wisse** es nicht.	

You may choose to use either general or special subjunctive in indirect discourse as long as the form is clearly recognizable as subjunctive. For this reason the special subjunctive is generally used only in the **er/es/sie-**form (e.g., **sie wisse),** which is clearly different from the indicative (e.g., **sie weiß**).

General subjunctive	Meine Freunde sagten, sie **wüßten** es nicht.	My friends said they *did*n't *know* (colloquial: *don't know*).
(Special subjunctive)	(Meine Freunde sagten, sie **wissen** es nicht.)	

As illustrated above, the general subjunctive must be used when the special subjunctive (e.g., **sie wissen**) is identical to the indicative (e.g., **sie wissen**).

1. Expressing skepticism

Red' keinen Unsinn/Stuß. Don't talk nonsense.
Ist das dein Ernst? Are you serious?
Hier ist was faul. There's something fishy here.
Meinst du? Wirklich? Meinst du das wirklich? Do you think so? Really? Do you really mean that?
Das ist ja komisch/eigenartig/merkwürdig. That's funny/strange.
Irgendetwas stimmt hier nicht. Something's wrong here.
Ist das wahr? Is that true?
Wer sagt das? Wer hat das gesagt? Who says that? Who said that?
Woher weißt du das? Wo/Von wem hast du das gehört? How do you know that? Where/From whom did you hear that?

2. Expressing insecurity or doubt

Das ist unwahrscheinlich. That's unlikely.
Das glaub' ich nicht. I don't believe that.
Es ist unwahrscheinlich, daß [sie das gesagt hat]. It's unlikely that [she said that].
Das ist zweifelhaft. That's doubtful.
Ich glaube nicht/ich bezweifle, daß [er das gesagt hat]. I don't believe [he said that].
Ich glaube das nicht. I don't believe that.
Das kann nicht sein. That can't be.

3. Expressing annoyance

Quatsch! / Unsinn! / Blödsinn! Nonsense!
Blödmann! / Dussel! / Idiot! Idiot!
Der hat wohl nicht alle Tassen im Schrank. He doesn't have all his marbles.
Bei der ist wohl eine Schraube los/locker. She's got a screw loose.
Hör mal. Listen.
Geh. Go on.
Also, wissen Sie. / Wirklich. / Tsk, tsk, tsk. Well, you know. / Really. / Tsk, tsk, tsk.
(Das ist doch) nicht zu glauben. (That is) not to be believed.
(Das ist) unerhört/unglaublich. (That is) unheard of/unbelievable.
(Das ist eine) Schweinerei. That's a mess, a dirty trick.
Das tut/sagt man nicht. One doesn't do/say such a thing.

Das kannst du doch nicht machen/sagen. You can't do/say that.
So eine Gemeinheit. That's mean.
Frechheit! The nerve!; She's/He's/You've got some nerve!
Also komm. Come on.

4. Stalling for time

Also. / Na ja. / Ja nun. Well. / Well, of course. / Well, now.
hmmmmmmmmm hmmmmmmmmmm
Laß mich mal nachdenken. Let me think about it.
Darüber muß ich (erst mal) nachdenken. I have to think about that (first).
Das kann ich so (auch) nicht sagen. I can't say that (either).
Das muß ich mir erst mal überlegen. I have to think about it.
Da muß ich erst mal überlegen. Let me think.

5. Being noncommittal

(Das ist ja) interessant. (That is) interesting.
hmmmmmmmmmm hmmmmmmmmmm
Wirklich? Really?
Ach ja? Oh really?
So so. Oh yes, I see.

6. Expressing good wishes

Ich halte/drücke [dir] die Daumen. I'll cross my fingers [for you].
Gesundheit! Bless you!
(Ich wünsche) guten Appetit/gesegnete Mahlzeit. (I hope you) enjoy your meal.
Prost! / Auf Ihr Wohl! / Zum Wohl! Cheers! / To your health!
Herzlichen Glückwunsch! Congratulations!
Herzlichen Glückwunsch zum Geburtstag! Happy birthday!
Ich wünsche Ihnen gute Reise! / Gute Reise! Bon voyage! Have a nice trip!
Gute Besserung. Get well soon.
Viel Glück! Good luck!
Viel Vergnügen/Spaß! Have fun!
Alles Gute! All the best! Best wishes!
Hals- und Beinbruch! Good luck! Break a leg!

7. Courtesy expressions

Bitte (sehr/schön?).   Please.
Danke (sehr/schön).   Thanks (very much).

8. Saying "you're welcome"

Bitte (sehr/schön).   You're (very) welcome.
Gern geschehen.   Glad to do it.
Nichts zu danken.   Don't mention it.

9. Expressing surprise

Ach nein!   Oh no!
(Wie) ist das (nur) möglich!   (How) is that possible?
Das hätte ich nicht gedacht.   I wouldn't have thought that.
Das ist ja prima/toll/klasse/stark/Wahnsinn!   That's great/fantastic/terrific, etc.!
Ich werd' verrückt.   I must be crazy.
(Das ist ja) nicht zu glauben!   (That's) unbelievable!
Kaum zu glauben.   Hard to believe.
Ich bin von den Socken/sprachlos.   I'm bowled over/speechless.
Um Himmels willen!   For heaven's sake!
Sag' bloß.   You don't say.
Was für 'ne Überraschung!   What a surprise!
Das haut/wirft mich um.   That bowls me over/knocks me out/blows me away.; *(neg.)* That's a bummer.

10. Expressing agreement (and disagreement)

Natürlich (nicht)! / Selbstverständlich (nicht)!   Naturally, of course (not)!
Klar.   Sure.
Warum denn nicht?   Why not?
Das kann (nicht) sein.   That can(not) be.
(Das) stimmt (nicht).   (That's) (not) right.
Richtig. / Falsch.   Right. / Wrong.
Das finde ich auch/nicht.   I think so, too./I don't think so.
Genau. / Eben.   Exactly. / That's right.
Du hast recht.   You're right.

11. Responding to requests

Bitte. / Selbstverständlich. / Natürlich. / Klar.   Glad to. / Of course. / Naturally.
Gern. / Machen wir. / Mit Vergnügen.   Glad to. / We'll do it. / With pleasure.
(Es tut mir leid, aber) das geht nicht.   (I'm sorry but) that won't work.
Das kann ich nicht [reparieren].   I can't [repair that].
Das habe ich nicht.   I don't have it.
Das ist zu schwer/groß/teuer.   That's too difficult/big/expensive.

12. Expressing regret

(Das) tut mir leid.   I'm sorry.
(Es) tut mir leid, daß [ich nicht kommen kann].   I'm sorry [I can't come].
Leider [kann ich morgen nicht].   Unfortunately [I can't tomorrow].
(Es) geht leider nicht.   That won't work, unfortunately.
Schade.   That's a shame. / Too bad.
(So ein) Pech.   That's tough luck.

13. Excusing oneself

Bitte entschuldigen Sie mich.   Please excuse me. / I beg your pardon.
Bitte verzeihen Sie mir [die Verspätung].   Please pardon [my delay].
Entschuldigung. / Verzeihung. / Entschuldigen Sie.   Excuse (pardon) me.
Entschuldigen Sie bitte, daß [ich erst jetzt komme].   Please excuse me [for arriving so late].
Das ist keine Entschuldigung.   That's no excuse.

14. Expressing indifference

(Das) ist mir egal.   That's all the same to me.
Es ist mir egal, ob [er kommt].   I don't care whether [he comes].
Das macht mir nichts aus.   It doesn't matter to me.
Das ist nicht meine Sorge.   That's not my problem.
Es macht mir nichts aus, daß [sie mehr verdient].   I don't care that [she earns more].
Macht nichts.   Doesn't matter.
Das ist mir wurscht.   I couldn't care less.
Das kannst du machen, wie du willst.   You can do as you please.
Das kannst du halten wie der Dachdecker.   You can do/take that as you wish.
Ich habe nichts dagegen. / Meinetwegen.   I have nothing against it.

15. Expressing admiration

Ach, wie schön! / Klasse!   Oh, how nice! / Great! / Terrific!
Phantastisch! / Toll! / Super! / Stark! / Irre! / Einsame Spitze!   Fantastic! / Great! / Super! / Incredible! / Really great!, etc.
Erstklassig! / Ausgezeichnet!   First-rate! / Excellent!
Das ist aber nett [von Ihnen/dir].   That's really nice [of you].
Die/Der ist nett.   She/He is nice.
Das sind nette Leute.   Those are nice people.

16. Expressing rejection

(So ein) Mist! (What) rubbish!

(Das ist) schrecklich! (That is) awful!

Das ärgert mich. That annoys me.

Der/Das/Die gefällt mir (gar) nicht. I don't like him/that/her (at all).

Ich mag sie/ihn nicht. I don't like her/him.

Ich kann sie/ihn nicht leiden. I don't like her/him.

Ich finde, sie/er ist langweilig/doof/uninteressant. I think she/he is boring/stupid/uninteresting.

Ich finde das schlecht/langweilig. I think that is bad/boring.

Ich finde sie/ihn nicht sympathisch/nett. I don't find her/him likeable/nice.

17. Expressing joy and pleasure

Wir freuen uns. We're pleased.

Wir freuen uns auf [seinen Besuch/die Ferien]. We're looking forward to [his visit/our vacation].

Wir sind begeistert. We are enthusiastic.

Wir sind froh (darüber), daß [er wieder arbeitet]. We're happy (about the fact) that [he's working again].

Es freut mich, daß [sie gekommen ist]. I'm happy that [she has come].

Das tun/kochen/essen wir gern. We like to do/cook/eat that.

Das macht mir/uns Spaß. I/We enjoy that. / That's fun.

Das machen wir zum Vergnügen. We do that for fun.

18. Expressing sadness

Ach (nein)! Oh (no)!

Wie schrecklich! How awful/horrible.

Mein Gott! / O je! My God!

Ich bin traurig, weil [sie/er nicht hier ist]. I am unhappy, because [she/he isn't here].

Ich bin sehr traurig darüber. I am very unhappy about that.

Ich bin deprimiert/frustriert. I am depressed/frustrated.

19. Making requests

Hättest du/Hätten Sie Lust [mitzukommen]? Would you like [to come along]?

Hättest du/Hätten Sie Zeit, [uns zu besuchen]? Would you have time [to come see us]?

Hättest du/Hätten Sie etwas [Zeit] für mich? Would you have some [time] for me?

Ich hätte gern [ein Pfund Äpfel]. I'd like [a pound of apples].

Könntest du/Könnten Sie [mein Auto reparieren]? Could you [repair my car]?

Würdest du/Würden Sie mir bitte helfen? Would you please help me?

Hättest du/Hätten Sie etwas dagegen? Would you mind?

Hast du/Hätten Sie etwas dagegen, wenn [ich mitkomme]? Would you mind if [I come along]?

Dürfte ich [ein Stück Kuchen haben]? May I/Is it OK if I [have a piece of cake]?

Macht es dir/Ihnen etwas aus? Do you mind?

Sei/Seien Sie so gut. Be so kind.

Ich möchte fragen, ob ich [mitkommen] darf/kann. I'd like to ask if I may/can [come along].

Könnte ich [um neun Uhr zu dir/Ihnen kommen]? Could I [come see you at nine o'clock]?

Ist es dir/Ihnen recht? Is it OK with you?

20. Asking for favors

Könntest du/Könnten Sie mir einen Gefallen tun und [mich mitnehmen]? Could you do me a favor and [take me along]?

Ich hätte eine Bitte: könntest/würdest du (könnten/würden Sie) [mich mitnehmen]? I have a request: could/would you [take me along]?

21. Making surmises

Ich glaube schon. / Ich denke ja. I think so.

Ich glaube (schon), daß [sie das gesagt hat]. I do believe [she said that].

Das dürfte/könnte wahr/richtig sein. That might/could be true/right.

Wahrscheinlich [stimmt das]. Probably [that's right].

Sicher. / Ich bin sicher. / Ich bin ziemlich sicher, daß [er das gesagt hat]. Sure. / I'm sure. / I'm quite sure that [he said that].

Ich vermute. / Ich nehme das an. I assume so.

Ich nehme an, daß [das stimmt]. I assume that [that's right].

Das scheint [nicht zu stimmen]. That appears [not to be right].

22. Expressing expectation

Hoffentlich. / Hoffentlich [kommt sie]. I hope. / I hope [she comes].

Ich hoffe (es) (sehr). I hope (so) (very much).

Ich hoffe, daß [er das Paket bekommen hat]. I hope [he received the package].

Ich freue mich auf [die Ferien]. I'm looking forward to [my vacation].

Ich kann es kaum erwarten. I can hardly wait.

23. Expressing fears

Ich befürchte/Ich fürchte, daß [sie nicht kommt].
I'm afraid [she's not coming].
Ich habe Angst, [nach Hause zu gehen]. I'm afraid [to go home].
Davor habe ich Angst. I'm afraid of that.
Ich habe Angst vor [dem Hund]. I'm afraid of [the dog].
[Der Hund] jagt mir Angst ein. [The dog] scares me.
Das ist mir unheimlich. It scares me.

24. Giving advice

Ich schlage vor, daß [wir um acht anfangen]. I suggest that [we begin at eight].
Ich rate dir/Ihnen, [zu Hause zu bleiben]. I advise you [to stay home].
Das würde ich dir/Ihnen (nicht) raten. I would (not) advise that.
Das würde ich (nicht) machen/sagen. I would (not) do/say that.

Das würde ich anders/so machen. I would do that differently/this way.
Das mußt du/müssen Sie so machen. You have to do it this way.
Ich zeige dir/Ihnen, [wie man das macht]. I'll show you [how one does that].
An [deiner/ihrer/seiner] Stelle würde ich [zu Hause bleiben]. If I were you/her/him], I'd [stay home].

25. Correcting misunderstandings

Das habe ich nicht so gemeint. I didn't mean it that way.
Das habe ich nur aus Spaß gesagt. I only said that in fun/jest.
Das war doch nicht so gemeint. It wasn't meant that way.
Das war nicht mein Ernst. I wasn't serious.
Nimm doch nicht alles so ernst. Don't take everything so seriously.

The following word lists will help you to increase the number of things you can say and write.

Audio-visual equipment

die **Boxen** (*pl.*)   speakers
die **Compact Disk**   compact disk
der **Farbfernseher**   color television
der **Kassettenrecorder**   cassette recorder
der **Kopfhörer**   headphone
der **Lautsprecher**   loudspeaker
das **Mikrophon**   microphone
der **Plattenspieler**   record player
der **Radiorecorder**   cassette radio
der **Schwarzweißfernseher**   black-and-white television
die **Stereoanlage**   stereo system
das **Tonband,** das **Band**   tape
das **Tonbandgerät**   (reel-to-reel) tape recorder
der **Tuner**   tuner
der **Verstärker**   amplifier
der **Videorecorder**   video recorder (VCR)
der **Walkman**   personal stereo

Body care and hygiene

die **Haarbürste**   hair brush
der **Haartrockner,** der **Föhn**   hair dryer
das **Handtuch**   hand towel
das **Make-up**   makeup
der **Rasierapparat**   razor
die **Schere**   scissors
die **Seife**   soap
der **Spiegel**   mirror
das **Taschentuch**   handkerchief
die **(elektrische) Zahnbürste**   (electric) toothbrush
die **Zahnpasta**   toothpaste

Buildings and other landmarks

die **Autobahnauffahrt (-ausfahrt)**   expressway on-ramp (off-ramp)
der **Bahnhof**   train station
die **Bahnlinie**   railroad line
der **Bauernhof**   farm
die **Brücke**   bridge
die **Bundesstraße**   federal highway

die **Burg**   fortress
das **Denkmal**   monument
die **Fabrik**   factory
der **Fernsehturm**   TV tower
der **Flughafen**   airport
der **Friedhof**   cemetery
der **Funkturm**   radio and TV tower
der **Fußweg**   footpath
die **Kapelle**   chapel
die **Kirche**/der **Dom**/das **Münster**   church/cathedral
das **Kloster**   monastery
die **Mühle**   mill
das **Museum**   museum
das **Parkhaus**   parking garage
die **Polizei**   police
die **Post**   post office
die **Ruine**   ruin
das **Schloß**   castle
die **Tiefgarage**   underground garage
der **Tunnel**   tunnel

Chores

(das) **Abendessen vorbereiten, machen**   to prepare supper
Fenster putzen   to clean windows
den **Hund**/die **Katze füttern**   to feed the dog/cat
(das) **Mittagessen kochen**   to cook dinner
Staub wischen   to dust
(die) **Wäsche bügeln**   to iron the wash, laundry
Wäsche, Kleider flicken   to mend clothes

(die) **Bäume beschneiden/pflanzen/fällen**   to prune/to plant/to cut down trees
das **Haus**/den **Zaun**/das **Boot streichen**   to paint the house/the fence/the boat
die **Hecke schneiden**   to trim the hedge
(das) **Holz sägen/spalten/hacken**   to saw/to split/to chop wood
(den) **Rasen mähen**   to mow the lawn
(den) **Schnee fegen, kehren/schippen**   to sweep/to shovel snow
(das) **Unkraut jäten**   to pull out weeds

Classroom objects

der **Filzstift** felt-tip pen
die **Folie** transparency
das **Klassenzimmer** classroom
die **Kreide** chalk
der **Kurs** course
die **Landkarte; die Wandkarte** map; wall map
der **Overheadprojektor** overhead projector
der **Papierkorb** wastebasket
das **Ringbuch** loose-leaf binder
der **Schwamm** sponge
das **Sprachlabor** language lab
die **Videokassette** videocassette
der **Videorecorder** video recorder (VCR)
die **(Wand)tafel** chalkboard

Clothing

das **Abendkleid** evening dress/gown
der **Anorak** jacket with hood, parka
der **Blazer** blazer
die **Daunenjacke** down jacket
der **Hosenrock** culottes
die **Kniestrümpfe** *(pl.)* knee socks
das **Kostüm** woman's suit
die **Latzhose** bib overalls
der **Mantel** coat
der **Overall** jumpsuit
der **Parka** parka
das **Polohemd** polo shirt
der **Regenmantel** raincoat
der **Rollkragenpullover** turtleneck
die **Sandalen** *(pl.)* sandals
der **Schal** scarf
der **Schlafanzug** pajamas
die **Sportschuhe** *(pl.)* sneakers
die **Strickjacke** (cardigan) sweater
das **Sweatshirt** sweatshirt
das **Trägerkleid** jumper
der **Trainingsanzug** sweat suit
die **Turnschuhe** *(pl.)* fitness/workout shoes
die **Weste** vest
der **Wintermantel** winter coat

Collectibles

sammeln to collect
alte Flaschen old bottles
Briefmarken stamps
Glas glass
Münzen coins
Pflanzen (getrocknet) plants (dried)
Puppen dolls
Silber silver
Streichholzschachteln matchboxes
Zinn pewter

College majors

Amerikanistik American studies
Anglistik English language and literature
Betriebswirtschaft business administration
Biologie biology
Chemie chemistry
Chinesisch Chinese
Englisch English
Französisch French
Germanistik German language and literature
Informatik computer science
Ingenieurwesen engineering
Italienisch Italian
Japanisch Japanese
Jura law
Kommunikationswissenschaft communications
Kunstgeschichte art history
Marketing marketing
Medizin medicine
Pädagogik/Erziehungswissenschaften education
Philosophie philosophy
Physik physics
Politik political science
Psychologie psychology
Publizistik journalism
Religionswissenschaft/Theologie religion
Rechnungswesen accounting
Romanistik Romance languages and literature
Russisch Russian
Sozialwissenschaften/Sozialkunde social studies
Soziologie sociology
Spanisch Spanish
Sprachwissenschaft/Linguistik linguistics
Theaterwissenschaft theater studies
Volkswirtschaft economics

Colors

dunkel[blau] dark [blue]
hell[blau] light [blue]
lila lilac
orange orange
purpur purple
rosa pink

Computer terminology

der **Anwender** program user
anzeigen to display
mit dem Computer arbeiten to work on the
    computer
auswählen to select a program
der **Bildschirm** screen
die **CD-ROM** CD-ROM
der **Computer** computer
der **Personalcomputer** personal computer

die **Diskette**   diskette
das **Diskettenlaufwerk**   diskette drive
der **Drucker**   printer
der **Laserdrucker**   laser printer
der **Matrixdrucker**   matrix printer
der **Tintenstrahldrucker**   ink jet printer
der **Typendrucker**   letter-quality printer
die **E-Mail**   E-mail; **eine Mail schicken/einen elektronischen Brief an jemanden schicken**   to send E-Mail
die **Festplatte**   hard disk
die **Floppy-Disk**   floppy disk
das **Internet**   Internet
laden   to load
ein **Programm laufen lassen**   to run a program
der **Monitor**   monitor
das **Netz**   network
das **Paßwort**   password
der **Positionsanzeiger**   cursor
programmieren   to program
die **Programmiersprache**   computer language
die **Software; das Softwarepaket**   software; software package
speichern   to store; **auf Diskette speichern**   to store on diskette
ein **700 MB Speicher**   a 700 megabyte memory
die **Tastatur**   keyboard
die **Taste; die Funktionstaste**   key; function key
der **Textverarbeiter, der Wortprozessor**   word processor

Directions

Asking directions

Wo ist [der Bahnhof]?   Where is the [train station]?
Wie weit ist es [zum Bahnhof]?   How far is it [to the train station]?
Wie komme ich am schnellsten [zum Bahnhof]?   What is the quickest way [to the train station]?
Wo ist hier in der Nähe [ein Café]?   Is there [a café] around here?
Wissen Sie den Weg nach [Obersdorf]?   Do you know the way to [Obersdorf]?
Wir wollen nach [Stuttgart]. Wie fahren wir am besten?   We're going to [Stuttgart]. What is the best route?

Giving directions

Da fahren Sie am besten mit [der U-Bahn].   It's best if you go by [subway].
Fahren Sie mit dem [Dreier]; Nehmen Sie den [Dreier].   Take number [3] [bus].
Fahren Sie mit der [Drei]; Nehmen Sie Die [Drei].   Take number [3] [subway or streetcar].
[Dort/An der Ecke/An der Kreuzung] ist die Haltestelle.   [Over there/on the corner/at the intersection] is the [bus] stop.
An der [ersten] Kreuzung gehen Sie [rechts].   At the [first] intersection turn [right].
Gehen Sie die [erste] Straße [links].   Take the [first] street [to the left].
Gehen Sie geradeaus.   Go straight ahead.
Bei der Ampel biegen Sie [rechts] ab.   At the traffic light turn [right].

Family

der **Enkel**   grandson
die **Enkelin**   granddaughter
das **Enkelkind**   grandchild
der **Halbbruder**   half brother
die **Halbschwester**   half sister
die **Schwiegermutter**   mother-in-law
der **Schwiegervater**   father-in-law
der **Schwager**   brother-in-law
die **Schwägerin**   sister-in-law

geschieden   divorced
ledig   single
verheiratet   married

Farewells and greetings

Adé.   'Bye. (*used in southern Germany and Austria*)
Auf Wiederhören.   Good-bye. (*on the telephone*)
Bis bald.   See you soon.
Bis dann!   See you later.
Ciao.   So long.
Grüezi.   Hello. (*used in Switzerland*)
Grüß Gott.   Good-bye. Hello. (*used in southern Germany and Austria*)
Mach's gut.   Take it easy.
Servus.   Good-bye! Hello! (*used in southern Germany and Austria*)

Film

der **Abenteuerfilm**   adventure movie
der **Actionfilm**   action movie
der **Horrorfilm**   horror film
der **Liebesfilm**   romance
der **Science-fiction-Film**   science fiction movie

die **Außenaufnahme**   location shot
das **Drehbuch**   (film) script
die **Filmfestspiele** (*pl.*)   film festival

die **Filmkomödie**   comedy film
die **Filmkritik**   movie criticism
die **(Film)leinwand**   (movie) screen
der **Filmmacher**/die **Filmmacherin**   filmmaker
der **(Film)schauspieler**/die **(Film)schauspielerin**
    movie actor/actress
die **(Film)szene**   (movie) scene
das **(Film)studio**   (movie) studio
der **Kameramann**/die **Kamerafrau**   cameraman/
    camerawoman
der **Regisseur**/die **Regisseurin**   director

Foods

Breakfast

das **Ei (weich gekocht)**   egg (soft-boiled)
das **Graubrot**   light rye bread
der **Honig**   honey
der **Joghurt**   yogurt
der **Kakao**   cocoa
die **Marmelade**   jam, marmalade
der **Pumpernickel**   pumpernickel bread
die **Schokolade**   hot chocolate
das **Schwarzbrot**   dark rye bread
der **Tomatensaft**   tomato juice
das **Vollkornbrot**   coarse, whole-grain bread
das **Weißbrot**   white bread

Main meal

die **Suppe**   soup
der **gemischte Salat**   vegetable salad plate
der **grüne Salat**   tossed (green) salad

der **Braten**   roast
das **Kalbfleisch**   veal
das **Kotelett**   chop
das **Rindfleisch**   beef
die **Roulade**   roulade
das **Schnitzel**   cutlet
das **Schweinefleisch**   pork
der **Speck**   bacon
der **Truthahn**   turkey

die **Bohnen** (pl.)   beans
der **Champignon**   mushroom
die **Erbsen** (pl.)   peas
die **Karotten, gelbe Rüben** (pl.)   carrots
der **Kohl**   cabbage
der **Mais**   corn
die **(gefüllte) Paprikaschote**   (stuffed) pepper
die **Pilze** (pl.)   mushrooms
der **Reis**   rice
das **Sauerkraut**   sauerkraut

der **Spargel**   asparagus
die **Zwiebel**   onion

das **Salz**   salt
der **Pfeffer**   pepper
der **Zucker**   sugar

Lunch/supper

die **(saure) Gurke**   (half-sour) pickle
das **Spiegelei**   fried egg
der **Thunfisch**   tuna fish
die **Wurst**/der **Aufschnitt**   sausage/cold cuts

Desserts and fruit

das **Eis**   ice cream
der **Karamelpudding**   caramel custard
das **Kompott**   stewed fruit
die **Schokoladencreme**   chocolate mousse
der **Vanillepudding**   vanilla pudding

die **Sahne**   cream
die **Schlagsahne**   whipped cream

die **Ananas**   pineapple
die **Erdbeeren** (pl.)   strawberries
die **Himbeeren** (pl.)   raspberries
die **Orange, Apfelsine**   orange
der **Pfirsich**   peach
die **Pflaume**   plum
der **Rhabarber**   rhubarb
die **Zitrone**   lemon
die **Zwetsch(g)e**   plum

Food preparation

backen   to bake
braten   to fry; to roast
grillen   to grill
kochen   to cook

Geographic terms

die **Anhöhe;** der **Hügel**   hill
der **Atlantik**   Atlantic (Ocean)
der **Bach**   brook
der **Berg**   mountain
das **(Bundes)land**   (federal) state in Germany and
    Austria
der **(Bundes)staat**   (federal) state in the U.S.A.
die **Ebbe**/die **Flut**   low tide/high tide
der **Fluß**   river
das **Gebirge**   mountain range
die **Gezeiten** (pl.)   tides
der **Gipfel**   peak

der **Gletscher**   glacier
die **Insel**   island
der **Kanal**   canal; channel
der **Kanton**   canton (*Switzerland*)
die **Küste**   coast
das **Meer**   sea
der **Pazifik**   Pacific (Ocean)
der **See**   lake
die **See**   sea
der **Strand**   beach
das **Tal**   valley
der **Teich**   pond
das **Ufer**   shore
der **Wald**   woods
die **Wiese**   meadow
die **Wüste**   desert

Hobbies

angeln   to fish
Blumen (z.B. Rosen, Dahlien, Lilien, Nelken)
   flowers (*e.g.,* roses, dahlias, lilies, carnations)
campen   to go camping
die **Gartenarbeit**   gardening
malen   to paint
schreiben [Gedichte, Geschichten, Romane, Dramen]
   to write [poems, stories, novels, plays]
zeichnen   to draw

Household

der **Backofen**   oven
die **Badewanne**   bathtub
die **Dusche**   shower
das **Mikrowellengerät**   microwave
das **Spülbecken/die Spüle**   kitchen sink
der **Trockner/der Wäschetrockner**   clothes dryer
das **Waschbecken**   washbasin

Jewelry

das **Armband**   bracelet
die **Halskette**   necklace
die **Kette**   chain
die **Ohrringe** (*pl.*)   earrings
der **Ring**   ring

Literature

dic **Anthologie**   anthology
das **Drama**   drama, play
das **Gedicht**   poem
die **Kurzgeschichte**   short story

der **Roman**   novel
die **Zeitschrift**   magazine
die **Illustrierte**   illustrated magazine

der **Autor/die Autorin**   author
der **Dichter/die Dichterin**   poet
der **Dramatiker/die Dramatikerin**   dramatist
der **Schriftsteller/die Schriftstellerin**   writer

Music and theater

das **Theaterstück;** die **Tragödie;** die **Komödie;** der
   Einakter   play; tragedy; comedy; one-act play
das **Musical**   musical comedy
die **Oper**   opera
die **Operette**   operetta

der **Dirigent/die Dirigentin**   conductor
der **Regisseur/die Regisseurin**   director
der **Sänger/die Sängerin**   singer
der **Schauspieler/die Schauspielerin**   actor/actress
der **Zuschauer/die Zuschauerin**   spectator

der **Beifall,** der **Applaus**   applause
die **Bühne**   stage
das **Foyer**   hallway, lobby
die **Inszenierung**   mounting of a production
das **Orchester**   orchestra
die **Pause**   intermission
das **Programmheft**   program
die **Vorstellung**   performance

dirigieren   to conduct
proben   to rehearse
singen   to sing
spielen   to play
üben   to practice

Musical instruments

das **Akkordeon**   accordion
die **Blockflöte**   recorder
die **Bratsche**   viola
das **Cello**   cello
das **Fagott**   bassoon
die **Flöte**   flute
die **Geige, Violine**   violin
die **Gitarre**   guitar
die **Harfe**   harp
die **Klarinette**   clarinet
das **Klavier**   piano
der **Kontrabaß**   double bass

die **Oboe** oboe
die **Orgel** organ
die **Posaune (+ blasen)** trombone (to play)
die **Pauke** kettle drum
das **Saxophon** saxophone
das **Schlagzeug** percussion (instrument)
die **Trommel** drum
die **Trompete (+ blasen)** trumpet (to play)
die **Tuba (+ blasen)** tuba (to play)
das **(Wald)horn (+ blasen)** French horn (to play)

Personal qualities and characteristics

Adjectives for mood or personality

ausgezeichnet excellent
elend miserable
erstklassig first-rate
furchtbar horrible
kaputt worn out, tired
klasse terrific
miserabel miserable
nervös nervous
phantastisch fantastic
prima excellent
schrecklich dreadful
toll great
traurig sad

Adjectives for personality

fies disgusting; unfair
klug smart
lahm slow, sluggish
langsam slow
praktisch practical
schlau clever, smart
verrückt crazy

Physical description of people

blond blond
dick fat
dunkel brunette
fett fat
gut aussehend handsome
häßlich ugly
hübsch pretty
mager thin, skinny
normal normal
schön beautiful
schwach weak
stark strong
vollschlank full-figured

Professions

ein **Angestellter**/eine **Angestellte** white-collar worker
der **Apotheker**/die **Apothekerin** pharmacist
der **Arzt**/die **Ärztin** physician
der **Betriebswirt**/die **Betriebswirtin** manager
der **Dolmetscher**/die **Dolmetscherin** translator
der **Elektriker**/die **Elektrikerin** electrician
der **Flugbegleiter**/die **Flugbegleiterin** flight attendant
der **Hochschullehrer**/die **Hochschullehrerin** college/university professor
der **Ingenieur**/die **Ingenieurin** engineer
der **Journalist**/die **Journalistin** journalist
der **Krankenpfleger**/die **Krankenschwester** nurse
der **Lehrer**/die **Lehrerin** teacher
der **Mechaniker**/die **Mechanikerin** mechanic
der **Musiker**/die **Musikerin** musician
der **Pfarrer**/die **Pfarrerin** clergyperson
der **Physiotherapeut**/die **Physiotherapeutin** physical therapist
der **Rechtsanwalt**/die **Rechtsanwältin** lawyer
der **Sekretär**/die **Sekretärin** secretary
der **Sozialarbeiter**/die **Sozialarbeiterin** social worker
der **Sozialpädagoge**/die **Sozialpädagogin** social worker (with college degree)
der **Steward**/die **Stewardeß** flight attendant
der **Tierarzt**/die **Tierärztin** veterinarian
der **Verkäufer**/die **Verkäuferin** salesperson
der **Volkswirt**/die **Volkswirtin** economist
der **Wissenschaftler**/die **Wissenschaftlerin** scientist
der **Zahnarzt**/die **Zahnärztin** dentist

Specialty shops

das **Blumengeschäft** florist shop
die **chemische Reinigung** dry cleaning shop
das **Eisenwarengeschäft** hardware store
das **Elektrogeschäft** appliance store
das **Feinkostgeschäft** delicatessen
das **Fotogeschäft** camera store
der **Juwelier** jeweler's; jewelry store
das **Kaffeegeschäft** store selling coffee
der **Kiosk** kiosk, stand
der **Klempner** plumber's shop
die **Konditorei** coffee and pastry shop
das **Möbelgeschäft** furniture store
der **Optiker** optician's shop
das **Schreibwarengeschäft** stationery store
das **Schuhgeschäft** shoe store
der **Schuhmacher**; der **Schuster** shoe repair (shop)
das **Sportgeschäft**; die **Sportausrüstungen** sporting goods store; sporting goods
der **Waschsalon** laundromat

Sports and games

das **Ballonfahren**   ballooning
das **Billard**   billiards
das **Bodybuilding**   bodybuilding
die **Dame**   checkers
das **Drachenfliegen**   hang gliding
das **Eishockey**   hockey
das **Fallschirmspringen**   parachute jumping
der **Federball**   badminton
der **Flipper**   pinball machine; **ich flippere**   I play the
   pinball machine
die **Gymnastik**   calisthenics
der **Handball, Hallenhandball**   handball
das **Hockey**   field hockey
die **Leichtathletik**   track and field
der **Radsport**, das **Radfahren**   bicycling
das **Rollerblading**   in-line skating, rollerblading
das **Rollschuhlaufen**   roller skating
das **Schlittschuhlaufen**   ice skating
das **Segelfliegen**   glider flying
das **Skateboardfahren**   skateboarding
das **Turnen**   gymnastics
der **Wasserball**   water polo
das **Windsurfen**   windsurfing

boxen   to box
fechten   to fence
jagen   to hunt
kegeln   to bowl
ringen   to wrestle
rudern   to row
schießen   to shoot

Table setting

die **Butterdose**   butter dish
der **Eierbecher**   egg cup
der **Eßlöffel**   tablespoon
das **Gedeck**   table setting
das **Gericht**   dish (food)
die **Kaffeekanne**/die **Teekanne**   coffeepot/teapot
das **Milchkännchen**   creamer (small pitcher for cream
   or milk)
die **Schüssel**   bowl
die **Serviette**   napkin
die **Speise**   dish (food)
der **Teelöffel**   teaspoon
der **Teller**   plate
die **Untertasse**   saucer
die **Zuckerdose**   sugar bowl

Transportation

die **Kutsche**   carriage
der **Pferdewagen**   horse-drawn wagon

der **LKW (= Lastkraftwagen)**/der **Laster**   truck
der **PKW (= Personenkraftwagen)**   passenger car
der **Anhänger**   trailer
der **Campingwagen**, der **Wohnwagen**   camper
   (pulled by a car)
der **Caravan**   camper (recreational vehicle)
der **Combi**   station wagon

die **Bergbahn**   mountain railway; cable car
die **Eisenbahn**   train, railway
der **Güterzug**   freight train

das **Boot**   boat
das **Containerschiff**   container ship
die **Fähre**   ferry
der **Frachter**   freighter
das **Kanu**   canoe
das **Motorboot**   motorboat
der **Passagierdampfer**   passenger ship
das **Ruderboot**   rowboat
das **Segelboot**   sailboat
das **Segelschiff**   sailing ship
der **Tanker**   tanker

der **Hubschrauber**   helicopter
der **Jet**   jet
der **Jumbojet**   jumbo jet
das **(Propeller)flugzeug**   propeller plane
das **Raumschiff**   spaceship
das **Segelflugzeug**   glider; sailplane

TV programs

das **Familiendrama**   soap opera
die **Fernsehkomödie**   sitcom (situation comedy)
die **Fernsehserie**   serial
die **Fernsehshow**, die **Unterhaltungsshow**   game
   show
der **Krimi**   detective or crime drama
die **Nachrichten** (*pl.*)   news
die **Quizsendung**, das **Fernsehquiz**   quiz show
die **Seifenoper**   soap opera
der **Spielfilm**   feature (film)
die **Sportschau**   sports program
der **Zeichentrickfilm**   cartoon

Weather expressions

der **Blitz**   lightning
Celsius   centigrade
der **Donner**   thunder
das **Gewitter**   thunderstorm
der **Hagel**   hail
das **Hoch**   high-pressure system
die **Kaltfront**   cold front

der **Landregen**   all-day rain
der **Luftdruck**   air pressure
der **Nebel**   fog
der **Niederschlag**   precipitation
der **Nieselregen**   drizzle
der **Schauer**   shower
der **Schneefall**   snowfall
der **Sprühregen**   drizzle
der **Tau**   dew
die **Temperatur**   temperature
das **Tief**   low-pressure system
die **Warmfront**   warm front
der **Wetterbericht**   weather report; **Was steht im
Wetterbericht?**   What's the weather report?
die **Wettervorhersage**   weather forecast
die **Windrichtung**   wind direction

bedeckt   overcast
bewölkt   cloudy; **stark bewölkt**   very cloudy
eisig   icy cold
heiter   fair
klar   clear, cloudless
neb(e)lig   foggy
schwül   humid
stürmisch   stormy
wolkenlos   cloudless
wolkig   cloudy

Es gießt (in Strömen).   It's pouring.
Es regnet Bindfäden.   It's raining cats and dogs.
Es ist naßkalt.   It's damp and cold.

Kapitel 3

Geburtsanzeige

Ammersee   the name of a lake in Bavaria
die **Eltern** *(pl.)*   parents
die **Geburtsanzeige**   birth announcement
ist gekommen   has arrived
das **Gewicht**   weight
die **Größe**   *here:* length
die **Schwester**   sister
überglücklich   overjoyed
die **Welt**   world

Kapitel 4

Krone

ab   as of
Achtung   attention
können   can
die **Öffnungszeiten**   store hours
seit   for
stressfreier   with less stress

Preisring-Markt

Edamer   type of Dutch cheese
Fanta   the name of a popular soft drink
griech. (= griechisch)   Greek
holl. (= holländisch)   Dutch
Mailänder   Milanese
das **Netz**   net
das **Rindergulasch**   beef for stew
Sarotti   the name of a brand of chocolate
die **Schokolade**   chocolate
der **Sekt**   champagne
Söhnlein Brillant   the name of a brand
of champagne
das **Sonderangebot**   special
die **Theke**   counter

Kapitel 5

Fernseh-Programm

ab 4   from age 4
das **Abenteuer**   adventure
der **Beruf**   profession

dt. (= deutsch)   German
fliegend   flying
das **Glücksrad**   Wheel of Fortune
Info (= Information)   information
Jede Menge Leben   Full House
das **Krankenhaus**   hospital
die **Nachrichten**   news
namenlos   nameless
polit (= politisch)   political
die **Presseschau**   current issues in the press
ran   come on!
das **Revier**   district
die **Reiter** *(pl.)*   cavalry
Riskier' was!   Take a Chance.
SAT 1 (= Satellit 1)   cable station 1
die **Schlagzeile**   headline
die **Schwarzwaldklinik**   The Black Forest Clinic
die **Serie**   series
die **Tagesschau**   daily news
trickreich   tricky
die **Umwelt**   environment
die **Volksmusik**   folk music
volkstümlich   traditional
die **Vorschau**   preview
das **Wunschkonzert**   request concert
ZDF (= Zweites Deutsches Fernsehen)   TV channel 2
der **Zeichentrickfilm**   cartoon

Kapitel 6

Restop Altea Motel

die **Ausflugsfahrt**   excursion
der **Ausgangspunkt**   starting point
äußerst   extremely
der **Badestrand**   beach
Bergsteigen   mountain climbing
bzw. (= beziehungsweise)   respectively
einladen   to invite
die **Erholung**   relaxation
erreichbar   accessible
die **Fahrtrichtung**   direction
hoteleigner   private (hotel's own)
die **Kulturstätte**   place of cultural interest (e.g., castle, museum)
die **Lage**   site, location
das **Loch**   hole

Mondsee the name of a lake and a town on the lake in Austria, about 30 km east of Salzburg
Salzkammergut an area in Austria, famous for its many lakes and alpine landscape
die **Schiffsrundfahrt** boat excursion
überraschen to surprise
die **Umgebung** environs, the area
die **Veranstaltung** event (e.g., concert)
das **Vergnügen** fun

3 Tage Budapest

die **Ankunft** arrival
das **Bad** bath
ca. (= circa) approximately
die **Dusche** shower
die **Ecke** corner
der **Einbettzuschlag** additional charge for single room
die **Halbpension** halfboard, i.e., including breakfast and one other meal
inbegriffen included
die **Leistung** service
lt. (= laut) according to
die **Nächtigung** overnight stay
der **Pauschalpreis** all-inclusive price
die **Reiseleitung** tour guide
die **Stadtrundfahrt** city tour
der **Stornoschutz** cancellation insurance
Verfügung: zur freien Verfügung free time
das **WC (= Wasserklosett)** toilet

Kapitel 7

Café an der Uni

die **Ananas** pineapple
die **Beilage** side dish
der **Champignon** mushroom
Fanta the name of a popular soft drink
Faß: vom Faß on tap
das **Gebäck** cake and pastries
gebrühter Tee brewed tea
das **Gericht** dish (food)
geöffnet open
die **Johannisbeere** currant
die **Kugel** scoop of ice cream
der **Pilz** mushroom
die **Preiselbeere** cranberry
die **Remoulade** a kind of mayonnaise (dressing)
die **Sahne** cream
die **Schlagsahne** whipped cream

das **Schnitzel** slice, cutlet
die **Schüssel** bowl
das **Spiegelei** fried egg
die **Speise** dish (food)
der **Thunfisch** tuna
der **Truthahn** turkey
Wahl: nach Wahl of your choice
Wiener Art Viennese style
Bitte treffen Sie an unserer Schauvitrine Ihre Wahl, und bestellen Sie bei Ihrer Bedienung! Please make your selection at the display case and order it from your server.
Alle Preise sind Inklusivpreise und enthalten Bedienungsgeld und Mehrwertsteuer. All prices include service charge and sales tax.

Jule Neigel Band

das **Olympiastadion** Olympic stadium

Oly Disco

der **Einlaß** entry
der **Eintritt** admittance
m (= Meter) meter
das **Olympiazentrum** the name of a subway station
der **Studentenausweis** student I.D.
U3 (= U-Bahnlinie 3) the subway line 3

Staatstheater am Gärtnerplatz

das **Dach** roof
der **Fiedler** fiddler
der **Vorverkauf** advance ticket sale

Konen

die **Baumwolle** cotton
bügelfrei no-iron
ein- und zweireihig single and double-breasted
frech snazzy
das **Leinen** linen
das **Markenfabrikat** brand name
pflegeleicht easy care
rein pure
schmal trim
Single sleeveless shirt
das **Sonderangebot** special
der **Streifen** stripe
uni plain (one color)
die **Viskose** viscose
vorwiegend predominantly
weit roomy

Kapitel 9

Stellenangebote *or* Stellenanzeigen

ab sofort   beginning immediately
aufgeschlossen   outgoing
die **Ausbildung**   training
die **Aushilfe**   temporary job
die **Bewerbung**   application
der **Elektroinstallateur/in**   electrician
f. = für
der **Festfahrer**   permanent employee (driver)
das **Fotofachlabor**   photo lab
Fotolaborant/in   photo lab technician
die **Gräfin**   countess
jhr. (= -jährig)   year-old
der **Kundenbereich**   customer service
der **Lebenslauf**   a short biography in narrative form
od. = oder
der **Raum**   area
der **Schichtdienst**   shift work
der **Schnellkurs**   crash course
selbständig   independent
Sprachkenntnisse   proficiency in a foreign language
das **Stellenangebot**   job offer
su. = suchen
tätig zu werden   to work
tüchtig   capable and hard-working
u. = und *or* **unter**
Wunsch: auf Wunsch   as you wish (your choice)
Zeugnisse   references
Zuschr. (= Zuschriften)   replies
Zwillingsmädchen   twin girls

Kapitel 10

Occasion unique à Yverdon

Occasion unique à Yverdon *(French)*   Unique opportunity in Yverdon
A luxury villa, early 19th century, including adjoining property of 16,317 square meters, as well as a farm requiring renovation. Unmatched view overlooking Neuchatel and lake, two minutes by car from center of city.
For more information, write: 22-120-5843, Est Vaudois. 1820 Montreux.

Bootsgarage am Luganersee

der **Anteil**   share
der **Aufzug**   hoist
das **Außenbad**   outdoor pool
Cheminée *(French)*   fireplace
die **Einstellhalle**   parking garage

das **Hallenbad**   indoor pool
inkl. (= inklusive)   inclusive
der **Lift**   elevator
Luganersee   Lake Lugano
die **Pergola** *(Italian)*   arbor
die **Zahlung**   payment

Pian San Giacomo

For sale: Chalet, consisting of 1 apartment with large living room, fireplace, 3 bedrooms, bathroom, large terrace.
1 apartment with living room, bedroom, bathroom, wood storage, laundry room, electric heating.
Beautiful garden with granite table, parking space, serene and sunny, open view, completely furnished.
5 minutes from the S. Bernardino racetrack. 40 minute drive on the expressway N13 from Lugano or Locarno.
Price: 395,000 francs. Call during evening hours (091) 54 20 21

Kapitel 12

Heiraten/Bekanntschaften

die **Bekanntschaft**   acquaintance
Bildzuschr. (= Bildzuschriften)   picture included with replies
ca. (= circa)   approximately
cm (= Zentimeter)   centimeter
die **Erscheinung**   appearance
freundl. = freundlich
gebildet   educated, cultured
gemeinsam   joint, together
großzügig   generous
Handeln   acting
das **Herz**   heart
das **Hirn**   brain; *here:* brains *(colloq.)*, mind
Küchenhilfe   kitchen help
J. = Jahre
jugendl. (= jugendlich)   youthful
liebenswert   lovable, amiable
m. = mit
mögl. (= möglichst)   if at all possible
das **Niveau**   class
Nr. (= Nummer)   number
reiselustig   fond of travel
schlk. (= schlank)   slim, slender
schüchtern   shy
selbständig   independent
symp. (= sympathisch)   likeable
Tel.-Ang. (= Telefonangabe)   telephone
der **Tierliebhaber**   a person fond of animals

treu   loyal, faithful
u. = und *or* **unter**
unt. = unter
verbringen   to spend (time)
Verlieben: zum Verlieben   to fall in love with
verwitwet   widowed
Zuschr. (= Zuschriften)   replies

Schiller hätte geweint

die **Auskunft**   information
das **Bildungsangebot**   courses offered
die **Einschreibung**   registration
Freude: vor Freude weinen   to weep with joy
nutzen   to use
die **Volkshochschule**   adult education

SUPPLEMENTARY DIALOGUES

The following dialogues contain phrases that may be particularly useful to you if you ever have the opportunity to travel or live in a German-speaking country.

Was steht in der Zeitung?

THOMAS: Was steht Neues in der Zeitung?
ULF: Keine Ahnung. Mich interessieren nur die Anzeigen.
THOMAS: Was suchst du denn?
ULF: Einen Job und eine Wohnung.

What's in the newspaper?

What's new in the newspaper?
No idea. I'm only interested in the classifieds.

What are you looking for?
A job and an apartment.

Auf einer Party

FRAU SCHWARZ: Frau Schiller, darf ich bekannt machen? Herr Busch.
FRAU SCHILLER: Guten Tag, Herr Busch.
HERR BUSCH: Guten Tag, Frau Schiller.

At a party

Ms. Schiller, I'd like you to meet Mr. Busch.

How do you do, Mr. Busch?
How do you do, Ms. Schiller?

Auf Wohnungssuche

VOLKER: *(nimmt Hörer ab)* Volker Hornung.
MARTIN: Ja, guten Tag. Ich rufe wegen der Anzeige im Tagesblatt an. Ist das Zimmer noch frei?
VOLKER: Nein, es tut mir leid. Wir haben es gestern abend vermietet. Aber die Leute in der Wohnung unter uns haben auch ein Zimmer zu vermieten.
MARTIN: Wissen Sie, wie hoch die Miete ist?
VOLKER: Nein, da sprechen Sie besser mit den Leuten selbst. Ihre Telefonnummer ist 781 66 54. Die Leute heißen Grüning. Das Zimmer ist auf jeden Fall groß, und es hat einen Balkon.
MARTIN: Das hört sich ja toll an. Also, vielen Dank. Ich rufe bei Grünings jetzt gleich an. Auf Wiederhören.

Apartment hunting

(lifts the receiver) Volker Hornung.
Yes, hello. I'm calling about the advertisement in the daily newspaper. Is the room still available?
No, I'm afraid not. We rented it out yesterday evening. But the people in the apartment downstairs also have a room for rent.
Do you know how much the rent is?
No, you'd better speak to them about that. Their telephone number is 781 66 54. Their name is Grüning. In any case the room is large, and it has a balcony.

That sounds great. Well thanks very much. I'll call Grünings right away. Good-bye.

In der Tankstelle

KUNDE: Volltanken, bitte.
TANKWART: Super oder Normal?
KUNDE: Normal. Und kontrollieren Sie bitte Ölstand und Reifendruck.

At the service station

Fill it up, please.
Super or regular?
Regular. And please check the oil and tires.

Auf der Post

KUNDIN: Ich möchte diesen Brief per Luftpost schicken.
BEAMTER: Nach Amerika? Bis 5 Gramm kostet er DM 2.
KUNDIN: Geben Sie mir bitte 5 Briefmarken zu 20 Pfennig und 5 zu 80 Pfennig. Kann ich dieses Paket hier aufgeben?
BEAMTER: Nein, die Paketannahme ist am Schalter nebenan.

Auf der Bank

KUNDE: Ich möchte gern Reiseschecks einlösen, Dollarschecks.
ANGESTELLTE: Bitte schön. Wieviel möchten Sie wechseln?
KUNDE: Fünfzig. Wie steht der Dollar heute?
ANGESTELLTE: Der Kurs für Reiseschecks ist 1,50 (eins fünfzig). Das sind also 75 Mark minus 3 Mark Gebühren.

Im Kaufhaus

KUNDIN: Darf ich bitte diese Jacke anprobieren?
VERKÄUFERIN: Selbstverständlich … Das Blau steht Ihnen gut, wirklich.
KUNDIN: Leider ist sie etwas zu eng.
VERKÄUFERIN: Hier habe ich die gleiche Jacke eine Nummer größer. Die müßte Ihnen passen.

Im Café

1. DAME: Sind diese zwei Plätze noch frei?
GAST: Ja, bitte.
OBER: Was wünschen die Damen?
2. DAME: Was können Sie uns denn empfehlen?
OBER: Der Apfelstrudel ist ausgezeichnet.
1. DAME: Zwei Stück bitte. Mit Sahne. Und zwei Kännchen Kaffee.
OBER: Aber gern.

Bei der Ärztin

PATIENT: Frau Doktor, ich habe immer solche Rückenschmerzen.
ÄRZTIN: Wie lange haben Sie die Schmerzen denn schon?
PATIENT: Seit zwei Wochen.
ÄRZTIN: Zeigen Sie mir mal genau, wo es weh tut.

At the post office

I'd like to send this letter air mail.

To America? The cost is 2 marks for up to 5 grams.
Please give me five 20-Pfennig stamps and five 80-Pfennig ones. Can I mail this package here?

No, the package window is the next one over.

At the bank

I'd like to cash some traveler's checks, dollar checks.

Fine. How much would you like to change?

Fifty dollars' worth. What's the exchange rate today?
The rate for traveler's checks is 1,50 (one fifty). So that comes to 75 marks, minus a 3 mark fee.

In the department store

May I please try on this jacket?
Of course . . . Blue looks good on you, really.

I'm afraid it's somewhat too tight.
Here, I have the same jacket a size larger. It should fit you.

In the café

Are these two seats free?
Yes, please sit down.
What would you like, ladies?
What would you recommend?
The apple strudel is excellent.
Two pieces, please. With whipped cream. And two pots of coffee.
Certainly.

At the doctor's

Doctor, my back aches all the time.

How long have you had the pain?

Two weeks.
Show me exactly where it hurts.

Im Hotel

TOURISTIN: Haben Sie noch ein Einzelzimmer frei?
EMPFANGSCHEFIN: Ja. Wir haben eins mit Dusche (im sechsten Stock).
TOURISTIN: Wieviel kostet es?
EMPFANGSCHEFIN: Hundert Mark. Mit Frühstück, natürlich.
TOURISTIN: Schön. Ich nehme es für eine Nacht.
EMPFANGSCHEFIN: Bitte sehr. Tragen Sie sich hier ein, bitte. Hier ist der Schlüssel.

In the hotel

Do you still have a single room available?
Yes. We have one with a shower (on the sixth floor).

How much is it?
One hundred marks. Breakfast is included, of course.

Fine. I'll take it for one night.
Fine. Please register here. Here's the key.

An der Theaterkasse

STUDENT: Ich möchte gern zwei Karten für den ersten Rang, für heute abend.
ANGESTELLTE: Tut mir leid. Ich habe nur noch Karten fürs Parkett.
STUDENT: Wie teuer sind die Karten? Ich habe einen Studentenausweis.
ANGESTELLTE: Dann bekommen Sie Ihre Karten fünfzig Prozent billiger.

At the theater box office

I'd like two tickets in the first balcony for this evening.
I'm sorry. I only have orchestra tickets left.

How much are the tickets? I have a student I.D.

Then you get a fifty percent discount.

Am Flughafen

FLUGGAST: Fliegt die Maschine direkt nach Istanbul?
ANGESTELLTER: Nein, sie macht eine Zwischenlandung in Athen. Möchten Sie Raucher oder Nichtraucher?
FLUGGAST: Nichtraucher, bitte.
ANGESTELLTER: Gang- oder Fensterplatz?
FLUGGAST: Ich hätte gern einen Fensterplatz.

At the airport

Does the plane go directly to Istanbul?
No, it makes a stop in Athens. Would you like smoking or non-smoking?

Non-smoking, please.
Aisle or window seat?
I would like a window seat.

Im Flugzeug

FLUGBEGLEITER: Wir bitten Sie, sich jetzt anzuschnallen und die Rückenlehnen senkrecht zu stellen.

In the airplane

Please fasten your seat belts and place your seat backs in the upright position.

Bei der Zugauskunft

TOURIST: Können Sie mir sagen, wann der nächste Zug nach München fährt?
BEAMTIN: Um 14 Uhr 20 fährt ein Intercity ab.

At the railway station information desk

Can you tell me when the next train leaves for Munich?
An Intercity-train leaves at 2:20 P.M.

Am Fahrkartenschalter

REISENDER: Einmal erster Klasse München, bitte.
BEAMTER: Hin und zurück oder einfach?
REISENDER: Einfach, bitte. Von welchem Bahnsteig fährt mein Zug ab?
BEAMTER: Gleis elf.

At the ticket window

One ticket to Munich, please. First class.
Round trip or one-way?
One-way, please. From which platform does my train leave?
Track eleven.

Im Zug

REISENDE: Warten Sie. Ich hebe den Koffer ins Gepäcknetz. *(Schaffnerin macht die Tür auf.)*

SCHAFFNERIN: (Ist) hier noch jemand zugestiegen? *(Reisende reicht ihr die Fahrkarte.)*

SCHAFFNERIN: Sie müssen in München umsteigen. Der Anschlußzug wartet auf Gleis 7.

REISENDE: Können Sie mir sagen, wo der Speisewagen ist?

SCHAFFNERIN: Ja, in der Mitte des Zuges.

In the train

Just a minute, I'll put the suitcase up on the rack. *(The conductor opens the door.)*

Has anyone here just gotten on? *(Passenger hands her the ticket.)*

You have to change trains in Munich. The connecting train will be waiting on Track 7.

Can you tell me where the dining car is?

Yes, in the middle of the train.

This vocabulary includes all the words used in *Deutsch heute* except numbers. The definitions given are generally limited to the context in which the words are used in this book. Chapter numbers are given for all words and expressions occurring in the chapter vocabularies and in the *Erweiterung des Wortschatzes* sections to indicate where a word or expression is first used. Recognition vocabulary does not have a chapter reference. The symbol ~ indicates repetition of the key word (minus the definite article, if any).

Nouns are listed with their plural forms: **der Abend, -e.** No plural entry is given if the plural is rarely used or nonexistent. If two entries follow a noun, the first one indicates the genitive and the second one indicates the plural: **der Herr, -n, -en.**

Strong and irregular weak verbs are listed with their principal parts. Vowel changes in the present tense are noted in parentheses, followed by simple-past and past-participle forms. All verbs take **haben** in the past participle unless indicated with **sein.** For example: **fahren (ä), fuhr, ist gefahren.** Separable-prefix verbs are indicated with a raised dot: **auf·stehen.**

Adjectives and adverbs that require an umlaut in the comparative and superlative forms are noted as follows: **warm (ä).** Stress marks are given for all words that are not accented on the first syllable. The stress mark follows the accented syllable: **Amerika'ner.** In some words, either of the two syllables may be stressed.

The following abbreviations are used:

abbr.	abbreviation	*dat.*	dative	*p.p.*	past participle
acc.	accusative	*decl.*	declined	*part.*	participle
adj.	adjective	*f.*	feminine	*pl.*	plural
adv.	adverb	*fam.*	familiar	*sg.*	singular
colloq.	colloquial	*gen.*	genitive	*subj.*	subjunctive
comp.	comparative	*m.*	masculine	*sup.*	superlative
conj.	conjunction	*n.*	neuter		

ab (*prep. + dat.*) after, from a certain point on; away; ~ **heute** from today on; ~ **und zu** now and then

ab·bauen to reduce

der Abend, -e evening 2; **Guten ~.** Good evening. 2; **zu ~ essen** to have (eat) dinner/supper 7

abend: gestern ~ last night 7; **heute ~** tonight, this evening 7

das Abendessen, - dinner, supper 4; **zum ~** for dinner 4; **Was gibt's zum ~?** What's for dinner? 4

abends evenings, in the evening 4

aber (*conj.*) but 2

ab·fahren (fährt ab), fuhr ab, ist abgefahren to depart (by vehicle) 8

die Abfahrt, -en departure

die Abfindung, -en severance pay

die Abgase (*pl.*) exhaust fumes

ab·holen to pick up 6

das Abitur' diploma from college-track high school (Gymnasium) 5

der Absatz, -e paragraph

absolut' absolutely, completely 11

ab·trocknen to dry dishes; to wipe dry 8

ab·waschen (wäscht ab), wusch ab, abgewaschen to do dishes 8

ach oh 1

Achtung! (*exclamation*) Pay attention!; Look out!

die Adres'se, -n address 1; **Wie ist deine/Ihre ~?** What is your address? 1

das Aero'bic aerobics 2; ~ **machen** to do aerobics 2

ähnlich similar 10

die Ahnung, -en hunch, idea 7; **Keine ~!** No idea! 7

akade'misch academic; **akademischer Beruf** profession requiring university education

alle all 5

allein' alone 6

allein'stehend single

allem: vor ~ above all 6

alles everything 3; all 4

allgemein general; **im allgemeinen** in general

die Alliier'ten (*pl.*) Allies (WW II)

der Alltag everyday life

die Alpen (*pl.*) Alps 6

als (*after a comp.*) than 3; as 6; (*conj.*) when 11

also well 1; therefore, so 3

alt (ä) old 1; **Wie ~ bist du/sind Sie?** How old are you? 1; **Ich**

bin [19] Jahre ~.   I'm [19] years old. 1

das **Alter**   age

das **Altglas**   old glass

am: ~ Freitag/Montag   on Friday/Monday 1

(das) **Ame'rika**   America 3

der **Amerika'ner, -/**die **Amerika'nerin, -nen** American person 3

amerika'nisch   American (*adj.*) 5

die **Amtssprache, -n**   official language

an (*+ acc./dat.*)   at; to 5; on 8

andere   other 3

anders   different(ly) 3

der **Anfang, ⸚e**   beginning

an·fangen (fängt an), fing an, angefangen   to begin 11; **mit [der Arbeit] ~**   to begin [the work]

an·geben (gibt an), gab an, angegeben   to give; name, cite

der/die **Angestellte** (*noun decl. like adj.*)   salaried employee, white-collar worker 12

die **Angli'stik**   English studies (language and literature) 5

die **Angst, ⸚e**   fear; **~ haben (vor +** *dat.*)   to be afraid (of) 8

an·kommen, kam an, ist angekommen (in + *dat.*)   to arrive (in) 8

die **Ankunft, ⸚e**   arrival

an·rufen, rief an, angerufen   to phone 7; **bei [dir] ~**   to call [you] at home 7

(sich) (*dat.*) **an·sehen (sieht an), sah an, angesehen**   to look at; **Ich sehe es mir an.**   I'm having a look at it. 13

(an)statt' (*+ gen.*)   instead of 9

die **Antwort, -en**   answer 7

antworten (*+ dat.*)   to answer (*as in* **Ich antworte der Frau.** I answer the woman.); **antworten auf** (*+ acc.*)   to answer (*as in* **Ich antworte auf die Frage.** I answer the question.) 12

die **Anzeige, -n**   announcement; ad 12

sich (*acc.*) **an·ziehen, zog an, angezogen**   to get dressed; **Ich ziehe mich an.**   I get dressed

10; **sich** (*dat.*) **an·ziehen**   to put on 10; **Ich ziehe [mir die Schuhe] an.**   I put on [my shoes]. 10

der **Anzug, ⸚e**   man's suit 7

der **Apfel, ⸚**   apple 4

der **Apfelsaft**   apple juice 4

die **Apothe'ke, -n**   pharmacy 4; **in die ~**   to the pharmacy 4

apothe'kenpflichtig   by prescription (drugs) only

der **Apothe'ker, -/**die **Apothe'kerin, -nen**   pharmacist

der **Apparat', -e**   apparatus, appliance 10

der **Appetit'**   appetite; **Guten ~!**   Enjoy your meal.

der **April'**   April 3

das **Äquivalent', -e**   equivalent; **äquivalent** (*adj.*)   equivalent

die **Arbeit**   work; die **Arbeit, -en** (school or academic) paper; piece of work 5

arbeiten   to work; to study 2; **am Computer ~**   to work at the computer 7; **bei einer [Firma] ~** to work at a [company] 9; **mit dem Computer ~**   to do work on a computer 9; **mit Wortprozessoren ~**   to do word processing 9

der **Arbeiter, -/**die **Arbeiterin, -nen**   worker 13

der **Arbeitgeber, -/**die **Arbeitgeberin, -nen**   employer

der **Arbeitnehmer, -/**die **Arbeitnehmerin, -nen**   employee, worker 13

das **Arbeitsamt**   government employment office

die **Arbeitsgruppe, -n**   study group

arbeitslos   unemployed, out of work 12

der **Arbeitsplatz, ⸚e**   job, position; workplace 9

die **Arbeitssuche**   job search

der **Architekt', -en, -en/**die **Architek'tin, -nen**   architect 9

die **Architektur'**   architecture

argumentie'ren   to argue

der **Arm, -e**   arm 10

die **Armbanduhr, -en**   wristwatch

die **Art, -en**   type, kind; manner;

auf diese ~ und Weise   in this way

der **Arti'kel, -**   article 5

der **Arzt, ⸚e/**die **Ärztin, -nen** (medical) doctor, physician 7

das **Aspirin'**   aspirin 4

der **Asylant', -en, -en/**die **Asylan'tin, -nen**   refugee

der **Asyl'bewerber, -/**die **Asyl'bewerberin, -nen**   applicant for asylum

das **Asyl'bewerberheim**   home for people seeking political refuge

das **Asyl'gesetz, -e**   law governing refugees

at'men   to breathe 14

auch   also 2

auf (*+ acc./dat.*)   on top of; to; on 8; **~ dem Weg**   on the way 4; **~ den Markt**   to the market 4; **~ [deutsch]**   in [German] 10; **~ Wiedersehen.**   Good-bye.

der **Aufenthalt, -e**   stay

die **Aufgabe, -n**   assignment; task, set of duties 9; die **Hausaufgaben** (*pl.*)   homework 9; **Hausaufgaben machen**   to do homework 11

auf·geben (gibt auf), gab auf, aufgegeben   to give up 9

auf·hören   to stop (an activity) 7

auf·listen   to list

auf·machen   to open 13

auf·nehmen (nimmt auf), nahm auf, aufgenommen   to accept

auf·passen   to watch out 9; **~ auf** (*+ acc.*)   to take care of 9

auf·räumen   to straighten up (a room) 8

auf·schreiben, schrieb auf, aufgeschrieben   to write down 11

auf·stehen, stand auf, ist aufgestanden   to get up; to stand up 7

auf·teilen (in + *acc.*)   to split up (into) 11

die **Aufteilung, -en**   division

auf·wachsen (wächst auf), wuchs auf, ist aufgewachsen   to grow up

das **Auge, -n**   eye 10

der **August'**   August 3

aus (*+ dat.*)   out of 6; to come/be

from (be a native of) 4; **Ich komme ~ [Kanada].** I come from [Canada]. 3

die **Ausbildung** training, education

der **Ausdruck, ⁻e** expression

auseinan'der apart, away from each other

aus·gehen, ging aus, ist ausgegangen to go out 7

ausgenommen except for

ausgesprochen really, very, exceptionally

das **Ausland** (*no pl.*) foreign countries 8; **im ~** abroad 8

der **Ausländer, -/die Ausländerin, -nen** foreigner 5

die **Ausländerfeindlichkeit** hostility toward foreigners

der **Ausländerhaß** xenophobia 13

ausländisch foreign 6

aus·machen to matter; **Es macht [mir] nichts aus.** It doesn't matter to [me]. 12

die **Ausnahme, -n** exception

aus·sehen (sieht aus), sah aus, ausgesehen to appear, look like, seem 7

der **Außenhandel** foreign trade 12

außer (+ *dat.*) besides, except for 6

außerdem besides, in addition, as well 7

der **Aussiedler, -/die Aussiedlerin, -nen** emigrant

der **Austauschstudent, -en, -en/ die Austauschstudentin, -nen** exchange student

aus·wandern, ist ausgewandert to emigrate

der **Ausweis, -e** identification card

sich (*acc.*) **aus·ziehen, zog aus, ausgezogen** to get undressed; **Ich ziehe mich aus.** I get undressed. 10; **sich** (*dat.*) **aus·ziehen** to take off; **Ich ziehe [mir die Schuhe] aus.** I take off [my shoes]. 10

der/die **Auszubildende** (*noun decl. like adj.*) trainee, apprentice

das **Auto, -s** automobile, car 6

die **Autobahn, -en** freeway, expressway 8

der **Autor,** *pl.* **Auto'ren/die Auto'rin, -nen** author

die **Autorate, -n** car payment

der **Bäcker, -/die Bäckerin, -nen** baker 4; **beim ~** at the baker's/bakery 4; **zum ~** to the baker's/bakery 4

die **Bäckerei, -en** bakery 4

das **Bad, ⁻er** bath; bathroom 8

der **Badeanzug, ⁻e** swimming suit 7

die **Badehose, -n** swimming trunks 7

baden to bathe 10; to swim

das **Badezimmer, -** bathroom

das **BAföG (= das Bundesausbildungsförderungsgesetz)** national law that mandates financial support for students

die **Bahn, -en** train; railroad 6

der **Bahnhof, ⁻e** train station 8

bald soon 3

die **Bana'ne, -n** banana 4

die **Band, -s** band (musical) 7

die **Bank, ⁻e** bench

die **Bank, -en** bank 9

die **Banknote, -n** bank note, bill

die **Bar, -s** bar, pub, nightclub 11

die **Barock'architektur** baroque architecture

der **Basketball** basketball 2

der **Bau** construction

der **Bauch,** *pl.* **Bäuche** abdomen 10

bauen to build 11

der **Bauer, -n, -n/die Bäuerin, -nen** farmer

der **Baum, ⁻e** tree 14

der **Baustein, -e** building block

der **Beamte** (*noun decl. like adj.*)/die **Beamtin, -nen** official, civil servant

beant'worten to answer (a question, a letter) 7

bedeu'ten to mean 9; **Was bedeutet das?** What does that mean?

die **Bedeu'tung, -en** significance; meaning

die **Bedie'nung** service (in a restaurant)

beein'flussen to influence 3

begin'nen, begann, begonnen to begin 10; **mit [der Arbeit] ~** to begin [(the) work]

behaup'ten to claim

der/die **Behin'derte** (*noun decl. like adj.*) handicapped person

bei (+ *dat.*) at 4; near, in the proximity of 6; while, during (*indicates a situation*); **~ der Uni** near the university 6; **~ [dir]** at [your] place/house/home 6; **~ [Ingrid]** at [Ingrid's] 4; **beim Bäcker** at the baker's/bakery 4; **beim Fernsehen** while watching TV; **~ [mir] vorbeikommen** to stop by [my] place 6; **~ uns** at our house; in our country

beibehalten to retain

beide both 8

das **Bein, -e** leg 10

das **Beispiel, -e** example; **zum Beispiel** (*abbrev.* **z.B.**) for example 3

bekannt' known, famous; **Das ist mir ~.** I'm familiar with that.

der/die **Bekann'te** (*noun declined like adj.*) acquaintance 10

bekom'men, bekam, bekommen to receive 4; **Kinder ~** to have children

bemer'ken to notice; to remark

die **Bemer'kung, -en** remark; observation

benut'zen to use 8

beob'achten to observe 8

bequem' comfortable

der **Bera'tungstermin, -e** consultation appointment

der **Berg, -e** mountain 6; **in die Berge fahren** to go to the mountains 6

berich'ten to report 11

der **Beruf', -e** profession, occupation 9

beruf'lich career related; professional

berufs'tätig working 9

die **Berufs'wahl** choice of profession

berühmt' famous 9

beschäf'tigen to occupy, keep busy 12; **sich beschäftigen (mit)** to be occupied (with) 12; **beschäftigt sein** to be busy 12

beschrei'ben, beschrieb, beschrieben to describe 9

beset'zen to occupy

der **Besit'zer, -/die Besit'zerin, -nen** owner

beson′ders especially, particularly 4

besprech′en (i), besprach, be-sprochen to discuss

besser (*comp. of* gut) better 4

(die) Besserung: Ich wünsche dir gute ~. I wish you a speedy recovery./Get well soon.

best- (-er, -es, -e) best 9

das Besteck′, -e a setting of knife, fork, and spoon; flatware 14

besteh′en to exist; ~ aus to consist of

bestel′len to order

bestimmt′ certain(ly), for sure 3

der Besuch′, -e visit 4; ~ haben to have company 4; zu ~ for a visit 6

besu′chen to visit 7; to attend (e.g., a seminar) 7

der Besu′cher, -/die Besu′cherin, -nen visitor

betref′fen (i), betraf, betroffen to deal with, concern

das Bett, -en bed 1; zu (ins) ~ gehen to go to bed

die Bevöl′kerung, -en population

die Bewe′gung, -en movement; progress

die Bewer′bung, -en application

das Bewußt′sein consciousness, awareness 14

bezah′len to pay (for) 4; das Essen ~ to pay for the meal 4

die Bibliothek′, -en library 2; in der ~ in/at the library 2

das Bier, -e beer 4

der Biergarten, ⸚ beer garden 8

das Bild, -er picture; photograph 1; image

die Bildung education; die Bildungskosten (*pl.*) education costs

billig cheap 4

bin am 1

die Biographie′, -n biography 5

die Biologie′ biology 5

bis (+ *acc.*) until, til 2; ~ auf (+ *acc.*) except for 14; ~ dann. See you then. 2

bißchen: ein ~ a little 2

bitte (*after* danke) You're welcome. 1; please 4; ~? May I help you? 1; ~ schön. You're

welcome.; ~ sehr. (*said when handing someone something*) Here you are.; Wie ~? (I beg your) pardon? 1

bitten, bat, gebeten (um + *acc.*) to request, ask (for) something

blaß pale 10

blau blue 1

bleiben, blieb, ist geblieben to stay, to remain 3

der Bleistift, -e pencil 1

der Blick, -e view

blond blond 10

bloß mere(ly), only

die Blume, -n flower 4

der Blumenmarkt, ⸚e flower market

die Bluse, -n blouse 7

der Boden, ⸚ floor 8; ground

der Bodensee Lake Constance

borgen to borrow 5

böse (auf + *acc.*) angry (at) 8; bad, mean; Sei [mir] nicht ~. Don't be mad at [me]. 8

brauchbar usable; Brauchbares something usable

brauchen to need 4

braun brown 1

der Brief, -e letter 10

der Brieffreund, -e/die Brief-freundin, -nen pen pal 10

der Briefträger, -/die Briefträ-gerin, -nen letter carrier

die Brille, -n eyeglasses 7; Tragen Sie eine ~? Do you wear glasses? 7

bringen, brachte, gebracht to bring 5

buchstabie′ren to spell

das Brot, -e bread; sandwich 4

das Brötchen, - bread roll 4

die Brücke, -n bridge 11

der Bruder, ⸚ brother 5

das Buch, ⸚er book 1

das Bücherregal, -e bookcase 1

die Büchertasche, -n book bag 1

die Buchhaltung bookkeeping

die Buchhandlung, -en bookstore 4

das Bühnenbild stage set, scenery

das Bundesland, ⸚er federal state

die Bundesrepublik Deutschland (BRD) Federal Republic of Germany (FRG) (*the official name of Germany*) 11

der Bundesstaat, -en federal state (in the U.S.A.)

der Bundestag lower house of the German parliament

der Bürger, -/die Bürgerin, -nen citizen

die Bürgerinitiative, -n citizens' action group

das Büro′, -s office 6

der Bus, -se bus 6

die Butter butter 4

bzw. (= beziehungsweise) or; respectively

das Café, -s café 6

der CD-Spieler, - (*also der* CD-Player, -) CD player 1

das Chaos chaos

der Chef, -s/die Chefin, -nen boss 9

die Chemie′ chemistry 5

(das) China China

circa (*abbr.* ca.) approximately

die Cola, -s cola drink 7

die Comics (*pl.*) comics 12

der Compu′ter, - computer 1; am ~ arbeiten to work at the computer 7; mit dem ~ arbeiten to do work on the computer 9

das Compu′terspiel, -e computer game 2

der Couchtisch, -e coffee table 8

der Cousin′, -s cousin (*m.*) (*pronounced* kuzě′)

da there 1; (*conj.*) since, because 10

dabei′ and yet; with it

dage′gen against it; on the other hand

daher therefore, for that reason 5

die Dame, -n lady

danach′ after it; afterwards 11

der Dank thanks 6; Vielen ~. Many thanks. 6

danke Thanks. 1; ~ sehr. Thank you very much.

danken (+ *dat.*) to thank

dann then 1; Bis ~. See you then. 2

das the (*n.*); that 1

daß (*conj.*) that 6

das **Datum,** *pl.* **Daten** date
dauern to last; to require time 12
dazu' to it, to that; in addition 14
decken to cover 8; **den Tisch ~** to set the table 8
dein your *(fam. sg.)* 1
die **Demonstration', -en** demonstration 11
demonstrie'ren to demonstrate 13
denen *(dat. pl. of demonstrative and relative pronoun)* them; which 13
denken, dachte, gedacht to think, believe 3; **~ an** (+ *acc.*) to think of/about 8
denn *(conj.)* because, for 6; *(flavoring particle adding emphasis to questions)* 4
die **Depression', -en** depression
deprimiert' depressed
der the *(m.)* 1
deshalb therefore, for that reason 5
das **Dessert', -s** dessert
deswegen therefore, for this reason 10
deutsch German *(adj.)* 3
(das) **Deutsch** German class 1; German (language) 2; **~ machen** to do German (homework) 2; **auf deutsch** in German 10
der/die **Deutsche** *(noun declined like adj.)* German person 3
die **Deutsche Demokra'tische Republik' (DDR)** German Democratic Republic (GDR)
(das) **Deutschland** Germany 3
der **Dezem'ber** December 3
der **Dialekt', -e** dialect 10
der **Dichter, -**/die **Dichterin, -nen** poet
dick fat 10; thick
die the *(f.)* 1
der **Dieb, -e**/die **Diebin, -nen** thief
die **Diele, -n** entrance hall
der **Dienstag** Tuesday 1
dies (-er, -es, -e) this, these 5
diesmal this time 12
das **Ding, -e** thing 12
dir *(dat.)* (to or for) you 6; **Und ~?** And you? (How about you?) *(as part of response to* **Wie geht's?***)* 2
die **Disco, -s** dance club 7
die **Disket'te, -n** disk, diskette 5

die **Diskussion', -en** discussion; debate
diskutie'ren to discuss
doch *(flavoring particle)* really; after all, indeed 4; Yes, of course; on the contrary *(response to negative statement or question)* 4; but still, yet 9; **Geh ~ zum ...** Well then, go to . . . 4
die **Donau** Danube
der **Donnerstag** Thursday 1
die **Doppelrolle, -n** double role
doppelt double, doubly
dort there 4
dorthin' (to) there
die **Dose, -n** can, tin; box 14
der **Dozent', -en, -en**/die **Dozen'tin, -nen** lecturer at a university
dran: ich bin ~ it's my turn 12
draußen outside 8
dritt- (-er, -es, -e) third 9
die **Drogerie', -n** drugstore 4
der **Drogerie'markt, ¨e** self-service drugstore
der **Drogist', -en, -en**/die **Drogi'stin, -nen** druggist
du you *(fam. sg.)* 1; **~!** Hey! 4; **~ meine Güte!** My heavens! 8
dumm (ü) dumb, stupid
dunkel dark 10
dünn thin 10
durch (+ *acc.*) through 4; divided by 1; by (means of which) 14
durch·arbeiten to work through; to study 5
durch·sehen (sieht durch), sah durch, durchgesehen to look through; to glance over; to examine 12
dürfen (darf), durfte, gedurft to be permitted, be allowed to; may 5
der **Durst** thirst 7; **~ haben** to be thirsty 7
(sich) duschen to shower 10
duzen to address someone with the familiar **du**-form

eben just, simply 7; even, smooth; *(flavoring particle) used to support a previous statement, express agreement; made as a final statement it implies the*

speaker has no desire to discuss a point further
ebenso likewise
echt genuine; **~?** *(slang)* Really?
die **Ecke, -n** corner 8
die **Ehefrau, -en** wife
ehemalig former
der **Ehemann, ¨er** husband
das **Ei, -er** egg 4; **Rühr~** scrambled egg; **Spiegel~** fried egg; **weichgekochtes ~** soft-boiled egg
die **Eidgenossenschaft, -en** confederation
eigen own 11
eigentlich actually 8
das **Eigentum** property
der **Eigentümer, -**/die **Eigentümerin, -nen** owner
die **Eigentumswohnung, -en** condominium
ein(e) a, an 2
einan'der one another, each other 8; **mit~** with each other 8
eindeutig unambiguous
der **Eindruck, ¨e** impression
einfach simple; simply 7
das **Einfami'lienhaus, ¨er** single-family house
der **Einfluß,** *pl.* **Einflüsse** influence
die **Einheit** unity; **Der Tag der deutschen Einheit** The Day of German Unity *(celebrated on October 3)*
einige some, several 6
der **Einigungsvertrag** Unification Treaty
ein·kaufen to shop 4; **~ gehen** to go shopping 4
die **Einkaufsstraße, -n** shopping street
die **Einkaufstasche, -n** shopping bag 4
das **Einkommen, -** income
ein·laden (lädt ein), lud ein, eingeladen to invite; to treat 7
einmal once, one time 6; **noch ~** again, once more 13
das **Einsatzgebiet, -e** area of application
die **Einwegflasche, -n** non-returnable bottle 14
der **Einwohner, -**/die **Einwohnerin, -nen** inhabitant 3

einzeln single, singly, individual(ly)

einzig- (-er, -es, -e) only, sole 13

das Eis ice cream

die Eisenbahn, -en railroad

eisern iron; **der Eiserne Vorhang** Iron Curtain

der Elch, -e moose

elegant' elegant

die Eltern (*pl.*) parents 5

der Empfangs'chef, -s/die Emp-fangs'chefin, -nen hotel receptionist

empfeh'len (ie), empfahl, emp-fohlen to recommend 11

das Ende, -n end, conclusion 5; **am ~** (in) the end 5; **zu ~** over, finished 11

endgültig final; definite

endlich finally 8

die Energie' energy 14

(das) Englisch English (language) 2; **auf englisch** in English

der Enkel, -/die Enkelin, -nen grandson/granddaughter

das Enkelkind, -er grandchild

entde'cken to discover

(sich) entschul'digen to excuse (oneself); **Entschuldigen Sie!** Excuse me!

die Entschul'digung, -en apology

die Entsor'gung (waste) disposal

die Entspan'nung, -en relaxation; **zur ~** for relaxation

entste'hen, entstand, ist ent-standen to come about

die Entwick'lung, -en development

er he, it 1

das Erd'geschoß the ground floor of a building

das Ereig'nis, -se occasion, event

die Erfah'rung, -en experience 9

erfin'den, erfand, erfunden to invent

der Erfolg', -e success

erfolg'reich successful

ergän'zen to complete

das Ergeb'nis, -se result

sich erin'nern (an + *acc.*) to re-member 11

sich erkäl'ten to catch a cold 10; **erkältet: ich bin ~** I have a cold 10

die Erkäl'tung, -en cold (illness)

10; **Was macht deine ~?** How's your cold? 10

erklä'ren to explain 4

erlau'ben (+ *dat. with persons*) to permit, allow

ernst serious 2

errei'chen to reach, achieve

erschei'nen, erschien, ist er-schienen to appear, seem

erst (*adv.*) not until, only, just 10; (*adj.*) first 10; **~ einmal** first of all

erstaunt' to be astonished, astounded

erstens first of all

der/die Erwach'sene (*noun decl. like adj.*) adult 13

erwar'ten to expect 9

die Erwei'terung, -en expansion, extension

erzäh'len (über + *acc.*/von) to tell (about) 2

der Erzie'hungsurlaub leave of absence for child rearing

es it 1; **~ gibt** (+ *acc.*) there is, there are 4

die Eßecke, -n dining area

das Essen, - meal; prepared food 4

essen (ißt), aß, gegessen to eat 4; **zu Abend ~** to have (eat) dinner 7

das Eßzimmer, - dining room 8

das Etikett', -e label

etwa approximately, about 3

etwas something 4; some, some-what 4; **noch ~** something else (in addition) 4

euch: bei ~ in your country

euer your (*pl. fam.*) 3

(das) Euro'pa Europe 3

die Europä'ische Union' European Union

ewig forever, eternally 7

das Exa'men, - comprehensive exam, finals 5; **~ machen** to graduate from the university 5

die Fabrik', -en factory 14

das Fach, ⸚er (academic) subject; field 5

der Fachbereich, -e subject area

das Fachgeschäft, -e specialty shop

das Fachwerkhaus, -häuser half-timbered house

fahren (ä), fuhr, ist gefahren to drive; to travel 6; **mit [dem Auto] ~** to go by [car] 6

der Fahrplan, ⸚e train schedule

das Fahrrad, ⸚er bicycle 6

der Fahrradweg, -e bicycle path

die Fahrschule, -n driving school

das Fahrverbot driving ban

der Fall, ⸚e case, situation; fall, demise 11

fallen (ä), fiel, ist gefallen to fall 11

falsch wrong, false 10

falten to fold

die Fami'lie, -n family 5

der Fan, -s fan; supporter (sports) 13

fänden (*subj. of finden*) would find

die Farbe, -n color 1; **Welche ~ hat ... ?** What color is . . .? 1

fast almost 8

faul lazy 2

faulenzen to lounge around, be idle 7

der Februar February 3

feiern to celebrate 7

der Feiertag, -e holiday

das Fenster, - window 1

die Ferien (*pl.*) vacation 5; **in den ~** on/during vacation 5; **in die ~ gehen/fahren** to go on vacation; **Seme'sterferien** semester break 5

die Ferienreise, -n vacation trip 8

der Fernsehbericht, -e TV report

das Fernsehen television (the in-dustry) 5

fern·sehen (sieht fern), sah fern, ferngesehen to watch TV 5

der Fernseher, - television set 1

die Fernsehsendung, -en televi-sion program 11

fertig finished 5; ready

fest firm(ly)

das Fest, -e party; celebration; feast; **auf dem ~** at the party; **ein ~ geben** to give a party 8

die Feststimmung festive atmos-phere

das Fieber fever 10

der Film, -e film 5

der Filmregisseur, -e/die Film-regisseurin, -nen movie director

finden, fand, gefunden to find 3;

to think, find 3; **Sie finden die Brötchen gut.** They like the rolls. 4; **Wie findest du das?** What do you think of that? 4

der **Finger, -** finger 10

die **Firma,** *pl.* **Firmen** company 6; **bei einer ~ arbeiten** to work for a company 9

der **Fisch, -e** fish 4

der **Fischmann, ⁝er**/die **Fischfrau, -en** fishmonger 4

fit fit

das **Fitneßtraining** fitness training

die **Flasche, -n** bottle; **eine ~ Mineralwasser** a bottle of mineral water 8

das **Fleisch** meat 4

fleißig industrious, hard-working 2

fliegen, flog, ist geflogen to fly 6

der **Flug, ⁝e** flight

der **Flugbegleiter, -**/die **Flugbeglei-terin, -nen** flight attendant

der **Flughafen, ⁝** airport

das **Flugzeug, -e** airplane 6

der **Flur, -e** entrance hall, hallway

der **Fluß,** *pl.* **Flüsse** river 14

folgen, ist gefolgt (+ *dat.*) to follow

folgend following

die **Forschung** research

der **Fotograf', -en, -en**/die **Foto-gra'fin, -nen** photographer

die **Fotografie', -n** photograph; photography

fotografie'ren to photograph 7

die **Frage, -n** question 2; **eine ~ stellen** to ask a question; **eine ~ an** (+ *acc.*) **stellen** to ask someone a question; **Sie stellt eine Frage an ihn.** She asks him a question.; *also* **eine ~** (+ *dat.*) **stellen** to ask someone a question; **Sie stellt ihm eine Frage.** She asks him a question. 10

fragen to ask, to question 4

fraglich questionable

der **Franken** frank; **Schweizer Franken (sFr.)** Swiss unit of currency

(das) **Frankreich** France

der **Franzo'se, -n, -n**/die **Franzö-sin, -nen** French person

franzö'sisch French (*adj.*)

(das) **Franzö'sisch** French (language)

die **Frau, -en** woman; wife 1; **Frau ...** Mrs. . . . ; Ms. . . . *(term of address for all adult women)* 1

die **Frauenpolitik** federal policy concerning women

frei free 5; **~ haben** to be off work 7; **~ sein** to be un-occupied 7

die **Freiheit, -en** freedom 9

der **Freitag** Friday 1

die **Freizeit** free time 7

die **Freizeitbeschäftigung, -en** leisure activity

fremd foreign; strange 13; **das ist mir ~** (*dat.*) that is strange to me 13

der **Fremdarbeiter, -**/die **Fremd-arbeiterin, -nen** foreign worker 13

das **Fremdenverkehrsbüro, -s** tourist office

die **Freude, -n** pleasure; **~ machen** to give pleasure 9

sich freuen (auf + *acc.*) to look forward (to); **~ (über** + *acc.*) to be pleased (about/with) 10

der **Freund, -e**/die **Freundin, -nen** friend 4; boyfriend/girlfriend

freundlich friendly 2

die **Freundlichkeit** friendliness

der **Frieden** peace 11

friedlich peaceful

frisch fresh 4

froh happy 2

früh early 6

der **Frühling** spring 3

das **Frühstück, -e** breakfast 4; **zum ~** for breakfast 4

sich fühlen to feel (ill, well, etc.) 10

führen to lead; carry in stock, have for sale

der **Führerschein, -e** driver's license 7

die **Führung** leadership

funktionie'ren to function, work

für (+ *acc.*) for 3

furchtbar terrible; very 2; horrible 3

sich fürchten (vor + *dat.*) to fear, be afraid (of) 10

fürchterlich horrible, horribly 10

der **Fuß, ⁝e** foot 6; **zu ~** on foot 6

der **Fußball** soccer 2

der **Fußballverein, -e** soccer club

die **Fußgängerzone, -n** pedestrian zone 8

die **Gabel, -n** fork 8

ganz complete(ly), whole; very 2; **~ gut** not bad, O.K. 2; **~ schön** really quite 10; **~ schön [blaß]** pretty [pale] 10; **im ganzen** altogether

gar: ~ nicht not at all 8

die **Gardi'nen** *(pl.)* curtains

der **Garten, ⁝** garden 1

der **Gast, ⁝e** guest 8

der **Gastgeber, -**/die **Gastgeberin, -nen** host, hostess

das **Gebäck'** pastries

das **Gebäu'de, -** building

geben (gibt), gab, gegeben to give 4; **es gibt** (+ *acc.*) there is, there are 4; **Was gibt's zum [Abendessen]?** What's for [dinner]? 4; **Was gibt's/gab es?** What is/was playing? 11; **Was gibt's Neues?** What's new? 12

gebo'ren, ist geboren born 13

gebrau'chen to use 7

der **Geburts'tag, -e** birthday 3; **Ich habe im [Mai] ~.** My birthday is in May. 3; **Wann hast du ~?** When is your birthday? 3; **zum ~** for one's birthday 3

die **Gefahr', -en** danger 11

gefähr'lich dangerous

gefal'len (gefällt), gefiel, gefallen (+ *dat.*) to please, be pleasing (to) 7; **Es gefällt [mir].** [I] like it. 7

das **Gefühl', -e** feeling

gegen (+ *acc.*) against 4; **~ [sechs] Uhr** around/about [six] o'clock 6

gegenü'ber (+ *dat.*) opposite; across from there; in opposi-tion to

der **Gegner, -** opponent

das **Gehalt', ⁝er** salary 12

gehen, ging, ist gegangen to go 2; **Es geht (nicht).** It will (won't) do./It's (not) O.K./It's (not) possible. 2; **Es geht nicht nur um [die Musik].** It's not just about [the music]. 13; **Geht das?** Is that OK? 6; **Mir geht es gut.** I'm fine. 10; **Wie geht es Ihnen?** How are you? *(formal)* 2; **Wie geht's?** How are you? *(informal)* 2; **zu Fuß ~** to walk 6

gehö'ren (+ *dat.*) to belong to 6

gelb yellow 1

das **Geld** money 4; **es geht um ~** it revolves around money 13

gelernt' trained

das **Gemü'se, -** vegetable 4

gemüt'lich comfortable, informal 6

genau' exact(ly) 7; **Genau!** That's right! 7

genau'so exactly the same 8

die **Generation', -en** generation

genug' enough 4

geöf'fnet open 13

gera'de just; straight 6

das **Gerät', -e** apparatus; tool; instrument

gera'ten, geriet, ist geraten get into a state; **in eine [Panik] ~** to get in a [panic]

das **Gere'de** talk; gossip

die **Germani'stik** German studies (language and literature) 5

gern gladly, willingly; *used with verbs to indicate liking, as in* **Ich spiele gern Tennis.** I like to play tennis. 2; **~ haben** to like, *as in* **Ich habe sie ~.** I like her. 4

das **Geschäft', -e** store; business 9

die **Geschäfts'frau, -en** businesswoman 9

die **Geschäfts'leute** *(pl.)* business people 9

der **Geschäfts'mann, ¨er** businessman 9

die **Geschäfts'zeit, -en** business hours

die **Geschich'te, -n** story; history 5

das **Geschirr'** dishes 8; **~ spülen** to wash dishes 8

der **Geschirr'spüler** dishwasher

die **Geschwin'digkeitsbegrenzung** speed limit

die **Geschwi'ster** *(pl.)* siblings 5

die **Gesell'schaft, -en** society; company 13

das **Gesetz', -e** law 14

das **Gesicht', -er** face 10

gespannt curious; eager

das **Gespräch', -e** conversation

der **Gesprächs'partner, -**/die **Gesprächs'partnerin, -nen** conversation partner

gestern yesterday 3; **~ abend** last night 7

gesund' (ü) healthy 7

geteilt' durch divided by (in division) 1

das **Getränk', -e** beverage 4

die **Gewalt'tätigkeit, -en** act of violence; violence

die **Gewerk'schaft, -en** labor union 13

die **Gewich'te** *(pl.)* weights; **~ heben** to lift weights 2

das **Gewicht'heben** weightlifting 2

giftig poisonous

die **Gitar're, -n** guitar 1

das **Glas, ¨er** glass 4

glauben (+ *dat. when used with a person*) to believe 2; **Ich glaube ja.** I think so. 2; **Ich glaube nicht.** I don't think so. 2

gleich immediately; in a minute 7; same; similar 7

gleichberechtigt entitled to equal rights 9

die **Gleichberechtigung, -en** equal rights 9

gleichzeitig at the same time

das **Glück** luck 9; happiness; **Viel ~!** Good luck! 12; **zum ~** fortunately 9

Glückwunsch: Herzlichen ~ (zum Geburtstag)! Happy birthday!

gnädig gracious; **gnädige Frau** Madam

das **Golf** golf 2

der **Grad** degree 3; **Es ist minus [10] ~.** It's minus [10] degrees. 3; **Wieviel ~ ist es?** What's the temperature? 3

das **Gramm** *(abbr.* **g)** gram (1 ounce = 28.35g) 4

grau gray 1

die **Grenze, -n** border, boundary 6; limit 11

(das) **Griechenland** Greece

das **Grillfest, -e** barbecue party

der **Groschen, -** 1/100 of the Austrian **Schilling**

groß (ö) large, big; tall (people) 1

(das) **Großbritan'nien** Great Britain

die **Größe, -n** size

die **Großeltern** *(pl.)* grandparents 5

die **Großmutter, ¨** grandmother 5

die **Großstadt, ¨e** city 14

der **Großvater, ¨** grandfather 5

grün green 1

der **Grund, ¨e** reason

das **Grundgesetz** constitution of Germany

die **Grundschule, -n** primary school (grades 1–4)

die **Gründung** establishment, founding

die **Grünen** *(pl.)* environmentalist political party

die **Gruppe, -n** group

gruppie'ren to group, organize

der **Gruß, ¨e** greeting; *(closing of a letter)* **viele Grüße** best regards 2; *(closing of a letter)* **liebe Grüße** best regards 10

Grüß dich! *(fam.)* Hi! 2

gültig valid

günstig favorable; reasonable (price)

die **Gurke, -n** cucumber 4

gut good, well; fine 2; **Mir geht es ~.** I'm fine. 10; **Na ~!** All right. 2

der **Gymnasiast', -en, -en**/die **Gymnasia'stin, -nen** student in a **Gymnasium**

das **Gymna'sium,** *pl.* **Gymnasien** college-track secondary school 5

die **Gymna'stik** calisthenics

das **Haar, -e** hair 10

haben (hat), hatte, gehabt to have 3; **Angst ~ vor** (+ *dat.*) to be afraid of 8; **Besuch ~** to have company 4; **Was hast du?** What is wrong with you?, What's the matter? 10

die **Habilitation'** postdoctoral thesis

das **Hähnchen, -** chicken 4

halb half 2; **~ [zwei]** half past

[one] 2; ~ **so groß** half as large 3

der **Halbbruder, ⸚** half brother

die **Halbschwester, -n** half sister

Hallo! Hello., Hi. 2

der **Hals, ⸚e** throat, neck 10

halten (hält), hielt, gehalten to hold 7; ~ **von** to think of, have an opinion about 7

die **Haltestelle, -n** stop (for bus, streetcar, subway)

die **Hand, ⸚e** hand 10

der **Handel** trade 6

der **Handschuh, -e** glove 7

die **Handtasche, -n** handbag, purse 7

hängen, hängte, gehängt to hang something, put 8

hängen, hing, gehangen to be hanging, be suspended 8

hart hard; difficult 9

der **Haß** hatred 13

häßlich ugly; hideous

hast has 1

hat has 1

hätte (*subj. of* **haben**) would have

der **Hauptbahnhof** main train station

das **Hauptfach, ⸚er** major (subject) 5

das **Hauptgericht, -e** main course, entrée

die **Hauptschule, -n** classes 1–9 (10), meant for students intending to learn a trade

die **Hauptspeise, -n** main course, entrée

die **Hauptstadt, ⸚e** capital 3

das **Haus,** *pl.* **Häuser** house 4; **nach Hause** (to go) home 4; **zu Hause** (to be) at home 6

die **Hausarbeit** housework; chore 8

die **Hausaufgaben** (*pl.*) homework 11; ~ **machen** to do homework

die **Hausfrau, -en** housewife 9

der **Haushalt** household; **den ~ machen** to take care of the house; to do the chores 9

der **Hausmeister, -/die Hausmeisterin, -nen** building superintendent

He! Hey!

heben: Gewichte ~ to lift weights 2

das **Heft, -e** notebook 1

die **Heimat** native country 13

die **Heirat** marriage 12

heiraten to marry, to get married 12

heiß hot 3

heißen, hieß, geheißen to be named, be called 1; **Wie heißt du?** What is your name? (*informal*); **Wie heißen Sie?** What is your name? (*formal*) 1; **Du heißt [Mark], nicht?** Your name is [Mark], isn't it? 1; **das heißt (d.h.)** that means, that is (i.e.); **es heißt** it says 9

die **Heizung** heating

helfen (i), half, geholfen to help 8; ~ **bei** to help with 8; **Hilfe!** Help!

hell light 10; bright

das **Hemd, -en** shirt 7

her (*prefix*) (*indicates motion toward speaker*) 8

herauf' up here

der **Herbst** autumn, fall 3; **im ~** in the fall 3

der **Herd, -e** cooking range 8

der **Herr, -n, -en** gentleman 1; **Herr ...** Mr. . . . (term of address) 1; ~ **Ober** (*term of address for a waiter*)

her·stellen to produce; to manufacture 12

herum' around 8

herum'·liegen, lag herum, herumgelegen to lie around 8

das **Herz, -ens, -en** heart

heute today 1; ~ **abend** this evening 2; ~ **morgen** this morning 2; ~ **nachmittag** this afternoon 2

heutzutage nowadays

hier here 3

hin (*prefix*) (*indicates motion away from speaker*) 8

hinein' into, in 12; **hinein·gehen, ging hinein, hineingegangen** to go in 12

hinter (+ *acc./dat.*) behind, in back of 8

hinterher' afterwards 14

der **Hinweis, -e** tip, hint

hmm hmm 3

das **Hobby, -s** hobby 7

hoch (höher, höchst-) high 5; **hoh-** *before nouns, as in* **ein hoher Preis** a high price 12

das **Hochdeutsch** High German, standard German

das **Hochhaus, -häuser** high-rise

die **Hochschule, -n** institution of higher education (e.g., university)

der **Hochschullehrer, -/die Hochschullehrerin, -nen** teacher at a university or college

hoffen to hope 9

hoffentlich (*colloq.*) hopefully; I hope so. 3

höflich polite

die **Höflichkeitsform** polite form

hoh- (-er, -es, -e) high (*the form of* **hoch** *used before nouns, as in* **ein hoher Preis** a high price) 12

die **Höhe, -n** height; **in ~ von** in the sum of

der/die **Homosexuel'le** (*noun decl. like adj.*) homosexual

hören to hear; to listen to 2; **Musik~** listening to music 2

die **Hose, -n** pants, trousers 7; die **kurze ~** shorts 7

der **Hund, -e** dog 8

der **Hunger** hunger 7; ~ **haben** to be hungry 7

husten to cough 10

der **Hut, ⸚e** hat 7

ich I 1; ~ **auch** me, too

die **Idee', -n** idea 7

Ihnen (*dat. of* **Sie**) (to) you; **Und Ihnen?** And you? (*as part of response to* **Wie geht es Ihnen?**) 2

ihr (*pron.*) you (*familiar pl.*) 2; (*poss. adj.*) her, their 3

Ihr (*poss. adj.*) your (*formal*) 1

illuso'risch illusory

die **Immatrikulation'** matriculation

immer always 4; ~ **mehr** more and more 9; **noch ~** still 11; **wie ~** as always 12

die **Immunologie'** immunology

in (+ *acc./dat.*) in 3; into; to 4
die Industrie', -n industry 9
die Informa'tik computer science 5
der Informa'tiker, -/die Informa'tikerin, -nen computer scientist 9
die Information', -en information 5
der Ingenieur', -e/die Ingenieu'rin, -nen engineer 5
das Institut', -e institute
das Instrument', -e instrument 10
intelligent' intelligent, smart 2
interessant' interesting 2
das Interes'se, -n interest
interessie'ren to interest 7; **sich interessieren (für)** to be interested (in) 10
interessiert' sein (an + *dat.*) to be interested (in)
international' international 6
das Interview, -s interview 6
interviewen to interview 6
der Interviewer, -/die Interviewerin, -nen interviewer 6
die Intoleranz' intolerance 13
die Investition', -en investment
inzwi'schen in the meantime 13
irgendwann sometime, at some point 10
isolie'ren insulate
ist is 1
(das) Ita'lien Italy
italie'nisch Italian (*adj.*)

ja yes 1; (*flavoring particle*) indeed, of course 4; **na ~** well now 6
die Jacke, -en jacket 7
das Jackett', -s (pronounced /zhakĕt'/) a man's suit jacket; sport coat 7
das Jahr, -e year 1; **Ich bin [19] Jahre alt.** I'm [19] years old. 1; **die [sechziger/achtziger] Jahre** the [1960s/1980s] 13; **vor [10] Jahren** [10] years ago 6
die Jahreszeit, -en season 3
das Jahrhun'dert, -e century 10
jährlich yearly, annually 14
das Jahrzehnt', -e decade
der Januar January 3

je ... desto ... the ... the ... (*with comp.*); **je größer desto besser** the bigger the better 14
die Jeans (*pl.*) jeans 7
jed- (-er, -es, -e) each, every 5; **jeder** everyone 5
jedenfalls at any rate
jedoch' (*conj. or adv.*) however, nonetheless 9
jemand (-en, -em) someone
jetzt now 3
der Job, -s job 5
jobben to have a temporary job (e.g., a summer job) (*colloq.*) 5
joggen to jog 2
das Jogging jogging 2; **~ gehen** to go jogging 2
der Journalist', -en, -en/die Journalis'tin, -nen journalist 9
der Jude, -n, -n/die Jüdin, -nen Jew
jüdisch Jewish
die Jugendherberge, -n youth hostel
der/die Jugendliche (*noun decl. like adj.*) young person 13
der Juli July 3
jung (ü) young 5
der Junge, -n, -n boy 1
der Juni June 3
der Juraprofessor, -en/die Juraprofessorin, -nen law professor

der Kabarettist', -en, -en/die Kabaretti'stin, -nen cabaret artist
der Kaffee coffee 4
das Kaffeehaus, -häuser café (in Austria); coffeehouse 6
der Kalen'der, - calendar 14
kalt (ä) cold 3
die Kamera, -s camera
der Kamm, -̈e comb 4
(sich) kämmen to comb 10; **Ich kämme mich./Ich kämme mir die Haare.** I comb my hair. 10
(das) Kanada Canada 3
kana'disch Canadian (*adj.*) 5
der Kanton', -e canton (a Swiss state)
kaputt' broken; exhausted (*slang*) 6

die Karot'te, -n carrot 4
die Karte, -n card; postcard 2; ticket 7; **die Karten** (*pl.*) playing cards 2
die Kartof'fel, -n potato 4
der Käse cheese 4
die Kasset'te, -n cassette
das Kasset'tendeck, -s cassette deck 1
der Kasten, -̈ box; crate; **ein 12er Kasten** a twelve pack
die Kategorie', -n category
die Katze, -n cat 8
kaufen to buy 4
die Kauffrau, -en merchant (*f.*)
das Kaufhaus, -häuser department store 4
die Kaufleute (*pl.*) merchants
der Kaufmann, -̈er merchant (*m.*)
kaum hardly
kein not a, not any 4; **~ ... mehr** no more ... 4
der Keks, -e cookie
der Keller, - cellar, basement
kennen, kannte, gekannt to know, be acquainted with [people, places, or things] 4
kennen·lernen to get to know; to make the acquaintance of 6
die Kettenerzählung, -en chain story
das Kilo(gramm) (*abbr.* kg) kilo(gram) (= 2.2 pounds) 4
der Kilometer, - (*abbr.* km) kilometer (= .062 miles) 3
das Kind, -er child 1
der Kindergarten, -̈ nursery school; kindergarten 9
das Kindergeld government's cash contribution to families with children, child allowance
das Kinn, -e chin 10
das Kino, -s movie theater 2; **ins ~ gehen** to go to the movies 2
die Kirche, -n church 13
klar clear; (*interj.*) of course, naturally 5
die Klasse, -n class 5; **die erste ~** first grade 5
der Klassiker, -/die Klassikerin, -nen author of a classical work
klassisch classic(al)

die **Klausur'**, **-en**   test 5; **eine ~ schreiben**   to take a test 5
das **Klavier'**, **-e**   piano; das **~konzert**   piano concerto; piano concert
das **Kleid**, **-er**   dress 7
die **Kleidung**   clothing 7; das **Kleidungsstück**, **-e**   article of clothing
klein   small; short *(of people)* 1
klettern, ist geklettert   to climb
das **Klima**   climate 3
klingeln   to ring 12
das **Kloster**, **-s**, **˙**   convent; monastery
der **Klub**, **-s**   club 13
die **Kneipe**, **-n**   bar, pub 7
das **Knie**, **-**   *(pl. pronounced* /Kni ə/) knee 10
der **Koch**, **˙e**/die **Köchin**, **-nen**   cook
kochen   to cook 7
der **Kochtopf**, **˙e**   pot for cooking; **am ~ stehen**   to stand at the stove
die **Kohle**, **-n**   coal
der **Kolle'ge**, **-n**, **-n**/die **Kolle'gin**, **-nen**   colleague 9
Köln   Cologne
kommen, kam, ist gekommen   to come 2; **~ aus ...**   to be from ...; **Woher kommst du?** Where are you from?/Where do you come from? 3; **Ich komme aus ...**   I come/am from ... 3
die **Kommo'de**, **-n**   chest of drawers 8
der **Kommunis'mus**   communism
kompliziert'   complicated 9
die **Komponen'te**, **-n**   component
der **Kompromiß'**, *pl.* **Kompromisse**   compromise 4
die **Konditorei'**, **-en**   pastry shop
die **Konjunktion'**, **-en**   conjunction
die **Konkurrenz'**, **-en**   competition
konkurrie'ren   to compete 12
können (kann), konnte, gekonnt   to be able to; can 5
könnte *(subj. of* **können**)   would be able to 12
das **Konzentrations'lager**, **-**   concentration camp
das **Konzert'**, **-e**   concert 6; **ins ~ gehen**   to go to a concert 6

der **Kopf**, **˙e**   head 10; **etwas geht [mir] durch den ~**   [I'm] thinking about something
die **Kopfschmerzen** *(pl.)*   headache 4
der **Kopie'rer**   copier
der **Körper**, **-**   body 10
korrigie'ren   to correct
kosten   to cost 5
das **Kostüm'**, **-e**   costume; ladies' suit
krank   sick, ill 2
das **Krankenhaus**, **-häuser**   hospital 7
die **Krankenkasse**   health insurance
der **Krankenpfleger**, **-**/die **Krankenpflegerin**, **-nen**   nurse
die **Krankenschwester**, **-n**   female nurse 8
die **Krankenversicherung**   health insurance
die **Krankheit**, **-en**   illness 10
kränklich   sickly
die **Krawat'te**, **-n**   necktie 7
der **Krieg**, **-e**   war 11
kriegen   to get 7
der **Krimi**, **-s**   mystery (novel or film) 5
die **Kritik'**   criticism; review 11
kritisch   critical 2
die **Küche**, **-n**   kitchen 4
der **Kuchen**, **-**   cake 4
das **Küchengerät**, **-e**   kitchen appliance
die **Küchenmaschine**, **-n**   mixer (*also used for* food processing)
der **Kugelschreiber**, **-**   ballpoint pen 1
kühl   cool 3
der **Kühlschrank**, **˙e**   refrigerator 8
der **Kuli**, **-s** (*colloq. for* **Kugelschreiber**)   ballpoint pen 1
kulminie'ren   to culminate
die **Kultur'**, **-en**   culture 13
kulturell'   culture, culturally 13
der **Kunde**, **-n**, **-n**/die **Kundin**, **-nen**   customer, client 12
die **Kündigung**, **-en**   dismissal
die **Kunst**, **˙e**   art; skill
die **Kunstgeschichte**   art history 5
der **Kurs**, **-e**   course 5
kurz   short, brief 6; die **kurze Hose**   shorts 7

die **Kürze**   brevity
die **Kurzgeschichte**, **-n**   short story
die **Kusi'ne**, **-n**   cousin *(f.)* 5

lächeln   to smile 8; **~ über** (+ *acc.*)   to smile about
lachen   to laugh 13; **~ über** (+ *acc.*)   to laugh about
der **Laden**, **˙**   store 4
das **Ladenschutzgesetz**   law that regulates business hours
die **Lampe**, **-n**   lamp 1
das **Land**, **˙er**   country, land 3; **aufs ~ fahren**   to go to the country
landen   to land
die **Landkarte**, **-n**   map
lang (ä)   long 5
lange *(adv.)*   for a long time 6
langsam   slow(ly) 14
langweilig   boring 7
lassen (läßt), ließ, gelassen   to leave; to let, permit; to have something done 13; **Laß uns gehen.**   Let's go. 13
der **Lastwagen**, **-**   truck 14
laufen (läuft), lief, ist gelaufen   to run; to go on foot, to walk 6
laut *(adj.)* loud; (*prep.* + *gen.* or *dat.*)   according to
das **Leben**   life 8
leben   to live 6
die **Lebensdauer**   life span; life (of a machine)
die **Lebensmittel** *(pl.)*   food; groceries 4
der **Lebensstandard**   standard of living 10
leer   empty 12
legen   to lay or put something in a horizontal position 8
lehren   to teach 9
der **Lehrer**, **-**/die **Lehrerin**, **-nen**   teacher 9
leicht   light; easy 9
die **Leichtathletik**   track and field
lcid: Es tut mir ~.   I'm sorry. 5
leider   unfortunately 3
leihen, lieh, geliehen   to lend 5
lernen   to learn; to study 5
lesen (ie), las, gelesen   to read 5
das **Lesestück**, **˙e**   reading selection
letzt   last 7

die **Leute** (*pl.*) people 4

das **Licht, -er** light

lieb (*adj.*) dear; **Liebe [Barbara], Lieber [Paul] ...** Dear [Barbara], Dear [Paul] . . . (*used at the beginning of a letter*) 2

die **Liebe** love

lieben to love

lieber (*comp. of* **gern**) preferably, rather 6

der **Liebesroman, -e** romance (novel) 5

der **Liebling, -e** favorite 4; darling; **Lieblings-** (*prefix*) favorite: das **Lieblingsgetränk** favorite drink 4

(das) **Liechtenstein** Liechtenstein

liegen, lag, gelegen to lie; to be situated, be located 3

die **Limona'de** carbonated, fruit-flavored drink; lemonade 4

links on/to the left 12

die **Lippe, -n** lip 10

der **Liter, -** (*abbr.* **l**) liter (= 1.056 U.S. quarts) 4

die **Literatur'** literature 5

der **Löffel, -** spoon 8

das **Lokal', -e** restaurant; bar 13

los loose; **Was ist ~?** What's wrong? 2

lösen to solve 14

die **Lösung, -en** solution 14

die **Luft** air 8; die **~verschmutzung** air pollution

die **Luftbrücke** airlift

die **Lust** desire; enjoyment 11; **~ haben** (+ **zu** + *inf.*) to be in the mood, to feel like doing something 11

lustig funny; merry; cheerful 2

machen to do; to make 2; **Deutsch ~** to do/study German (homework) 2; **Examen ~** to graduate from the university 5; **(Es) macht nichts.** (It) doesn't matter. 8; **Mach schnell!** Hurry up! 8

das **Mädchen, -** girl 1

der **Magen, ⸚** stomach 10; die **~schmerzen** (*pl.*) stomachache 10

die **Mahlzeit, -en** meal; **~!** Enjoy your meal.

der **Mai** May 3

mal time; times (in multiplication) 1; **drei~** three times; **mal (= einmal)** once; sometime 7; (*flavoring particle that softens a command and leaves the time indefinite*) **Sagt ~ ...** Tell me . . . 7; **Moment ~!** Just a minute! 12

die **Mama** mom 5

man one, people, (*impersonal*) you 1

manch (-er, -es, -e) many a (*sg.*); some (*pl.*) 5

manchmal sometimes 4

der **Mann, ⸚er** man 1; husband

der **Mantel, ⸚** outer coat 7

die **Margari'ne** margarine 4

die **Mark** mark; die **Deutsche ~ (DM)** (basic monetary unit in Germany) 4

der **Markt, ⸚e** market 4; **auf den ~** to the market 4

die **Marmela'de** marmelade, jam 4

der **März** March 3

die **Maschi'ne, -n** machine 9

maschi'ne·schreiben, schrieb Maschine, maschinegeschrieben to type

die **Mathe** (*short for* **Mathematik**) math 5

die **Mathematik'** mathematics 5

die **Mauer, -n** (exterior) wall 11

mehr (*comp. of* **viel**) more 3; **immer ~** more and more 9; **~ oder weniger** more or less; **kein ... ~** no more . . . 4; **nicht ~** no longer, not anymore 5

mehrere several; various 13

mein my 1

meinen to mean; to think, have an opinion 8

die **Meinung, -en** opinion; **meiner ~ nach** in my opinion 14

meist (*superlative of* **viel**) most 5; die **meisten (Leute)** most of (the people) 5

meistens most of the time, mostly

die **Mensa, -s** university cafeteria

der **Mensch, -en, -en** person, human being 2; **~!** Man!/Wow!

merken to notice; to realize 12

das **Messer, -** knife 8

das **Metall', -e** metal 14

der **Meter, -** (*abbr.* **m**) meter (= 39.37 inches)

der **Metzger, -** butcher 4

die **Metzgerei', -en** butcher shop, meat market 4

(das) **Mexiko** Mexico

mieten to rent

die **Mietwohnung, -en** rental apartment

der **Mikrowellenherd, -e** microwave (oven)

die **Milch** milk 4

die **Million', -en** million 3

die **Minderheit, -en** minority

mindestens at least

das **Mineral'wasser** mineral water 4

minus minus 3

die **Minu'te, -n** minute 2

mit (+ *dat.*) with 4; **~ dem [Auto] fahren** to go by [car] 6

der **Mitarbeiter, -/die Mitarbeiterin, -nen** employee 12

die **Mitbestimmung** co-determination

mit·bringen, brachte mit, mitgebracht to bring along 5

der **Mitbürger, -/die Mitbürgerin, -nen** fellow citizen

miteinan'der with each other 8

mit·fahren (fährt mit), fuhr mit, ist mitgefahren to drive/ride along 6

mit·gehen, ging mit, ist mitgegangen to go along 7

das **Mitglied, -er** member 10

die **Mitgliedschaft** membership

das **Mittagessen** midday meal 4; **zum ~** for the midday meal, for lunch 4

die **Mittagspause** lunch break; the time during which a store closes for lunchtime

mitten: ~ in ... in the middle of . . .

der **Mittwoch** Wednesday 1

die **Möbel** (*pl.*) furniture 8

das **Möbelstück, ⸚e** piece of furniture

möchte (*subj. of* **mögen**) would like 5

modern' modern 5

mögen (mag), mochte, gemocht to like 5

möglich possible 7

die **Möglichkeit, -en** possibility

der **Moment', -e** moment 12; **im ~** at the moment 12; **~ mal!** Just a minute! 12

der **Monat, -e** month 3

der **Montag** Monday 1; **am ~** on Monday 2; **~ in acht Tagen** a week from Monday

morgen tomorrow 3

der **Morgen** morning 2; **Guten ~.** Good morning. 2

morgens mornings, every morning 4

das **Motorrad, -̈er** motorcycle 6

das **Motto, -s** motto 13

müde tired 2

der **Müll** garbage, trash 14

der **Müllberg, -e** pile of garbage, trash heap

die **Müll-Lawine** public garbage disposal crisis (*literally,* avalanche of garbage)

multikulturell' multicultural 13

der **Mund, -̈er** mouth 10

die **Münze, -n** coin

das **Musical, -s** musical 7

die **Musik'** music 2; **~hören** listening to music 2

der **Mu'siker, -/die Mu'sikerin, -nen** musician 9

müssen (muß), mußte, gemußt to have to; must 5

müßte (*subj. of* **müssen**) would have to

das **Musterbeispiel, -e** prime example, paradigm

die **Mutter, -̈** mother 5

der **Mutterschutz** mothers' rights regarding maternity leave

die **Muttersprache, -n** native language

die **Mutti, -s** mom 5

die **Mütze, -n** cap 7

na: ~ gut! All right. 2; well (*interjection*); **na ja** well now 6

nach (+ *dat.*) after 2; to (*with cities and countries used without an article,* e.g., **nach Berlin; nach Deutschland**) 3; **~ Hause** (to go) home 4

der **Nachbar, -n, -n/die Nachbarin, -nen** neighbor 2

das **Nachbarland, -̈er** neighboring country 3

nachdem' (*conj.*) after

nach·denken, dachte nach, nachgedacht (über) (+ *acc.*) to think (about), reflect (on)

nachher afterwards 5

der **Nachmittag, -e** afternoon 2

der **Nachname, -ns, -n** last name

die **Nachricht, -en** message; **Nachrichten** (*pl.*) newscast

die **Nachspeise, -n** dessert

nächst next 8

die **Nacht, -̈e** night 2; **Gute ~.** Good night. 2

der **Nachtisch, -e** dessert

der **Nachttisch, -e** bedside table 8

die **Nähe** nearness, proximity; vicinity; **in der ~** near at hand

der **Name, -ns, -n** name 6

nämlich after all; that is (to say); you know; you see 7

die **Nase, -n** nose 10

naß (nasser or **nässer)** wet 3

der **National'rat** National Council (*Switzerland*)

natür'lich natural(ly) 2; of course

der **Natur'wissenschaftler, -/die Natur'wissenschaftlerin, -nen** (natural) scientist

neben (+ *acc./dat.*) beside, next to, besides 8

nebenan' next door

das **Nebenfach, -̈er** minor (subject) 5

der **Neffe, -n, -n** nephew 5

negativ negative

nehmen (nimmt), nahm, genommen to take 4

nein no 1

nennen, nannte, genannt to name 9

nervös' nervous

nett nice 2

neu new 1; **Was gibt's Neues?** What's new? 12

neugierig curious

der **Neuschnee** newly fallen snow

(das) **Neuschott'land** Nova Scotia

die **Neutralität'** neutrality

nicht not 2; **~?** (*tag question*) don't you?; isn't it? 1; **Du**

heißt [Monika], ~? Your name is Monika, isn't it? 1; **~ mehr** no longer, not anymore 5; **~ nur ... sondern auch** not only . . . but also 6; **~ so [kalt]** not as [cold] 3; **~ wahr?** isn't that so? 2; **noch ~** not yet 3

die **Nichte, -n** niece 5

der **Nichtraucher, -/die Nichtraucherin, -nen** non-smoker

nichts nothing 2; **~ Beson'deres** nothing special 2; **(Es) macht ~!** (It) doesn't matter. 8

nie never 11

(das) **Niederdeutsch** Low German (term for dialects spoken in northern Germany)

(die) **Niederlande** (*pl.*) the Netherlands

niedrig low 12

niemand no one 7

noch still; in addition 3; **~ ein ... another . . . ; ~ einmal** again, once more 13; **~ immer** still 11; **~ nicht** not yet 3; **Sonst ~ einen Wunsch?** Anything else? 4; **sonst ~ etwas** something else 4; **was ~** what else? 8

der **Norden** north 3

nördlich to the north 3

(das) **Norwegen** Norway

der **Notdienst** emergency service

die **Note, -n** grade; note 5

die **Notiz', -en** note 5

der **Novem'ber** November 3

die **Nudeln** (*pl.*) noodles 4

der **Numerus clausus** limited number of university positions for study in certain subjects

die **Nummer, -n** number 1

das **Nummernschild, -er** license plate

nur only 2

ob (*conj.*) whether, if 8

oberflächlich superficial 8

das **Obst** fruit 4

obwohl' (*conj.*) although 6

oder or 2; **~?** Or don't you agree? 7; **Du kommst doch, ~?** You're coming, aren't you? 7

offen open 4; frank 13

öffentlich public 8

öffnen to open 11

oft often 2

ohne (+ *acc.*) without 4

das **Ohr, -en** ear 10

der **Ökolo'ge, -n, -n**/die **Ökolo'-gin, -nen** ecologist

O.K. okay, O.K. 2

der **Okto'ber** October 3

die **Oma, -s** grandma 5

der **Onkel, -** uncle 5

der **Opa, -s** grandpa 5

das **Open-Air-Konzert** outdoor concert 13

die **Oper, -n** opera 6; **in die ~ gehen** to go to the opera 6

die **Oran'ge, -n** orange 4

der **Oran'gensaft** orange juice 4

ordnen to arrange, put in order

die **Ordnung** order; **in ~** that is all right, O.K. 7

der **Ort, -e** place (geographical) 10

das **Ortsmünztelefon, -e** pay phone for local calls

der **Ostblock** the eastern block

der **Osten** east 3

(das) **Österreich** Austria 3

der **Österreicher, -**/die **Österrei-cherin, -nen** Austrian person 3

österreichisch Austrian (*adj.*) 6

östlich eastern

der **Ozean, -e** ocean 3

der **Ozonwert** ozone level

paar: ein ~ a few 4; **alle ~ Minu-ten** every few minutes

die **Packung, -en** package

der **Papa, -s** dad 5

das **Papier', -e** paper 1

die **Pappe** cardboard 14

der **Pappteller, -** paper plate 14

der **Park, -s** park 8

das **Parterre'** the ground floor of a building

die **Partnerschaft, -en** partnership

die **Party, -s** party 4; **auf eine ~** to a party; **auf einer ~** at a party

passen (paßt) (+ *dat.*) to fit; to be appropriate

passie'ren, ist passiert (+ *dat.*) to happen 8; **Was ist dir passiert?** What happened to you? 8

passiv passive(ly) 7

die **Pause, -n** break, rest; inter-mission

die **Person', -en** person

der **Personal'chef, -s**/die **Personal'chefin, -nen** head of the human resources (per-sonnel) department 9

persön'lich personal(ly)

die **Pfandflasche, -n** returnable bottle, money-back bottle 14

der **Pfennig, -e** 1/100 of the German Mark

die **Pflanze, -n** plant 1

die **Pflicht, -en** chore; duty 14

das **Pfund, -e** (*abbrev.* **Pfd.**) pound (= 1.1 U.S. pounds) 4

die **Philosophie'** philosophy 5

die **Physik'** physics 5

der **Phy'siker, -**/die **Phy'sikerin, -nen** physicist 9

das **Picknick, -s** picnic; **~ machen** to have a picnic 5

die **Pizza, -s** pizza 7

der **Plan, ⁝e** plan 6; schedule

das **Plastik** plastic 14

das **Plastikbesteck, -e** a setting of plastic knife, fork, and spoon; plastic flatware 14

der **Platz, ⁝e** place; seat; space 5; **~ nehmen** to take a seat 13

pleite broke, out of money 8

plötzlich suddenly

die **Podiumsdiskussion, -en** panel discussion

die **Politik'** politics; political sci-ence 12

der **Poli'tiker, -**/die **Poli'tikerin, -nen** politician 9

poli'tisch political(ly) 11

das **Polohemd, -en** polo shirt 7

die **Pommes frites** (*pl.*) French fries 7

das **Porträt', -s** portrait

positiv positive

die **Post** mail; post office 12

das *or* der **Poster, -** poster 1

die **Postleitzahl, -en** postal code

praktisch practical(ly); for all practical purposes 2

der **Präsident', -en, -en**/die **Präsi-den'tin, -nen** president 11

die **Praxis** (a professional) prac-tice

präzis' precise(ly)

der **Preis, -e** price 12

die **Premie're, -n** premiere

prima fantastic, great (**prima** takes *no adj. endings*) 11

privat' private 5

pro per 14

die **Probe, -n** rehearsal 7

proben to rehearse

probie'ren to try; to (put to the) test; (*food*) to taste

das **Problem', -e** problem 6

das **Produkt', -e** product 10

produzie'ren to produce 14

der **Profes'sor**, *pl.* **Professo'ren**/die **Professo'rin, -nen** professor 1

das **Prozent'** percent 5

der **Prozent'satz** percentage 5

die **Prüfung, -en** test, examina-tion 5

die **Psychologie'** psychology 5

der **Pulli, -s** sweater 7

der **Punkt, -e** dot, spot, point; period 9

pünktlich punctual 8

putzen to clean 8; **Ich putze mir die Zähne** I'm brushing my teeth 10

die **Qualität', -en** quality 10

der **Quatsch** nonsense; **~!** Nonsense! 12

die **Rabenmutter, ⁝** unfit mother

der **Rabenvater, ⁝** unfit father

das **Rad, ⁝er** (*short for* **Fahrrad**) bike, bicycle 6; wheel

rad·fahren (fährt Rad), fuhr Rad, ist radgefahren to (ride a) bi-cycle, to bike 7

der **Radfahrer, -**/die **Radfahrerin, -nen** cyclist, bike rider 7

das **Radio, -s** radio 1

die **Radtour, -en** bicycle trip

der **Rappen, -** 1/100 of the Swiss Frank

(sich) rasieren to shave 10

der **Rassis'mus** racism 13

das **Rätoromanisch** Rhaeto-Romanic

der **Ratschlag, -schläge** advice, piece of advice

der **Rauch** smoke 8

rauchen to smoke 14

der **Raucher, -**/die **Raucherin,**

-nen smoker

der **Raum, ¨e** room; space

raus (*contraction of* **heraus**) out

die **Real'schule, -n** school from 5th to 10th grade that prepares students for careers in business, health fields, etc.

rechnen to calculate; **~ mit** to count on

das **Recht, -e** right; law; **~ auf +** *acc.* right to

recht haben to be right; **Du hast recht.** You're right. 8

rechts on/to the right 12

der **Rechtsanwalt,** *pl.* **Rechtsan-wälte**/die **Rechtsanwältin, -nen** lawyer 9

die **Rechtswissenschaft** (study of) law

recyceln to recycle 14

das **Recycling** recycling 14

reden (**über +** *acc.*) to talk/speak (about) 8

das **Referat', -e** report; seminar paper 5

regelmäßig regular(ly)

regeln to apply; to regulate

die **Regelstudienzeit** limit on time to complete university studies

der **Regen** rain 3

der **Regenmantel, ¨** raincoat 7

der **Regenschirm, -e** umbrella 7

die **Regie'** direction (theater, TV)

regie'ren to govern

die **Regie'rung, -en** government 11

die **Regie'rungsform** form of government

das **Regie'rungsgebäude, -** government building

regnen to rain 3

reich rich

das **Reich** empire; das **Dritte ~** the Third Reich

das **Reichstagsgebäude** German parliament building in Berlin

reif ripe

die **Reinigung** cleaning

die **Reise, -n** trip, journey 8

reisen, ist gereist to travel 6

der/die **Reisende** (*noun decl. like adj.*) traveler, passenger

der **Reisepaß,** *pl.* **Reisepässe** passport

relativ' relative 3

reparie'ren to repair 14

der **Repor'ter, -**/die **Repor'terin, -nen** reporter 7

der **Rest, -e** rest, remaining part 7

das **Restaurant, -s** restaurant 8

das **Rezept', -e** prescription; recipe

richtig correct, right 6

riechen, roch, gerochen to smell 4

der **Rinderbraten** roast beef 4

der **Rock, ¨e** skirt 7

der **Rockfan, -s** rock fan 13

die **Rockmusik** rock (music) 6

der **Rockmusiker, -**/die **Rockmusi-kerin, -nen** rock musician 13

der **Roggen** rye

der **Rohstoff, -e** raw material 12

der **Rolladen, -läden** window shutters that unroll vertically

die **Rolle, -n** role; **eine ~ spielen** to play a role

das **Rollenspiel, -e** role play

der **Roman', -e** novel 5

die **Rosi'ne, -n** raisin

rot red 1

der **Rotwein, -e** red wine 4

der **Rücken, -** back 10; die **Rückenschmerzen** (*pl.*) back-ache 10

die **Rückmeldung** registration subsequent to the first one (university)

die **Rückreise, -n** return trip

die **Ruhe** peace and quiet

der **Ruhetag, -e** the day on which a restaurant is closed

ruhig calm, easygoing, quiet 2

das **Rührei, -er** scrambled egg

(das) **Rumänien** Rumania

der **Russe, -n, -n**/die **Russin, -nen** Russian person

(das) **Rußland** Russia

die **Sache, -n** thing 8; affair, concern 8; (*pl.*) clothes 8

der **Saft, ¨e** juice 4

die **Saftflasche, -n** bottle of juice 14

sagen to say, tell 3; **sag mal** tell me 7

der **Salat, -e** lettuce; salad 4

sammeln to collect 9

der **Samstag** (*in southern Germany*)

Saturday 1

samstags Saturdays, every Saturday 4

der **Satz, ¨e** sentence 12

sauber clean 8

sauber·machen to clean 8

das **Schach** chess 2

schade that's too bad, a pity, a shame 10

schaden (+ *dat.*) to harm

der **Schaffner, -**/die **Schaffnerin, -nen** conductor (on a train or streetcar)

der **Schauplatz, ¨e** scene

der **Schein, -e** glow; (*type of offi-cial document*) der **Geldschein** bill; der **Seminarschein** cer-tificate of attendance for one semester of a course

scheinen, schien, geschienen to shine 3; to appear, seem 14

schenken to give (as a gift) 6

das **Schiff, -e** ship 6

der **Schilling, -e** shilling; **öster-reichischer ~ (öS)** Austrian unit of currency

der **Schinken, -** ham 4

der **Schirm, -e** umbrella 7

schlafen (ä), schlief, geschlafen to sleep 6; **bei jemandem ~** to sleep at someone's house

das **Schlafzimmer, -** bedroom 8

schlagen (ä), schlug, geschlagen to hit, beat; to whip

das **Schlagobers** (*Austrian*) whipped cream

die **Schlagsahne** whipped cream

die **Schlange** snake; line **~ stehen** to stand in line

schlank slender 9

schlecht bad, badly 2; **Mir ist ~.** I feel nauseated. 10

schlechter (*comp. of* **schlecht**) worse 10

schließen, schloß, geschlossen to close 4

schließlich finally, after all 10

das **Schloß,** *pl.* **Schlösser** castle, palace; lock

schmecken (+ *dat.*) to taste 7; **Es schmeckt [mir].** It tastes good to [me]. 7; **Hat es geschmeckt?** Did it taste good? 7

der **Schmerz, -en** pain 10

(sich) schminken to put on make-up; **ich schminke mich** I put on make-up; **Ich schminke mir die Augen.** I put on eye make-up. 10

schmutzig dirty

der **Schnee** snow 3

schneien to snow 3

schnell fast, quickly 7; **Mach ~!** Hurry up! 8

schon already 4

schön nice, beautiful 3; **ganz ~** really quite 10

der **Schornstein, -e** smokestack

der **Schrank, ⸚e** wardrobe 8

der **Schraubenverschluß, -ver-schlüsse** screw top or cap

schreiben, schrieb, geschrieben to write 1; **~ an** (+ *acc.*) to write to; **~ über** (+ *acc.*) to write about 8; **~ von** (+ *dat.*) to write about; **Wie schreibt man das?** How do you spell that? 1

die **Schreibmaschine, -n** typewriter 9; **~ schreiben** to type 9

der **Schreibtisch, -e** desk 8

der **Schuh, -e** shoe 7

die **Schule, -n** school 5

die **Schulklasse, -n** (school) class

der **Schultag, -e** school day

schützen to protect 11

schwach weak 10

die **Schwangerschaft** pregnancy; der **Schwangerschaftsurlaub** maternity leave

schwarz black 1

schwätzen to talk, gossip

(das) **Schweden** Sweden

schweigen to be silent

die **Schweiz** Switzerland 3

der **Schweizer, -/die Schweizerin, -nen** Swiss person 3

Schweizer Swiss (*adj.*) 10

(das) **Schweizerdeutsch** Swiss German

schwer hard, difficult 5; heavy

die **Schwester, -n** sister 5

Schwieger- (*prefix meaning* in-law); **~tochter** daughter-in-law

schwierig difficult 9

schwimmen, schwamm, ist geschwommen to swim 2

der **See, -n** lake 14

die **See, -n** sea

segeln to sail

sehen (ie), sah, gesehen to see 5

sehr very (much) 2

sei (**du**-*imperative of* **sein**); **~ [mir] nicht böse.** Don't be mad [at me]. 8

die **Seife** soap

die **Seifenoper, -n** soap opera

sein his; its 3

sein (ist), war, ist gewesen to be 2

seit (+ *dat.*) since (*time or date*) 5; for (*time period*) 5; **~ wann** since when, (for) how long 5; **~ kurzer Zeit** recently

seitdem since then

die **Seite, -n** side; page 13

der **Sekretär, -e**/die **Sekretä'rin, -nen** secretary 1

selber oneself, myself, itself, etc. 14

selbst oneself, myself, itself, etc. 8

selbstverständlich of course, it goes without saying

selten seldom 10

das **Seme'ster, -** semester 5

die **Seme'sterferien** (*pl.*) semester break 5

das **Seminar', -e** seminar 5

die **Seminar'arbeit, -en** seminar paper 5

der **Seminar'schein, -e** certificate of attendance for one semester of a course

die **Semmel, -n** bread roll

die **Sendung, -en** broadcast 11

der **Septem'ber** September 3

der **Sessel, -** easy chair 8

setzen to set or put something down 8; **sich setzen** to take/have a seat

das **Shampoo', -s** shampoo

die **Shorts** (*pl.*) shorts 7

sicher safe; secure; certain(ly) 9

sie she, it 1; they 2

Sie you (*formal*) 1

die **Siegermacht, ⸚e** victor in war, winner

siezen to address someone with the formal **Sie**-form

sind are 1

der **Sinn** meaning, purpose

die **Situation', -en** situation 10

der **Sitz, -e** headquarters, seat 10

sitzen, saß, gesessen to sit 8

die **Sitzung, -en** session

der **Ski, -er** (**Ski** *is pronounced* **Schi**) ski 6; **Ski fahren** (*also* **Ski laufen**) to ski 6; **zum Ski-fahren gehen** to go skiing 10

der **Smog** smog 14

so so, thus, this way 1; **~ ... wie** as . . . as 3; **~?** Is that so? Really? 5

sobald (*conj.*) as soon as 9

die **Socke, -n** sock 7

das **Sofa, -s** sofa 8

sofort' immediately

sogar' even 11

der **Sohn, ⸚e** son 5

solch (-er, -es, -e) such a (*sg.*); such (*pl.*) 5

der **Soldat', -en, -en**/die **Solda'tin, -nen** soldier 11

sollen (soll), sollte, gesollt to be supposed to; to be said to 5

der **Sommer** summer 3

das **Sonderangebot, -e** special offer

sondern (*conj.*) but, on the contrary 6; **nicht nur ... ~ auch** not only . . . but also 6

der **Sonnabend** (*in northern Germany*) Saturday 1

die **Sonne** sun 3

die **Sonnenbrille, -n** sun glasses 7

sonnig sunny 3

der **Sonntag** Sunday 1

sonst otherwise 4; **~ noch etwas?** Anything else? 4; **~ noch einen Wunsch?** Would you like anything else? 4

die **Sorge, -n** care, worry 12; **sich Sorgen machen (um)** to worry (about) 12

die **Sorte, -n** type, kind

sowie' (*conj.*) as well as

sozial' social; das **sozia'le Netz** social "safety net," social legislation

die **Sozial'hilfe** social welfare

die **Spaghet'ti** spaghetti 4

(das) **Spanien** Spain

spanisch Spanish (*adj.*)

die **Spannung, -en** tension

sparen to save (e.g., money, time) 12

der Spaß enjoyment; fun 9; **an der Arbeit ~ haben** to enjoy one's work 9; **Es/Das macht ~** It/That is fun. 9; **der Spaß, ¨e** joke 9

spät late 2; **Wie ~ ist es?** What time is it? 2; **später** later 2

spazie'ren·fahren (ä), fuhr spazieren, ist spazierengefahren to go for a drive 7

spazie'ren·gehen, ging spazieren, ist spazierengegangen to go for a walk 5

der Spiegel, - mirror 8

das Spiegelei, -er fried egg

das Spiel, -e game 13

spielen to play 2

der Spielfilm, -e feature film

die Spielzeit season (theater)

der Sport sport(s) 2; **~ treiben** to engage in sports 2

der Sportverein, -e sports club

die Sprache, -en language 10

sprachlich with regard to language, linguistically

sprechen (i), sprach, gesprochen to speak 6; **~ mit** to speak to/with (someone); **~ über** (+ *acc.*) to speak about 8; **~ von** (+ *dat.*) to speak about/of 8

spülen to rinse; to wash 8; **Geschirr ~** to wash dishes 8

die Spülmaschine, -n dishwasher 8

der Staat, -en state; country 5

staatlich (*abbrev.* **staatl.**) public, government-owned 5

die Stadt, ¨e city 3; **das ~viertel** city district

der Stammbaum, -bäume family tree

der Stand, ¨e stand

stark (ä) strong 6

starr motionless

statt (+ *gen.*) instead of 9

der Staub dust 8; **~ wischen** to dust 8

staubsaugen, staubsaugte, staubgesaugt to vacuum 8

das Steak, -s steak 7

stecken to stick, put or insert something into something else 8

stehen, stand, gestanden to stand; to be located 8; **es stand in der Zeitung ...** it said in the newspaper . . . 11

stehen·bleiben, blieb stehen, ist stehengeblieben to stop 14

stehlen (ie), stahl, gestohlen to steal

steigen, stieg, ist gestiegen to rise, climb

die Stelle, -n job; position 9; place, spot

stellen to stand, place, put something (upright) 8; **eine Frage ~** + *dat.* to ask someone a question 10; **eine Frage an** + *acc.* **~** to ask someone a question 10

das Stellenangebot, -e job offer (ad)

sterben (i), starb, ist gestorben to die 11

die Stereoanlage, -n stereo system

das Stichwort, ¨er key word, cue

der Stiefel, - boot 7

die Stiefmutter, ¨ stepmother 5

der Stiefvater, ¨ stepfather 5

stimmen to be correct; **Das stimmt.** That's right. 6

das Stipen'dium, *pl.* **Stipendien** scholarship, grant 5

der Stock, *pl.* **Stockwerke** floor/story (above ground level) of a building

stolz (auf + *acc.*) proud (of) 13

der Strand, ¨e beach

die Strandkleidung beach clothes

die Straße, -n street 1

die Straßenbahn, -en streetcar 6

der Streik, -s strike 12

streng strict 14

der Strom electricity

die Strumpfhose, -n pantyhose 7

das Stück, -e piece 4; piece (of music); play (theater) 7

der Student', -en, -en/die Studen'tin, -nen student 1

der Studen'tenausweis, -e student identification card

das Studen'tenheim, -e dormitory 5

das Studienbuch book in which courses one has attended are entered

der Studiengang, ~ gänge course of study

die Studiengebühren (*pl.*) administrative fees at the university; tuition

der Studienplatz, ¨e opening for student in a particular course of study at a university

studie'ren to study; to go to college 2; **~ an/auf** (+ *dat.*) to study at (a college) 8

das Studium studies 5

der Stuhl, ¨e chair 1

die Stunde, -n hour 7; lesson; class; **die Klavier~** piano lesson

das Substantiv, -e noun

suchen to look for 4

der Süden south 3

südlich to the south 3

super super, great 7

der Supermarkt, ¨e supermarket 4; **in den ~** to the supermarket 4

surfen to surf

süß sweet; nice

die Tablet'te, -n tablet, pill 4

der Tag, -e day 1; **Guten ~./~.** Hello.; Hi. 2; **eines Tages** one day; **[Montag] in acht Tagen** a week from Monday

das Tagebuch, ¨er diary

tagen to be in session, to meet

die Tagesreise a day's journey

täglich daily

tagsüber during the day

der Tankwart, -e/die Tankwartin, -nen gas station attendant

die Tante, -n aunt 5

der Tante-Emma-Laden, ¨ mom-and-pop store

tanzen to dance 2

die Tasche, -n bag; pocket 4; handbag, purse 7

die Tasse, -n cup 4

die Technologie', -n technology

der Tee tea 4

das Teil, -e component; share

der Teil, -e part 11

teilen to divide (up); (*math*) **~ durch** to divide by

die Teilzeitbeschäftigung, -en part-time work

das Telefon', -e telephone 1

telefonie'ren (mit jemandem)   to telephone (someone) 12

die Telefon'nummer, -n   telephone number 1; **Wie ist deine/Ihre ~?**   What's your telephone number? 1; **Wie ist die ~ von ... ?**   What is the telephone number of . . . ? 1

die Telefon'zelle, -n   telephone booth

das Tempolimit   speed limit 14

das Tennis   tennis 2

der Teppich, -e   rug, carpet 8

der Termin', -e   appointment; **einen ~ bei jemandem haben**   to have an appointment with someone 12

der Termin'kalender, -   appointment calendar

teuer   expensive 5

das Thea'ter, -   theater 6; **ins ~ gehen**   to go to the theater 6; **die ~karte, -n**   theater ticket

das Thema, pl. Themen   theme, topic 7

tippen   to type 9

der Tisch, -e   table 1; **den ~ decken**   to set the table 8

das Tischtennis   table tennis, Ping-Pong 2

die Tochter, ⸚   daughter 5

die Toilette, -n   toilet; men's/ ladies' room

tolerant'   tolerant 2

toll   great, fantastic 7

die Tomate, -n   tomato 4

die Tonne, -n   drum, container; ton 14

das Tor, -e   gate

die Torte, -n   layered-cake with a cream or fruit filling 4

der Tourist', -en, -en/ die Touri'stin, -nen   tourist 6

die Tradition', -en   tradition 13

tragen (ä), trug, getragen   to carry; to wear 7

die Traube, -n   grape 4

träumen (+ von)   to dream (of)

traurig   sad

(sich) treffen (i), traf, getroffen   to meet 8; **Ich treffe mich mit Freunden.**   I'm meeting friends.

der Treffpunkt, -e   meeting place;

rendezvous

die Treppe, -n   staircase

trinken, trank, getrunken   to drink 4

das Trinkgeld   tip

trocken   dry 3

trotz (+ gen.)   in spite of 9

trotzdem   nevertheless 9

tschüs   so long, good-bye (informal) 1

das T-Shirt, -s   T-shirt 7

tun, tat, getan   to do 7; **weh ~ (+ dat.)**   to hurt 10

die Tür, -en   door 1

der Türke, -n, -n/die Türkin, -nen   Turk

die Türkei'   Turkey

turnen   to do gymnastics

typisch   typical

die U-Bahn, -en (abbr. for Untergrundbahn)   subway 6

über (+ acc./dat.)   about 4; over, above; across 8

überall   everywhere 8

überglücklich   ecstatic

überhaupt'   altogether, in general; **~ nicht**   not at all

übernach'ten   to spend the night, to stay (in hotel or with friends) 6

übrig   remaining, leftover

übrigens   by the way

die Uhr, -en   clock 1; **Wieviel ~ ist es?**   What time is it? 2; **um [zehn] ~**   at [ten] o'clock 2; **Um wieviel ~?**   At what time? 2

um (+ acc.)   at 2; around 4; **~ [zehn] Uhr**   at [ten] o'clock 2; **~ wieviel Uhr?**   At what time? 2; **Er ging ~ die Ecke.**   He went around the corner.; **~ ... zu (+ inf.)**   (in order) to 10; **Es geht nicht nur ~ [die Musik].**   It's not just about [the music]. 13

der Umstand, ⸚e   circumstance, situation; **unter Umständen**   perhaps, maybe

umständlich   involved 14; **Das ist [mir] zu umständlich.**   That's too much bother/trouble [for me]. 14

die Umwelt   environment 14

das Umweltbewußtsein   environmental awareness 14

umweltfreundlich   environment-friendly, eco-friendly 14

der Umweltsünder, -/die Umweltsünderin, -nen   environmental culprit

die Umweltumfrage, -n   environmental survey, poll

unbedingt   without reservation, absolutely 11

und   and 1; plus (in addition) 1; **~ dir/Ihnen?**   And you? (How about you?) 2

der Unfall, ⸚e   accident

unfreundlich   unfriendly 2

(das) Ungarn   Hungary

ungefähr   approximately 13

unglaub'lich   unbelievable, unbelievably 8

ungleich   different

die Uni, -s (colloq. for Universität) 2

die Universität', -en   university 2

uns   us 4

unser   our 3

unsicher   insecure; unsafe 12

unten   downstairs; below 6

unter (+ acc./dat.)   under, beneath; among 8; **~ anderem**   among other things

unterbre'chen (unterbricht), unterbrach, unterbrochen   to interrupt

unterhal'ten (unterhält), unterhielt, unterhalten   to entertain; **sich unterhalten**   to converse 11; **~ über (+ acc.)**   to converse about 11

der Unterschied, -e   difference 8

unzufrieden   dissatisfied

die Urgroßeltern (pl.)   great-grandparents

der Urlaub   vacation; **in or im or auf ~ sein**   to be on vacation; **in ~ fahren**   to go on vacation

die USA (pl.)   U.S.A. 3

usw. (= und so weiter)   and so forth

die Vase, -n   vase 8

der Vater, ⸚   father 5

der Vati, -s   dad 5

verän'dern   to change

die Verän'derung, -en   change

verant'wortlich (für) responsible (for) 11

die **Verant'wortung, -en** responsibility 9

das **Verb, -en** verb

der **Verband, ⁻e** association

verbin'den, verband, verbunden to combine

verbrau'chen to use up (water, gasoline, etc.) 14

verbrin'gen, verbrachte, verbracht to spend (time)

verdie'nen to earn 5

der **Verein', -e** club

verein'baren to arrange

vereint' unified

die **Verfas'sung, -en** constitution 9

verfol'gen to pursue; to follow; to persecute

verges'sen (vergißt), vergaß, vergessen to forget 10

verglei'chen, verglich, verglichen to compare

die **Vergnü'gung, -en** pleasure

verhaßt' hated

verhei'ratet married 9

verkau'fen to sell 12

der **Verkäu'fer, -/die Verkäu'ferin, -nen** salesperson

der **Verkehr'** traffic 14

das **Verkehrs'mittel, -** means of transportation 8

verlas'sen (verläßt), verließ, verlassen to leave, abandon 11

verlet'zen to injure, hurt 10; **Ich habe mir den Arm verletzt.** I've hurt my arm.; **Ich habe mich verletzt.** I hurt myself. 10

verlie'ren, verlor, verloren to lose 12

vermie'ten to rent (out)

der **Vermie'ter, -/die Vermie'terin, -nen** landlord/landlady

vermis'sen (vermißt) to miss someone or something

die **Verpa'ckung, -en** packaging 14

verrückt' crazy 14

verschie'den various

die **Verschmut'zung** pollution 14

verschö'nern to beautify

verschrot'ten to turn to scrap

versor'gen to provide for

verständ'lich understandable

versteh'en, verstand, verstanden to understand 6

versu'chen to try 11

verü'ben to commit

verur'sachen to cause 14

verwandt' related

der/die **Verwand'te** *(noun declined like adj.)* relative 10

verwech'seln to confuse or mistake something or someone for something or someone else

verwer'ten to make use of 14

der **Vetter, -n** cousin *(m.)* 5

das **Video, -s** video 5

der **Videorecorder, -** VCR, video cassette recorder

das **Videospiel, -e** video game 2

viel (mehr, meist-) much 2; **viele** many 4; **Viel Glück!** Good luck! 12; **viele Grüße** *(closing in a personal letter)* regards

vielleicht' maybe, perhaps 2

das **Viertel, -** a fourth, quarter 2; district of a city; **~ vor [zwei]** quarter to [two]; **~ nach [zwei]** quarter past [two] 2

der **Viktua'lienmarkt** an outdoor market in Munich

die **Vitamin'tablette, -n** vitamin pill 4

die **Voka'bel, -n** vocabulary word

voll full 8

der **Volleyball** volleyball 2

von (+ *dat.*) of 1; from 3; by [the person doing something]

vor (+ *acc./dat.*) before 2; in front of 8; **~ allem** above all 6; **~ [zehn] Jahren** [ten] years ago 6

vorbei' over; gone 11

vorbei'·kommen, kam vorbei, ist vorbeigekommen to come by 6; **bei [mir] ~** to come by [my] place 6

vor·bereiten to prepare 5; **sich ~ (auf + *acc.*)** to prepare oneself (for) 12

vorbereitet prepared; **Ich bin (nicht) gut vorbereitet.** I'm (not) well prepared. 5

die **Vorbereitung, -en** preparation 14

vor·haben to intend, have in mind 7

der **Vorhang, ⁻e** drape; curtain; der **Eiserne ~** the Iron Curtain

vorig last, previous; **voriges Jahr** last year

die **Vorlesung, -en** lecture 5

der **Vorname, -ns, -n** first name 8

die **Vorspeise, -n** appetizer

sich *(dat.)* **vor·stellen** to imagine 13; **Ich stelle mir das so vor, ...** I imagine that like this . . . 13

die **Vorstellung, -en** concept; notion; performance

der **Vorteil, -e** advantage

das **Vorurteil, -e** prejudice

die **Vorwahl, -en** area code

der **Wagen, -** car; wagon 6

die **Wahl** vote; choice, selection

wählen to choose; to elect

der **Wahlslogan, -s** election slogan

wahnsinnig crazy

wahr true 10; **nicht ~?** isn't that so? 10

während *(prep.)* (+ *gen.*) during 9; *(conj.)* while 13

wahrschein'lich *(adj.)* probable; *(adv.)* probably

der **Wald, ⁻er** forest 8

die **Wand, ⁻e** (interior) wall 1

der **Wanderer, -/die Wanderin, -nen** hiker

wandern, ist gewandert to hike; **~ gehen** to go walking/hiking 2

die **Wanderung, -en** hike 7; **eine ~ machen** to go on a hike 7

wann when 1; **seit ~** since when, (for) how long 5

war *(past tense of* **sein***)* was 3

die **Ware, -n** wares, merchandise, goods 12

wäre *(subj. of* **sein***)* would be 12

warm warm 3; **schön ~** nice and warm 3

warten (auf + *acc.*) to wait (for) 6

warum why 4

was what 2; **~ für (ein) ...** what kind of (a) . . . 2; **~ für ein Wetter!** Such weather! 3; **~ gab es?** What was playing? 11; **~ gibt's Neues?** What's new? 12; **~ gibt's zum [Abendessen]?** What's for [dinner]? 4; ~ **hast du?** What's wrong? 10; ~ **ist los?** What's wrong? 2; ~ **noch?** What else? 8

die **Wäsche** laundry 8; ~ **waschen** to do the laundry 8

waschen (ä), wusch, gewaschen to wash 8; **sich** ~ to wash oneself 8; **Ich wasche [mir] die Hände.** I'm washing [my] hands. 10

die **Waschmaschine, -n** washing machine 8

das **Wasser** water 4; **ein** ~ a bottle/glass of mineral water 7; die **~verschmutzung** water pollution

der **Wasserski, -er** water ski 6; **Wasserski fahren** to waterski 6

das **WC (das Wasserklosett)** toilet

wechseln to change 9

weg away 12

der **Weg, -e** way 4; **auf dem** ~ on the way 4

wegen (+ gen.) on account of, because of 9

weg·werfen (wirft weg), warf weg, weggeworfen to throw away 14

weh tun (+ dat.) to hurt 10; **Die Füße tun mir weh.** My feet hurt. 10

weil (conj.) because 6

die **Weile** while; **eine ganze** ~ a long time 12

der **Wein, -e** wine 4

das **Weingeschäft, -e** wine shop

weiß white 1

der **Weißwein, -e** white wine 4

weit far 8

weiter farther, further 3

der **Weizen** wheat

welch (-er, -es, -e) which 1; **Welche Farbe hat ... ?** What color is . . . ? 1; **Welcher Tag ist heute?** What day is today? 1

die **Welt, -en** world 10

der **Weltkrieg, -e** world war 10

wem (dat. of wer) (to or for) whom 6

wen (acc. of wer) whom

die **Wendung, -en** expression

wenig little 5; **ein** ~ a little 5;

wenige few 5

weniger minus (in subtraction) 1; less

wenigstens at least 13

wenn (conj.) when, whenever 4; if 5

wer who 2

der **Werbespot, -s** ad on TV or radio

die **Werbung** advertising

werden (wird), wurde, ist geworden to become 5; **will** (auxiliary verb of the fut. tense): **Das wird sie sicher finden.** She will certainly find it. 13

werfen (i), warf, geworfen to throw 14

das **Werkzeug, -e** tool

wessen (gen. of wer) whose 9

der **Westen** west 3

westlich western 11

das **Wetter** weather 3; **Was für ein ~!** Such weather! 3; **Wie ist das ~?** How's the weather? 3

wichtig important 6

wie how 1; as 3; ~ **alt bist du?** How old are you?; ~ **bitte?** I beg your pardon? 1; ~ **geht es Ihnen?** How are you? 2; ~ **geht's?** How are you? 2; ~ **immer** as always 12; ~ **ist das Wetter?** How is the weather? 3; ~ **ist deine Telefonnummer?** What is your telephone number? 1; ~ **lange** for how long; ~ **schreibt man das?** How do you spell that? 1; ~ **spät ist es?** What time is it?; ~ **wär's mit ... ?** How about . . . ?

wieder again 3; **immer** ~ again and again

die **Wiederho'lung, -en** review; repetition

Wiedersehen: Auf ~. Good-bye. 2

wiederum in turn; on the other hand

die **Wiedervereinigung** reunification 11

Wien Vienna

wieviel' how much 1; ~ **Grad ist es?** What's the temperature? 3; ~ **macht das?** How

much/What does that come to? 4; **wie viele** how many? 1

der **Wind** wind 3

windsurfen to windsurf; ~ **gehen** to go windsurfing 7

der **Winter** winter 3

wir we 2

wirklich really 3

die **Wirklichkeit** reality 9

die **Wirtschaft** economy 6

wirtschaftlich economically 10

die **Wirtschaftswissenschaft** economics

wissen (weiß), wußte, gewußt to know (a fact) 5

die **Wissenschaft, -en** science 9

der **Wissenschaftler, -/die Wissenschaftlerin, -nen** scientist 9

wo where 3

die **Woche, -n** week 1

das **Wochenende, -n** weekend 4; **Schönes ~!** Have a nice weekend! 4

woher where from 3; ~ **kommst du?** Where are you from? 3

wohin where (to) 6

wohl probably; indeed 6; well 10

wohnen to live, reside 3; **bei jemandem** ~ to live at someone else's residence

das **Wohnhaus, -häuser** residential building; apartment building

die **Wohnung, -en** dwelling; apartment 8

das **Wohnzimmer, -** living room 8

wollen (will), wollte, gewollt to want to; intend to 5

wollte (subj. of wollen) would want

das **Wort, ¨er** word 1; **das ~ haben** to have the floor; **Worte** words (in context)

der **Wortprozessor, -en** word processor; **mit dem ~ arbeiten** to do word processing 9

der **Wortschatz** vocabulary

wozu' what for, to what purpose, why

der **Wunsch, ¨e** wish 4; **Sonst noch einen ~?** Anything else? 4

wünschen to wish 6

würde (subj. of werden) would 12; **Ich ~ das nicht empfehlen.**

I wouldn't recommend that.

die **Wurst, ∺e** sausage 4; lunch meat

das **Würstchen, -** frankfurter 4

die **Würze, -n** spice

z.B. (*abbr. for* **zum Beispiel**) e.g. (for example) 5

die **Zahl, -en** number, numeral 1

zahlen to pay 5; **~ , bitte.** I'd like to pay, please (*in a restaurant*).

die **Zahlung, -en** payment; **in ~ nehmen** to take in trade

der **Zahn, ∺e** tooth 10

der **Zahnarzt, ∺e**/die **Zahnärztin, -nen** dentist 9

die **Zahnbürste, -n** toothbrush

die **Zahnpaste/Zahnpasta** toothpaste

die **Zahnschmerzen** (*pl.*) toothache 10

zeigen to show 9

die **Zeile, -n** line

die **Zeit, -en** time 5; **zur ~** at the moment 12

zeitgenössisch contemporary

die **Zeitlang: eine ~** a while

die **Zeitschrift, -en** magazine; journal 14

die **Zeitung, -en** newspaper 4; **Es**

stand in der ~. It said in the newspaper. 11

zelten to camp in a tent 6

das **Zentral' institut** department or school in university

das **Zentrum,** (*pl.*) **Zentren** center

zerstör'en to destroy 11

das **Ziel, -e** goal 10

ziemlich quite, rather, fairly 3

der **Zigeu'ner, -**/die **Zigeu'nerin, -nen** gypsy

das **Zimmer, -** room 1

zu (+ *dat.*) (*prep.*) to (*with people and some places*) 4; **~ Abend essen** to eat dinner 7; **~ Besuch** for a visit 6; **~ Ende** over, finished 11; **~ Fuß gehen** to walk 6; **~ Hause** (to be) at home; **um ... ~** (+ *inf.*) (in order) to 10; **zur Zeit** at the moment 12

zu too 3

zueinan'der to each other

zuerst' first of all; at first 6

zufrie'den satisfied, content

der **Zug, ∺e** train 6

das **Zuhau'se** home

die **Zukunft** future 12

zum (*contraction of* **zu dem**) to or for the

zumin'dest at least

zunächst' at first

zurück' back, in return 5

zurück'·bringen, brachte zurück, zurückgebracht to bring back

zurück'·fliegen, flog zurück, ist zurückgeflogen to fly back 13

zurück'·nehmen (nimmt zurück), nahm zurück, zurückgenommen to take back 14

zurück'·tragen (trägt zurück), trug zurück, zurückgetragen to take or carry back 14

zurück'·zahlen to pay back 5

zusam'men together 2

der **Zusam'menhang, ∺e** connection

zuviel' too much 5

zwar to be sure, it's true, indeed 8

zweit- second

zwingen, zwang, gezwungen to force, compel 11

zwischen (+ *acc.*/*dat.*) between, among 8

The English–German end vocabulary contains the words included in the active vocabulary lists and the *Erweiterung des Wortschatzes* section of the chapters. Not included from the active lists are numbers, articles and pronouns. The plural forms of nouns are given. Strong and irregular weak verbs are indicated with a raised degree mark (°). Their principal parts can be found in the Reference Section. Separable-prefix verbs are indicated with a raised dot: **mit·bringen.**

abdomen der Bauch, ⸚e
able: to be ~ to können°
about über
above all vor allem
abroad im Ausland
absent: to be ~ fehlen
absolute(ly) absolut; unbedingt
accident der Unfall, ⸚e
account: on ~ of wegen
acquaintance der/die Bekannte (*noun decl. like adj.*); **to make the ~ of** kennen·lernen
actually eigentlich
addition: in ~ noch, dazu
address die Adresse, -n; **What is your ~?** Wie ist deine/Ihre Adresse?
adult der/die Erwachsene (*noun decl. like adj.*)
advertisement die Reklame, -n; die Anzeige, -n
aerobics das Aerobic
afraid: to be ~ (of) Angst haben (vor + *dat.*), (sich) fürchten (vor + *dat.*)
after nach (*prep.*); nachdem (*conj.*); **~ all** schließlich
afternoon der Nachmittag, -e; **this ~** heute nachmittag
afternoons nachmittags
afterwards nachher
again wieder; noch einmal
against gegen
ago: [ten years] ~ vor [zehn Jahren]
air die Luft
airplane das Flugzeug, -e
airport der Flughafen, ⸚
all alle; **at ~** überhaupt; **~ day** den ganzen Tag
allowed: to be ~ to dürfen°

almost fast
alone allein
Alps die Alpen (*pl.*)
already schon
also auch
although obwohl
always immer
America (das) Amerika
American (*adj.*) amerikanisch; **~ (person)** der Amerikaner, -/ die Amerikanerin, -nen
among unter
and und; **~ so on** und so weiter
angry böse; **Don't be ~ with me.** Sei mir nicht böse; **to feel ~** sich ärgern
answer die Antwort, -en; **~ [the woman]** [der Frau] antworten; **to ~ the question** auf die Frage antworten, die Frage beantworten
any einige; etwas; **I don't have any . . .** Ich habe kein ...
anyone jemand
anything: ~ else? Sonst noch etwas?
apartment die Wohnung, -en
apology die Entschuldigung, -en
apparatus der Apparat, -e
appear scheinen°; erscheinen°
apple der Apfel, ⸚; **~ juice** der Apfelsaft
appliance das Gerät, -e
appointment der Termin, -e
approximately ungefähr
April der April
architect der Architekt, -en, -en/die Architektin, -nen
arm der Arm, -e
arrive an·kommen°
art die Kunst, ⸚e; **~ history** die

Kunstgeschichte
article der Artikel, -
artificial künstlich
as als; wie; **~ . . . ~** so ... wie; **~ always** wie immer
ask fragen; **~ for** bitten° um; **to ~ him a question** ihm/an ihn eine Frage stellen
aspirin das Aspirin
assignment die Aufgabe, -n
astonished erstaunt
at an; auf; **~ (a place)** bei; **~ [seven]** um [sieben]
attic der Dachboden
August der August
aunt die Tante, -n
Austria (das) Österreich
Austrian österreichisch (*adj.*); **~ (person)** der Österreicher, -/ die Österreicherin, -nen
author der Autor, -en/die Autorin, -nen
automobile das Auto, -s
autumn der Herbst
awareness das Bewußtsein
away weg; ab

back der Rücken, -; **~ache** die Rückenschmerzen (*pl.*); (*adv.*) zurück
bad schlecht; schlimm; böse; **not ~** ganz gut; **too ~** schade
badly schlecht
bag die Tasche, -n
bake backen°
baker der Bäcker, -/die Bäckerin, -nen
bakery die Bäckerei, -en; **at the ~** beim Bäcker; **to the ~** zum Bäcker
balcony der Balkon, -s

ballpoint pen der Kugelschreiber, - [der Kuli, -s (*colloq.*)]
banana die Banane, -n
band die Band, -s
bank die Bank, -en
bar die Bar, -s; die Kneipe, -n
basement der Keller, -
basketball der Basketball
bath das Bad, ¨er
bathe baden
bathing: ~ suit der Badeanzug,
  ¨e; ~ **trunks** die Badehose, -n
bathroom das Bad, ¨er; die
  Toilette, -n
be sein°; ~ **so kind.** Sei/Seien
  Sie so gut.
beautiful schön
because weil; denn; ~ **of**
  wegen
become werden°
bed das Bett, -en; **to make the ~**
  das Bett machen
bedroom das Schlafzimmer, -
beer das Bier; ~ **garden** der
  Biergarten, ¨
before vor; vorher; bevor
begin an·fangen°; beginnen°;
  ~ **the work** mit der Arbeit
  anfangen
beginning der Anfang, ¨e
behind hinter
believe glauben; **I ~ so.** Ich
  glaube schon/ja.
belong to gehören
beside bei; neben; außer; außer-
  halb
besides außerdem; außer
best best; ~ **of all** am besten
better besser
between zwischen
bicycle das Fahrrad, ¨er; **to ride a**
  ~ mit dem Fahrrad fahren
big groß
bike das Rad, ¨er; ~ **trip** die
  Radtour, -en
biology die Biologie
birthday der Geburtstag, -e;
  When is your ~ ? Wann hast
  du Geburtstag?; **for one's ~**
  zum Geburtstag
black schwarz
blond blond
blouse die Bluse, -n
blue blau

body der Körper, -
book das Buch, ¨er
book bag die Büchertasche, -n
bookcase das Bücherregal, -e
bookstore die Buchhandlung, -en
boot der Stiefel, -
border die Grenze, -n
boring langweilig
born geboren; **I was born in
  1977.** Ich bin 1977 geboren.
borrow borgen
boss der Chef, -s/die Chefin,
  -nen
both beide; beides
bother stören
bottle die Flasche, -n
boy der Junge, -n, -n; ~**friend**
  der Freund, -e
bread das Brot, -e
breakfast das Frühstück; **for ~**
  zum Frühstück; **to eat ~**
  frühstücken
breathe atmen
bridge die Brücke, -n
bright hell
bring bringen°; ~ **along**
  mit·bringen°
broke (out of money) pleite
broken: ~ down kaputt
brother der Bruder, ¨; **brothers
  and sisters** die Geschwister
  (*pl.*)
brown braun
brush: to ~ [my] teeth [mir] die
  Zähne putzen
build bauen
bus der Bus, -se
business das Geschäft, -e
businessman der Geschäftsmann,
  pl. Geschäftsmänner
businesspeople die Geschäfts-
  leute (*pl.*)
businesswoman die Geschäftsfrau, -en
busy: to be ~ beschäftigt sein; **to
  keep ~** (sich) beschäftigen
but aber; sondern
butcher der Metzger, -/die
  Metzgerin, -nen
butcher shop die Metzgerei, -en;
  at the ~ beim Metzger; **to
  the ~** zum Metzger
butter die Butter
buy kaufen

by (close to) bei, an (+ *dat.*),
  neben (+ *dat.*); ~ **[car]** mit
  [dem Auto]

café das Café, -s
cafeteria (university) die Mensa,
  -s *or* Mensen
cake der Kuchen, -; die Torte, -n
call nennen°; an·rufen°; **to ~
  [your] home** bei [dir]
  anrufen
called: it's ~ (es) heißt
calm ruhig
camera der Fotoapparat, -e; die
  Kamera, -s
camp campen; **to ~ in a tent**
  zelten
can können°
can die Dose, -n
Canada (das) Kanada
Canadian (person) der Kanadier,
  -/die Kanadierin, -nen
cap die Mütze, -n
capital die Hauptstadt, ¨e
car das Auto, -s; der Wagen, -
card die Karte, -n; **(playing) cards**
  die Karten (*pl.*)
cardboard die Pappe
care die Sorge, -n; **to ~ for**
  sorgen für; **to take ~ of something** auf etwas auf·passen
carpet der Teppich, -e
carrot die Karotte, -n
carry tragen°
cassette die Kassette, -n
cassette deck das Kassettendeck, -s
castle das Schloß, *pl.* Schlösser
cat die Katze, -n
CD player der CD-Spieler, -; der
  CD-Player, -
celebration die Feier, -n; das
  Fest, -e
cellar der Keller, -
century das Jahrhundert, -e
certain(ly) bestimmt; sicher
chair der Stuhl, ¨e; **easy ~** der
  Sessel, -
change wechseln
cheap billig
check: The ~, please. Zahlen,
  bitte.
cheerful lustig
cheese der Käse

chemistry die Chemie
chess das Schach; **~ game** das Schachspiel
chest of drawers die Kommode, -n
chicken das Hähnchen, -
child das Kind, -er
chin das Kinn
chocolate die Schokolade, -n
chore die Pflicht, -en; **household chores** die Hausarbeit; **to do the chores** den Haushalt machen
Christmas das Weihnachten; **Merry ~!** Frohe *or* Fröhliche Weihnachten!
church die Kirche, -n
cigarette die Zigarette, -n
circle der Kreis, -e
citizens' action group die Bürgerinitiative
city die Stadt, ¨e; **old part of the ~** die Altstadt; **~ hall** das Rathaus, ¨er
class die Klasse, -n; **German ~** die Deutschstunde
classical klassisch
clean sauber; **to ~** putzen; auf·räumen; sauber·machen
clear klar
client der Kunde, -n, n/die Kundin, -nen
climate das Klima
clock die Uhr, -en
close eng; nah(e)
close: to ~ schließen°; zu·machen
clothing die Kleidung; **article of ~** das Kleidungsstück, -e
coat der Mantel, ¨; **sport ~** das Jackett, -s; der Sakko, -s
coffee der Kaffee; **for (afternoon) ~** zum Kaffee; **to go for ~** Kaffee trinken gehen; **~house** das Kaffeehaus, ¨-er; **~ table** der Couchtisch, -e
cola drink die Cola
cold kalt; die Erkältung, -en; **to catch a ~** sich erkälten
colleague der Kollege, -n, -n/die Kollegin, -nen
collect sammeln
college das College, -s; **to go to ~** studieren; auf/an die Universität gehen

color die Farbe, -n; **What ~ is . . . ?** Welche Farbe hat … ?
comb der **Kamm,** ¨e; **to ~ (one's hair)** (sich) kämmen
come kommen°; **to ~ along** mit·kommen°; **to ~ by** vorbei·kommen°
commercial (TV or radio) der Werbespot, -s; die Reklame, -n
compact disc die Compact Disc, -s; die CD, -s
company die Gesellschaft, -en; die Firma, *pl.* Firmen; **to have ~** Besuch haben
compete konkurrieren
complete(ly) ganz; voll
compromise der Kompromiß, *pl.* Kompromisse
computer der Computer, -; **~ game** das Computerspiel, -e; **~ science** die Informatik; **~ language** die Programmiersprache, -n
concept die Vorstellung, -en
concert das Konzert, -e
concerto das Konzert, -e
condition der Zustand, ¨e
consciousness das Bewußtsein
constitution die Verfassung, -en
container (garbage receptacle) die Tonne, -n
contrary: on the ~ sondern; doch
cook kochen
cool kühl
corner die Ecke, -n
correct richtig
cost kosten
cough husten
could könnte
country das Land, ¨er; der Staat; **in our ~** bei uns; **in the ~** auf dem Land(e); **out into the ~** ins Grüne; **to the ~** aufs Land
course der Kurs, -e; die Vorlesung, -en; die Veranstaltung, -en
course: of ~ natürlich; klar; selbstverständlich
courtyard der Hof, ¨e
cousin *(female)* die Kusine, -n; **~** *(male)* der Vetter, -n
cover decken
cozy gemütlich

crazy verrückt
create schaffen°
criticism die Kritik, -en
crooked schief
cucumber die Gurke, -n
cultural(ly) kulturell
culture die Kultur, -en
curious neugierig; gespannt
customer der Kunde, -n, -n/die Kundin, -nen

dad der Vati, -s
daily täglich
dance: to ~ tanzen
dance club die Disco, -s
dancing: I'm going ~. Ich gehe tanzen.
danger die Gefahr, -en
dangerous gefährlich
dark dunkel
darling der Liebling, -e
data die Tatsachen *(pl.)*
date das Datum; **What's the ~ today?** Den wievielten haben wir heute?; Der wievielte ist heute?
daughter die Tochter, ¨
day der Tag, -e; **one/some ~** eines Tages; **all ~** den ganzen Tag; **days of the week** die Wochentage *(pl.)*
dear lieb (-er, -e, -es)
December der Dezember
decide (sich) entscheiden°; beschließen°; **to make a decision (after reflecting on it)** sich entscheiden
decorate dekorieren
deed die Tat, -en
degree der Grad
demonstrate demonstrieren
demonstration die Demonstration, -en
dentist der Zahnarzt, ¨e/die Zahnärztin, -nen
depart ab·fahren°
department store das Kaufhaus, -häuser
depend on ab·hängen von
describe beschreiben°
desire die Lust
desk der Schreibtisch, -e
dessert der Nachtisch, -e
destroy zerstören

develop (sich) entwickeln
development die Entwick-
lung, -en
dialect der Dialekt, -e
die sterben°
difference der Unterschied, -e
different verschieden; anders;
something ~ (et)was anderes
difficult schwer; schwierig
difficulty die Schwierigkeit, -en
dining room das Eßzimmer, -
dinner das Abendessen, -; **for ~**
zum Abendessen; **to eat ~**
zu Abend essen
discussion die Diskussion, -en
dishes das Geschirr
dishwasher die Spülmaschine, -n;
der Geschirrspüler, -
diskette die Diskette, -n
distorted schief
district das Viertel, -; **city ~** das
Stadtviertel, -
disturb stören
divide teilen; auf·teilen (in + *acc.*)
divided by [in mathematics]
geteilt durch
do machen; tun°; **to ~ a task**
eine Arbeit machen; **to ~**
chores den Haushalt machen
doctor der Arzt, ⁻e/die
Ärztin, -nen; **to go to the ~**
zum Arzt gehen
dog der Hund, -e
doll die Puppe, -n
done fertig; **to have something ~**
etwas machen lassen
door die Tür, -en
dormitory das Studentenheim, -e
downstairs unten
dream: to ~ of träumen (von)
dress das Kleid, -er; **to ~** (sich)
an·ziehen°; **I get dressed.** Ich
ziehe mich an.
drink das Getränk, -e; **to ~**
trinken°
drive fahren°; **to ~ along**
mit·fahren; **to ~ away**
weg·fahren°; **to go for a ~**
spazieren·fahren°
driver der Fahrer, -/die Fah-
rerin, -nen
dry trocken; **to ~ (dishes)**
ab·trocknen
dumb dumm; **something ~**

etwas Dummes
during während
dust der Staub; **to ~** Staub
wischen
duty die Pflicht, -en
dwelling die Wohnung, -en

each jed- (-er, -es, -e)
ear das Ohr, -en
early früh
earn verdienen
east der Osten
easy leicht
easygoing ruhig
eat essen°
economic wirtschaftlich
economy die Wirtschaft
educate aus·bilden
education die Erziehung; die
Ausbildung; das Schulwesen
egg das Ei, -er
else: what ~ ? was noch?; **some-**
thing ~ ? sonst noch etwas?
employed berufstätig
employee der Arbeitnehmer,
-/die Arbeitnehmerin, -nen;
der Mitarbeiter, -/die
Mitarbeiterin, -nen
employer der Arbeitgeber, -/die
Arbeitgeberin, -nen
empty leer
end das Ende, -n; **in/at the ~**
am Ende
energy die Energie
engage: to ~ in sports Sport
treiben
engineer der Ingenieur, -e/die
Ingenieurin, -nen
England (das) England
English (*adj.*) englisch; **~**
language (das) Englisch
enjoy: to ~ something Spaß an
einer Sache haben
enjoyment die Lust; das
Vergnügen; der Spaß
enough genug
entrance hall der Flur, -e
environment die Umwelt; **envi-**
ronment-friendly umweltfreundlich; **~al awareness**
das Umweltbewußtsein
especially besonders
etc. usw.
eternal(ly) ewig

even sogar; **~ if** auch wenn
evening der Abend, -e; **Good ~.**
Guten Abend.; **this ~** heute
abend
evenings abends
every jed- (-er, -es, -e)
everyone jeder
everything alles
everywhere überall
exactly genau; **~ the same**
genauso
examination die Klausur, -en; die
Prüfung, -en; **comprehensive**
~ das Examen, -; **to take an ~**
eine Klausur schreiben
examine durch·sehen°; prüfen
example das Beispiel, -e; **for ~**
zum Beispiel (z.B.)
excellent(ly) ausgezeichnet
except außer
excuse die Entschuldigung, -en;
~ me! Entschuldigung!
expect erwarten
expensive teuer
experience die Erfahrung, -en
explain erklären
explanation die Erklärung, -en
expressway die Autobahn, -en
eye das Auge, -n

face das Gesicht, -er
fact die Tatsache, -n
factory die Fabrik, -en
fairly ganz; ziemlich
fall der Herbst; **to ~** fallen°
false falsch
familiar bekannt
family die Familie, -n
famous bekannt; berühmt
fantastic phantastisch; toll; prima
far weit
farmer der Bauer, -n, -n/die
Bäuerin, -nen
farmhouse das Bauernhaus,
-häuser
farther weiter
fast schnell
fat dick
father der Vater, ⁻
favorite Lieblings-; **~ (program)**
(die) Lieblings(sendung)
fear die Angst, ⁻e; **to ~** sich
fürchten (vor + *dat.*); **to ~ for**
Angst haben um

feast das Fest, -e
February der Februar
Federal Republic of Germany die Bundesrepublik Deutschland (BRD)
feel sich fühlen; **to ~ like** Lust haben; **I don't ~ like working.** Ich habe keine Lust zu arbeiten.; **I don't ~ like it.** Dazu habe ich keine Lust.
feeling das Gefühl, -e
fence der Zaun, ⸚e
fever das Fieber
few wenig(e); **a ~** ein paar
fight kämpfen
film der Film, -e
finally endlich, schließlich
find finden°
fine fein; gut; **I'm ~.** Es geht mir gut.
finger der Finger, -
finished fertig; zu Ende
first erst; **at ~** zuerst; **~ of all** erst einmal, erstens
first name der Vorname, -ns, -n
first-rate klasse, spitze, ausgezeichnet
fish der Fisch, -e
fit passen
flatware das Besteck, -e
floor der Boden, ⸚; **~ (of a building)** der Stock, pl. Stockwerke; **first ~** das Erdgeschoß
flower die Blume, -n
fluent(ly) fließend
fly fliegen°
food das Essen; die Lebensmittel (pl.)
foot der Fuß, ⸚e; **to go on ~** zu Fuß gehen°; laufen°
for für (prep.); denn (conj.); **(time)** seit; **~ a year** seit einem Jahr
force zwingen°
foreign fremd
foreigner der Ausländer, -/die Ausländerin, -nen
forest der Wald, ⸚er
forever ewig
forget vergessen°
forgetful vergeßlich
fork die Gabel, -n
(the) former jen- (-er, -es, -e); ehemalig

formerly früher
fortunately zum Glück
fourth das Viertel, -
France (das) Frankreich
frank(ly) offen
free frei; **for ~** umsonst, gratis
freeway die Autobahn, -en
freezer der Gefrierschrank, ⸚e
French (adj.) französisch; **~ (language)** (das) Französisch
French fries die Pommes frites (pl.)
fresh frisch
Friday der Freitag
friend der Freund, -e/die Freundin, -nen
friendliness die Freundlichkeit
friendly freundlich
from von; **~ (native of)** aus; **Where do you come ~?** Woher kommst du?
fruit das Obst
full voll
fun das Vergnügen; der Spaß; **That's ~.** Es macht Spaß.
funny lustig
furnished möbliert
furniture die Möbel (pl.); **piece of ~** das Möbelstück, -e
further weiter
future die Zukunft

game das Spiel, -e
garage die Garage, -n
garbage der Müll
garden der Garten, ⸚
gasoline das Benzin
general: in ~ überhaupt, allgemein
gentleman der Herr, -n, -en
genuine echt
German (adj.) deutsch; **~ (person)** der/die Deutsche (noun decl. like adj.); **~ (language)** (das) Deutsch; **to do ~ (homework)** Deutsch machen; **I'm doing ~.** Ich mache Deutsch.; **~ Mark** D-Mark; **~ studies (language and literature)** die Germanistik
German Democratic Republic die Deutsche Demokratische Republik (DDR)
Germany (das) Deutschland

get bekommen°; kriegen; **to ~ up** auf·stehen°; **to ~ together** zusammen·kriegen, sich treffen°
girl das Mädchen, -; **~friend** die Freundin, -nen
give geben°; **to ~ (as a gift)** schenken; **to ~ up** auf·geben°
glad froh
gladly gern
glove der Handschuh, -e
go gehen°; **to ~ along** mit·gehen; **to ~ along with [you]** mit [dir] mitgehen; **to ~ by [car]** mit [dem Auto] fahren°
goal das Ziel, -e
golf das Golf
gone weg
good gut; **~ Gracious/Heavens!** Du meine Güte!
good-bye Auf Wiedersehen.; Tschüs. (colloq.)
government die Regierung, -en
grade die Note, -n; **[seventh] ~** [die siebte] Klasse
grandfather der Großvater, ⸚
grandmother die Großmutter, ⸚
grandparents die Großeltern (pl.)
grape die Traube, -n
gray grau
great toll, ausgezeichnet, prima
green grün
greeting der Gruß, ⸚e
groceries die Lebensmittel (pl.)
group die Gruppe, -n
grow wachsen°
guest der Gast, ⸚e; der Besucher, -/die Besucherin, -nen
guilty schuldig; **not ~** unschuldig
guitar die Gitarre, -n

hair das Haar, -e
half die Hälfte, -n; halb
hall der Flur, -e
hand die Hand, ⸚e
handbag die (Hand)tasche, -n
hang hängen°
happen passieren°; **What happened to you?** Was ist dir passiert?
happy froh, glücklich
hard hart; schwer

hardly kaum
hard-working fleißig
has hat
hat der Hut, ¨e
hatred der Haß; ~ **of foreigners** der Ausländerhaß
have haben°; **to ~ to** müssen°; **to ~ something done** etwas machen lassen°; ~ **some cake.** Nehmen Sie etwas Kuchen.
head der Kopf, ¨e
headache die Kopfschmerzen *(pl.)*
healthy gesund
hear hören
heavy schwer
hello Guten Tag.; Grüß dich.; Hallo. *(informal)*
help helfen°; **to ~ with [work]** bei [der Arbeit] helfen; ~! Hilfe!; ~ **me!** Hilf mir!
here hier, da; ~ **[toward the speaker]** her; ~ **you are** bitte sehr
Hey! Du!; He!
Hi! Tag!
high hoch
hike die Wanderung, -en; **to ~** wandern
history die Geschichte
hobby das Hobby, -s
hold halten°
holiday der Feiertag, -e
home: at ~ zu Hause; **(to go) ~** nach Hause; **at the ~ of** bei
homeland die Heimat
homework die Hausaufgaben *(pl.)*; **to do ~** die Hausaufgaben machen
homosexual der/die Homosexu- elle *(noun decl. like adj.)*
hope die Hoffnung, -en; **to ~** hoffen; **to ~ for** hoffen auf *(+ acc.)*; **I ~** hoffentlich
horrible furchtbar; fürchterlich; schrecklich
horribly furchtbar; fürchterlich; schrecklich
hospital das Krankenhaus, ¨er
hot heiß
hour die Stunde, -n
house das Haus, ¨er
household der Haushalt
housework die Hausarbeit

how wie; ~ **are you?** Wie geht es Ihnen?/Wie geht's?
however aber
human being der Mensch, -en, -en
hunch die Ahnung, -en
hunger der Hunger
hungry: to be ~ Hunger haben; **to get ~** Hunger bekommen/ kriegen
hurt weh tun°
husband der (Ehe)mann, ¨er

ice das Eis
ice cream das Eis
idea die Idee, -n; die Vorstellung, -en; die Ahnung; **No ~!** Keine Ahnung!
idle: be ~ faulenzen
if wenn; ob; **even ~** wenn auch
ill krank
illegible unleserlich
illness die Krankheit, -en
image das Bild, -er; die Vorstel- lung, -en
imagine sich *(dat.)* vor·stellen; ~ **that!** Stell dir das vor!
immediately gleich
important wichtig; **to be ~** eine Rolle spielen
impression der Eindruck, ¨e
improve verbessern
in(to) in; hinein
indeed in der Tat
independent unabhängig
individual einzeln
industrious fleißig
industry die Industrie, -n
inflation die Inflation
influence beeinflussen°
inhabitant der Einwohner, -/die Einwohnerin, -nen
injure verletzen
innocent(ly) unschuldig
in order to um ... zu
insecure unsicher
insert stecken
in spite of trotz
instead of (an)statt
instrument das Instrument, -e
intelligent intelligent
intend to vor·haben°; wollen
interested: to be ~ (in) (sich) interessieren (für)

interesting interessant
international international
intolerance die Intoleranz
invite ein·laden°
is ist; **isn't it?** nicht?; nicht wahr? *(tag question)*; **Your name is [Monica], isn't it?** Du heißt [Monika], nicht?

jacket die Jacke, -n
January der Januar
jeans die Jeans *(pl.)*
job der Beruf, -e; der Job, -s; die Stelle, -n; **to have a ~** berufs- tätig sein; **to have a temporary ~** jobben
jogging das Jogging
join in mit·machen (bei + *dat.*)
journalist der Journalist, -en, -en/die Journalistin, -nen
juice der Saft, ¨e
July der Juli
June der Juni
just eben; erst; gerade

key der Schlüssel, -
kilogram das Kilo(gramm)
kilometer der Kilometer, -
kind gut, nett; **be so ~** sei/seien Sie so gut/nett; **what ~ of per- son** was für ein Mensch
kindergarten der Kindergarten
kitchen die Küche, -n; ~ **appli- ance** das Küchengerät, -e; ~ **range** der Herd, -e
knee das Knie, -
knife das Messer, -
know (a fact) wissen°; **to ~ (be acquainted)** kennen°; **to get to ~** kennen·lernen; **to ~ [German]** Deutsch können

lack fehlen
lake der See, -n
lamp die Lampe, -n
land das Land, ¨er
language die Sprache, -n
large groß
last letzt; ~ **night** gestern abend; **to ~** dauern
late spät
later später; **until ~** bis später, tschüs, bis dann, bis bald
laugh lachen

laundry die Wäsche
law das Gesetz, -e; **~ (field of study)** Jura *(no article)*
lawyer der Jurist, -en, -en/die Juristin, -nen; der Rechtsanwalt, ⸚e/die Rechtsanwältin, -nen
lay legen
lazy faul
lead führen
learn lernen
least: at ~ wenigstens
leave lassen°; weg·fahren°; ab·fahren°
lecture die Vorlesung, -en
left: on/to the ~ links
leg das Bein, -e
leisure time die Freizeit
lend leihen°
lesson die Stunde, -n; **piano ~** die Klavierstunde, -n
let lassen°
letter der Brief, -e
lettuce der (Kopf)salat, -e
library die Bibliothek, -en
lie liegen°
life das Leben, -
light *(adj.)* leicht ; **~ (in color)** hell
like: would ~ to möchte; **to ~** gern haben; mögen; gefallen°; **What do you ~ to do?** Was machst du gern? **I ~ to swim.** Ich schwimme gern. **How do you ~ the cheese?** Wie findest du den Käse?
likewise ebenso; auch
lip die Lippe, -n
listen: to ~ to music Musik hören
literature die Literatur
little klein; wenig; **a ~** ein bißchen, ein wenig
live leben; wohnen
living room das Wohnzimmer, -
living standard der Lebensstandard
located: to be ~ liegen°
lock das Schloß, *pl.* Schlösser
long lang; lange; **a ~ time** lange
longer: no ~ nicht mehr
look: to ~ at an·sehen°, an·schauen; **to ~ like . . .** wie . . . aus·sehen°; **to ~ for** suchen; **to ~ forward to** sich freuen auf (+ *acc.*)

lose verlieren°
lot: a ~ viel
loud laut
lounge around faulenzen
love die Liebe; **to ~** lieben; **in ~** verliebt
low niedrig
luck das Glück; **Good ~!** Viel Glück!; **to be lucky** Glück haben
lunch das Mittagessen; **for ~** zum Mittagessen; **to have ~** zu Mittag essen°
lunch meat die Wurst, ⸚e

machine die Maschine, -n
magazine die Zeitschrift, -en
major subject das Hauptfach, ⸚er
mail die Post
main Haupt-; **~ train station** der Hauptbahnhof, ⸚e
make machen
mama die Mama
man der Mann, ⸚er; **~!** Mensch!
manner die Art
many viele; **how ~** wie viele; **too ~** zu viele
map die Landkarte, -n
March der März
margarine die Margarine
market der Markt, ⸚e
marmalade die Marmelade
marriage die Heirat, -en
married verheiratet
marry heiraten
math die Mathe
mathematics die Mathematik
matter aus·machen; **it doesn't ~** (es) macht nichts; **it doesn't ~ to [me]** es macht [mir] nichts aus
May der Mai
may dürfen°; **that ~ well be** das mag wohl sein
maybe vielleicht
meal das Essen
mean meinen; bedeuten; **What does that ~?** Was bedeutet das?
meaning die Bedeutung, -en
meanwhile inzwischen
meat das Fleisch
meat market die Metzgerei, -en

medicine das Medikament, -e
meet (sich) treffen°; kennen·lernen; **I'm meeting friends.** Ich treffe mich mit Freunden.
member das Mitglied, -er
merchandise die Ware, -n
merchant der Kaufmann, ⸚er/ die Kauffrau, -en; *(pl.)* die Kaufleute
mere(ly) bloß
merry lustig
microwave oven der Mikrowellenherd, -e
milk die Milch
million die Million, -en
mind: to have in ~ vor·haben°
mineral water das Mineralwasser
minor subject das Nebenfach, ⸚er
minute die Minute, -n; **Just a ~, please!** Einen Moment, bitte!
mirror der Spiegel, -
Miss Fräulein
missing: to be ~ fehlen
mixer (food processor) die Küchenmaschine, -n
modern modern
mom die Mutti, -s; die Mama
moment der Moment, -e; **at the ~** im Moment, zur Zeit
Monday der Montag
Mondays montags
money das Geld
month der Monat, -e
more mehr; **no ~ . . .** kein ... mehr; **~ and ~** immer mehr; **~ or less** mehr oder weniger
morning der Morgen; **Good ~.** Guten Morgen.; **this ~** heute morgen
mornings morgens
most of the time meistens
mostly meistens
mother die Mutter, ⸚
motorcycle das Motorrad, ⸚er
motto das Motto, -s
mountain der Berg, -e
mouth der Mund, ⸚er
movie der Film, -e; **~ theater** das Kino, -s
movies das Kino, -s; **to the ~** ins Kino
Mr. Herr

Mrs. Frau
Ms. Frau
much viel; **how ~** wieviel; **too ~** zuviel
multicultural multikulturell
music die Musik
music lesson die Musikstunde, -n
musical das Musical, -s
musical instrument das Musik-instrument, -e
musician der Musiker, -/die Musikerin, -nen
must müssen°
mystery (novel or film) der Krimi, -s

name Name, -ns, -n; **first ~** der Vorname, -ns, -n; **last ~** der Nachname, -ns, -n; **What is your ~?** Wie heißen Sie?; **to ~** nennen°; **Your ~ is [Mark], isn't it?** Du heißt [Mark], nicht?
named: to be ~ heißen°
napkin die Serviette, -n
narrow eng
natural(ly) klar; natürlich; selbst-verständlich
nature die Natur
near bei; **~by** in der Nähe, nah(e)
neck der Hals, ⁻e
need brauchen
neighbor der Nachbar, -n, -n/die Nachbarin, -nen
neighboring country das Nach-barland, ⁻er
nephew der Neffe, -n, -n
nervous nervös
never nie
nevertheless trotzdem
new neu; **What's ~?** Was gibt's Neues?
newspaper die Zeitung, -en
next nächst
nice nett; schön
niece die Nichte, -n
night die Nacht, ⁻e; **last ~** gestern abend; **Good ~.** Gute Nacht.
no nein; kein; nicht; **~ longer** nicht mehr; **~ more . . .** kein ... mehr
noodles die Nudeln (pl.)

no one niemand
nonsense der Quatsch
north der Norden
nose die Nase, -n
not nicht; **isn't that so?** nicht?; **~ at all** gar nicht; **~ any, no** kein; **~ only . . . but also . . .** nicht nur ... sondern auch ...
note die Notiz, -en
notebook das Heft, -e
nothing nichts; **~ special** nichts Besonderes
notice bemerken, merken
novel der Roman, -e
November der November
now jetzt; nun; **~ and then** ab und zu
number die Zahl, -en
numeral die Zahl, -en
nurse der Krankenpfleger, -/die Krankenpflegerin, -nen; **~ (fe-male only)** die Kranken-schwester, -n
nursery school der Kinder-garten, ⁻

observe beobachten
obtain bekommen; kriegen
occupied: to be ~ beschäftigt sein
occupy beschäftigen
occur (to come into one's mind) einfallen°
ocean der Ozean, -e
October der Oktober
of von
offer an·bieten°
office das Büro, -s
often oft
oh ach, ah; **~ I see** ach so; **~ my** o je; **~ well** naja
OK okay (O.K.); ganz gut; **It's (not) ~.** Es geht (nicht).
old alt; **I'm [19] years ~.** Ich bin [19] Jahre alt. **How ~ are you?** Wie alt bist du?
on an; auf; **~ account of** wegen
once einmal; mal; **~ more** noch einmal
one (pronoun) man; **~ another** einander
oneself selbst, selber
only nur; erst; bloß
open offen, geöffnet; **to ~** auf·machen; öffnen

opera die Oper, -n
opinion die Meinung, -en; **What's your ~?** Was hältst du davon?
or oder
orange die Orange, -n; **~ juice** der Orangensaft
orchestra das Orchester, -
order die Ordnung; **in ~** in Ordnung; **to ~** bestellen
organization die Organisation, -en
organize organisieren
other ander- (-er, -es, -e)
otherwise sonst; anders
out of aus
outside draußen
over (time) vorbei; **~ (position)** über
own (adj.) eigen; (verb) besitzen°

packaging die Verpackung, -en
page die Seite, -n
pain der Schmerz, -en
paint malen; streichen
pale blaß
pants die Hose, -n
pantyhose die Strumpfhose, -n
paper das Papier; **~ (theme, es-say)** die Arbeit, -en; **~ plate** der Pappteller, -
paperback das Taschenbuch, ⁻er
pardon: I beg your ~? Wie bitte?
parents die Eltern (pl.)
park der Park, -s
part der Teil, -e; **in ~** zum Teil; **to play a ~** eine Rolle spielen
participate (in) mit·machen (bei); **I ~ in a game.** Ich mache bei einem Spiel mit.
particular besonder-
particularly besonders
party die Party, -s; die Feier, -n; das Fest, -e; die Fete, -n; **at a ~** auf einem Fest; **to give a ~** ein Fest geben; **to go to a ~** auf ein Fest gehen
passive passiv
patio die Terrasse, -n
pay: to ~ for bezahlen; zahlen; **to ~ back** zurückzahlen
peace der Frieden
pedestrian der Fußgänger, -/die Fußgängerin, -nen; **~ zone** die Fußgängerzone, -n

pen der Kugelschreiber, - [der Kuli, -s *(colloq.)*]

pencil der Bleistift, -e

people die Leute *(pl.)*; die Menschen *(pl.)*; die Einwohner *(pl.)*; man

per pro

percent das Prozent

perhaps vielleicht

period der Punkt, -e

permit lassen°

permitted: to be ~ dürfen°

person der Mensch, -en, -en; die Person, -en

pharmacy die Apotheke, -n; **to the ~** in die Apotheke

philosophy die Philosophie

photograph das Bild, das Foto; **to ~** fotografieren

physics die Physik

piano das Klavier, -e; **~ lesson** die Klavierstunde, -n

pick up ab·holen

picnic das Picknick, -s

picture das Bild, -er

piece das Stück, -e

Ping-Pong das Tischtennis

pity: what a ~ schade

place der Platz, ̈-e; die Stelle, -n; der Ort, -e; **to my ~** zu mir; **at my ~** bei mir

plan der Plan, ̈-e; **to ~** vor·haben°; planen

plant die Pflanze, -n; **to ~** pflanzen

plastic das Plastik

play das Theaterstück, -e; **to ~** spielen

please bitte; **to ~** gefallen°

pleased: to be ~ (about) sich freuen (über + *acc.*)

pleasure die Freude, -n; die Lust; das Vergnügen

pocket die Tasche, -n

point der Punkt, -e

police die Polizei

political(ly) politisch

politician der Politiker, -/die Politikerin, -nen

portion der Teil, -e

position die Stelle, -n

possible möglich; **It's (not) ~.** Es geht (nicht).; **That would (not) be ~.** Das ginge (nicht).

post office die Post; **to go to the ~** auf die *or* zur Post gehen

postal code die Postleitzahl, -en

postcard die Postkarte, -n

poster das/der Poster, -

potato die Kartoffel, -n

pound das Pfund, -e

practical(ly) praktisch

prefer: I ~ to work. Ich arbeite lieber.

prejudice das Vorurteil, -e

preparation die Vorbereitung, -en

prepare (for) (sich) vor·bereiten (auf + *acc.*)

present das Geschenk, -e

president der Präsident, -en, -en/die Präsidentin, -nen

pretty schön; **~ pale** ganz schön blaß

price der Preis, -e

private(ly) privat

probably wahrscheinlich

produce her·stellen, produzieren

product das Produkt, -e

profession der Beruf, -e

professor der Professor, -en/die Professorin, -nen

program das Programm, -e; **TV *or* radio ~** die Sendung, -en

programmer der Programmierer, -/die Programmiererin, -nen

promise versprechen°

protect schützen

proud(ly) stolz

psychology die Psychologie

pub die Kneipe, -n; die Gaststätte, -n; die Wirtschaft, -en

public öffentlich; staatlich

pullover der Pulli, -s; der Pullover, -

punctual(ly) pünktlich

pure rein

purse die Handtasche, -n

put legen; stellen; stecken; setzen; hängen

quality die Qualität, -en

quarter das Viertel, -

question die Frage, -n

questionable fraglich

quick schnell

quiet ruhig; still

quite ziemlich

racism der Rassismus

radio das Radio, -s

railroad die Bahn, -en

rain der Regen; **to ~** regnen

raincoat der Regenmantel, ̈

range (kitchen) der Herd, -e

rare(ly) selten

rather ziemlich; **~ than** lieber als

raw material der Rohstoff, -e

reach erreichen

read lesen°

ready fertig

real echt; richtig

reality die Wirklichkeit

really wirklich; richtig; echt *(slang)*; **~ neat** echt toll

reason der Grund, ̈-e; **for that ~** daher; darum; deshalb; deswegen; aus diesem Grund

reasonable (price) günstig

receive bekommen°

recently vor kurzem; neulich; seit kurzer Zeit

recommend empfehlen°

record die Platte, -n

record player der Plattenspieler, -

recover (from) sich erholen (von)

recuperate sich erholen

recycle recyceln

recycling das Recycling

red rot

refrigerator der Kühlschrank, ̈-e

rehearsal die Probe, -n

related verwandt

relative der/die Verwandte *(noun decl. like adj.)*

remain bleiben°

remaining übrig

remember (someone/something) sich erinnern (an + jemand/etwas)

rent die Miete, -n; **to ~** mieten; vermieten

repair reparieren

report das Referat, -e; **to ~** berichten

reporter der Reporter, -/die Reporterin, -nen

request bitten° (+ um)

responsibility die Verantwortung, -en

responsible verantwortlich

rest der Rest, -e; **to ~** sich aus·ruhen

restaurant das Restaurant, -s; die
Gaststätte, -n; **town hall ~**
der Ratskeller, -
return zurück·fahren°; zurück·ge-
hen°; zurück·kommen°; **to
~ (something)** (etwas) zu-
rück·nehmen°
reunification die Wiedervereinigung
rich reich
ride: to ~ a bike mit dem Fahrrad fahren°, rad·fahren°
right das Recht, -e; **Is it all ~ with
you?** Ist es dir recht?; **to be ~**
recht haben; **you're ~** du hast
recht; **that's ~** genau; richtig;
~ to Recht (auf + *acc.*); **equal
rights** die Gleichberechtigung; **on/to the ~** rechts
ring klingeln
rinse spülen
river der Fluß, *pl.* Flüsse
roast beef der Rinderbraten
rock: ~ music die Rockmusik; ~
musician der Rockmusiker, -
/die Rockmusikerin, -nen
role die Rolle, -n
roll das Brötchen, -
romance (novel) der Liebesroman, -e
room das Zimmer, -
rug der Teppich, -e
run laufen°
running das Jogging

sad traurig
safe sicher
sail: to ~ segeln
salary das Gehalt, ̈er
same gleich; **It's all the ~ to me.**
Das ist mir egal.
sandwich das [Wurst]Brot, -e
satisfied zufrieden
Saturday der Samstag; der Sonnabend
Saturdays samstags
sausage die Wurst, ̈e
save (time, money, etc.) sparen
say sagen
schedule der Stundenplan, ̈e
school die Schule, -n
science die Wissenschaft, -en; die
Naturwissenschaft, -en

scientist der Wissenschaftler, -/
die Wissenschaftlerin, -nen
season die Jahreszeit, -en
seat der Platz, ̈e; **Is this ~ taken?**
Ist hier frei?; **to ~ oneself**
sich setzen°
secretary der Sekretär, -e/die Sekretärin, -nen
see sehen°
seem scheinen°
seldom selten
self: oneself, myself, itself, etc.
selbst, selber
sell verkaufen
semester das Semester, -
seminar das Seminar, -e; ~
room das Seminar, -e; ~
report die Seminararbeit, -en
send schicken
sentence der Satz, ̈e
separate: to ~ trennen
September der September
serious ernst; **Are you ~?** Ist
das dein Ernst?
serve dienen
set setzen; **to ~ the table** den
Tisch decken
several einige; mehrere
shampoo das Shampoo
shave (sich) rasieren
shine scheinen°
ship das Schiff, -e
shirt das Hemd, -en
shoe der Schuh, -e
shop das Geschäft, -e; der Laden, ̈; **to ~** ein·kaufen
shopping: to go ~ ein·kaufen
gehen
shopping bag die Einkaufstasche, -n
short kurz; **~ (people)** klein
shorts die Shorts (*pl.*)
show zeigen
shower die Dusche, -n; **to ~**
(sich) duschen
sick krank
side die Seite, -n
significance die Bedeutung
similar ähnlich; gleich
simple einfach
simply einfach
since seit (*prep.*); da (*conj.* =
because); **~ when** seit wann
sing singen°

singer der Sänger, -/die Sängerin,
-nen
single einzeln
single-family home das Einfamilienhaus, ̈er
sister die Schwester, -n
sit sitzen°; **to ~ down** sich setzen
situated: to be ~ liegen°
situation die Situation, -en
ski der Ski, -er; **to ~** Ski lau-
fen°, Ski fahren°
skirt der Rock, ̈e
sleep schlafen°; **to ~ at [a
friend's] house** bei [einem
Freund] schlafen
slow(ly) langsam
small klein
smart intelligent
smell riechen°
smile (about) lächeln (über +
acc.)
smog der Smog
smoke der Rauch; **to ~** rauchen
snow der Schnee; **to ~**
schneien
so so; also; **Isn't that ~?** Nicht?;
~ that damit; **~ long.**
Tschüs.; **I believe ~.** Ich
glaube schon/ja.
soap die Seife
soccer der Fußball
society die Gesellschaft, -en
sock die Socke, -n
sofa das Sofa, -s
soft drink die Limonade, -n
software die Software
soldier der Soldat, -en, -en/die
Soldatin, -nen
solution die Lösung, -en
solve lösen
some etwas; einige; manch (-er,
-es, -e); **at ~ point** irgendwann
someone jemand
something etwas/was; **~ like
that** so was
sometime irgendwann
sometimes manchmal
somewhat etwas
son der Sohn, ̈e
song das Lied, -er
soon bald; **as ~ as** sobald
sorry: I'm ~ (es) tut mir leid
south der Süden

space der Platz, ⸚e

spaghetti die Spaghetti (pl.)

Spanish (language) (das) Spanisch

speak sprechen°

speechless sprachlos

spell buchstabieren; **How do you ~ that?** Wie schreibt man das?

spend (money) aus·geben°; **to ~ (time)** verbringen°; **to ~ the night** übernachten

spite: in ~ of trotz

splendid großartig

spoon der Löffel, -

sport der Sport; **to engage in sports** Sport treiben°

spring der Frühling

stairs die Treppe, -n

stand stehen°; **to ~ up** auf·stehen°; **to ~/put upright** stellen

standard German (das) Hochdeutsch

state (in Germany) das Land, ⸚er; **~ (in the U.S.A.)** der Staat, -en

state-owned staatlich

stay: to ~ bleiben°

steak das Steak, -s

step der Schritt, -e; die Stufe, -n

stepfather der Stiefvater, ⸚

stepmother die Stiefmutter, ⸚

steps die Treppe, -n

stereo system die Stereoanlage, -n

still noch; immer noch; noch immer

stomach der Magen

stomachache die Magenschmerzen (pl.)

stop auf·hören (mit); halten; stehen·bleiben°

store das Geschäft, -e; der Laden, ⸚

story die Geschichte, -n

straight gerade

straighten up auf·räumen

strange merkwürdig

street die Straße, -n; **~car** die Straßenbahn, -en

stress der Streß

strict(ly) streng

strike der Streik, -s; **to ~** streiken

stroll spazieren

strong stark

student der Student, -en, -en/die Studentin, -nen

studies das Studium

study studieren; lernen; arbeiten; durch·arbeiten

stupid dumm

subject (academic) das Fach, ⸚er

subway die U-Bahn

such solch (-er, -es, -e); **~ a** so ein

suddenly plötzlich

suit (man's) der Anzug, ⸚e; **(woman's) ~** das Kostüm, -e; **to ~** passen

summer der Sommer

sun die Sonne, -n

sun glasses die Sonnenbrille, -n

Sunday der Sonntag

Sundays sonntags

superficial oberflächlich

supermarket der Supermarkt, ⸚e; **to the ~** in den Supermarkt; **at the ~** im Supermarkt

supper das Abendessen; **for ~** zum Abendessen; **to have ~** zu Abend essen

supposed: to be ~ to sollen°

sure sicher; bestimmt; **(agreement) ~!** Natürlich!

surf surfen

surprise überraschen

suspense: to be in ~ gespannt sein

sweater der Pulli, -s; der Pullover, -

swim schwimmen°

swimming: to go ~ schwimmen gehen°; **~ suit** der Badeanzug, ⸚e; **~ trunks** die Badehose, -n

Swiss (adj.) Schweizer; **~ (person)** der Schweizer, -/die Schweizerin, -nen

switch (to change) wechseln

Switzerland die Schweiz

table der Tisch, -e; **bedside ~** der Nachttisch, -e

table tennis das Tischtennis

take nehmen°

take along mit·nehmen°

take care of (someone) auf·passen

(auf + acc.)

take off sich (dat.) [etwas] aus·ziehen°; **I take off my shoes.** Ich ziehe mir die Schuhe aus.

talk sich unterhalten°; **to ~ (about)** reden (über); sprechen° (über + acc./von)

tall (people) groß

task die Aufgabe, -n

taste schmecken; probieren

tasty lecker

tax die Steuer, -n

teacher der Lehrer, -/die Lehrerin, -nen

telephone das Telefon, -e; **to ~** telefonieren; an·rufen°

telephone number die Telefonnummer, -n; **What is your ~?** Wie ist deine/Ihre Telefonnummer?

television das Fernsehen; **~ set** der Fernseher, -; **color ~** der Farbfernseher, -; **~ program** die Fernsehsendung, -en; **to watch ~** fern·sehen°

tell sagen; erzählen; **to ~ (about)** erzählen (über + acc./von)

tennis das Tennis

terrace die Terrasse, -n

terrible schlimm; furchtbar; schrecklich

test die Klausur, -en; **to take a ~** eine Klausur schreiben°

than als (after a comparison)

thank danken; **~ you very much** danke sehr/schön

thanks danke; der Dank; **~ a lot, many ~** vielen Dank

that daß; jen- (-er, -es, -e)

theater das Theater, -; **to go to the ~** ins Theater gehen; **~ play** das Theaterstück, -e; **movie ~** das Kino, -s

then dann; da

there da; dort; dahin; **~ is/are** es gibt

thereby dadurch

therefore also; deshalb; daher; darum; deswegen

these diese

thin dünn, schlank

thing das Ding, -e; die Sache, -n

think denken°; meinen; **What do**

you ~? Was meinst du?
What do you ~ of the cake?
Was hältst du von dem Ku-
chen?; **I don't ~ so.** Ich
glaube nicht.
third das Drittel, -
thirst der Durst
thirsty: to be ~ Durst haben°
this dies (-er, -es, -e)
throat der Hals, ⸚e
throw werfen°; **to ~ away** weg·
werfen°
Thursday der Donnerstag
thus also
ticket die Karte, -n
tie: neck~ die Krawatte, -n; **to ~**
binden°
tight eng
time die Zeit, -en; das Mal, -e;
mal; **at this ~** zur Zeit; **at
that ~** damals; **at the same ~**
zur gleichen Zeit; **for a long ~**
lange; **a short ~ ago** vor kurzem, neulich; **What ~ is it?**
Wieviel Uhr ist es?/Wie spät
ist es?; **At what ~?** Um wieviel Uhr?; **Have a good ~!**
Viel Vergnügen!
times mal; **[three] ~** [drei] mal
tinker basteln
tired müde; kaputt
to an; auf, in; nach; zu
today heute; **What day is it ~?**
Welcher Tag ist heute?
together zusammen
tolerant tolerant
tomato die Tomate, -n
tomorrow morgen; **day after ~**
übermorgen
tonight heute abend
too zu; **me ~** ich auch; **~ little**
zu wenig; **~ much** zuviel
tool das Gerät, -e; das Werkzeug, -e
tooth der Zahn, ⸚e; **to brush [my]
teeth** [mir] die Zähne putzen
toothache die Zahnschmerzen (*pl.*)
tour die Tour, -en
tourist der Tourist, -en, -en/die
Touristin, -nen
town hall restaurant der Ratskeller, -
trade der Handel; **foreign ~** der
Außenhandel
tradition die Tradition, -en

traffic der Verkehr
train der Zug, ⸚e; die Bahn; ~
station der Bahnhof, ⸚e
translation die Übersetzung, -en
transportation: means of ~ das
Verkehrsmittel, -
travel fahren°; reisen
tree der Baum, ⸚e
treat einladen°
trip die Reise, -n, die Fahrt, -en;
die Tour, -en; **bike ~** die
Radtour, -en
trousers die Hose, -n
truck der Lastwagen, -
true wahr
try versuchen; probieren
T-shirt das T-Shirt, -s
Tuesday der Dienstag
Tuesdays dienstags
turn: to have one's ~ dran sein;
it's your ~ du bist dran
TV das Fernsehen; **~ set** der
Fernseher, -; **~ program** die
Fernsehsendung, -en
type: to ~ tippen; **to be able to ~**
Schreibmaschine schreiben
können
typewriter die Schreibmaschine, -n

umbrella der Regenschirm, -e;
der Schirm, -e
unbelievable unglaublich
uncle der Onkel, -
under unter
understand verstehen°
undress (sich) aus·ziehen°; **I get
undressed.** Ich ziehe mich
aus.
unemployed arbeitslos
unfortunately leider
unification die Vereinigung
unified vereinigt; vereint
union die Gewerkschaft, -en
university die Universität, -en;
die Uni, -s; **to attend a ~** an/auf
die Universität gehen; **at the ~**
an/auf der Universität
unsafe unsicher
until bis; **~ now** bisher; **~ later**
bis später; tschüs; bis dann; bis
bald
up to bis zu
U.S.A. die USA (*pl.*); **to the ~** in
die USA

use benutzen; gebrauchen; **to ~
up** verbrauchen
utensil das Gerät, -e

vacation der Urlaub; die Ferien
(*pl.*); **~ trip** die Ferienreise,
-n; **on/during ~** in Urlaub/in
den Ferien; **to go on ~** in
Urlaub/in die Ferien fahren°;
to be on ~ in Urlaub/in den
Ferien sein°
vacuum der Staubsauger, -; **to ~**
staub·saugen
vain: in ~ umsonst
vase die Vase, -n
VCR der Videorecorder, -
vegetable das Gemüse, -
very sehr; ganz
vicinity: in the ~ in der Nähe
video das Video, -s
video camera die Videokamera,
-s
video game das Videospiel, -e
video recorder der Videorecorder, -
village das Dorf, ⸚er
visit der Besuch; **to ~**
besuchen
visitor der Besucher, -/die Besucherin, -nen
volleyball der Volleyball

wait (for) warten (auf)
walk der Spaziergang, ⸚e; **to
take a ~** einen Spaziergang
machen; **to go for a ~** spa-
zieren·gehen°
walking: to go ~ wandern/
spazieren gehen°
wall die Wand, ⸚e; die Mauer, -n
want (to) wollen°
war der Krieg, -e; **world ~** der
Weltkrieg, -e
warm warm
was war
wash die Wäsche; **to ~** (sich)
waschen°; **to ~ dishes**
ab·waschen°; Geschirr spülen
washing machine die Waschmaschine, -n
watch die (Armband)uhr, -en;
to ~ an·sehen°; **to ~ TV**
fern·sehen°; **to ~ out** auf·
passen
water das Wasser

water ski der Wasserski, -er; **to ~** Wasserski fahren°

way der Weg, -e; **on the ~** auf dem Weg; die Art; **this ~** so; auf diese Weise

weak schwach

wear tragen°

weather das Wetter; **~ report** der Wetterbericht, -e

Wednesday der Mittwoch

week die Woche, -n; **a ~ from [Monday]** [Montag] in acht Tagen

weekend das Wochenende; **on the ~** am Wochenende

weightlifting das Gewichtheben

welcome: you're ~ bitte (sehr)

well gut; wohl; **I'm not ~.** Mir geht's schlecht.; **~ (interjection)** na!, nun!; **~ now, oh ~** na

well known bekannt

west der Westen

wet naß

what was; **~ kind (of), ~ a** was für (ein)

when wann; wenn; als

where wo; **~ (to)** wohin; **~ do you come from?** Woher kommst du?

whether ob

which welch (-er, -es, -e)

while während

white weiß

who wer

whole ganz

whom wen (*acc. of* wer); wem (*dat. of* wer)

whose wessen

why warum

willingly gern

wind der Wind

window das Fenster, -

windsurfing: to go ~ windsurfen gehen°

wine der Wein, -e

winter der Winter

wish wünschen; **I ~ I had . . .** Ich wollte, ich hätte ...

with mit; **~ it** damit; **~ me** mit mir; **to live ~ a family** bei einer Familie wohnen

woman die Frau, -en

wonder: to ~ about gespannt sein

woods der Wald, ̈-er

word das Wort, ̈-er

word processor der Wortprozessor, -en; **to do word processing** mit dem Wortprozessor arbeiten

work die Arbeit; **to do the ~** die Arbeit machen; arbeiten; **to ~ through** durch·arbeiten; **It doesn't ~.** Es geht nicht.; **It works.** Es geht.

worker der Arbeiter, -/die Arbeiterin, -nen; der Arbeitnehmer, -/die Arbeitnehmerin, -nen

workplace der Arbeitsplatz, ̈-e

world die Welt, -en; **~ war** der Weltkrieg, -e

worry die Sorge, -n; **to ~ about** sich kümmern um; sich sorgen machen (um)

worth wert

worthwhile wert; **to be ~** sich lohnen

would würde; **~ like** möchte; **How ~ it be?** Wie wär's?

wow Mensch!

write schreiben°; **to ~ to someone** jemandem/an jemanden schreiben; **to ~ down** auf·schreiben

writer der Schriftsteller, -/die Schriftstellerin, -nen

wrong falsch; **What's ~?** Was ist los?; **What is ~ with you?** Was hast du?

xenophobia der Ausländerhaß

year das Jahr, -e

yearly jährlich

yellow gelb

yes ja

yesterday gestern

yet noch; schon; **not ~** noch nicht

young jung

youth die Jugend; der/die Jugendliche (*noun decl. like adj.*)

zip code die Postleitzahl, -en

PERMISSIONS AND CREDITS

Texts

pp. 284-285: Adaptation of Fölsing, Ulla, "Porträt: Gisela Anton." In *Kultur-Chronik,* 3/1994, 2.

pp. 384-385: Adaptation of Gartner, Guido, "Die Kündigung, nur noch drei Tage." In *Kultur-Chronik,* 4/1994, 27-29.

pp. 320: Matter, Mani, "Heidi." In *Us emer lääre Gygechaschte,* Zürich: © Benziger Verlag AG, 1972.

pp. 456: Hohler, Franz "Der Verkäufer und der Elch." In *Kontakt mit der Zeit,* ed. Dieter Stöpfgeshoff, Munich: Max Hueber Verlag, 1981.

Realia

p. 5: Allgemeiner Deutscher Automobil-Club e. V., München, Deutschland.

p. 105: Courtesy of Preisring-Markt.

p. 109: Courtesy of Dallmayr, München.

p. 182: Courtesy of Restop Altea.

p. 209: Courtesy of Staatl. Mineralbrunnen Siemens Erben, Mainz.

p. 211: "Jule Neigel Band." In *Live in Concert,* 4/95.

p. 211: Studenten im Olympiazentrum e.V., Geschäftsleitung Discothek, Helen-Meyer-Ring 9, 80809 München.

p. 224: Modehaus KONEN, München.

p. 278: Hannes Keller AG Computer-Zentrum Zürich.

p. 317: Schweizer Bankverein/Swiss Bank Corporation, Basel.

p. 404: Courtesy of Münchner Volkshochschule, München.

p. 427: Triumph Adler AG, Nürnberg.

p. 447: © Manfred von Papen.

p. 452: Courtesy of OKA.

Photos

Kapitel 1: facing p. 1 & p. 4: David R. Frazier Photolibrary; p. 9, top: Stuart Cohen; p. 9, bottom & p. 10: David R. Frazier Photolibrary.

Kapitel 2: pp. 20, 23, & 27: David R. Frazier Photolibrary; pp. 37, 38, & 39: Ulrike Welsch; p. 42: Stuart Cohen; p. 48: David R. Frazier Photolibrary.

Kapitel 3: p. 54: Ulrike Welsch; p. 63: Stuart Cohen; p. 64: Ulrike Welsch; p. 65, top: David R. Frazier Photolibrary; p. 65, bottom: Ulrike Welsch; p. 67:

Kathy Squires; p. 72: Ulrike Welsch; p. 77, top: Bildarchiv Foto Marburg/Art Resource.

Kapitel 4: p. 88: Kathy Squires; p. 92, top: Ulrike Welsch; p. 92, bottom: David R. Frazier Photolibrary; p. 94: David R. Frazier Photolibrary; p.100: Ulrike Welsch; pp. 101 & 103: David R. Frazier Photolibrary; p. 104: Ulrike Welsch; pp. 106: Stuart Cohen; p. 116: Ulrike Welsch.

Kapitel 5: p. 130: Kathy Squires; pp. 133, 135, & 137: Ulrike Welsch; p. 141: Kathy Squires; pp. 142 & 145: Ulrike Welsch; p. 159: David R. Frazier Photolibrary; p. 162: Beryl Goldberg.

Kapitel 6: p. 166: David R. Frazier Photolibrary; p. 170: Kathy Squires; p. 171: David R. Frazier Photolibrary; p. 173: Kathy Squires; p. 175: David R. Frazier Photolibrary; p. 178: Stuart Cohen; pp. 179 & 180: David R. Frazier Photolibrary.

Kapitel 7: p. 202: Ulrike Welsch; pp. 206, 208, & 210: David R. Frazier Photolibrary; p. 212: Musik + Show/A. Keuchel; p. 214: David R. Frazier Photolibrary; p. 219: Kathy Squires; p. 223: Bildarchiv Huber; p. 233: Bildarchiv Engelmeier; p. 235: Beryl Goldberg; p. 238: Kathy Squires.

Kapitel 8: pp. 240 & 243: Stuart Cohen; p. 244: Ulrike Welsch; p. 247: Engraving of the Francis Daniel Pastorius homestead, Germantown, PA, by Max Zeitler, 1908. Reproduced from Marion D. Learned, *The Life of Francis Daniel Pastorius* (Philadelphia: Wm. J. Campbell, 1908), courtesy of The Balch Institute for Ethnic Studies Library; pp.

249 & 251: David R. Frazier Photolibrary; p. 252: Ulrike Welsch; p. 254: David R. Frazier Photolibrary; pp. 262 & 270: Ulrike Welsch.

Kapitel 9: p. 276: Ulrike Welsch; p. 282: Bildarchiv Engelmeier; p. 283: David R. Frazier Photolibrary; p. 287, left & center: German Information Center; p. 287, right: Bettmann Archive; pp. 289 & 291: David R. Frazier Photolibrary; p. 301: Ulrike Welsch; p. 303: Action Press; p. 305: David R. Frazier Photolibrary.

Kapitel 10: p. 310: Judy Poe; p. 316: The Picture Cube/Stephen Saks; p. 320: Keystone Press AG Archive; p. 322: The Stock Market/G. Anderson; p. 323: Keystone Press AG Archive; p. 324: Swiss National Tourist Office; p. 335: The Stock Market/Robin Prange.

Kapitel 11: p. 344: Ulrike Welsch; p. 349, top: German Information Center; p. 349, bottom: Kathy Squires; p. 352: Bettmann Archive; p. 356: Sipa Press; p. 358: Stuart Cohen; p. 366: Photoreporters/dpa.

Kapitel 12: pp. 378 & 385: Stuart Cohen; p. 386: Ulrike Welsch; p. 388: Photoreporters/dpa; p. 390: David R. Frazier Photolibrary; p. 393: Ulrike Welsch; p. 401: Beryl Goldberg.

Kapitel 13: pp. 412, 418, 433, & 434: Ulrike Welsch; p. 424: Photoreporters/dpa.

Kapitel 14: p. 438: Stuart Cohen; p. 444: David R. Frazier Photolibrary; p. 446: Ulrike Welsch; p. 449: Photoreporters/dpa.

Illustrations

Penny Carter: pp. 118, 172, 398.

Chris Demarest: pp. 35, 52, 215, 330.

Anna Veltfort: pp. 12, 14, 15, 24, 25, 58, 75, 96, 116, 125, 143, 161, 170, 216, 217, 251, 252, 254, 255, 256, 259, 261, 279, 280, 313, 314, 315, 326, 327, 369, 370, 459.